Examination Guide for *United States History*

In the *United States History: Beginnings Through Reconstruction* program, content is comprehensive, and the presentation is motivating. The program places special attention on blending content, skill development, and visual presentation at an appropriate reading level. Numerous features bring the experience of the people of the United States into sharper focus in a lively manner.

1 — The **Prologue** introduces the text and stresses reasons for studying history.

20-21, 328-329 — **Unit Openings** provide colorful visual overviews with an introductory paragraph describing the general topics to be studied in the unit.

22, 234 — **Chapter Openers** contain a colorful photograph and a brief introductory paragraph that previews chapter content.

83, 369 — **Chapter Organization** consists of numbered sections and subsections to provide an outline, and review questions at the end of each section to reinforce learning.

157-158, 245-246 — **Primary Sources** give vivid examples of historical evidence, demonstrating that history concerns the experiences of real people.

23, 235 — **Key Terms** and **Concepts** appear in boldface type when first introduced and are defined in context.

247, 359 — **Paintings**, **Drawings**, and **Photographs**, many in full color, have captions with a question that relates the illustration to text content.

237, 273, 368 — **Maps**, all in full color, with captions, provide visual content showing the relationships among geographic and political, social, and economic factors.

167, 291, 355 — Full-color **Graphics** include charts, graphs, tables, and diagrams, with captions, that illustrate statistical and narrative information.

106, 337 — Color-coded **Profiles** of famous and not-so-famous people from a variety of backgrounds help students remember that history is the story of people.

78, 339 — Color-coded **Skill Features** and **Concept Features** employ analytical methods basic to building social studies skills while highlighting particular events and ideas.

88-95, 394-401 — Color-coded **City Sketches** depict various aspects of American urban life as they relate to the unit topics and chapter material.

182-183, 371-372 — **Chapter Reviews** provide a summary of main points, a vocabulary list, recall and analytical questions, and an exercise to sharpen geography and social studies skills.

96-97, 326-327 — **Unit Reviews** provide a time line of important events covered in the unit, a list of major generalizations, analytical questions, suggested projects, and a bibliography.

436 — The **Epilogue** at the end of the text sums up the course.

437-532 — The **Appendix** includes a **Readings** section; an **Atlas** with reference maps and a graphics section with data on the American population, society, political system, and economy; the **Declaration of Independence**; and an annotated **Constitution.**

531-544 — A **Glossary** contains all the important historical and concept terms.

545 — A comprehensive **Index** provides a ready reference

TEACHER'S ANNOTATED EDITION
UNITED STATES HISTORY

Volume 1

BEGINNINGS THROUGH RECONSTRUCTION

For a people to be without history, or to be ignorant of its history, is as for a person to be without memory . . .

Henry S. Commager

Henry N. Drewry
Lecturer of History, Princeton University

Robert P. Green, Jr.
Associate Professor of Education, Clemson University

Thomas H. O'Connor
Professor of American History, Boston College

Laura L. Becker
Assistant Professor of History, Florida International University

Robert E. Coviello
Social Studies Department Chairperson, Walpole High School

CHARLES E. MERRILL PUBLISHING CO.
A BELL & HOWELL COMPANY
Columbus, Ohio
Toronto London Sydney

ISBN 0-675-02041-7

Published by
CHARLES E. MERRILL PUBLISHING CO.
A Bell & Howell Company

Columbus, Ohio 43216

Printed in the United States of America

2T

Table of Contents

Introduction _____ 5T
    Program Objectives   **5T**
    Program Components   **5T**

Program Use _____ **19T**

General Teaching Methods _____ **27T**

Teaching Strategies _____ **31T**

    Introduction _____ **31T**

    Unit I _____ **34T**
        Chapter 1   **34T**
        Chapter 2   **38T**
        Chapter 3   **41T**
        City Sketches   **44T**
        Unit I Review   **45T**

    Unit II _____ **46T**
        Chapter 4   **46T**
        Chapter 5   **49T**
        Chapter 6   **52T**
        Chapter 7   **55T**
        City Sketch   **58T**
        Unit II Review   **59T**

    Unit III _____ **61T**
        Chapter 8   **61T**
        Chapter 9   **65T**
        Chapter 10   **67T**
        City Sketch   **69T**
        Unit III Review   **70T**

    Unit IV _____ **72T**
        Chapter 11   **72T**
        Chapter 12   **75T**
        Chapter 13   **78T**
        City Sketches   **80T**
        Unit IV Review   **82T**

    Unit V _____ **83T**
        Chapter 14   **83T**
        Chapter 15   **86T**
        Chapter 16   **89T**
        City Sketches   **93T**
        Unit V Review   **94T**

    Conclusion _____ **95T**
        City Sketch   **98T**

    Readings _____ **100T**

Reading List _____ **108T**
    For Teachers   **108T**
    For Students   **112T**

Notes   **115T**

Survey Form _____ **119T**

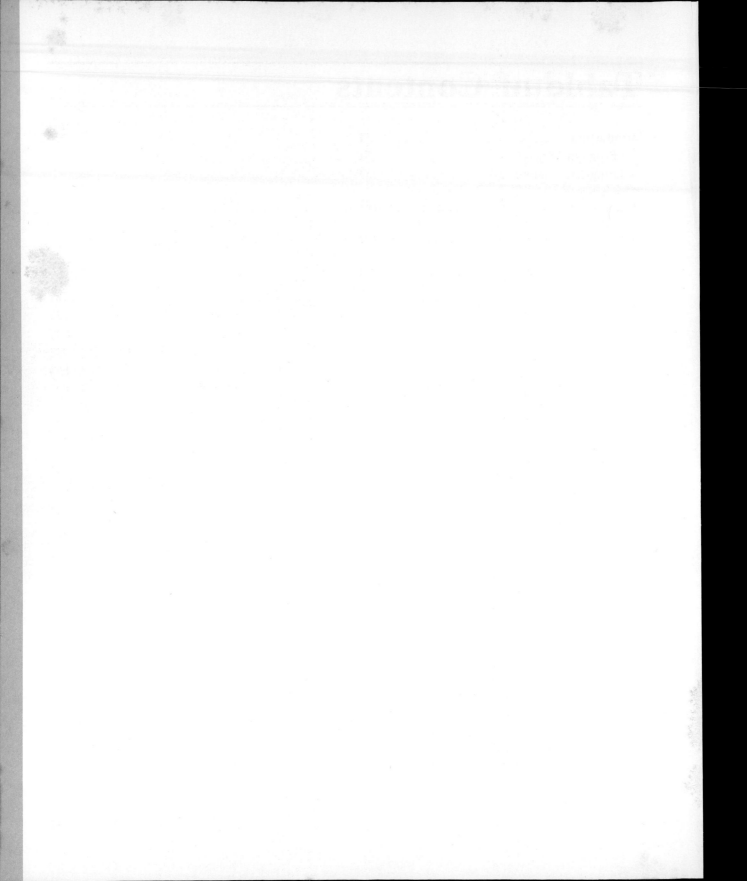

Introduction

The United States was born a product of the Western European liberal tradition and the democratizing influence of a New World. At the heart of the nation's experience has been agreement over the basic principles of its society and political system: individual rights, government by consent of the governed, and equality of opportunity. The strength of these basic beliefs has rarely wavered, although the extent to which each is manifested has changed from era to era. Social and economic factors, sectional allegiances, and ideological predilections have all had an impact. Conflict and controversy have arisen. But the American tradition has been one of progress in fulfilling the promise of these basic beliefs. *United States History* is a record of that progress.

Program Objectives

United States History: Beginnings Through Reconstruction is designed to achieve the following objectives:

1. Help students gain insights into relationships among people, ideas, and events as they learn and use significant facts of America's history.
2. Help students sharpen social studies skills.
3. Help students develop an appreciation of history and its study.

Program Components

Historians and educators designed the *United States History: Beginnings Through Reconstruction* program for middle and junior high school students. This first volume provides students with a comprehensive and in-depth coverage of American history through Reconstruction. While developing significant facts about America's history, the program aims to improve student study skills, to instill an appreciation of history, and to help students gain insights into relationships among the people, ideas, and events that have shaped present-day American society.

The **Student Edition** contains all of the basic content, concepts, skills, terms, and generalizations expected in a junior high school American history program. Each of the units is organized chronologically, using time and place in developing historical perspective. Unit titles describe what the United States has meant to its people at different times in its history.

In addition to the chapter narratives, special, color-coded features focus on the social, economic, political, and geographic aspects of the American story. There are city sketches which follow each unit of related material. Special features within each chapter expand the coverage in the text. These include biographical profiles, skill features, and concept features. The chapters also include many excerpts from primary and secondary sources, full-color maps, and numerous photographs, charts, graphs, and diagrams. An appendix at the end of the Student Edition contains primary and secondary readings, an atlas, historical data graphs, the texts of the Declaration of Independence and the Constitution of the United States with detailed annotations, a glossary, and an index.

United States History: Beginnings Through Reconstruction has a controlled reading level, appropriate concepts and skill development, concise explanations of terms within the narrative, and short chapters with student questions in the margins that highlight important points. To reinforce narrative material, there are caption, section, chapter, and unit questions. These range in degree of difficulty from simple recall to thoughtful analysis.

The **Teacher's Resource Book** to accompany *United States History: Beginnings Through Reconstruction* is a unique, time-saving teacher aid designed to assist teachers in the teaching of American history. It provides effective tools for teaching content, reinforcing skills, enriching lessons, and evaluating student performance.

The Teacher's Resource Book contains five sections beginning with teacher lecture notes, an in-depth outline of content based on the heading structure of *United States History*. Also included in this section is a section-by-section commentary. The second section contains outline maps which may be duplicated and used by students for a variety of map exercises. The third section contains skill-building student activities which correspond to and reinforce the content of the student text. The fourth section consists of chapter quizzes and unit tests. The last section provides a list of audio-visual resources.

The **Teacher's Annotated Edition** of *United States History: Beginnings Through Reconstruction* contains a complete Student Edition with annotations that are printed in blue on the text pages. These provide additional detail and include ways for emphasizing various facts, events, and movements. The Teacher's Guide section provides suggestions for general teaching procedures and references to additional resources. It offers teaching strategies, objectives, and answers to caption, section, chapter, and unit questions. The Teacher's Annotated Edition has been organized to reduce teacher preparation time and to allow for easy adaptation to individual teaching styles and students' needs.

Prologue

The Prologue introduces *United States History: Beginnings Through Reconstruction* with a discussion of reasons for studying American history.

PROLOGUE

History can help a person learn about the past, understand the present, and prepare for the future. Most current political, economic, and social conditions in the United States took a long time to develop and are continuing to change. History traces the development, following all the twists and turns that affected it along the way.

To begin to understand the present American political system, for example, consider some of the major political developments in the nation's past and ask questions about them. What was life in the colonies like under British rule? Why were the colonists unhappy with British rule? What kind of government did Americans set up for themselves? How did a free and open society in the United States affect the way that government worked? What divided the American people, leading to a civil war? How did Americans restore the unity of their country after the ordeal of the Civil War?

Similarly, the American economic system and American society can be considered. What values did the American people derive from their rural society and their agricultural way of life? How did these values affect their political ideas and their social attitudes? Why did the United States decide to change from an agrarian economy to an industrial economy? How did the economy influence immigration? Why was there conflict among races of people? In what ways did the industrial economy of the North conflict with the plantation economy of the South?

Even the most far-reaching study of history may not provide complete answers. There are some historical facts that are clear, simple, and upon which historians easily agree. There are other aspects of history that are not clear and upon which historians may never agree. These usually concern judgments involving correct and incorrect decisions. The important thing is that history raises questions and aids in providing a structure for answering them. Evaluating facts and weighing evidence are valuable skills for making sound and reasonable decisions.

United States History: Beginnings Through Reconstruction tells the story of the United States and its people. It follows a development from America's distant past to the Reconstruction period that came after the Civil War. It provides a framework for learning about the way things were, understanding the way things are, and preparing for the way things may be in the United States.

The Prologue is designed for the students as an introduction to this text as well as an introduction to the study of American history.

Unit Openers

Unit title

Unit number

Introductory paragraph develops an initial understanding of major unit theme.

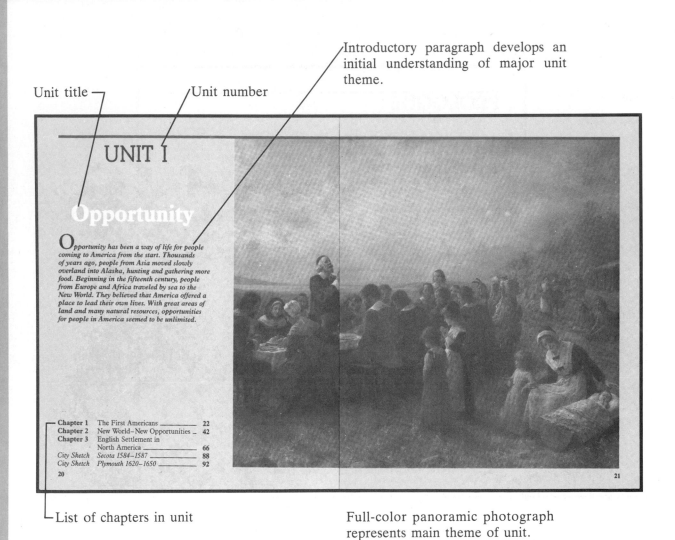

UNIT I

Opportunity

Opportunity has been a way of life for people coming to America from the start. Thousands of years ago, people from Asia moved slowly overland into Alaska, hunting and gathering more food. Beginning in the fifteenth century, people from Europe and Africa traveled by sea to the New World. They believed that America offered a place to lead their own lives. With great areas of land and many natural resources, opportunities for people in America seemed to be unlimited.

Chapter 1   The First Americans ———— 22
Chapter 2   New World–New Opportunities — 42
Chapter 3   English Settlement in
             North America ———— 66
City Sketch Secota 1584–1587 ———— 88
City Sketch Plymouth 1620–1650 ———— 92

20

21

List of chapters in unit

Full-color panoramic photograph represents main theme of unit.

Chapter Openers

Brief introductory paragraph previews chapter content. ⟶

Chapter title ⟶   Chapter number

From Ocean to Ocean   13

John Charles Frémont, the "Pathfinder," became a living sign of the spirit of manifest destiny. His adventures inspired many Americans to go west. What did people hope to find in the area west of the Mississippi River?

298   From Ocean to Ocean

With the Louisiana Purchase in 1803, the United States gained its first area of land west of the Mississippi River. In the years following, Americans began to move into these lands as well as others in the West. Large areas of land were added to the United States in the 1840's and 1850's. Soon the nation extended from the Atlantic Ocean to the Pacific Ocean. Except for Alaska and Hawaii, the United States grew to its present size during these years.

1. The Westward Movement

Americans had begun to explore the lands west of the Mississippi River before many areas to the east of it were settled. The Lewis and Clark expedition of 1804 to 1806 gave people in the United States their first information about the Louisiana Territory. Soon other Americans were exploring and settling lands in the West. Moving across the Mississippi River into the huge area of the West presented exciting challenges and new problems to Americans and the United States.

1.1 Leading the Way West.   The United States followed up the Lewis and Clark expedition with others. In 1806, Lieutenant Zebulon Pike traveled up the Arkansas River to the Rocky Mountains in Colorado. Pike's report gave new information about the West. It added to American interest in trade with the Spanish in New Mexico.

Another expedition was led by Major Stephen Long in 1819 and 1820. Long explored the Great Plains along the Platte River to the Rocky Mountains. Both Pike and Long reported that the Great Plains were not fit for settlement because of the lack of rainfall and trees. This led to the common belief that the Great Plains was a "Great American Desert." For years, people were not interested in settling there.

Fur traders and trappers were an even more important source of information about the West. After the United States gained Louisiana, Americans became important in the western fur trade. Prior to that time, the French and Spanish had competed with the British for furs.

The trappers went into the mountains and river areas of the West for beaver. Some time during the year, they met with a representative of a fur-trading company to sell their furs. These furs were later sold by the companies to customers in the East or in Europe. Over the years, the trappers came to know the streams, rivers, mountain passes, and trails of nearly every area in the West. Such trappers as Jim Bridger and Jedediah Smith guided early settlers through the Rocky Mountains to Oregon and California.

Use a topographical map to trace Pike's travels and to consider the nature of the land into which he went.

Where did Pike explore?

What were the early reports about the Great Plains?

Note that the fur trade was forced farther west as the line of settlement moved west.

From Ocean to Ocean   299

Full-color photograph gives visual dimension to chapter theme.

Narrative Organization

boundary between Georgia and Spanish Florida at the 31st parallel. Many Americans were very pleased with the Pinckney Treaty.

3.4 Washington's Farewell. President Washington prepared to leave office in 1796. During his two terms, he had helped establish the new government on a solid foundation. But Washington was troubled. Matters with France were growing worse. The French had been angered by the Jay Treaty. Under the terms of the treaty of 1778, France and the United States were allies. Great Britain was France's enemy.

President Washington was concerned over the possibility of war with France. In a Farewell Address written in September 1796, he urged future leaders to keep the United States independent when dealing with other nations. Washington said:

> *The great rule of conduct for us in regard to foreign nations is, in extending our commercial relations to have with them as little political connection as possible. . . .*
> *It is our true policy to steer clear of permanent alliances with any portion of the foreign world, so far, I mean, as we are now at liberty to do it. . . .*

Washington went on to admit that temporary alliances are sometimes necessary. Permanent alliances were to be avoided, however.

1. What war in Europe threatened United States neutrality?
2. How did the European war affect American trade?
3. What advice did Washington give in his Farewell Address?

4. The Adams Presidency

The United States faced many challenges follow[ing the] first time under the Constitution, George Washington [had led] the country. During the years from 1788 to 1796, h[e had shown] government had proved it could work. A pattern ha[d been set that] promised success in dealing with the future.

4.1 The Election of 1796. The presidential [election of 1796] was the first between political parties. John Ada[ms and Thomas] Pinckney ran for the Federalists. Thomas Jefferson an[d Aaron Burr ran] for the Democratic-Republicans. The vote was very clo[se. Many voters] were angry about the Jay Treaty and gave their [support to]

204 Testing the New Government

Type is readable in a one-column format.

Chapter material is enriched with frequent excerpts from primary sources.

Review questions after each section reinforce student understanding.

Important terms are printed in boldface type and immediately defined or explained in context.

these new lands. One event which drew people to the West was the discovery of gold. In 1848, James Marshall found gold on the property of John Sutter in California. Word spread rapidly. By 1849, large numbers of people were making their way from the East to California by ship or overland. This movement was called the **gold rush**. During 1849, more than 80,000 people came to California from Europe, Mexico, China, and the United States. They were known as **"forty-niners"** because of the year in which most of them came. Gold mining camps were quickly set up in the mountain valleys of central California. San Francisco grew up as an important trading center and source of supplies.

At first, there seemed to be a great deal of gold. Miners often found it near the surface of the earth where it was easy to mine. Only a few people, however, became rich mining for gold. Many were disappointed and returned home. Some left to try their luck in other gold or silver booms in Nevada, Colorado, and later in Montana. Others settled down to farming or business. As a result of the gold rush, the population of California increased rapidly. It became a state in 1850. Similar opportunities would soon bring people to other areas of the West.

1. Who started the trade between Americans and the people of New Mexico?
2. Who set up the first American settlement in Texas?
3. Who were the military leaders in the Mexican War?
4. What brought people to California in 1849?

4. Indians and the Westward Movement

The movement of people and the expansion of the United States into the lands west of the Mississippi River had a great influence on the Indians of the area. At first, there was little contact between the Indians and the newcomers. As time went on, there was greater contact with the growing numbers of trappers, miners, and settlers moving into the West. This affected the Indians' ways of life and caused the loss of more and more Indian land.

4.1 Changes in Indian Life. The Spanish exploration and settlement in the West had brought many changes in the Indians' ways of life. One of the most important changes came with the introduction of horses into North America. The Spaniards brought horses with them when they explored the Great Plains in the 1500's. Through raids and trading with the Spaniards and each other, many groups of Indians

From Ocean to Ocean **313**

Marginal student notes in the form of questions indicate important information to be learned.

Major section heads are numbered for easy identification.

Heading structure provides an outline of content.

Chapter title appears on each page for easy reference.

Chapter Reviews

Main Points reinforces content by listing key points of the chapter in a concise, straightforward format.

Building Vocabulary reviews important people, places, laws, treaties, organizations, and terms in the order of their presentation in the chapter.

Remembering the Facts provides review and reinforcement of chapter content.

Chapter 3 Review

Main Points

1. England was slow to enter the race for colonies in the New World because of political unrest at home.
2. During the reign of Queen Elizabeth I, England became the leading European naval power.
3. Between 1607 and 1732, England established colonies along the east coast of North America.
4. The English colonies were set up by joint stock companies, by proprietors, or by the English government.
5. English colonies were settled by people looking for land, money, and religious freedom.
6. The Glorious Revolution in England put an end to the English plan to centralize the colonial government.

Building Vocabulary

1. Identify the following:

John Cabot	Powhatan	John Winthrop	William Penn
Parliament	House of Burgesses	Roger Williams	Dr. Alexander Hamilton
Sir Francis Drake	Puritans	Anne Hutchinson	James Oglethorpe
Spanish Armada	Mayflower Compact	Toleration Act	Dominion of New England
Jamestown			

2. Define the following:

manufacturing	charter	vetoed	meeting houses
armada	investors	rituals	proprietors
joint stock companies	legislature	compact	proprietary colonies
			royal colony

Remembering the Facts

1. ...ed English efforts to ...lonies in the New World?
2. ...ngland begin to settle ...North America?
3. ...e English colonies were set ...? as royal colonies?
4. ...dians aid settlers at ...and Plymouth?
5. Which colonies were started by people who left the Massachusetts Bay Colony?
6. Which English colony was first settled by the Dutch? How did the English government gain control of it?
7. How did England try to organize the governing of the colonies?
8. How did the Glorious Revolution in England affect the colonies?

...ettlement in North America

Understanding the Facts

1. Why was tobacco important to the colony of Virginia?
2. Why did the Pilgrims, Puritans, and Quakers disagree with the Church of England?
3. Why was the Mayflower Compact important?
4. Why did people leave the Massachusetts Bay Colony?
5. Why did England want control of New Netherland and New Sweden?
6. Why did England plan to centralize the northeastern colonial governments under the Dominion of New England?

Using Maps

Longitude and Latitude. Because of the huge size of the earth, a way of easily identifying locations is needed. One way to do this is to draw two types of imaginary lines circling the globe. When maps are drawn, these lines are added, too.

One set of these lines runs north and south from north pole to south pole. These are called meridians, or lines of longitude. The distance between them is measured in degrees east or west of the prime (original) meridian. The prime meridian is labeled 0°. Since England was a world leader in exploration and mapmaking when the system was set up, the prime meridian runs through England.

The second set of lines runs east and west, but they do not come together at any one point. These are called parallels, or lines of latitude. The prime parallel is the equator, and it is labeled 0°. Latitude is measured in degrees according to the distance north or south of the equator.

By using these lines, we can identify any place on the earth as being at some degree east or west longitude and some degree north or south latitude.

Examine the map on page 83, and answer the following questions.

1. Between which lines of north latitude is the colony of Virginia?
2. Which line of west longitude runs along the eastern coast of Virginia?
3. Which parallel divides the Pennsylvania colony from the Maryland colony?
4. What is the one colony which lies entirely west of 80° west longitude?
5. Which colonies are crossed by the parallel at 40° north latitude?
6. Between which parallels do the English colonies lie?

Understanding the Facts helps students gain further insight into chapter concepts through analysis, synthesis, and evaluation.

Using Maps, Using Diagrams, Using Line Graphs, and Using Pie Graphs give students practice in basic social studies skills.

English Settlement in North America 87

11T

Unit Reviews

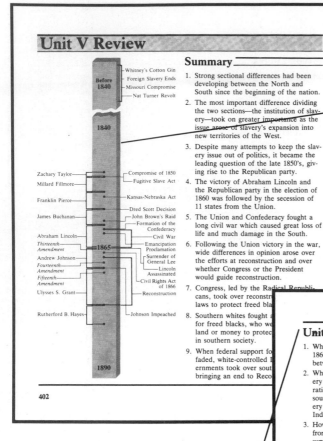

Unit V Review

Time line (Before 1840 – 1890)

Before 1840
- Whitney's Cotton Gin
- Foreign Slavery Ends
- Missouri Compromise
- Nat Turner Revolt

1840

Zachary Taylor
Millard Fillmore

Franklin Pierce

James Buchanan

Abraham Lincoln
Thirteenth Amendment
Andrew Johnson
Fourteenth Amendment
Fifteenth Amendment
Ulysses S. Grant

Rutherford B. Hayes

- Compromise of 1850
- Fugitive Slave Act
- Kansas-Nebraska Act
- Dred Scott Decision
- John Brown's Raid
- Formation of the Confederacy
- Civil War
- Emancipation Proclamation
- Surrender of General Lee
- Lincoln Assassinated
- Civil Rights Act of 1866
- Reconstruction
- Johnson Impeached

1865

1890

402

Summary

1. Strong sectional differences had been developing between the North and South since the beginning of the nation.

2. The most important difference dividing the two sections—the institution of slavery—took on greater importance as the issue arose of slavery's expansion into new territories of the West.

3. Despite many attempts to keep the slavery issue out of politics, it became the leading question of the late 1850's, giving rise to the Republican party.

4. The victory of Abraham Lincoln and the Republican party in the election of 1860 was followed by the secession of 11 states from the Union.

5. The Union and Confederacy fought a long civil war which caused great loss of life and much damage in the South.

6. Following the Union victory in the war, wide differences in opinion arose over the efforts at reconstruction and over whether Congress or the President would guide reconstruction.

7. Congress, led by the Radical Republicans, took over reconstr[uction]... laws to protect freed bla[cks]...

8. Southern whites fought a[gainst]... for freed blacks, who we[re]... land or money to protec[t]... in southern society.

9. When federal support fo[r]... faded, white-controlled [gov]ernments took over south[ern]... bringing an end to Reco[nstruction]...

The Summary highlights major generalizations developed in the unit.

Time lines highlight the chronology of major events in the unit.

Unit Questions

1. Why did westward expansion before 1860 contribute to the sectional crisis between the North and the South?

2. Why did many Americans feel that slavery clashed with the ideas in the Declaration of Independence? How did white southerners deal with the ideas of slavery and the ideals of the Declaration of Independence?

3. How was the Republican party different from the Whigs or Democrats in its support? How was this important in 1860?

4. What were the major reasons why the North was able to win the war?

5. What was the position of the Confederacy toward President Lincoln's belief that the Union was perpetual? Did the position of the Southern states change during Reconstruction and how?

6. How did the Republican party use reconstruction for its own advantage?

7. What were the successes and failures of the war and reconstruction as far as the rights of blacks were concerned?

Review questions reinforce learning through questions that tie together major points presented in the unit.

Suggested Activities

1. Write a brief statement showing how each of the following people might have reacted to news of the Dred Scott decision: a slave, a slave owner, a free black, and an abolitionist.

2. Locate poems and songs written during or about the Civil War. Try to include those which were about people from both the South and the North. Select several, and present them to the class.

3. Organize a discussion or class debate on the following—Do you think that reconstruction should have been controlled by Congress or the President?

Suggested Activities provide individual and group projects that give students the opportunity to examine unit concepts in greater depth.

Suggested Readings

Davis, Burke. *Mr. Lincoln's Whiskers.* New York: Coward, McCann, & Geoghegan, Inc., 1979. Discusses Lincoln's election as President and advice given him to grow a beard.

Ellis, Keith. *The American Civil War.* New York: G. P. Putnam, Sons, 1971. Discusses the leaders, battles, and events of the war.

Keith, Harold. *Rifles for Watie.* New York: Thomas Y. Crowell Co., 1957. The story of a young soldier during the Civil War.

Sterling, Dorothy. *The Trouble They Seen: Black People Tell the Story of Reconstruction.* Garden City, New York: Doubleday, 1976. Blacks give eyewitness accounts of reconstruction to Congress.

Suggested Readings provide a list of works suitable for in-depth study as well as student enjoyment.

403

Special Features

Concept features abstract generalizations about history through the examination of specific events. ——

Each type of feature is color-coded for easy reference.

The Profiles focus in on famous and not-so-famous people in American history. ——

Skill features provide the means for using students' understanding of history by performing tasks common to the social studies. ——

Questions reinforce learning. ——

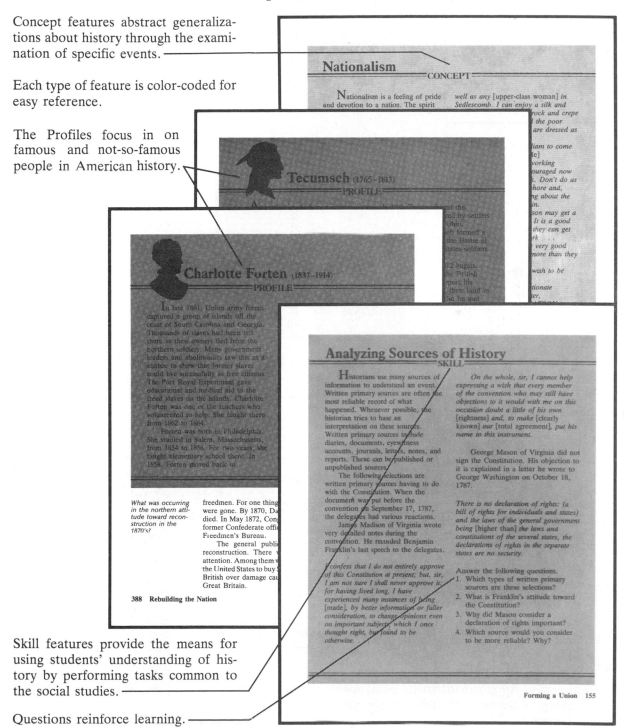

Nationalism
CONCEPT

Nationalism is a feeling of pride and devotion to a nation. The spirit

well as any [upper-class woman] in Sedlescomb. I can enjoy a silk and
rock and crepe
the poor
are dressed as

iam to come
e]
orking
ouraged now
k. Don't do as
hore and,
g about the
in.
son may get a
It is a good
they can get
rk
very good
more than they

wish to be

tionate
er,

Tecumsch (1765–1813)
PROFILE

d the
ed by settlers
Ohio,
h formed a
the Battle of
tates soldiers

12 begun,
e British
port his
their land in
So he and

Charlotte Forten (1837–1914)
PROFILE

In late 1861, Union army forces captured a group of islands off the coast of South Carolina and Georgia. Thousands of slaves had been left there as their owners fled from the northern soldiers. Many government leaders and abolitionists saw this as a chance to show that former slaves could live successfully as free citizens. The Port Royal Experiment gave educational and medical aid to the freed slaves on the islands. Charlotte Forten was one of the teachers who volunteered to help. She taught there from 1862 to 1864.

Forten was born in Philadelphia. She studied in Salem, Massachusetts, from 1854 to 1856. For two years, she taught elementary school there. In 1858, Forten moved back to

What was occurring in the northern attitude toward reconstruction in the 1870's?

freedmen. For one thing
were gone. By 1870, Da
died. In May 1872, Con
former Confederate offic
Freedmen's Bureau.

The general public
reconstruction. There
attention. Among them
the United States to buy
British over damage cau
Great Britain.

388 Rebuilding the Nation

Analyzing Sources of History
SKILL

Historians use many sources of information to understand an event. Written primary sources are often the most reliable record of what happened. Whenever possible, the historian tries to base an interpretation on these sources. Written primary sources include diaries, documents, eyewitness accounts, journals, letters, notes, and reports. These can be published or unpublished sources.

The following selections are written primary sources having to do with the Constitution. When the document was put before the convention on September 17, 1787, the delegates had various reactions.

James Madison of Virginia wrote very detailed notes during the convention. He recorded Benjamin Franklin's last speech to the delegates.

I confess that I do not entirely approve of this Constitution at present; but, sir, I am not sure I shall never approve it; for having lived long, I have experienced many instances of being [made], by better information or fuller consideration, to change opinions even on important subjects which I once thought right, but found to be otherwise.

On the whole, sir, I cannot help expressing a wish that every member of the convention who may still have objections to it would with me on this occasion doubt a little of his own [rightness] and, to make [clearly known] our [total agreement], put his name to this instrument.

George Mason of Virginia did not sign the Constitution. His objection to it is explained in a letter he wrote to George Washington on October 18, 1787.

There is no declaration of rights: (a bill of rights for individuals and states) and the laws of the general government being [higher than] the laws and constitutions of the several states, the declarations of rights in the separate states are no security.

Answer the following questions.
1. Which types of written primary sources are these selections?
2. What is Franklin's attitude toward the Constitution?
3. Why did Mason consider a declaration of rights important?
4. Which source would you consider to be more reliable? Why?

Forming a Union 155

City Sketches

CITY SKETCH
Washington, D.C. 1800-1825

The United States government moved to the new federal city of Washington in 1800. In that year, the young city was a clear example of the difference that can exist between dreams and reality. In the dreams of government leaders, Washington was a magnificent capital with lovely parks, beautiful public buildings, and grand avenues. In reality, it was a small village of rough fields, half-finished buildings, and muddy paths.

There had been years of debate in Congress over the location of the nation's capital. No state wanted any other state to have special influence over the federal government. Congress had met in eight different cities, four different states. Moving became more difficult as the quantity of needed records grew. A compromise was finally reached that settled the question of a permanent location for the capital city. When southerners agreed to let the federal government assume the state debts of the Revolution, northerners agreed to have the capital along the banks of the Potomac River.

Two states gave land to the government to form the federal District of Columbia. There, only Congress had control. The District was free of any single state's influence. The capital, built in the District, was available to people from the North, the South, and the rapidly growing West.

Plans

President Washington selected the French engineer, Pierre Charles L'Enfant, to design the federal city in 1791. L'Enfant had come to America to serve in the Revolution. He wanted very much to design a great capital for the new nation. And on paper, his plans for the city of Washington were beautiful. The survey work of marking the District's boundaries was done by Americans Andrew Ellicott and Benjamin Banneker. Banneker, a free black from Baltimore, was also an astronomer, mathematician, and scientist. The boundaries of the District of Columbia included the cities of George Town in Maryland and Alexandria in Virginia. The capital city itself was located next to George Town, on the Maryland side of the Potomac River. Later Alexandria and the lands across the Potomac were returned to Virginia.

L'Enfant planned Washington so that the three branches of the federal government were located in three separate areas of the

252 Washington, D.C.

The City Sketches appear at the end of each unit, before the unit review.

Some units have two City Sketches that can be compared and contrasted.

The City Sketches help to humanize history by blending primary source materials with author narrative.

---

city, according to their different constitutional duties. The building for the legislature, the Capitol, was on the highest point of land. A mile and a half away was the President's House, in the center of the executive area. From both of these, streets went out into the rest of the city. Pennsylvania Avenue was planned as a broad, stately connection between them. It would serve for ceremonial processions and would add dignity to the communication between the Congress and the President. The judicial building was in a third section of the city, away from the main areas of traffic. The different [ ] would be designed by different architects. By law, there could be no slave labor [ ] build the capital. Some slaves were [ ] to do this work and earned money for [ ] freedom.

Money Problems

President Washington and the [ ] sessions of Congress did not set aside [ ] money for building the city because [ ] thought it would pay for itself. Government leaders expected many people to [ ] the area and buy expensive lots [ ] homes and businesses. Profits from [ ] sales would be used to pay for [ ] streets and buildings. That idea did [ ]. Few people came to the city at first, [ ] fewer of them invested their money [ ] total number of people working [ ] federal government at that time [ ] small. It was not easy for others [ ] living in Washington. There was [ ] business in providing for the needs [ ] who worked for the government. Carpenters, stonemasons, and people in the [ ] trades even had difficulty finding steady [ ] Life in the new federal city was certain [ ]

254 Washington, D.C.

---

be satisfied and content, inconvenience. . . .

Determined as she [ ] mention some of the problems [ ] huge, unfinished house [ ] letters.

The house is upon a grand [ ] requiring about thirty servants [ ] keep the apartments in [ ] perform the ordinary business [ ] stables. . . . The lighting [the lamps] from the kitchen to parlors [ ] tax indeed [so may candles] . . . we are obliged to keep [fires to] secure us from daily agues [chills and fevers]. . . . bells [to call the servants are wholely] wanting, not one single [bell] hung through the whole house, and [these] are all you can obtain. This is so [great an] inconvenience, that I know not what [ ]

George Washington inspects the unfinished [President's] House with architect James Hoban. Who [wanted the] President to live in the White House? [ ]

During the War of 1812, 4,000 British soldiers [ ] and burned Washington. How did the burning [affect the] future growth of the city?

described the dangers of traveling [ ] Thomas Law, a friend, had built a [ ]

This out-of-the-way-house to which [ ] removed, was separated from the [in-] habited part of the city by fields [and] grounds broken up by deep gulleys [and] over which there was occasionally [a] road. The election of President being [then] was then pending, one vote given [ ] would decide the question between [Jeffer-] son and Mr. Burr. Mr. Bayard [of Delaware] held that vote. The different influential [ ] leading members [of Congress] were [often] given by Mr. Law. The night was [cold and] rainy, and on their attempt to return [the] coachman lost his way, and until day [break were] driving about this waste and broken [ground,] and if not overturned into the deep [gulleys,] momentarily in danger of being so, [ ] which would most probably have cost [ ] the gentlemen their lives, and as it is [ ]

256 Washington, D.C.

Bayard and three other members of Congress who had a leading and decisive influence in this difficult crisis of public affairs, the loss of either, might have turned the scales . . . and Mr. Burr [would have] been elected to the Presidency.

Slow Growth

Congress seldom provided funds for work on the public properties. The experiment of establishing a magnificent federal city seemed to be a failure. Political scientist James Sterling Young suggests that the main problem was a lack of interest on the part of most Americans in a government that was located out of their way.

For the government of Jefferson's day [ ] was not, by any candid [honest] view [ ] the important institutions in America [ ] city—important in a social presence [ ] important in its impact upon the everyday life [ ] of the citizens. It was, for one thing, [ ] an unfamiliar social presence in [ ] whose ways of living and whose organization [ ] of affairs had developed over a century [ ] any national governmental institution.

What government business there was [was] not, most of it, of a sort to attract [ ] widespread, sustained [long lasting] [ ] interest.

Growth was so slow for the capital [that] some people continued to believe [that the] federal government should move [to a] larger city. To many people, the burning of Washington's government buildings [by] British forces in 1814 seemed to be [a final] blow. Margaret Smith expressed the [feel-] ings in her writings:

Thursday. . . . This morning on [com-] ing we were greeted with the sad news [that our] city was taken, the bridges and public [buildings] burnt, our troops flying in every direction. [Our] little army totally dispersed [scattered]. . . . I do not suppose Government will ever return to Washington. All the [ ] property was invested in that place [is now] reduced to poverty. . . .

Tuesday [August] 30. Here we are, once more restored to our home. . . . The blast has passed by, without devastating this spot. . . . The poor capitol! nothing but its blackened walls remained! 4 or 5 houses in the neighborhood were likewise in ruins. . . . We afterwards looked at the other public buildings, but none were so thoroughly destroyed as the House of Representatives and the Presi-

The federal city in 1824 had many grand buildings like the Capitol. It also had many muddy streets. What problems faced lawmakers and their families from around the country who came to live and work in Washington?

begun on the center section, Washington still had no street lights, no sewer system, no city water system. Water was carried from wells in the center of the city or from the nearby creek. There were still open fields where cattle and hogs ran free. But there was a stronger feeling that the federal capital of Washington, D.C., was in place to stay.

John Quincy Adams moved into the White House just 25 years after his parents had lived in it. There was still no fence, but the grounds had been made smoother for walking. Most of the White House rooms were finished enough to be used. Louisa Adams, unlike Abigail, could use the great "audience-room" for public receptions instead of drying the family's clothes in it. A quarter of a century had passed since the government first moved to the District of Columbia. There was

still a very strong contrast between the original dream and the reality of the capital city, but a beginning had been made. Washington, as a city, would move a little closer to the dream in the years to come.

1. What was L'Enfant's plan for the capital city?
2. Name the main street which connects the Capitol building and the President's House.
3. How did Congress expect to pay for the building of the capital city?
4. Where did most of the lawmakers live during their stay in Washington?
5. How was Washington affected by the War of 1812?
6. Compare the President's House which Abigail Adams lived in to that of her daughter-in-law, Louisa Adams.

Washington, D.C.   257

Color-coded for easy reference.

Questions reinforce learning.

These features depict various aspects of the development of American urban life from the tiny Indian village of Secota to the sprawling megalopolis of Houston.

14T

Photographs and Cartoons

Numerous photographs and cartoons, most in full color, promote visual perception of ideas.

Captions identify photographs and cartoons.

This cartoon is titled "The Horse America, Throwing His Master." It was published in the 1770's. Do you think it was drawn by a British or colonial cartoonist? Why?

Parliament repealed the act in March 1766. British merchants complained that Americans had stopped buying their goods, and they pressured British officials to change the law. The boycott had worked. But the British government did not completely back down. Parliament passed the Declaratory Act which let the colonists know that the British government had the right to pass laws for the colonies in all cases.

1.4 The Townshend Acts.   Relations between Britain and the colonies began to improve until George III selected new advisors. In 1767, Charles Townshend, a member of the group, proposed a series of taxes that would help raise money from the colonies. These were the Townshend Acts. New naval courts were set up, and taxes were placed on lead, paper, paint, glass, and tea. Townshend also proposed that money collected be used to pay certain British officials in the colonies. In the past, these officials depended upon money voted to them by the colonial legislatures. Because the colonial legislatures controlled the salaries, they had a great deal of influence on British officials.

A new round of protests began over the passage of the Townshend Acts. New boycotts of British goods were started. Letters of protest were sent to Parliament. The Massachusetts legislature called for the other colonial legislatures to unite against the Townshend Acts. The colonists protested that they should not be taxed by Parliament since they were not represented there. They also viewed as dangerous the paying of officials with money raised from the new taxes.

As the conflicts between the British and the colonists increased, the American people divided into two groups. Those colonists who

What were the provisions of the Townshend Acts?

national government. With this plan, larger states would have more power.

The Virginia Plan showed clearly that many delegates were open to changing the structure of the government and not just revising the Articles of Confederation. But smaller states, like New Jersey, were against the Virginia Plan. New Jersey's William Paterson presented his own resolution. His plan, called the New Jersey Plan, insisted representation in the legislature remain the same as under the Articles. Each state would be represented equally.

2.2 The Great Compromise.   The issue of representation was a difficult one. It was settled by *compromise*—a settlement of differences by each side giving up part of what it wants. The delegates decided to have two houses of congress: the Senate and the House of Representatives. Each state was to have two Senators which were to be selected by its legislature. Small and large states, therefore, would be

What is a compromise?

As delegates signed the Constitution, Benjamin Franklin (center) observed a rising sun on the president's chair and a new day for the country. Not every delegate shared his view. Why did some delegates not sign the Constitution?

Caption questions relate the visual to the narrative.

156   Forming a Union

Graphics

A variety of full-color illustrations, including maps, tables, charts, graphs, and diagrams, correspond directly to the chapter narrative and visually reinforce concepts.

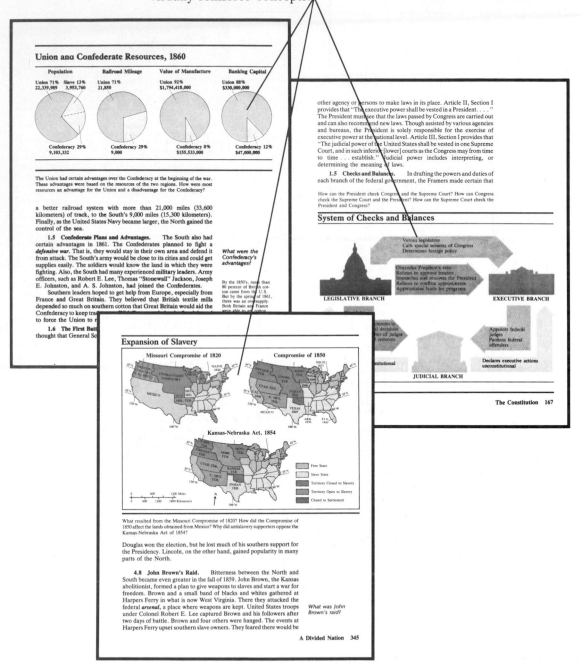

Union and Confederate Resources, 1860

Population	Railroad Mileage	Value of Manufacture	Banking Capital
Union 71% Slave 13% 22,339,989 3,953,760	Union 71% 21,850	Union 92% $1,794,418,000	Union 88% $330,000,000
Confederacy 29% 9,103,332	Confederacy 29% 9,000	Confederacy 8% $155,533,000	Confederacy 12% $47,000,000

The Union had certain advantages over the Confederacy at the beginning of the war. These advantages were based on the resources of the two regions. How were most resources an advantage for the Union and a disadvantage for the Confederacy?

a better railroad system with more than 21,000 miles (33,600 kilometers) of track, to the South's 9,000 miles (15,300 kilometers). Finally, as the United States Navy became larger, the North gained the control of the sea.

1.5 Confederate Plans and Advantages. The South also had certain advantages in 1861. The Confederates planned to fight a *defensive war*. That is, they would stay in their own area and defend it from attack. The South's army would be close to its cities and could get supplies easily. The soldiers would know the land in which they were fighting. Also, the South had many experienced military leaders. Army officers, such as Robert E. Lee, Thomas "Stonewall" Jackson, Joseph E. Johnston, and A. S. Johnston, had joined the Confederates.

Southern leaders hoped to get help from Europe, especially from France and Great Britain. They believed that British textile mills depended so much on southern cotton that Great Britain would aid the Confederacy to keep trade. . . .

1.6 The First Batt[le.] . . . thought that General Sc[ott] . . .

What were the Confederacy's advantages?

By the 1850's, more than 80 percent of British cotton came from the U.S. But by the spring of 1861, there was an oversupply. Both Britain and France were able to get cotton

other agency or persons to make laws in its place. Article II, Section I provides that "The executive power shall be vested in a President. . . ." The President must see that the laws passed by Congress are carried out and can also recommend new laws. Though assisted by various agencies and bureaus, the President is solely responsible for the exercise of executive power at the national level. Article III, Section I provides that "The judicial power of the United States shall be vested in one Supreme Court, and in such inferior [lower] courts as the Congress may from time to time . . . establish." Judicial power includes interpreting, or determining the meaning of laws.

1.5 Checks and Balances. In drafting the powers and duties of each branch of the federal government, the Framers made certain that

How can the President check Congress and the Supreme Court? How can Congress check the Supreme Court and the President? How can the Supreme Court check the President and Congress?

System of Checks and Balances

Vetoes legislation
Calls special sessions of Congress
Determines foreign policy

Overrules President's veto
Impeaches and removes the President
Refuses to approve treaties
Refuses to confirm appointments
Appropriates funds for programs

LEGISLATIVE BRANCH

EXECUTIVE BRANCH

[...]ndments to [...]l decisions [...]er of judges [...] removes

Appoints federal judges
Pardons federal offenders

[...]nstitutional

Declares executive actions unconstitutional

JUDICIAL BRANCH

The Constitution   167

Expansion of Slavery

Missouri Compromise of 1820

Compromise of 1850

Kansas-Nebraska Act, 1854

	Free State
	Slave State
	Territory Closed to Slavery
	Territory Open to Slavery
	Closed to Settlement

What resulted from the Missouri Compromise of 1820? How did the Compromise of 1850 affect the lands obtained from Mexico? Why did antislavery supporters oppose the Kansas-Nebraska Act of 1854?

Douglas won the election, but he lost much of his southern support for the Presidency. Lincoln, on the other hand, gained popularity in many parts of the North.

4.8 John Brown's Raid. Bitterness between the North and South became even greater in the fall of 1859. John Brown, the Kansas abolitionist, formed a plan to give weapons to slaves and start a war for freedom. Brown and a small band of blacks and whites gathered at Harpers Ferry in what is now West Virginia. There they attacked the federal *arsenal*, a place where weapons are kept. United States troops under Colonel Robert E. Lee captured Brown and his followers after two days of battle. Brown and four others were hanged. The events at Harpers Ferry upset southern slave owners. They feared there would be

What was John Brown's raid?

A Divided Nation   345

Epilogue

The Epilogue provides a concise wrap-up for the students to this course of American history by outlining some of the major changes which have occurred in the development of the American nation.

Epilogue

The Epilogue provides a concise wrap-up for the students to this course of American history by outlining some of the major changes which have occurred in the development of the American nation.

For nearly 400 years, Americans experienced periods of political, economic, and social change. In spite of enormous challenges, they adapted to preserve a spirit of independence and to protect an ideal for democratic government.

During the 1600's and 1700's, most Americans lived on farms of varying size scattered along the Atlantic coast of North America. Colonial life centered around small villages and towns. Only a few larger cities served as trade centers. From this rural, agrarian society came one nation in 1776. With the Constitution, life in America reorganized around federal and state capitals, and concerns slowly became more national.

By the early 1800's, not only was American political life changing but also American economic life was changing. Labor that had been done mostly by hand or animal power was being done with the force of steam. By the 1900's, electricity and gasoline power provided the force to drive machines. Steamboats, trains, automobiles, and airplanes became the products of a continuing industrial revolution in the United States.

As the United States aged, it grew dramatically. The lure of the country's natural resources—land, lumber, water, minerals—drew more people to the United States and across the continent that the country occupied. Total population rose, the number of cities increased, and American life continued to change. From a small, rural republic, the United States grew into an industrial giant with worldwide influence and concerns.

The attitudes of the American people kept pace with the physical expansion of the country. Americans believed progress and opportunity were unlimited. By the twentieth century, Americans called for equality for all people. Many thought that it was within the power of the United States to abolish poverty, wipe out hunger and disease, and see that all people were secure in their old age. They sought an American dream for the world.

But continued opportunity had its challenges. Midway through the twentieth century, perhaps signaled by the explosion of the atomic bomb in 1945, the United States entered a new phase. After a history of plenty, Americans began to experience scarcity. Once again the American people have had to adapt to preserve and protect their ideals and principles to the realities of a changing world.

436

Appendix

Includes an Atlas with full-color reference maps and a graphics section that provides data on the American population, society, political system, and economy.

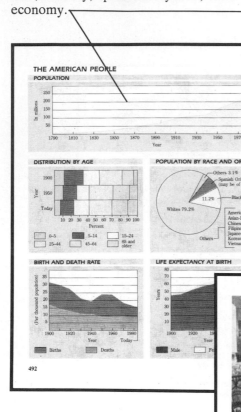

THE AMERICAN PEOPLE
POPULATION

In millions
Year: 1790 1810 1830 1850 1870 1890 1910 1930 1950 1970 Today.

DISTRIBUTION BY AGE

Year: 1900, 1950, Today
Percent: 10 20 30 40 50 60 70 80 90 100

- 0–5
- 5–14
- 15–24
- 25–44
- 45–64
- 65 and older

POPULATION BY RACE AND ORIGIN

Others 3.1%
Spanish Origin 6.5% (may be of any race)
Whites 79.2%
11.2% — Blacks

Others —
American Indian
Asian-Indian
Chinese
Filipino
Japanese
Korean
Vietnamese

BIRTH AND DEATH RATE

(Per thousand population)
1900 1920 1940 1960 1980 Today.
Year

- Births
- Deaths

LIFE EXPECTANCY AT BIRTH

Years
1900 1920 19

- Male
- Fe

492

MINERAL RESOURCES AND DEPOSITS

Aluminum
Anthracite Coal
Bituminous Coal
Bauxite
Beryllium
Chromium
Cobalt
Copper
Gold
Iron Ore
Lead
Magnesium
Manganese

Mercury   Nickel   Sulphur   Uranium
Molybdenum   Oil   Tin   Vanadium
Natural Gas   Silver   Tungsten   Zinc

INDUSTRY AND MANUFACTURING

Aerospace
Apparel
Chemicals and Allied Products
Electric and Electronic Equipment
Fabricated Metal Products
Food Processing
Furniture
Iron and Steel
Lumber and Wood Products
Machinery
Paper Products
Petroleum and Coal Products
Primary Metals Industry
Printing and Publishing
Rubber and Plastic Products
Stone, Clay and Glass Products
Textiles
Tourism
Transportation Equipment

Manufacturing Value, 1980
$10 Billion
$20 Billion
$30 Billion
$40 Billion
More than $40 Billion

491

A selection of Readings, based on primary and secondary sources, corresponds directly to the narrative of the text and provides added insight into the politics, culture, and life of the United States.

the Constitution is void and that courts, as well as other departments, are bound by that instrument.

From William Cranch, ed., *Reports of Cases Argued and Adjudged in the Supreme Court of the United States* (Washington, D.C.: Government Printing Office, 1804), Vol. 1, p. 137.

Questions

1. According to Chief Justice John Marshall, what is the duty of the judicial department?

2. If a law conflicts with the Constitution, which will be supported by the Supreme Court?

3. How does judicial review check the power of the executive and legislative branches of the United States government?

UNIT III
Democracy

Testing the New Government   8

Washington's First Inaugural

George Washington became President of the United States on April 30, 1789. The first President under the Constitution was inaugurated in New York, the temporary capital of the new government. One of the many witnesses to the events of that day was Pennsylvania Senator William Maclay. He recorded his observations in a diary, from which the following passage is taken.

The President was conducted out of the middle window into the gallery [overlooking Wall Street], and the oath was administered by the Chancellor [the highest judicial officer in the state of New York]. Notice that the business done was communicated to the crowd by proclamation, etc., who gave three cheers, and repeated it on the President's bowing to them.

George Washington takes the presidential oath.

to the law, disregarding the Constitution, or conformably to the Constitution, disregarding the law, the court must determine which of these conflicting rules governs the case. This is of the very essence of judicial duty. If, then, the courts are to regard the Constitution, and the Constitution is superior to any ordinary act of the legislature, the Constitution, and not such ordinary act, must govern the case to which they both apply. . . .

It is also not entirely unworthy of observation that in declaring what shall be the supreme law of the land, the Constitution itself is first mentioned, and not the laws of the United States generally, but those only which shall be made in pursuance of the Constitution have that rank.

Thus, the particular phraseology of the Constitution of the United States confirms and strengthens the principle, supposed to be essential to all written constitutions, that a law repugnant to

458 Readings

Program Use

Introducing the Text

Besides the teacher, the students' most important classroom aid in the study of history is the textbook. Students should be familiar with the layout of the text so that they can make the best possible use of its content. A class reading and discussion of the **Preface** is one way to introduce students to the text design. The order of information in the Preface carries students through an explanation of the various parts of the text. As sections of the Preface are read in class, cite examples of each item mentioned, and have the students turn to them in their texts. Reading through the **Table of Contents** may also be helpful in showing the organization of 16 chapters in five units of study. For a more thorough examination of a rationale for the study of American history, use the **Prologue**, and lead the students in a discussion. The Prologue serves as an introduction to the text content. The **Epilogue** at the end of the text sums up the course.

Encourage the students to be familiar with the **Appendix** as a reference source. In it, the **Readings** section contains letters, diaries, songs, newspaper and magazine articles, and excerpts from historical documents, speeches, and other narratives; the **Atlas** provides map resources and historical data in a graphics format; the **Declaration of Independence** outlines the guiding philosophy for the creation of the United States; and the annotated **Constitution of the United States** presents the American plan of government with explanation.

At the end of the book, the **Glossary** provides an overview of the main terms used in the text, and the **Index** locates topics or people of continuing concern through different time periods.

Setting the Scene

The chapters of the text are grouped into five units which divide the course content into manageable parts. Each unit is organized around a theme reflecting an important concept appropriate to the period under study. Set the scene for each unit to prepare students for the information to be gained in the chapters. Use the **Unit Openings** to introduce students to the who, what, when, and where facts of the period. Unit Openings contain pictures—paintings, drawings, photographs, and original artwork—representing major social, economic, and political concerns. Each Unit Opening also contains an introductory paragraph explaining the unit theme.

For each chapter, there is also an opening. A colorful **Chapter Opener** to the material sets the tone for reading the narrative with an illustration, caption, and caption question.

Using the Text

Before assigning chapter material, consider the type of reading involved. Determine the quantity most appropriate for the reading abilities of the students. Decide the order in which the students are to read such material as chapter narratives, biographical profiles, skill features, concept features, and city sketches. Also instruct students to study any illustrations within the assigned material.

The *United States History* content is presented in a lively narrative style designed to maintain student interest. It has a controlled reading level, using both the Dale-Chall and Fry reading formulas for level consistency. Special elements within the narrative help students to read with understanding and retention. **Key Terms** appear in boldface type and are defined in context when first introduced. Chapter organization consists of **Numbered Sections** and **Subsections.** Throughout the narrative, marginal **Student Notes** in the form of questions indicate important information to be learned. They should help students to know the key points being made. Encourage students to read section and subsection headings and student notes before and after reading the chapter narrative. This can serve as a preview to the material as well as a review.

United States History contains biographical **Profiles** of famous and not-so-famous people in American history. Some Profiles feature the lives of two people for comparison. There is no Profile for Chapter 1 because of the limited specific information about individuals living in America before the arrival of Europeans in the fifteenth century. Students should be aware that the Profiles are consistent with unit and chapter themes and content.

In each of the chapters, there is a color-coded skill or concept feature. The **Skill Features** provide the means for using the students' understanding of history by performing tasks common to the social studies. The **Concept Features** abstract generalizations about history through the examination of specific events.

There are **City Sketches** in the textbook. Found at the end of each unit, these color-coded features depict various aspects of the development of American urban life from the tiny Indian village of Secota to the sprawling megalopolis of Houston. These sketches relate to the unit theme and chapter material.

Chapter content—including the chapter narratives, biographical profiles, skill features, concept features, and city sketches—contains many **Primary**

Sources, firsthand accounts of American history. Students may need preparation regarding the quoted material before it is assigned for reading. Quoted material is recognized by its quotation marks, indented blocks of type, or blocks of italic type. Ellipses [which are sets of periods . . .] indicate material deleted, and brackets [like this] contain definitions for preceding words. Students may need some practice reading quoted material, and hearing the teacher read some of it could help them to grasp the proper technique. Some students can be assigned larger portions of quoted material from the original sources found in the **Acknowledgements.**

Along with primary sources, there are also numerous paintings, drawings, and photographs to illustrate the material. Students are introduced to interpreting them in the Skill Feature "Analyzing Pictures" in Chapter 2.

Pictorial illustrations in *United States History* offer a sampling of the development of painting, drawing, and photography during the course of United States history. **Paintings** include examples from John White's watercolors of Secota to Aaron Douglas's mural. **Drawings** also capture the emotions of life at times during American history. Significant **Photographs** include daguerreotypes from the early 1800's to color pictures of the moon. Encourage students to be familiar with not only the picture and its meaning but also the producer of the picture. Students can locate the sources of many of the pictures by using the listing of **Photo Credits.**

In addition to pictures, there are many other kinds of illustrations in *United States History*. These include **Maps, Tables, Pie Graphs, Bar Graphs, Line Graphs, Flow Charts, Skewed Diagrams,** and **Charts.** There are **Skill Exercises** for using these illustrations. They are included in the end-of-chapter material as an aid in sharpening geography and social studies skills that are so necessary for understanding history. Each map exercise emphasizes a different aspect of map work or reinforces a learned skill. Collectively, they provide a base for understanding the physical characteristics of the land and how maps are used to illustrate history. Throughout the book, there are over 50 maps that contain scale, directionals, longitude/latitude indicators, and color to highlight key subject material. Several Skill Exercises are provided to help students develop an ability to gain and understand information from the study of charts, tables, graphs, and diagrams. These appear in Chapters 7, 12, and 15.

Reviewing Content_____

For each chapter assignment, the teacher can determine the exact material to be learned. There are **Feature Questions** offered within each skill or concept feature. For the chapter content, illustration **Caption Questions, Chapter Section Questions,** and **Chapter Reviews** are included. Chapter Reviews contain five sections which summarize the **Main Points** of the chapter material and ask students to **Build Vocabulary** by identifying key people, places, laws, treaties, and organizations and by defining key words and terms; to check their abilities for **Remembering the Facts** presented in the narrative; to check their abilities for **Understanding the Facts** in relation to other facts and trends; and to sharpen their skills in **Using Maps, Using Diagrams, Using Line Graphs, Using Pie Graphs, Using Bar Graphs,** and **Using Tables.** Encourage students to look over the feature, caption, section, and review questions before they begin assignments to give sharper focus and direction to their reading.

For each unit, review material is given under the title **Unit Review.** Each Unit Review contains a **Time Line** depicting a chronology of key events in the unit on the right side and presidential administrations and ratification dates of constitutional amendments on the left side. Students are introduced to time lines in the Skill Feature "Reading Time Lines" in Chapter 3. Unit Time Lines aid in the students' development of a sense of events happening within a time perspective. The information given on the Time Lines is only from that material considered in the unit. This explains why certain events, and presidential administrations in particular, are not repeated for the same time period in different units.

The Unit Reviews contain **Summary Points** providing brief statements on the major unit trends and events. **Unit Questions** relate to material appearing in different chapters in the unit and are keyed to the understanding of the unit aims. **Suggested Activities** in the Unit Reviews are intended to enrich student learning and supplement the unit material. These individual and group activities can be used when they fit the resources available and should be structured to conform to the needs of the students. Some of these activities require more direction than others, including instruction on where to find the required information. Some sources are included in the list of **Suggested Readings,** also part of the Unit Review material. For other sources, students may need to know how to use the resources of the school or local library.

References to skills used in *United States History: Beginnings Through Reconstruction*

Social Studies Skills

	Introduction	Chapter 1	Chapter 2	Chapter 3	Chapter 4	Chapter 5	Chapter 6	Chapter 7	Chapter 8	Chapter 9	Chapter 10	Chapter 11	Chapter 12	Chapter 13	Chapter 14	Chapter 15	Chapter 16	Conclusion
Understanding Map Projections	●																	
Reading the Chapter		●																
Analyzing Pictures			●															
Reading Time Lines				●														
Checking Points of View					●													
Reading Primary and Secondary Sources						●												
Analyzing Sources of History							●											
Recognizing Main Ideas									●									
Reading for Detail											●							
Checking Fact and Opinion													●					
Asking Questions																●		
Drawing Conclusions																	●	

Social Studies Concepts

	Introduction	Chapter 1	Chapter 2	Chapter 3	Chapter 4	Chapter 5	Chapter 6	Chapter 7	Chapter 8	Chapter 9	Chapter 10	Chapter 11	Chapter 12	Chapter 13	Chapter 14	Chapter 15	Chapter 16	Conclusion
Responsibility								●										
Nationalism										●								
Creativity												●						
Mobility														●				
Sectionalism															●			
Pluralism																		●

Using Maps, Diagrams, and Graphs

	Introduction	Chapter 1	Chapter 2	Chapter 3	Chapter 4	Chapter 5	Chapter 6	Chapter 7	Chapter 8	Chapter 9	Chapter 10	Chapter 11	Chapter 12	Chapter 13	Chapter 14	Chapter 15	Chapter 16	Conclusion
Directions	●								●									
Reference Maps		●																
Thematic Maps			●														●	●
Longitude and Latitude				●										●				
Keys and Legends					●													
Tracing Routes						●				●								
Scale							●											
Reading Diagrams								●										
Demographic Maps												●						
Using Line Graphs													●					
Comparing Maps											●				●			
Reading Pie Graphs																●		

Supplementing the Text

A **Teacher's Resource Book** supplements the material and skill exercises provided in the textbook. The components of the **Teacher's Resource Book** are:

1. **Teacher Lecture Notes:** an outline of content based on the heading structure of the text and a section-by-section commentary.
2. **Outline Maps:** a selection of maps that may be duplicated and used for a variety of map exercises.
3. **Exercises and Activities:** worksheets that may be duplicated and used to provide additional analytical practice for the students. These activities particularly reinforce the chapter contents of the text and offer development exercises under such titles as "The Chapter in Brief," "Working With Maps," "Working With Charts," "Elements of History," and "You and History."
4. **Evaluation:** quizzes and tests that provide an objective basis for evaluating student progress that can be combined with the teacher's own more subjective methods of evaluation. The tests include chapter quizzes and unit examinations. Test items include true and false, multiple choice, chronological order, fill-in, and using skills questions.
5. **Audiovisual Listings:** a selection of materials from a wide variety of media.

Teaching the Course

To aid in planning classroom presentation, the **Teacher's Annotated Edition** of *United States History* consists of a **Teacher's Guide** bound into an annotated printing of the student text. The blue-printed, marginal annotations suggest a point to be emphasized, provide additional historical information, indicate references to similar material in other parts of the text, and point out recurring themes presented in the text. Other annotations are used to explain the various elements of the student text.

The Teacher's Guide in the Teacher's Annotated Edition is divided into five major sections—Introduction, Program Use, General Teaching Methods, Teaching Strategies, and Reading List.

The **Introduction** serves to acquaint teachers with the program rationale, objectives, and components. Because the student text is the most important component, its main features are explained and illustrated with sample pages.

The **Program Use** section lists and explains in further detail the elements of the program and how to use them.

The **General Teaching Methods** section is a "how to" section, providing guidelines for several strategies that are particularly effective in teaching American history. For example, it may be of value to have students debate historically significant issues. This section gives guidelines for conducting debates.

Teaching Strategies include a section for each unit with learning objectives, an analysis of the unit opener, suggestions for how to use the unit review, additional unit projects, and suggested responses for unit review questions; a section for each chapter with learning objectives, teaching ideas, including how to present and use the Profile and Skill and Concept Features, and suggested responses for feature questions, caption questions, chapter section questions, and chapter review questions; and a section for each City Sketch with learning objectives, teaching ideas, and responses for the questions.

The **Reading List** section includes a suggested reading list for teachers with titles of books, series, periodicals, and reference works that the teacher can use throughout the course. An annotated student reading list of fiction and nonfiction books written for an advanced elementary and junior high school reading level is also included. This list supplements the titles given in the Suggested Readings section of the Unit Reviews.

Evaluating the Student

A teacher evaluates a student in order to determine the degree to which learning objectives have been achieved and to know more about the student as an individual. Evaluation for appraisal of academic achievement and for diagnosis of learning difficulties can be in the form of prepared tests or informal questioning. Both can be written or oral. The **Teacher's Resource Book** evaluation section provides written tests for formal evaluation. The student text provides sufficient feature, caption, chapter section, chapter review, and unit review questions to informally evaluate the student. These questions can be used during class to provide a motivator for discussion or as part of a method of review.

Evaluating the Program

Perhaps one of the best ways to ensure that effective learning-teaching materials are produced is to let authors and publishers know how the classroom teacher feels about the ones currently in use. Please help in the planning of revisions and new programs by completing and mailing the form found on the last two pages of the Teacher's Guide. After removing the *United States History* **Survey Form** from the book, fold and staple it so that the Charles E. Merrill Publishing Company label shows. The authors and publishers appreciate hearing from you.

General Teaching Methods

The following strategies are designed to reinforce or supplement the teaching ideas provided in the Teaching Strategies section. They are especially suitable for enhancing more active student participation in the study of history.

Brainstorming

Brainstorming involves students in a free and open exchange of ideas. Besides generating ideas about a particular topic or problem, brainstorming fosters student creativity and thinking. When brainstorming is used prior to a reading activity, it gives students ideas to look for in their reading and thus enhances reading comprehension. It is an activity in which all students can participate, regardless of academic ability.

To conduct a brainstorming session, follow these suggestions:

1. Set aside a limited amount of time and keep up the pace.
2. Allow students to say anything that comes to mind and jot it on the chalkboard.
3. Do not criticize ideas, be receptive.
4. Try to lead students to build upon other's ideas.

Audiovisual Materials

Audiovisual materials include films, filmstrips, tapes, records, cassettes, picture files, cartoon files and maps. Literally thousands of materials are available commercially, and many can be created by teachers and students. These materials may provide an overview of major historical eras and events as well as indepth study of an important concept or theme. They are especially suitable for students who have difficulty reading. At the same time, they reinforce concepts and information for others.

When teachers use films and filmstrips, it is useful to keep some suggestions of audiovisual educational experts in mind:

1. Always preview the material. Look for major ideas and ways to tie in these ideas with previously-covered topics.
2. Place on the chalkboard or in a handout the major ideas or names of which you want students to be aware. Tell the students to watch for this information. Most audiovisual specialists advise students *not* to take notes during the presentation of the film or filmstrip.
3. Debrief the class using your list of names and ideas. This is the point at which students should take notes. Here the whole class can participate, with

the teacher addressing questions with simple or more obvious answers to slower students. In this manner, all of the students are reinforced for paying attention.

Visual materials (tables, maps, graphs, cartoons, etc.) are also an important part of modern textbooks. They break up the print and reduce the reading level, but they also supplement the narrative. The teaching ideas in this manual frequently focus the teacher's attention on these valuable resources. Often students will be asked to *analyze* a visual. The teacher may aid the students in their analyses by directing them through the following steps:

1. Note details.
2. Look for relationships between details.
3. Draw inferences or generalizations from these relationships.
4. Make a statement summarizing these inferences or generalizations.

Games and Simulations

Games and simulations are techniques which require active student participation. For this reason, advocates declare that better learning takes place. Gaming and simulation are actually separate dimensions of the same student-oriented technique. They may be combined in simulation games. [1]

Games. The most simple game is the learning game. In the case of the learning game, a student plays a game to win—there are specific rules and procedures—but needs no prior knowledge. The student learns new information by playing the game. One such game teaches students how bills become laws. A simple board game, it requires the student to advance his or her piece, representing a bill, by the roll of the die. Pitfalls abound, however, on the path from introduction to signature by the President, as the bill might be "pigeon-holed," "vetoed," or meet a similar fate. If the bill lands on a space with one of these pitfalls, the student must return to start. By playing the game, the student becomes familiar with the steps in the legislative process.

A little more sophisticated is the instructional game. This type of game combines competition and rules with drill and practice. The students must know a certain amount of information, and the game drills them on this knowledge. Any number of popular games or sports have been adapted to the classroom for instructional gaming. The title of the old "Who, What, and Where" game suggests the suitability of these activities for history drill. In each adaptation, the class is divided into teams and that team accumulating the higher (or highest) number of correct answers wins.

Simulations. The most basic component of simulations is role-playing. In role-playing, students assume the role of another person in the reenactment of

---

[1]For a complete discussion of these techniques, see Ron Stadsklev, *Handbook of Simulation Gaming in Social Education* (Institute of Higher Education Research and Services, The University of Alabama, 1974).

an historical event or problem. Make sure students playing roles have enough background information to accurately portray their individual's opinions. Do not let the role-play drag on. Stop it when you feel the crucial points have been covered or when students "run out of gas." Have the whole class review the major points made.

A more sophisticated form of simulation is the "social simulation." The social simulation combines role-playing with a forum for social interaction and decision-making. In designing a social simulation, the teacher should take the following steps:[2]

1. Select a problem or issue with alternative solutions.
2. Determine simulated groups, their positions, and how the class decision will be made.
3. Provide students with background information or allow them time for its development.
4. Provide some forum in which the various groups will present their cases. Have the class (or decision-making group) make its decision based upon these presentations.
5. Establish limits for behavior, time, research activities, etc.

A social simulation might be devised around an historical issue such as the Senate's consideration of the Versailles Treaty after World War I. The class could be the Senate divided into a number of positions. Two obvious positions would be isolationists and supporters of Wilson and the concept of a League of Nations. The class as a whole would vote to ratify or reject the treaty.

Simulation Games. Simulation games combine all the features of the previously mentioned activities. As such, they are time-consuming to produce. A great number, however, are available commercially and should be considered.

Debate

Debating involves students in orally defending and/or attacking viewpoints on a specific topic, theory, or principle. The goal of each debater is to convince others that his or her position is either correct or the most persuasive. The process helps students gain skill in using structured oral communication to persuade others to change their positions or points of view. Debating may be a one-on-one or a group activity. Either way, the whole class can be involved because students who do not take part directly in the debate are still involved in the learning process as they listen to new information, consider the arguments, make judgments about the quality of the presentations, and come to decisions about a conclusion.

To initiate the debate, select a topic or issue about which there is a diversity of opinion. Have students indicate their positions on the issue, and

---

[2]Adapted from Jo Michalski, "Developing A Social Simulation, 'The Land Use Simulation'" in *Handbook of Simulation Gaming in Social Education* (Institute of Higher Education Research and Services, The University of Alabama, 1974).

then divide them into groups according to position or viewpoint. Explain that each group will have a certain amount of time in which to present its views and the justification for those views to the rest of the class. Allow each group time to analyze and solidify its position and prepare the strongest and most valid arguments possible. This will probably require additional reading or research.

Give each group (or a spokesperson for each group) an opportunity to present its argument, allowing for rebuttal. As arguments can get heated, it is best to set a specific time frame within which all argument and discussion must be contained. After each viewpoint has been debated, survey the class to determine if the debate has led any students to change their position on the issue.

Case Studies

A case study is used to supplement material in the text by focusing on a particular problem, topic, or issue for which alternative solutions or courses of action existed. Students should take the following steps:

1. Identify the problem or conflict situation.
2. Review (analyze and evaluate) alternative positions or courses of action. Here the teacher may want to use a range of materials, including primary (anthologies of documents are readily available) and secondary sources.
3. Choose a course of action or position and develop a defense of that position or course.
4. Present their positions orally or in writing.

Case studies are especially useful if teachers want their students to practice inquiry and higher-level thinking skills. This strategy may be implemented any time there is an issue or conflict to be considered.

Teaching Strategies

Educational objectives and ideas for motivating lessons make up this teaching strategies section. **Learning Objectives** are written in terms of actions that the student should exhibit if the listed objectives are achieved. Each list includes goals for content knowledge and understanding, as well as for Skill Features, Concept Features, and Using Map and Graph exercises. **Teaching Ideas** stress actions for the teacher in order to motivate student learning. The teaching ideas given are suggestions for covering content in *United States History: Beginnings Through Reconstruction.* Teachers should choose and adapt those which are most appropriate to their situations and set up their own specific lesson plans to fit individual teaching styles.

Introduction *(The Land)*

Learning Objectives
The student should be able to:

1. name the major physical regions of the United States.
2. describe the geographic characteristics of each region.
3. describe the influence of the Ice Age on the Western Hemisphere.
4. identify the original home and the route taken by the first people in the Western Hemisphere.

Teaching Ideas

- Distribute to each student an outline map of the United States showing the present states. Explain to students that the states are shown only for purposes of helping them get a better sense of where various places are located and that the state divisions did not exist at the time. Discuss the geographic features of each of the physical regions as they are dealt with in the textbook. As each region is discussed students should identify and mark it on their outline maps.

- Draw a straight line on the chalkboard that is five or six feet long. Ask students to think of it as a line stretching between the Pacific and Atlantic Oceans at sea level (36 degrees north latitude). Refer to a large physical wall map of the United States, point out the imaginary line of 36 degrees north latitude, and ask students to provide information which you can use to draw a second line that reflects the distance, or elevation, above sea level (above the straight line) or below sea level (below the straight line) encountered by a person traveling across this country by foot, car, or boat at 36 degrees latitude. When finished relate the areas reflected to the various physical regions previously discussed. This exercise might be repeated with lines representing 40 degrees north latitude or 30 degrees north latitude to show that as one moves north or south the physical features will differ slightly.

Answers

Page 2: *(illustration)* Each physical region, with its own geographical character, has allowed the American people to develop a varied culture based on survival in that region.

Page 4: *(illustration)* The Interior Plains.

Page 6: *(illustration)* North Carolina and Tennessee.

Page 7: *(illustration)* Minor landforms include valleys, deltas, sandy beaches, peninsulas, bays, and bayous.

Page 9: *(illustration)* The soil is made up of chernozem and a mixture of chernozem and podzol.

Page 10: *(illustration)* Bryce Canyon is located in the Intermontane Plateaus and Basins region. Big Sur is located in the Pacific Coastal Ranges region.

Page 11:
1. The Coastal Plains, the Appalachian Highlands, the Interior Plains, the Interior Highlands, the Rocky Mountains, the Intermontane Plateaus and Basins, and the Pacific Coastal Ranges.
2. Mississippi River.
3. The forty-eight states of the United States that share a common boundary. Alaska and Hawaii are not included when using this term.

Page 12: *(illustration)* The Southeast—southern Florida, the Southwest—southern Texas, the West Coast—central and southern California.

Page 13: Skill Feature *(Understanding Map Projections)*
1. Land masses differ in shapes and sizes due to projection distortion.
2. Asia, Australia, Greenland
3. Because of the projection distortion.
4. The Mercator projection (page 51).
5. Cylindrical projection—advantage, can show large land areas on a small map; disadvantage, distortion of size and shape is greater in the far northern and far southern latitudes. Concial projection—advantage, has less distortion than the cylindrical projection map, good for regional maps especially around the middle latitudes; disadvantage, limiting in use.

Page 14: Plants vary due to the altitude. Broadleaf deciduous trees are found at low elevations, whereas, needle leaf conifers are found in higher elevations. Tundra grasses and mosses grow on the high mountain tops.
The dry desert areas have sparse vegetation, consisting largely of scrub grasses and desert plants like cactus.

Page 15:
1. Tropical moist climates; dry climates; moist, mild winter climates; moist, cold winter climates; polar climates.
2. Due to different latitudes and variations in altitude.
3. Because the Rocky Mountains block moisture from the west.

Page 16:   *(illustration)* The oceans were lower, more land was exposed such as the land bridge that connected Asia with North America.

Page 17:   1. Between Asia and North America now covered by the Bering Strait.
2. Radiocarbon dating.
3. Asian people from Mongolia.

Page 18:   Chapter Review *(Remembering the Facts)*
1. 1,606 miles (2,585 kilometers); 2,898 miles (4664 kilometers).
2. The northern shoreline has many natural harbors whereas the southern shoreline has fewer natural harbors with more sandy beaches.
3. Missouri and Mississippi Rivers; the Interior Plains.
4. The Central Plains and the Great Plains.
5. The Rockies are higher in elevation. The Rockies are to the west of the Appalachian Highlands.
6. The Superior Highlands and the Ozark Plateau.
7. Eight—The Northeast, Southeast, Midwest, Great Plains, Southwest, West Coast, Alaska, and Hawaii.
8. Its varied latitudes and altitudes.
9. The Southeast, Southwest, and the West Coast.
10. Tens of thousands of years ago.

Page 19:   Chapter Review *(Understanding the Facts)*
1. Many differences exist including the low flat lands of the eastern coastal plains, the low mountains and high hills of the Appalachian Highlands, swamps and marshes of southern Florida in the Coastal Plain region, the high-level plains of the Interior region, the high mountains of the Rockies, the canyons and plateaus of the Intermontane region, and the desert conditions with below sea level elevation in California.
2. The American people have had to adapt their living styles according to the physical surroundings. Many examples can be listed.
3. The east coast rises from the water level with a plain landform whereas the west coast has a rocky, rugged coast line that rises from the water level with high cliffs and little beach areas.
4. One, the Ice Age provided the means to travel by way of the land bridge; and two, the Ice Age forced the people to travel in order for them to find food and survive.
5. As their homelands began to dry up, the animals there moved away to find food, and so the first Americans also went searching for food.
6. By studying and measuring the radiocarbon left in remains, the scientists can estimate the age of the remains.

Page 19:   Chapter Review *(Using Maps)*
1. West.
2. East.
3. South.
4. South or Southeast.
5. Southwest.
6. North.

Unit I—Opportunity

Learning Objectives

The student should be able to:

1. name various kinds of opportunities available to people who came to the Western Hemisphere.
2. describe how and why various groups of people came to the Western Hemisphere over time and where each group chose to live.
3. identify the effects of the arrival of Europeans in the fifteenth century on the people living in the Western Hemisphere.

Teaching Ideas

● Write the word OPPORTUNITY on the chalkboard. Ask students what the word means to them, and list their responses. Discuss how different degrees of opportunity can be available to different people, how different opportunities can exist at different times, and how different views of opportunity can cause conflict between groups of people.

● Read the unit opening paragraph to the class, and have the students look carefully at the illustration (pages 20-21). The illustration is a rendering of the first Thanksgiving Day, celebrated at Plymouth, Massachusetts in 1621. The painting shows Indians and Pilgrims, and children as well as men and women, gathered as a Pilgrim gives thanks. The land beyond them is vast and unrestricted. Discuss with the students how this illustration represents the concept OPPORTUNITY.

● After study of the unit, discuss the word OPPORTUNITY again in light of the unit of study. Use the Unit Review (pages 96-97) to conclude the teaching of the unit and prepare students for the unit test.

Chapter 1 *(The First Americans)*

Learning Objectives

The student should be able to:

1. outline the chapter as an aid to reading with understanding.
2. describe the way early people came to live in the Western Hemisphere over long periods of time.
3. describe the effects of environment and agriculture on the way people lived.
4. identify various groups of early people in the Western Hemisphere.
5. distinguish among various cultures in different parts of the Western Hemisphere.
6. identify and read a reference map.

Teaching Ideas

● Write the word HISTORY on the chalkboard, and ask the students to define it. When a clear definition has been developed, identify this word as an important term which will be useful in understanding this and future chapters. The definition of history should imply that it is concerned with people, time, and place, and students should approach its study with the questions who, when, and where in mind. When those answers are known, students should consider other questions—how, why, and with what result. Lead the students through the exercise outlined in the Skill Feature, "Reading the Chapter" (page 27). Students should be encouraged to use it in all their reading.

- Draw a long line the length of the chalkboard. Label the line PEOPLE ON EARTH. Label the left end point THE FIRST PEOPLE and the right end point TODAY. Very close to the right end point, put a slash, labeling it 1776. Several inches from 1776, yet a great distance from THE FIRST PEOPLE, draw a slash, labeling it LAND BRIDGE. Explain that the period of United States history is very short when compared to the time people have lived on the earth, and that the period of time since the land bridge migration is also relatively short. Discuss where people lived before the land bridge migration and why they moved. Explain the idea that there was a continuous migration of people over Asia from the time of the first people on the earth until people reached the Western Hemisphere and spread throughout the Americas.

- Write the word FOOD on the chalkboard, and ask the students how they get the food they eat. Trace the line of food suppliers back to farmers. Ask the students where people got their food before there were farms. Discuss the advantages and disadvantages of hunting and gathering and the planned growing of food, agriculture. Discuss the benefits of a reliable food source. Review the pertinent materials in the text about the Mayan, Aztec, and Inca civilizations in Middle and South America.

- Ask the students what class would be like without the school building. Ask what would happen if the weather unexpectedly changed. Discuss why shelter is necessary. Have the students list the types of shelters mentioned in Section 3 (pages 30-39). Also have them list where these shelters were found and who were the people who made them. Discuss the relationship between shelter and the environment in which the shelter is used. Review in detail the pertinent text material.

Answers

Page 22: (*illustration*) They settled in different places along the trails that first brought them; Canada, Pacific Northwest, moving south into Middle and South America.

Page 24: (*illustration*) The changing climate, the movement of animals that the people hunted, and the type of plants that the people gathered or grew.

Page 25: 1. Asia.
2. To adjust to the areas in which they lived.
3. By hunting, gathering wild plants, and agriculture.

Page 25:	(illustration) Spirits of the sun, rain, and animals.
Page 27:	Skill Feature (Reading the Chapter) 1. The First Americans. 2. The First Arrivals, People of Middle and South America, and People of North America. 3. The Southwest, the Plains, the Great Basin and California, the Northwest Coast, the Far North, the Arctic, and the Eastern Woodlands.
Page 28:	(illustration) The Aztecs traded with a variety of other peoples, and jewelry was a valuable trade item.
Page 29:	(illustration) Machu Picchu was a walled, fortified city in the mountains for protection; roads were for transportation and communication, keeping the Inca ruler in touch with all parts of the large empire.
Page 30:	1. Mayas, Aztecs, and Incas. 2. Mayas on the Yucatán Peninsula in Middle America; Aztecs in central and southern Mexico; Incas in the Andes Mountains of South America. 3. Mayas had a 365-day calendar, a system of numbers, and picture writing; Aztecs built canals, streets, pyramids, made pottery and jewelry, and wove cloth; Incas domesticated animals for food and clothing, built roadways, bridges, and canals, and developed an organized form of government.
Page 31:	(illustration) For protection.
Page 33:	(illustration) For fishing and trading along the waterways.
Page 35:	(illustration) A similar environment.
Page 37:	(illustration) People in the western Plains trapped buffalo by herding them over cliffs.
Page 39:	(illustration) Burial was given importance by making it part of a religious ceremony.
Page 39:	1. In the Southwest, people included the Pima, Papago, Pueblo, Hopi, Zuñi, Apache, and Navaho; in the Plains, the Dakota, Pawnee, Mandan, Osage, Omaha, Blackfoot, Crow, Cheyenne, and Comanche; in the Great Basin and California, the Ute, Paiute, Shoshoni, Nez Percé, Modoc, Chumash, Yokut, and Pomo; in the Northwest Coast, the Haida, Tlingit, Chinook, and Nootka; in the Far North, the Tanaina, Cree, Ottawa, and Ojibwa; in the Arctic, the Aleut and Eskimo; in the Eastern Woodlands, the Fox, Miami, Shawnee, Sauk, Huron, Winnebago, Choctaw, Chickasaw, Cherokee, Creek, Powhatan, Natchez, Seminole, Cayuga, Onondaga, Oneida, Mohawk, and Seneca. 2. Basic differences were in types of shelter, location, religion, government, diet, language, and modes of travel. 3. To fight common enemies, solve common problems, and to stop fighting among neighboring groups.
Page 40:	Chapter Review (Remembering the Facts) 1. Southwest, Plains, Northwest, Far North, Eastern Woodlands. 2. By hunting caribou, moose, elk, bison, and other large animals.

3. By fishing, hunting small animals, gathering wild plants.
4. Agriculture.
5. Mayas, Aztecs, and Incas.
6. On the Yucatán Peninsula in Middle America; in central and southern Mexico; in the Andes Mountains of South America.
7. The Mayas ate mostly corn; the Aztecs ate corn, beans, squash, and peppers; the Incas ate grains, potatoes, and llama meat.
8. Southwest, Plains, Great Basin and California, Northwest Coast, Far North, Arctic, and Eastern Woodlands.
9. Stone, adobe, animal skins, brush, wooden posts and boards, tree bark, sod, driftwood, whale bones, and blocks of snow.
10. To show the history of a family and the titles of the family leader.

Page 41: Chapter Review (*Understanding the Facts*)
1. In order to survive, people had to adapt to new ways of living and doing things.
2. Depending on the physical surroundings and the long-term weather, people of an area adjusted their ways of life, shelters, food, and beliefs.
3. It was a very strong force in their lives. Religious leaders and spirits of nature guided everyday life, and ceremonies were used to influence nature, improving agriculture.
4. Many languages were spoken by the Plains people, and sign language allowed communication among them.
5. The League joined the participating groups in a bond of peace, uniting them to fight common enemies and solve common problems.

Page 41: Chapter Review (*Using Maps*)
1. A continent is any one of the largest landmasses on the earth; an island is land, smaller than a continent, surrounded by water; a peninsula is a stretch of land jutting out into water; a mountain is a landmass, higher than a hill, rising above the land around it; a plain is a large area of nearly level land with few trees.
2. They are all masses of land.
3. An ocean is a large body of water which covers three fourths of the earth's surface; a sea is a body of water, smaller than an ocean, mostly surrounded by land; a lake is an inland body of water, smaller than a sea; a river is a stream of water of considerable size which flows into another river, lake, sea, or ocean.
4. They are all bodies of water.
5. Size; size.
6. For land, students might mention such things as hills, mesas, valleys, and isthmuses; for water, they might mention bays, ponds, creeks, and canals.
1. Part of the Western Hemisphere, including the southern part of North America, all of Middle America, and the northwest part of South America.
2. Capital cities, major cities, roads, and areas controlled by the Mayas, Aztecs, and Incas.
3. Features created by people.
4. To locate features created by people in reference to natural features.

Learning Objectives

The student should be able to:

1. describe the reasons for European overseas exploration in the fifteenth century.
2. name most of the major European explorers and their areas of exploration.
3. identify the areas of the Western Hemisphere claimed by various European nations.
4. list European interests in the New World exploration and colonization.
5. describe the colonial activities of Spain, France, and other European countries.
6. interpret information from pictures.
7. identify and read a thematic map.

Teaching Ideas

- Have the students consider the possibility that the United States might set up a colony in space. Ask if any of them would volunteer to go. Have the students explain why they would or would not volunteer for the mission. Discuss and list some of the elements for the mission including technological needs, training and preparation, funding, and mission goals. Compare these elements with those of the fifteenth-century European explorers. Have the students use the pertinent text material to list the elements for missions of overseas explorations in the 1400's and 1500's.

- Write on the chalkboard CHRISTOPHER COLUMBUS WAS THE ONLY GREAT EXPLORER IN HISTORY WHO WHEN HE LEFT, DIDN'T KNOW WHERE HE WAS GOING, WHEN HE GOT THERE, DIDN'T KNOW WHERE HE WAS, AND WHEN HE GOT BACK, DIDN'T KNOW WHERE HE HAD BEEN. Read the statement out loud, and discuss each part with the students, providing information to support or refute it. Consider the cases of explorers before and after Columbus. Have the students turn to the chart "European Explorers" (page 50) and the map "Major European Explorations" (page 51). Review in detail the list of explorers and their areas of exploration. Include in the discussion other pertinent information from the text.

- Instruct the students to draw two columns in their notebooks, labeling one FRANCE and the other SPAIN. Have the students use the chapter sections concerning French and Spanish colonization in the New World to write down the activities of both countries. After allowing a sufficient amount of time for the students to gather information, discuss the similarities and differences of France and Spain in the New World. Also compare the extent of the colonial activity of the French and Spanish people with that of the Dutch and Swedes.

- Instruct the students to read the Profile of La Salle (page 60). Write on the chalkboard PROFILE and BIOGRAPHY. Define each, with profile meaning a concise sketch of a person's life and biography meaning a detailed account of a person's life. Ask the students why the material on La Salle is a profile and not a biography. Ask why La Salle might have been selected for the Profile in this chapter about explorers. Explain that the Profiles in *United States History* focus on that aspect of a person's life that relates to the content of the chapter. Review in detail the information about La Salle, and profile some of the other explorers mentioned in the chapter. This approach can be used with other Profiles studied throughout the text.

Answers

Page 42:   (*illustration*) It details European and African coasts, but the outline of the American coast is less well-defined.

Page 44:   (*illustration*) European and Middle Eastern traders met at Azov, Trebizond, Damascus, and Alexandria; Middle Eastern and Asian traders met at Kashgar and Canton.

Page 45:   (*illustration*) They made it possible to determine exact locations.

Page 47:   (*illustration*) Columbus did not expect to find huge lands in the Western Hemisphere; Magellan knew the lands were there when he planned his expedition.

Page 48:   1. A series of religious wars in the Middle East called Crusades.
2. Land routes through the Middle East were controlled by the Ottoman Turks who monopolized the trade causing high prices and less profits for European traders.
3. It was the most able of the seagoing nations. Its sailors had been to the Madeira and Canary islands, as well as the Azores in the Atlantic. The school started by Prince Henry the Navigator increased sea-travel knowledge among Portuguese sailors.
4. He believed that he had come to the Indies Islands, off the southeast coast of Asia.

Page 51:   (*illustration*) These countries were united under strong leaders; they had large armies and treasuries to pay to have explorers find new trade and set up colonies.

Page 52:   (*illustration*) They had horses, guns, cannons, and armor.

Page 54:   (*illustration*) In the photograph, the Spanish missionaries are teaching Christianity to the Indians, and the Indians are teaching them about crops. Most of the Spaniards seem to be interested in what is beyond the Indians.

Page 55:   Skill Feature (*Analyzing Pictures*)
1. Many kinds of people explored the area.
2. They were considered lower in rank than the Spaniards.
3. Their roles included prayer, work, teaching, and exploration.

Page 56:
1. Middle America, southern North America, and South America.
2. Gold, silver, and land.
3. By forming colonies with governments in the New World headed by viceroys directly representing the Spanish crown.
4. Christianity and Spanish ways of farming and making goods.

Page 57:
(illustration) A wooded land where many Indians lived and hunted abundant animals, an exciting place to go.

Page 58:
(illustration) The French attempted to cooperate and trade with the Indians, while the Spaniards took Indian land and gold and made Indians slaves.

Page 61:
1. Giovanni da Verrazano.
2. Eastern Canada and northern New York.
3. Furs, the Northwest Passage, and land.
4. Robert Cavelier, Sieur de la Salle.

Page 62:
(illustration) Land claims were based on previous explorations, and Spain and France did more exploring.

Page 63:
(illustration) By building protective walls.

Page 63:
1. Along the Hudson River.
2. Along the Delaware River.

Page 64:
Chapter Review *(Remembering the Facts)*
1. To trade for goods produced in India, China, and Southeast Asia.
2. Spain.
3. On an island that is part of the group in the Caribbean Sea now called the Bahamas.
4. Ponce de León explored Florida; Balboa reached the Pacific Ocean; Magellan led an expedition to sail around the world; Cortés explored and conquered Mexico; Pizarro explored and conquered Peru; de Soto explored southeastern North America to the Mississippi River; Coronado explored southwestern North America.
5. The Spaniards marched into the cities with horses, guns, and cannons; the Aztec and Inca peoples tried to cooperate and trade with the Spaniards, but they were defeated.
6. Gold, silver, and land for empire.
7. Verrazano sailed along the Atlantic coast of North America; Cartier explored the St. Lawrence Valley; Champlain explored and settled the St. Lawrence Valley.
8. Furs, a Northwest Passage to Asia, and land for empire.

Page 65:
Chapter Review *(Understanding the Facts)*
1. Improvements in ships, maps, and navigation, as well as the cut-off of trade between Europe and Asia by the Ottoman Turks.
2. The Portuguese planned to reach Asia by sailing along the coast of Africa and east across the Indian Ocean. Columbus planned to sail west across the Atlantic Ocean.
3. Spain had a strong navy, it had started exploration early, and it was supported legally in its claims by the pope.

40T

4. Early voyages failed to report any signs of gold and silver, and there were civil wars in France.

5. Spain destroyed civilizations, took land, and enslaved people. France tried to cooperate with people, not interfering with their use of land. Both Spain and France tried to convert the people to Christianity.

6. The Dutch came to establish fur trading centers; the Swedish came to take part in the fur trade.

Page 65:   Chapter Review *(Using Maps)*
1. 1650.
2. Spanish—orange; French—green; Dutch—brown; English—cream.
3. Spanish.
4. Spanish.
5. Spanish, French, Dutch, Swedish, and English.

Chapter 3 *(English Settlement in North America)*

Learning Objectives

The student should be able to:
1. list the reasons for England's late entry into the race for colonies in the New World.
2. describe the methods for establishing colonies.
3. order the original English colonies in North America.
4. distinguish among the types of colonies.
5. describe the ways English colonies were governed.
6. identify and read a time line.
7. distinguish between longitude and latitude.

Teaching Ideas

- Write on the chalkboard ENGLAND WAS LATE ENTERING THE INTERNATIONAL RACE FOR COLONIES BECAUSE. . . . Ask the students to complete this sentence in their notebooks in as many ways possible, using the pertinent text material. Discuss the student responses, and list the major reasons on the chalkboard. Have the students write down the major reasons listed on the chalkboard and arrange them in the order of importance, with 1 being the most important, 2 being less important than 1, and so on. Again discuss the student responses, and write on the chalkboard the two major reasons for England's late entry into the colonial land race.

- Divide the class into 13 groups, and assign each group one of the original 13 colonies. Instruct the students to write WHO, WHEN, WHERE, HOW, WHY, and WITH WHAT RESULT in their notebooks, allowing enough space between the words to write the answers. Instruct the students to use their texts and to work together to answer the questions. After allowing a sufficient amount of time, review the findings of each group. Ask for similarities about the colonies. Ask how each question could be answered for all of the colonies in general. This should include for WHO, people who had religious, political, and economic motives from many walks of life and from many areas; for WHEN, between 1607 and 1732; for WHERE, along the Atlantic coast of North America from what is now Maine to Georgia; for HOW, by a variety of means including joint stock companies, action by proprietors, and grants by the king; for WHY, seeking new opportunities for wealth, freedom to worship, or adventure; and for WITH WHAT RESULT, England joined France and Spain in gaining an empire in North America. Write the word GENERALIZE on the chalkboard, and explain its meaning—to make a summary statement.

- Select one student to list in order on the chalkboard his or her class schedule for the day. Then draw a line on the chalkboard, labeling the line A CLASS DAY. Label the endpoints BEGINNING and END, left and right respectively. Along the line from left to right, write the student's class schedule in order, using a slash along the line for each class. Explain that this is a time line, and discuss its meaning and uses. Review the material in the Skill Feature, "Reading Time Lines" (page 78).

Answers

Page 66:   *(illustration)* They hoped to gain land, wealth, and world recognition.

Page 69:   *(illustration)* Explorations served as the basis for any land claims.

Page 69:   1. John Cabot.
2. Taking cargoes from Spanish ships and sinking them.
3. Roanoke Island, Virginia.

Page 71:   *(illustration)* Answers will vary but may include land, "excellent fruites by planting," and excitement.

Page 72:   *(illustration)* The ocean made it accessible to England for trade, and the river provided a means into the interior.

Page 74:   *(illustration)* To prevent possible trouble since their settlement was north of the lands mentioned in their charter.

Page 76:   *(illustration)* To move away from the restricted life in Puritan-controlled Massachusetts Bay Colony.

Page 77:   1. By joint stock companies.
2. Disease and lack of food.
3. Puritans and Separatists.
4. It was the first proprietary colony, and it protected religious freedom.

Page 78:   Skill Feature *(Reading Time Lines)*
1. Virginia.
2. Georgia.
3. The seventeenth century.
4. It was founded almost 50 years after the one before it.

	1. Four.
	2. Henry was John's great-grandfather.
Page 81:	*(illustration)* Colonists concentrated their efforts on growth rather than on defense.
Page 82:	1. England took the area from the Dutch.
	2. The Society of Friends (Quakers).
	3. James Oglethorpe, as a refuge for English debtors.
Page 83:	*(illustration)* Expansion increased with population growth; answers will vary but may include more opportunity for land and greater freedom.
Page 85:	1. A colony under direct control of the crown.
	2. To organize and unify the colonies.
Page 86:	Chapter Review *(Remembering the Facts)*
	1. Civil war over the throne in England.
	2. First unsuccessful attempt by Walter Raleigh in 1587 at Roanoke Island; first successful attempt in 1607 at Jamestown.
	3. Joint stock companies included Virginia and Massachusetts; proprietary colonies included Maryland, Maine, New Hampshire, Carolina, New Jersey, Pennsylvania, Delaware, Georgia, Rhode Island, and Connecticut; royal colonies included New York.
	4. Indians taught the settlers to plant and traded with them. Squanto in Plymouth taught Pilgrims about Indian ways in the wilderness; Powhatan traded with the settlers in Virginia.
	5. Rhode Island by Roger Williams and Connecticut by Thomas Hooker.
	6. New York had been New Amsterdam; in 1664, English ships took it over without firing a shot.
	7. By setting up the Dominion of New England.
	8. Plans for the Dominion of New England were stopped.
Page 87:	Chapter Review *(Understanding the Facts)*
	1. It was the first profit-making colonial crop.
	2. They opposed the idea of an established church.
	3. It was the first example of constitutional government in the New World.
	4. Because of restrictions on life in Massachusetts, including the necessity of being a Puritan before being allowed to participate in government.
	5. To control the Atlantic coast from Spanish Florida in the south to French Canada in the north.
	6. For greater control of the colonies and for a strong, unified area on the border of French Canada.
Page 87:	Chapter Review *(Using Maps)*
	1. Between 36°N and 40°N.
	2. 76°W.
	3. 40°N.
	4. Georgia.
	5. Pennsylvania and New Jersey.
	6. Between 30°N and 48°N.

City Sketches *(Secota 1584-1587; Plymouth 1620-1650)*

Learning Objectives
The student should be able to:
1. describe town life in Secota and Plymouth.
2. identify the similarities and differences in the lives of some Indians and English colonists in the sixteenth and seventeenth centuries.

Teaching Ideas
- Ask the students what the expression "A picture is worth a thousand words" means to them. Discuss the expression and the importance of pictures in adding to understanding. Refer to the Skill Feature, "Analyzing Pictures" (page 55). Using the list for picture analysis, consider each picture in the City Sketches of Secota and Plymouth. Review the material in the text, and discuss the similarities and differences of these cities.

- Have the students consider what might have been included in time capsules left by the peoples of Secota and Plymouth in the fifteenth and sixteenth centuries. Instruct the students to review the material in the text, and then construct a list of these items. Ask what these items might tell about life in these cities.

Answers

Page 89: *(illustration)* The buildings form a pattern, the fields are separate from the buildings, and there are pathways.

Page 90: *(illustration)* Nets, spears, and traps.

Page 91: *(illustration)* People wanted to avoid pain after death for actions while alive.

Page 91:
1. In the eastern part of what is now North Carolina.
2. They cast spells, gave knowledge about enemies' movements, and were considered very important.
3. Male chieftains wore their hair long and tied it in a knot close to their ears; they wore birds' feathers and pearl bracelets, dressed in cloaks of cured skins, and painted their bodies. Women wore deerskin dresses, their hair was short in the front and somewhat longer in the back, and much of their bodies were chalked.
4. Corn, grains, beans, peas, and fish.
5. Their chief god had created the world and then had made other gods to help him create and rule everything else.

Page 93: *(illustration)* Harbor waters were rough, it was not easy to get to land, it took longer to build shelters, and finding food was difficult.

Page 94: *(illustration)* They taught them how to plant food and to fish.

Page 95: *(illustration)* Secotan buildings were made of small poles, covered with bark or mats woven of long rushes; Plymouth buildings were made of logs and boards.

Page 95:
1. On the *Mayflower,* because it took a long time to get houses built on land.
2. First governor of Plymouth and historian of Pilgrims.
3. Investors in the Plymouth Company.
4. Much the same—corn, grains, and fish.
5. Plymouth had longer, colder winters; Plymouth colonists were also closer to the ocean and exposed to the cold ocean winds.

Unit I Review *(Unit Questions)* ————————————————

Page 97:
1. To adjust to the environment in the areas in which they settled.
2. Improvements in ships, maps, and navigation; the rise of nation states and expanding economies.
3. Gold first attracted Europeans; they remained interested because of potential wealth, slaves, and a possible route along the coast to Asia.
4. Columbus did not calculate the existence of both North and South America.
5. Weapons, armor, and horses.
6. Opportunities for wealth and adventure and a way to get to Asia.
7. It had claims to the land from earlier explorations. It also had started making settlements after the Spaniards and French had claimed much land in North America.
8. English settled for land for empire, French for furs and land, and Spaniards for gold and land.
9. The distance from England, different environments and life-styles from England, and desire to be separate from some of the restrictions on life in England, which had led colonists to come to the New World.

Unit II—Independence

Learning Objectives

The student should be able to:

1. describe the meaning of the word independence as it applies to a national government.
2. order the steps by which the 13 English colonies became the independent nation of the United States.
3. name the major provisions of the United States government established under the Constitution.

Teaching Ideas

- Ask the students to name their favorite holiday, and ask why it is their favorite. List the more popular choices on the chalkboard. Take a quick vote to determine the class favorite. Point out the position of the Fourth of July. Ask why other holidays might be more popular. Discuss the meaning of the Fourth of July and why it is celebrated. Discuss the terms Independence Day and independence. Distinguish between national and personal independence.

- Read the unit opening paragraph to the class, and have the students look carefully at the illustration (pages 98-99). Baron von Steuben, a Prussian soldier, trains American soldiers during the terrible winter at Valley Forge. The artist depicts the soldiers as disciplined and purposeful despite the cold and hunger they endured at Valley Forge. Discuss with the students how this painting represents the concept INDEPENDENCE.

- After study of the unit, ask the students what independence means to them and what it meant to the people in the colonies and in the new United States.

Chapter 4 *(Colonial Society)*

Learning Objectives

The student should be able to:

1. order the major colonial ethnic groups according to percents of the total population.
2. describe colonial society.
3. distinguish between indentured servants and slaves.
4. distinguish between importing and exporting.
5. distinguish among the activities of the regions in the colonies.
6. identify the threats to the safety of the colonists.
7. identify a point of view.
8. distinguish between a key and a legend on a map.

Teaching Ideas

- Take two pieces of paper of equal size. Place one on a desk, and tear the other into several pieces. Hold up the whole piece of paper to represent the total colonial society, and hold up the torn papers to represent the segments that make up the whole society—the various ethnic groups. Review in detail the pertinent text material relating to the ethnic makeup of the colonial population.

- Obtain a copy of the Classified Section of a local newspaper. Duplicate and read out loud some of the help wanted advertisements. Review the structure of most of the ads—job title, name of employer, job description, job qualifications, salary, and place to apply for the job. Review the pertinent text material on colonial work roles. Instruct the students to write a help wanted advertisement for a colonial newspaper, using the structure outlined above, the text material, and their own ideas. Discuss the student advertisements for each job and the elements of each job description, evaluating them in terms of accuracy and realism.

- Write the word ENVIRONMENT on the chalkboard. Remind the students that this term was defined in Chapter 1. Review the definition, and ask the students how the environment influenced the way the colonists lived. Review the pertinent text material concerning the regions in the colonies.

- Bring into class a few small items produced or manufactured in foreign countries. These might include a toy from Japan, a leathergood from Spain, or a tea bag from China or India. Explain that a certain country produces a certain good because that country has all the elements needed to make production worthwhile. These elements are natural resources, technology, and workers. Also explain that if a country lacks one of these elements, it can either import the element or import the good if it is needed in that country. Review the pertinent text material concerning colonial trade and economy, including the map "Colonial Trade Routes" (page 110) and the map "Colonial Economy" (page 116).

Answers

Page 100:   (*illustration*) By farming.

Page 103:   (*illustration*) About 150 percent, or 2.5 times; English were 48 percent, Africans were 20 percent, Scots were 11.2 percent, Germans were 7 percent, Dutch were 2.7 percent, French were 1.4 percent, and Swedes and Finns were 0.6 percent.

Page 103:   1. From England, Scotland, Ireland, Germany, Holland, Sweden, Finland, France, and countries in West Africa.
2. English settled all along the Atlantic coast, Scots settled in Pennsylvania and the Appalachian area, Germans settled in Pennsylvania, Dutch settled in New York, Swedes and Finns settled in the Delaware Valley, and Africans and French settled in all the colonies.

3. Slave ships were greatly crowded, slaves were poorly fed, and thousands died.

Page 104: *(illustration)* Each provided something that most settlers could not make themselves.

Page 105: *(illustration)* They did not have machinery to do the work.

Page 107: *(illustration)* Religion was very important and affected their daily lives.

Page 108:
1. Land.
2. Most were farmers; some were merchants, artisans, and manufacturers.
3. The family and religion.

Page 109: *(illustration)* To train Congregationalist ministers; to train ministers.

Page 110: *(illustration)* The 13 colonies, the Guinea Coast of Africa, and the West Indies; rum, slaves, and molasses.

Page 111: *(illustration)* Answers will vary but may include carpenters and blacksmiths.

Page 112: *(illustration)* Tobacco, rice, and indigo.

Page 113:
1. Answers will vary but may include climate, soil, land formation, political system, economic system, and social patterns.
2. The New England Colonies had Harvard, Yale, and Dartmouth; the Middle Colonies had the College of New Jersey (Princeton), Philadelphia College (University of Pennsylvania), Columbia, and Rutgers; the Southern Colonies had William and Mary.
3. Tobacco, rice, and indigo.

Page 115: Skill Feature *(Checking Points of View)*
1. Crevecoeur, that Indians lived a good way of life; Nevins, that Indian life is based on power.
2. Popular opinion of their time.
3. Historians are affected by the time when they are writing and what experiences they have had with the subject.
4. Answers will vary but may include ideas such as causes of events, results of events, and influences on events.

Page 116: *(illustration)* The New England Colonies had mostly industry; the Middle Colonies blended industry and farming; the Southern Colonies had mostly farming.

Page 118: *(illustration)* Both countries wanted to expand their empires in North America.

Page 119:
1. The settlers were taking Indian land.
2. Everything produced in the colonies was for the benefit of England, and colonial manufacturing was limited.
3. While France was extending its empire, it was claiming the same land in North America as Britain.

Page 120: Chapter Review *(Remembering the Facts)*
1. Europeans to find religious freedom, to escape from poverty, and to find new ways to improve their lives; Africans came as slaves.
2. English and Africans.

3. By farming.
4. It provided a cheap and readily available source of labor.
5. The right to vote and participate in government, limited to owning property.
6. The New England Colonies; the Middle Colonies.
7. In the 1600's, along the eastern foothills of the Appalachian Mountains; in the 1700's, along the Ohio Valley.
8. To protect member colonies from attacks by the Indians and the French and Dutch.
9. They avoided the laws by smuggling.
10. Pitt used money and the army more wisely.

Page 121: Chapter Review *(Understanding the Facts)*
1. Each culture added to the whole of an American culture.
2. Indentured servants worked for a set period of time; slaves were the property of their owners.
3. Because they varied in geographic area and climate.
4. The Indians, the British crown, and the French.
5. By regulating the colonial economy to produce and trade for the benefit of Britain.
6. By defeating the French in numerous battles around the world, including Quebec.

Page 121: Chapter Review *(Using Maps)*
1. Orange.
2. Cream.
3. Green.
4. The Middle Colonies.
5. The New England Colonies.
6. The New England Colonies.
7. Charleston, South Carolina, and New Bern, North Carolina.
8. Lumber.

Chapter 5 *(Winning Freedom)* _____

Learning Objectives

The student should be able to:
1. describe British colonial policies after 1763.
2. order the events leading to the American Revolution.
3. identify the Declaration of Independence.
4. name most of the major American leaders during the Revolution.
5. distinguish between American and British advantages and disadvantages in the war.
6. identify the major events of the war for independence.
7. list the major results of the American Revolution.
8. distinguish between primary and secondary sources.
9. identify and trace a route on a map.

Teaching Ideas

- Write on the chalkboard ARE YOU AMERICAN OR BRITISH? Ask the students why this question was difficult for many colonists to answer after the French and Indian War. Review in detail Section 1 (pages 123-132), using the table "Events Leading to the Revolution" (page 129) as a guide to British and American actions.

- Instruct the students to label a page in their notebooks with the title BOSTON MASSACRE. Instruct the students to write WHO, WHEN, WHERE, HOW, WHY, and WITH WHAT RESULT in their notebooks, allowing enough space between the words to write answers.

- Tell the students that a common way of sharing news and information in the colonial days was by the town crier, a public official who made public proclamations. This person read the news out loud in a public area. When the Declaration of Independence was issued, many people found out about it through the town criers. Have one student at a time read out loud parts of the Declaration of Independence (pages 506-508). As it is being read, have the students list the specific grievances mentioned, and then review the pertinent text material.

- Write the following on the chalkboard:

  DATELINE PHILADELPHIA—BRITISH FAVORED AS WAR BEGINS

  DATELINE BOSTON—A WIN AT CONCORD, A LOSS AT BUNKER HILL

  DATELINE SARATOGA—GENTLEMAN JOHNNY BOWS TO LOCALS

  DATELINE FT. PITT—CLARK TAKES THREE OUT WEST

  DATELINE YORKTOWN—WASHINGTON WINS THE BIG ONE

  DATELINE PARIS—THE UNITED STATES GAINS PEACE

  Ask the students to explain each of these fictional headlines. Discuss the who, when, where, how, why, and with what result of each story behind the headline while reviewing in detail the pertinent text material.

- Ask the students "How revolutionary was the American Revolution?" Ask the students why, and list their responses on the chalkboard. Discuss the concept of revolution and the degrees of change possible in any revolt. Review in detail the results of the Revolution. Ask the students again "How revolutionary was the American Revolution?" Compare their answers after reviewing the results with those already on the chalkboard.

Answers

Page 122: *(illustration)* Britain decided to tighten its controls on the colonies.

Page 124: *(illustration)* It was a law taxing the use of newspapers, pamphlets, contracts, wills, and certain other printed materials.

Page 126: *(illustration)* Answers will vary but may include the idea that a colonial cartoonist portrayed a mean rider using weapons as a whip.

Page 127: *(illustration)* It portrayed the British as being murderous.

Page 129: *(illustration)* Important issues and events included the Proclamation of 1763, the Sugar Act, the Stamp Act, the Townshend Acts, the Tea Act, and the Intolerable Acts; British policies responded only to the immediate problems; much of the colonial protest was boycotting; the war might have been prevented by British recognition of long-range colonial problems and/or by colonial submission to British demands.

Page 131: Skill Feature *(Reading Primary and Secondary Sources)*
1. The primary source is Revere's own writing; the secondary source is the poem "Paul Revere's Ride."
2. Revere's own writing.
3. It is recorded by the person who did the action.

Page 132:
1. Restrictions on movement west and on trade and manufacturing.
2. They felt the British actions were improper and illegal and an attempt to ruin the colonial economy.
3. They tarred and feathered loyalists who did not join the boycott.

Page 133: *(illustration)* Jefferson wrote that government got its authority from the people, and if government did not protect the rights of the people, then the people could overthrow the government and create a new one.

Page 136: *(illustration)* Saratoga and Oriskany; Philadelphia.

Page 137: *(illustration)* Marquis de Lafayette of France.

Page 138: *(illustration)* October 19, 1781.

Page 139: *(illustration)* The French fleet blocked the British from the sea.

Page 140: *(illustration)* Spain; along the Atlantic coast to the Mississippi River; the Pacific Northwest and areas in the northwest, northeast, and southwest parts of the United States.

Page 140:
1. George Washington.
2. It brought France into the war on the side of the colonies.
3. Yorktown.

Page 142: *(illustration)* Some were forced to move out of the country, more participated in government, prisoner's conditions improved, more land ownership was possible, many were in debt, and many things were the same.

Page 143:
1. Fear of limitless authority.
2. Many fought in the war, but few, if any, benefited.
3. It was in debt to its allies, and too much printed money lowered the value of money already in use.

Page 144: Chapter Review *(Remembering the Facts)*
1. With boycotts and demonstrations of protest.
2. In Philadelphia, to determine a unified way to meet the crisis of the Intolerable Acts.

3. To enforce the boycott of British goods and to scare British officials stationed in the colonies; to organize opposition to the British.
4. The signing of the Declaration of Independence.
5. British advantages included a well-trained, fully-equipped army and a large navy; British disadvantages included unfamiliar and rugged ground and poor roads and communication. Colonial advantages included home ground, closeness to supplies, and experience with their weapons; colonial disadvantages included lack of training and discipline and limited number of supplies.
6. France, Spain, and Holland.
7. It ended the war, recognized American independence, set the United States' boundaries, and gave fishing rights.
8. A change in leadership from British to American, the establishment of state governments, and more political participation by citizens.
9. Nothing changed.

Page 145: Chapter Review *(Understanding the Facts)*
1. Because of needs Britain had after the war, including the need for money to pay war debts.
2. Trade and industry were both limited in general, and specific items were limited by specific legislation.
3. Patriots supported a possible break with Britain, while loyalists hoped that the colonies could remain loyal.
4. With the aid of French financial and military support.
5. For women and blacks, nothing changed; for white men, there were changes in political participation, leadership, and authority in state governments, changes in social attitudes toward human rights, and economic changes in available land for settlement, less restrictions on trade and industry, but also inflation and war debts.

Page 145: Chapter Review *(Using Maps)*
1. Blue arrows.
2. British.
3. West.
4. Valley Forge, Pennsylvania.
5. About 525 miles or 830 kilometers.
6. South.
7. The French navy blocked the mouth of the Chesapeake Bay.

Chapter 6 *(Forming a Union)* _____

Learning Objectives
The student should be able to:
1. distinguish between the Land Ordinance of 1785 and the Northwest Ordinance.
2. describe the problems of the Articles of Confederation.
3. identify the compromises in the making of the Constitution.

4. distinguish between the views of the Federalists and the Anti-Federalists.
5. distinguish between the Articles of Confederation and the Constitution.
6. list some of the freedoms guaranteed by the Bill of Rights.
7. distinguish among various sources of history.
8. identify and read the scale on a map.

Teaching Ideas

- Tell the students that there are many ways of evaluating performance. In sports like track, performance is measured by speed; in gymnastics, performance is measured by form and grace; and in baseball, performance is measured by the statistical average of various areas over an entire season. Explain to the students that to evaluate the performance of the United States government under the Articles of Confederation, we must balance its strengths and weaknesses. Instruct the students to make two columns in their notebooks, labeling one STRENGTH and one WEAKNESS. Review the pertinent text material, and instruct the students to note what they feel are strong and weak actions of the government. Discuss the results, and ask the students to assign a letter grade (A for superior, B for good, C for acceptable, D for unacceptable, and F for failure) to the government under the Articles. Take a quick vote to establish a class opinion. Ask whether the government under the Articles needed to be revised and why.

- Write on the chalkboard GOVERNMENT SHOULD BE. . . . Ask the students what they think the ideal government should be. Instruct them to complete this sentence in their notebooks. Discuss the responses. Ask the students if they think that the delegates to the Constitutional Convention shared the same view of what government should be. Review the pertinent text material, and instruct the students to list the areas of compromise that made the writing and ratifying of the Constitution possible.

- Instruct the students to turn to the Bill of Rights (pages 522-524) in the annotated Constitution. Instruct the students to list the headings for the first ten amendments. Consider each element of the Bill of Rights by reviewing the pertinent text and appendix materials.

Answers

Page 146: *(illustration)* By the Articles of Confederation.

Page 148: *(illustration)* For land.

Page 149: *(illustration)* It was northwest of the main body of the United States; Ohio, Indiana, Illinois, Michigan, and Wisconsin.

Page 150: *(illustration)* By knowing the trails and routes through the unfamiliar lands.

Page 152: *(illustration)* It brought the economic problems of the country into sharper focus and showed the weakness of the Articles of Confederation in maintaining a strong economy. This all led to the framing of a new constitution.

Page 154:
1. The Land Ordinance of 1785 and the Northwest Ordinance of 1787.
2. By stationing forts in the Northwest Territory.
3. Each state controlled its own trade.
4. State tax laws.

Page 155: Skill Feature *(Analyzing Sources of History)*
1. Notes and a letter.
2. He felt that it may be an imperfect document, but every member of the convention should sign it.
3. It meant a security of those rights by the national government.
4. The letter; the notes are Franklin's words filtered though the interpretation of Madison as he recorded them.

Page 156: *(illustration)* Because there was no declaration of rights in the document.

Page 158:
1. The Virginia Plan was for representation based on size, while the New Jersey Plan was for equal representation for all states.
2. It set up two houses of Congress, combining parts of the Virginia and New Jersey plans.
3. Three fifths of the number of slaves would be counted to determine the representation and taxation.

Page 158: *(illustration)* To have a stronger building (nation).

Page 159: *(illustration) The Federalist Papers.*

Page 160: *(illustration)* Delaware; Rhode Island; Delaware, New Jersey, and Georgia; by less than ten votes in New York and Rhode Island.

Page 161:
1. They wanted to keep their liberties and the rights of the states more secure—a weak central government seemed safer to them.
2. To express the Federalist views in support of the new Constitution.
3. Nine.
4. A list of definite individual rights (the first ten amendments to the Constitution).

Page 162: Chapter Review *(Remembering the Facts)*
1. The Articles of Confederation.
2. The Northwest Territory was to be examined and measured, and lots were to be sold.
3. When there were 5,000 free adult males of voting age in the territory, they could elect a legislature; when there were 60,000 free settlers in the territory, they could apply to the national government for statehood.
4. Answers will vary but may include that government under the Articles could not maintain a strong economy, could not tax, and could not control trade.
5. To improve the Articles of Confederation; an entirely new plan of government was written.
6. By compromise.
7. Ratified in 1788 and into effect in 1789.
8. Answers will vary but may include freedom of speech, freedom of religion, freedom of the press, trial by jury, right of assembly, right to bear arms, and protection from cruel and unusual punishments.

Page 163: Chapter Review *(Understanding the Facts)*
1. Under the Articles, there was a weak central government in which the freedom and independence of each state was protected.
2. It had no strong central organization.
3. The Virginia Plan was used for representation by size in the House of Representatives, and the New Jersey Plan was used for equal representation in the Senate.
4. Where the authority should be—in state or central government; guarantees for individual liberties and states' rights; and authority of the convention to change or do away with the Articles.
5. To guarantee individual rights.

Page 163: Chapter Review *(Using Maps)*
1. 250 miles; 400 kilometers.
2. Between about 40°N and 48°N.
3. Between about 92°W and 84°W.
4. 500 miles or 800 kilometers.
5. About 250 miles or 400 kilometers.
6. Lake Michigan; about 300 miles or 480 kilometers.
7. Ohio, Indiana, Illinois, Michigan, and Wisconsin.

Chapter 7 *(The Constitution)*

Learning Objectives
The student should be able to:
1. list the basic principles of the United States government.
2. name the branches of the United States government.
3. distinguish among the authority of the branches of the government.
4. describe the system of checks and balances among the branches.
5. distinguish between the organization of government under the Articles of Confederation and the Constitution.
6. list the powers of federal and state government under the Constitution.
7. describe the methods for changing the Constitution.
8. distinguish between rights and responsibilities.
9. identify and read a diagram.

Teaching Ideas
- Instruct the students to read the Declaration of Independence (pages 506-508), listing the grievances mentioned. Instruct the students to list the basic principles of the United States government, using the pertinent text material. Compare and discuss the grievances of 1776 and the principles of government of 1789.
- Write on the chalkboard MAKING LAWS, ENFORCING LAWS, INTERPRETING LAWS. Explain to the students that these are the elements of governing. Ask why the job of governing is divided three

ways. Explain the separation of powers under the Constitution. Review in detail the pertinent text material concerning the branches of government.

- Ask the students to think about what driving would be like without traffic laws. Discuss the problems that would be created and the need for this and other kinds of laws. Review in detail the powers of the federal and state governments to make laws.

- Instruct the students to list the headings for the amendments to the Constitution (pages 522-530). Review briefly the meaning of each amendment. Explain that these are changes or additions to the original document. Review the pertinent text material on changing the Constitution. Write on the chalkboard WHO, WHEN, WHERE, HOW, WHY, and WITH WHAT RESULT to aid in the review.

Answers

Page 164: *(illustration)* A constitution; British political philosophy and ideals of the Revolution.

Page 166: *(illustration)* The legislative branch makes the laws, the executive branch enforces the laws, and the judicial branch interprets the laws.

Page 167: *(illustration)* The President checks Congress by vetoing legislation, calling special sessions of Congress, and determining foreign policy; the President checks the Supreme Court by appointing federal judges and pardoning federal offenders. Congress checks the Supreme Court by establishing lower courts, proposing amendments to the Constitution, fixing the number of judges, and impeaching and removing judges; Congress checks the President by overruling vetoes, refusing to approve treaties, impeaching and removing the President, refusing to confirm appointments, and appropriating funds for programs. The Supreme Court checks the President by declaring executive actions to be unconstitutional; the Supreme Court checks Congress by declaring laws to be unconstitutional.

Page 168:
1. Popular sovereignty, limited government, federalism, separation of powers, and checks and balances.
2. Yes, power to rule is given by the people and limited by the people.
3. Separation of powers divided the functions or powers of government, and the checks and balances ensures this separation.

Page 169:
1. The basic principles are the root of the Constitution; the others are important but not so basic.
2. National law.
3. To recognize and respect minority rights.

Page 170: *(illustration)* Members must be at least 25 years of age, citizens of the United States for 7 years, and residents of the states from which they are elected.

Page 171: *(illustration)* Changes in the number of houses, voting, and congressional authority; the executive was the Committee of States; the Supreme Court had certain areas of original jurisdiction.

Page 173: Concept Feature *(Responsibility)*
1. To use freedom of speech and press in responsible ways; to use guns in accordance with the law and not to infringe on the rights of others; to support freedom of speech and press even when disagreeing with the specific things being said or written; not to use the privacy guaranteed in the freedom from unreasonable search and seizure to carry on illegal activities; to be fair in determining reasonable bails and fines; to show up for trial when released on bail.
2. Answers will vary but may include the idea that a contract exists between the governed and those governing. This is seen in both the Constitution and the Declaration of Independence. Under this contract, if one party fails to live up to its obligation (of being responsible), the other party is released from its obligation (of protecting freedoms).
3. Answers will vary but may include the idea that if the majority has to continuously be forced to live up to its responsibilities, this ceases to be rule by the majority and endangers the existence of democratic rights.

Page 176:
1. The House of Representatives and the Senate.
2. The electoral college.
3. The Supreme Court.

Page 177: *(illustration)* Federal powers include coining money, conducting foreign relations, and regulating interstate commerce; state powers including creating local governments, providing public education, and directing automobile operation; shared powers include levying taxes, providing for public welfare, and defining and punishing crimes; powers denied to the federal government include taxing exports, suspending writ of habeas corpus, and granting titles of nobility; powers denied to the states include coining money, entering into treaties, and voiding contracts.

Page 178:
1. Expressed, implied, and inherent.
2. Concurrent.
3. Exclusive.

Page 179: *(illustration)* Four.

Page 180:
1. Changes can be proposed by two-thirds vote in each house of Congress or by a national convention; changes can be approved by three fourths of all state legislatures or by three fourths of special state conventions.
2. The Supreme Court defines and extends the meaning of the Constitution.

Page 181: *(illustration)* By continuous informal changes.

Page 182: Chapter Review *(Remembering the Facts)*
1. The people of the United States.
2. Limited government.
3. Central and state governments.
4. Legislative, executive, and judicial.
5. The President checks Congress by vetoing legislation, calling special sessions of Congress, and determining foreign policy. The President checks the Supreme Court by appointing federal judges and pardoning

federal offenders. Congress checks the Supreme Court by establishing lower courts, proposing amendments to the Constitution, fixing the number of judges, and impeaching and removing judges. Congress checks the President by overruling vetoes, refusing to approve treaties, impeaching and removing the President, refusing to confirm appointments, and appropriating funds. The Supreme Court checks the President by declaring executive actions to be unconstitutional. The Supreme Court checks Congress by declaring laws to be unconstitutional.

6. In their qualifications for membership, terms of office, and types of powers.
7. Commander in chief.
8. Delegated.
9. Reserved.
10. Amendments.
11. In Congress or a national convention.

Page 183: Chapter Review *(Understanding the facts)*
1. In form—three branches, bicameral legislature.
2. It had a strong central government.
3. Checks and balances.
4. The process for change is included in Article V.

Page 183: Chapter Review *(Using Diagrams)*
1. Checks and balances.
2. Legislative, executive, and judicial.
3. By using arrows.
4. By refusing to confirm the appointment.
5. Executive.
6. Legislative.
7. Each branch restrains the power of the other branches.

City Sketch *(Philadelphia 1750-1775)*

Learning Objectives

The student should be able to:
1. list the reasons for Philadelphia's growth in the colonial period.
2. describe the influence of individual leaders in the development of Philadelphia as a city.

Teaching Ideas

- Write on the chalkboard the following figures showing the population of the five largest cities in the colonies in 1750 and 1790:

YEAR	BOSTON	PHILADELPHIA	NEW YORK	CHARLESTON	BALTIMORE
1750	15,731	13,400	13,300	8,000	100
1790	18,038	42,444	33,131	16,359	13,503

Review in detail the material in the text, including the map of the mid-Atlantic area (page 184). Ask the students for reasons people were attracted to Philadelphia in larger numbers than to other cities. The reasons should include the good location for trade, good harbor, easy access to the interior colonial frontier, good local leadership, Quaker beliefs in the equality of people, and the availability of education. Point out the location of Baltimore on the map, and ask students why its population may have grown so quickly.

- Write on the chalkboard and read out loud:

    A PENNY SAVED IS A PENNY EARNED.
    A BIRD IN THE HAND IS WORTH TWO IN THE BUSH.

Explain that Benjamin Franklin included many such bits of advice in his *Poor Richard's Almanac,* which he edited between 1732 and 1758. The almanac sold 10,000 copies a year and became very widely read in the colonies. Discuss the meaning of each saying. Point out that Franklin was a practical person giving practical advice. Instruct the students to list examples from the text that show Franklin was a practical problem solver. These could include the organization of a volunteer fire department to battle the ever-present danger of fire. Ask the students to what problems Franklin might be directing his problem-solving efforts if he were living today.

Answers

Page 185:   *(illustration)* It had access to the Delaware Bay and ocean trade, while internal rivers provided means of transportation.

Page 186:   *(illustration)* Spectacles; Hannah Breintnall.

Page 187:   *(illustration)* He promoted the Pennsylvania Academy, the public library, the volunteer fire department, street cleaning, the hospital, and the night patrols.

Page 189:   *(illustration)* Jobs and business.

Page 189:   1. English Quakers.
2. Shipping and trade.
3. He promoted the Pennsylvania Academy, the public library, the volunteer fire department, street cleaning, the hospital, and the night patrols.
4. There was cheaper land outside the city which also avoided noise and traffic.

Unit II Review *(Unit Questions)* _____

Page 191:   1. Most African settlers were free people in Africa and were enslaved in the colonies; most Europeans had many restrictions on life or were in debt in Europe and were free in the colonies.
2. The English colonies were located over a large geographic area with varied climates, soil, and land formations.

3. The British government viewed the colonies as existing for the support of the home country; the colonies preferred greater freedom to carry on their own trade.

4. To maintain economic freedom against the oppressive rule of Britain.

5. Colonial forces fought on their home ground, the fighting was spread over a huge area, and the colonists were aided by a French alliance against the British.

6. Social effects included a greater emphasis on human rights; politically, state governments were created; and economically, the creation of one of the largest countries in the world made it more active in world trade and manufacturing.

7. The Atlantic coast in the east to the Mississippi River in the west, with the Great Lakes and Canada in the north and Spanish-owned Florida in the south.

8. Authority was given to the states, making the central government too weak to dominate them.

9. With no strong central organization, problems among states and with foreign nations were difficult to solve.

10. Supporters of the Constitution tried to convince the people that the Constitution would provide a much better government. Those opposed felt that the new constitution would destroy the rights of the states and individual liberties of the people.

Unit III—Democracy

Learning Objectives

The student should be able to:
1. describe the organizing and operating of the government under the Constitution.
2. name the major American political and cultural leaders during the late 1700's and early 1800's.
3. identify the major events influencing democracy in the United States.

Teaching Ideas

- Conduct an election for a class mascot. Ask for several nominations, and list them on the chalkboard. Instruct the students to vote for their choice. Use either secret ballot or a show of hands. List the total number of votes for each choice. Discuss the idea of majority rule and the concern for the rights of the minority. Write DEMOCRACY on the chalkboard, and discuss the term.

- Read the unit opening paragraph to the class, and have the students look carefully at the illustration (pages 192-193). The painting, "Fourth of July Celebration in Center Square, Philadelphia, 1819," by John Lewis Krimmel shows patriotic posters over the tent doorways, the flag of the United States, and a flag emblazoned with the words "Virtue, Liberty, Independence." Less than 40 years after Independence, celebrating the Fourth had become a national tradition. Discuss with the students how this illustration represents the concept DEMOCRACY.

- After study of the unit, draw a graph outline on the chalkboard, numbering from 10 to 1 down the left side and writing 1790-1840/POLITICAL; 1790-1840/SOCIAL; and 1790-1840/ECONOMIC across the bottom. Ask the students if it is possible to measure democracy in a country. Discuss the graph outline. Ask the students to list those elements that might be considered indicators of political, social, and economic democracy. These should include greater participation in elections, freedom of movement within the country and society, and more opportunities to make a better living. Discuss the two time periods listed on the graph, 1790 and 1840, in relation to the indicators. Agree on criteria for measuring these indicators. Ask the students to rate democracy for each indicator and for each time period. Record the class consensus on the graph on the chalkboard. Use the Unit Review (pages 258-259) to conclude the teaching of the unit and prepare students for the unit test.

Chapter 8 *(Testing the New Government)*

Learning Objectives

The student should be able to:
1. describe the contributions of George Washington as first President.

2. name the major political leaders in the early years of the government under the Constitution.
3. identify the main economic and political events during the Washington, Adams, and Jefferson administrations.
4. describe the development of political parties.
5. identify main ideas in material assigned for reading.
6. identify and read directions on a map.

Teaching Ideas

- Write on the chalkboard the following statement by Thomas Jefferson about George Washington: HIS MIND WAS GREAT AND POWERFUL, WITHOUT BEING OF THE VERY FIRST ORDER; HIS PENETRATION STRONG . . . AND SO FAR AS HE SAW, NO JUDGMENT WAS EVER SOUNDER. HE WAS SLOW IN OPERATION, BEING LITTLE AIDED BY INVENTION OR IMAGINATION, BUT SURE IN CONCLUSION. . . . HIS INTEGRITY WAS MOST PURE, HIS JUSTICE THE MOST INFLEXIBLE I HAVE EVER KNOWN. . . . HE WAS, INDEED, IN EVERY SENSE OF THE WORDS, A WISE, A GOOD, AND A GREAT MAN. Read the statement out loud, and discuss each part with the students, providing information to clarify Jefferson's words. Ask the students what Jefferson was saying about Washington as a leader. Discuss the term LEADERSHIP, and ask the students to list qualities of leadership. Review the pertinent text material concerning the Washington administration, and discuss it in relation to Jefferson's description and the students' list of leadership qualities.

- Tell the students that the class will be conducting an interview today with someone representing former Washington Cabinet members Alexander Hamilton and Thomas Jefferson. Instruct each student to prepare at least five questions to ask the representative, having each question directed to either Hamilton or Jefferson. Instruct the students to review the pertinent text material. Allow ample time to review the material and write the questions. Announce to the class that the teacher will be representing the former Secretaries. Call on students to ask their questions, and answer each question with historical accuracy. Emphasize that the answers illustrate either Hamilton's or Jefferson's point of view. Conclude the lesson by listing on the chalkboard the differences between the two people.

- Ask the students how they can tell the difference between a Democrat and a Republican today. Ask them how it was possible to tell the difference between a Federalist and a Democratic-Republican in the early days of the federal government under the Constitution. Instruct the students to read the table "Political Parties in the 1790's" (page 206). Discuss the differences, and review in detail the pertinent text material on the development of political parties.

- Instruct the students to label a page in their notebooks ISSUES AND ANSWERS. Instruct the students to draw three columns on the page, and label the columns WASHINGTON, ADAMS, and JEFFERSON. Instruct the students to review the text material, and list in each column the major issues of each administration. Discuss the issues, and review the answers that each President offered.

Answers

Page 194: *(illustration)* Answers will not vary but may include debt, inflation, an uncertain constitution, and a not-yet unified country.

Page 196: *(illustration)* Randolph was Attorney General, Jefferson was Secretary of State, Hamilton was Secretary of the Treasury, and Knox was Secretary of War.

Page 197:
1. George Washington.
2. Jefferson was Secretary of State, and Hamilton was Secretary of the Treasury.
3. The Supreme Court.

Page 199: *(illustration)* A place for the government to deposit its money, to lend money to government and private citizens, and to provide a sound currency.

Page 200: *(illustration)* Western Pennsylvania.

Page 201:
1. So the United States would establish future credit.
2. It was a place for the government to deposit its money, to lend money to government and private citizens, and to provide a sound currency.
3. They thought the taxes unfair in cutting profits.
4. Federalists and Democratic-Republicans.

Page 202: *(illustration)* It brought them closer to war.

Page 203: Skill Feature *(Recognizing Main Ideas)*
1. The main idea is that the House of Representatives is a place for serious business.
2. The reader must determine it.
3. It is not stated.
4. Yes.

Page 204:
1. War between France and Great Britain.
2. Britain began seizing American ships and impressing its sailors.
3. To avoid permanent foreign alliances.

Page 205: *(illustration)* Adams was a Federalist, and Jefferson was a Democratic-Republican.

Page 206: *(illustration)* It was too pro-British; for the commercial ties and fear of France; a Massachusetts banker; a Kentucky blacksmith.

Page 207:
1. John Adams.
2. France.
3. To stop the Democratic-Republicans from gaining too much power.
4. Thomas Jefferson.

Page 208:	(illustration) Jefferson, a Democratic-Republican.
Page 210:	(illustration) Americans hoping to resettle in the West; it almost doubled.
Page 211:	(illustration) 1804 to 1806.
Page 211:	1. Government costs were cut.
	2. *Marbury* v. *Madison*.
	3. Captain Meriwether Lewis and Captain William Clark.

Page 212: Chapter Review *(Remembering the Facts)*

1. State legislatures chose electors who elected him.
2. 1789 in New York.
3. District and circuit courts.
4. To repay war debts, to establish a central bank of the United States, to pass a protective tariff, and to pass an excise tax.
5. The Democratic-Republicans; the Federalists.
6. Britain pulled out of the Northwest Territory, the United States paid debts to British citizens, Americans paid damages for British ship seizures, and the Canadian boundary was surveyed and set.
7. The right to navigate the Mississippi River and to use freely the port at New Orleans.
8. France's attempt to gain a bribe from American commissioners.
9. In the House of Representatives.
10. The right of the Supreme Court to declare an act of Congress unconstitutional.
11. The Louisiana Purchase; about 50 people including guides, soldiers, trappers, and volunteers.

Page 213: Chapter Review *(Understanding the Facts)*

1. It set many precedents.
2. To protect the rights of people and protect them from harm by the government or other people.
3. It provided a place for depositing government money, granted loans, and provided for a sound currency.
4. They believed it to be unconstitutional.
5. From differences of opinion over foreign and domestic policies.
6. It made it possible to ship goods down the Mississippi River through the port of New Orleans and on to overseas markets.
7. To stop the growth of the Democratic-Republican party.
8. It showed that one political party could be defeated and the opposition could take over peacefully.

Page 213: Chapter Review *(Using Maps)*

1. West.
2. Southwest.
3. Northwest.
4. West.
5. Northeast.
6. About 700 miles (1100 kilometers).
7. About 2,000 miles (3,200 kilometers).

Chapter 9 *(The Growth of Nationalism)*

Learning Objectives

The student should be able to:

1. describe the influence of a European war on the United States in the early 1800's.
2. list the causes and results of the War of 1812.
3. name the major American political and cultural leaders in the early 1800's.
4. describe the effects of nationalism on American politics, courts, foreign affairs, and culture.
5. identify and trace routes on a map.

Teaching Ideas

* Write on the chalkboard the heading WAR OF 1812 and under it the subheadings CAUSES and RESULTS. Ask the students to complete lists for both of these. As items are listed, discuss each cause and result. Review the pertinent text material in detail to add points not presented by the class. When the lists are complete, ask the students to make some general statements about the War of 1812 based on the information on the chalkboard. Ask the students to evaluate the war by answering the following questions: (1) Was the War of 1812 unavoidable? (2) Did the war solve the problems which caused it? (3) How did the feeling of nationalism affect the conflict?

* Instruct the students to read the Profile of Tecumseh (page 217) and the Concept Feature, "Nationalism" (page 227) that quotes Mary Jane Watson's letter to her grandparents. Discuss each reading in detail. Tell the students that both concern nationalism. Ask the students to define nationalism and relate the term to elements of the readings. Review in detail the pertinent text material concerning American nationalism.

* Hand out copies of the poem "The Star-Spangled Banner" by Francis Scott Key. Discuss each part of the poem. Review in detail information concerning the national anthem (page 220). Tell the students that the poem is an obvious example of patriotic literature. Review in detail the text material concerning nationalism and American literature, art, and architecture.

Answers

Page 214: *(illustration)* Answers will vary but may include that it fostered feelings of nationalism.

Page 216: *(illustration)* Nothing, as it hurt American trade.

Page 218: 1. Great Britain.
2. It hurt American trade more than it did foreign trade.
3. Great Britain.

Page 219: *(illustration)* To capture the other's local seat of government; to stop trade in and out of the United States.

Page 220: *(illustration)* Answers will vary but may include the idea that it inspires feelings of patriotism.

Page 221: *(illustration)* Answers will vary but may include the idea that they inspire feelings of patriotism.

Page 223:
1. Put-in-Bay, the Thames, and New Orleans.
2. December 24, 1814.
3. New England.

Page 224: *(illustration)* On the rivers.

Page 227: Concept Feature *(Nationalism)*
1. She likes it.
2. She writes only about its good points, praising them highly.
3. To make her point.

Page 228:
1. In the types of bills passed—the charter for the Second Bank of the United States, a new protective tariff, and money for roads and canals.
2. *Fletcher* v. *Peck*—laws by states could be voided; *McCullough* v. *Maryland*—national laws are superior; *Gibbons* v. *Ogden*—national government could regulate trade.
3. In the Monroe Doctrine and expansion.

Page 229: *(illustration)* The Monroe Doctrine.

Page 230: *(illustration)* By painting scenes of Indian life.

Page 231:
1. American settings, including the Hudson Valley and the frontier.
2. American themes, including landscapes and people.
3. Roman and Greek.

Page 232: Chapter Review *(Remembering the Facts)*
1. Britain seized American ships bound for France.
2. To avoid war and to stop the British and French from harming trade.
3. The Battle of Tippecanoe.
4. Put-in-Bay, the Thames, New Orleans.
5. It was an area with a Federalist majority that made its living by sea trade, and war with Britain cut that trade.
6. It ended the fighting and returned all boundaries to the way they had been.
7. A central bank of the United States, a protective tariff, and improved transportation.
8. The United States was not to interfere in European affairs, and Europeans were not to interfere in affairs in the Western Hemisphere.
9. Washington Irving.
10. A group of artists who painted views of the Catskill Mountains and the Hudson River in New York; Thomas Doughty.

Page 233: Chapter Review *(Understanding the Facts)*
1. Because British interference was greater than French on the seas and in the frontier areas.

2. It caused a failure to coordinate an invasion of Canada and a major battle to occur after the peace treaty.
3. Federalist opposition to the war was seen as traitorous.
4. After it, American policies and culture were no longer dictated by Europe.
5. It became more American in nature.
6. It brought a time of strong national pride.

Page 233:   Chapter Review *(Using Maps)*
1. With blue lines.
2. With red lines.
3. Ohio.
4. The Thames and York (Toronto).
5. About 175 miles or 280 kilometers.
6. South.
7. About 50 miles or 80 kilometers.
8. Ft. McHenry and Bladensburg.
9. East.
10. South.

Chapter 10 *(The Age of Jackson)* _____

Learning Objectives

The student should be able to:
1. distinguish between nationalism and sectionalism.
2. describe the reasons for the split in the Democratic-Republican party after 1824.
3. identify the major events of the Jackson Presidency.
4. list ways in which the United States became more democratic.
5. name groups of people not affected by expanded democracy.
6. identify details in a reading assignment.
7. distinguish between information on two maps.

Teaching Ideas

- Ask the students to name their favorite professional sports team. List the choices on the chalkboard. Point out that one may be more popular than the others because it is the local team. Ask what team would be the favorite if the students had grown up in another part of the country. Discuss the idea of team loyalty in geographic terms. Write SECTION-ALISM on the chalkboard. Discuss the idea of loyalty to the political ideals of a geographic section of the country. Review in detail the pertinent text material.

- Administer a 20-question quiz concerning the important elements of the Jackson administration. Do not collect or grade the quiz. Use the quiz as an outline to review the pertinent text material in greater detail.

● Instruct the students to open the text to the picture "Choctaw Removal" by Valjean Hessing (page 247). Refer to the Skill Feature, "Analyzing Pictures" (page 55). Using the list for picture analysis, discuss the picture. Review in detail the pertinent text material concerning President Jackson and the Indians.

Answers

Page 234: *(illustration)* Because Jackson was so important to the politics of this time.

Page 236: *(illustration)* Over the tariff, business, manufacturing, transportation, and cheaper land prices; each represented a different sectional view.

Page 237: *(illustration)* Part of the West and South; New England; in the House of Representatives, Clay supported Adams; more solid in the West and South (Georgia, Illinois, Kentucky, Louisiana, Missouri, Ohio, and Virginia).

Page 238:
1. John Quincy Adams, Andrew Jackson, Henry Clay, and William Crawford.
2. The North wanted to protect home industries, and the South wanted easy, direct foreign trade.
3. The new Democratic party.

Page 240:
1. He had lived on the frontier and had been a soldier.
2. Blacks, women, and white males who did not own property.
3. He appointed members of his own party to government jobs.

Page 241: *(illustration)* Nullification.

Page 243: Skill Feature *(Reading for Detail)*
1. A British actor.
2. The roads were rough, hard, marshy, and had many ruts; the coach was boat-shaped, wet, and hot.
3. 1832.
4. Between New York and Philadelphia.
5. She was not at all pleased.

Page 244: *(illustration)* Whether or not there should be a central bank of the United States.

Page 245:
1. For political reasons, as well as to stop bills that he thought were unconstitutional.
2. In the South.
3. They differed over the right of a state to resist federal authority.
4. Dispute over the tariffs of 1828 and 1832.

Page 247: *(illustration)* Some states and the federal government took over their lands.

Page 248:
1. A policy of removal to lands west of the Mississippi River.
2. The Court decision said that Georgia had no authority over the Cherokees.
3. Jackson did not enforce the Supreme Court decision.

Page 249: *(illustration)* About 50 percent; qualifications for suffrage allowing more people to vote and increased total population; 18 percent; 82 percent; 14 percent.

Page 249:   1. The Whig party.
2. William Henry Harrison.
3. The Democrats were blamed for the panic.

Page 251:   Chapter Review *(Remembering the Facts)*
1. By the House of Representatives.
2. The Democrats and the National-Republicans.
3. He was a popular choice of common people, city workers, and farmers.
4. Changes in voting qualifications.
5. He opposed it.
6. He did not like banks and thought paper money was of no value.
7. Removal from lands east of the Mississippi River.
8. All groups opposed these efforts, some like the Sac and Fox offered armed resistance, others like the Cherokee tried legal means.
9. To oppose Democratic policies.
10. A period of slow economic activity with prices low and many people out of work.

Page 251:   Chapter Review *(Understanding the Facts)*
1. Different sections had different ideas and concerns.
2. Clay gave his support to Adams and was rewarded with an appointment as Secretary of State.
3. To protect the government from dishonesty and to bring greater democracy in the government.
4. As a nationalist with regard to tariffs and the nullification crisis; as a supporter of states' rights with regard to the bank issue and the Maysville Road veto.
5. He felt the Indians were blocking settlement.
6. Democrats were blamed for the depression allowing the Whigs to win.
7. Jackson left office, and the Democrats were defeated in 1840.

Page 251:   Chapter Review *(Using Maps)*
1. 1828.
2. 1828.
3. Connecticut, Delaware, Massachusetts, Vermont, New Hampshire, and Rhode Island.
4. In the South and West.
5. In New England.
6. In 1824, New York, Delaware, Maryland, Illinois, and Louisiana; in 1828, Maine, Maryland, and New York.

City Sketch *(Washington, D.C. 1800-1825)*

Learning Objectives
The student should be able to:
1. identify the reasons for the location of the nation's capital.
2. describe the plan for the city of Washington.
3. order the events in building the new city.

Teaching Ideas

- Ask the students to list the reasons for the location of the nation's capital at the present site of Washington, D.C. Discuss the advantages and disadvantages. Point out that one of the advantages included its central location to all sections of the country. Ask the students why this advantage has become less important since its building. Consider these reasons in suggesting a location for a new capital city in the United States today.

- Draw a diamond figure on the chalkboard. Label it WASHINGTON, D.C. Draw lines dividing the figure from top to bottom and left to right. Label the appropriate sections NORTHEAST, NORTHWEST, SOUTHEAST, and SOUTHWEST. Tell the students that streets running east and west were given the letters of the alphabet. Streets running north and south were given numbers. Avenues with state names run at angles through the city. All addresses carry the designation of the section of the city in which it is located. Discuss the advantages and disadvantages to this plan. Discuss the students' local city or town. Ask the students to draw a simple form of its plan. Review in detail the reasons behind the plan of Washington. Ask the students if there seem to be any reasons for the plan of the local town or city. Discuss the term CITY PLANNING.

Answers

Page 253: *(illustration)* They served for ceremonial processions and to add dignity to the communication between the branches of government.

Page 254: *(illustration)* John Adams.

Page 255: *(illustration)* It slowed it down.

Page 257: *(illustration)* No street lights, no sewer system, and no city water supply.

Page 257:
1. The three branches of government would be located in three separate areas of the city, according to their different constitutional duties.
2. Pennsylvania Avenue.
3. Through the sale of private land in the area.
4. In boarding houses.
5. It was burned.
6. For Louisa Adams, the grounds were smoother for walking, the audience room was used for public receptions instead of for drying clothes, and the house was more finished.

Unit III Review *(Unit Questions)*

Page 259:
1. The need for unification, a sound economy, and respect from foreign countries.
2. Literature, painting, and music gave vivid accounts of everyday life in the United States.
3. Answers will vary but may include the idea that neither side won because the war did not decide the issues which had caused it.

4. Answers will vary but may include the idea that people can be proud of their country and their section at the same time.

5. Washington set precedents for the office, Jefferson doubled the physical size of the United States, and Jackson's election was a victory for the common people leading to a greater participation in government for many people.

6. To prevent any one state from having special influence over the federal government; it was a planned city designed specifically to be the federal capital.

7. Federalists formed around the policies of Washington and Hamilton, Democratic-Republicans formed in opposition to Federalists and around the policies of Jefferson, National-Republicans formed around the policies of John Quincy Adams, and Whigs formed to oppose Jackson's policies.

8. Jackson favored Indian removal to benefit settlers, and he opposed the authority of the Supreme Court.

Unit IV—Expansion

Learning Objectives

The student should be able to:
1. list the ways that the United States expanded in the first half of the nineteenth century.
2. identify the major events influencing American expansion.
3. name the people who contributed to American expansion.

Teaching Ideas

- Write the word EXPANSION on the chalkboard. Have the students consider the possibility that the United States had never physically expanded beyond the boundaries of the original 13 states. Direct the students to the map "United States Expansion, 1853" (page 310). List the states of the Union without physical expansion. List the states that would not be part of the United States today. Have the students consider how life in the United States would be different today without its physical expansion. Discuss other kinds of expansion the United States has experienced, including industry and population.

- Read the opening paragraph to the class, and have the students look carefully at the illustration (pages 260-261). The illustration is a section of a mural painted by John Steuart Curry. When the Washington government made available the fertile land of Oklahoma (" the Beautiful Land"), scores of overeager "sooners" jumped the gun, and entered Oklahoma territory. They had to be evicted by federal troops, who on occasion, would shoot their horses. On April 22, 1889, ready for the legal opening, some 50,000 settlers poured in on lathered horses or careening vehicles. Discuss with the students how this may represent the concept EXPANSION.

- Divide the class into eight groups, assigning each group one question from the Unit Questions (page 327). Encourage each group to work together to answer the assigned question. After sufficient time, review the questions. Select one student from each group to answer for the group. Use the Unit Review (pages 326-327) to conclude the teaching of the unit and prepare students for the unit test.

Chapter 11 *(The Promise of America)*

Learning Objectives

The student should be able to:
1. identify ways in which Americans attempted to perfect their lives in the 1820's and 1830's.
2. name the major reformers and their areas of concern.
3. name the major contributors to American literature in the first half of the 1800's.

4. describe creativity.
5. identify and read a demographic map.

Teaching Ideas

- Select three students to each draw a line, a circle, and a square on the chalkboard. Explain that the ideal line is perfectly straight, the ideal circle is perfectly round, and the ideal square is perfectly even on all sides. Ask the class to select a perfect line, circle, and square from those on the chalkboard. Discuss the term PERFECTION, and review in detail the text material concerning the desires of many Americans in the early 1800's to perfect themselves and their society.

- Write on the chalkboard THE GREATEST PROBLEMS FACING AMERICA TODAY ARE. . . . Instruct the students to write down their responses. Discuss the responses, and ask the students if they feel that something can be done about the problems. Discuss the possible ways to solve the problems. Instruct the students to use the text to list the problems that faced American society in the early 1800's. Discuss the list, and review the information from the text concerning the ways Americans attempted to solve these problems.

- Prepare a list of all names included in this chapter. Tell the students that today the class is going to play "name association." Instruct the students that the game is played by the teacher giving a name and a selected student responding with what made that person famous. Tell the students that some names might be used more than once. Begin slowly, using some names studied in past chapters (for example, George Washington, Christopher Columbus, and Andrew Jackson). Include names from this chapter, and gradually pick up speed selecting names and students to answer. Encourage rapid responses. Keep the game moving and rather short. After the game, review with the entire class all the names on the prepared list. Review in detail the pertinent text information about the names on the list.

Answers

Page 262: (*illustration*) Answers will vary but may include that Thoreau did what it was believed possible for all Americans to do.

Page 264: (*illustration*) Charles Finney.

Page 265: (*illustration*) To gain perfection through shared work, property, and wealth.

Page 265: 1. Many churches taught that people had a duty to improve themselves.
2. The Church of Jesus Christ of the Latter-Day Saints (Mormons) and Millerites.
3. The idea that every person is worthwhile and that people have the ability to guide their own lives.

Page 268: (*illustration*) It worked for the perfection of society.

Page 269: (*illustration*) Political, economic, and social rights for women.

Page 270: *(illustration)* Most students would be familiar with these objects; reading and writing.

Page 271: *(illustration)* The Female Seminary of Troy, New York, and Mount Holyoke Female Seminary in Massachusetts.

Page 273: *(illustration)* In the northeast; in the south and west.

Page 274:
1. People who wanted to do away with slavery.
2. People began to pay attention to the cause of women's rights.
3. Public tax money was used, more schools were built, and better teacher training and better books were used.
4. Dorothea Dix.

Page 275: Concept Feature *(Creativity)*
1. He thinks one can use one's mind to build one's own world.
2. He says that the creative person should be considered great.

Page 276: *(illustration)* Authors wrote about America and its people, using different forms and new ideas and themes.

Page 277:
1. America.
2. Ralph Waldo Emerson, Henry David Thoreau, and Margaret Fuller.
3. Answers will vary but may include *Walden, The Scarlet Letter, The House of Seven Gables, Moby Dick, The Pit and the Pendulum, The Murders in the Rue Morgue, Leaves of Grass, The Courtship of Miles Standish, Song of Hiawatha,* and *Voices of Freedom.*

Page 278: Chapter Review *(Remembering the Facts)*
1. Greater democracy and a spirit of equality.
2. They believed the power to perfect is within each person.
3. They wanted to attempt to remake society.
4. William Lloyd Garrison founded *The Liberator,* Theodore Weld formed the Liberty party, James G. Birney was a presidential candidate, Elijah Lovejoy was an abolitionist publisher, and Frederick Douglass and Sojourner Truth were former slaves who spoke out against slavery.
5. They could not vote or hold public office, own property if married, or enter certain professions or schools.
6. There was increased demand for public tax-supported schools to educate better citizens.
7. They were usually treated as criminals and often kept in cages.
8. To shift the emphasis from punishment to reform.
9. Answers will vary but may include Hawthorne, Melville, Poe, Whitman, Longfellow, and Whittier.

Page 279: Chapter Review *(Understanding the Facts)*
1. Revivalists taught that with God's help, it was possible for people to live better lives.
2. Because of their beliefs.
3. Answers will vary but may include that some lasted because of a common bond, such as religion.
4. Most Americans at that time accepted slavery.

5. The goals of each reform group were basically the same, an improved society by making its institutions better.
6. Citizens needed to be able to read, write, and understand issues in order to vote.
7. Some people linked alcohol to crime, poverty, and other problems.
8. Their subjects included the evils in people's lives, the struggle between good and evil, and the belief in the power of the individual to overcome evil.

Page 279: Chapter Review *(Using Maps)*
1. The Northeast.
2. North.
3. The West.
4. Varied.
5. North Carolina.
6. Yes.

Chapter 12 *(New Ways and New People)* ————————————————

Learning Objectives

The student should be able to:
1. order events in the development of industry in the United States.
2. name major inventors and inventions.
3. identify means of transportation in the early 1800's.
4. describe the benefits and problems of city life in the early 1800's.
5. describe the effects of increased foreign immigration.
6. distinguish between fact and opinion.
7. identify and read a line graph.

Teaching Ideas

- Divide the class into groups of five students each. Supply each group with five pieces of scrap paper. Instruct students that each group is to fold each piece of paper five times. Tell the students that each group is in competition with the others in order to be the first to fold all five pieces of paper. Instruct the students that the teacher will signal them to start. When a group is finished, the people in the group should raise their arms. Before the teacher gives the signal to start, instruct the students to discuss as a group the best way to fold the paper in the shortest amount of time. Each student may make one fold and pass the paper on to another, or each student may fold one piece of paper completely. Allow ample time for group discussion. Signal the students to begin. After the competition, discuss the various techniques used. Write on the chalkboard INDUSTRY. Review in detail the development of industry in the United States.

- Instruct the students to turn to the map "Major Railroads in the 1850's" (page 289). Have the students consider a trip from New Orleans, Louisiana, to Montpelier, Vermont. Instruct students to study the map and write out an itinerary for the trip, listing city-by-city stops along main and secondary lines. Discuss the student itineraries, and have the students estimate the length of time for the trip on a train traveling about 15 miles per hour. Review in detail the pertinent text material.

- Read out loud the Profile of Margaret Gaffney Haughery (page 293). The Profile contains examples of many aspects of life which are discussed in the chapter. Ask the students to identify and list the elements of life mentioned in the Profile. List them on the chalkboard. The list should include Haughery being an immigrant from Ireland, moving west from Maryland to New Orleans, finding opportunity in the city for business, making use of steam-powered machinery, and contributing money to help a reform cause. Discuss the material, particularly that concerning city life, immigration, and business, in detail.

Answers

Page 200: (illustration) Making goods in new ways changed the ways people made their livings and where they lived, and it changed the lives of people used to farming their own land and making their own decisions.

Page 282: (illustration) They provided the needed supply of unskilled labor.

Page 283: Skill Feature (Checking Fact and Opinion)
1. Approximate number, age, and salary.
2. He pitied them.
3. The cautiousness of the proprietor, the use of children as workers, and the working conditions.
4. Water-wheels powered the machinery, the factory produced finished cotton.
5. Answers will vary but may include the idea of studying the material carefully to look for words that indicate opinion.

Page 285: (illustration) Whitney's cotton gin, Goodyear's way to cure rubber, Morse's telegraph, Howe's original sewing machine, Kelly's way to make steel, McCormick's reaper, Page's revolving disc harrow, and Heath's mechanical binder.

Page 285:
1. Samuel Slater.
2. Lowell, Massachusetts.
3. The cotton gin, the process of vulcanization, the telegraph, the sewing machine, and the reaper.
4. Coal.

Page 286: (illustration) Buffalo and Albany, New York.

Page 287: (illustration) *Clermont;* more boats were used for river transportation.

Page 288: (illustration) Walking, the horse and carriage, and the steamboat; in the North.

Page 290:
1. To make it easier and cheaper to get raw materials to factories and goods to markets.
2. To get produce to people cheaply and quickly.
3. The South.

Page 291:	*(illustration)* It increased rapidly; 13 percent; Ireland and Germany.
Page 292:	*(illustration)* Cincinnati.
Page 293:	1. New York.

Page 293:
1. New York.
2. More jobs and schools, libraries, and operas and plays.
3. Larger cities stretched their borders beyond the point where water, sewage, and other services were available; there were crowded tenements, and the air was clouded by factories.

Page 294: *(illustration)* Better pay.

Page 295:
1. Ireland and Germany.
2. Irish in eastern cities and Germans in the Middle West.
3. The American party, also known as the Know-Nothings.

Page 297: Chapter Review *(Remembering the Facts)*
1. In most of them, buildings were dirty and pay was poor.
2. Interchangeable parts.
3. They helped its growth.
4. Patents.
5. Canals, railroads, and steamboats.
6. Building reservoirs, adding street lighting and night watches, and forming police and fire departments.
7. Immigrants from Ireland and Germany.
8. Nativists feared competition for jobs from immigrants who worked for lower wages.

Page 297: Chapter Review *(Understanding the Facts)*
1. Slater's reproduction of British textile machinery and New England merchants' investments in textile manufacturing rather than importing at the time of the War of 1812.
2. People worked in factories, not in their homes; they used machines that were power-driven, not hand-driven; the making of products was divided into separate tasks for many people, instead of all at once by one person.
3. The cotton gin.
4. Tasks could be done easier and faster.
5. Much of the new machinery was made of iron.
6. Greater needs for iron, timber, and coal.
7. New towns were built near factories, and old cities grew larger where factories were built.
8. It increased by immigrants attracted to job opportunities.

Page 297: Chapter Review *(Using Line Graphs)*
1. Population growth in the United States between 1790 and 1860.
2. About 4 million.
3. About 10 million.
4. About 17 million.
5. About 7 million.
6. It increased.
7. The rate of growth would not be that great.

Chapter 13 *(From Ocean to Ocean)* _____

Learning Objectives

The student should be able to:

1. name Americans who explored the lands west of the Mississippi River.
2. describe the reasons for American interest in Oregon.
3. order the events leading to the annexation of Texas.
4. list the causes and results of the Mexican War.
5. describe the effects of the gold discovery in California.
6. describe the effects of American expansion on Indian life.
7. describe mobility in relation to westward expansion.
8. identify and read latitude and longitude.

Teaching Ideas

● Write the word WEST on the chalkboard. Ask students to list words that are associated with it. Discuss the student responses. Ask students to describe where the West is. Explain that the West has had different meanings at different times. The Appalachian Mountains, the Mississippi Valley, the Rocky Mountains, and the Pacific coast all have been considered to be the West at one time or another. Define MANIFEST DESTINY as the fate of the United States to stretch from ocean to ocean and include the West. Review in detail the pertinent text material.

● Instruct the students to turn to the picture of Independence Rock (page 301). Read the caption out loud. Ask the students why they think travelers wanted to document their journey. Discuss student responses. Ask students for other ways to document a trip. Responses should include diaries and journals. Define a diary as a daily record of personal experiences and a journal as a record of events and experiences as they happen. Diaries and journals of people involved in history-making events are among the most important records in history. They often reflect political, economic, and social conditions of the time. Some public leaders kept diaries and journals, but even more revealing at times have been those records kept by private citizens. Instruct the students to write a brief account of a day in the life of a traveler on the Oregon Trail. Refer the students to the map "Routes to the Far West" (page 302) for the location of the trail in order to place the writer at some point along the trail. Also instruct the students to review the pertinent text material, including the quotation from Francis Parkman's *The Oregon Trail* (page 303). Allow ample time for the students to review the material and write. Discuss the student accounts of life on the trail, evaluating them in terms of accuracy and realism.

● Instruct the students to write WHO, WHEN, WHERE, HOW, WHY, and WITH WHAT RESULT in their notebooks, allowing enough space between the words to write the answers. Instruct the students to use their texts to answer these questions for the Mexican War. After allowing sufficient time, review the student findings.

- Draw a circle on the chalkboard. Divide the circle appropriately and label each portion of the circle as follows:

> UNITED STATES (1783) 28%
> LOUISIANA TERRITORY (1803) 28.3%
> MEXICAN CESSION (1848) 18.1%
> TEXAS (1845) 13.3%
>
> OREGON COUNTRY (1846) 9.7%
> FLORIDA (1819) 2.4%
> OTHER 0.2%

Label the pie graph PERCENT OF EXPANSION. Discuss the pertinent text material concerning territorial growth of the United States from its independence to the 1850's.

Answers

Page 298: *(illustration)* Land, wealth, and adventure.

Page 300:
1. Meriwether Lewis and William Clark, Zebulon Pike, Stephen Long, and various fur trappers and traders.
2. A magazine editor in 1845 first used the term.
3. Business people, settlers, and American leaders.

Page 301: *(illustration)* 2,000 miles or 3,200 kilometers, four to six months.

Page 302: *(illustration)* Ft. Leavenworth, Ft. Kearney, Ft. Laramie, Ft. Hall, Ft. Boise, and Ft. Vancouver; almost 700 miles or 1,120 kilometers; Nauvoo, Illinois, and Salt Lake City; Santa Fe and Yuma; Santa Fe to Los Angeles; the Humboldt River.

Page 303:
1. From Independence, Missouri, to Oregon Country.
2. Great Britain, Russia, Spain, and the United States.
3. Great Britain.

Page 304: *(illustration)* Many Indians who lived there lost land, and many died of disease and lack of food.

Page 307: *(illustration)* Because of the bravery of the 187 Texans who held out against the 4,000 attacking Mexican soldiers.

Page 308: *(illustration)* Great Britain and the United States; by treaty in 1846.

Page 309: *(illustration)* Because of border conflict and American desire to expand.

Page 310: *(illustration)* By treaty, purchase, cession, and annexation; four; by purchase.

Page 311: *(illustration)* 1848.

Page 312: Concept Feature *(Mobility)*
1. Husband and wife packing up, blacksmith, carpenter, mason, and baker all off to the mines.
2. Laborers and boys became rich from the gold they found.
3. Possibly not at all, or at least not so fast.

Page 313:
1. William Becknell.
2. Stephen Austin.
3. Zachary Taylor, Winfield Scott, Stephen Kearney, and John C. Frémont.
4. People came in wagons and ships to find gold.

Page 314:
(illustration) Horses were faster and more mobile; they permitted the people to travel over larger areas of land; buffalo provided the people with food, clothes, and shelter.

Page 315:
1. Horses made hunting buffalo and traveling over large areas easier.
2. It set the boundaries of Indian land, leading to reservations.

Page 316: Chapter Review *(Remembering the Facts)*
1. They supplied information about the West and guided settlers.
2. Merchants wanted ports on the Pacific, settlers wanted to live on the fertile lands in Oregon and California, and American leaders wanted to keep Europeans from gaining control of the area.
3. The Oregon Trail.
4. The missions were broken up.
5. Loyalty to Mexico and the practice of the Catholic religion.
6. War; annexation.
7. The United States paid Mexico $15 million for all the land north of the Rio Grande and the Gila River.
8. The discovery of gold.
9. They made it easier to hunt buffalo and to travel.
10. It limited the boundaries of Indian lands.

Page 317: Chapter Review *(Understanding the Facts)*
1. Opportunities for land, wealth, and adventure.
2. Spain, France, Russia, Great Britain, and Mexico.
3. Because of Mexico's restrictions on slavery and immigration; because most of the people were Americans.
4. The annexation of Texas, a border dispute, and a Mexican invasion.
5. It affected the Indians' ways of life and caused the loss of more Indian land.
6. Limitation.

Page 317: Chapter Review *(Using Maps)*
1. North.
2. British Canada and the Russian Territory.
3. British Canada and the United States.
4. Mexico and the United States.
5. About 450 miles or 720 kilometers.

City Sketches *(New Orleans 1845-1855; San Francisco 1845-1855)* ———

Learning Objectives

The student should be able to:
1. describe city life in New Orleans and San Francisco.
2. distinguish between the economic bases of New Orleans and San Francisco.

3. distinguish between the growth of New Orleans and San Francisco before 1845.

Teaching Ideas

● Direct students to the maps of New Orleans (page 318) and San Francisco (page 322). Ask the students to compare the geographical locations. Discuss the responses. Review the text material, and list further points to compare and contrast on the chalkboard. These should include origins, ethnic makeup of the populations, and growth. Ask students how each was affected by United States expansion. Discuss responses.

● Have the students consider the possibility that huge gold and silver deposits might be found on the moon. Ask students how this might affect future plans to settle the moon and other areas of space. Review how gold affected the settlement of the area around San Francisco. List specific examples on the chalkboard.

Answers

Page 319: *(illustration)* Tobacco, flour, cotton, and sugar.

Page 320: *(illustration)* Black, Indian, Irish, French, Spanish, West African, West Indian, and Anglo-American peoples.

Page 321: *(illustration)* French.

Page 321:
1. About 100 miles or 160 kilometers from where the Mississippi River emptied into the Gulf of Mexico.
2. A wall of earth to hold back water.
3. Black, Indian, Irish, French, Spanish, West African, West Indian, and Anglo-American peoples.
4. Spanish, music, singing, dancing, and manners.

Page 323: *(illustration)* Mining pans, shovels, gambling saloons, restaurants, and hotels.

Page 324: *(illustration)* There were very few homes and little family life.

Page 325: *(illustration)* Banking and trade.

Page 325:
1. Spanish missionaries.
2. It is located on a natural deep-water channel connecting the bay to the ocean.
3. The gold rush.
4. All the canvas tents and wooden buildings.
5. To maintain law and order in the city.
6. Both are near water, trade-centered, and international in flavor.
7. A mix of peoples came to both cities; they came to San Francisco for gold and to New Orleans for jobs.

Unit IV Review *(Unit Questions)*

Page 327:
1. American literary figures began writing about America and its peoples.
2. They all were influenced by the democratic spirit and the spirit of perfection.

3. A need to get raw materials to factories and goods to markets added to a need for better transportation. As the factory system grew, towns were built near factories, and older towns grew where factories were started.
4. The Northeast; the South and the West, because they were agriculturally based.
5. Oregon, Texas, California, and the Southwest; by treaty, annexation, and purchase.
6. Answers will vary but may include the ideas that Jefferson supported self-reliance, the perfection of individuals, and reform movements, and that Hamilton supported industrial development, physical expansion of the country, and increased role of business and government.
7. Answers will vary but may include reflections of Jackson's proslavery and antiforeign sentiments.
8. New Orleans was a French city in origin and became the third largest United States city, San Francisco was a Spanish outpost that grew as a result of the discovery of gold; New Orleans as a major port and San Francisco as a banking and trade center.

Unit V—Division

Learning Objectives

The student should be able to:
1. identify the factors leading to division in the United States.
2. describe the ways in which division occurred.
3. identify the steps taken to reunite the nation.

Teaching Ideas

- Have the students recall the text material concerning the geographic regions in the colonies (pages 108-113). Direct the students to the material in the text. Discuss the similarities and differences of each region compared to the others. List on the chalkboard the major differences. Write the word DIVISION on the chalkboard. Have the students recall other times when Americans have been divided. These should include the debates over the Constitution, the time of the Hartford Convention, and the Nullification Crisis. Discuss the reasons for division in the United States up to this time in the 1800's.

- Read the unit opening paragraph to the class, and have the students look carefully at the illustration (pages 328-329). The illustration is a section of a painting by James Walker, *Gettysburg—The First Day,* On the fields near Gettysburg, Meade with 92,000 men in blue met in combat with 75,000 grey-clad soldiers. The battle lasted three days before the Confederates were defeated. Discuss with the students how this battle may represent the concept DIVISION.

- After study of the unit, direct the students to the Unit Review Time Line (page 402). Instruct the students to list the events leading to the Civil War, adding any other events not included on the Time Line. Instruct the students to use the text material to write a date for each event. Discuss the length of time over which the country had been dividing. Have the students consider ways that the Civil War might have been prevented. Ask the students if division ended with Reconstruction. Use the Unit Review (pages 402-403) to conclude the teaching of the unit and prepare students for the unit test.

Chapter 14 *(A Divided Nation)*

Learning Objectives

The student should be able to:
1. identify the social, economic, and political differences of the North and the South.
2. describe slavery.
3. distinguish between northern and southern attitudes toward slavery.
4. describe the efforts to compromise on the issue of the expansion of slavery.

5. order the events leading to southern secession.
6. describe the effects of sectionalism.
7. distinguish among information on three maps.

Teaching Ideas

- Write a chart outline on the chalkboard with AREAS OF DIFFER-ENCE, NORTH, and SOUTH across the top. Under AREAS OF DIFFERENCE, list SOCIAL, ECONOMIC, and POLITICAL. Instruct the students to write the chart outline in their notebooks, allowing enough space to complete it. Review the pertinent text material in discussing the sectional differences between North and South.

- Write on the chalkboard SLAVERY MEANS. . . . Ask the students to complete this sentence in their notebooks in as many ways as possible, using the pertinent text material. Discuss the student responses, and list the major meanings on the chalkboard. Review in detail the pertinent text material.

- Direct the students to the Concept Feature, "Sectionalism" (page 339). Select a student to read out loud the portion of David Wilmot's speech given in the feature. Select another student to read out loud the portion of Robert Toomb's speech. Discuss the speeches, using the feature questions as a guide. Explain that the speeches represent the sectional views of the North and the South on the issue of the expansion of slavery. Write the word COMPROMISE on the chalkboard. Remind the students that this term was defined in Chapter 6 (page 156). Ask the students how the slavery issue had been compromised. Review the pertinent text material, including the map "Expansion of Slavery" (page 345).

- Write the following on the chalkboard:

  > FUGITIVE SLAVE ACT
  > *UNCLE TOM'S CABIN*
  > "BLEEDING KANSAS"
  > REPUBLICAN PARTY
  > DRED SCOTT CASE
  > JOHN BROWN'S RAID
  > ELECTION OF 1860

Have the students consider how Jefferson Davis, representing a view from the South, and Abraham Lincoln, representing a view from the North, would comment on each element of the list. Review in detail each element, including the facts and the sectional views of each.

Answers

Page 330: *(illustration)* Taxes, government spending, federal banks, tariffs, and the rise of industry.

Page 332: *(illustration)* There was no machinery that could do it.

Page 333: 1. The North.
2. The South.
3. The South.

Page 335: *(illustration)* By auction.

Page 336: *(illustration)* They were returned to slavery and usually punished.

Page 338: 1. The cotton gin.
2. It increased from 1.5 million to over 3 million.
3. They felt it was a way to control blacks and a way to allow blacks and whites to live together.
4. To end slavery.

Page 339: Concept Feature *(Sectionalism)*
1. The spread of slavery to the territories.
2. Wilmot was from the free state of Pennsylvania; Toombs was from the slave state of Georgia.
3. Slim.

Page 341: 1. The Free-Soil and Liberty parties.
2. To bring the question of slavery's expansion to the country's attention.
3. The North—California admitted as a free state, popular sovereignty in the territories, and the end of slave trade in the District of Columbia; the South—the Fugitive Slave Act and popular sovereignty.

Page 341: *(illustration)* In the antislavery North.

Page 343: *(illustration)* Those for and against the expansion of slavery.

Page 345: *(illustration)* Missouri was a slave state, Maine was a free state, and no slavery was allowed above 36°30′ in the Louisiana Purchase territory; Texas was a slave state, California was a free state, New Mexico was open to slavery, and Utah was closed to slavery; because the question of expanded slavery above 36°30′ was a possibility.

Page 346: 1. It permitted federal law officers to help return runaway slaves to the South.
2. 1854.
3. It supported southern views of the spread of slavery.

Page 347: *(illustration)* The North; the deep South; Lincoln opposed the spread of slavery, while Breckinridge favored it.

Page 348: *(illustration)* 1861.

Page 348: 1. Abraham Lincoln, Stephen Douglas, John C. Breckinridge, and John Bell.
2. South Carolina, Mississippi, Florida, Alabama, Georgia, Louisiana, and Texas.

Page 349: Chapter Review *(Remembering the Facts)*
1. Political—the North felt the federal government was supreme, and the South felt the state governments were supreme; social—the North was more urban and immigrant, and the South was more rural and heavily slave; economic—the North was industrial favoring higher taxes, more government spending, federal banks, and protective tariffs, and the South was

agricultural favoring lower taxes, less government spending, state banks, and no tariffs.
2. Over 3 million.
3. By slave codes or laws.
4. By slowing down work, revolting, and running away.
5. They wanted to end slavery; some wanting to stop its spread into new territories or states, some wanting to end all slavery, and others wanting equal treatment for blacks.
6. The Missouri Compromise and the Compromise of 1850; they were both temporary solutions.
7. The Kansas-Nebraska Act said that people could decide about slavery in each territory; the Dred Scott decision suggested that slavery could not be kept out of the territories.
8. It was opposed to the spread of slavery.
9. The election of Lincoln as President.

Page 350:   Chapter Review *(Understanding the Facts)*
1. The federal government threatened slavery, so many slaves states accepted the view of a state's right to support slavery.
2. With it, the workers were able to prepare more cotton for shipment to textile mills in a shorter time. Amounts of cotton from the South increased, and planters profited.
3. Slaves' lives were regulated by slave codes, and they were treated as property.
4. They did not want to lose support from all areas of the country.
5. Both the North and the South were no longer willing to compromise.

Page 350:   Chapter Review *(Using Maps)*
1. Thematic maps.
2. Seven (Michigan, Wisconsin, Iowa, Florida, Arkansas, Texas, and California).
3. The number was even.
4. More free states.
5. More free states.
6. Larger.
7. They gained.
8. They gained.

Chapter 15   *(The Civil War)*

Learning Objectives
The student should be able to:
1. list the states that made up the Confederacy.
2. order the events leading to the Civil War.
3. distinguish between Union and Confederate war plans and advantages.
4. identify the major events of the Civil War.
5. name most of the major Union and Confederate leaders.

6. describe the effects of the war on the home front.
7. identify a speech as a primary source.
8. identify and read a pie graph.

Teaching Ideas

- Write the following list on the chalkboard:

  BANKING CAPITAL
  EQUIPMENT
  LEADERSHIP
  LOCATION
  NAVY
  POPULATION
  RAILROAD MILEAGE
  VALUE OF MANUFACTURE
  TOTAL ADVANTAGE

  Next to this list, make two columns, one headed UNION and the other headed CONFEDERACY. Use this chart as a guide to reviewing the advantages of both the North and the South before the Civil War. As each element is discussed, place a check in the appropriate column for either the Union or the Confederacy. Review the pertinent text material and the pie graphs "Union and Confederate Resources, 1860" (page 355).

- Divide the class into four groups. Assign the groups the following dates: April 1861 to April 1862, April 1862 to April 1863, April 1863 to April 1864, and April 1864 to April 1865. Using the pertinent text material, have the students in each group prepare a list of the major Civil War events in their assigned time period. Review and discuss in detail each group's list. Ask the members of each group to determine the most significant events during each time period. Have the students make general statements about each phase of the Civil War.

- Direct the students to the portion of the letter Abraham Lincoln wrote to Horace Greeley in 1862 (page 360). Read the quote out loud. Ask the students what Lincoln's reasons for fighting the war seemed to be. Direct the students to the Skill Feature, "Asking Questions" (page 367). Read the Gettysburg Address out loud. Ask the students what Lincoln's reasons for fighting the war seemed to be a year later, in 1863. Discuss other reasons for fighting the war. Have the students consider the various reasons for fighting the war, and discuss the results of the Civil War.

Answers

Page 351: *(illustration)* Answers will vary but may include the issue of states' rights, to preserve the Union, and because of sectional differences.

Page 353: *(illustration)* The Union area is shown in green, the Confederate area is shown in cream.

Page 354: *(illustration)* Answers will vary but may include that they would enable the coordinated movement of the army as one unit and permit messages and commands to get from leaders to the fronts.

Page 355: *(illustration)* More people meant more people to fight, more railroads meant better transportation for moving supplies, more manufacture meant more war materials, more money meant better financial support for the war—as these advantages worked for the Union, they were disadvantages for the Confederacy which lacked these resources.

Page 356:
1. April 12, 1861, at Fort Sumter, South Carolina.
2. Arkansas, North Carolina, Tennessee, and Virginia.
3. Missouri, Kentucky, Delaware, and Maryland.
4. France and Great Britain.

Page 357: *(illustration)* The *Virginia* withdrew, and the blockade held.

Page 358: *(illustration)* The blockade was in use, the South was invaded, and the Mississippi was taken over by the Union; Bull Run and Richmond; to prevent the South from sending out cotton and bringing in supplies.

Page 359: *(illustration)* Lee's army was forced to withdraw to Virginia, and it gave Lincoln a victory to accompany his Emancipation Proclamation.

Page 360:
1. Fort Henry and Fort Donelson.
2. The First Battle of Bull Run, the Seven Days Battles, and the Second Battle of Bull Run.
3. Nearly 200,000 blacks, most of whom were slaves, joined the Union forces.

Page 361: *(illustration)* People raised money, gathered food, collected clothing, and rolled bandages.

Page 363: *(illustration)* By bounties and the draft.

Page 364:
1. They set up volunteer aid societies, acted as spies, served as nurses, and helped to provide food and other supplies.
2. Industries that made iron, cannons, movable bridges, and locomotives.
3. They sold bonds, issued paper money, took out loans, and passed taxes.

Page 365: *(illustration)* Gettysburg, Pennsylvania; about 70 miles or 110 kilometers.

Page 366:
1. Fredricksburg, Chancellorsville, Gettysburg, and Vicksburg.
2. Gettysburg.
3. It split the South and gave control of the Mississippi River to the Union.

Page 367: Skill Feature *(Asking Questions)*
1. Question answered by the material—To save the Union.
2. Question answered by the material—A battle where men had been killed in action.
3. Question raised by the material.
4. Question answered by the material—To win the war and save the nation.
5. Question raised by the material.
6. Question raised by the material.

Page 368: *(illustration)* He had split the South and gained control of the Mississippi River; to further divide the South and destroy Southern supplies; the Wilderness, Cold Harbor, Spotsylvania Courthouse, and Petersburg.

Page 369: *(illustration)* The preservation of the Union.

Page 370: 1. Ulysses S. Grant.
2. April 9, 1865, at Appomattox Courthouse, Virginia.
3. April 14, 1865.

Page 371: Chapter Review *(Remembering the Facts)*
1. He did not plan to end slavery where it already existed.
2. The Union planned to blockade the South, split it at the Mississippi River, and invade it; the South planned to fight a defensive war to be close to their sources of supplies.
3. Both countries depended on the South for cotton.
4. All slaves in Confederate lands.
5. It involved much of the population on both sides in various roles from fighting to making weapons.
6. The Republican party.
7. April 9, 1865.
8. Answers will vary but may include Fredericksburg, Chancellorsville, Gettysburg, and Vicksburg.
9. His assassination.

Page 372: Chapter Review *(Understanding the Facts)*
1. Because of Lincoln's call for troops to fight the Confederacy.
2. It had the advantages of population, railroads, manufacture, and banking.
3. It had more experienced leaders, it hoped for European aid, and it planned to fight a defensive war.
4. To hold the support of abolitionists.
5. They sold bonds, printed more paper money, and taxed the states.
6. They hired someone else to serve for them.
7. The South invaded the North and suffered a major defeat; the North held off the invasion and forced the South to retreat.
8. He believed he was helping the Confederate cause.

Page 372: Chapter Review *(Using Pie Graphs)*
1. None.
2. All.
3. The Union.
4. The Union.

Chapter 16 *(Rebuilding the Nation)* _____

Learning Objectives

The student should be able to:
1. distinguish between the reconstruction plans of Presidents Lincoln and Johnson.

2. outline the congressional reconstruction plan.
3. identify the main points of the constitutional amendments ratified during Reconstruction.
4. order the events leading to President Johnson's impeachment.
5. list the ways southern whites responded to reconstruction.
6. describe the activities and conditions of southern blacks during Reconstruction.
7. order the events leading to the Compromise of 1877.
8. demonstrate the ability to draw a conclusion.
9. identify and read a thematic map.

Teaching Ideas

- Write on the chalkboard REBUILDING THE NATION, FREED SLAVES, and TREATMENT OF THE SOUTH. Tell the students that these were the three main issues facing American leaders after the Civil War. Also write on another part of the chalkboard POLICY and PROGRAM. Define each, with policy meaning an official attitude toward an issue and program meaning an official plan of action. Review in detail the pertinent text material concerning Reconstruction attitudes and plans. Have the students distinguish among the various policies and programs concerning the major issues of Reconstruction.

- Instruct the students to read the Profile of Charlotte Forten (page 388). Ask the students why Forten moved to Port Royal. Ask why it was necessary for people from the North to go to the South to teach former slaves. Write EDUCATION on the chalkboard. Ask why slave owners denied slaves an education. Ask how important it was for former slaves to be able to read and write. Ask how important it is for citizens to be able to read and write in a democracy. Review in detail the material concerning the other functions of the Freedmen's Bureau.

- Tell the students that an on-the-street interview is one way in which views of private citizens are expressed in a public forum. Local newspapers and television news programs often use this method as a way of establishing a public opinion. Instruct the students to review the text material concerning the Reconstruction period. Instruct them to prepare at least five questions to be part of an on-the-street interview conducted during the late 1860's and 1870's. One way for the students to determine the important topics for possible questions is to consider the chapter narrative headings and subheadings. The questions might include "What do you think of the work of the Freedmen's Bureau?" or "Do you think President Andrew Johnson should stay in office?" Allow ample time for the students to review the material and prepare the questions. While the students are working, write the following on the chalkboard:

    THADDEUS STEVENS
    CHARLOTTE FORTEN
    JOHN T. TROWBRIDGE

EDWIN STANTON
JONATHAN C. GIBBS
A BLACK ALABAMA SHARECROPPER
A WHITE GEORGIA LABORER
A WHITE NEW YORK STATE LEGISLATOR
A FORMER CONFEDERATE GENERAL
AN ARMY OFFICER IN OCCUPIED MISSISSIPPI

Discuss the student questions, and have the students consider how each of the people listed on the chalkboard would answer their questions.

Answers

Page 373: *(illustration)* Plans were made by President Lincoln, President Johnson, and the Radical Republican Congress.

Page 375: *(illustration)* To find jobs and avoid the black codes.

Page 377: Skill Feature *(Drawing Conclusions)*
1. His view was that whites had lost money, jobs, and land.
2. His view was that blacks were also worse off after the war.
3. Based on this information, people were hungry, poor, and had no jobs.
4. One person has limited experience and cannot understand all aspects of a situation.

Page 378:
1. They could not agree over which branch of the government should direct reconstruction.
2. Those wanting to make major changes, including Charles Sumner, Benjamin Wade, Thaddeus Stevens, and Henry Winter Davis.
3. He did not like planters and cared little about the freed slaves, but he cared about states' rights, and his plan was similar to Lincoln's.

Page 379: *(illustration)* To become better citizens.

Page 381: *(illustration)* March 1867; when state constitutions were accepted by Congress and enough of the new legislatures had approved the Fourteenth Amendment, they could be readmitted; to see that the states held constitutional conventions.

Page 379: *(illustration)* To become better citizens.

Page 381: *(illustration)* March 1867; when state constitutions were accepted by Congress and enough of the new legislatures had approved the Fourteenth Amendment, they could be readmitted; to see that the states held constitutional conventions.

Page 382: *(illustration)* Johnson was found not guilty.

Page 382:
1. All needy people in the South, with the freed slaves as its main concern.
2. They could not vote, testify against whites in court, serve on juries, or hold certain jobs.
3. Tennessee.
4. Radicals charged Johnson with breaking the Tenure of Office Act.

Page 383: *(illustration)* Blanche K. Bruce, Hiram P. Revels, Jonathan C. Gibbs, and Francis L. Cardozo.

Page 385: *(illustration)* Many opposed the new Republican governments and carpetbaggers, scalawags, and untrained blacks in government.

Page 386: *(illustration)* Beatings, killings, and black codes.

Page 386:
1. Land, education, and the rights to vote and hold public office.
2. The Republicans.
3. They opposed the new Republican governments and anyone else seeking to help freed slaves gain equal rights.
4. To scare blacks and their supporters.

Page 390: *(illustration)* Tilden; Tilden; 20 disputed electoral votes; a congressional commission decided the election.

Page 391:
1. He favored Radical reconstruction and black rights.
2. They hurt the Republican party which had lost most of its power in the South.
3. 1877.
4. The last Radical governments in the South were no longer protected by the federal government, they were later taken over by Democrats, and blacks lost their political rights and economic opportunities.

Page 392: Chapter Review *(Remembering the Facts)*
1. Southern whites had to take a loyalty oath, and new state governments had to recognize the freedom of slaves (Confederate leaders were not part of the plan).
2. All slaves in the United States.
3. He succeeded Lincoln after the assassination; southern whites should take a loyalty oath, Confederate leaders and people who had $20,000 in cash or property would need a special pardon, seceded states would hold elections for constitutional conventions to repeal their acts of secession, to adopt the Thirteenth Amendment, and to refuse to pay Confederate debts.
4. The Freedmen's Bureau was set up to help needy southerners, the Civil Rights Acts were passed to protect political freedom of the freed slaves, and Reconstruction acts were passed, which set up military districts to return the states to the Union after new legislatures approved the Fourteenth Amendment.
5. To aid all needy people in the South, although freed slaves were its main concern.
6. No state could deprive a citizen of life, liberty, or property without due process of law.
7. Voting and holding public offices; South Carolina and Louisiana.
8. It kept them from controlling southern state governments by threats, beatings, and sometimes killings.
9. Crédit Mobilier and the "Whiskey Ring."
10. Northern Republicans got a President, and southern Democrats got the last federal troops and federal control out of the South.

Page 393: Chapter Review *(Understanding the Facts)*
1. Presidential reconstruction was thought by some to be too soft, while congressional reconstruction was thought by some to be too hard.

2. Because of Johnson's past record.
3. Eleven articles of impeachment, most dealing with Johnson's failure to follow the Tenure of Office Act; Johnson was voted "not guilty."
4. To limit the rights of blacks.
5. To be full citizens; they felt freed blacks would destroy the South.
6. Land was an economic base, and without it, blacks could not gain equality.

Page 393: Chapter Review *(Using Maps)*
1. States and military districts.
2. Black representation, years of readmission, members of state constitutional conventions.
3. III.
4. I.
5. Tennessee; it was readmitted before districts were established.
6. South Carolina.
7. One, South Carolina.
8. Southern whites.

City Sketches   *(New York 1860-1865; Atlanta 1860-1865)*

Learning Objectives
The student should be able to:
1. distinguish between the origins of New York and Atlanta.
2. describe the roles of New York and Atlanta in the Civil War.
3. identify the ways people in the two cities were affected by the war.

Teaching Ideas
- Divide the class in half. Assign one group Atlanta and the other New York. Have the students consider themselves in their assigned city in the year 1865. Tell the students that they will be writing a letter to a friend in the other city. Instruct the students to review the text material and write a letter describing life and recent events in their assigned city during the Civil War. Allow sufficient time for the students to write a one-page letter. Select students to read their letters out loud. Discuss them in terms of accuracy and realism.

- Write on the chalkboard JULY 13, 1863 and SEPTEMBER 4, 1864. Instruct the students to scan the text material. Ask why these dates are important to people living at the time in New York and Atlanta. Discuss the causes and results of the events of each day—the first day of the New York draft riots and the day Sherman's soldiers entered Atlanta. Review in detail the pertinent text material.

Answers
Page 395:   *(illustration)* The *Tribune,* the *Times,* and the *Sunday Times;* to report the activities and news of the war.

Page 396: *(illustration)* Some felt people were drafted for political reasons.

Page 397: *(illustration)* Many families lost relatives, and many people from New York returned from the war wounded.

Page 397:
1. New Amsterdam.
2. Many men in uniform, flags draped in many places.
3. To them, army service meant pay and proof of their loyalty.
4. A large, cheering crowd had gathered, and people embraced one another and cried.

Page 399: *(illustration)* Atlanta was a base for Confederate supplies, transportation, and communication. It was a railroad center and a major southern manufacturing city.

Page 400: *(illustration)* To destroy this base of supply.

Page 401: *(illustration)* They began building again.

Page 401:
1. Railroad promoters named it.
2. They destroyed it; they maintained law and order and helped in the rebuilding.
3. They had little money, and their property had been destroyed.
4. New York had free, public education, Atlanta had mostly expensive, private education.
5. Both served as supply and manufacturing centers and sent many soldiers to the fighting.

Unit V Review *(Unit Questions)*

Page 403:
1. The status of the western territories (free or slave) became an issue.
2. The Declaration of Independence states that all men are created equal; southern whites argued that slavery was important to their economy; that it had existed in many societies in the past, and that working conditions in northern factories were worse than those of southern plantations.
3. Both Democrats and Whigs would not take a stand on slavery, while Republicans founded their party on antislavery.
4. The North had more people and raised larger armies, had the most factories which produced war supplies, had a better railroad system, and had more money to finance the fighting.
5. By the act of secession, the Confederacy opposed Lincoln's belief that the Union was perpetual; this view changed with the South's hope to gain better treatment in supporting plans for reconstruction.
6. Republicans protected the rights and freedoms of blacks and stood to gain their support in helping the Republicans stay in power.
7. Slavery was ended, blacks became citizens, and they gained the right to vote. Often these rights were limited by codes passed in state legislatures. Whatever gains resulted from the Civil War appeared in many cases to be limited in practice.

Conclusion *(Reconstruction to the Present)* _____

Learning Objectives

The student should be able to:

1. identify the major social, economic, and political changes in the United States since Reconstruction.
2. identify the major changes that have occurred in American foreign policy since Reconstruction.
3. describe important factors which influenced each of the major changes in domestic life and foreign affairs.
4. locate on a map the areas of the world in which the United States was involved in military conflicts since Reconstruction.
5. identify the actions taken by government and by individuals and groups to make America a more democratic country.

Teaching Ideas

- Divide the class into groups of five or six students each. Instruct each group to prepare a report for the class in which they provide information on the changes taking place between 1865 and 1985 in some aspect of American life. Instruct students to make use of the last chapter of the textbook and other resources. If available, audiovisual materials may be used in presentation of the reports. Report topics could include the following: Men's Fashions, Women's Fashions, Children's Fashions, Travel by Land and Sea, The American Military, Communication, Recreation, Working Conditions, Recordkeeping, and Data Processing.

- Write the word CHANGE on the chalkboard. Ask students what the word means to them and list their responses. Discuss how people change and how conditions in an area change. Ask students if they have ever returned to visit a place where they had not been for a long time and how they felt upon their return. Discuss the responses. Have students imagine the plight of someone lost in space for 30 or 40 years and returned to earth today not knowing what has happened in the years between taking off and returning.

- Conduct a role-playing exercise in which the whole class is a team that will be the first to set up a space colony. Assign each student a role and devote one or two class periods to role-playing the planning to go into space and the establishment of the colony either on the moon, on a planet, or in an orbit around the earth. When the role playing is complete discuss the similarities and differences in the role-playing experiences and the real life experiences of the people who established the first colonies in North America.

Answers

Page 405:   *(illustration)* Wide, open spaces for settlement, happy people, good houses, public schools, and available transportation.

Page 407: Concept Feature *(Pluralism)*

1. Italians, Russians, Poles, Hungarians, Greeks, and Asiatics; he believed that they were least likely to be assimilated and would remain alien to the great body of the people of the United States.
2. He said that some of the nation's best citizens began life in the United States in this way.
3. Answers will vary but may include that people from many countries had been the founders of the democratic United States.

Page 408:

1. First came miners, then ranchers, and finally homesteaders.
2. The gains of guaranteed rights to blacks began to erode with strict voting privileges and with states' segregation laws which were supported as constitutional by the Supreme Court.
3. The Populists, union organizations, some church groups and social organizations, muckrakers, and the Progressives.
4. Among the reforms were new local and state governments under commissions or city managers, direct primary, workman's compensation, Sherman Antitrust Act, Pure Food and Drug Act, conservation laws, Federal Trade Commission, and the Clayton Antitrust Act.

Page 411: *(illustration)* The League of Nations.

Page 412:

1. To survive world competition, to sell goods around the world, and to invest in other lands.
2. To allow ships to travel from one ocean to another ocean without the need to sail around South America.
3. German submarines sinking without warning unarmed American ships.
4. Some Senators were angry because they were not consulted before finalizing the treaty. Others feared the League of Nations could draw the United States into future wars to protect foreign nations.

Page 413: *(illustration)* Black life in the 1920's in a predominantly white America.

Page 416: *(illustration)* He saw it as too restricting.

Page 416:

1. Anyone who was "different" in beliefs, practices, or behavior, especially foreigners.
2. Because of new prosperity and convenience appliances, people had more time to do things "for fun." Many sought a more exciting and fast-paced life. The automobile made travel quicker and easier.
3. American farmers produced more crops than could be sold, so prices fell. Industrial production began to slow. Many Americans speculated and risked their life savings in the stock market.
4. At reform—improving American life and safeguarding against future depressions.

Page 418: *(illustration)* Office of Price Administration set prices and controlled consumption; War Production Board supervised industrial production; and relocation centers were an attempt to protect America from foreigners living in America.

Page 420: *(illustration)* Our foreign policy centers around the cold war and the means short of military action to stop the spread of communism into other countries. Through the years since World War II the United States adopted different policies to continue cold war efforts such as containment, coexistence, and detente.

Page 421:
1. German invasion of Poland in September 1939.
2. The Japanese sneak attack on Pearl Harbor, December 7, 1941.
3. The bombing of Hiroshima and Nagasaki with the new weapon—the atomic bomb.
4. The North Korean army invading South Korea in an effort to unite the country under communist rule.

Page 422: *(illustration)* A peace settlement was reached, however, fighting continued until Vietnam was reunited under one communist rule in 1975.

Page 424: *(illustration)* The Twenty-fourth Amendment, the Civil Rights Act of 1964, the Equal Employment Opportunity Commission, the Voting Rights Act, and the Open Housing Act of 1968.

Page 427: *(illustration)* New technology such as television, automatic manufacturing processes, computers, and the automatic copying machine.

Page 427:
1. Containing communism to limit the spread of communism.
2. Reagan has a conservative attitude towards government policies so his federal economic program includes reducing government controls and government spending, and encouraging more private giving for social services.
3. The Economic Opportunity Act, the Civil Rights Act of 1964, the Voting Rights Act of 1965, and the Open Housing Act of 1968.
4. Answers will vary but may include changes such as more urban, less rural living; mass exodus to the suburbs left declining inner cities; more people moved to the sun belt regions of the United States.

Page 429: Chapter Review *(Remembering the Facts)*
1. By passing a law requiring all voters to pay a poll tax and pass a literacy test before voting.
2. A large labor supply, an abundance of natural resources, new manufacturing inventions, and good transportation.
3. Reform groups such as the Populists and Progressives helped to enact laws that regulated big business—the Interstate Commerce Act of 1887 and the Sherman Antitrust Act of 1890.
4. Freedom of the seas in peace and war, an end to secret treaties and alliances, equal trading rights for all nations, and a League of Nations.
5. Growth of new industries.
6. Many Americans lost their life savings and many their jobs, banks closed, and factories shut down.
7. War production workers.
8. Tension and a lack of cooperation between the United States and the Soviet Union.

9. Through court action, boycotts, sit-ins, demonstrations, marches, and protests.
10. Space explorations, cures for diseases, new inventions in manufacturing processes, and computers.

Page 429: Chapter Review *(Understanding the Facts)*
1. The gains immediately after the Civil War were almost completely erased by voting discrimination and segregation laws that were practiced from the late 1800's, into the 1900's, until court and attitude changes began in the 1950's, continuing into the 1960's and 1970's when new laws were passed to protect the rights of blacks.
2. Economic expansion for overseas markets and sources for raw materials, expansion of American influence around the world; yes; the policies now include a greater American influence around the world in an attempt to contain communism from expanding.
3. Answers will vary but may include that some gains in reform were made but not all of the requested reforms made it into law; some groups of people did not benefit from the reforms that were enacted such as blacks and other minorities.
4. The New Deal program emphasized high taxes and large-scale government spending for social programs. Reagan's economic policies are the opposite as he is determined to limit the federal government's role in spending, regulating, and taxing.
5. Answers will vary but may include that since the many protests, new laws have been passed to gain rights for blacks and other minorities.
6. Answers will vary but may include that the 1920's began the more exciting and fast-paced life that seems to be the style of today. Since the 1920's more new inventions have continued to free people from time-consuming tasks and allow more leisure time.

Page 429: Chapter Review *(Using Maps)*
1. Lumber and textiles.
2. The Midwest.
3. So that the processing can be done close to the source of the product to lower costs.
4. Mining.
5. In the Northeast.

City Sketch *(Houston 1960-1985)*

Learning Objectives

The student should be able to:
1. list the reasons for Houston's progress in the last three decades.
2. distinguish between the results of growth and change in Houston.

Teaching Ideas

● Direct the students to the map of Houston (page 430). Instruct the students to list the advantages and disadvantages to its location. Explain that the advantages outweighed the disadvantages. Ask the students to describe the geographic factors that influenced the growth of the city. Have the students list specifically the industries that were attracted to Houston.

- Have the students recall the discussion concerning trends in the Conclusion chapter. Ask the students what trends does Houston appear to be following. Review in detail the pertinent text material concerning life in Houston and the problems caused by rapid growth.

Answers

Page 431:   *(illustration)* Petroleum and the Houston Ship Channel.

Page 432:   *(illustration)* 1961.

Page 433:   *(illustration)* The money oil brings in attracts more workers and pays for buildings and expansion.

Page 434:   *(illustration)* It has created traffic problems.

Page 435:   *(illustration)* 25 percent of Houston's streets are unlighted, 400 miles of streets are unpaved, and 29 percent of the people live in substandard housing.

Page 435:
1. As a center for the cattle industry.
2. Petroleum.
3. Because of its excellent land, air, and sea transportation.
4. The lack of zoning laws and rapid growth.
5. Housing, paving streets, lighting streets, and traffic control.
6. Its economy is very strong, and it has many resources.

Readings

Each of the 53 readings, which appear in the Appendix of *United States History,* is followed by several questions. Some ask students to recall information presented in the reading. Others involve higher levels of critical thinking and might be used for initiating class discussion. The following answers are suggested responses to the questions in the Readings section.

Answers to Readings

UNIT I—Opportunity

Chapter 1 (*The First Americans*)

Page 438:   *After the Ice Age*
1. Answers will vary, but might include camels and bears.
2. Many animals could not adapt to living in warm climates.

Page 439:   *Secrets of the Mayas*
1. To improve farming.
2. To build such a massive canal network, the Mayas needed a strong bureacracy. With a collapse of the unifying bureacracy came the collapse of civilization.

Page 439:   *An Indian's View*
1. They believed that they came from the land.
2. They believed that they came from the land of the Great Plains, and were the first people there.

Chapter 2 (*New World—New Opportunities*)

Page 440:   *Columbus sees America*
1. Nothing. They thought that they saw a light, but it was an illusion.
2. Answers will vary, but might include that it began further exploration and settlement of the Americas.

Page 441:   *Cortes Meets Montezuma*
1. It was very friendly and respectful.
2. Answers will vary, however, it should be pointed out that what appears as friendliness can also be interpreted as caution.

Page 442:   *Marquette on the Mississippi*
1. Future explorers could use Marquette's descriptions to guide them and to let them know what conditions to expect.
2. At approximately 43 degrees of latitude. Marquette's maps were not as accurate as those today, and/or the course of the river changed over the years.

Chapter 3 (*English Settlement in North America*) ————————————————

Page 443: *Lost Colony Mystery Solved?*
1. Chiefly on the oral traditions of the Lumbee people.
2. Answers will vary, but might include the possibility that expeditions from Jamestown could have passed them on to the Lumbees.

Page 444: *Discovering an Edible America*
1. Those similar to the fruits and plants in their homeland.
2. Josselyn had never seen a similar hornet's nest.

Page 445: *Religious Toleration in Maryland*
1. It did not provide religious toleration for people who were non-Christians.
2. Written into the act were specific references to "his or her."

UNIT II—Independence ————————————————

Chapter 4 (*Colonial Society*) ————————————————

Page 446: *City Life*
1. Local government named and numbered streets, established fire codes, enforced local laws, and provided street lighting among other services.
2. Answers will vary, but might include the idea that most large cities no longer depend upon volunteer police and/or fire protection.

Page 447: *Massachusetts School Law*
1. To be able to read the scriptures.
2. Either the children's parents or masters, or the town's inhabitants.

Page 447: *Albany Plan of Union*
1. These might include one general government, colonies retain their own constitutions, and a plan for a common defense.
2. Answers will vary, but may include the following: the crown was to appoint the president-general, and there was a provision for collecting taxes.

Page 448: *Disunity in the Colonies*
1. Competition for trade.
2. Civil War and possibly extermination by the Indians and the blacks.
3. Answers will vary, but might include the idea that the tone of Burnaby's book does not suggest a serious attitude toward the American Revolution.

Chapter 5 (*Winning Freedom*) ————————————————

Page 449: *The Edenton Tea Party*
1. Everything in their power to preserve peace and happiness in their country. Specifically, they resolved to boycott British tea and other goods.
2. These women were probably relatives who shared the same names.

Page 449: *In the Name of Liberty*
1. Because the family members were loyalists.
2. They were trying to frighten the loyalists and convey a message of dissatisfaction.

Page 451: *Debate on American Independence*
1. Answers will vary, but may include the following: (a) The middle colonies were not yet ready to separate from Britain; (b) Some colonies had forbidden their delegates to consent to a Declaration of Independence; and (c) It was legally impossible for any colony to declare another colony independent from Britain.
2. Answers will vary, but may include the following: (a) America's bond of allegiance to the King had been broken when he ended his American colonial protection; (b) A Declaration of Independence allowed European powers to negotiate with and acknowledge the legitimacy of America; and (c) A Declaration of Independence allowed France to immediately assist America in the war with Britain.

Page 452: *Winter at Valley Forge*
1. Lack of food, clothing, and shelter; anxiety; fatigue.
2. He was too actively involved in the events.

Chapter 6 (*Forming a Union*) _____

Page 453: *Northwest Ordinance*
1. Freedom of religion.
2. It assured their right to a trial by jury.
3. Schools and education should be encouraged.

Page 454: *Objections to the Constitution*
1. The power to revise the Articles of Confederation.
2. The right of supreme power or sovereignty.
3. Antifederalists reasoned that a federal government located far away from many of its citizens could not adequately represent their welfare or enforce its own laws.
4. They produced a great fear of national government that is too strong and/or that does not represent the true welfare of its citizens.

Page 455: *Federalist Number 15*
1. The inability of government to get out of debt, weakness in relations with foreign governments, inactivity in promoting commerce and controlling prices, and the influence of private interests in government.
2. It is a national humiliation that will lead the country to disaster.

Chapter 7 (*The Constitution*) _____

Page 456: *Popular Sovereignty*
1. The people.

2. (a) One person; (b) a body that is not formed upon the principle of representation, and (c) the people.
3. Liberty, caution, diligence, loyalty, and an opportunity to bring forward the talents and abilities of all of the citizens.

Page 457: *The United States Constitution as a Model for Other Nations*
1. It created the possibility for a peaceful, legal, and legitimate government revolution.
2. Answers will vary, but may include that it was the first constitution, and it was widely distributed abroad.

Page 458: *Judicial Review*
1. To explain and interpret the law. Also, to determine which of two or more conflicting rules will stand.
2. The Constitution.
3. It allows the courts to nullify any unconstitutional acts of Congress or actions of the President.

UNIT III—Democracy _____

Chapter 8 *(Testing the New Government)* _____

Page 459: *Washington's First Inaugural*
1. The crowd, cheers, and general celebration.
2. He was very nervous and used ineffective motions.

Page 460: *Hamilton's Opinion on the Bank Issue*
1. They are equally effective.
2. Whether the power in question is a means to achieving a previously accepted objective or specified power. In addition, it must be determined that the power is not forbidden by any provision of the Constitution.
3. The bank was a *means* of achieving several of the accepted objectives of the federal government, including the collection of taxes, trade with foreign countries, trade between the states, and trade with Indian tribes.

Page 460: *Jefferson's Opinion on the Bank Issue*
1. The powers specifically granted by the Constitution and those prohibited to the states.
2. He believed that a national bank was unconstitutional. He also feared that it would lead to unlimited national power.
3. No. He felt that such a bank could only be considered constitutional if it was *necessary* to carry out previously granted federal powers.

Page 461: *Lewis and Clark Journals*
1. The high points covered with snow.
2. He saw that he was near to the source of the Missouri River, but realized that he would have to cross the mountains to reach the Pacific.

Chapter 9 *(The Growth of Nationalism)*

Page 462: *Our National Anthem*
   1. The American Flag.
   2. Answers will vary, but might include the lyrics and the beat.

Page 463: *The Monroe Doctrine*
   1. The American continents.
   2. He said that the United States would not interfere with the existing European colonies.
   3. The United States did not interfere in the internal concerns of any European powers. It considered any European government in power to be the legitimate government of that country.
   4. Monroe feared that extensive European colonization close to the United States would pose a threat to U.S. safety. In addition, he felt that the smaller American colonies were entitled to their chosen form of government.

Page 464: *In Defense of American Ways*
   1. Dwight feels that Americans are only impolite when they are provoked. Americans are so seldom too inquisitive that the criticisms are not justified.
   2. Dwight says that Americans are better educated and more religious.

Chapter 10 *(The Age of Jackson)*

Page 465: *Jackson's Inaugural*
   1. He was in the crowd until he was forced to retreat to his lodgings to protect himself.
   2. Answers will vary, but might include that she was disappointed in the actions of the crowd.

Page 466: *Nullification Ordinance*
   1. To protect U.S. manufacturers. (If foreign products have an added tax, U.S. citizens will be more likely to buy products made here.)
   2. They said that the taxes were both unnecessary and unconstitutional.
   3. Secede from the Union and organize a separate government.

Page 467: *Trail of Tears*
   1. Most rode on horseback or walked. Those who were sick rode in wagons.
   2. Answers will vary, but might include fatigue, inclement weather, lack of shelter, and illness or death.

UNIT IV—Expansion

Chapter 11 *(The Promise of America)*

Page 468: *The Liberator*
   1. Answers will vary, but might include uncompromising.
   2. The danger of fire.

Page 469: *For a National Language*
1. A uniform national language.
2. It would reach all classes of children and teach them the same spellings and pronunciations before they had learned incorrect spellings and pronunciations elsewhere.
3. To prevent the formation of dialects and help to create a stable and uniform language.

Page 470: *Temperance Crusade*
1. Illness, crime, poverty, and unnecessary death.
2. The formation of temperance societies.

Chapter 12 *(New Ways and New People)*

Page 471: *Working Women of Lowell*
1. Before 1840, women had no property rights. They were forced to be dependent upon husbands and/or other relatives. Today, women have the same property and economic legal rights as men. In some situations, however, women are still not afforded the same economic opportunities as men.
2. Among others, the right to earn and spend their own money.

Page 472: *On the National road*
1. The softness and rough texture.
2. Stone bridges.

Page 472: *City Tenant Housing*
1. Answers will vary, but may include overcrowding, unsanitary conditions, and unsafe buildings.
2. They could not afford to live elsewhere.

Chapter 13 *(From Ocean to Ocean)*

Page 474: *Narcissa Whitman's Diary*
1. They supplied milk.
2. High water and strong currents.

Page 474: *Travis's Last Appeal*
1. Answers will vary, but might include that it reveals courage and a desire to fight for freedom.
2. Travis wanted to face Santa Anna at the Alamo rather than have the war spread into the other Texas settlements.

Page 475: *Smallpox Destroys the Mandans*
1. By way of two infected crew members of the Fur Company's steamer.
2. The Mandan village was surrounded by several Sioux war parties. This prevented any Mandans from escaping the disease. In addition, the Mandans had no natural resistance to the disease.

UNIT V—Division

Chapter 14 (A Divided Nation)

Page 476: *Rebirth of Slavery*
1. The Industrial Revolution and the invention of the cotton gin.
2. Slavery would not have been profitable.

Page 477: *Slave Auction*
1. Answers will vary, but it should be noted that most people used slaves as a source of inexpensive labor.
2. The first black indentured servants arrived at Jamestown, Virginia Colony, in 1619.

Page 477: *"Darling Nelly Gray"*
1. She was sold to a planter in Georgia.
2. He had to escape slavery so that he could earn the money to buy Nelly Gray's freedom.

Page 478: *In Defense of the South*
1. The American Revolution.
2. Yes, because the South was opposing what it viewed to be a "tyrant".

Chapter 15 (The Civil War)

Page 479: *On the Eve of War*
1. She definitely favored secession.
2. Georgia was not part of the United States.

Page 480: *A Patriotic Song of the South*
1. Slaves.
2. In order of secession, South Carolina, Alabama, Mississippi, Georgia, Florida, Texas, Louisiana, Virginia, Arkansas, North Carolina, and Tennessee.

Page 481: *A Patriotic Song of the North*
1. By motivating soldiers to fight for the Union.
2. To the Union, freedom meant the abolition of slavery. To the Confederacy, freedom meant a lack of governmental oppression and the restoration of states' rights.

Page 482: *Civil War Medical Corps*
1. Generally a lack of resources.
2. Answers will vary, but might include that proper medicines were not available in most field hospitals.

Page 483: *Coming to Terms*
1. (a) That all states recognize the federal government's authority; (b) that all laws concerning slavery would remain in effect; and (c) that all groups hostile to the United States government would disband.

2. Neither side was willing to compromise on the key issues of slavery and federal power.

Chapter 16 *(Rebuilding the Nation)*

Page 484:   *Columbia in Ruins*
1. All public buildings.
2. By fire.

Page 485:   *Lincoln's Reconstruction Policy*
1. The South had no authorized government which could form a treaty with the federal government.
2. Lincoln felt that Louisiana would adopt the Union viewpoint sooner if it was admitted to the Union than if it was rejected by the Union. He also pointed out that Louisiana would provide another vote for the Thirteenth Amendment.
3. It adopted a Free State constitution, gave the benefits of a public education equally to blacks and whites, and voted for the ratification of the Thirteenth Amendment.

Page 486:   *Texas Rejoins the Union*
1. The Texas legislature abolished or would soon abolish slavery.
2. With the readmittance of Texas, the Union was complete once again.

Reading List

For Teachers

The following books, series, periodicals, and reference works are recommended for teachers' use throughout the course of *United States History*. Books and series contain standard and current scholarship designed to offer a sampling of the major works by American historians. Periodicals and reference works contain sources for additional information and materials to consult for clarification.

Books

Beard, Charles A. *An Economic Interpretation of the Constitution of the United States.* New York: Macmillan Publishing Co., Inc., 1935.

Becker, Carl L. *The Declaration of Independence: A Study in the History of Political Ideas.* New York: Random House, Inc., 1958.

Billington, Ray A. *Westward Expansion: A History of the American Frontier.* New York: Macmillan Publishing Co., Inc., 1974.

Birdsall, Stephen S. and Florin, John W. *Regional Landscapes of the United States and Canada.* New York: John Wiley & Sons, 1981.

Blassingame, John W. *The Slave Community: Plantation Life in the Ante-Bellum South.* New York: Oxford University Press, Inc., 1979.

Boorstin, Daniel J. *The Americans: The Democratic Experience.* New York: Random House, Inc., 1973.

Catton, Bruce. *A Stillness at Appomattox.* New York: Doubleday Publishing Co., 1953.

Clancy, Herbert J. *The Democratic Party: Jefferson to Jackson.* New York: Fordham University Press, 1962.

Cochran, Thomas C. *Business in American Life.* New York: McGraw-Hill Book Co., 1972.

Commager, Henry S. *The American Mind: An Interpretation of American Thought & Character Since the 1800's.* New Haven: Yale University Press, 1950.

Corwin, Edward S. *The Constitution and What It Means Today.* Princeton: Princeton University Press, 1974.

Curtin, Philip D. *The Atlantic Slave Trade: A Census.* Madison: University of Wisconsin Press, 1969.

DeConde, Alexander. *History of American Foreign Policy.* New York: Charles Scribner's Sons, 1978.

Degler, Carl N. *Out of Our Past: The Forces That Shaped Modern America.* New York: Harper & Row, Publishers, Inc., 1970.

Donald, David. *Lincoln Reconsidered.* New York: Alfred A. Knopf, Inc., 1956.

Drewry, Henry N., and Drewry, Cecelia H. (eds.). *Afro-American History, Past to Present.* New York: Charles Scribner's Sons, 1971.

Driver, Harold E. *Indians of North America.* Chicago: University of Chicago Press, 1969.

Dulles, Foster R. *Labor in America: A History.* Arlington Heights, Illinois: AHM Publishing Corp., 1968.

Ferrell, Robert H. *American Diplomacy.* New York: W. W. Norton & Co., Inc., 1975.

Foner, Eric. *Free Soil, Free Labor, Free Men: The Ideology of the Republican Party Before the Civil War.* New York: Oxford University Press, Inc., 1971.

Franklin, John Hope. *From Slavery to Freedom: A History of Negro Americans.* New York: Alfred A. Knopf, Inc., 1980.

Garland, Hamlin. *A Son of the Middle Border.* Lincoln: University of Nebraska Press, 1979.

Genovese, Eugene D. *Roll, Jordan, Roll: The World the Slaves Made.* New York: Random House, Inc., 1976.

Handlin, Oscar. *The Uprooted.* Boston: Little, Brown & Co., 1973.

Higham, John. *Strangers in the Land.* New York: Atheneum Publishers, 1963.

Hofstadter, Richard. *American Political Tradition: And the Men Who Made It.* New York: Alfred A. Knopf, Inc., 1973.

Jensen, Merrill. *New Nation: A History of the United States During the Confederation 1781-1789.* New York: Random House, Inc., 1967.

Livermore, Shaw, Jr. *Twilight of Federalism: the Disintegration of the Federalist Party—1815-1830.* Princeton: Princeton University Press, 1962.

Meier, Matt S., and Rivera, Feliciano. *The Chicanos: A History of Mexican Americans.* New York: Hill & Wang, 1972.

Miller, Perry. *The New England Mind: The Seventeenth Century.* Cambridge: Harvard University Press, 1953.

Morison, Samuel Eliot. *Admiral of the Ocean Sea.* Boston: Little, Brown & Co., 1942.

Morison, Samuel Eliot. *European Discovery of America: The Northern Voyages.* New York: Oxford University Press, Inc., 1971.

Mumford, Lewis. *City in History: Its Origins, Its Transformations, & Its Prospects.* New York: Harcourt Brace Jovanovich, Inc., 1961.

Nevins, Allan. *Emergence of Modern America, 1865-1878.* St. Clair Shores, Michigan: Scholarly Press, Inc., 1927.

North, Douglass C. *Economic Growth of the United States, 1790-1860.* New York: W. W. Norton & Co., Inc., 1966.

Nye, Russell B. *Society and Culture in America: 1830-1860.* New York: Harper & Row, Publishers, Inc., 1974.

O'Connor, Thomas H. *The Disunited States: The Era of Civil War & Reconstruction.* New York: Harper & Row, Publishers, Inc., 1979.

Parrington, Vernon L. *Main Currents in American Thought.* 3 Vols. New York: Harcourt Brace Jovanovich, Inc., 1963.

Quarles, Benjamin. *Allies for Freedom: Blacks & John Brown.* New York: Oxford University Press, Inc., 1974.

Randall, James G., and Donald, David. *The Civil War and Reconstruction.* Lexington, Massachusetts: D. C. Heath & Co., 1969.

Rayback, Joseph G. *History of American Labor.* New York: Free Press, 1966.

Rossiter, Clinton. *Seedtime of the Republic.* New York: Harcourt Brace Jovanovich, Inc., 1953.

Schlesinger, Arthur M., Jr. *Age of Jackson.* Boston: Little, Brown & Co., 1945.

Smith, Page. *Daughters of the Promised Land: Women in American History.* Boston: Little, Brown & Co., 1970.

Stampp, Kenneth M. *The Peculiar Institution.* New York: Alfred A. Knopf, Inc., 1956.

Van Doren, Carl. *The Great Rehearsal: The Story of the Making and Ratifying of the Constitution.* New York: Viking Press, 1971.

Ward, John W. *Andrew Jackson: Symbol for an Age.* New York: Oxford University Press, Inc., 1962.

Washburn, Wilcomb E. *The Indian in America.* New York: Harper & Row, Publishers, Inc., 1975.

Wertheimer, Barbara M. *We Were There: The Story of Working Women in America.* New York: Pantheon Books, Inc., 1977.

Williams, William A. *The Tragedy of American Diplomacy.* New York: Dell Publishing Co., Inc., 1972.

Wills, Garry. *Inventing America: Jefferson's Declaration of Independence.* New York: Doubleday Publishing Co., 1978.

Wright, Louis B., and Fowler, Elaine. *Everyday Life in the New Nation: 1787-1860.* New York: G. P. Putnam's Sons, 1972.

Series

Boorstin, Daniel J. (ed.). *The Chicago History of American Civilization Series.* Chicago: University of Chicago Press.

Commager, Henry S., and Morris, Richard B. (eds.). *The New American Nation Series.* New York: Harper & Row, Publishers, Inc.

Donald, David (ed.). *The Making of America Series.* New York: Hill & Wang.

Gabriel, Ralph H. (ed.). *The Yale Pageant of America.* New Rochelle, New York: United States Publishers Association.

Handlin, Oscar (ed.). *American Problem Studies.* New York: Holt, Rinehart & Winston.

Johnson, Allen, and Nevins, Allan (eds.). *The Yale Chronicles of America.* New Rochelle, New York: United States Publishers Association.

Reference

American Heritage Pictorial Atlas of the United States. New York: McGraw-Hill Book Co., 1966.

Bailey, Thomas A. (ed.). *The American Spirit: United States History as Seen by Contemporaries.* 2 Vols. Lexington, Massachusetts: D. C. Heath & Co., 1978.

Bemis, Samuel F., and Griffin, G. G. *A Guide to the Diplomatic History of the United States 1775-1921.* Magnolia, Massachusetts: Peter Smith.

Commager, Henry S. (ed.). *Documents of American History.* 2 Vols. Englewood Cliffs, New Jersey: Prentice-Hall, Inc., 1973.

Concise Dictionary of American Biography. New York: Charles Scribner's Sons, 1980.

Freidel, Frank, and Showman, Richard K. (eds.). *The Harvard Guide to American History.* 2 Vols. Cambridge: Harvard University Press, 1974.

James, Edward T., and James, Janet W. (eds.). *Notable American Women.* 4 Vols. Cambridge: Harvard University Press, 1971.

Morris, Richard B., and Morris, Jeffrey B. (eds.). *Encyclopedia of American History.* New York: Harper & Row, Publishers, Inc., 1976.

National Geographic Society (ed.). *The World of the American Indian.* Washington: National Geographic Society, 1974.

Ploski, Harry A., and Marr, Warren. *The Negro Almanac.* New York: Bellwether Publishing Co., 1976.

United States Bureau of the Census. *Historical Statistics of the United States: Colonial Times to 1970.* 2 Vols. United States Government Printing Office, 1975.

Periodicals

American Heritage: The Magazine of History. Bi-monthly. American Heritage Publishing Co., Inc., 383 W. Center Street, Marion, OH 43302.

The American Historical Review. 5 times a year. American Historical Association, 400 A Street, S.E., Washington, D.C. 20003.

American History Illustrated. 10 times a year. Telegraph Press, P. O. Box 1831, Harrisburg, PA 17105.

The Historian: A Journal of History. Quarterly. Phi Alpha Theta National Honor Society in History, c/o 2812 Livingston Street, Allentown, PA 18104.

The History Teacher. Quarterly. Society for History Education, Inc., Department of History, California State University, Long Beach, 1250 Bellflower Blvd., Long Beach, CA 90840.

The Journal of American History. Quarterly. Organization of American Historians, 112 North Bryan Street, Bloomington, IN 47401.

Social Education. Monthly. National Council for the Social Studies, 3615 Wisconsin Ave., N.W., Washington, D.C. 20016.

For Students

This list contains titles covering the scope of American history. Each book has a reading level of advanced elementary or junior high school, and standard works of literature included on the list have been adjusted to a seventh grade reading level. This list supplements those works of fiction and nonfiction in the Suggested Readings section of the Unit Reviews.

Books

Alderman, Clifford L. *Rum, Slaves and Molasses: The Story of New England's Triangular Trade.* New York: Macmillan Publishing Co., Inc., 1972. Facts and opinions about trade in New England in the early 1800's.

Aldrich, Bess S. *A Lantern in Her Hand.* Mattituck, New York: Amereon Ltd., 1928. Adventures on the Nebraska frontier.

Altsheler, Joseph A. *The Star of Gettysburg.* Mattituck, New York: Amereon Ltd., 1976. Adventures of Confederate soldiers from Fredericksburg to Gettysburg.

Anticaglia, Elizabeth. *Heroines of Seventy-Six.* New York: Walker & Co., 1975. Chronicles the involvement of 14 women in the Revolution.

Avi. *Night Journeys.* New York: Pantheon Books, Inc., 1979. A river adventure set in the Pennsylvania colony in 1767.

Baker, Betty. *Settlers and Strangers: Native Americans of the Desert Southwest & History as They Saw It.* New York: Macmillan Publishing Co., Inc., 1977. Traces the story of the pueblo-dwelling Indians.

Baker, Betty. *A Stranger and Afraid.* New York: Macmillan Publishing Co., Inc., 1972. Story of Indian conflicts during the time of the sixteenth-century conquistador explorations in the Southwest.

Beatty, Jerome, Jr. *From New Bedford to Siberia.* New York: Doubleday Publishing Co., 1977. True story of a voyage on a whaling ship in the 1800's.

Beatty, John, and Beatty, Patricia. *Who Comes to King's Mountain?* New York: William Morrow & Co., Inc., 1975. The American Revolution in South Carolina.

Blumenthal, Shirley, and Ozer, Jerome S. *Coming to America: Immigrants from the British Isles.* New York: Delacorte Press, 1980. Discusses the first group of people to settle the English colonies.

Boyd, James. *Drums.* New York: Charles Scribner's Sons, 1936. Story of the Revolution in the southern colonies and at sea.

Brown, Dee. *Lonesome Whistle: The Story of the First Transcontinental Railroad.* New York: Holt, Rinehart & Winston, 1980. Discusses the plans to build the railroad and the immigrants who did the work.

Burchard, Peter. *The Deserter: A Spy Story of the Civil War.* New York: Coward, McCann & Geoghegan, Inc., 1974. Adventures aboard a Confederate ship.

Chidsey, Donald B. *Mr. Hamilton and Mr. Jefferson.* New York: Elsevier/ Nelson Books, 1975. Political life in the late 1700's.

Faber, Doris. *The Perfect Life: The Shakers in America.* New York: Farrar, Straus & Giroux, Inc., 1974. Story of achievements and failures by Shakers in attempting to live a perfect life.

Finlayson, Ann. *Greenhorn on the Frontier.* New York: Frederick Warne & Co., Inc., 1974. Adventures of two orphans traveling in western Pennsylvania before the Revolution.

Fisher, Leonard E. *The Factories.* New York: Holiday House, Inc., 1979. Relates the development of industry in America.

Freedman, Florence B. *Two Tickets to Freedom: The True Story of Ellen & William Craft, Fugitive Slaves.* New York: Simon & Schuster, Inc., 1971. Story of a dramatic escape from slavery.

Garland, Hamlin. *Main-Travelled Roads.* New York: New American Library, Inc., 1962. Highlights the problems of returning Union soldiers after the Civil War.

Haskins, James. *James Van der Zee: The Picture-Takin' Man.* New York: Dodd, Mead & Co., 1979. Portrait of a photographer of black history.

Hergesheimer, Joseph. *Three Black Pennys.* New York: Alfred A. Knopf, Inc., 1949. Story of the steel industry in Chicago.

Highwater, Jamake. *Many Smokes, Many Moons.* Philadelphia: J. B. Lippincott Co., 1978. The cultural traditions of the American Indians.

Hilton, Suzanne. *The Way It Was—1876.* Philadelphia: Westminister Press, 1975. Old prints, photographs, and facts about life in the last century.

Howard, Elizabeth. *North Wind Blows Free.* New York: William Morrow & Co., Inc., 1949. Concerns the Underground Railroad.

Hungerford, Edward Buell. *Forge for Heroes.* Chicago: Follett Publishing Co., 1966. Recounts the dark days of the Revolution during the winter at Valley Forge.

Irwin, Constance. *Strange Footprints on the Land: Vikings in America.* New York: Harper & Row, Publishers, Inc., 1980. A European exploration of America 500 years before Columbus.

Keller, Charles. *Laughing: A Historical Selection of American Humor.* Englewood Cliffs, New Jersey: Prentice-Hall, Inc., 1977. Humorous stories from American history.

Kjelgaard, Jim. *The Lost Wagon.* New York: Dodd, Mead & Co., 1955. Dangers and adventures of a family along the Oregon Trail.

La Farge, Oliver. *Laughing Boy.* Boston: Houghton Mifflin Co., 1929. A Navaho love story.

Lawrence, Mildred. *Touchmark.* New York: Harcourt Brace Jovanovich, Inc., 1975. Life in Boston before and during the Revolution.

Lawson, Don. *The Changing Face of the Constitution.* New York: Franklin Watts, Inc., 1979. Examines the flexible nature of the United States Constitution.

Meltzer, Milton. *In Their Own Words: A History of the American Negro, 1619-1865.* New York: Thomas Y. Crowell Co., 1964. Excerpts from primary sources.

Mitgang, Herbert. *The Fiery Trial: A Life of Lincoln*. New York: Viking Press, 1979. A look at Lincoln's life from today's perspective.

Monjo, Ferdinand N. *Vicksburg Veteran*. New York: Simon & Schuster, Inc., 1973. Fictional accounts of the Battle of Vicksburg.

O'Dell, Scott. *The King's Fifth*. Boston: Houghton Mifflin Co., 1966. Adventure of Spanish explorers on an expedition to the Cities of Gold.

Ortiz, Victoria. *Sojourner Truth, A Self-Made Woman*. Philadelphia: J. B. Lippincott Co., 1974. Biography of a former slave.

Perl, Lila. *Hunter's Stew and Hangtown Fry: What Pioneer America Ate and Why*. Boston: Houghton Mifflin Co., 1977. The history of the frontier with a history of American foods.

Perrin, Linda. *Coming to America: Immigrants from the Far East*. New York: Delacorte Press, 1980. Discusses Asian immigration to the United States.

Roach, Marilynne. *Down to Earth at Walden*. Boston: Houghton Mifflin Co., 1980. Henry David Thoreau's simple life at Walden Pond in the early 1800's.

Slater, Abby. *In Search of Margaret Fuller: A Biography*. New York: Delacorte Press, 1978. Life of the famous transcendentalist.

Snow, Richard F. *Freelon Starbird*. Boston: Houghton Mifflin Co., 1976. Story of one young soldier's involvement in the Revolution.

Steele, William O. *Wilderness Tattoo: A Narrative of Juan Ortiz*. New York: Harcourt Brace Jovanovich, Inc., 1972. Adventures of a Spanish explorer in the New World.

Talbot, Charlene J. *An Orphan for Nebraska*. New York: Atheneum Publishers, 1979. Success story set in Nebraska in the 1870's.

Tunis, Edwin. *Colonial Living*. New York: Thomas Y. Crowell Co., 1976. Concerns various topics of the period.

Twain, Mark. *Life on the Mississippi*. New York: ANSCO School Publishers, 1969. Account of the early steamboat days.

Vance, Marguerite. *The Jacksons of Tennessee*. New York: E. P. Dutton, 1953. Story based on the lives of Rachel and Andrew Jackson.

Young, Alida E. *Land of the Iron Dragon*. New York: Doubleday Publishing Co., 1978. Novel about the Chinese people who worked to build the Central Pacific Railroad in the middle 1800's.

Notes

Notes

Notes

Notes

1 2 3 4 5 6 7 8 9 10 11 12 13 14 15—95 94 93 92 91 90 89 88 87 86 85

United States History: Beginnings Through Reconstruction _____

Circle the number that corresponds most nearly to your opinion of each of the following items of *United States History: Beginnings Through Reconstruction.* Please also star (*) three factors that most influence your evaluation or choice of text.

Student Text	Excellent	Very Good	Satisfactory	Fair	Poor	Comments
1. Annotated Constitution	1	2	3	4	5	_____
2. Appendix Materials	1	2	3	4	5	_____
3. Approach	1	2	3	4	5	_____
4. Boldfaced Terms	1	2	3	4	5	_____
5. Chapter Openers	1	2	3	4	5	_____
6. Chapter Reviews	1	2	3	4	5	_____
7. City Sketches	1	2	3	4	5	_____
8. Concept Development	1	2	3	4	5	_____
9. Concept Features	1	2	3	4	5	_____
10. Content	1	2	3	4	5	_____
11. Coverage of people and events	1	2	3	4	5	_____
12. End-of-Section Questions	1	2	3	4	5	_____
13. Factual Accuracy	1	2	3	4	5	_____
14. Graphic Illustrations	1	2	3	4	5	_____
15. Organization	1	2	3	4	5	_____
16. Photographs	1	2	3	4	5	_____
17. Prologue	1	2	3	4	5	_____
18. Readability	1	2	3	4	5	_____
19. Skill Features	1	2	3	4	5	_____
20. Unit Openers	1	2	3	4	5	_____
21. Unit Reviews	1	2	3	4	5	_____
22. Using Skills	1	2	3	4	5	_____
23. Visual Impact	1	2	3	4	5	_____

Teacher's Annotated Edition

	Excellent	Very Good	Satisfactory	Fair	Poor	Comments
1. Teachability	1	2	3	4	5	_____
2. Introduction	1	2	3	4	5	_____
3. Program Use	1	2	3	4	5	_____
4. General Teaching Methods	1	2	3	4	5	_____
5. Teaching Strategies	1	2	3	4	5	_____
6. Reading Lists	1	2	3	4	5	_____

Teacher's Resource Book

	Excellent	Very Good	Satisfactory	Fair	Poor	Comments
1. Teacher Lecture Notes	1	2	3	4	5	_____
2. Outline Maps	1	2	3	4	5	_____
3. Exercises and Activities	1	2	3	4	5	_____
4. Evaluation	1	2	3	4	5	_____
5. Audiovisual List	1	2	3	4	5	_____

Circle the appropriate information.

1. Grade level of students	7	8	9	10	11	12
2. Enrollment of that grade	1-50		51-100	101-200		200 +
3. Total school enrollment	1-200		201-500	501-1000		1000 +
4. Locale of school	rural		small town	suburban		large city
5. Ability level of class	below average			average		above average
6. Appropriateness of text for your class	easy			about right		difficult
7. Number of years text used	1		2	3	4	5
8. May we quote you?	Yes	No				

Name _____ Position _____

School _____City _____ State _____ Zip _____

Date _____

Fold

BUSINESS REPLY CARD
FIRST CLASS   PERMIT NO 284   COLUMBUS OHIO

NO POSTAGE
NECESSARY
IF MAILED
IN THE
UNITED STATES

Postage will be paid by:

CHARLES E. MERRILL PUBLISHING CO.
A Bell & Howell Company
Managing Editor, Elhi Social Studies
1300 Alum Creek Drive
Columbus, Ohio 43216

UNITED STATES HISTORY

Volume 1

BEGINNINGS THROUGH RECONSTRUCTION

For a people to be without history, or to be ignorant of its history, is as for a person to be without memory . . .

Henry S. Commager

Henry N. Drewry
Lecturer of History, Princeton University

Robert P. Green, Jr.
Associate Professor of Education, Clemson University

Thomas H. O'Connor
Professor of American History, Boston College

Laura L. Becker
Assistant Professor of History, Florida International University

Robert E. Coviello
Social Studies Department Chairperson, Walpole High School

CHARLES E. MERRILL PUBLISHING CO.
A BELL & HOWELL COMPANY
Columbus, Ohio
Toronto   London   Sydney

AUTHORS

Henry N. Drewry is Lecturer with the rank of Professor of History at Princeton University. He taught social studies for 14 years in secondary schools. A coauthor of numerous professional articles and books, Drewry is the recipient of the Harvard University Prize for Distinguished Secondary School Teaching. He is Director of the Princeton University Teacher Preparation Program and spends sabbaticals in secondary schools teaching social studies.

Robert P. Green, Jr., is an Associate Professor of Education at Clemson University, South Carolina, where he teaches social studies methods to undergraduate and graduate students and supervises student teachers. An author of numerous articles on social studies education, Dr. Green is a consultant to school systems and has served as a consultant/contributor to educational publishers.

Thomas H. O'Connor is a Professor of American History and former chairperson of the Department of History at Boston College. He has written many articles and books, including *The Disunited States: The Era of Civil War and Reconstruction* and *Lords of the Looms*. Dr. O'Connor is a member of the Commission on the Bicentennial of the United States Constitution.

Laura L. Becker is an Assistant Professor of History at Florida International University in Miami, Florida, where she teaches both undergraduate and graduate courses in United States history. Dr. Becker has published articles on American history in professional and academic journals and has written and hosted a series of public radio programs on women in America.

Robert E. Coviello is Chairperson of the Social Studies Department of Walpole High School in Walpole, Massachusetts, where he teaches courses in United States history, economics, and international relations. Experienced in curriculum development, Coviello is a consultant to school systems and has served as a consultant/contributor to educational publishers.

ISBN 0-675-02040-9

Published by
CHARLES E. MERRILL PUBLISHING CO.
A Bell & Howell Company
Columbus, Ohio 43216

REVIEWERS

Dorothy Bachmann
Social Studies Consultant
Educational Development Center
Paramus, New Jersey

Linda Barone
Social Studies Teacher
Utica Free Academy
Utica, New York

William J. Burkhardt
Curriculum Coordinator
Northeast Junior High School
Bethlehem, Pennsylvania

Ethel Calloway
Social Studies Department Chairperson
John Tyler High School
Tyler, Texas

Dorothea B. Chandler
Curriculum Consultant, Retired
Torrance Unified School District
Torrance, California

Walter Gordinier
History Instructor
Nazareth Academy
Rochester, New York

Irene W. Kanter
Assistant Principal
Anderson High School
Austin, Texas

Dona McSwain
Social Studies Department Chairperson
West Stanley High School
Oakboro, North Carolina

Darrell Ochoa
Social Studies Consultant
Edgewood Independent School District
San Antonio, Texas

Dr. Catherine C. Pickle
Curriculum Consultant
Memphis City Schools
Memphis, Tennessee

Diane Rasserty
Social Studies Department Chairperson
South Seminole Middle School
Casselberry, Florida

William Rayner
Social Studies Teacher
Altimira School
Sonoma, California

Dr. Paul R. Rivers
Social Studies Supervisor
Baltimore County Public Schools
Towson, Maryland

Mel D. Rosen
President, California Council
    for the Social Studies
Van Nuys, California

Richard Ross
Social Studies Teacher
Ada Middle School
Ada, Oklahoma

Carl H. Sears
Curriculum Director
Elmhurst Public Schools
Elmhurst, Illinois

STAFF
Project Editor: William M. Nies; *Editors:* Thomas Photos, Donald Lankiewicz, Lynette Hoffman, Myra Immell, Jacquelyn Whitney; *Production Editor:* Kimberly Munsie; *Project Designer:* Kip M. Frankenberry; *Project Artist:* Catharine Bookwalter White; *Artist:* Barbara White; *Map Artist:* June Barnes; *Photo Editor:* Elaine Comer Shay

PREFACE

The actions that people did or did not take in the past have made your present and will influence your future—just as you are the makers of American history for tomorrow's citizens. So this study of America is mostly a study of its people—their needs, wants, hopes, and choices. It was written to help you see more clearly the connections among people, places, events, and ideas.

United States History: Beginnings Through Reconstruction consists of 16 chapters grouped into 5 units as well as a Prologue, Introduction, Conclusion, and Epilogue. The Prologue stresses reasons for studying American history. The Introduction discusses the geography of the United States. The Conclusion highlights Reconstruction to the present. The Epilogue summarizes changes that have occurred in the development of the nation.

The text is organized on a unit-chapter basis. Each unit opens with a colorful two-page photograph and a listing of the chapters in the unit. Each unit title describes what the United States has meant to its people at different times in its history. Each chapter begins with a photograph and a paragraph that serve as a thought-provoking introduction to the theme of the chapter.

Within the text, facts and concepts are presented in a readable narrative replete with high-interest excerpts from primary and secondary sources. Chapters are divided into sections and subsections that contribute to easier reading and understanding. Concept terms appear in boldface type and are defined or explained in context.

Throughout the text, there are a number of special features. Skills highlight processes important to understanding the significance of history. Concepts develop recognition of major themes and generalizations. Profiles help to humanize history. City Sketches add greater dimension to social, cultural, and economic aspects of American life.

Photographs are used extensively to reinforce or expand chapter content. Precisely executed maps, graphs, charts, and diagrams, all in color, provide supportive data and clarify important historical relationships.

United States History: Beginnings Through Reconstruction also contains numerous study aids. Review questions at the end of each main section will help you check your understanding of important facts. Comprehensive chapter reviews provide a variety of exercises designed to reinforce comprehension. Unit reviews include a time line of key events, a list of major generalizations, analytical questions, suggested activities, and an annotated bibliography.

An Appendix includes several special features. A Readings section, organized on the text's unit-chapter basis and tied to its narrative, will help you understand more about the people and events that made history. A full-color Atlas contains general reference maps and a graphics section to aid you in learning more about the population, government, economy, and society of the United States. The Declaration of Independence and an annotated Constitution are included to aid you in understanding more about the American political system.

TABLE OF CONTENTS

Prologue   1

Introduction   The Land   2

    1. Geographical Features   3
    2. Weather and Climate   11
    3. Prehistoric Times   15
    4. Conclusion   17

UNIT I

Opportunity   20

Chapter 1   The First Americans   22

    1. The First Arrivals   23
    2. People of Middle and South America   25
    3. People of North America   30
    4. Conclusion   39

Chapter 2   New World–New Opportunities   42

    1. Backgrounds and New Beginnings   43
    2. Spain in the New World   48
    3. France in the New World   56
    4. Other Europeans in the New World   61
    5. Conclusion   63

Chapter 3   English Settlement in North America   66

    1. English Backgrounds   67
    2. First Permanent Colonies   69
    3. Later Colonies   77
    4. Governing the Colonies   82
    5. Conclusion   85
    City Sketch **Secota** *1584-1587*   88
    City Sketch **Plymouth** *1620-1650*   92

UNIT II

Independence   98

Chapter 4   Colonial Society   100

    1. The People of the English Colonies   101
    2. Life in the English Colonies   103
    3. Regions in the Colonies   108
    4. From Conflict to Unity   113
    5. Conclusion   119

Chapter 5   Winning Freedom   122

    1. The Road to Rebellion   123
    2. The War for Independence   132
    3. The Meaning of Freedom   141
    4. Conclusion   143

Chapter 6   Forming a Union   146

    1. The Period of Confederation   147
    2. Making the Constitution   154
    3. The Struggle for Ratification   158
    4. Conclusion   161

Chapter 7   The Constitution   164

    1. Basic Principles   165
    2. Other Principles   168
    3. Branches of Government   169
    4. Division of Powers   176
    5. The Changing Constitution   179
    6. Conclusion   181
    City Sketch **Philadelphia** *1750-1775*   184

UNIT III

Democracy   192

Chapter 8   Testing the New Government   194

    1. The Beginning   195
    2. The Economy   197
    3. Foreign Affairs   201

Chapter 12	New Ways and New People	280
1.	The Rise of Industry	281
2.	A System of Transportation	286
3.	The Growth of Cities	290
4.	The Changing Population	294

Chapter 13	From Ocean to Ocean	298
1.	The Westward Movement	299
2.	On to Oregon	300
3.	The Southwest and California	304
4.	Indians and the Westward Movement	313
5.	Conclusion	315
City Sketch	**New Orleans** *1845-1855*	318
City Sketch	**San Francisco** *1845-1855*	322

4.	The Adams Presidency	204
5.	Jefferson in Office	208
6.	Conclusion	211

Chapter 9	The Growth of Nationalism	214
1.	The United States and Neutral Rights	215
2.	The War of 1812	218
3.	The National Spirit	223
4.	The Creation of a National Culture	228
5.	Conclusion	231

Chapter 10	The Age of Jackson	234
1.	The Return of the Two-Party System	235
2.	Jacksonian Democracy	238
3.	Jackson's Use of Presidential Power	240
4.	Jackson and the Indians	245
5.	The Impact of Jackson Politics	248
City Sketch	**Washington, D.C.** *1800-1825*	252

UNIT IV

Expansion 260

Chapter 11	The Promise of America	262
1.	The Spirit of Perfection	263
2.	Reforming American Society	267
3.	American Literature in the Reform Years	274
4.	Conclusion	277

UNIT V

Division 328

Chapter 14	A Divided Nation	330
1.	Sectional Differences	331
2.	The Peculiar Institution	333
3.	Slavery and Politics	338
4.	The Road to Disunion	341
5.	The Final Break	346
6.	Conclusion	348

Chapter 15	The Civil War	351
1.	The Opening Guns	352
2.	From Plans to Action	356
3.	The War on the Home Front	360
4.	The High Point of the Confederacy	364
5.	The Road to Appomattox	366
6.	Conclusion	370

Chapter 16	Rebuilding the Nation	373
1.	President Versus Congress	374
2.	Congressional Reconstruction	378
3.	Reconstruction and the Postwar South	383
4.	The End of Reconstruction	387
5.	Conclusion	391
City Sketch	**New York** *1860-1865*	394
City Sketch	**Atlanta** *1860-1865*	398

Conclusion Reconstruction to the Present   404

    1. The Watershed Years   404

    2. Rise to World Power   408

    3. Prosperity and Depression   412

    4. The World in Conflict   417

    5. Contemporary America   421

    6. Conclusion   427

    City Sketch **Houston** *1960-1985*   430

Epilogue   436

Appendix

    Readings   437

    Atlas and Historical Data   487

    Declaration of Independence   506

    Constitution of the United States   509

Glossary   531

Index   545

Acknowledgments   565

Photo Credits   567

Maps

Physical Regions of the United States	4
General Regions of the United States	12
Land Bridge	16
Routes of the Early People	24
Mayas, Aztecs, and Incas	29
People of North America	35

Trade Routes in the 1400's	44
Major European Explorations	51
European Claims in North America, 1650	62
Major English Explorations	69
Land Grants, 1606	71
Settlement in the Thirteen Colonies	83
Secota	88
Plymouth	92
Colonial Trade Routes	110
Colonial Economy	116
The Major Campaigns of the Revolutionary War (1775-1777)	136
The Major Campaigns of the Revolutionary War (1778-1781)	139
North America in 1763	140
North America in 1783	140
The Northwest Territory	149
Philadelphia	184
Election of 1800	208
Exploring the Louisiana Purchase, 1806	210
Major Campaigns of the War of 1812	219
Principal Roads and Canals by 1840	225
Election of 1824	237
Election of 1828	237
Washington, D.C.	252
Population Density by 1850	273
Major Railroads in the 1850's	289
Routes to the Far West	302
Oregon Boundary	308
United States Expansion, 1853	310
New Orleans	318
San Francisco	322
Expansion of Slavery	345
Election of 1860	347
Union and Confederacy	353
Early Civil War (April 1861-July 1862)	358
War in the East (1862-1863)	365
Last Phases of the War (1863-1865)	368
Reconstruction of the South	381
Election of 1876	390
New York	394
Atlanta	398
United States Acquisitions, 1858-1917	409
The United States Economy	415
Houston	430
United States	488
Climate	490
Land Use	490
Mineral Resources and Deposits	491
Industry and Manufacturing	491
The World	496
North America	498
South America	499
Eurasia	500
Africa	502

Charts, Graphs, and Diagrams

Landforms	7
European Explorers	50
The Colonies	84

vii

Colonial Population 1630-1780	103
Percent of Nationality Groups, 1775	103
Events Leading to the Revolution	129
Ratification of the Constitution	160
System of Checks and Balances	167
Plans of Government	171
Division of Powers	177
Amending the Constitution	179
Political Parties in the 1790's	206
Voter Participation, 1824-1840	249
Percent of Eligible Voters, 1840	249
Population Growth, 1790-1860	291
Total Estimated Population, 1860	291
Union and Confederate Resources, 1860	355
Population	492
Distribution by Age	492
Population By Race and Origin	492
Birth and Death Rate, 1900-Today	492
Life Expectancy at Birth	492
Education	493
Health Care Expenditures	493
Census of Religious Groups	493
Gross National Product	494
Median Income of Families	494
America at Work	494
Purchasing Power of the Dollar	494
Consumer and Wholesale Prices	494
Public Employees	495
Federal Government Receipts and Expenditures	495
Expenditures by State and Local Government	495
The States of the Union	503
Presidents and Vice Presidents	504
Third Party Movements	505
Political Parties in Power	505

Skill Features

Understanding Map Projections	13
Reading the Chapter	27
Analyzing Pictures	55
Reading Time Lines	78
Checking Points of View	115
Reading Primary and Secondary Sources	131
Analyzing Sources of History	155
Recognizing Main Ideas	203
Reading for Detail	243
Checking Fact and Opinion	283
Asking Questions	367
Drawing Conclusions	377

Concept Features

Responsibility	173
Nationalism	227
Creativity	275
Mobility	312
Sectionalism	339
Pluralism	407

Using Maps, Diagrams, and Graphs

Directions and Relative Location	19
Reference Maps	41
Thematic Maps	65
Longitude and Latitude	87
Keys and Legends	121
Tracing Routes	145
Scale	163
Reading Diagrams	183
Direction and Distance	213
Tracing Routes	233
Comparing Maps	251
Demographic Maps	279
Using Line Graphs	297
Longitude and Latitude	317
Comparing Maps	350
Reading Pie Graphs	372
Thematic Maps	393
Thematic Maps	429

Profiles

LaSalle (1643-1687)	60
Dr. Alexander Hamilton (1712-1756)	80
Anne Bradstreet (1612-1672)	106
Phillis Wheatley (1753?-1784)	106
Thomas Paine (1737-1809)	134
Daniel Shays (1747?-1825)	153
James Madison (1751-1836)	175
John Marshall (1755-1835)	175
Benjamin Banneker (1731-1806)	198
Tecumseh (1765-1813)	217
John Floyd (1783-1837)	239
Sarah Grimké (1792-1873)	266
Angelina Grimké (1805-1879)	266
Margaret Gaffney Haughery (1813-1882)	293
Mariano Guadalupe Vallejo (1808-1890)	305
Frederick Douglass (1817-1895)	337
Clara Barton (1821-1912)	362
Charlotte Forten (1837-1914)	388
Sandra Day O'Connor (1930-)	425
Geraldine A. Ferraro (1935-)	425

PROLOGUE

History can help a person learn about the past, understand the present, and prepare for the future. Most current political, economic, and social conditions in the United States took a long time to develop and are continuing to change. History traces the development, following all the twists and turns that affected it along the way.

To begin to understand the present American political system, for example, consider some of the major political developments in the nation's past and ask questions about them. What was life in the colonies like under British rule? Why were the colonists unhappy with British rule? What kind of government did Americans set up for themselves? How did a free and open society in the United States affect the way that government worked? What divided the American people, leading to a civil war? How did Americans restore the unity of their country after the ordeal of the Civil War?

Similarly, the American economic system and American society can be considered. What values did the American people derive from their rural society and their agricultural way of life? How did these values affect their political ideas and their social attitudes? Why did the United States decide to change from an agrarian economy to an industrial economy? How did the economy influence immigration? Why was there conflict among races of people? In what ways did the industrial economy of the North conflict with the plantation economy of the South?

Even the most far-reaching study of history may not provide complete answers. There are some historical facts that are clear, simple, and upon which historians easily agree. There are other aspects of history that are not clear and upon which historians may never agree. These usually concern judgments involving correct and incorrect decisions. The important thing is that history raises questions and aids in providing a structure for answering them. Evaluating facts and weighing evidence are valuable skills for making sound and reasonable decisions.

United States History: Beginnings Through Reconstruction tells the story of the United States and its people. It follows a development from America's distant past to the Reconstruction period that came after the Civil War. It provides a framework for learning about the way things were, understanding the way things are, and preparing for the way things may be in the United States.

The Prologue is designed for the students as an introduction to this text as well as an introduction to the study of American history.

1

Introduction
The Land

One reason America is a land of opportunity is because of its abundant and varied natural resources. What effect has its geography had on the United States?

Each chapter opens with a large photograph of a subject important to the overall chapter.

To appreciate fully the culture, society, and institutions of the American people, it is necessary to understand the unique geographical features in which the American people live. Many of the reasons the United States emerged as a highly developed country are directly related to the diversity and variety of its physical regions and the richness of its natural resources.

Chapters are organized on a formal outline basis in order to help students better work with the content. Chapters are divided into sections, and sections are divided into subsections, all of which are numbered for ease of reference.

1. Geographical Features

The United States of America is the world's fourth largest country in area, with a land mass of 3,536,855 square miles (9,156,918 square kilometers). The United States is spread over a huge area of North America, stretching some 2,898 miles (4,664 kilometers) from Maine in the east to California in the west, not to mention its non-coterminous area—Alaska and Hawaii. From the northern border of North Dakota to the southern border of Texas, the United States extends 1,606 miles (2,585 kilometers).

Where does the United States rank among all nations in area?

There is as much physical variety within the United States as can be found in any other country on Earth. There are huge forests, large areas of flat, grassy plains, and wide deserts. Moving from the Atlantic Seaboard in the east to the Pacific Coast in the west, the United States can be divided into seven major physical regions. These are: (1) the Coastal Plains, (2) the Appalachian Highlands, (3) the Interior Plains, (4) the Interior Highlands, (5) the Rocky Mountains, (6) the Intermontane Plateaus and Basins, and (7) the Pacific Coastal Ranges.

Compare the land area of the United States with the four other largest countries.
1. Soviet Union
2. Canada
3. China
4. United States
5. Brazil

1.1 The Coastal Plains. A lowland area sweeps north and south from Massachusetts to Texas. It forms a plain along the coasts of the Atlantic Ocean and the Gulf of Mexico. This coastal plain extends for more than 2,000 miles (3,219 kilometers) from one end to the other and is divided into two parts—the Atlantic Coastal Plain and the Gulf Coastal Plain.

What are the two parts of the coastal plains?

The Atlantic Coastal Plain follows along the Atlantic coastline from Cape Code in Massachusetts to the Florida Peninsula. It is narrow in the north but becomes more than 200 miles (322 kilometers) wide as it moves south.

The Atlantic coastline is irregular in the north. There the plain extends to the foothills of the Appalachian Mountains. In this region there are many natural harbors. Some of the more important ones are Massachusetts Bay, Long Island Sound, New York Bay, Delaware Bay, and Chesapeake Bay. A **bay** is a body of water that is partly enclosed by

To aid readability and understanding, key terms and concepts appear in boldface type when first presented and are defined in context.

The Land 3

Physical Regions of the United States

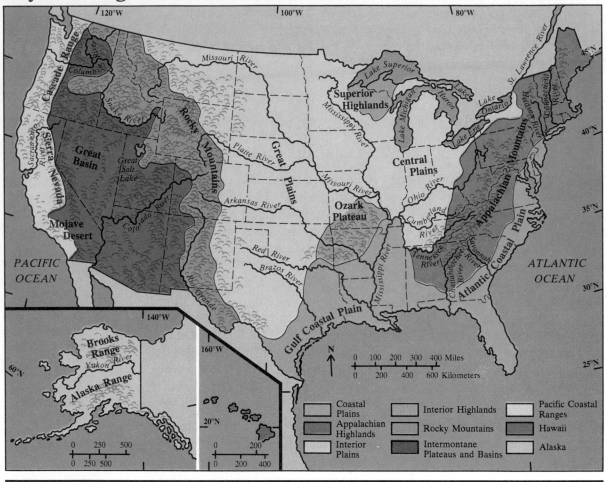

All maps appear in full color. Color is used to highlight important data. Longitude, latitude, and scale are included on all maps.

The United States is now politically divided into fifty states and physically divided into nine regions. What physical region covers most of the central part of the coterminous United States?

land but has a wide outlet to the sea, whereas a **sound** is a long, narrow inlet of the sea.

Along the southern part of the Atlantic Plain there are fewer natural harbors. Sandy beaches are found along much of the shoreline. Offshore islands from Virginia to Georgia are separated from the mainland by marshes and lagoons. A **lagoon** is a shallow body of water connected to larger one. Albemarle and Pamlico Sounds both lie along the coast of North Carolina.

What is a lagoon?

4   The Land

Mixed forests of **conifers** (cone-bearing evergreens) and broadleaf **deciduous trees** (trees that shed their leaves) are the natural vegetation of the northern part of the Atlantic Coastal Plain. The vegetation of the southern part is mostly coniferous forests. Marshes are common, and there are many slow-moving rivers crossing that portion of the plain. The plain's most southern part includes the Everglades Swamp in Florida.

The Gulf Coastal Plain is a much wider band of flat land and gently-rolling hills. It varies in width from 150 miles (241 kilometers) to about 600 miles (966 kilometers). At one point, the Gulf Coastal Plain extends far inland to where the Ohio River flows into the Mississippi River.

The Mississippi River, the longest river in North America, empties into the Gulf of Mexico in southern Louisiana. There it has made a huge **delta,** or a low flat land area shaped like a triangle at the mouth of the river. This part of the Gulf Coastal Plain is made up of marshes and bayous. A **bayou** is made up of many small marshy creeks and river tributaries which flow through a delta region.

1.2. The Appalachian Highlands.   Just west of the Atlantic Coastal Plain is the Appalachian Highlands, which takes its name from the Appalachian Mountains. The highlands stretch about 1,200 miles (1,931 kilometers) from north to south. That is, the highlands run southwest from northern Maine to central Alabama.

The southeastern edge of the highlands is known as the Piedmont. This is a low plateau that varies in altitude from 500 to 1,000 feet (152 to 305 meters) above sea level. The land drops off sharply from the Piedmont to the plain, creating steep waterfalls along fast-moving rivers. The line where this drop takes place is called the **fall line.**

West of the coastal plain in the northeast and the Piedmont in the southeast are the Appalachian Mountains. The Appalachian Mountains are made up of many low, rounded peaks clustered into different ranges. These include the Catskills of New York, the Pocono Mountains of northeastern Pennsylvania, the Allegheny Mountains that stretch from central Pennsylvania to Virginia, the Blue Ridge Mountains that extend from Pennsylvania to Georgia, and the Great Smoky Mountains that run along the border between Tennessee and North Carolina.

North of the Mohawk River Valley in New York, the landscape of the Adirondack Mountains is characterized by sharp mountains and a plateau dotted with hundreds of lakes. In far northern New York, the landscape becomes flat or rises in gently rolling hills. This is part of the St. Lawrence River Valley. The major mountain areas of New England

Where is the Everglades Swamp located?

Examples of deciduous trees are ash, beech, birch, maple, chestnut, and oak.

What is a delta?

A delta is formed by soil carried down by a river and deposited at its mouth as the river broadens and slows in the low-lying coastal flatlands.

How does the fall line affect water on a river?

Discuss the importance of the fall line to early settlement, e. g., the falls provided water power.

The word *ridge* in Blue Ridge means that these mountains rise from the Piedmont as a steep rock wall. *Blue* refers to the bluish appearance of the coniferous trees covering the mountains.

are the White Mountains of New Hampshire and Maine, the somewhat lower Green Mountains of Vermont, and the Berkshire Hills of western Massachusetts.

In between the different ranges which make up the Appalachian Mountains is an area sometimes called the Great Valley. In some places, the Great Valley is known by other names. In Pennsylvania it is called the Lehigh Valley, in Virginia the Shenandoah Valley, and in Tennessee the Cumberland Valley.

West of the Appalachian Mountains is the Appalachian Plateau. The plateau covers an area of about 1,000 miles (1,609 kilometers) from north to south and 200 miles (322 kilometers) from east to west. It really consists of two parts—the Allegheny Plateau that is located north of Virginia and the Cumberland Plateau that runs from Kentucky to Alabama.

As is true of most of the eastern United States, the Appalachian Highlands are part of an area of extensive forest—both conifers and deciduous broadleafs. Despite much clearing of trees during western expansion, many areas of the highlands remain covered by trees today. Conifers are found mostly in Maine and the southern sections of the highlands. Forests of many kinds of broadleaf deciduous trees cover the rest of the area.

What valleys are part of the Great Valley?

A plateau is a raised plain of relatively level surface. The word comes from the French meaning flat or platter.

The Great Smoky Mountains are among the highest, most rugged, and thickly forested mountains in the Appalachian Highlands. These mountains are usually covered by a smoky mist or haze. What two states use these mountains as a border between them?

Chapter illustrations are accompanied by a caption and question which relates to the text narrative.

Landforms

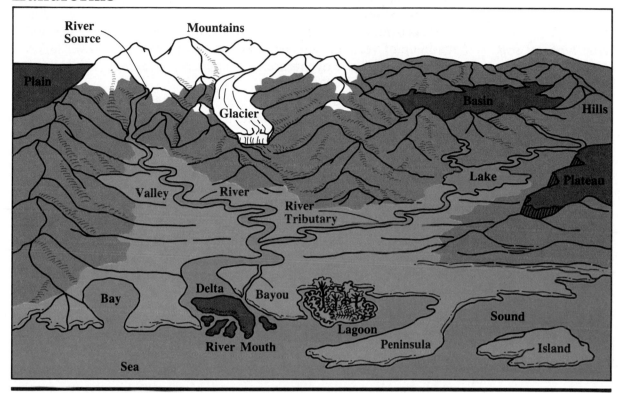

All four major landforms—plains, plateaus, mountains, and hills—can be found in the United States. Many minor landforms make up the small details of the major landform areas. What are some of the minor landforms?

1.3. The Interior Plains.   A huge plains region covers the United States between the Appalachian Mountains and the Rocky Mountains. The region is divided into the generally flat Central Plains, just west of the Appalachian Highlands, and the Great Plains which rise gradually from the Mississippi and Missouri River Basins westward toward the Rocky Mountains.

The Central Plains include lowland parts of central and western Kentucky and Tennessee, the Great Lakes region, and the Upper Mississippi and Lower Ohio and Missouri River Basins. Elevations change from about 500 feet (152 meters) in the east to about 2,000 feet (610 meters) in the west. Prairie grasses form the natural vegetation of this area. There are forests on the hills and in the river valleys.

West of the river basins, the elevations slowly increase from 2,000 feet (610 meters) to over 5,000 feet (1,524 meters) toward the Rocky

Glaciers carved out the Great Lakes of the Central Plains. They comprise the largest group of fresh water lakes in the world.

What type of natural vegetation is found in the Central Plain?

What types of soil
are found in the
Great Plains region?

Ask students to determine
how different plant life at
each altitude influences a
different animal popula-
tion and human settle-
ment.

Why did the early
Spaniards have
difficulty traveling?

What accounts for
the many caverns in
the Ozark Plateau?

Point out that the conti-
nental divide runs along
the main ridge of the
Rocky Mountains. Rivers
and streams flow in oppo-
site directions from the divide to the oceans.

In which direction
do the Rocky
Mountains stretch?

Mountains. This area is the Great Plains, also called the High Plains. Many long rivers flow eastward from the Great Plains and empty into the Mississippi River. They flow through large sections of dry, almost treeless land, once covered with prairie and steppe grasses. The soil is made up of very fertile **chernozem** (rich topsoil with a lower layer of lime) and a mixture of chernozem and **podzol** (a leached, acidic bottom ground soil).

The part of the Great Plains lying along the Upper Missouri River is known as the Missouri Plateau. In the Dakotas and Montana are highlands made up of scattered groupings of hills. In the Black Hills of South Dakota, Harney Peak reaches an altitude of 7,242 feet (2,207 meters), making it the highest peak in the United States east of the Rocky Mountains.

From South Dakota to Texas, much of the Great Plains is high, dry, very flat land. The treeless landscape has such a look of sameness that legend has it that Spaniards traveling in western Texas during the colonial period had great difficulty finding their way. They had to place markers along their trail in order to get a sense of direction. Over time, the land became known as the *Llano Estacado,* or "staked plain."

1.4   The Interior Highlands.   In the central United States, two separate highland regions rise above the plains. These are the Superior Highlands and the Ozark Plateau.

The Superior Highlands are located around Lake Superior in northern Minnesota, Wisconsin, and Michigan. Coniferous forests cover rocky plateaus. There are many lakes among the hills. The Mesabi Range in Minnesota is one of the longest chains of hills in that area.

The Ozark Plateau is located between the Missouri and the Arkansas Rivers, west of the Mississippi River. The land is gently rolling in some places and has rugged mountains in other places. The rock base of much of the area is limestone that has been eroded by water. As a result, there are more than 400 underground caverns running through the plateau region.

1.5.   The Rocky Mountains.   West of the Great Plains is the Rocky Mountains region. The Rocky Mountains extend from Canada in the north to New Mexico and western Texas in the south. The Rocky Mountain region occupies an area over 1,000 miles (1,609 kilometers) long and between 125 and 375 miles (201 to 603 kilometers) wide.

Like the Appalachian Mountains, the Rockies stretch from north to south. The Rocky Mountains, however, are much more rugged and much higher than the Appalachian Mountains. Many peaks are over 14,000 feet (4,268 meters) high. Plants are greatly affected by altitude. Broadleaf deciduous trees are found at low elevations, whereas needle-

Great herds of American bison, or buffalo, once roamed the Interior Plains, grazing on the abundant prairie and steppe grasses. What kind of soil is found in this region?

leaf conifers are found in higher elevations. Mountaintops not covered by snow are capped by tundra grasses and mosses.

1.6 Intermontane Plateaus and Basins. West of the Rocky Mountains lies an area of intermontane plateaus and basins. The term **intermontane** means "between mountains." The region lies between the Rocky Mountains and the mountain ranges along the Pacific Coast.

The intermontane area is long and broad, stretching from Washington south to the Mexican border. Much of the region lies in a "rain shadow" of the Pacific mountains. The mountains block rain, and, as a result, the lowland areas are very dry. Vegetation is sparse, consisting largely of scrub grasses and desert plants.

Except for the Colorado and the Columbia Rivers and their tributaries, the region has **interior drainage.** That is, water from the highlands flows into lakes or rivers in the area itself rather than out to sea. However, the Columbia River flows west into the Pacific Ocean, and the Colorado River flows south into the Gulf of California.

Some of the most beautiful landscapes in the country are found in the intermontane region. Perhaps the best known is the Grand Canyon, one of the most impressive land formations in the world. Additionally, the Mojave Desert and the Great Basin of Oregon, Utah, and Nevada lie within the region, and the Great Salt Lake lies within the Great Basin. Death Valley, in southeastern California, is the lowest spot in the United States. It lies at 282 feet (86 meters) below sea level.

1.7 The Pacific Coastal Ranges. The most western of the physical regions of the **coterminous United States** (the United States

What does intermontane mean?

As air reaches a mountain range it is forced to rise, the air cools, and precipitation is released. The side of the mountain over which the air rises receives a lot of precipitation. The opposite inland side receives little precipitation.

What is meant by interior drainage?

The Colorado River formed the Grand Canyon over a period of millions of years by wearing away the layers of granite, sandstone, and shale in its path.

excluding Alaska and Hawaii) is made up of the Pacific Coastal Ranges. Like the Rocky Mountains, the Pacific Coastal Ranges extend from Canada in the north to the Mexican border in the south. The area is about 200 miles (322 kilometers) wide from east to west. It has some of the highest mountains, as well as some of the richest farmland, in the United States.

The interior range includes the Cascade Mountains in Washington and Oregon and the Sierra Nevada Mountains in California. Within the Sierra Nevada is Mount Whitney, the highest peak in the coterminous United States, at 14,494 feet (4,418 meters). Mount Rainier in Washington, at 14,410 feet (4,392 meters) above sea level, is in the Cascade Range. Also in the Cascades are active volcanoes, such as Mount St. Helens which has erupted several times in recent years.

Closer to the Pacific Coast is a second range of mountains stretching from Washington to California. In general, there are few good natural harbors along the West Coast. However, the most important are Puget Sound in Washington, as well as San Francisco and San Diego Bays in California.

Between the Pacific mountain ranges are hills, lower mountains, and valleys. The Puget Trough runs south from Puget Sound as far as Eugene, Oregon. The Willamette River Valley is part of this trough. In central California, the California Trough, better known as the Central

What is the name of the highest mountain in the coterminous United States?

Have students gather news photos of the May 18, 1980, eruption of Mount St. Helens. Point out the direct influence on the surrounding environment.

Located in southern Utah, Bryce Canyon (left) contains some of the most oddly shaped and beautifully colored rocks. Rugged rock cliffs (right) are found around Big Sur in California. In what regions are these two locations found?

or San Joaquin Valley, extends between two ranges for almost 450 miles (724 kilometers) in length. In extreme southern California, the Imperial Valley extends south into Mexico. All of these valleys have rich soil and are important farm areas.

1. What are the seven major physical regions?
2. Into which river do most rivers flow eastward from the Great Plains?
3. What is meant by the term "coterminous" United States?

2. Weather and Climate

Part of the United States lies north of the Arctic Circle, part lies south of the tropic of Cancer, and part lies within the middle latitudes of the northern hemisphere. These different latitudes, combined with variations in altitude, give the United States many different climates. In the coterminous United States east of the Rocky Mountains, climate changes most dramatically from north to south. West of the Rocky Mountains, elevation is a very important influence.

Although the United States has areas within it that represent each of the five major world climate groups (tropical moist climates; dry climates; moist, mild winter climates; moist, cold winter climates; and polar climates), it is easier to describe the general climates of the United States by examining its geographical subdivisions.

2.1 The Northeast. The Northeast is made up of the New England and Middle Atlantic states. The region has great variance in climate. The northern parts of New England are much colder than the Middle Atlantic states because of differences in altitude, in latitude, and in nearness to the ocean. Climate is an important factor in determining what crops will grow, and when these crops should be harvested. Because of the cold climate, the average length of the **growing season** (the time when it is possible to grow crops) in the north is only four months. By comparison, the growing season in the southern parts of the region is nearly seven months long.

2.2 The Southeast. The Southeast includes the area roughly south of the Ohio River and east of the Mississippi River. Summers in this region are hot and humid. Winters, with the exception of southern Florida, are generally moist and cool to mild. Rain falls throughout the year, but rain is heaviest during the summer. The growing season in the Southeast lasts from 7 to 11 months.

Southern Florida has a tropical and moist climate. Even in the coldest month of January, temperatures average above 70°F (21°C). This region is so warm that its growing season lasts all year long.

Where are important farm areas found?

End-of-section questions provide immediate reinforcement of key ideas.

Have students bring in a weather report map from a daily newspaper to use as a review of the information in this section.

Refer students to the map on page 12 to locate each of the major climatic regions of the United States.

What factors contribute to the cold climate in New England?

Explain that climate depends on several factors: prevailing winds, closeness to the ocean, altitude, and distance from the equator.

General Regions of the United States

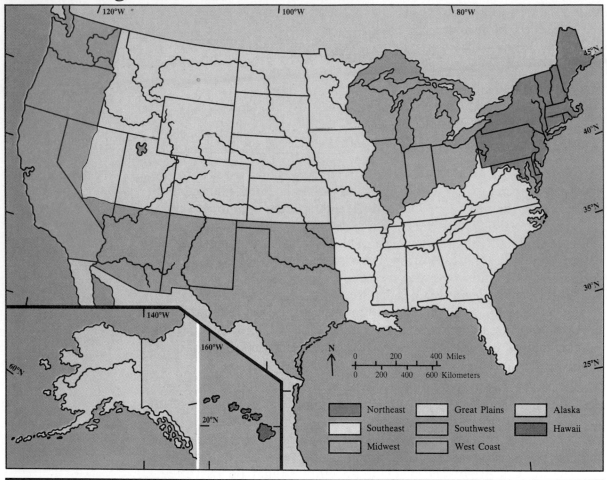

The states of the United States can be grouped into regions that share common climatic characteristics, as well as historical and economic characteristics. Where would you find a growing season that lasts all year?

Explain that rainfall averages include all types of precipitation—rain, snow, sleet, or hail.

Why is there a drought-free growing season?

2.3 The Midwest. North of the Ohio River and east of the Great Plains, the winter climate is moist and cold. South of the Great Lakes, summers are hot, and winters are cold with at least one month of average high temperatures below 32°F (0°C). Rainfall averages 20 to 50 inches (51 to 127 centimeters) a year. Because of regular rainfall, the area is assured of a drought-free growing season that lasts about seven months. East and west of the Great Lakes, summers are cooler, and winters are longer. In these areas, the growing season lasts only about six months.

Understanding Map Projections
SKILL

If a tennis ball is cut into two pieces and one half is flattened on a table, it cannot be flattened totally without more cutting. Mapmakers have the same problem. A mapmaker tries to show the surface of a round earth on the flat map. When only a small part of the earth's surface is shown, there is no problem. Adjustments must be made when a large area or the whole earth is shown.

In making adjustments from a round to a flat surface, mapmakers use a variety of systems, or projections. Each projection shows certain areas accurately, but none show true scale for every part of the earth. Only a globe is an accurate reflection of the earth.

One type of projection is cylindrical. To make one, a cylinder of paper is wrapped around a globe. The light projects the globe's features onto the paper. Distortion is least where the paper touches the globe. The best known cylindrical projection is the Mercator projection. The map on page 51 is an example of a Mercator projection.

Another projection is conical. The name comes from the fact that the projection is made onto a cone of paper. Again, there is least distortion where the paper cone touches the globe. Maps of the United States are often conical projections. The map on page 12 is an example of a conical projection.

Study a globe and the maps on pages 44 and 51, then answer the following questions.
1. How do the maps differ?
2. What same areas on the maps appear to have different sizes?
3. Why do certain land areas appear different on a map than they do on a globe?
4. Which map distorts the large land areas most?
5. What are the advantages and the disadvantages of using each projection?

Cylindrical Projection

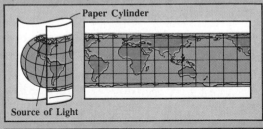

Conical Projection

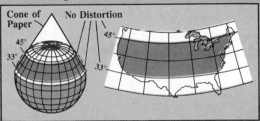

Acting as a partial rain barrier, the Rocky Mountains (left) receives an ample supply of average rainfall. However, desert areas in the Southwest (right) have this country's driest climate. What kind of vegetation is found in each area?

Why is there little rainfall in the Great Plains?

Point out that varied climate conditions have different economic benefits and drawbacks for each region. Have the students list some of these after reading the section.

2.4 The Great Plains. The climate of the Great Plains is generally **semi-arid** (partly dry with limited moisture). Because the Rocky Mountains block moisture from the west, rainfall is light, averaging only 8 to 20 inches (20 to 51 centimeters) a year. In the plains region, the range of temperatures is greater than anywhere else in the United States. Summers are very hot, and winters are very cold. In Bismarck, North Dakota, for example, the average high temperature in January is only 18°F (-8°C). In July, on the other hand, it goes as high as 83°F (28°C). That is a difference of 65°F (18°C). In the eastern part of the Great Plains, the growing season runs as long as six months, while in the western part, the growing season is usually not more than four months.

2.5 The Southwest. In the Southwest, there are great differences in climate and temperature, depending on the altitude of a particular location. The highest parts of the Rocky Mountains, for example, are extremely cold most of the year. Rainfall averages as much as 30 inches (76 centimeters) a year, but moisture often falls either as snow or frozen rain.

The low-lying basins in the intermontane region, on the other hand, have a generally hot and dry climate. This climate is found in parts of Nevada, Arizona, and New Mexico, as well as in western Texas. The average rainfall is less than 8 inches (20 centimeters) a year. Summers are hot, but the winters are surprisingly cool to cold. As a result of extreme temperature variation, the growing season lasts only from five to seven months.

In the southernmost regions of the Southwest, particularly southern Texas, the climate is much milder. Winters are mild and wet, while summers are very hot. The growing season also is longer. In parts it lasts nearly all year long.

Lead a discussion on how the physical regions of the United States might have influenced the determination of state boundaries.

2.6   The West Coast.   On the Pacific Coast, the summers are very warm, and the winters are generally moist and mild. The coastal mountains that run from Washington through Oregon and northern California cause warm winds blowing in from the Pacific Ocean to dump moisture over these three states. As a result, these coastal states receive from 60 to more than 80 inches (152 to over 203 centimeters) of rain a year. The heavy rainfall of the region, combined with the warm winds, provide a growing season of more than seven months.

Why does the Pacific Coast receive heavy rainfall?

In central and southern California, there is a Mediterranean climate. Summers there are dry and hot, while winters are mild and rainy. Like southern Florida and southern Texas, the growing season is about all year long.

1. What are the five major world climates?
2. Why does the United States have different climates?
3. Why is the climate of the Great Plains generally semi-arid?

3. Prehistoric Times _____

To this point, the discussion of the geography of the United States has centered on its landscape, weather, and climate as known today. Tens of thousands of years ago, however, when many of the physical features were being formed, things were much different.

Point out that the "face" of the earth is constantly changing. Students might suggest ways in which the landscape of their community has changed or is changing. Changes can be slow or fast.

3.1   The Ice Age.   Tens of thousands of years ago, the Western Hemisphere looked different than it does today. For one thing, it was much larger in size. At that time, one-third of the earth's surface was covered by ice. This was the result of a part of the earth's history known as the Ice Age. During the Ice Age, the general climate of the earth slowly grew freezing cold. The moisture escaping from the oceans and the seas, which usually returns as rain, fell mostly as snow. This snow became packed into **glaciers,** or heavy, giant sheets of solid ice which move slowly across the land. With less rain falling, the oceans became lower than before, and much of the earth that was normally covered by water became dry land.

Compare the length of the Ice Age with the age of the United States as an aid to students in establishing time perspective.

3.2   The Land Bridge.   The last Ice Age began about 70,000 B.C., reached its peak about 40,000 B.C., and came to an end about 10,000 B.C. At different times during the last Ice Age, glaciers covered much of Europe, Asia, and North America. Because the oceans were much lower than they are today, the Western Hemisphere was much larger and extended over a greater portion of the globe. South America was much closer to Africa, while North America was joined to Asia by a wide strip of land called a **land bridge.** This land bridge is now covered by the Bering Strait.

Though the land mass of the Western Hemisphere was greater, the one thing it lacked was people. Modern scientists claim that only giant creatures, such as dinosaurs, roamed the frozen plains. There were no humans to be found in this part of the world. It was not until the glaciers started to melt, and the temperatures of earth began to rise, that humans made their first appearance on the North American continent.

About 42,000 years ago, ice covered one-third of the earth's surface. The level of the oceans was lower, too. How did the Ice Age help make it possible for people to come from Asia to North America?

Why was the Western Hemisphere much larger during the Ice Age?

Explain that the Ice Age discussed in this section is only the latest in a series of such phenomena.

Land Bridge

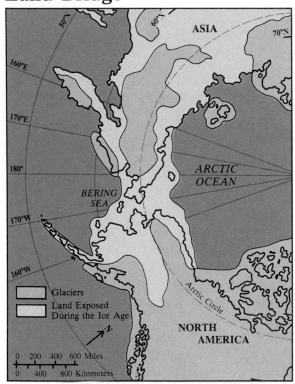

Through a method known as **radiocarbon dating,** it is possible to measure the amount of radioactive carbon left in such remains as bones, wood, and cloth. By using radiocarbon dating, scientists believe that humans have been in North America at least 11,000 or 12,000 years. In fact, there are some scholars who believe that the first people may have arrived as early as 40,000 or 50,000 years ago.

3.3   The First People.   Who were these first people? If there were no humans originally in the Western Hemisphere, then from where did they come? By all accounts, the first settlers were from Mongolia. They left their homes in what is now the Gobi Desert during the late stages of the last Ice Age. As that area began to dry up, the animals there moved away to find more fertile grazing lands. Desperate for food, the Mongolians headed eastward into the rising sun in search of better hunting grounds.

Clothed in warm skins and thick hides, they lived off the land and fought their way through hostile tribes they met along the way. Finally, the wanderers reached the land bridge, crossed over the Bering Strait from eastern Siberia, and entered the peninsula of Alaska.

There are some scientific experts who believe that small groups of people from islands in the eastern Pacific Ocean might have sailed to the western coast of South America at a much later period. Most authorities agree, however, that the first people to inhabit the Western Hemisphere were those who came across the land bridge from Asia to Alaska.

1. Where was the land bridge which the early people used to cross into the Western Hemisphere?
2. What method makes it possible to measure the age of items such as bones, wood, and cloth?
3. Who were the first people to inhabit the Western Hemisphere?

What does radiocarbon dating measure?

Refer students to the world map in the Atlas. Have students estimate the mileage from the Gobi Desert to the West Coast of the United States to help them realize the time involved for the emigrations to take place.

Why did the people move?

Most historians agree that the Bering Strait was the major, if not the only, entry point to the Americas. However, trans-Pacific migrations have not been ruled out.

Who else might have settled in South America?

4. Conclusion _____

Many people have the impression that the United States has little background and history. Other parts of the world are seen as having ancient cultures and old civilizations. The United States, by contrast, is seen as a recent discovery, a "new" world. Actually, the land and the people that form the roots of American history stretch far back into the past. The United States of today is only a small part of a long and colorful history.

Introduction Review

Main Points

1. The United States is located on the continent of North America. As a large country, it has a land mass of more than 3,500,000 square miles (9,100,000 square kilometers).

2. Many different climate zones exist in the United States due to its size and variation in elevation.

3. The United States contains a wide range of different geographical features. Its seven major physical regions are the Coastal Plains, the Appalachian Highlands, the Interior Plains, the Interior Highlands, the Rocky Mountains, the Intermontane Plateaus and Basins, and the Pacific Coastal Ranges.

4. Climate and types of soil are two major factors in determining what crops can be grown in any region of the United States.

5. Over tens of thousands of years the physical features of the United States changed to produce what we see today. These changes took place, in part, because of the Ice Age.

6. The first people to come to America crossed a land bridge from Asia during the late stages of the Ice Age.

Building Vocabulary

1. Identify the following:

Appalachian Highlands	Death Valley	Arctic Circle
Llano Estacado	Tropic of Cancer	Ice Age

2. Define the following:

bay	bayou	growing season
sound	fall line	coterminous United States
lagoon	chernozem	semi-arid
conifers	podzol	glaciers
deciduous trees	intermontane	land bridge
delta	interior drainage	radiocarbon dating

Remembering the Facts

1. What is the distance across the United States north to south? East to west?

2. How does the shoreline of the northern part of the Atlantic Coastal Plain compare with the southern shoreline?

3. Which is the longest river in North America? In what physical regions of the United States is it located?

4. Into what two areas is the huge Interior Plains region divided?

Each chapter ends with a Chapter Review to aid students in retaining the material just studied.

5. Are the Rocky Mountains higher or lower than the Appalachian Mountains? Which is to the west of the other?
6. What two separate regions make up the Interior Highlands?
7. How many geographical regions of the United States are there? What are they?

8. What two factors about the United States cause it to have many different climates?
9. Which geographic regions of the United States have areas with the longest growing season?
10. During what time period did the first people come to America, and how did they arrive?

Understanding the Facts

1. What differences exist in the physical features of the United States?
2. How do the differences in physical features and climate affect the lives of the American people?
3. How do the east and west coastal regions physically differ from each other?

4. What geographical subdivisions have the greatest seasonal weather and climate changes? Why?
5. Why did the first Americans leave their original homes to travel to a new land?
6. How can modern scientists tell how long human beings have been in America?

Using Maps

Directions and Relative Location. It is important to know direction in order to use a map properly. North is the direction toward the North Pole. On most maps, north is usually at the top. Many maps show a direction indicator for north.

Once you know north, you also know that east is to the right, west is to the left, and south is opposite to north. For more precise directions, you can use the indicator to find northeast, northwest, southeast, and southwest. These are located between the four basic directions.

You can use directions to talk about the relative location of places on a map. Relative location means the location of a place relative to, or compared with, another place. For example, the Great Salt Lake is southeast of the Cascade Range.

Check your understanding of direction and relative location by using the map on page 4 to answer the following questions.

1. Which direction from the Appalachian Mountains is the Great Plains?
2. Which direction from the Pacific Coastal Ranges is the Atlantic Coastal Plain?
3. Which direction provides the most direct route from Lake Erie to the Savannah River?
4. What direction does the Mississippi River flow?
5. What is the relative location of the Mojave Desert to the Superior Highlands?
6. What is the relative location of Lake Superior to the Gulf Coastal Plain?

To develop map skills, exercises using chapter maps appear at the end of the Chapter Review.

UNIT I

Opportunity

Opportunity has been a way of life for people coming to America from the start. Thousands of years ago, people from Asia moved slowly overland into Alaska, hunting and gathering more food. Beginning in the fifteenth century, people from Europe and Africa traveled by sea to the New World. They believed that America offered a place to lead their own lives. With great areas of land and many natural resources, opportunities for people in America seemed to be unlimited.

Chapter 1	The First Americans	22
Chapter 2	New World–New Opportunities	42
Chapter 3	English Settlement in North America	66
City Sketch	*Secota 1584–1587*	88
City Sketch	*Plymouth 1620–1650*	92

The First Americans 1

After the last Ice Age, Asiatic people left their homes in search of food. Crossing over the Bering Strait on the land bridge, these wanderers became the first people to arrive in America. Where did these first arrivals settle?

Tens of thousands of years ago humans finally came upon the empty land of the Western Hemisphere. It would be up to them to transform its wilderness, to cultivate its soil, to build communities, and to plan the future of their social life together. It would take thousands of years to do all these things, but it would all be part of American history.

Clarify the terms Western Hemisphere and North and South America.

1. The First Arrivals _____

When the first Asiatic people crossed from Siberia to Alaska, they did not stay in one place. They moved through the frozen areas of northern Canada into the warmer climate of what is now the United States. By about 9000 B.C., many of the hunters and their families had come as far south as Arizona and New Mexico. At that time, the Southwest was a fertile region with plenty of water and many kinds of animals. Some people remained in this area. Others continued to travel southward across Mexico and Central America into what is now South America. In each area, people developed different *cultures*—ways of life—to adjust to the areas in which they lived.

What is a culture?

1.1 Early Life in the North.   The various Asiatic groups in time settled down in different places along the trails that first brought them down into the North American continent. Those who stayed in the northern parts of what today is Canada found the climate too cold and the ground too hard for farming. Therefore, they hunted caribou, moose, elk, bison, and other large animals. These animals not only provided meat for the family, but furs for clothing, skins for boots, and bones for tools.

Have students speculate on the types of houses, clothing, and tools of groups that settled in each climate region.

1.2 Early Life in the South.   Some people moved further south and settled in the Pacific Northwest. Living close to rivers, lakes, and the ocean, they were able to move about a great deal. They were also able to enjoy a diet of fish, as well as small game and wild plants. Other people moved into the woodlands and valleys of the eastern sections of the United States. Here they hunted small animals, fished, gathered wild plants, and made tools.

What kind of food did people eat to survive?

Still others went further south and settled in the Southwest. By the time they arrived, many rivers had dried up, and the region had become semi-arid. Water was scarce, animals were few, and food was hard to get. The people in this region were forced to live mainly on nuts, roots, and berries. They hunted small game and made baskets to gather food.

1.3 The Beginning of Farming.   Because there were no longer large animals to hunt, those people who settled in the regions known today as Mexico, Central America, and the northern sections of South

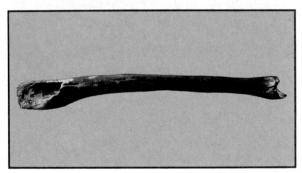

Routes of the Early People

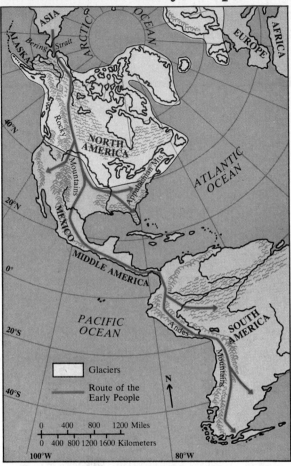

When scientists tested this caribou-bone scraper (bottom) found in Alaska, they proved that people lived there by 25,000 B.C. The duck decoy (top) was probably made in the Great Basin about 2500 B.C. What factors affected where the early Americans lived and what tools they made for hunting and working?

Point out how the first inhabitants used natural resources to satisfy their needs.

America stopped moving around. They settled in warm areas where the rainfall is often heavy and the soil is very fertile.

In these warmer climates, the early people developed *agriculture*—the planned growing of food. As early as 8000 B.C., those in what is now Mexico learned to plant seeds and grow some kinds of food for themselves. Corn, beans, and squash were among the first plants grown. They soon became the people's basic plant foods. Pumpkins, gourds, potatoes, and avocados were also grown. Later there were many other crops, including tobacco which the people smoked, chewed, and sometimes ate.

People gained more control over their food supply when they learned to grow plants. Groups settled near fields and gardens and formed small villages. There they grew enough food to store some for later use. Because they no longer had to spend as much time searching for food, people could work on other things. As life became more complex, some of the larger groups developed organized societies. This was a long and gradual process that took thousands of years.

How did people gain more control over their food supply?

Have students explore the importance of farming by raising the question whether civilization could have been possible without it.

1. The first Americans came from what land?
2. Why did the early people in the Western Hemisphere develop different cultures?
3. How did the early people get food?

2. People of Middle and South America

Between 300 and 1500 A.D., three groups of people in Middle and South America rose to power. The groups all had large populations and highly developed societies. While they were alike in some ways, each developed its own unique culture.

2.1 The Mayas.   From about 300 to 900 A.D., the Mayas formed a great culture in Middle America. They had settled in the area of the Yucatán Peninsula (now southeast Mexico, Guatemala, and Honduras). There they made their living by farming, mostly growing corn. Most Mayas lived in one-room houses with thatched roofs.

Where did the Mayas settle?

One of the ancient cultures of Middle America was that of the Mayas, who built large, stone pyramids that served as religious centers. Religion was an important aspect of Mayan life. What kinds of things did Mayas worship?

The First Americans 25

Religion was the strongest force in the lives of the Mayas. They worshiped things in nature such as spirits of the sun, rain, and animals. Groups of Mayas lived near scattered religious centers, each ruled by a priest. In these centers, the Mayas built huge stone pyramids. On the flat tops of these were small temples and sculptures.

The priests ruled the everyday lives of the people. The Mayan farmers supported the priests with their crops, and this gave the priests time to work out new ideas. The Mayan priests were very interested in measuring time. They studied the movement of the sun, moon, stars, and planets, and from this, they formed an accurate, 365-day calendar. The priests set up a system of numbers based on twenty with the place value of zero. The Mayas also had a system of writing in which small pictures stood for words.

Mayan culture began to lose strength about 800 A.D. There may have been an epidemic or some natural disaster. The farms may have worn out the soil so it did not produce as many crops for food. Or there may have been wars among groups of Mayas or with outsiders. By about 1000 A.D., the Mayas had abandoned many of their religious centers. Some people drifted into the dense jungles while others stayed in the northern part of the Yucatán Peninsula.

2.2   The Aztecs.   During the next few hundred years, another society rose to power. Its culture included large cities with many people and a well-ordered government. It began with a small group of hunter-warriors in the center of Mexico. In time, they took over nearby groups and formed an *empire*—many different peoples and lands ruled by one government or leader. The Aztec empire, led by a ruler who was all-powerful, later covered most of central and southern Mexico.

In the early 1300's, the Aztecs set up a capital city, Tenochtitlán, built on an island in a lake. The people found a way to bring fresh water to the city from springs on the mainland. They built canals and raised streets of hard earth running through the city. The major canals and roads led to a central square, where the Aztecs built large pyramids with temples and sculpture on their flat tops. They put their markets, shops, government buildings, and great stone palaces around the square. The Aztecs had many flower gardens and a zoo with hundreds of kinds of birds and animals. By the early 1500's, nearly 100,000 people lived in the capital city.

Most Aztecs lived by farming. Corn was their most important crop, but they also grew beans, squash, peppers, cotton, and tobacco. The farmers grew enough food for themselves and for the government leaders and others in the capital. Aztec *artisans*—skilled workers—made pottery and wove cloth. They made jewelry from gold, silver, and

Reading the Chapter
SKILL

One way to make your study of history easier is to look at the structure of the reading material. Begin with a careful look at the title of each chapter. Look at the sections and the subsections which divide it. The title and the headings form a guide to the ideas you should get from the reading. In this way, the outline previews the reading like a preview of a movie or a television program. Going through the outline before you read lets you know what to expect. After you read the material, use the outline to check your recall.

Use this chapter as an example. Follow the outline formed by the title, section headings, and subsection headings.

Title—The First Americans
Section heading—
1. The First Arrivals
Subsection headings—
1.1 Early Life in the North.
1.2 Early Life in the South.
1.3 The Beginning of Farming.
Section heading—
2. People of Middle and South America
Subsection headings—
2.1 The Mayas.
2.2 The Aztecs.
2.3 The Incas.

Section heading—
3. People of North America
Subsection headings—
3.1 The Southwest.
3.2 The Plains.
3.3 The Great Basin and California.
3.4 The Northwest Coast.
3.5 The Far North.
3.6 The Arctic.
3.7 The Eastern Woodlands.

You should be able to answer the following questions before you read the chapter.

1. What is the chapter about?
2. What is discussed in each of the three major sections?
3. Into what groups are the people of North America divided?

Looking over the outline can also raise some questions that reading the chapter will answer. Here are some possible questions.

1. When did people first come to the Western Hemisphere?
2. Who were the Mayas, Aztecs, and Incas?
3. Which people lived in the various geographic areas of North America?

By examining the title, section headings, and subsection headings, you can better understand the chapter. Follow this structure as you read each chapter in this book.

This two-headed serpent is a piece of Aztec jewelry probably worn across the chest. Artisans used turquoise as well as gold, silver, and jade for carving. Why was jewelry important in the Aztec economy?

jade. Aztec traders contacted many peoples and brought goods such as rubber, cacao, gold, and jewels into the Aztec capital.

Religion was a very important part of Aztec life. The people had many gods, and one of the most powerful was the war and sun god. The Aztecs believed that they must make human sacrifices to this god so that the sun would rise each morning. Thousands of people each year were put to death for that reason.

Why did the Aztecs make human sacrifices?

The Aztecs fought many wars to expand their empire. They took over new lands and forced the people to send goods to Tenochtitlán every year. The Aztecs also fought to get captives for the sacrifices. Some of the conquered peoples were angry about sending their wealth and their people as sacrifices to the Aztec capital. Sometimes they rebelled, and by the early 1500's, the empire began to weaken.

2.3 The Incas. Sometime after 1200, another great empire was formed in the Western Hemisphere. The Incas lived in the Andes Mountains of South America. By the middle of the 1400's, they ruled lands stretching in a narrow strip over 2,000 miles (3,200 kilometers) long from what is now southern Colombia to the middle of Chile. The heart of the Inca empire was in the mountains of Peru.

What things did the Incas raise?

Inca farmers grew many kinds of crops, among them grains and potatoes. They also raised llamas for meat and wool. All the land was controlled by the government. Most people, living in small stone houses, farmed the land for themselves and the government. The government in turn made sure that no one went hungry. Some of the land farmed by the Incas got little rain, so they built stone-lined canals to bring water to those fields.

The Incas also worshiped the sun, and they believed that their ruler was a direct descendant of the sun. As a living god, the ruler could do no wrong. The ruler's wishes were laws that directed the daily lives of the people. Under the ruler was a council of state with four members. Each was in charge of one quarter of the empire. There were many other levels of officers down to the village leaders. The government kept a *census*, or count, of the number of people in each part of the empire.

Cuzco was the capital city of the Incas. It had a central square with temples and palaces around it. Inca artisans carefully shaped the stones in these buildings so that they fit together perfectly without cement. Sometimes they decorated buildings with thin sheets of gold. The artists

What did the Incas believe about their ruler?

Raise the question of why it is important to keep track of the number of people in a country. Ask students if they know how often a census is taken in the United States. Have them find out what uses are made of it.

The Inca city of Machu Picchu (left) stretched along a ridge in the Andes Mountains. A highway system crisscrossed the Inca empire (right). How did these engineering accomplishments help make the Inca powerful?

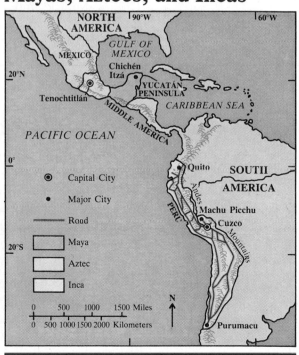

Mayas, Aztecs, and Incas

also used gold, as well as silver, copper, and bronze, to make ornaments. The Inca crafts included pottery and cloth woven from cotton and wool.

How did the Incas link their empire together?

The government built a chain of highways to link all parts of the empire. These carefully built roads crossed the high Andes Mountains. The Incas hung strong vine bridges across deep valleys and dug tunnels through the steepest mountains. They put inns and way stations along the routes. Over these roads, the Incas sent runners in a message service. In this way, the ruler kept in touch with all parts of the land.

Note the differences in the way the Incas treated people outside the empire from the way the Aztecs treated such groups.

Some groups of people willingly joined the Inca empire. Others were added to it by war. New members were carefully drawn into Inca life. They were taught the Inca religion and offered the same benefits and duties as other Incas. Groups who would not accept the Inca plan were moved to areas where they were not dangerous to the empire. Government leaders tried not to cause hardships because of the move.

What led to unrest in the Inca empire?

The Incas had the largest and most highly organized group in the Americas with an all-powerful ruler. In the early 1500's, the Inca ruler died without stating who should rule next. A bitter fight broke out between two groups, each claiming the throne for its leader. In the following years, there was unrest throughout the Inca empire.

1. What three groups of people developed great cultures in Middle and South America?
2. Where did each of the three great cultures develop?
3. What are some of the accomplishments of each group?

3. People of North America

It is a good idea to keep a map of the United States displayed during study of this section. Make the point that the political boundaries as we know them did not exist but are used only for reference.

For hundreds of years, the people of Middle and South America built their great cultures. At about the same time (from 100 B.C. to 1500 A.D.), other groups lived in the area that is now the United States and Canada. These people were spread out across the land, from the hot south to the cold north, from the Pacific to the Atlantic. Their cultures also were influenced by the *environment*—surrounding land, water, and air—in which they lived.

What influenced the cultures of the peoples living in North America?

3.1 The Southwest. Most of the land is hot and dry in the southwest part of what is now the United States (Arizona, New Mexico, Utah, and Colorado). It has thin, rocky soil. In the northern part of this area are steep-walled canyons and flat-topped hills. The southern part is flat desert country.

The Hohokam were one of the early peoples who lived in this area. They probably had migrated from northwest Mexico around 300 B.C. By 100 B.C., they were settled near the middle of Arizona. The Hohokam farmed the land, building long canals to bring water from the rivers to the dry fields. Many years later, the Hohokam were followed on the land by the Pima and Papago peoples.

North of the Hohokam lived another group known as the Anasazi, "the Old Ones." About 900 A.D., these people began to construct apartmentlike buildings in which villages of people lived. The group later was given the name Pueblo, from a Spanish word for village. The buildings, also later called *pueblos*, were very large, sometimes several stories high. They were made of stone or *adobe* (sun-dried brick) and were built into steep cliff walls or on *mesas*—the flat tops of high hills. People entered their pueblos by climbing ladders to openings in the flat roofs. The ladders could be pulled inside for protection.

Each pueblo formed a separate town independent from the others. Two of the Pueblo groups were the Hopi of Arizona and the Zuñi of

Who were the Hohokam?

Use each of the groups discussed in this section to demonstrate the influence of environment on culture. Be sure to include dwellings in the discussion.

What was used to build the pueblos?

The Hopi people lived in these cliff pueblos in Arizona around 1150 A.D. They climbed up and down the cliff by toeholds cut in rock. They farmed nearby fields and hunted. Why did the Hopi build villages in cliffs?

New Mexico. In each group, a council of elders chosen by the priests set up rules and judged crimes. The Pueblos were a peaceful farm people, fighting only to protect themselves and their homes. Their major crops were corn, beans, and squash. They also grew cotton and wove cloth and blankets of many colors. The Pueblos made many kinds of baskets and pottery with black-on-white designs. Pueblo men and women shared the farm work equally. Women had a special place in Pueblo life, for they controlled the fields and were the leaders of their families.

What was the role of women in Pueblo life?

Water was very important to the Pueblo people. Their land was hot and dry, and they needed rain to make their crops grow. The Pueblos had many religious ceremonies to ask for rain during the year. These were held in the *kiva*, a round underground room. The kiva also was used as a meeting and working room for the men of the village.

How did the Apaches differ from the Pueblos?

Two other groups moved into the Southwest by about 1200 A.D. The Apaches and the Navahos came from northern Canada. They were warlike peoples who often raided the Pueblos, taking food and goods. The Apaches moved throughout the Southwest, not staying long in any one place. Their homes, called *wickiups*, were frames of thin poles covered with animal skins. They could be put up and down quickly.

Wars of conquest were rare. The usual reasons were prestige, revenge, plunder, and the desire for slaves.

The Navahos gradually began to settle near the Pueblos. They lived in *hogans*—small, round houses of mud and logs. The Navahos learned farming and weaving from the Pueblos. They also borrowed many parts of the Pueblo religion. One of these was the art of sand painting. To do this, the Navahos took sand, bits of minerals, and seeds of many colors and arranged them into a picture. They used these paintings in the ceremonies they held to cure sickness.

What and where is the Great Plains?

3.2 The Plains.   Near the center of North America is a large area known as the Great Plains. It stretches from southern Canada to southern Texas. The eastern part of this area has rich soil. The western part, where the soil is not so rich, is a broad grassland.

Many different groups of people lived in this land. Among those who lived in the eastern part were the Dakota and other Sioux, and the Pawnee, Mandan, Osage, and Omaha peoples. They were farmers and hunters who set up small villages along rivers and streams. They made their homes of log frames covered with dirt and brush. The women took care of the crops, growing corn, beans, squash, and tobacco. The men hunted deer, elk, buffalo, and other big game.

What did the peoples of the Great Plains hunt?

The Blackfoot, Crow, Cheyenne, and Comanche lived in the western Plains. Their homes, known as *tipis*, were cone-shaped. They were made of poles covered with buffalo hides. These people hunted buffalo for food, clothing, and fuel. Sometimes hunters dressed in animal skins and crept up on their prey. Other times they tried to drive

The Indians never tamed the buffalo or used them as beasts of burden. They used them to provide meat, fur, and leather.

Mandan people built villages along rivers and streams. Women fished and planted gardens. Men hunted and traded. Why were boats important in the everyday lives of the Mandan?

herds over cliffs or into narrow valleys where they were trapped. After the kill, the people carried the buffalo meat and skins to their homes or camps on *travois*—small platforms, each fastened to two poles. Sometimes the people used dogs to pull the travois.

The many groups living on the Plains often met each other as they hunted and traveled across the area. They sometimes traded food and other goods. Many languages were spoken by the Plains peoples. So they developed a set of hand signals for important words or phrases. This sign language allowed them to communicate with those who spoke a different language.

Their religions, centered around spiritual power, were very important to the Plains people. Sometimes people fasted for several days so that they might see visions of spirits. Every year, some groups gathered for the Sun Dance, a ceremony to keep away enemies and famine. As part of it, the men danced in a circle always facing the sun. Sometimes men tortured themselves to show how brave they were.

3.3 The Great Basin and California. The Great Basin is a large area between the Rocky Mountains and the Sierra Nevada Mountains. It covers much of the present state of Nevada, as well as parts of California, Idaho, Utah, and Wyoming. The land is mostly a

How did the different peoples of the Great Plains communicate with each other?

There were some 300 distinct languages among North American Indians. The languages of American Indians can be divided into ten groups. For instance, the Dakota and the Cherokee belong to the same language group, although they belong to different cultural groups.

desert, too dry for farming. Only a few groups of people lived in this area, among them the Ute, Paiute, Shoshoni, and Nez Percé. These people lived in small family groups. They were always on the move, searching for food. They found pine nuts, seeds, and roots from a few wild plants. They also ate insects, rabbits, and other small animals.

Why did many groups live in California but only a few in the Great Basin?

Between the Great Basin and the Pacific coast, in the California area, the land is very different. The weather is mild, and many groups of people lived there, including the Modoc, Chumash, Yokut, and Pomo. These people lived in brush shelters and settled in small villages. Food was easy to get in the California area. The people hunted small game and caught fish. There were many kinds of wild plants, and the people ate seeds, berries, nuts, and roots. Acorns, one of their main foods, were gathered, pounded into flour, and washed to remove their acid. The flour was then used to make a kind of bread or mush.

The people of the Great Basin-California area made baskets and used them to gather, store, and sometimes cook foods. They wove the rushes used to make the baskets in many styles, sometimes with very tiny stitches. They often decorated the baskets with patterns of beads, feathers, and shells.

3.4 The Northwest Coast. The Northwest Coast stretches along the Pacific Ocean from northern California to southern Alaska. It is rich in natural resources. Dense forests grow in the mild, rainy climate. Many groups of people, such as the Haida, Tlingit, Chinook, and Nootka, lived there. They built strong houses of wooden posts and boards. The houses were large enough for as many as 50 people.

What was the main source of food for the peoples of the Northwest Coast?

The Northwest Coast people lived in small villages close to the ocean beaches. They made huge seagoing canoes up to 60 feet (18 meters) long. The people got most of their food by hunting sea animals and by fishing, generally for salmon. There was plenty of food, and the people sometimes traded some of it for goods from other groups.

The great forests were very close to the villages, and the people had many uses for wood. Besides their homes and canoes, they made carved boxes, wooden tools, and ceremonial masks. Outside their houses, they put large wooden posts called **totem poles**. These were carved with figures of faces and animals. The poles showed the history of the family and the titles of the family leader.

Village society was generally divided into four groups, based on wealth. The slaves were at the lowest level. They were people who had been captured in war. Next came the average people and above them, the nobles. At the top were the chiefs, the richest people in the villages.

What was a potlatch?

A chief sometimes gave a special feast, called a **potlatch**, which lasted for several days. During it, the chief gave away or destroyed many things such as canoes, blankets, and large sheets of copper. The potlatch proved how rich the chief was, and he kept his high level in the village.

3.5 The Far North. From the middle of Alaska stretching across Canada to the Atlantic is the Far North—a land of long winters and short summers. There are many lakes and streams there, as well as huge evergreen forests. A few groups of people lived in this area, the Tanaina, Cree, Ottawa, and the Ojibwa who are also called Chippewa. Small bands lived and hunted in family groups. They set up wood frame homes and covered them with bark, brush, or animal skins.

Who lived in the Far North?

Most of the Far North is very cold, and plants are scarce. People there lived on meat, sometimes pounded, mixed with berries, and dried. They hunted moose, deer, and beaver, and they caught fish. In the summers, the people used canoes made of wood poles and bark. In the winters, they had wooden snowshoes for traveling on the snow.

The people of North America formed many groups with varied ways of life. The major cultures are divided according to geography. What did the peoples within each section have in common?

People of North America

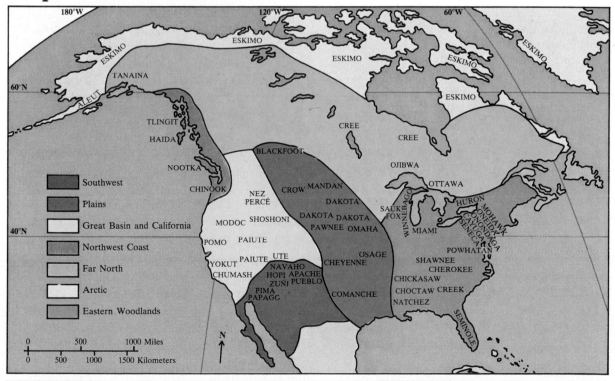

A discussion of why people live in such harsh climates will help to stress the attachment of people to a particular environment and way of life.

3.6 The Arctic.

The land of North America that is nearest to the North Pole is known as the Arctic. In the west, it begins with the Aleutian Islands off the southern coast of Alaska. It stretches around Alaska and across northern Canada to Greenland in the Atlantic Ocean. The Arctic is one of the coldest areas of the world. Snow covers the land up to nine months each year. Most kinds of plants and animals cannot live so far north.

Two groups of people found ways to live in this harsh land. A small group called the Aleuts lived on the bare, foggy Aleutian Islands. They were a branch of a larger group, the Eskimos, who lived all across the area of the Arctic. The two groups had many of the same ways of living. But their languages and some of their customs were different.

What were the differences between the Aleuts and the Eskimos?

The people of the Arctic lived near the sea, and from it they got most of their food. They caught fish and hunted sea animals like whales, seals, and walrus. The people used two kinds of boats, both made of wood frames covered with animal skins. One of them, the *kayak*, was like a canoe and held one or two hunters. The other, the *umiak*, could hold about ten people. The Eskimos also tamed and used dogs to pull sleds across the ice and snow. In the Arctic, there was little wood that could be used for fires. So the people there sometimes ate meat raw.

For what did Arctic people use animals?

The Arctic people used the animals they killed for many things besides food. The skins were used for the many layers of clothing the people wore in the great cold. The people made goggles of bone with narrow slits to protect their eyes from the bright sun on the snow. They also used bone and ivory to make harpoons, hooks for fishing, knives, and needles. The Eskimos carved lamps from soft rock found in the Arctic area and burned seal oil in them. They used the lamps for light, heat, and some cooking.

The Arctic people built houses to protect them from the weather. Most Eskimos used animal skin tents in the short summers. In the cold winters, they made houses of sod, stone, and driftwood. Some of them built houses from blocks of snow. The Aleuts sometimes built houses under the ground, like basements. These had frames of whale bones or driftwood and were covered with grasses.

What were some Eskimo beliefs?

The people who lived in the Arctic had little contact with the people to the south. The Eskimos lived in small family groups which sometimes joined together for hunting. Eskimos believed that they should help each other to live in the harsh climate. It was important to them that each person live in peace with others in the group. The Aleuts lived in small villages on the islands. Each village was led by a chief, and all villages on an island were governed by one ruler. The Aleuts had slaves, most often people taken from nearby islands during raids.

3.7 The Eastern Woodlands. The area known as the Eastern Woodlands stretches from the Great Lakes and the St. Lawrence River in the north to the Gulf of Mexico in the south. From east to west, it covers the area between the Atlantic coast and the Mississippi River. The northern part has cold winters, and the whole area has warm summers. There are lots of rivers in the Eastern Woodlands, and plenty of rain falls on the land.

Many groups of people lived in this wide area. Different groups known together as the Iroquois lived in the northeast. Others like the Fox, Miami, Shawnee, Sauk, Huron, and Winnebago lived in the Great Lakes area. The Choctaw, Chickasaw, Cherokee, Creek, Powhatan, Natchez, and Seminole peoples lived in the southeast. And some groups lived in the center area in the Ohio and Mississippi river valleys. The Eastern Woodlands people got their food by hunting, fishing, farming, and gathering parts of wild plants. Many of them grew corn, beans, squash, and tobacco. Those who lived in the Great Lakes area harvested a kind of wild rice that grows there. And in the north, people made maple sugar from the sap of maple trees.

Most of the groups of the Eastern Woodlands lived in villages ruled by chiefs. Some people built fences around their villages for defense. They were made of logs set together on end and pointed on the top. Most people lived in *wigwams*, small, rounded buildings covered with sheets of bark. A few groups made their homes from poles and clay. The

Where was the Eastern Woodlands?

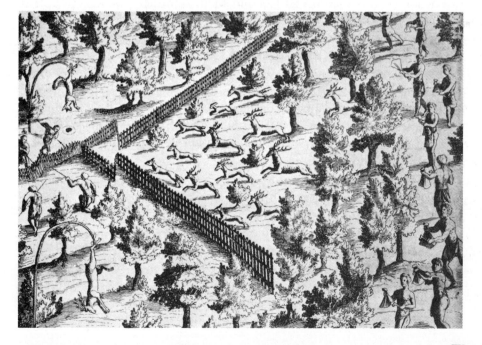

Deer provided many of the Eastern Woodlands people with clothing, food, and tools. The Huron hunted deer using traps. How was this way of hunting similar to the way buffalo were hunted in the western Plains?

The First Americans **37**

Iroquois homes were large, rectangular buildings called **long houses**. They built them with wood poles and bark. A dozen or more related families lived in a long house, each with its own separate section.

The Eastern Woodlands people made many beautiful and useful things. Wood was carved into bowls and tools, and some pottery was made. In the southeast, the people wove cane and wicker baskets. People near the Great Lakes hammered copper to make works of art and small figures used in their ceremonies. The Ohio and Mississippi valley groups were well known for their crafts. These people made bowls, jars, and figures using bone, shells, and copper. Many of their pieces were shaped like animals.

Religion was important to the people of the Eastern Woodlands. Beliefs in spirits of nature guided their lives. Their feasts and ceremonies were often tied to the growing of food. For example, the Green Corn Dance of the Creek people honored the first corn crop of the year. Groups in the north were guided by dreams of supernatural beings. Many groups had dances and ceremonies to cure sickness. Members of one Iroquois group wore carved and painted wood masks as they worked to cure those who were ill.

Groups in the central part of the Eastern Woodlands built large hills of earth as part of their religion. As early as 600 A.D., the Hopewell people in the Ohio Valley area built these **mounds** in round, square, or animal shapes. The Hopewells used the mounds as places to bury their dead, sometimes as many as 1,000 in each. Around 1000 A.D., people in the Mississippi Valley were building temple mounds. These flat-topped mounds had small temples or chiefs' houses on them.

Some Eastern Woodlands villages, like those of the Creek people, had central plazas with meeting houses, public squares, and fields where ceremonies were held. Iroquois villages had groups of long houses. Women had an important role in Iroquois life. They controlled the land and the houses, both of which passed from mother to daughter. Iroquois women chose the **sachems**, or chiefs.

War was common among the people of the area. Sometimes groups fought to show how brave they were. At other times, they fought to capture slaves. The Iroquois adopted some of the slaves, but they also put many others to death. To fight common enemies or solve common problems, some Eastern Woodlands groups formed **alliances**—unwritten partnerships for a specific purpose. Most of these did not last.

By about 1400, Iroquois leaders wanted to stop the bitter fighting among neighboring groups. So leaders of five groups in what is now New York formed the League of the Iroquois. These allies were the Cayuga, Onondaga, Oneida, Mohawk, and Seneca peoples. Each of

This serpent mound was built by Hopewell people 400 years ago. It winds a quarter-mile. Mounds were used for burial and other religious purposes. How do the mounds show the Hopewell people's concern with death?

them sent chiefs to a general council. There they discussed wars and other matters of the Woodlands peoples. Anyone could speak at the meeting. Each chief had one vote, and all of them had to agree before action was taken. The council handled only matters that involved all of its members. It could not bother the governing of any separate group. By the middle of the 1500's, the League of the Iroquois was one of the largest and strongest groups in the lands north of Mexico.

1. Who were some of the people living in the various geographic sections of North America?
2. How did ways of life differ among the people of North America?
3. Why was the League of the Iroquois formed?

4. Conclusion

The idea of America as a new land with a short history is obviously false. The Western Hemisphere is very old and has changed in geography and climate as conditions on the earth have changed. For tens of thousands of years, many groups of people, each with their own special habits, customs, languages, and ways of life lived there. They were living all across the land of North and South America when the first Europeans sailed westward across the Atlantic Ocean.

Chapter 1 Review

Main Points

1. Over a long period of time, the early peoples moved to all parts of North and South America.
2. These early peoples developed ways of living dictated by the climate and the animals in the area.
3. The early people obtained their food by hunting, fishing, and picking nuts, roots, and berries.
4. People gained control over their food supply when they learned to grow plants. Because they did not have to spend so much time searching for food, some people settled together forming villages, towns, and cities.
5. Between 300 and 1500 A.D., the Mayas, Aztecs, and Incas developed advanced societies in Middle and South America.
6. The cultures of the early Americans were influenced by their environment.
7. The early peoples in North America lived in the following geographical areas: the Southwest, the Plains, the Great Basin and California, the Northwest Coast, the Far North, the Arctic, and the Eastern Woodlands.

Building Vocabulary

1. Identify the following:

Mayas	Cuzco	Sioux
Aztecs	Hohokam	Sun Dance
Tenochtitlan	Pueblo	Eskimos
Incas		League of the Iroquois

2. Define the following:

cultures	pueblos	tipis	umiak
agriculture	adobe	travois	wigwams
empire	mesas	totem poles	long houses
artisans	kiva	potlatch	mounds
census	wickiups	kayak	sachems
environment	hogans		alliances

Remembering the Facts

1. Into what sections of the Western Hemisphere did the early people move and settle?
2. How did the early people who settled in the north obtain their food?
3. How did the early people in the Southwest obtain the food they needed?
4. What new way of providing food was developed among the early people in the Western Hemisphere?

Each chapter ends with a Chapter Review to aid students in retaining the material just studied.

5. What were the three great cultures of Middle and South America?
6. Where did the Mayas live? the Aztecs? the Incas?
7. What kinds of food did they eat?

8. In what seven geographic areas did the early people in North America live?
9. What did early people in North America use to build their homes?
10. What was the purpose of totem poles?

Understanding the Facts

1. Why did the people living in different areas develop different cultures?

2. How did geography and culture affect the lives and cultures of the peoples of North and South America?

3. How important was religion among the early people in the Americas?
4. Why did the people living on the Plains develop a sign language?
5. Why was the League of the Iroquois important?

Using Maps

Reference Maps. A map which shows various features such as oceans, continents, lakes, rivers, mountains, countries, and cities is called a reference map. To help readers, people who draw maps use symbols for the different features which the map shows. Symbols are used to show features created by people as well as natural features. The meaning for each symbol is found in the map key.

Before you look at a specific reference map, answer the following questions about geography in general.

1. What is a continent? an island? a peninsula? a mountain? a plain?
2. What do continents, islands, peninsulas, mountains, and plains have in common?
3. What is an ocean? a sea? a lake? a river?
4. What do oceans, seas, lakes, and rivers have in common?

5. How do continents differ from islands? How do oceans differ from seas?
6. Can you name any types of land or water areas that are not listed here?

After you have answered these questions, study the reference map and its key on page 29. Then answer the following questions.

1. What area of the world does the map show?
2. What is represented by each of the different symbols in the key?
3. Do the symbols which make up the key show features created by people or natural features?
4. Why is it important to be able to locate the geographic features shown on a reference map?

To develop map skills, exercises using chapter maps appear at the end of the Chapter Review.

New World– New Opportunities

Juan de la Cosa was a navigator on one of the ships during Columbus' first voyage in 1492. In 1500, he drew one of the earliest known maps of the New World. How accurate does the map appear to be?

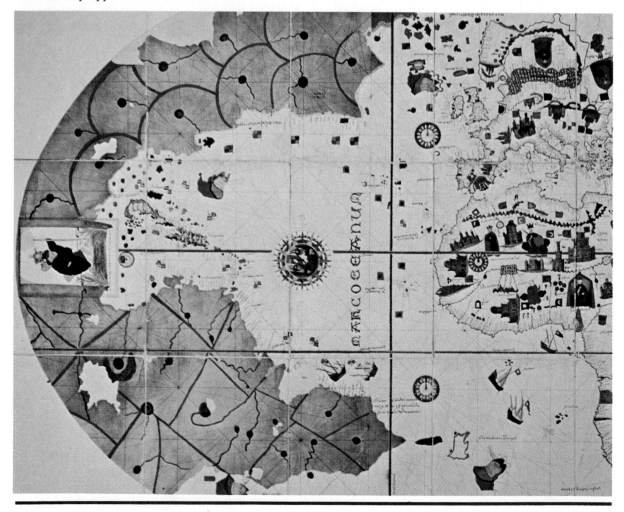

The Western Hemisphere is very large, and people have lived on the lands there for many thousands of years. But most of the people in Europe during the 1400's knew nothing of that area or its peoples. Most Europeans of that time had no idea how big the world is. Their maps showed Africa as a small peninsula and Asia as a large landmass. But they did not show the lands of the Western Hemisphere at all.

Since the earth is round, no half is any more east or west than the other half. Explain to students that use of the term "Western Hemisphere" is a result of the early Europeans sailing west to reach the area.

1. Backgrounds and New Beginnings

Some Europeans had explored less known areas of the world as early as the 800's. One of the first groups to sail far into the Atlantic Ocean came from the northern countries that are now Denmark, Sweden, and Norway. These Norse (North) people are also called Vikings. Sailing west in their sturdy ships, the Vikings found the islands of Iceland and Greenland and left settlers on them. About the year 1000, a group led by Leif Ericson sailed west from Greenland. They came to the coast of North America and stayed there for a short time. Little news of these adventures reached other people, however. During the next few hundred years, most Europeans were interested in the lands around and east of the Mediterranean Sea.

Who were the Vikings, and what did they do?

The foundations of some buildings were excavated at L'Anse-aux-Meadows in Newfoundland in 1961. Artifacts found there indicate that they were built by the Vikings.

1.1 The Growth of Trade. From about 1100 to 1250, Europeans took part in religious wars in the Middle East. In these wars, called Crusades, Christians tried to drive Muslims out of such Holy Land cities as Jerusalem and return them to Christian rule. The wars were not generally successful, but they helped to bring about great changes in the world. European soldiers came home knowing more about the geography and peoples of the Middle East. They also brought with them spices, silks, fine cottons, and other goods from these eastern Mediterranean lands. The goods were rare and costly in Western Europe at the time, because they came from the faraway lands of India, China, and Southeast Asia.

What were the Crusades?

Use a map of the world to locate for the class the Middle East. Point out its strategic location as the crossroads for three continents.

A strong trade grew between Europe and Asia in the 1300's. To take part in the trade, Western Europeans dealt with traders of the Middle East and Central Europe. The Middle East merchants had a *monopoly* (exclusive control of the trade) because they alone knew the safe routes to the Far East. In turn, they traded only with a few merchants in Europe, mostly those of Venice and Genoa in Italy. The goods changed hands many times along the trade routes. Each time, the

Why was there a monopoly on trade between Europe and Asia?

Trade Routes in the 1400's

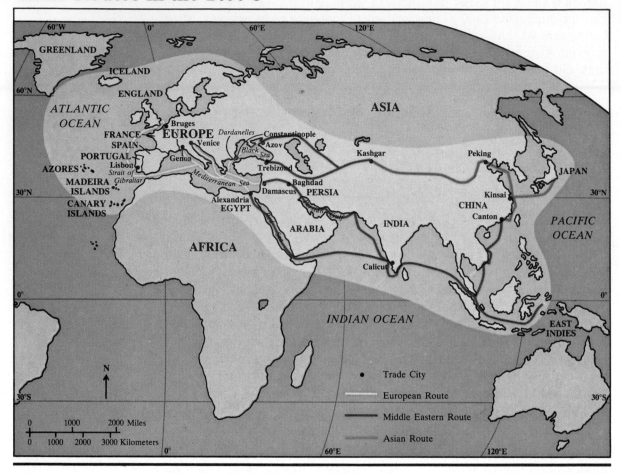

A system of water and land routes of trade linked the known world in the 1400's. Merchants controlled each of the many routes. In which cities did Asian, Middle Eastern, and European traders exchange goods?

prices were raised to cover the merchant's costs and to add some profit. Western Europeans wanted to avoid high prices by trading directly with Asian merchants. They could increase their own profits by finding a new route to the Far East.

Little was done about finding a new route until the early 1400's. Then a group of Muslims known as the Ottoman Turks rose to power. They took over the Middle East, swept through North Africa, and put Eastern Europe in danger. In 1453, the Turks captured Constantinople, a city at the crossroads of Asia and Europe. Trade was endangered because the Turks controlled much of the land and the known sea routes between Europe and the Far East. Western Europeans became more determined to find their own routes to Asia.

1.2 A New Route to the Far East. By the 1450's, some countries in Europe were changing from a collection of small kingdoms into large national states. Countries like Portugal, Spain, France, and England were slowly becoming unified under strong leaders. They had their own separate languages and systems of laws. They had large national armies and rich treasuries. Some of them could pay to have explorers find new trade and to set up *colonies*. These are settlements in other lands made by people still tied to the rule of their home countries. In the early 1400's, too, there were great improvements in sails and shipbuilding. New kinds of sailing tools made travel into unknown areas much safer than before.

What was happening in Europe during the 1400's?

Portugal was the most able of the western seagoing countries. Its sailors had been to the Madeira and Canary islands as well as the Azores in the Atlantic Ocean. The son of the Portuguese king, Prince Henry the Navigator, started a school in 1419. Navigators, sailors, ship captains, mapmakers, and others came there to study the sea and to try out new sailing tools. Using their ideas, Portuguese sea captains took ships south along the coast of Africa. The Portuguese had two aims. One was to find

The Portuguese made every attempt to keep secret the activities and discoveries of their explorers to Africa, fearing competition, especially from Spain.

Explorers used the astrolabe (left) and stars to determine latitude and time. The compass (right) was used for direction. How did these new kinds of sailing tools make ocean travel safer?

The southern tip of Africa is called the Cape of Good Hope.

Who was the first European to sail around Africa?

What were the Middle Kingdoms?

The approximate dates of these kingdoms were: Ghana, 8th-11th century; Mali, 12th-14th century; and Songhai, 14th-16th century.

A bulletin board with pictures can help to show the rich diversity of African culture at this time and help to dispel some commonly held misconceptions about Africa.

What did Columbus want to do?

a route around Africa to Asia and the Far East trade. The other was to find the source of African gold which long had been a part of the Mediterranean trade.

In 1488, Bartolomeu Dias successfully rounded the southern tip of Africa and returned to Portugal. Ten years later, Vasco da Gama led three ships around the tip, crossed the Indian Ocean, and reached the northwest coast of India. After many years of searching, the Portuguese had found their own route to Asia.

1.3   The African Continent.   Europeans had known very little about Africa south of the Sahara Desert. As the Portuguese slowly made their way down its coast, they found that Africa was not a small peninsula. It was a huge land of many peoples, languages, and cultures. Some Africans had strong kingdoms with important cities of trade and learning. At different times, the kingdoms of Ghana, Mali, and Songhai rose to power. They lay in the center of important trade routes that ran from North Africa to the West African coast. For that reason, they were known as the Middle Kingdoms. Their people had richly developed cultures. Gold, salt, ivory, leather, iron, and other African goods passed through their markets. The Muslim traders who came from North Africa also brought the ideas and teachings of their religion to the Middle Kingdoms. Many people there accepted parts of the Muslim religion, adding them to their own religious beliefs.

In Africa, the Portuguese raided and took what they wanted from small camps or villages that were not protected. When they came to areas under powerful kingdoms, they worked to set up peaceful trade. In 1441, a Portuguese sea captain returned from Africa with a valuable cargo. He had captured several Africans to sell as slaves. The slave trade, an old way of life in Europe and in Africa, was very profitable. Other sailors and merchants in Portugal became interested in this new source of slaves. Within ten years, Portugal became the European center for trade in African goods and in African slaves.

1.4   The Voyages of Columbus.   Portuguese explorers found a way to reach Asia by sailing south then east around Africa in 1498. Earlier, a sailor named Christopher Columbus had suggested another route. Columbus wanted to sail directly west from Europe to reach Asia. Some people at that time believed that such a voyage was possible. They knew that the earth was round, but they did not know how big it really is. Columbus expected to find China and India about 2,400 miles (3,840 kilometers) to the west, on the other side of the Atlantic. Actually, China and India are over 10,000 miles (16,000 kilometers) west, with the huge lands of the Western Hemisphere and the Pacific Ocean in the way.

Christopher Columbus (left) was certain that Asia could be reached by sailing west from Spain. Fernando Magellan (right) proved it could be done. Why did Columbus fail to reach Asia while Magellan succeeded?

Columbus was an Italian who had worked as a sailor and mapmaker in Portugal. He tried to get the Portuguese to finance a trip to prove his idea. They refused. A few years later, Columbus was able to get the help he needed from Spain's rulers, Queen Isabella and King Ferdinand. At sunrise on August 3, 1492, three small ships—the *Niña*, the *Pinta*, and the *Santa María*—sailed from the harbor of Palos, Spain. They were bound for Asia.

After a short stay at the Canary Islands in September, the ships sailed west into the Atlantic. Five weeks later, a lookout from one of the ships spotted land. On October 12, 1492, Columbus and his sailors went ashore to an island they named San Salvador. It is part of the group in the Caribbean Sea now called the Bahamas. Columbus believed that he had come to the Indies Islands off the southeast coast of Asia. He called the people he found living there Indians. From that island, Columbus sailed to some of the others in the Caribbean. He did not find the Asian cities of trade that he expected, but Columbus took some of the Indians back to Spain.

The islands that Columbus reached are now called the West Indies, and he returned there three times in the next ten years. The news of his travels spread to other countries in Europe. "When treating of this country," wrote an Italian historian in 1494, "one must speak of a new world, so distant is it. . . ." A few years later, Amerigo Vespucci also

New World—New Opportunities   47

explored the area for Portugal. He believed that these lands were part of a new continent which "it is proper to call a new world." In 1507, a German mapmaker gave the name America to these lands in honor of Vespucci, who had identified them as separate continents.

For whom was America named?

Before 1500, most European countries were Catholic. The pope often acted as a neutral arbiter in international disputes.

1.5 Dividing the World. Soon after Columbus' first trip, ships from both Spain and Portugal were sailing far west into the Atlantic. These two countries were strong rivals. To prevent trouble between them, the Spanish rulers asked for help from the pope, the head of the Catholic church. Both Spain and Portugal were Catholic countries, and their rulers agreed to follow the pope's decision.

So in 1493, Pope Alexander VI drew an imaginary line, called the Line of Demarcation, around the world. Newly found lands not under control of a Christian leader to the west of the line would go to Spain; those lands east of it would go to Portugal. A year later, the two countries signed the Treaty of Tordesillas setting the line at 370 leagues (about 1,250 miles or 2,000 kilometers) west of the Cape Verde Islands in the Atlantic. A Portuguese sea captain, Pedro Alvarez Cabral, was blown off course on a voyage around Africa. He landed on the east coast of South America in 1500. Because of the treaty, Portugal was able to claim the area, now called Brazil. The lands found by explorers for Spain became an empire over much of the Western Hemisphere.

Who drew the Line of Demarcation? For what reason?

This is why the language of Brazil is Portuguese, while Spanish is spoken in other parts of South America.

How did Portugal come to claim Brazil?

Discuss what attitudes Europeans held toward the people of the New World as reflected in the decision of the pope to divide the land between Spain and Portugal.

1. What events led to greater trade between Europeans and the people of the eastern Mediterranean?
2. Why were European nations interested in finding an all-water route to Asia?
3. How was Portugal able to take the lead in searching for new routes to Asia?
4. Why did Christopher Columbus call the people he met in the New World "Indians"?

2. Spain in the New World_____

Spain's rulers encouraged their people to follow the western routes of Columbus. They wanted to find the route to Asia, but they became even more interested in making claims on the new lands across the Atlantic. Almost all the news brought back from these lands had reports of great amounts of gold to be found there.

2.1 Early Spanish Explorations. On his first trip to the New World, Columbus also had landed on the island which is divided today between Haiti and the Dominican Republic. He had named it Española (Hispaniola) and had written this description of it:

> Its mountains and plains, and meadows, and fields, are so beautiful and rich for planting and sowing, and rearing cattle of all kinds, and for building towns and villages. The harbors on the coast, and the number and size and wholesomeness of the rivers, most of them bearing gold, surpass anything that would be believed by one who had not seen them.

Columbus had set up a post on the island. It served as a base for Spaniards who explored other islands and the nearby mainland. In 1496, they built a new city named Santo Domingo and used it as the Spanish capital of the area.

Columbus made a total of four trips to the New World before his death in 1506, at the age of 55.

In 1508, Juan Ponce de León sailed with soldiers to the island of Puerto Rico and took it over. By 1511, the Spaniards had taken several islands to settle, including Jamaica and Cuba. Ponce de León explored other areas and, in 1513, reached a land he named Florida (from the Spanish word meaning "full of flowers"). He searched there for gold and other treasures and tried to set up a Spanish settlement. The Indians of Florida drove the Spaniards out and killed Ponce de León in 1521. In 1565, the Spaniards started a settlement in Florida near the place where Ponce de León had first landed. Named St. Augustine, it was the first lasting European settlement in what is now the United States.

What was the first permanent European settlement in what is now the United States?

While Ponce de León and others searched the islands of the Caribbean, Vasco Nuñez de Balboa landed on the shore of what is now Panama in Central America. With soldiers, he traveled across Panama and reached the Pacific Ocean in 1513. Balboa and his force were the first Europeans to see this great ocean from its American shore. Their travels across Panama showed that the land was narrow in some places. This encouraged other explorers to keep looking for a way to reach Asia by going through or around America.

2.2 The Voyage of Magellan. One of those explorers was Fernando Magellan. Magellan and his crew set out from Spain with five ships in September 1519. They reached Brazil and sailed south along its coast. By the following spring, Magellan found the strait which now bears his name at the tip of South America. The ships sailed through it and headed north into the Pacific Ocean to the Philippine Islands. Magellan was killed there, and most of his ships were wrecked. Another captain, Sebastián del Cano, brought the one remaining ship through the Indian Ocean and around Africa to Europe. On September 6, 1522, the *Victoria* and its valuable cargo of spices arrived in Spain after a

Who led the voyage which sailed around the world?

In circumnavigating the globe, Magellan gave Spain its first claim to the Philippine Islands.

European Explorers

Explorers	Dates of Activity	Achievements
Bartolomeu Dias	1488	Sailed around the southern tip of Africa
Vasco da Gama	1498–1503	Reached India by sailing around the southern tip of Africa
Amerigo Vespucci	1497–1504	Explored the eastern coast of South America
Pedro Alvarez Cabral	1500	Landed in Brazil
Christopher Columbus	1492–1504	Explored the West Indies and the Caribbean
Vasco Nuñez de Balboa	1513	Reached the Pacific Ocean
Juan Ponce de León	1513–1521	Explored Florida
Hernando Cortés	1519–1536	Explored and conquered Mexico
Fernando Magellan	1519–1522	Led first expedition to sail around the world
Francisco Pizarro	1530–1537	Explored and conquered Peru
Hernando de Soto	1539–1542	Explored southeastern North America to the Mississippi River
Francisco de Coronado	1540–1542	Explored southwestern North America
Giovanni da Verrazano	1524	Sailed along the Atlantic coast of North America
Jacques Cartier	1534–1541	Explored St. Lawrence River valley
Samuel de Champlain	1603–1615	Explored St. Lawrence River valley
Louis Joliet and Jacques Marquette	1673	Explored along Mississippi River
La Salle	1669–1682	Explored from the Great Lakes to lower Mississippi River
Henry Hudson	1609–1611	Explored Hudson River and Hudson Bay areas

Major European Explorations

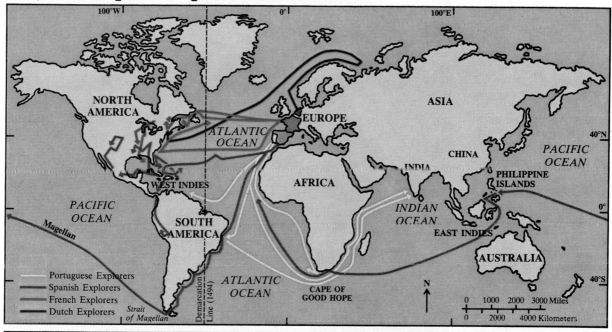

The governments of Portugal, Spain, France, and Holland supported the early voyages of exploration which led to colonization and settlement. Why did so many explorers start from just a few countries?

Detailed information that expands and reinforces the text narrative appears in colorful tables, charts, graphs, and diagrams.

voyage around the world. The trip begun by Magellan proved that Christopher Columbus was right. Europeans could reach the Far East by sailing west.

2.3 The Conquest of Mexico and Peru. In the same year that Magellan sailed from Spain, Hernando Cortés and 700 soldiers sailed from Cuba to the coast of Mexico. They landed near what is now Vera Cruz. Cortés wanted the Aztec land and gold for himself and Spain.

On his way into Mexico, Cortés met other Indians ruled by Montezuma and the Aztecs. Some of them, hoping for freedom, joined Cortés. The army moved on, invited by Montezuma to visit Tenochtitlán. Many Aztecs thought that Cortés might be the god mentioned in their histories. If so, they believed, no defense was possible against him. The Spaniards also marched to the city with horses, guns, and cannons—things unknown to the Indians.

Montezuma is also known as Moctezuma. Cortés was thought to be the god Quetzalcoatl.

What did the Aztecs think about Cortés?

Tenochtitlán was a wonderful sight to the Spaniards with its palaces, streets, water systems, and busy markets. They were amazed by the gold and silver used by the Aztecs, who did not seem to value it as

An Aztec artist drew this picture of the Spanish conquest of Mexico in the early 1500's. In what ways did the Spaniards hold an advantage in the fighting?

Because the Inca empire was so highly organized, Pizarro weakened the whole structure by destroying its leader.

How did Spain gain control of much of South America?

highly as the Spaniards did. Cortés put Montezuma into prison where the Aztec ruler died. By 1521, the Spanish army had defeated the Aztecs and taken over their empire. Mexican gold and silver were soon on their way to Spain. The Spaniards destroyed Tenochtitlán, with its places of human sacrifice, and built their own Mexico City in its place.

In 1530, another *conquistador* (Spanish for "conqueror") set out from a base in Panama. Francisco Pizarro led an army of 180 soldiers south. They cut their way through the jungles to the mountains of northern Peru. The army reached the Inca empire in 1532, and Pizarro captured its ruler, Atahualpa. Atahualpa gave the Spaniards great amounts of gold and silver for his freedom, but they murdered him. The army took over the government and began sending Inca treasure to Spain. Pizarro visited the Inca capital of Cuzco in the mountains. But in 1535, he chose a place on the coast to begin the Spanish city of Lima. In a short time, Spanish rule was spread over much of South America.

2.4 Expanding the Empire.   News of the treasures taken by Cortés and Pizarro led others to the New World. Some searched for gold in the lands north of the Caribbean and across the Gulf of Mexico.

In 1539, Hernando de Soto took 600 soldiers into Florida. They marched west through the lands that later became Georgia and Alabama and reached the Mississippi River in May 1541. The army crossed the river and moved on, returning to it the following spring. There de Soto died of a fever, and the soldiers buried his body in the Mississippi. Explorations by de Soto had failed to turn up gold or silver. But they did give Spain a claim to the entire Gulf area and the lower part of the Mississippi Valley.

Francisco Vásquez de Coronado looked for gold farther west. He was searching for the "Seven Cities of Cibola." These were supposed to be whole cities made of gold. Beginning in 1540, Coronado's army traveled through the lands which later became Arizona, New Mexico, Texas, Oklahoma, and Kansas. They did reach the pueblos of the Zuñi Indians, but there was no gold. They were, however, the first Europeans to see the Grand Canyon, and their travels added a great sweep of land to the empire claimed by Spain.

How did Spain gain control of the Southwest?

2.5 Spanish Colonies. Spain set up many government offices at different times to look after its claims in the New World. One of these, the Council of the Indies, was formed in Spain in 1524. It made laws, administered justice, directed the army, and took care of finances for the empire. To govern the lands and people in the Americas more closely, Spain later formed colonies there. One, called New Spain, was formed in 1535, and its capital was Mexico City. It covered the West Indies, the Philippines, Venezuela, and all the lands claimed north of Panama. Another colony was Peru, formed in 1542, with its capital at Lima. It covered Panama and all the Spanish claims in South America except Venezuela. The governments in the colonies were headed by *viceroys* who were direct representatives of the Spanish crown.

Who looked after Spanish claims in the New World?

The crown owned the land in the colonies, according to European ideas, by claims and conquest. So the Spanish rulers also could give parts of it away. They gave large areas to the explorers and to other Spaniards who came to the New World. The Indians who lived on the lands were made to farm the fields and work the mines. In return, the Spanish owners were to give the Indians food, shelter, and clothing. They also were to protect and teach them. This plan soon became a system in which a few Spaniards owned huge areas of land worked by many Indian slaves.

American Indians had no natural immunities to diseases brought by Europeans, such as measles and smallpox. Epidemics were a major reason for the decrease in size of the Indian population.

A great number of Indians died fighting the Spaniards. Others died from European diseases or from slave work. The land system in the Spanish colonies depended on large numbers of workers to be profitable. By the early 1500's, most of the Caribbean Indians were dead, and the landowners wanted more slaves. So Spain allowed sea

What did the Spanish land system in the New World require?

New World—New Opportunities 53

Spain's empire in the New World was first settled by soldiers and missionaries. Estevanico, a black guide, and others led explorers and settlers through unknown areas. What seems to be the relation between the Spaniards and the Indians?

captains to bring them directly from Africa to the West Indies. Many African kingdoms did not want to supply this greater number of slaves. But the European countries used their stronger weapons and armies to capture slaves and enforce their wishes. By 1560, there were nearly 100,000 African slaves in the New World.

2.6 Spanish Missions. Catholic priests were among the first people to follow the explorers to the New World. They came as *missionaries*—church workers sent to teach the Indians Christianity and to make them members of the Catholic church. The missionaries also taught the Indians Spanish ways of farming and making goods. Some, like Father Bartolomé de las Casas, tried to protect the Indians from cruel soldiers and landowners. But in most cases, they failed.

What did the missionaries do?

As the Spanish empire spread in the late 1500's and 1600's, the plan of setting up missions went with it. By the late 1600's, there were missions in Arizona and the southern part of California. Father Eusebio Kino, sometimes called "the priest on horseback," set up several missions there. In the late 1700's, Father Junípero Serra added to the mission chain as far north as what is now San Francisco.

How large was the Spanish empire in the New World?

By the middle of the 1500's, Spain had established the outlines of a colonial empire in the New World which was larger in size than the empires of Egypt, Persia, Greece, or Rome. From the Mississippi River, Florida, and Mexico in the north, to Cape Horn in the south,

Analyzing Pictures
SKILL

The pictures that appear all the way through this book contain special information. They aid your understanding of each chapter. The pictures identify the focus of the material, and they make the book more interesting.

Look carefully at each picture to analyze its content. The steps you can take to analyze the picture are simple.

1. Look at the picture to get a general sense of what the subject is about.
2. Read the caption which goes with each picture.
3. Decide if the picture is a drawing, a painting, or a photograph. (There will be no photographs before the mid-1800's when photography was developed.)
4. Decide, if possible, whether a drawing or a painting was done by someone who lived at the time or someone who lived at a later time.
5. Decide whether a picture is a posed portrait or an unposed photograph.
6. Consider the main theme and the general message of the picture.
7. Identify the main focus of the picture.
8. Consider how the figures in the picture support the main theme.
9. Consider how the use of color or lack of color supports the theme of the picture.
10. Decide why you think the picture is used at its location in the book.

Using such a list can make understanding pictures easier. As an example, use the above list to analyze the picture on page 54. Also, consider the following questions.

1. Two of the figures are soldiers. One is black; the other is white. What does this tell about the people who explored the area?
2. Three of the figures are Indians. What does their position in the picture tell about the way they were viewed by the artist and by the other figures in the picture?
3. Three of the figures are Catholic missionaries. What does this picture tell about their roles and importance to Spanish exploration?

As you look at the other pictures in this book, develop your own lists of questions.

from the Caribbean islands in the east, to the California missions in the west, Spain controlled the Atlantic and the Pacific.

1. Where did the Spaniards explore in the New World?
2. What did the Spanish explorers hope to find in Mexico and Peru?
3. How did the Spaniards control the large areas they took over in the New World?
4. What did the missionaries teach the Indians?

3. France in the New World

Portugal and Spain were the first Western European countries to make gains in their search for new routes to the Far East. By the middle of the 1500's, Portugal had set up many valuable trading posts in Africa and Asia. During the same years, Spain explored the lands across the Atlantic and brought back large amounts of gold and silver. News of these adventures quickly reached other European countries. Their rulers wanted a part of the Asian and African trade. They also became very interested in the lands and treasures of the New World.

3.1 Early French Voyages. Spain used soldiers, ships, and settlements to protect the areas it claimed in the New World, especially in Middle and South America. Spain's defenses were weak farther north. In 1523, Francis I, king of France, hired Giovanni da Verrazano to search that area for a route, a Northwest Passage, through North America to Asia. Verrazano reached the coast of North Carolina in the spring of 1524 and sailed up to what is now New York Harbor. He did not find a Northwest Passage but went as far as Nova Scotia before returning to France.

What were the early French explorers seeking?

From 1534 to 1541, Jacques Cartier made three trips to North America for France. He, too, was looking for the Northwest Passage. Cartier explored the area around the Gulf of St. Lawrence and the St. Lawrence River. He did not find a way to the Pacific. The lands he explored were called Canada by the Indians who lived there. Cartier claimed these lands for the French king.

Cartier traveled down the St. Lawrence past "Mont Real" and reached the lowest part of the rapids which he called "La Chine" (China).

After Cartier's trips, French exploration came to a sudden halt for two reasons. First, Verrazano and Cartier had failed to report any signs of gold or silver. The French government did not want to spend more money on costly trips without some proof that they would bring treasure. Second, France was caught up in civil wars that lasted nearly

40 years. In 1589, a powerful leader defeated his rivals and came to the throne as Henry IV. Under his rule, France again turned its interest to North America.

3.2 French Settlements. The reports of Verrazano and Cartier had carried news of the forests, fish, and great numbers of fur-bearing animals in North America. Leaders in the fur business in France were very interested in these reports. With the king's permission, they hired Samuel de Champlain in 1603 to lead a group who would start fur-trading posts in eastern Canada. Beginning that year, Champlain made several such trips through Canada. He founded a settlement at Quebec in 1608, setting up a trading post and building a fort there. He also made allies of Huron and other northern Indians.

In the spring of 1609, Champlain's group explored the area south of the St. Lawrence River with some Huron and other Indian warriors. They moved into northern New York, reaching a lake which Champlain named for himself. Near there, the group met some members of the Mohawk family of the Iroquois—longtime enemies of the other northern Indians. There was a short fight with no clear winners, although the Mohawk were greatly surprised by the French guns. From then on, the Iroquois thought of the French as enemies, too.

The French found the League of the Iroquois to be powerful enemies. Because of them, the French did not move south to explore and settle the Atlantic coast area that is now the United States. Instead,

Who founded the first French settlements in Canada?

Refer students to the map on page 35, showing approximate locations of some Indian groups, including the five that made up the League of the Iroquois.

Why did the French not explore and settle the Atlantic coast area?

The French began to settle Canada in the 1600's. This map makes more sense turned upside-down, with Florida in the bottom left corner. What did the French artist hope to show in the detail of this picture?

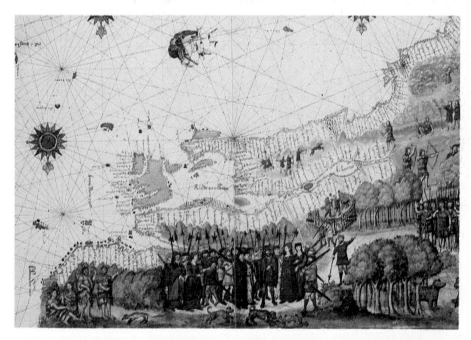

they moved west along the St. Lawrence River. Champlain also explored the Ottawa River farther west and crossed into Georgian Bay. He entered Lake Huron in 1615 before returning east by way of Lake Ontario. Champlain spent the next 20 years encouraging other French people to live and work in Canada.

3.3 French Missions.   Catholic missionaries were among those who followed Champlain to Canada. They set up missions as the Spaniards had done, working first from a base near the northwest tip of Lake Huron. They worked well with the Hurons but were not as successful with other Indians, especially the Iroquois. The Iroquois looked upon the French missionaries as great enemies. They tortured and killed some of them, like Father Isaac Jogues, and set out to destroy their allies. By the middle of the 1660's, the Iroquois had destroyed the mission base and had scattered the Hurons into the forests. The Hurons were never again a powerful Indian group, but the missionaries did not leave the Indian lands. They believed strongly that it was their duty to make the Indians members of the Catholic church.

With whom did the French missionaries work?

3.4 New France.   The French government was eager to make lasting settlements in North America. To do this, it gave control of the area to a private group called the Company of New France in 1627. It was also called the Company of the Hundred Associates because 100 people paid to start the company. The company agreed to bring 300 settlers a year to the New World in return for a monopoly on the fur trade there.

The plan under the company did not work very well. In 1663, the French king took back control of the lands called New France and

French missionaries and fur traders traveled the St. Lawrence River, the Great Lakes, and the Mississippi River, exploring and expanding New France. How did French relations with the Indians differ from that of the Spaniards?

appointed three officials to run it from Quebec. A governor, usually a French noble, was generally in charge. An *intendant* was head of the sovereign council, the appointed lawmaking and judicial body. A bishop took care of all church matters. Several of the people who held these offices turned out to be able leaders. Jean Talon, the first intendant, helped the fur traders and farmers. He also improved defenses against the Iroquois. Count Frontenac served as governor from 1672 to 1682. He was able to defeat the Iroquois, ending their threat to French settlements. Frontenac also encouraged exploration into western lands.

Who ran New France under the king?

3.5 Into the Great West. As eastern Canada became more settled by the French, missionaries and fur traders moved farther west. They heard stories from the western Indians about a large body of water. The French thought it might be the Northwest Passage. Explorers set out to find it and to add lands to the empire of France.

Two explorers, Father Jacques Marquette and Louis Joliet, set out to find the Northwest Passage in 1673. Starting at the top of Lake Michigan, they traveled down to the Mississippi by way of the Fox and Wisconsin rivers. Marquette and Joliet made their way down the Mississippi more than 1,000 miles (1,600 kilometers), to where it was joined by the Arkansas River. There they decided that the river would take them south to the Gulf of Mexico instead of west to the Pacific Ocean. They returned to Lake Michigan by way of the Illinois River.

Who were the first French to explore the Mississippi?

Another French explorer, Robert Cavelier, Sieur de la Salle, also traveled in the Great Lakes area. He explored a little of the Ohio land south of Lake Erie and saw Niagara Falls between it and Lake Ontario. La Salle took the Illinois River from south of Lake Michigan to the place where it joins the Mississippi. Traveling down that river, he reached the point in 1682 where it flowed into the Gulf of Mexico. La Salle claimed the lands on both sides of the Mississippi and the rivers which joined it for France. He named the area Louisiana in honor of the French king.

It is interesting to find the names of places throughout the Mississippi Valley derived from the French. Perhaps this can serve as the basis for a discussion of French influence on other aspects of American culture.

3.6 The Nature of New France. By the end of the 1600's, France claimed a three-part empire in North America. The northern area, Canada, ran from Nova Scotia west along the St. Lawrence to the Great Lakes. The southern part, Louisiana, ran north and south from the central Mississippi Valley to the Gulf of Mexico. The middle area took in the rest of the lands between the Mississippi and Ohio rivers. These lands were not as large as the huge Spanish empire in the New World. But the French had the largest empire in North America. It had thousands of rivers and lakes, making travel easy and communications quick. The French built forts along the borders of their empire.

What was the nature of New France?

La Salle (1643–1687)

PROFILE

At age 23, Robert Cavelier, Sieur de la Salle, settled in New France. There he traded furs and farmed near Montreal. From his Indian trading partners, he heard stories of the great rivers and lakes to the west.

La Salle had a strong spirit of adventure and a desire to expand the boundaries of New France. He sold his land in 1669 to finance a trip to explore the Ohio River. For the next 18 years, La Salle and a party of explorers traveled through the Great Lakes area and down the Mississippi River. La Salle reached the mouth of this great river in 1682 and claimed the entire Mississippi Valley for France. He named this huge territory Louisiana in honor of King Louis XIV of France.

La Salle wanted to establish a colony at the mouth of the river. So he returned to France, gathered 200 colonists, and sailed for America in 1684. The ships sailed too far west and landed on the Texas coast. When La Salle tried to lead the settlers over land to the Mississippi River, they could not find the way. After many difficulties, the colonists rebelled and returned to France.

Because of La Salle, France held a great empire in the heart of North America. Eventually, other explorers moved into the Mississippi Valley, and France established permanent settlements.

Profile Features appear throughout the text, containing brief sketches of famous and not-so-famous people in American history.

Compare the treatment of Indians by the French and Spaniards and have students note the reasons for this treatment.

The French government screened all French people who wanted to go to North America. It made sure they were loyal to France and to the Catholic faith. New France did not have a large population. Some French people stayed along the Atlantic coastline and fished in the waters of Newfoundland and Labrador. Others farmed the land in small family plots. Many French people worked closely with the enormous network of Indian groups whose canoes carried valuable furs up and down the rivers and lakes to the various trading posts. French settlers who hunted and trapped alone in the deep forests of the far north became known as *coureurs de bois* (French for "forest runners"). Many of them joined Indian groups and followed Indian ways of life.

Although the number of French settlers remained small, they had strong unity and order. This gave the French an advantage against other

European countries which were interested in colonies. The French could also count upon large numbers of northern Indians to help them. They got along well with most Indians. The French were interested mostly in the fur trade, not in making the Indians work mines or fields. With a loyal band of settlers, a number of Indian allies, and a network of forts, the French intended to remain in North America for a long time.

What advantages did the French have in colonizing the New World?

1. Who was the first French explorer in the New World?
2. Where did the French make settlements?
3. What did French settlers hope to find in the New World?
4. Who claimed the Mississippi River Valley for France?

4. Other Europeans in the New World_____

While Spain and France were carving out their empires in the New World, other European nations were also eager to get their share of whatever wealth and resources America might have to offer. There was still some territory left unexplored along the Atlantic coast. It lay between the Spanish holdings in Florida and the French trading posts along the St. Lawrence River.

4.1 The Dutch in North America. During the late 1500's and early 1600's, the Dutch carried on a very busy trade with Asia. They formed the Dutch East India Company in 1602 to manage it. Like other Europeans, the Dutch were interested in a faster, western route to Asia. In 1609, the company hired Henry Hudson to cross the Atlantic and search for the Northwest Passage. Hudson sailed his ship, the *Half Moon*, along the coast of North America and into a river which he named for himself. Although Hudson failed to find a route to Asia, the Dutch claimed the land along the Hudson River. They sent others to explore the area. The Dutch built a fort and trading post at the northern end of the river (now Albany, New York) in 1614. Another post was built on Manhattan Island at the southern end of the Hudson.

In 1621, the Dutch West India Company was formed to handle trade and settlements in America and Africa. Three years later, Dutch ships brought families to settle in the American colony they called New Netherland. They made several settlements along the Hudson and on the islands around its mouth. In 1626, Peter Minuit bought Manhattan Island from the Indians for about $24 in trading goods. The name

If possible, display a large map of the East Coast of North America. Discuss with the class why it would be easy for ships entering the Chesapeake Bay, New York Harbor, or the Gulf of St. Lawrence to think they were perhaps near a northwest passage to Asia.

How did the Dutch acquire claims in the New World?

Who was responsible for the Dutch settlements in the New World?

European Claims in North America 1650

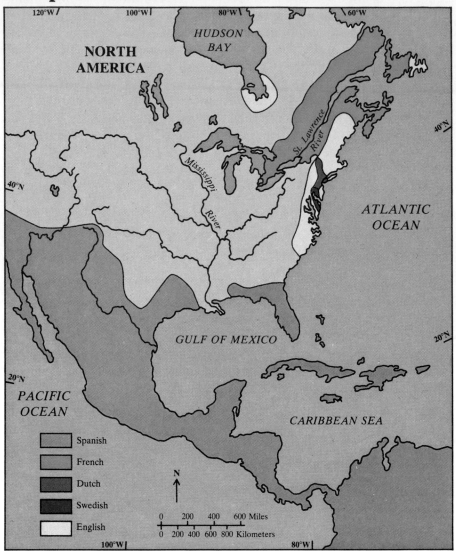

NORTH AMERICA

HUDSON BAY

St. Lawrence River

Mississippi River

ATLANTIC OCEAN

GULF OF MEXICO

PACIFIC OCEAN

CARIBBEAN SEA

120°W 100°W 80°W 60°W
40°N
40°N
20°N
20°N
100°W 80°W

Spanish	
French	
Dutch	
Swedish	
English	

N

0   200   400   600 Miles
0   200 400 600 800 Kilometers

The Spanish, French, Dutch, Swedish, and English had land claims in North America by 1650. Why were some countries able to claim more land than other countries?

Manhattan was changed to New Amsterdam. It became the capital of New Netherland and was a major Dutch trading center. The company and the people were interested most in the fur trade. The population of New Netherland remained small.

How long did the Swedes have a colony in the New World?

4.2 New Sweden.   People from Sweden also came to North America in the late 1630's. They built a few forts and settlements along the Delaware River, just south of New Netherland. The Dutch had

While the Spaniards searched for gold and the French searched for furs, the Dutch wanted new lands for trade centers. Ports like this one in New Amsterdam were links in a worldwide network of Dutch trading companies. How did the settlers in New Amsterdam improve harbors to protect their ships?

claimed this land but had not settled it. The main Swedish settlement was Fort Christina (now Wilmington, Delaware), and the colony they called New Sweden grew up around it.

Few people came from Sweden to the colony. Those who did planned to work in the fur trade. That caused trouble between New Sweden and New Netherland during the 1640's. In 1655, the Dutch took over New Sweden and ended Swedish rule in North America.

1. Where did the Dutch settle in the New World?
2. Where was New Sweden?

5. Conclusion

During the 1500's and 1600's, most of the major Western European powers made settlements in the Americas. The Portuguese claimed Brazil, and the Spaniards ruled an empire from western South America to California. French land claims swept from the Gulf of St. Lawrence to the Gulf of Mexico. Both the Dutch and the Swedes had settled colonies along the Hudson and Delaware rivers. The English also thought about overseas colonies in the late 1500's. They turned to the only area that was not protected by major settlements—the Atlantic coast of what is now the United States.

Chapter 2 Review

Main Points

1. During the 1400's, most Europeans did not know about the land and peoples of the Western Hemisphere.
2. The desire for more trade led Europeans to seek new routes to Asia after the Ottoman Turks cut off routes through the Middle East in 1453.
3. In the late 1400's, Portuguese navigators reached Asia by sailing around Africa.
4. Christopher Columbus landed in the Western Hemisphere when he attempted to reach Asia by crossing the Atlantic Ocean.
5. Spain led all other European nations in exploring the Western Hemisphere.
6. Portugal, France, Holland, Sweden, and England joined Spain in establishing settlements on the continents called the Americas.
7. European interests in the New World included gold, trade, land for colonies, and the desire to teach Christianity to the Indians.
8. With strong weapons and armies, Europeans were able to take the land of the peoples they met in America.

Building Vocabulary

1. Identify the following:

   Leif Ericson
   Crusades
   Middle Kingdoms
   Christopher Columbus
   Indians
   Line of Demarcation

   Fernando Magellan
   Montezuma
   Francisco Pizarro
   Council of the Indies
   Northwest Passage

   Samuel de Champlain
   Company of New France
   La Salle
   Henry Hudson
   Fort Christina

2. Define the following:

   monopoly
   colonies
   conquistador

   viceroys
   missionaries

   intendant
   coureurs de bois

Remembering the Facts

1. Why did Europeans want to go to Asia?
2. What country supported Christopher Columbus in his search for an all-water route to Asia?
3. Where did Columbus land on his first voyage to the New World?
4. What was the major accomplishment of Juan Ponce de León? Vasco Nuñez de

Balboa? Fernando Magellan? Hernando Cortés? Francisco Pizarro? Hernando de Soto? Francisco Vásquez de Coronado?

5. What did the Spanish explorers do when they met the Aztec and Inca peoples in Middle and South America? What did the people there do?

6. What were the main interests of Spain in coming to the New World?

7. What was the major accomplishment of Giovanni da Verrazano? Jacques Cartier? Samuel de Champlain?

8. What were the main interests of France in the New World?

Understanding the Facts

1. What developments in Europe and the Middle East led Europeans to seek an all-water route to Asia?

2. How did Christopher Columbus' plan to reach Asia differ from the Portuguese plan?

3. Why was Spain successful in establishing an empire in the New World?

4. Why did French exploration in North America stop for a while after the voyages of Cartier?

5. How were the Spaniards and the French different in the treatment of the people they met in the New World?

6. Why did the Dutch come to North America? Why did the Swedes?

Using Maps

Thematic Maps. A map used to show information about a specialized subject is called a thematic map. The subject could be economic, political, social, cultural, or almost anything that can be expressed geographically. Areas of the map are usually colored to show elements of the subject of a thematic map.

The theme of the map on page 62 is the American land claims of various European nations. Answer the following questions about this thematic map.

1. What is the date of the land claims shown on this map?

2. Which color represents the area under Spanish control? French control? Dutch control? English control?

3. Which nation had the largest claims in North America?

4. Which nation claimed land in the Caribbean?

5. Which nations had claims to part of what is now the United States?

English Settlement in North America

3

English activity in exploration increased toward the end of the sixteenth century. Many people in England wanted to share in the glory of expansion. How did the English hope to benefit from exploration?

England is located on an island separated from the continent of Europe by a narrow channel. Part of its coast also faces the Atlantic Ocean. English leaders knew that Spain was building a rich empire across the ocean during the 1500's. They were eager to share in the wealth of the New World. But for much of the sixteenth century, their attention was centered on events in England and in Europe.

1. English Backgrounds

During the last half of the 1400's, the English had been caught up in several civil wars over the throne. The Wars of the Roses, as they were called, ended in 1485, and the noble who finally won was Henry Tudor. He came to the throne as King Henry VII and worked to restore law and order to the country. He also encouraged English business and trade and improved the country's money system.

What were the Wars of the Roses?

1.1 Claims and Conflicts.   Henry VII showed interest in the New World shortly after the first voyage of Christopher Columbus. He hired an Italian sea captain called John Cabot in 1497 to explore part of the new lands for England. Cabot sailed to the shores of Newfoundland and traveled the coast as far south as what is now Delaware. Henry VII did not have money to follow up Cabot's explorations. But from those voyages, England later made its claims to the lands which one Spanish official had called "the cold and frozen North."

Which English monarch first showed interest in the New World?

During the reign of Henry's son, Henry VIII, there was also great unrest in England over religion. Like most Europeans, the English people were members of the Catholic church headed by the pope in Rome. In the 1520's, Henry VIII had a disagreement with the pope. As a result, Henry persuaded Parliament (the English lawmaking body) to break church ties between England and Rome. In 1534, Parliament passed the acts that set up the Church of England, or the Anglican church, and made the English monarch its head. In the next years, there was much bitter conflict in many parts of the kingdom. Some people wanted to remain Catholic, some followed the Church of England, and some adopted other forms of Protestant worship.

Help students realize the importance of religion and religious issues at the time. It was believed that everyone should belong to the same religion for a nation to be strong.

1.2 The Rule of Elizabeth.   In 1558, Queen Elizabeth I, one of Henry's daughters, came to the throne of England. She was a strong ruler who firmly established the power of the crown. She worked to create religious as well as political unity in the country. Elizabeth made the Church of England a single, national church. All loyal English

What did Elizabeth I do?

people were expected to belong to it. She also strengthened the English economy. She encouraged *manufacturing*—making goods by hand or machine—and promoted the sale of English wool to other countries.

Elizabeth also supported the growth of English sea power. For some time, England had been a rival of Spain, Europe's leading sea power and a strong Catholic country. In the mid-1500's, conflict between the two countries grew. With Elizabeth's approval, English sea captains raided Spanish treasure ships returning from the Americas, taking their cargoes. Sir John Hawkins and Sir Francis Drake were two of the most successful of these English "sea dogs," or raiders. Setting out in 1577, Drake sailed through the Strait of Magellan, north along the Pacific coast to what is now San Francisco Bay, and on around the world. He was the first English captain to do so, and he brought much gold and silver from Spanish ships back to England with him.

Drake raided many Spanish ships along the coast of Peru and near Panama before sailing north to present-day California, which he named New Albion and claimed for England.

1.3   Early Exploration and Settlement.   During the late 1500's, England became richer, safer, and stronger. More English sailors explored and mapped the lands along the north Atlantic coast of North America. In 1576, Martin Frobisher sailed to Baffin Land, west of Greenland, and entered what is now called Frobisher Bay. John Davis explored most of Baffin Bay in 1585. A few years later, John Knight explored much of Newfoundland and Labrador. All of these sea captains were searching for the Northwest Passage to Asia. They did not find it, but they did claim the areas they explored for England.

What explorers established English claims in parts of Canada?

Little by little, Queen Elizabeth took more interest in North America. In 1583, she sent Sir Humphrey Gilbert and five ships to find a place on the coast of North America for settlement. A colony there could serve as a base for England against Spain. Gilbert's ships arrived safely in Newfoundland. The plans for a settlement, however, were put off when Gilbert was lost at sea on his return trip. The following year Elizabeth asked Sir Walter Raleigh to look in other parts of North America for lands suited for colonies.

For whom was Virginia named?

Raleigh sent several groups to explore the lands farther south. He named part of the area Virginia in honor of Queen Elizabeth, who was called the "Virgin Queen." In 1587, Raleigh sent about 150 men and women led by John White to start a settlement on Roanoke Island. There a baby named Virginia Dare was born—the first English child born in the New World. The first supply ships from England did not return to Roanoke for three years. When they arrived, all the colonists were gone. Searchers found only the letters CRO cut into a tree and the word CROATOAN carved into a doorpost.

"Virginia" was used to describe much of the English claim along the East Coast of North America. It had no clearly defined boundaries. The Pilgrims also set out to start a colony in Virginia.

The supply ships for the "lost colony" had been delayed by events in Europe. The rivalry between England and Spain over the years had

Major English Explorations

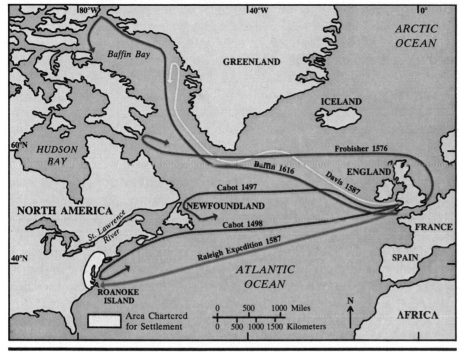

Most English explorers of the late 1500's and early 1600's were looking for a way around or through North America. They searched for the Northwest Passage. Only Raleigh's expedition led to settlement. How were the other explorations later used by the English to claim more of North America?

grown into war. King Philip II of Spain was very angry about the sinking of Spanish ships and the stealing of their gold by English "sea dogs." In 1588, he sent a great *armada*—fleet of warships—against England. The Spanish Armada, once in the narrow channel, was scattered by heavy storms. The guns of the smaller English ships greatly damaged the heavy Spanish vessels. With the defeat of the Spanish Armada, England became Europe's major naval power.

How did England become Europe's major naval power?

1. Which explorer provided the basis for England's claim to land in the New World?
2. What actions by the English led to war with Spain?
3. Where was the first English settlement in the New World?

2. First Permanent Colonies

The English still had not established a lasting settlement in the New World when Queen Elizabeth died in 1603. The English crown passed to her cousin, James Stuart, who was also King James VI of Scotland. He took the title James I of England and ruled both kingdoms. The new king was unpopular with the rich English nobles and had little money of his own. He wanted New World trade and settlements, but he could not pay to start colonies. Instead, he encouraged private (nongovernment) trading companies to do so.

2.1 Joint Stock Companies. Most individuals, like the king, could not afford to start colonies by themselves. They chose to form groups called *joint stock companies*. In these, the head of the group asked the king for a *charter*. It was an official paper giving permission for settlements and trade in a certain area. It also allowed the company to sell shares to raise money for settlement. The *investors*—people who bought shares in the company—expected to make a profit from the trade carried on by the settlers. The charter also set some of the rules for the colony, often allowing the company to set the rest.

In 1606, James I granted a charter forming two joint stock companies known together as the Virginia Company. They were to settle the lands claimed by England in North America. One joint stock company, the London Company, was granted rights to settlement of the southern area including what is now North Carolina and Virginia. The other company was the Plymouth Company. It was given the northern region, most of which is now known as New England.

2.2 The Jamestown Settlement. The London Company was the first to make a lasting English settlement in North America. It sent a group of 105 colonists to explore the area around the Chesapeake Bay. There, in the spring of 1607, the colonists started a settlement and called it Jamestown in honor of the king. It was the beginning of the colony of Virginia.

Disease and lack of food killed more than two thirds of the colonists in their first few months. Those who lived seemed more interested in searching for gold and silver than in planting crops. Two supply ships from England arrived in Jamestown the next year, but the settlers still faced very hard times. The colony survived mostly because of Captain John Smith. Smith was a soldier who served as the colony's leader. He forced the settlers to work, especially at growing their own food. Smith also bargained for food from the powerful chief of the Powhatan Indians. The chief, called Powhatan by the settlers, controlled 200 villages near Jamestown. The Indians could have crushed the settlers, but Powhatan chose to trade rather than to make war.

As time passed, the London Company sent more farmers to the Virginia colony. They planted crops and raised herds of animals on the

What is a joint stock company?

Now might be a good time to point out how each of the European powers, especially France, Spain, and England, had first become interested in the New World while looking for a northwest passage to Asia, but later had become interested in the area for its economic benefits.

What was the first permanent English settlement in the New World?

Who was the leader of the Jamestown colony?

Land Grants, 1606

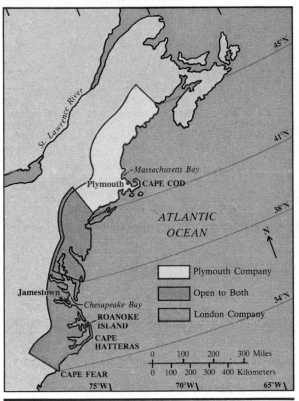

Plymouth Company
Open to Both
London Company

NOVA BRITANNIA,
OFFERING MOST
Excellent fruites by Planting in
VIRGINIA.

Exciting all such as be well affected
to further the same.

Both the Virginia Company and the London Company tried to attract settlers to their land in the New World. This advertisement was published in 1609. What did these companies have to offer a future settler?

lands they got from the Indians. About 1612, a settler named John Rolfe began planting fields of Indian tobacco. In a few years, tobacco became an important crop that brought high prices in England. Rolfe married Pocahontas, the daughter of Powhatan, in 1614. For a while, relations between the Indians and the settlers were friendly. The Virginia colony grew as thousands of men and women came to settle there. Then beginning in 1619, disease swept through the colony, killing nearly 4,000 settlers. During this time, the Powhatan Indians and the colonists fought over the land. After many battles, the colonists slowly gained control of the area.

During the early years, a lasting government began to take form in Virginia. By their charter, the owners of the London Company in England had the right to name a governor and a council to run the colony. All land belonged to the company, and the settlers worked it for

What crop became important for the Virginia economy?

Compare the English policy of sending large numbers of colonists to the New World with the policies of France and Spain. Also, have students be aware of economic differences among the colonies of the three nations.

Jamestown was well established by the 1630's. Trade with the Indians and the firm leadership of John Smith had helped it survive. How was its location near water also important to its growth?

What was the first legislature in the English colonies?

the company. The land policy did not work well, and in 1619, the company began granting land to individuals. That same year, the settlers were also given a voice in the running of the colony's government. They elected representatives to a *legislature*—lawmaking body—called the House of Burgesses. These people could pass laws, but those laws could be *vetoed,* or put aside, by the governor. The laws could also be vetoed by the London Company. Although its power was limited, the House of Burgesses was the first representative form of government in North America.

The London Company made little profit from the Virginia colony. Its leaders in England ran the company badly and quarreled bitterly among themselves. In 1624, James I took away their charter and brought Virginia under direct royal control. From then on, the king named the governor as well as members of the governor's council. The House of Burgesses continued as the elected legislature.

2.3 The Plymouth Colony.   The Plymouth Company became the Council for New England in 1620, with the right to grant land to settlers for colonies. The first people to take advantage of this left England for America not only for money and land, but also for the kind of religious freedom they could not find in their homeland.

Many English people did not like the forms of worship that Queen Elizabeth had established for the Church of England. They believed that she had kept too many *rituals,* or forms of service, from the

Catholic church. Some who joined the national church wanted to work to make it better or to "purify" it. Because of this, they became known as Puritans. Others wanted to separate from the church, and they were known as Separatists. James I looked upon persons who were not followers of the Church of England as dangerous troublemakers. He made life so hard for the Separatists that a group of them left England in 1608. They settled in Holland where they stayed for 11 years.

How did Puritans and Separatists differ?

The Separatists heard about the success of the Jamestown colony in Virginia. After returning from Holland to England, they received a charter to start a settlement in that area of America, too. In 1620, the *Mayflower* set sail from England with 35 Separatists and 66 other passengers aboard. These people were also called Pilgrims because they were travelers in a strange land. They were headed for Virginia, but strong winds blew their ship farther north. They landed in New England just north of Cape Cod Bay, in what is now Massachusetts.

The other passengers on board were settlers and indentured servants, sent by people who provided money to start the colony.

The Pilgrim leaders, including William Bradford and Captain Miles Standish, realized that they had not reached Virginia. Some of the people were upset, saying that they had only been given the right to settle and set up a government in Virginia. In order to prevent any possible trouble, 41 passengers of the *Mayflower* signed a **compact,** or agreement, to set up a civil government and to obey its laws. This Mayflower Compact was the basis for government in the colony. It said:

What established the basis of government for Plymouth?

> *We, whose names are underwritten . . . Having undertaken for the Glory of God, and Advancement of the Christian Faith, and the Honor of our King and Country, a Voyage to plant the first colony in the northern Parts of Virginia; Do . . . solemnly and mutually in the Presence of God and one another, covenant and combine ourselves together into a civil Body Politic, for our better Ordering and Preservation . . . .*

The Compact was signed by the adult male members on the ship, both Puritans and others.

In late 1620, the Pilgrims began building a small settlement. They called it Plymouth after the town in England from which they had sailed. Their first winter was a hard one. Half the colonists died from the cold, illness, or the lack of food. Their lives became somewhat easier in the spring. They began to plant the large fields left by Indians who had died in an epidemic. They received help from Squanto, a Pawtuxet Indian. Squanto had been taken to England earlier by an explorer. He had lived there for a time and could speak English. Squanto stayed with the Pilgrims, teaching them useful Indian ways of living in the wilderness. The settlers also made a peace treaty with Massasoit, chief of the nearby Wampanoag Indians. It lasted for over 40 years.

Help students to realize the feelings which the people must have had, moving into a strange new land. Perhaps some can relate their own feelings about moving to a new area.

Who aided the Pilgrims?

In time, the Pilgrims got an official land grant from the Council of New England. They governed themselves for the next 70 years with

Forty-one passengers of the *Mayflower* signed the Mayflower Compact on November 21, 1620. Why did the Pilgrims need the agreement?

almost no outside control. Plymouth became a small, independent settlement in New England with its own elected governor and council. Life was never easy in Plymouth, but the settlers made a fair living by farming, fishing, and trading.

2.4 Massachusetts Bay Colony.   A number of educated and wealthy Puritans in England formed the Massachusetts Bay Company in 1629. They received a charter and a grant of land in America. The Puritans took their charter with them when they left for America. They did not want to be controlled by people in England, as the colonists in Jamestown had been. The Puritans wanted to be independent and to govern themselves according to their own ideas.

Why did the Puritans come to the New World?

More than 1,000 settlers arrived in Massachusetts in 1630. They founded Boston and several other towns. Many of these settlers died during the first hard winter, and some returned to England in the spring. People came to the colony in great numbers in the next few years, however. By 1640, the population was about 16,000.

Of the 20,000 or so people who migrated to the colony, only about 4,000 were members of Puritan congregations. Many other people left England because of debts, a desire for land, and to look for better opportunities in America.

The Puritans practiced in Massachusetts the type of religious life they had wanted in England. They set up a congregational form of worship. In it, each congregation was an independent group which chose its own minister and decided its own local church policies. The Puritan places of worship were called *meeting houses*. They were used for both religious services and day-to-day activities of government.

John Winthrop, the governor, and the other leaders tried to keep Massachusetts government in the hands of a small group of important Puritans. The legislature was called the General Court. It passed a law in 1631 that only members of the Congregational church could become voters. Few people were allowed to become church members, so the number of voters was limited. Beginning in 1634, the voters in each town chose three people to represent them in the General Court. This set up a form of representative government.

How did the Puritans restrict political rights?

2.5   Rhode Island and Connecticut.   There were many restrictions on life in the Massachusetts Bay Colony. Because of this, many settlers decided to leave and start their own settlements elsewhere. One of the first to go was Roger Williams. He had been a minister in Salem, a town north of Boston. Williams believed that people should be able to worship as they pleased and that the church and the government should be separate. He also spoke out against taking land from the Indians.

Who was the first to speak out against Puritan practices?

Massachusetts leaders were angered by Williams and decided to send him back to England in 1635. Williams and five friends fled into the forests and made their way south to Narragansett Bay. Williams bought a nearby piece of land from the Narragansett Indians and started a settlement he called Providence. Religion was not used as a basis for voting, and people did not have to pay taxes to support the church.

Some other people from Massachusetts followed Williams into the area south of Boston. One of them was Anne Hutchinson, whose religious views also upset the Boston leaders. Hutchinson founded a settlement to the south of Providence. Before long, there were several settlements in the area. Roger Williams went to England in 1643. He received a charter for the various settlements the next year, and they became the colony of Rhode Island.

How did Rhode Island become a colony?

Other groups from Massachusetts moved west toward the Connecticut Valley. The Reverend Thomas Hooker led a group who established Hartford and several other towns. Their plan for government was called the Fundamental Orders of Connecticut. It allowed more voters to take part in the affairs of the settlement than did Massachusetts Bay. Other Massachusetts Puritans founded the town of New Haven in 1637. The king of England granted a charter in 1662 which joined New Haven and Hartford and set up the colony of Connecticut.

The Fundamental Orders of Connecticut may have been the first written constitution in history to create a government. Use its mention as a basis for discussing the advantages of a written constitution.

2.6   The Colony of Maryland.   Charters to set up colonies such as Virginia and Plymouth had been given by English kings to private groups. The kings also gave charters to some of their rich friends. These people became known as *proprietors,* and they were given large areas of land in America. There they founded *proprietary colonies.* The

What was a proprietary colony?

Thomas Hooker and his followers (left) moved into Connecticut in 1636. Anne Hutchinson (right) moved to Rhode Island in 1638. Why did both people leave the Massachusetts Bay Colony?

Who founded the first proprietary colony?

Have students compare Maryland and Massachusetts Bay on the issue of religious freedom.

proprietors most often stayed in England. They chose officials to lead their colonies and had direct control over them.

The first proprietary colony founded in North America was Maryland. It was a result of efforts of a Catholic English noble. George Calvert, the first Lord Baltimore, wanted land in America to gain wealth for his family and to be a refuge for fellow Catholics from England. Charles I granted the Calvert family a large piece of land north of the Potomac River near Virginia in 1632. It became the proprietary colony of Maryland.

The first group of some 200 colonists arrived in Maryland in the spring of 1634. From the beginning, the colony did well. The climate and soil were ideal for farming. A representative assembly gave the people a voice in the running of their colony. People of many religions came to live in Maryland. By the mid-1600's, there were more Protestants than Catholics. To protect religious freedom for both groups in Maryland, the Toleration Act was passed in 1649. It granted freedom of worship to all people who believed in Jesus Christ. Catholics lost much of their political power, however, as the number of Protestants grew in Maryland.

2.7 Maine and New Hampshire. As early as 1622, the areas north of Massachusetts had been settled by people from that colony. In 1629, the area was given to two English citizens who later became proprietors. Sir Ferdinando Gorges received most of Maine, while John Mason got New Hampshire. The king wanted these territories in safe, trustworthy hands for two reasons. He wanted to control the huge forest areas of Maine and New Hampshire. Great amounts of lumber, tar, pitch, and resin were needed by the English navy for building and repairing ships. The king also hoped that the two colonies would weaken the power of Puritan Massachusetts.

Why did the crown want Maine and New Hampshire to be proprietary colonies?

Things in Maine and New Hampshire did not work out as the English hoped. Over the years, Massachusetts Bay slowly and quietly bought up the holdings of the Gorges family. It took over Maine as well as the colony of Plymouth in 1691. Massachusetts also tried to buy New Hampshire from members of the Mason family. To prevent this, New Hampshire was changed in 1679 from a proprietary colony to a ***royal colony,*** one under the direct control of the king. It was the first royal colony in New England.

How did Massachusetts gain control of Maine?

1. How were the first settlements financed?
2. What hardships did the first settlers face?
3. Which two religious groups formed settlements in Massachusetts?
4. How was the colony of Maryland different from the other early colonies?

3. Later Colonies

While the first English colonies were being started in North America, relations between Charles I and Parliament broke down. Both sides raised armies and began a civil war in 1642. The forces of Parliament slowly gained power and defeated the royal army in 1646. Charles I was executed in 1649. For the next 11 years, England did not have a king. The leader was a member of Parliament, a Puritan named Oliver Cromwell. His title was "Lord Protector." During this period, no new colonies were founded in America. Those which had already been set up were allowed to handle their own affairs. Then in 1658, Cromwell died. English leaders invited the oldest son of Charles I to be king in 1660. He took the throne as Charles II. The period that followed proved to be a very active time of English colonization in America.

The civil war in England led to struggles between the supporters of the king and those of Parliament in the colonies. This was especially true in Virginia and Maryland.

What caused a break in the English colonization of America?

Reading Time Lines
SKILL

Knowing the relation of time to events is important to studying history. Time lines can help to show that relation. The first time line below marks the period during which England started its colonies in North America. Each of the 13 colonies is labeled at a particular section of the time line when it was founded. Study the time line, and answer the following questions.

1. Which colony was founded first?
2. Which of the colonies was last?
3. In which century were most of the colonies founded?
4. How is Georgia different from the rest of the colonies?

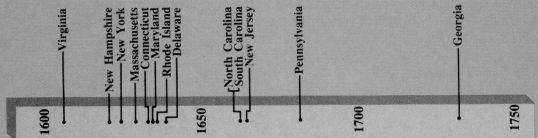

Time in relation to people is often expressed in generations. The time line below covers the same period of time as the one above. It is about several generations of the Adams family of Massachusetts. Beginning with Henry Adams in England, it continues to the birth of John Adams, who became the second President of the United States.

1. How many generations of the Adams family lived during this time?
2. How was John Adams related to Henry Adams?

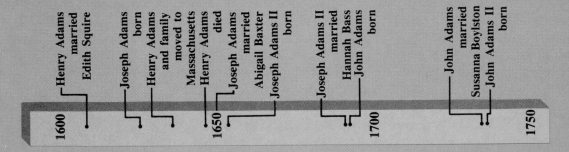

3.1 The Carolina Grant. Three years after Charles II took the throne of England, he granted eight nobles a large piece of land in America. This proprietary colony of Carolina ran from the southern border of Virginia to the northern border of Spanish Florida. The proprietors expected to make money as landowners, managing large estates producing olives, wine, silk, turpentine, and pitch.

Many people moved into the area of Carolina to live. The northern part was settled mostly by people who came from Virginia. They set up small farms, and tobacco was the main crop. The southern part of Carolina was settled mostly by people who were sent to the colony by the proprietors in England. Some founded the port settlement of Charles Town (later Charleston). The area grew rapidly and developed an active trade with England, the West Indies, and other colonies. The southern section broke away from the proprietors in 1719 and became the royal colony of South Carolina. Ten years later, the king took back the whole grant, and North Carolina also became a royal colony.

3.2 New York and New Jersey. By the early 1660's, the Dutch still held the areas of New Netherland and what had been New Sweden. This kept England from controlling the entire Atlantic coast from Spanish Florida in the south to French Canada in the north. Charles II set about to change that situation. He gave his brother James, the Duke of York, title to the entire area from Connecticut south to Maryland in 1664. He then sent four ships across the Atlantic Ocean to take the area from the Dutch.

The Dutch settlers first learned of these plans when the people living in New Amsterdam saw the powerful English ships anchored in their harbor. Seeing that fighting was useless, the Dutch allowed the English to take over. The English let the Dutch keep their own language, religion, customs, and ways of life.

Both the colony of New Netherland and the town of New Amsterdam were renamed New York in honor of the Duke. James, in turn, gave the area between the Hudson and Delaware rivers to two friends, Lord John Berkeley and Sir George Carteret. This area became the colony of New Jersey. It soon attracted many nearby settlers because of its generous land terms. With the addition of New York and New Jersey, the English empire in North America ran in a single, unbroken line along the Atlantic coast from Maine to South Carolina.

3.3 Pennsylvania. After England took New York and New Jersey, it was 17 years before another English colony was set up in America. The colony of Pennsylvania, chartered in 1681, was the work of William Penn. Penn was a member of the Society of Friends, or

Have students be alert to the reasons for the establishment of these later colonies, and have them compare them with earlier ones.

Who settled the Carolinas?

New Netherland was made up of Dutch, English, Swedes, Finns, and many other people. Many were not happy with Dutch rule. They were mostly concerned with having a government which could protect their trade rights.

For whom was New York named?

Dr. Alexander Hamilton (1712–1756)
═══PROFILE═══

In the 1700's, travel in the colonies was not easy. Every trip took careful planning. Transportation and roads were poor, and there were few maps. Each colony had different money, and robberies were frequent.

On the morning of May 30, 1744, Dr. Alexander Hamilton, a medical doctor, and a servant named Dromo set out from Annapolis, Maryland, to tour the colonies. They traveled on horseback, and their trip took them as far north as York in Maine. On the way, they visited Baltimore, Philadelphia, Trenton, New York, Providence, Boston, and New Haven. By the time they returned on September 27, Hamilton and Dromo had seen more of the colonies than most of the people living in America.

Hamilton described the trip as covering about 1,600 miles (2,560 kilometers).

Hamilton kept careful records of the people he met and the places he visited. He described the growing unity in colonial America. Americans of different colonies appeared to him to be more alike than people in different parts of some European countries.

After the trip, Hamilton continued to practice medicine, and he served in Maryland's colonial legislature. Hamilton is best remembered, however, for writing about his travels. When it was published, his book was one of the most accurate first-hand accounts of colonial life in the mid-1700's.

Quakers. This group believed that people did not need established churches or ministers to worship God. They did not approve of war and refused to serve in the army. They also refused to pay taxes to the government or the Church of England. Because of their beliefs, Quakers were often persecuted.

Who settled Pennsylvania?

William Penn asked Charles II for land in America where Quakers and people of other faiths could worship God in their own ways. The king owed a debt to Penn's father and gave Penn a grant of land west of the Delaware River in 1681. It was called Pennsylvania (Penn's woods).

Settlers from many countries with many religions came to Pennsylvania. Quakers from England, Presbyterians from Scotland,

William Penn signed treaties with the Indians and tried to honor them. How did peace between the Delaware Indians and the Pennsylvania colonists affect the growth of the colony?

Catholics from Ireland, Huguenots (Protestants) from France, Calvinists from Holland, Lutherans from Germany, and many others established settlements there. Only eight years after its founding, Pennsylvania had over 11,000 settlers. They produced large amounts of wheat, flour, beef, and pork. The main city, Philadelphia, was a settlement of brick houses, with a planned system of streets. Philadelphia was the largest and busiest city in the English colonies by 1750.

Why was Penn given a land grant?

3.4 Delaware. Pennsylvania had no outlet to the Atlantic Ocean. So William Penn got a grant from the Duke of York in 1682 for an area called Delaware, first settled by the Swedes. Delaware was governed by the leaders of Pennsylvania for almost 20 years. People from Delaware elected their own representative assembly in 1701. For some years after that, the two colonies were separate but shared the same governor.

Why did Penn seek a grant from the Duke of York?

3.5 Georgia. The last English colony in North America was established 50 years after Pennsylvania was founded. James Oglethorpe, an English reformer, wanted to create a refuge for people who were in English prisons because they could not pay their debts. The English government saw this as a chance to set up a military defense against the Spaniards in Florida. So in 1732, George II granted Oglethorpe a charter for the land between the Savannah River and the Florida border. The colony, named Georgia after the king, grew slowly. Some of the debtors refused to work and ran away. Oglethorpe's plans to produce wine and silk failed to work out, and the people spent much

Discuss the practice of putting people into prison for debts. How does the law handle debtors today?

Why did Georgia grow slowly?

time fighting the Spanish. In 1752, the king took over, and Georgia became a royal colony.

1. How did England gain control of New York and New Jersey?
2. Which group established the colony of Pennsylvania?
3. Who founded the colony of Georgia? Why?

4. Governing the Colonies_____

During the early 1600's, England did not have a definite plan for governing the colonies. Jamestown, Plymouth, Massachusetts Bay, Rhode Island, and Connecticut all began without direct involvement of the crown. As years went by, most of these colonies took care of their own affairs. The proprietary colonies, too, were not firmly controlled by the English government. Although the king personally appointed the proprietors and was supposed to approve all decisions, he seldom knew what was going on across the ocean. In a short time, colonies like Maryland and New Hampshire had few close ties with the crown.

4.1 Royal Colony Government. By 1660, the English colonial system in America was made up of many different settlements spread out along the Atlantic coast. It was a loose grouping with no real unity. Charles II decided to take a more active role by forming royal colonies. In these, the governor and the members of the council (the upper house) were chosen by the crown. The assembly (the lower house) was elected by the colonists. The governor, with the council and the assembly, governed the colony by the crown's rules. In this way, the crown took part directly in the governing of a royal colony.

Even with the growing number of royal colonies, England was having trouble with so many different colonies spread over such a great area. The people were used to leading their own lives and making their own rules. They had run their own assemblies and selected their own representatives. They chose their own church leaders, built their own ships, and set up their own defense. They often failed to pay their taxes to England. They fought with governors they did not like and refused to obey English laws. These problems were more common in the New England colonies which were not royal colonies. They had strong local assemblies and did not regard the authority of England very highly.

4.2 The Dominion of New England. Charles II died in 1685 and was succeeded by his brother James, the Duke of York. James II

Point out the implications of distance and communications between England and the colonies.

What did Charles II do to gain more control over the colonies?

Why did the British have trouble governing the colonies?

Students should be aware that the English government had to take care of colonies in the West Indies and in Nova Scotia and Newfoundland, as well as trade routes all over the world.

Settlement in the Thirteen Colonies

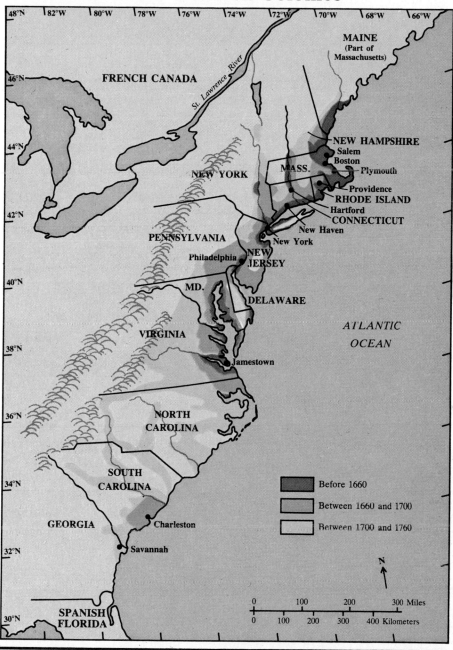

By 1760, about 95 percent of the colonists lived in rural areas, usually on farms or in small villages. The other 5 percent lived in cities. How was expansion affected by a growth in population? What might have motivated settlers to move farther west over this period of time?

The Colonies

Colony Date Founded	Original Founder	Reasons Founded	Type of Government
Virginia 1607	London Company	Expand trade	Charter (1606–1624) Royal (1624)
Maine 1622	Ferdinando Gorges John Mason	Profit for founders from trade and fishing	Proprietary (1622–1691) Part of Massachusetts (1691–1820)
New Hampshire 1622	Ferdinando Gorges John Mason	Profit for founders from trade and fishing	Proprietary (1622–1641) Part of Massachusetts (1641–1679) Royal (1679)
New York 1624	Peter Minuit	Expand Dutch trade	Dutch Colony (1624–1664) Proprietary (1664–1685) Royal (1685)
Massachusetts 1629	Massachusetts Bay Company (Puritans)	Expand trade Religious freedom	Charter (1629–1691) Royal (1691)
Connecticut 1633	Thomas Hooker	Expand trade Religious freedom	Self-governing Charter (1662)
Maryland 1634	George Calvert	Profit for founder from selling land Religious freedom	Proprietary (1634–1691) Royal (1691–1715) Proprietary (1715)
Rhode Island 1636	Roger Williams	Religious freedom	Self-governing Charter (1644)
Delaware 1638	Swedish South Company	Expand Swedish trade	Swedish Colony (1638–1655) Dutch Colony (1655–1664) Proprietary (1664–1682) Part of Pennsylvania (1682–1701) Self-governing Charter (1701)
North Carolina 1663	Anthony Cooper John Colleton William Berkeley	Profit for founders from trade and selling land	Proprietary (1663–1719) Royal (1719)
South Carolina 1663	Anthony Cooper John Colleton William Berkeley	Profit for founders from trade and selling land	Proprietary (1663–1719) Royal (1719)
New Jersey 1664	John Berkeley George Carteret	Profit for founders from selling land	Proprietary (1664–1702) Royal (1702)
Pennsylvania 1681	William Penn	Profit for founder from selling land Religious freedom	Proprietary (1681)
Georgia 1732	James Oglethorpe	Profit for founder Refuge for debtors Military defense	Proprietary (1732–1752) Royal (1752)

immediately went ahead with a plan to reorganize the colonies. The governments of New York, New Jersey, Connecticut, Rhode Island, Plymouth, Massachusetts Bay, New Hampshire, and Maine were joined to form the Dominion of New England. This was meant to create a strong, unified area on the border of French Canada. It was also supposed to bring Puritan colonies like Massachusetts under control.

Have students recall why the various New England colonies were set up and point out the growth of representative government in them. This will help them to better understand the clash with Andros.

The Dominion of New England was headed by a powerful governor, Sir Edmund Andros, appointed by the king. Andros was assisted by a council whose members were also appointed. He was a capable manager, but his style quickly made bitter enemies. Andros angered important Puritan leaders in Boston by refusing to accept Congregationalism as the official religion. He angered citizens by limiting them to one town meeting a year. He angered almost everyone when he raised taxes without going through the local assemblies.

How did Andros anger the people?

4.3   The Glorious Revolution.   Events in England put a sudden stop to the Dominion of New England. The English people drove out the unpopular James II in 1688. They asked his daughter Mary and her husband William to be joint rulers. This change was called the "Glorious Revolution." When news of it reached the colonies, some people in Boston rose up against Governor Andros. In April 1689, they put him and his council in prison and the Dominion ended.

What was the Glorious Revolution?

William and Mary agreed to give Massachusetts a new charter, but they made some changes. Although they insisted that the governor still be appointed by the crown, they did agree that the council could be chosen by the lower house. They also did away with the religious requirements for voting in the Bay Colony. The right to vote and to hold office became based on property ownership rather than on church membership. For the most part, however, things went back to the way they had been in Massachusetts and the other colonies.

The Glorious Revolution guaranteed important rights for the English people, including the people in the colonies. The Declaration of Rights of 1689 said that the crown could not pass tax laws without the consent of Parliament, could not keep an army in peacetime, and other basic rights.

1. What was a royal colony?
2. Why was the Dominion of New England created?

5. Conclusion

English plans for colonial organization and unity had failed by the early 1700's. The English colonies throughout North America were still as separate and divided as they had been during the 1600's. Each colony generally kept to itself and had its own government. Religions, points of view, and ways of doing things often differed. The colonies had no central government, capital city, or ruler—except the ruler of England who lived 3,000 miles (4,800 kilometers) away across the Atlantic.

Chapter 3 Review

Main Points

1. England was slow to enter the race for colonies in the New World because of political unrest at home.
2. During the reign of Queen Elizabeth I, England became the leading European naval power.
3. Between 1607 and 1732, England established colonies along the east coast of North America.
4. The English colonies were set up by joint stock companies, by proprietors, or by the English government.
5. English colonies were settled by people looking for land, money, and religious freedom.
6. The Glorious Revolution in England put an end to the English plan to centralize the colonial government.

Building Vocabulary

1. Identify the following:

   John Cabot
   Parliament
   Sir Francis Drake
   Spanish Armada
   Jamestown

   Powhatan
   House of Burgesses
   Puritans
   Mayflower Compact

   John Winthrop
   Roger Williams
   Anne Hutchinson
   Toleration Act

   William Penn
   Dr. Alexander Hamilton
   James Oglethorpe
   Dominion of New
     England

2. Define the following:

   manufacturing
   armada
   joint stock
     companies

   charter
   investors
   legislature

   vetoed
   rituals
   compact

   meeting houses
   proprietors
   proprietary colonies
   royal colony

Remembering the Facts

1. What delayed English efforts to establish colonies in the New World?
2. When did England begin to settle colonies in North America?
3. Which of the English colonies were set up by joint stock companies? by proprietors? as royal colonies?
4. How did Indians aid settlers at Jamestown and Plymouth?
5. Which colonies were started by people who left the Massachusetts Bay Colony?
6. Which English colony was first settled by the Dutch? How did the English government gain control of it?
7. How did England try to organize the governing of the colonies?
8. How did the Glorious Revolution in England affect the colonies?

Understanding the Facts

1. Why was tobacco important to the colony of Virginia?
2. Why did the Pilgrims, Puritans, and Quakers disagree with the Church of England?
3. Why was the Mayflower Compact important?
4. Why did people leave the Massachusetts Bay Colony?
5. Why did England want control of New Netherland and New Sweden?
6. Why did England plan to centralize the northeastern colonial governments under the Dominion of New England?

Using Maps

Longitude and Latitude. Because of the huge size of the earth, a way of easily identifying locations is needed. One way to do this is to draw two types of imaginary lines circling the globe. When maps are drawn, these lines are added, too.

One set of these lines runs north and south from north pole to south pole. These are called meridians, or lines of longitude. The distance between them is measured in degrees east or west of the prime (original) meridian. The prime meridian is labeled 0°. Since England was a world leader in exploration and mapmaking when the system was set up, the prime meridian runs through England.

The second set of lines runs east and west, but they do not come together at any one point. These are called parallels, or lines of latitude. The prime parallel is the equator, and it is labeled 0°. Latitude is measured in degrees according to the distance north or south of the equator.

By using these lines, we can identify any place on the earth as being at some degree east or west longitude and some degree north or south latitude.

Examine the map on page 83, and answer the following questions.

1. Between which lines of north latitude is the colony of Virginia?
2. Which line of west longitude runs along the eastern coast of Virginia?
3. Which parallel divides the Pennsylvania colony from the Maryland colony?
4. What is the one colony which lies entirely west of 80° west longitude?
5. Which colonies are crossed by the parallel at 40° north latitude?
6. Between which parallels do the English colonies lie?

Secota 1584-1587

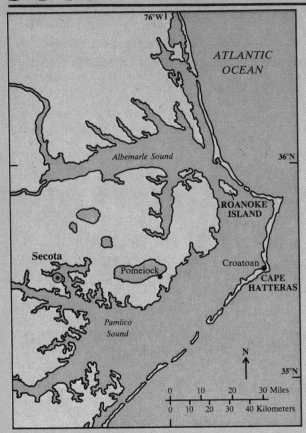

Secota was a Powhatan Indian town near Roanoke Island in what is now the eastern part of North Carolina. In 1584, it was part of the land which Queen Elizabeth asked Sir Walter Raleigh to colonize for England. Raleigh hired Arthur Barlowe to lead the first group of English explorers to the area.

At different times, several groups were sent to explore and settle the area which became Virginia and North Carolina. John White drew pictures of the Indians, their towns, and the plants, fish, and birds which he saw on his trips. Barlowe, White, and a third explorer, Thomas Hariot, wrote down their descriptions of the new land for the people back in England. By reading the descriptions and looking at the pictures, Americans today can get an idea of how some earlier Americans, the Indians, lived in the 1580's.

Early Towns

Their towns are small and few, . . . a village may contain but ten or twelve houses— some perhaps as many as twenty. . . .

The houses are built of small poles . . . covered from top to bottom either with bark or with mats woven of long rushes. . . .

In one part of the country a . . . chief . . . may govern a single town, but in other parts the number of towns under one chief may vary to two, three, six, and even to eight or more. The greatest [chief] we met governed eighteen towns, and he could [get together] seven or eight hundred warriors. The language of each chief's territory differs from that of the others. . . .

Secota

Those of their towns which are not fenced in are usually more beautiful [like] Secota. The houses are farther apart and have gardens. . . . They also have groves of trees where they hunt deer, and fields where they sow their corn. In the cornfields they set up a little hut on a [platform], where a watchman is stationed. . . . He makes a continual noise to keep off birds and beasts. . . .

They also have a large plot . . . where they meet with neighbors to celebrate solemn feasts. . . . In the [smaller gardens] they sow pumpkins . . . and just outside the town is the river . . . from which they get their water.

City Sketches depict cultural, social, and economic aspects of American life at given points in time. City Sketches appear at the end of each unit, before the Unit Review. Some units, such as this one, have two City Sketches. They can be compared and contrasted. See Teacher's Guide for learning objectives, teaching ideas, and answers for City Sketches.

The People

The chieftains of Virginia wear their hair long, tied in a knot close to the ears. . . . One long bird's feather is stuck into the [top] and a short one above each ear. They hang large pearls in their ears. . . . Their [faces and bodies] are painted. . . . Around their necks they have a chain of pearls . . . and upon their arms they wear bracelets. . . .

They are dressed in cloaks made of finely cured skins. . . .

The women of Secota [dress in] deerskins. . . . Their hair is cut short in front, somewhat longer at the back, and falls softly to their shoulders. . . . Their foreheads, cheeks, chins, arms, and legs are chalked, and the pattern of a chain is pricked or painted around their necks. . . .

The priests of the town . . . are [very old] and have greater experience than the ordinary [people]. Their hair [also] is cut in a crest on the top of their heads; the rest of it is short and falls over their foreheads like a fringe. Earrings adorn their ears. They wear a short cloak made of fine rabbit skins. . . .

They have sorcerers . . . whose [spells] often go against the laws of nature. For they are very familiar with devils, from whom they [get] knowledge about their enemies' movements.

[These men] shave their heads entirely, except for the crest, which they wear as the others do. A small black bird is [tied] above one of their ears as a badge of office. . . .

The [people] pay great attention to the sorcerer's words, which they often find to be true.

Planting Crops

The soil in the fields around Secota was very rich. Because of the long warm seasons, the Indians were able to bring in three crops of corn a year. To prepare the land for planting: *They simply break the upper part of the ground to raise up the weeds, grass, and old stubs of cornstalks with their roots. . . . After the weeds have dried in the sun for a day or two,*

John White, governor of Roanoke Island, was also an artist. His watercolors provide a look into the everyday lives of the people of Secota. How does White's painting show Secota was a well-planned town?

Their greene corne.

[they are] *scraped up into many small heaps and burned. . . .*

Then they sow the seed. For corn they begin in one corner of the plot and make a hole with a [stick]. They put four grains into each hole . . . and cover them with soil. The seeds are planted in rows. . . . between the holes . . . the [Indians] sometimes set beans and peas. . . .

Secota Cooking

Their women have the greatest skill in making large earthen pots, which are so fine that not even [the English] can make any better. These are carried around from place to place just as easily as our own brass kettles. They set them up on a pile of earth and then put wood underneath and [light] it, taking great care that the fire burns evenly on all sides. They fill the pot with water, then put fruit, meat, and fish into it, and let it boil together as in a [stew]. . . . When it is cooled, they serve it in small dishes. . . .

Catching Fish

They have a [special] way of fishing in their rivers. As they have neither steel nor iron, they [tie] the sharp, hollow tail of a certain fish . . . to reeds or to the end of a long rod, and with this point they spear fish both by day and by night. . . . And they make traps with reeds or sticks set in the water. . . .

It is a pleasing picture to see these people wading and sailing in their shallow rivers. They [do not] desire to pile up riches. . . .

Shown here are various ways the Secotans caught fish. The lighted fire in the canoe attracted the fish at night. What other methods did they use?

Religion and Law

The people of Secota had many gods. Some were more important to them than others. They believed that their chief god had always lived. He had created the world and then had made other gods to help him create and rule everything else.

Then he made the sun, the moon, and the stars. . . . The [Indians] say that the waters of the world were made first and that out of these all creatures . . . were formed.

As to the creation of [people], they think that the woman came first. She [had] children fathered by one of the gods, and in this way the [Indians] had their beginning. But how many ages or years have passed since then, they do not know, for they have no writing or any means of keeping records of past time. . . .

Temples were set up where the Indians worshiped their gods. They made human shapes of the gods, or idols, and prayed and sang to them.

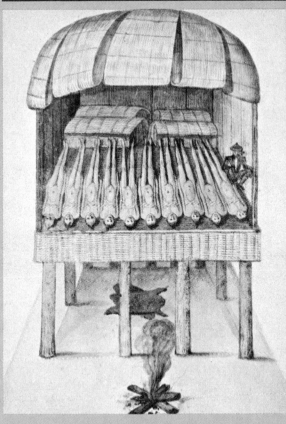

The bodies of dead chiefs were placed on platforms like this. How was the concern for death used to maintain law and order in Secota?

Their religion taught them that humans have souls which do not die. After the body died, the soul of a good person would go to heaven. The soul of a bad person would go to a pit called Popogusso, at the farthest end of the world. There it would burn forever. Most of the bodies were buried, but for the chiefs:

. . . *they build a* [platform] *nine or ten feet high. . . . They cover this with mats and upon them lay the dead bodies of their chiefs* [after the bodies are specially treated]. *. . . Near the bodies they place their idol, for they are* [sure] *that it keeps the bodies of their chiefs from all harm.*

Under the [platform] *lives one of their priests, who is in charge of the dead and* [says] *his prayers night and day. He sleeps on deerskins spread on the ground, and if it is cold, he lights a fire.*

. . . the belief in heaven and the fiery pit makes the [people obey] *their governors and behave with great care, so that they may avoid* [pain] *after death and enjoy bliss. Evil-doers have to pay for their crimes in this world, nevertheless.* [Stealing] *. . . and other wicked acts are punished with fines, beatings, or even with death. . . .*

A Strange Sickness

As the English people stayed on in Virginia, the Indians of Secota and some of the other towns began to turn against them. At the same time, strange things began to happen in the towns which were visited by the English. Hariot wrote that:

. . . within a few days [after we left a town] *the people began to die very fast. In some towns twenty people died, in some forty, in some sixty. . . . And the strange thing was that this occurred only in towns where we had been. . . . The disease . . . was so strange a one that they did not know anything about it or how to cure it. . . .*

[The Indians believed] *that more of our* [people] *would yet come to this country to kill them and to take away their homes.*

1. Where was Secota located?
2. What role did the sorcerers play?
3. What did the people of Secota look like? What did they wear?
4. What did the people of Secota eat?
5. How did the people of Secota believe the world was created?

Plymouth 1620~1650

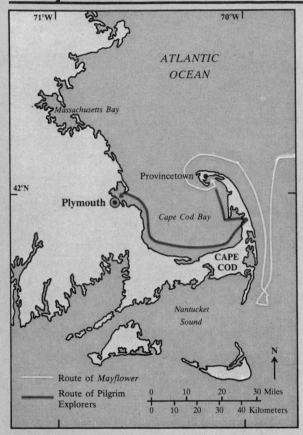

ATLANTIC
OCEAN

Massachusetts Bay

Provincetown

Plymouth

Cape Cod Bay

CAPE
COD

Nantucket
Sound

N

Route of *Mayflower*

Route of Pilgrim
Explorers

0   10   20   30 Miles
0   10   20   30   40 Kilometers

After 65 days at sea, the *Mayflower* reached the coast of America at the beginning of winter in 1620. The crew, knowing they were too far north, sailed down the coast toward Virginia. The weather was so terrible that they turned back to Cape Cod Bay.

Using small boats from the ship, some of the passengers explored the land for a place to live. They finally found an area they named Plymouth where much of the land had already been cleared by Indians. It had a river and a hill where they could build a fort for safety. The passengers decided to settle there.

The *Mayflower* stayed for the rest of the winter because of the weather and the need for repairs. Many of the passengers lived aboard the crowded ship while they were building houses on the land. Among those settlers who came to Plymouth in 1620 were:

Captain Myles Standish and Rose his wife. . . .

Francis Cooke and his son John; but his wife and other children came afterwards. . . .

Mr. William Mullins and his wife and two children, Joseph and Priscilla; and a servant, Robert Carter. . . .

A Record

William Bradford, a Separatist, was chosen by the Pilgrims to be governor of Plymouth in 1621. He wrote a history, or record, of the many years of hardship that the Pilgrims faced in America. That history still exists today, and from it, people can learn who the Pilgrims were and what happened to them. Bradford was a leader in the settlement for more than 35 years. Much of the information on the following pages comes from his record.

A Hard Beginning

The settlers had a very hard time at first. They had only a few small boats, and the winter winds and rains made the harbor's water very rough. It was not easy to move their goods to land, and it took weeks to get their small houses built.

But that which was most sad . . . was, that in two or three months' time half of their company died, especially in January and February, being the depth of winter, and [needing] *houses and other comforts; being* [sick] *with . . . diseases which this long voyage . . . had brought upon them. So as there died some times two or three of a day . . . of 100 and odd persons,* [only about] *fifty remained. . . .*

All this while the Indians [were watching] *them, and would sometimes show themselves . . . but when any approached near them, they would run away. . . .*

Spring

But about the 16th of March, a certain Indian came boldly amongst them and spoke to them in broken English, which they could well understand. . . . His name was Samoset. He told them also of another Indian whose name was Squanto . . . who had been in England and could speak better English. . . .

Samoset came to visit the Pilgrims again and brought Squanto, Chief Massasoit, and others with him. The Pilgrims and the Indians

The Pilgrims landed in bad weather in the winter of 1620. What special problems did a winter landing present to the Pilgrims?

exchanged gifts and made speeches which Squanto translated. The visit ended after a peace treaty with Massasoit was signed. When the other Indians returned to their homes, Squanto stayed with the Pilgrims to help them learn about the new land.

New Ways for New Land

In a small village like Plymouth, everyone had to work hard for food—hoeing corn and other crops in the summer, digging clams and catching fish in the winter. The Pilgrims were not very skilled in farming and fishing at first. For example, Plymouth Harbor was filled with fish, but they had not brought hooks small enough to catch them. Squanto taught the Pilgrims Indian ways to fish and farm. He showed them where and how to trap and catch fish. He also taught them how and when to plant corn in hills, using fish for fertilizer. Governor Bradford wrote about Squanto's ways.

All which they found true by trial and experience. Some English seed they sowed, as wheat and [peas], *but it came not to good, either by the badness of the seed or lateness of the season or both, or some other* [trouble].

More Problems

Since they were poor people, the Pilgrims had needed help to come to the New World. The Plymouth Company's investors had paid for the voyage and for supplies. But, in return, the settlers had to spend their first seven years working for the company as a group, with common land and property. All of the profits, or extras, from their farming, fishing, and trading went back to London. And the Pilgrims did not like working common fields to fill a common warehouse, with no time to work for themselves and their families.

Pilgrims and Indians celebrated the first Thanksgiving in the New World. How did the Indians help the Plymouth colonists survive?

For the young men, that were most able and fit for [labor] *and service,* [were unhappy] *that they should spend their time and strength to work for other men's wives and children without any* [extra credit]. . . . *this was thought* [unfair]. . . .

In 1623, the common use of land began to change. That year, each family was given a piece of land for planting corn. Bradford wrote that:

This had very good success, for it made all hands very [busy], *so as much more corn was planted than otherwise. . . . The women now went willingly into the field, and took their little ones with them to set corn; which before would* [make believe] *weakness and inability. . . .*

Beginning to divide the land among families settled one problem. The trouble of paying back the Plymouth Company lasted for years. The settlers were not good enough at fishing to make a lot of profit, although the demand for dried cod was great in Europe. Most of their profit came from fur trading with the Indians from Cape Cod to Maine. In 1626, their debt was set at about $9,000. By the time they finally paid it off in 1648, the Pilgrims had sent the Plymouth Company furs and other goods worth about $100,000!

Growing

Plymouth, though small, was becoming a stronger settlement by 1627. The chief trading agent of the Dutch West India Company was very pleased with it during his visit that year. He reported that:

New Plymouth lies on the slope of a hill stretching east towards the sea-coast. . . . The houses are constructed of clapboards, with gardens also enclosed behind and at the sides with clapboards, so that their houses and courtyards are arranged in very good order, with a stockade against sudden attack; and at the ends of the streets there are three wooden gates. In the center, on the cross street, stands the Governor's house, before which is a square stockade upon which four patereros [guns] *are mounted, so as to enfilade* [cover] *the streets.*

Troubled Times

In the 1630's, many Puritans came to settle in the Boston area. The Pilgrims did make some money by selling cattle and other goods to the new people. But the growth of towns to the north of Plymouth, around the better Boston Harbor, also had a bad effect on the Pilgrim settlement. Soon, fewer ships came into their harbor, and trade fell off. Their fields, worked by the Indians long before the Pilgrims had arrived, were not so rich as some of the newer land. And as children grew up, there was no more land for

Plymouth buildings had walls of rough pine logs filled in with clay. How do the buildings of Plymouth compare to those of Secota?

Captain Standish his wife died in the first sickness and he married again and [has] four sons living and some are dead. . . .

Francis Cooke is still living, a very old man, and [has] seen his children's children have children. After his wife came over with other of his children; he [has] three still living by her, all married and have five children, so their increase is eight. And his son John which came over with him is married, and [has] four children living. . . .

Mr. Mullins and his wife, his son and his servant died the first winter. Only his daughter Priscilla survived, and married with John Alden [a Mayflower passenger]; who are both living and have eleven children. And their eldest daughter is married and [has] five children. . . .

Governor Bradford himself died in 1659, but Plymouth did continue. The town grew slowly and, in 1691, became part of the larger Massachusetts Bay Colony. As for the children of the Pilgrims, they also continued to grow in number. Some of them moved out into every part of America.

them near their parents. Some of the first settlers and many of their children began to move farther away. New towns and churches were started in other parts of the settlement. In 1644, the people talked about moving the whole settlement to better land on Cape Cod. Finally, some of the Pilgrim families did move to a place called Nauset. Governor Bradford wrote:

And thus was this poor church [Plymouth] left, like [a] mother grown old and forsaken of her children . . . her [older people] being most of them worn away by death, and these of later time being like children [married] into other families, and she like a widow left only to trust in God. Thus, she that had made many rich became herself poor.

Catching Up

In 1650, Bradford reported again on the families who had first come to Plymouth:

1. Where did many of the passengers of the *Mayflower* live during the first winter in Plymouth? Why?
2. Who was William Bradford?
3. Who paid for the Pilgrims' trip to the New World?
4. Compare the diet of the Indians of Secota to that of the Pilgrims of Plymouth.
5. Locate Secota and Plymouth on the maps. From their general locations, compare their climates. What problems would the colonists of Plymouth have that the Indians of Secota would not have?

Unit I Review

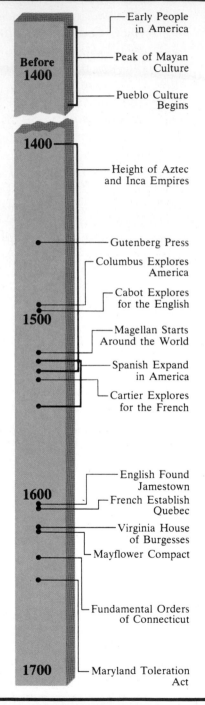

Early People in America

Peak of Mayan Culture

Before 1400

Pueblo Culture Begins

1400

Height of Aztec and Inca Empires

Gutenberg Press

Columbus Explores America

Cabot Explores for the English

1500

Magellan Starts Around the World

Spanish Expand in America

Cartier Explores for the French

English Found Jamestown

1600

French Establish Quebec

Virginia House of Burgesses

Mayflower Compact

Fundamental Orders of Connecticut

1700

Maryland Toleration Act

Summary

1. People first entered the Western Hemisphere across a land bridge between Asia and North America.

2. Over centuries, these people settled in all areas of North and South America.

3. Some of the early people established high levels of civilization and strong political units while others lived in small villages or moved from place to place as hunters.

4. European interest in the Western Hemisphere began with ocean voyages in the fifteenth century.

5. In 1492, Christopher Columbus landed in America while looking for an all-water trade route to Asia.

6. Europeans soon realized that Columbus had discovered a New World, with opportunities for adventure, riches, and land for empire.

7. In taking advantage of New World opportunities, Europeans conquered some groups of Indians and took the land of other groups.

8. Spain became the leading nation in exploring the New World, establishing a large empire in Central and South America and in the southwestern part of what is now the United States.

9. Portugal and France also set up empires, while Sweden and Holland had small areas of North America.

10. The English were late in entering the race for land in the New World, but in 1607, they began colonies along the Atlantic coast of North America.

Each unit is completed by a Unit Review which provides an important summary of the unit themes, as well as unit questions and suggested student activities and readings to enrich and enhance learning.

Unit Questions

1. Why did the early people in the Western Hemisphere develop different cultures in the areas of North and South America where they settled?
2. What developments in Europe made it possible to begin sea voyages to unknown parts of the world in the fifteenth century?
3. How did Europeans become interested in Africa in the fifteenth century? Why did they remain interested in the years which followed?
4. What was wrong with the plan of Christopher Columbus to reach Asia by sailing west across the Atlantic Ocean?
5. What were some of the reasons that Europeans were able to enslave Indians and Africans?
6. What attracted people in the Old World to the New World?
7. Why did the English settle along the Atlantic coast of North America?
8. What were some of the differences in the groups of people and the reasons for settlement in the English, French, and Spanish colonies in America?
9. What were some of the reasons for the growth of a spirit of independence among the English colonies in North America during the 1600's?

Suggested Activities

1. Compare the reports of the first space explorers with the reports of the early explorers to the New World.
2. Select one group of Indian people. Describe the area in which they lived, and show how the environment influenced their way of life.
3. Examine atlases and list the titles of three reference maps and three thematic maps of North America.
4. Gather information on the Dutch or Swedish colonies in North America. Report on how you think these colonies might have survived against the English.

Suggested Readings

Armstrong, Virginia. *I Have Spoken: American History Through the Voices of the Indians*. Chicago: Swallow, 1971. Opinions of the European settlement of the New World are given from the points of view of various American Indians.

Brown, Richard. *The Human Side of American History*. Boston: Ginn & Company, 1962. Personal accounts of great and small events in American history.

Lavine, Sigmund. *The Houses the Indians Built*. New York: Dodd, Mead, & Co., 1975. Differences in the cultures of various Indian groups are shown through a study of their homes, buildings, and shrines.

Loeb, Robert. *Meet the Real Pilgrims: Everyday Life on Plimouth Plantation in 1627*. Garden City, New York: Doubleday, 1975. Looks at the lives of the Pilgrims in early New England.

UNIT II

Independence

Independence was a spirit that became evident early in the history of the American people. Far from established rules and restrictions on life in the Old World, people began to make their own laws and develop their own ways of doing things in the New World. When the freedom to be independent was threatened, American people fought to defend and preserve it. The spirit of independence contributed to the emergence of a new nation, government, and culture that was separate from the old.

Chapter 4   Colonial Society ————— 100
Chapter 5   Winning Freedom ————— 122
Chapter 6   Forming a Union ————— 146
Chapter 7   The Constitution ————— 164
City Sketch   *Philadelphia 1750–1775* ——— 184

Colonial Society 4

Bethlehem, Pennsylvania, was the main settlement in North America of one of the Protestant groups, the Moravians. This view of it was drawn in 1757. How did most settlers in the English colonies make a living?

The English took more than 100 years to build their colonial empire in North America. Starting with Jamestown in 1607, they founded a string of colonies along the Atlantic coast. By the 1730's, the English had 13 colonies, stretching from French Canada in the north to Spanish Florida in the south. The 13 English colonies were different from each other in many ways. They had their own local governments and their own ways of life. The people who settled in the colonies had come to the New World for many different reasons. All of these people added to the growth and variety of American culture.

People in the colonies were a mix of ethnic, racial, religious, social, and economic backgrounds. This is an important point and will be referred to many times throughout the text.

1. The People of the English Colonies_____

People from several countries *immigrated* to (came to live in) the English colonies of North America. By 1700, the colonies had about 250,000 people. This number increased ten times in the next 75 years. By 1775, the population of the English colonies was about 2.5 million. Most of the people were white Europeans who wanted to come to the New World. They hoped to have religious freedom, to escape poverty, and to find new ways of improving their lives. Some who arrived in the colonies were forced to come. This was especially true of the black people from Africa.

How much did population grow over time?

1.1 The English. About 60 percent of the white settlers in the English colonies were of English nationality. They brought many English ways with them, and their language became the common one in the colonies. Most of them belonged to one of the Protestant religious groups.

Refer students to the charts on page 103 for population totals and a breakdown by group.

The largest group of settlers were members of the middle class. They lived in *rural* (country) areas, where they farmed small plots of land. Some worked as blacksmiths, carpenters, or stonecutters. Some lived in the few *urban* (city) areas along the Atlantic coast, where they worked in shops, on ships, or with machines. A small number of colonists from England were members of the upper class. In the northern colonies, they became merchants, ministers, doctors, and lawyers. In the southern colonies, they were wealthy *planters*, owners of large farms known as plantations.

What were English settlers like?

1.2 The Scots. The next largest group of English-speaking white settlers (about 14 percent) were Scots. Many came from southern Scotland, where they had worked as weavers and mechanics. The largest single group of Scots in America were the so-called Scotch-Irish. They were Scots whom the English government had forced to resettle in the province of Ulster in northern Ireland. They had been treated harshly by the English and hated by the Irish. They sought peace and safety in America. Most of the Scots who first came to America settled in Pennsylvania. In the early 1700's, some moved farther southwest, toward the mountain valleys of the Appalachians.

Why did Germans come to America?

1.3   The Germans.   One of the largest groups of non-English-speaking Europeans to come to the 13 colonies (8.7 percent) were Germans. The Germans left their homeland in the early 1700's to escape war and hunger. Most settled in Pennsylvania's Susquehanna Valley around Lancaster and York. Sometimes they were called Pennsylvania Dutch because the German word for "German" is *Deutsch*. The political freedom offered by Pennsylvania, together with the richness of the land, provided opportunities for many Germans to become successful. Most became well-to-do farmers. A few made a profitable living making and selling wagons and hardware.

1.4   Other European Settlers.   In addition to the Germans, there were several other groups of non-English-speaking European settlers. The Dutch (3.4 percent), located mostly in the Hudson Valley region of New York, contributed many things to American life. Their brick houses with tile roofs were stronger than the wooden planks and shingles of most colonial houses. Their pottery, kitchenware, and iron hardware were both well designed and useful. The French settled in many colonies. Making up about 1.7 percent of the population, they provided America with many artists and artisans. Swedes and Finns, 0.7 percent of all colonists, established settlements throughout the Delaware Valley. They developed ways to build log cabins that later became popular among settlers moving farther west.

What were some contributions of non-English-speaking European settlers?

1.5   The Africans.   The beginning of the black population in the English colonies came in 1619 when a Dutch ship left 20 Africans in Jamestown. Before the end of the century, many more Africans were brought to the colonies. They were captured in wars or kidnapped by slave traders along the coast of West Africa. Their trip to America was a terrible ordeal. Slave ships were horribly crowded, and people were poorly fed. Thousands of Africans died on the ships before reaching America.

When did blacks first come to America?

During the colonial period, Africans became the largest single non-English group in the English colonies. In 1700, there were more than 25,000 slaves. By 1750, there were over 235,000. And in 1775, there were some 500,000 slaves in the English colonies—about 20

A more detailed discussion of slavery is contained in Chapter 14, Section 2. Students should be aware that the slavery question will be of major importance as they continue in the text.

Colonial Population, 1630–1780

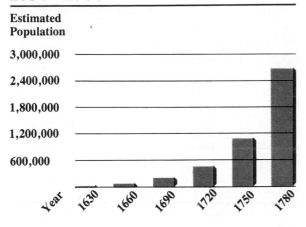

Estimated Population

3,000,000	
2,400,000	
1,800,000	
1,200,000	
600,000	

Year   1630   1660   1690   1720   1750   1780

Percent of Nationality Groups, 1775

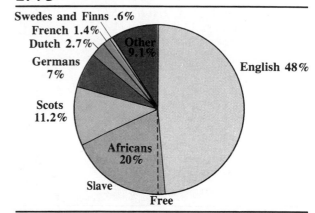

Swedes and Finns .6%
French 1.4%
Dutch 2.7%
Germans 7%
Scots 11.2%
Africans 20%
Other 9.1%
English 48%
Slave   Free

Total colonial population increased 100 times between 1630 and 1720. How much did it increase between 1750 and 1780? What percent of the total population did each nationality group make up?

percent of the total population. Just as the white population had grown ten times between 1700 and 1775, so had America's black population.

1. From what countries did the various people in the English colonies come?
2. Where did the people of various national backgrounds settle in the colonies?
3. How did the trip to the New World of blacks differ from that of whites?

Discuss the problem of slavery as it fit with the ideas of freedom upon which many colonies were founded.

2. Life in the English Colonies

The people who came to live in the various parts of the English colonies had many different manners and customs. Gradually, the immigrants to the New World began to form a way of life that was different in many ways from the one they had in the Old World. They began to shape an American way of life.

2.1 Work Roles. The vast majority of white settlers in the English colonies worked as farmers. Land formed the economic base of

What did the vast majority of colonists do for a living?

Colonial Society   103

Skilled working people like those shown here were in great demand in the colonies. Hat makers (left) or a weaver (right) could make a good living. Why was each important to settlers living in the colonies?

colonial America. Where the soil was fertile and the climate favorable, farmers prospered. Where the soil was rocky and the climate cold, the land produced little beyond what a family needed to eat.

Since most people lived on farms, colonial cities remained small in size. They were important, however, as trade centers. Through them came manufactured goods from other English colonies and from England. Merchants were key figures in colonial cities. They brought in goods the colony needed and sold what the colony produced. Mills, factories, and iron-making furnaces were set up in many cities to produce goods for trade. Producers hired artisans to make shoes, furniture, silverware, and tools. The most important manufacturing activity, centered in New England, was shipbuilding.

What was an indentured servant?

Many people who came to the English colonies did not arrive as farmers, merchants, artisans, or manufacturers. They came as *indentured servants.* These were people who bound themselves to work for someone in America for a set number of years, usually five to seven. In exchange for their labor, the servants' passage was paid to the colonies by the person for whom they were to work. Once the term of service was completed, the servant was free. Most indentured servants were people who wanted to go to America but did not have enough money to make the trip. Gottlieb Mittelberger, who came from Germany in 1750, described the buying of indentured servants:

This is how the [sale of] human beings on board ship takes place. Every day Englishmen, Dutchmen, and . . . Germans come . . . on board the newly arrived vessel that has brought people from Europe and offers them for sale. From among the healthy they pick out those suitable for [their] purposes. . . . When an agreement has been reached, adult persons . . . bind themselves to serve for three, four, five, or six years, according to their health and age. The very young, between the ages of ten and fifteen, have to serve until they are twenty-one, however.

Many parents . . . must . . . sell their children as if they were cattle. Since the fathers and mothers often do not know where or to what masters their children are to be sent, it frequently happens that . . . parents and children do not see each other for years on end, or even for the rest of their lives.

Have students consider the use of indentured servants and slaves as evidence of the need for labor in the colonies.

The first Africans to come to the English colonies came as indentured servants. They helped to provide the workers needed on large farms, especially in the southern colonies. These servants were supposed to work out their terms of service and then get their freedom, just as the white

Many people who came to the colonies arrived as indentured servants. With the demand for more workers, black people from Africa were imported as slaves. Why did large farms, like this tobacco plantation, need so many workers?

Anne Bradstreet (1612–1672)
Phillis Wheatley (1753?–1784)
PROFILE

Few women were well known during colonial times. Most were known because of their husbands. There were some exceptions. Two of these were Anne Bradstreet and Phillis Wheatley. Both were born in the Old World, both lived in Massachusetts, and both were well educated. Both were also poets who were popular in America and Britain.

Bradstreet was born in Britain in 1612. In 1630, she sailed for America with her parents and husband. Bradstreet found life in Massachusetts Bay Colony to be difficult. Bradstreet maintained a house at the edge of the wilderness and raised eight children. She also found time to write poetry.

Bradstreet's early poems reflected mostly her Puritan religion. Later she wrote more personal poems. In a poem praising Queen Elizabeth I, Bradstreet expressed some thoughts on being a woman.

She hath wip'd off the aspersion
  [slander] of her Sex,
That women wisdom lack to play the
  Rex [ruler]. . . .

In 1650, a book of Bradstreet's poems was printed in Britain. *The Tenth Muse Lately Sprung Up in America* was the first volume published by an American poet.

Phillis Wheatley was born in Africa about 1753. In 1761, John and Susannah Wheatley bought her as a slave in Boston. The Wheatleys taught her to read and write. She also learned history, geography, and the Latin classics.

In 1766, Wheatley wrote her first poem. It was to King George III when he repealed the Stamp Act.

And may each clime with equal
  gladness see
A monarch's smile can set his subjects
  free!

In 1773, Wheatley was freed and went to Britain where she met other writers. There her first book, *Poems on Various Subjects*, was published. At the time, there were few volumes of poems by Americans, and this was the first by a black woman.

Wheatley was not a typical slave. Neither Anne Bradstreet nor Phillis Wheatley were typical women. Few women and almost no slaves were as well educated. Still fewer became published poets. Bradstreet and Wheatley were the exceptions.

servants did. A Virginia law in 1661 made black indentured servants' terms of service "continuous." This meant most Africans became servants for life. A 1663 Maryland law made black indentured servants *slaves*, people who were the property of their owners.

How did blacks become slaves?

2.2 Outlooks.   The family was the cornerstone of colonial society. Most family groups in America were very large, especially those on the farms. A single household might contain a father, mother, brothers, sisters, grandparents, uncles, aunts, and cousins. Because of war, sickness, accidents, and the lack of proper medical care, the death rate was very high. It was common for a person to marry two or three times. And it was not unusual to have a household of 14 or 15 people. For farmers, a large household meant a steady source of labor.

What were features of the colonial family?

Under the English system of laws in the colonies, women had few political or civil rights. Women did not have the right to vote and could not participate in government. Generally, they were limited by law in owning property. Women, however, took on a great many responsibilities. Many worked alongside their husbands on the farms. Some managed farms by themselves when their husbands died or were away at war. A number of women operated taverns and inns. A few colonial

Old Burton Church, Virginia, is a typical eighteenth-century colonial building. This scene shows wealthy landowning families arriving for religious services. What part did religion play in the lives of the colonists?

governments did allow women to own property, inherit money, and hold licenses to operate businesses.

One of the most important influences on colonial life was religion. In some colonies, religious leaders were also the government leaders. Religion for most colonists was something that affected their daily lives. In colonial society, particularly in the Puritan colonies, emphasis was placed on hard work. It was considered a serious offense to waste time. English colonists believed that God rewarded those who worked hard and punished those who did not.

1. What was the economic base of colonial America?
2. How did people in the colonies make their livings?
3. What were some of the influences on colonial life?

How important was religion in colonial America?

3. Regions in the Colonies

Students should look for ways in which the physical environment affected ways of life in the colonies, much as they studied its affect on Indian life.

There were many reasons why settlers in the English colonies shared similar ways of life. There were also reasons why some parts of the colonies were quite different from other parts. The English colonies were not all located in one small geographic area. They did not all have the same kind of climate, soil, and land formations. The colonies ran all the way from the Canadian border with its cool temperatures to Spanish Florida with its warm climate. This area contained three major regions—the New England Colonies, the Middle Colonies, and the Southern Colonies. In each of these, the people developed their own political systems, economic structures, and social patterns.

Into what regions were the English colonies divided?

3.1 The New England Colonies. The colonies in the New England region—Connecticut, Rhode Island, New Hampshire, and Massachusetts including Maine—had certain features in common. The people there were almost all of English background. Congregationalism, with strict Puritan beliefs, was the major form of worship. Congregations built meeting houses and elected their own ministers. Religion and politics were local matters in New England. Each town ran its own affairs. The *town meeting*, a gathering of all eligible voters, was the usual way in which political issues were debated and laws passed. Most adult males participated. Those who were not members of the Congregational church, however, were not allowed to vote.

What colonies made up the New England Colonies?

Education was considered very important in the New England Colonies. The colonists believed that their children should be able to

Why was education important to New England colonists?

Harvard College was founded in Cambridge, Massachusetts, in 1636. It was the first college in colonial America. Why was it established? What was the purpose of most colonial colleges founded later?

read and understand the Bible. In 1647, Massachusetts passed a law providing for a tax-supported public school system. Even before that, in 1636, Harvard College was founded in Cambridge, Massachusetts, near Boston. It was the first English colonial college, and it was built to train Congregationalist ministers. In 1701, Yale College in New Haven, Connecticut, and in 1769, Dartmouth College in Hanover, New Hampshire, were founded for the same reason.

Many of the people in the New England Colonies had small farms. They worked the land usually with the help of family members, including children. Much of the land was hard and rocky and not easy to farm. Farms produced little more than the people who lived there needed. So, many people also found work in seaport towns. Shipbuilding and fishing became important to the New England economy, and foreign trade increased greatly.

Student assignments on the soil, climate, and other physical features of the three regions can be of benefit. These should include such information as average temperature in selected months, as well as average yearly rainfall.

People in New England traded with such European countries as England, Portugal, Spain, and France. Trade with the British, French, and Spanish West Indies was also important. Molasses was brought into New England from the West Indies. Much of it was made into rum. Rum was shipped across the Atlantic Ocean to Africa. On the coast of West Africa, it was exchanged for slaves, and the slaves were shipped back across the Atlantic to the West Indies. There the slaves were sold, and part of the income was used to buy more molasses which was then

With whom did the people of New England trade?

Colonial Society   109

Colonial Trade Routes

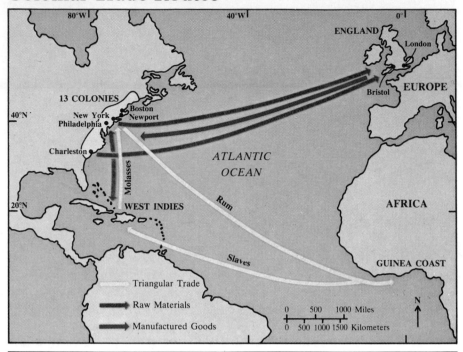

The flow of trade between the colonies and England involved raw materials from the colonies for goods made in England. Notice also the triangular trade routes. What three areas did this trade connect? What goods were traded?

brought to New England. This routine became known as the *triangular trade*.

What colonies made up the Middle Colonies?

3.2 The Middle Colonies.   The people in the Middle Colonies—New York, New Jersey, Pennsylvania, and Delaware—were quite different in their national backgrounds and religious beliefs. The Scots were mostly Presbyterian. The largest religious group among the Germans, Finns, and Swedes was Lutheran. The Dutch were Reformed, Lutheran, and Catholic. Most of the French were Huguenots (Protestants). Quakers, Baptists, and Methodists were mainly English and Welsh. The Jews who settled in New York and Philadelphia in the 1600's were Spanish and Portuguese.

Differences in nationality and religion prevented close political cooperation in the Middle Colonies. Town meetings were not used. Instead, decisions were usually made by government officials in an elected colonial assembly.

Who ran education in the Middle Colonies?

Public education in the Middle Colonies was not widespread. There were a number of schools and academies, usually run by private or church groups. Several schools of higher education were founded in the 1700's. The College of New Jersey, started in 1746 by the

Presbyterians, later became Princeton University. The Philadelphia College was chartered in 1754 and later became the University of Pennsylvania. The Church of England set up Columbia University in New York City in 1754. And the Dutch Reformed Church founded Rutgers University in 1766 in New Jersey.

Farming was the main way of making a living in the Middle Colonies. The size of the farms varied. There were the huge estates of the Dutch in New York. There were the small farms of the Germans and the Scots in Pennsylvania. Because all the farms produced mostly grains—corn, wheat, rye, barley—the Middle Colonies became known as the "Bread Colonies."

What was grown in the Middle Colonies?

The land of the Middle Colonies was more fertile than that in New England. It produced more than enough for the people who lived there to use. Farmers sold their surplus goods. Three important rivers—the Hudson, Delaware, and Susquehanna—which cut through the area were ways for farmers to move these goods to the merchants in the coastal cities of New York City, Philadelphia, and Baltimore.

During the colonial period, manufacturing in the Middle Colonies was usually done by people in their homes. Family members spun and wove textile goods, and artisans worked with iron, glass, and paper. Outside the home, other industries grew up. Sawmills produced large amounts of lumber, mills provided flour, and ovens baked bricks for building homes.

Trade between the colonies was as great as overseas trade, as ships moved up and down the coast, taking the goods of one colony to another. Those colonies which lacked good ports had to send their goods to nearby colonies before they could be exported.

A ready supply of trees helped shipbuilding become a profitable industry in the colonies. Shipyards in the New England and Middle colonies built ships for trade and fishing. What kinds of skilled people did a community need to build ships?

Rice Hope, a Carolina plantation, was typical of the large farms in the South. Dr. William Read owned Rice Hope. What were the major crops grown by planters like Dr. Read?

What colonies made up the Southern Colonies?

3.3 The Southern Colonies.   In the Southern Colonies—Maryland, Virginia, North Carolina, South Carolina, and Georgia—one religion and one social group dominated the area. The Church of England (in America known as the Episcopal church) was the leading religion. Political life was directed by planters.

The scattering of people over the large area of the Southern Colonies made it difficult to organize a public school system. Children of planters were usually taught at home by tutors. The other children worked on the farms and received little formal education. The only college in the Southern Colonies was William and Mary, founded in Williamsburg, Virginia, in 1693.

Farming was by far the most important way of life in the Southern Colonies. There were many small farms throughout the area, especially in the western valleys. Farmers there grew corn, grains, fruits, and vegetables. They usually worked their own land and lived on what they grew.

Who controlled southern political and business life?

A handful of planters ruled the southern political and business life. They controlled most of the farming and the *exporting* (sending out goods) and *importing* (bringing in goods) from other countries. The tobacco, rice, and *indigo* (a vegetable dye used on cloth) grown on the plantations of the Southern Colonies were in great demand in England. The planters made a large profit on these crops because they did not have to pay the slaves who were forced to work their large plantations. The wealth of most planters was in land and slaves. But they often had little cash for the things they needed. So, although southern planters were wealthy, they were also generally in debt.

Make students aware that the importance to the Southern Colonies of exports will come up again later, during the study of sectionalism.

112   Colonial Society

3.4   The Western Frontier.   The number of people in the three major regions grew rapidly. As this happened, more and more settlers moved west into the fresh lands on the outer limits of the colonies, called the *frontier*. In the 1600's, this meant the eastern foothills of the Appalachian Mountains. By the early 1700's, people from Pennsylvania, Virginia, and North Carolina pushed farther west. They passed through gaps in the Alleghenies and the Blue Ridge Mountains and moved into the lands of the Ohio Valley.

Where was the frontier?

Life on the frontier was hard and rugged. There were no luxuries, fine manners, or fancy clothes. Most frontier settlers lived isolated lives. Families had to rely on themselves for their material and spiritual needs. They cleared their own land and built their own one-room cabins. They made their furniture, raised their food, and made most of their clothes. There were no schools, and children had little formal education. Frontier families were usually very large. Children had regular duties on the farm and in the home.

The idea of frontier will be a continuing one. Point out, as study progresses, how the frontier changed from generation to generation.

What was life like on the frontier?

1. How were the geographic regions of the colonies different from one another?
2. What early colleges were established in each region?
3. What colonial products were in demand in England?

4. From Conflict to Unity

Threats and dangers from outside often cause people with different points of view to work together for their common safety. This is what happened to many of the English colonies in North America. People there still had different religions, different local political systems, and different ways of life. But they found they had to work together if they were to solve common problems.

What dangers did the people in the English colonies face?

4.1   The Settlers and the Indians.   Most settlers in the English colonies fought with many Indian groups almost from the moment they arrived. As more settlers came to the colonies, they took over land where the Indians had lived and hunted for hundreds of years. The Indians saw the land being taken away and their ways of life being destroyed. So they often fought back. In 1622, Indians killed nearly one third of the settlers at Jamestown. The settlers answered the attack with a long series of wars against the Indian groups in Virginia. They destroyed Indian crops and burned their villages to the ground.

The land conflict will be a continuing theme in Indian-white relations.

What was the basic cause of trouble between the Indians and colonists?

In New England, the Pequot Indians united in 1637 to drive out the settlers along the Connecticut River. The colonists struck back, killing over 500 men, women, and children in a Pequot camp. In 1643, the colonists of Massachusetts Bay, Plymouth, Connecticut, and New Haven joined together in the New England Confederation. A *confederation* is a loose union of people or groups for shared support and action. The New England Confederation was formed to protect the member colonies against the French and Dutch settlements as well as against the Indians. It was an early example of colonists working together for protection.

Several Indian groups in New England joined together under a Wampanoag chief known as "King Philip." In the summer of 1675, they set out to drive the settlers from the land. The Indians attacked settlement after settlement. After the death of King Philip in the spring of 1676, the fighting gradually ended. But the war made longtime enemies of the northeastern Indians and the New England settlers.

Students should realize the consequences for Indians of the expansion of settlement. These included entire groups being destroyed and survivors merging with other Indian groups or moving farther west. This last often brought conflict between groups of Indians over land.

In Pennsylvania, William Penn and his Quaker followers established good relations with the Indians at first. The settlers usually abided by the terms of treaties. But later they, too, found it easy to force the Indians west. When the Scots and other groups began moving into the western lands during the early 1700's, fighting became more frequent between the settlers and the Indians there. Conflict between the two groups continued all through the colonial period. It provided a powerful force in pulling colonists together for their common defense.

4.2 The Colonists and the Crown. During the time of settlement, the English did not pay much attention to their colonies. The colonists were allowed to handle their own affairs. After King Charles II came to the throne in 1660, however, the English government decided to set up stricter rules and regulations. It wanted to use the colonies to increase wealth in England. The government began to follow a policy of *mercantilism.* According to this policy, the colonists were to produce raw materials not found in England. They were supposed to sell these raw materials only to England. In addition, the colonies were not to make anything they could buy from England.

What was the basic
cause of trouble be-
tween the colonies
and England?

Be sure that students understand that mercantilism was a means for England to make a profit from its colonies.

To enforce this policy, many laws were passed in England to control colonial trade. The Navigation Acts of the 1660's listed such colonial products as tobacco, cotton, indigo, and turpentine which must be exported to England only. The English government ruled that colonists could import only English goods. All goods traded between the colonies and England had to be carried on English or colonial ships. One of the most profitable businesses in the colonies was the sugar trade with the West Indies. In an effort to stop the colonists from trading with

Checking Points of View
SKILL

Historians have seen the American Indian from many points of view. Their attitudes are usually based on the popular opinion of their time. Here are two selections written at different times in American history.

Michel Guillaume Jean de Crèvecoeur in 1775 described what sometimes happened in the colonies after the French and Indian War. During the war, Indians captured some of the colonists' children.

Many an anxious parent I have seen last war, who at the return of the peace, went to the Indian villages where they knew their children had been carried . . . ; when to their [great] sorrow, they found them so perfectly Indianized, that many . . . chose to remain; and the reasons they gave me would greatly surprise you: the most perfect freedom, the ease of living, the absence of those cares . . . which so often [are with] us . . . made them prefer that life of which we entertain such dreadful opinions. . . .

Allan Nevins had another way of looking at the Indians in 1927.

They were physically of fine [build], strong and active. . . . Their chief [kind] of wealth consisted of their herds of ponies and of their weapons. . . . they were quite unable to understand the desire of the white man to [take over] any part of the earth. Their government was simple and, in a sense, democratic, [made up of] a leadership of chiefs who [gained] their [offices] by skill and courage and whose [authority] was most [strictly] exercised in time of war or other emergency.

These proud, stern, and really [frightening] peoples . . . had many faults but . . . [their] courage and [bravery] touched even their enemies to [admire them]. . . .

Having read these selections, answer the following questions.

1. What does each historian seem to be saying about the Indians?
2. What would make them each have a different point of view?
3. What can you say about people who write history, after reading these descriptions?
4. Can you think of other subjects over which historians might have different opinions?

Colonial Economy

82°W	**76°W**	**70°W**

MAINE
(Part of Mass.)

N.H.

Portsmouth

N.Y.

Albany

MASS.

Boston

CONN.

Newport

R.I.

New London

New York

PA.

N.J.

Philadelphia

40°N

MD.
Baltimore

DEL.

ATLANTIC
OCEAN

VA.

Norfolk

New
Bern

36°N

N.C.

	New England Colonies
	Middle Colonies
	Southern Colonies

S.C.

N
↑

0	100	200 Miles
0	100	200	300 Kilometers

GA.

Charleston

32°N

Savannah

	Trade Centers		Rum		Rice
	Tobacco		Fur		Glass
	Iron		Grain		Lumber
	Paper		Cattle		Fishing
	Shipbuilding		Indigo		Naval Stores

The colonies could not export enough raw materials to pay for the manufactured goods from England they needed. So colonists set up their own industries. How did the colonies differ in economic development?

the French and Spanish West Indies, England passed the Molasses Act of 1733. It made the colonists pay more for sugar, molasses, and rum imported from any place outside English territory.

Mercantilist laws also put restrictions on colonial manufacturing. The Woolen Act of 1699 stopped the colonists from exporting wool products. The Hat Act of 1732 and the Iron Act of 1750 also limited manufacturing. These laws were designed to keep colonial manufacturers from competing with English manufacturers.

Mercantilism hurt some colonial economic interests, but it also benefited them in several ways. Some colonists had a monopoly on the sale of several major crops—tobacco, rice, and indigo. Merchants took part in a trade that was closed to other countries. And during the era of almost constant wars at sea, colonial ships were protected by the powerful English navy.

How did mercantilism benefit the colonists?

Despite these benefits, merchants, traders, and leaders in business had reacted against the English laws by finding ways to avoid them by the early 1700's. Colonies carried on their own trade with foreign countries. They imported manufactured goods directly into the colonies. They used their own ships to smuggle tea from Holland, textiles from France, wine from Portugal, and molasses and sugar from the West Indies. The colonists were slowly uniting against the economic rules laid down by the English government.

In 1707, England and Scotland became Great Britain. Thereafter it is correct to refer to Britain and the British.

4.3 The British and the French.   The third major threat to British colonial security was the presence of the French in North America. They had started building their empire at the same time the British started theirs. In 1608, one year after the founding of Jamestown, the French had started a settlement at Quebec. Both countries wanted to extend their empires, and they sometimes claimed the same lands in North America.

Why was there friction between the French and the British in North America?

In the late 1600's and early 1700's, the British and the French engaged in a series of wars to see which would be the leading world power. The fighting took place in many parts of the world—in Europe, India, the West Indies, and North America. In America, these wars became known as King William's War (1689–1697), Queen Anne's War (1702–1713), and King George's War (1744–1748). The French and their Indian allies raided frontier settlements in the Middle Colonies and New England. Colonists, in turn, attacked French posts along the Canadian border.

The rivalry between Britain and France finally became a worldwide struggle that once again involved Europe and India, as well as North America. The fighting began in America over the question of whether France or Britain owned the Ohio Valley. In the spring of 1754, the

The Ohio Valley was most important because of profitable fur trade centered there. The British hoped to have their allies the Iroquois, keep control of the area. The Iroquois were valuable fighters on the side of Britain in the war.

governor of Virginia, Robert Dinwiddie, sent 21-year-old George Washington and a small military force to stop the French from building Fort Duquesne, near present-day Pittsburgh, Pennsylvania. The French with Indian allies drove Washington off, and the French and Indian War began.

To discuss action and defense, leaders from Maryland, Pennsylvania, New York, and the New England colonies met at Albany, New York, in June 1754. At this meeting, Benjamin Franklin of Pennsylvania suggested a Plan of Union. Under this plan, the colonies would join together under a president general named by the king. A grand council would also be created, elected by the colonial assemblies. Together with the king and the president general, it would make laws for the colonies.

Franklin's Plan of Union was turned down by the colonies and by the English government. The colonial governors did not want to lose power to a president general. The colonial assemblies did not want to share their authority with those outside their own areas. The king did not want still another set of leaders in America. So the colonies remained as separate as before. When fighting broke out in 1754, the colonists found themselves at war with the French.

What was Franklin's Plan of Union?

Where did the French and Indian War begin?

In 1775, French soldiers and their Indian allies attacked a British force under the command of General Braddock (center) in Western Pennsylvania. What caused a conflict between the French and the British?

At first, the French and Indian War went badly for the British and the colonists. British General Edward Braddock and his soldiers were sent against the French at Fort Duquesne in 1755. Braddock and his soldiers, however, never got there. On the way, the French surprised them, firing from behind trees and bushes. Braddock was killed, and the British were defeated. This loss opened up the entire frontier to attacks by the French and their Indian allies. The British government and the colonies could not agree upon a course of action.

Things changed greatly in 1758, when William Pitt was put in charge of the British war effort. By using money and the army wisely, Pitt was able to change the course of the war. British forces took the offensive. They defeated the French in a number of battles during 1758 and 1759. In the fall of 1759, British General James Wolfe defeated General Louis Montcalm and his French forces on the Plains of Abraham, a plateau near the city of Quebec. The British captured Quebec, and the following spring, they captured Montreal. After suffering serious defeats in Europe, India, and the West Indies as well, France finally agreed to surrender.

What events led to defeat of the French by the British?

In 1763, Britain and France signed the Treaty of Paris. It officially ended the series of wars around the world and set down peace terms. According to the treaty, Britain received from France all of Canada and all the lands east of the Mississippi River. Britain also got all of Spanish Florida, since Spain had helped France in the war. Spain had been given Louisiana in 1762 to encourage it to join the war on the side of France. The Treaty of Paris marked the end of France as a colonial power in North America.

What were the terms of the Treaty of Paris of 1763?

1. Why was there conflict between the Indians and the settlers?
2. How did mercantilism affect the colonies?
3. Why were the French a threat to British colonial security?

5. Conclusion

There was rejoicing in the colonies over the end of the French and Indian War. The French were no longer a threat. Britain had succeeded in defending its claim to all the land of North America east of the Mississippi River. Its empire now extended from Hudson Bay in the north to the tip of Florida in the south. The young English king, George III, was hailed by the colonists. Yet in the next dozen years, events in colonial America would lead to war between Britain and the colonies.

Chapter 4 Review

Main Points

1. People who settled in the English colonies came from many different parts of Europe and Africa.
2. Most Europeans who immigrated to the colonies wanted to come. Most Africans came against their wills.
3. All of the people in the colonies contributed to a new American culture.
4. English culture most influenced the colonial way of life.
5. Life in the colonies varied with the differences in geography.
6. The English colonies can be divided into three groups—New England Colonies, Middle Colonies, and Southern Colonies.
7. Fear of the Indians, French, and Spanish and disagreements with the English encouraged unity among the colonists.
8. The French and Indian War began in 1754. After several defeats, the French surrendered and signed the Treaty of Paris in 1763.

Building Vocabulary

1. Identify the following:

   Anne Bradstreet
   Phillis Wheatley
   New England Colonies
   Congregationalism
   Middle Colonies

   "Bread Colonies"
   Southern Colonies
   New England Confederation
   King Philip
   Fort Duquesne

   Franklin's Plan of Union
   General Edward Braddock
   General James Wolfe
   General Louis Montcalm
   Treaty of Paris

2. Define the following:

   immigrated
   rural
   urban
   planters
   indentured servants

   slaves
   town meeting
   triangular trade
   exporting

   importing
   indigo
   frontier
   confederation
   mercantilism

Remembering the Facts

1. Why did Europeans settle in the English colonies? Why did Africans?
2. What were the two largest national groups in the English colonies?
3. How did most of the people in the colonies make a living?
4. Why was a large family an advantage in colonial society?

5. Which rights did men have under English law that women did not?
6. In which region of the colonies was public education most widespread? Which region grew mostly grain?
7. Where was the colonial frontier in the early 1600's? in the 1700's?

8. Why was the New England Confederation formed?
9. How did the colonists react to mercantilism?
10. How was William Pitt able to change the course of the French and Indian War?

Understanding the Facts

1. Why did the American culture develop differently from those cultures of the people who settled the colonies?
2. How did indentured servants differ from slaves?
3. Why did the colonial regions develop various ways of doing some things?

4. What threats and dangers caused the colonists to seek to unite in some of their actions?
5. How did the English hope to profit from the colonies?
6. How did the British win the French and Indian War?

Using Maps

Keys and Legends. Thematic maps contain various codes or keys to provide information or tell the story of the theme. A list of the keys with their meanings is called a legend.

Examine the map on page 116 and read the legend in the lower right corner. The legend contains keys which give information on the three major regions of the colonies and the various major products of the colonies.

On the map, the keys show the map symbols for the location of a region, a country, or an item. Notice that some of the keys are symbols and some are colors. After you have studied the map, answer the following questions.

1. Which color on the map shows the Southern Colonies?
2. Which color shows the Middle Colonies?
3. Which color shows the New England Colonies?
4. Which region in colonial America produced the most iron?
5. In which region were most of the trading centers located?
6. Which colonial region was closest to good fishing waters?
7. Which trading centers were closest to the supplies of naval stores?
8. What was produced in quantity in all regions of colonial America?

Winning Freedom 5

England's colonial empire was more loosely controlled than those of other European nations during the Age of Colonization. By the mid-1700's, the colonists and the British government had drifted quite a bit apart. Why?

The end of the French and Indian War in 1763 marked a turning point in relations between Britain and its American colonies. Britain decided to tighten its controls over the colonies, and the colonists disagreed with the change in policy. Each side found it hard to see the other's point of view. In the years that followed, the colonists and the British government drifted farther apart.

1. The Road to Rebellion

To the people of the colonies, the British victory in the French and Indian War brought a new feeling of security. The French threat had been ended, and the power of the Indians along the frontier had been greatly weakened. Victory also meant to American colonists that they no longer had to depend on the British military for their defense. Most colonists were proud of being part of the British Empire. But when the war was over, they looked forward to living their own lives as free as possible from Britain.

For more than a century and a half, the British government had been too busy to control the colonies strictly. There had been political quarrels in Britain and a series of wars with France for almost 75 years. After 1763, Britain was at peace, and it turned its attention to the American colonies.

Following victory in the French and Indian War, what did the colonists expect?

1.1 New British Policies. Britain changed the way it treated the colonies because of the needs it had after the French and Indian War. The war had cost a great deal of money, and the British government faced large debts. Many leaders in Britain felt that the colonies should help pay a part of the debts. They said that the war had been fought in large measure to protect the colonies from the French and their Indian allies.

The British government also had to decide how to handle the land west of the Appalachian Mountains. British traders and merchants wanted the Indians to control it to guarantee them a continued supply of furs. The British government wanted to stop the spread of settlement west of the mountains. Keeping the colonies along the Atlantic coast would make them easier to control and would reduce Indian-white tensions.

In 1763, George III formed a new group of advisors under the leadership of George Grenville. With the king's support, Grenville introduced new policies for the colonies. One idea was to have the

What did the British do?

Several groups of Indians in the Ohio Valley rose against the English in 1763. This was called Pontiac's Conspiracy, after a chief of the Ottawa who led it. Many British forts were captured before peace was made in 1766. The fighting showed the fear of the Indians of further loss of their land to the English colonies.

colonies strictly obey the Navigation Acts. These laws, passed in the late 1600's, were to limit colonial trade only to Britain. The colonies had been trading with other areas, and this was illegal. In addition, Grenville introduced a new series of laws. These laws together are known as the Grenville Acts.

Clarify for students why the British favored the Proclamation, why it was beneficial to the Indians, and why it was opposed by most colonists.

1.2   The Grenville Acts.   The Grenville Acts included several separate parts. Three of these resulted in much disagreement between Britain and the colonies. The first was the Proclamation of 1763. It prevented colonists from settling west of the Appalachian Mountains. Indian groups living in the area were to be left to themselves in order to protect the valuable fur trade.

The second was the Sugar Act of 1764. Grenville wanted to raise more money from colonial trade. So he placed a tax on sugar, wines, and coffee and set up a plan to enforce the collection of the tax on

Some people in Boston burned stamps to protest the Stamp Act (left). The Sons of Liberty used signs (bottom right) to keep people from using them. Examples of British stamps are shown here (top right). What was the Stamp Act?

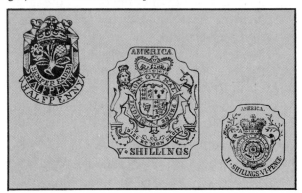

molasses. More British navy ships were to patrol the American coast to stop smuggling. People caught smuggling were to be tried in naval courts rather than civil courts. The naval courts had no juries. In the past, colonial civil juries often did not convict people accused of smuggling.

The third major part of the Grenville Acts was the Stamp Act, passed in 1765. According to this, people had to buy stamps to put on all newspapers, pamphlets, contracts, wills, and certain other printed materials. The money raised from the sale of the stamps was to be used to help pay for British soldiers stationed in the colonies.

What acts were included in the Grenville Acts?

1.3 The Colonial Response. The British leaders felt they were right in passing the Grenville Acts. The colonies, on the other hand, felt that the British government took improper steps to control them. A storm of protest broke out in the colonies over the Grenville Acts. Many colonists insisted that Britain was trying to ruin colonial trade. They also felt they had the right to settle on land west of the Appalachian Mountains. And colonists protested against what they thought was illegal British taxation.

Part of the disagreement was over the meaning of representation in government. Voters in England selected the members of Parliament to represent all the people of the British Empire. These members did not represent a certain town, county, or area. This was called *virtual representation.* In the colonial legislatures, the idea of *direct representation* had developed. This meant that people of a certain area selected a representative who worked for that area. No American colonists sat in Parliament. Therefore, the colonists felt that they were not represented. In attacking the Stamp Act, Patrick Henry of Virginia stated that "taxation without representation is tyranny!"

What was at the core of the disagreement between the colonies and Britain?

Focus attention on the differences between the two types of representation. Ask students what type is used in the U.S. today.

The one part of the Grenville Acts which created the most protest was the Stamp Act. It was the first act passed that was not a tax on trade. Rather, it was a *direct tax,* or one which must be paid to the government and is not included in the price of goods. Colonial merchants and leaders were determined to force the British government to repeal the act.

What is a direct tax?

Measures were taken against the policies of the British government. The colonists organized a *boycott*—they refused to buy British goods. People were told not to buy the tax stamps. Also groups were formed to scare tax officials. Delegates from nine colonies met in New York City in October 1765 to discuss the Stamp Act. This meeting was known as the Stamp Act Congress. The congress stated that no taxes had ever been passed for the colonies except by their own legislatures. They called upon the British government to repeal the Stamp Act.

What is a boycott?

The Stamp Act Congress was important as a sign of growing colonial unity.

This cartoon is titled "The Horse America, Throwing His Master." It was published in the 1770's. Do you think it was drawn by a British or colonial cartoonist? Why?

Parliament repealed the act in March 1766. British merchants complained that Americans had stopped buying their goods, and they pressured British officials to change the law. The boycott had worked. But the British government did not completely back down. Parliament passed the Declaratory Act which let the colonists know that the British government had the right to pass laws for the colonies in all cases.

1.4 The Townshend Acts. Relations between Britain and the colonies began to improve until George III selected new advisors. In 1767, Charles Townshend, a member of the group, proposed a series of taxes that would help raise money from the colonies. These were the Townshend Acts. New naval courts were set up, and taxes were placed on lead, paper, paint, glass, and tea. Townshend also proposed that money collected be used to pay certain British officials in the colonies. In the past, these officials depended upon money voted to them by the colonial legislatures. Because the colonial legislatures controlled the salaries, they had a great deal of influence on British officials.

What were the provisions of the Townshend Acts?

A new round of protests began over the passage of the Townshend Acts. New boycotts of British goods were started. Letters of protest were sent to Parliament. The Massachusetts legislature called for the other colonial legislatures to unite against the Townshend Acts. The colonists protested that they should not be taxed by Parliament since they were not represented there. They also viewed as dangerous the paying of officials with money raised from the new taxes.

Into what groups did the colonists divide?

As the conflicts between the British and the colonists increased, the American people divided into two groups. Those colonists who supported a possible break with Britain were called *patriots*. Those who remained loyal to England were called *loyalists*. In some colonies, patriot groups known as the Sons of Liberty were formed to enforce the boycott of British goods and to scare British officials stationed in the colonies.

On the night of March 5, 1770, a crowd of people led by the Sons of Liberty gathered in the streets of Boston and threw snowballs at a British guard. Other soldiers arrived to help the guard and were attacked by members of the crowd with sticks and pieces of ice. Some of the soldiers shot into the crowd, killing three people and wounding several others. A trial later determined that the soldiers were acting in self-defense. Patriot leaders, like Samuel Adams of Massachusetts, used the so-called Boston Massacre to increase dislike of the British. The clash had little impact outside of Massachusetts, however.

At the same time as the Boston Massacre, new leaders in Parliament forced a repeal of the Townshend Acts except for the tax on tea. The tea tax was kept to let the colonies know that the British leaders felt that they had the right to pass such laws. With the repeal came a period of calm for the next three years.

Make students aware that "loyalist" and "patriot" depend upon a person's point of view and each had a particular meaning in this period.

What was the Boston Massacre?

Lawyer John Adams defended the British soldiers in the trial.

Paul Revere's engraving of the Boston Massacre appeared in *The Boston Gazette* in 1770. Note the "Butcher's Hall" sign over the customs house to the right. How did this engraving turn many colonists against the British?

The passage of the Tea Act illustrates a political action taken for economic reasons. Have students look for other such actions during their study of the Revolution.

1.5   The Boston Tea Party.   In 1773, the British government passed a law aimed at saving the East India Company from going bankrupt. This huge trading company was important in India and elsewhere in the British Empire. British officials feared that if it went bankrupt, it might hurt the British economy. So Parliament passed the Tea Act.

Under the plan, the company could ship 17 million pounds of unsold tea directly for sale in America. Other importers of tea had to land their product in England first and had to sell it to merchants there for resale. This added to the cost of the tea. Parliament wanted the East India Company to be able to sell its tea much cheaper than anyone else. The idea that the East India Company was to have a monopoly of the tea trade angered merchants in the colonies. They asked themselves what was to keep the British leaders from giving the same advantages to other companies for other goods.

From South Carolina to Massachusetts, there were riots and even destruction of East India Company tea. On the night of December 16, 1773, the Boston Sons of Liberty, dressed as Mohawk Indians, dumped the tea cargo from three ships into Boston harbor. This famous "Tea Party" was the patriots' response to the British tea policy.

When was the Boston Tea Party?

Refer students to the use of language to show growing conflict between the colonies and Britain. Have them consider such terms as "Boston Massacre," "Intolerable Acts," along with "patriots" and "loyalists."

1.6   The Intolerable Acts.   The British leaders were shocked and angered by the Boston Tea Party. Many feared that the destruction of the tea was a direct threat to the authority of the government. They felt that the colonies must be shown that Britain did not intend to put up with those kinds of actions without an answer.

Members of Parliament moved in the spring of 1774 to punish Massachusetts for destroying the tea. A series of laws were passed that became known in the colonies as the Intolerable Acts. These measures closed the port of Boston to shipping until the people had paid for the tea they had destroyed. Parliament also put Massachusetts under control of the royal governor, suspending the colonial legislature. The laws prevented any British official from being tried in a colonial court. They also made it possible for British troops to be *quartered*—given a place to live—in private homes.

What were some provisions of the Intolerable Acts?

Another law, the Quebec Act, angered colonists even further. This law permitted French Canadians to keep their laws, their language, and their Catholic religion. It also stated that lands west of the Appalachian Mountains and north of the Ohio River belonged to Canada, not to the American colonies. This law was meant to keep the colonists from moving into the Ohio Valley.

Why did the Quebec Act anger the colonists?

1.7   The Continental Congress.   The passage of the Intolerable Acts pushed the colonists further away from Britain. American leaders called for a meeting to discuss ways to deal with the British government. The Virginia House of Burgesses asked each colony to send delegates to Philadelphia for a Continental Congress which could plan the next move.

Representatives from every colony except Georgia met in the First Continental Congress in September 1774. They were deeply worried by the British actions but were divided in their ideas for meeting the crisis.

Where did the First Continental Congress meet?

Georgia's strongly loyalist governor, James Wright, managed to keep opinions divided among Georgia's colonists for some time.

Which issues and events were important in pushing the British and the colonists into war? How were British policies short-sighted? How were the colonists economically motivated? How could the war have been prevented?

Events Leading to the Revolution

British Actions	Year	Colonial Actions
Parliament issued the Proclamation of 1763	1763	Colonists ignored the proclamation and continued to move westward
Parliament passed the Sugar Act to raise money from colonial imports	1764	Colonists protested new taxation without colonial representation in Parliament
Parliament imposed the Stamp Act to help pay for the British troops stationed in the colonies	1765	Colonists organized a boycott of British goods and the Sons of Liberty were formed to enforce the boycott
Parliament repealed the Stamp Act and passed the Declaratory Act to assert its authority	1766	Colonists welcomed the repeal of the Stamp Act and did not protest the Declaratory Act
Parliament passed the Townshend Acts to raise more money from colonial imports	1767	Colonists organized new boycotts after violent protests in Massachusetts
Parliament stationed more soldiers in Boston	1768	Colonists in 12 of the 13 colonies refused to import British goods
Parliament repealed the Townshend Acts except for a tax on tea	1770	Colonists clashed with British soldiers in Massachusetts, leading to the so-called Boston Massacre
Parliament passed the Tea Act, giving the monopoly on the tea trade to the East India Company	1773	Colonists protested the act and members of the Boston Tea Party destroyed a cargo of tea on a British ship
Parliament passed acts to close the Boston port, to suspend the Massachusetts charter, to house soldiers in colonial homes, and to prevent colonists from moving into the western frontier	1774	Colonists answered the so-called Intolerable Acts by calling a Continental Congress and by establishing a Continental Association to enforce a boycott of British goods
Parliament declared Massachusetts in a state of rebellion and sent soldiers to Lexington and Concord, Massachusetts	1775	Colonists called a Second Continental Congress and established a Continental Army

Some like James Duane of New York and Joseph Galloway of Pennsylvania hoped to ask the king for help. If George III would aid them, they would remain in the British Empire. They believed there were still some advantages to being tied to England and under Parliament's rule. Patriots like John Adams of Massachusetts and Patrick Henry of Virginia took the view that Parliament had no authority over the colonies. Even these patriots, however, were willing to try to make peace before starting to fight.

What steps did the First Continental Congress take?

The First Continental Congress took two major steps. As some delegates wished, a letter of grievances was sent to the king. The letter accepted the British leaders' right to govern colonial trade, but it asked the leaders to repeal laws which had been passed since 1763. These were the laws to which the Americans objected.

In a more extreme move, the First Continental Congress created a Continental Association. It was to enforce a boycott of British goods until Parliament repealed the Intolerable Acts. Some patriots burned British goods and tarred and feathered loyalists who would not join the boycott. Imports from England dropped to almost nothing.

1.8   The Final Break.   George III and the British leaders were determined not to back down again. They wanted British soldiers in America to enforce the laws. Early in 1775, British General Thomas Gage in Boston learned that patriots were collecting guns and ammunition and storing them at Concord, Massachusetts, near Boston. Gage, recently made governor of the colony, planned to take military action to stop them.

Why did the British march on Lexington and Concord?

See more on Revere's ride in the Skill Feature for this chapter on page 131.

On the evening of April 18, Gage sent 800 soldiers to seize the military supplies. Patriots in Boston heard of the move and sent Paul Revere and William Dawes to warn the patriots at Concord. The British soldiers arrived at Lexington, a town between Boston and Concord, at dawn. They were met there by 70 *minutemen*—patriot soldiers who could be ready for duty at a moment's notice. Shooting broke out, and eight minutemen were killed. At Concord, there was more fighting, but it ended by noon and the British were turned back to Boston. Meanwhile all the minutemen of the countryside had been called to arms. On the 15-mile march back to Boston, they shot at the British from behind trees and stone walls. The British march became a retreat.

What did the Second Continental Congress do in the spring of 1775?

With the fighting at Lexington and Concord, a war had started. A Second Continental Congress met in Philadelphia on May 10, 1775. The delegates named George Washington of Virginia as commander-in-chief of colonial armed forces, the Continental Army. For those still hoping for peace, the delegates sent to George III one last appeal—the Olive Branch Petition. George turned it down, and he declared that the

Reading Primary and Secondary Sources
SKILL

Among the important sources of information for historians are written records. They establish facts and help to interpret meaning. These records may be firsthand, or primary, sources which tell the author's own ideas. Others are secondhand, or secondary, sources which tell about other people's ideas. The two selections that follow tell about Paul Revere's part in the battles of Lexington and Concord.

Henry Wadsworth Longfellow wrote the poem "Paul Revere's Ride" in 1860.

Listen, my children, and you shall
   hear
Of the midnight ride of Paul Revere,
On the eighteenth of April, in
   Seventy-five;
Hardly a man is now alive
Who remembers that famous day and
   year.
He said to his friend, "If the British
   march
By land or sea from the town to-night,
Hang a lantern aloft in the belfry arch
Of the North Church tower as a signal
   light,—
One, if by land, and two, if by sea;
And I on the opposite shore will be,
Ready to ride and spread the alarm
Through every Middlesex village and
   farm,

For the country folk to be up and to
arm."

Another source about Revere's ride is Paul Revere's own writing.

I set off upon a very good horse; it was then about 11 o'clock, and very pleasant. After I had passed Charlestown Neck, . . . I saw two men on horseback, under a tree. When I got near them, I discovered they were British officers. One tried to get ahead of me, and the other to take me. I turned my horse very quick, and galloped towards Charlestown Neck, and then pushed for the Medford Road. The one who chased me, trying to cut me off, got into a clay pond, near where the new tavern is now built. I got clear of him, and went through Medford, over the bridge, and up to Menotomy. In Medford, I awaked the captain of the Minutemen; and after that, I alarmed almost every house, till I got to Lexington.

Answer the following questions.

1. Which of the accounts is a primary source? Which is a secondary source?
2. Which of the accounts is a more reliable report of the event?
3. Why is it more reliable?

Americans were rebels. The time for appeals was over. The Second Continental Congress became a government for the patriots in revolt.

1. What were the restrictions the British placed on the colonists after 1763?
2. Why did the colonists object to British taxes?
3. How did patriots act toward the colonists who supported Britain?

2. The War for Independence

By early 1776, the independence cause was gaining support. Some colonists remained loyal to Britain, perhaps a majority in some areas. But a large number of patriots agreed with a pamphlet written by Thomas Paine called *Common Sense*. In it, Paine set down reasons why the colonies should become independent. Paine concluded, " 'Tis time to part."

See the Profile on Thomas Paine on page 134.

2.1 The Declaration of Independence. On June 7, 1776, Richard Henry Lee of Virginia presented a resolution in the Second Continental Congress stating that "these United Colonies are, and of right ought to be, free and independent states. . . ." While the delegates talked about this idea, they named a committee of five to justify what American colonists were doing in their fight with Britain. Thomas Jefferson of Virginia, John Adams of Massachusetts, Robert Livingston of New York, Benjamin Franklin of Pennsylvania, and Roger Sherman of Connecticut made up the committee. Jefferson himself completed the final writing of what is known as the Declaration of Independence.

Who drafted the Declaration of Independence?

Jefferson wrote that all people are created equal and that all people have certain basic rights which no government can take away. He stated that all governments get their authority from the people. This was in opposition to the British government view that governments got their authority from one person, a king or queen. Jefferson also wrote that if a government did not protect the rights of the people, then the people could overthrow that government and make a new one. According to Jefferson, since George III did not protect their rights, the American colonists had the right to declare their independence.

What ideas were expressed in the Declaration of Independence?

Discuss the meaning of independence and the reasons given in the Declaration by the colonists for declaring independence. See the complete text of the Declaration in the appendix.

On July 4, 1776, the delegates of the Second Continental Congress formally approved the Declaration of Independence. Copies of it were

Thomas Jefferson (right) composed the Declaration of Independence. Benjamin Franklin (left) and John Adams (center) made several suggestions, but it remained mostly Jefferson's work. What ideas about government did Jefferson write?

sent to all the colonies to inform the people. The colonists considered themselves independent, but they still had to fight and win a war to prove it.

2.2 The Early War. Both the Americans and the British had certain advantages and faced certain problems when war began. The colonial forces were fighting on their home ground and were close to their supplies. Many Americans knew how to handle weapons, which they used for hunting. On the other hand, they were seldom trained to fight in groups and to follow military commands. They also had a limited supply of guns and ammunition.

The British army was well trained and fully equipped. Their navy was the largest and the best in the world. Still, America was 3,000 miles (4,800 kilometers) from Britain. The British soldiers were far from

List on the board the advantages and disadvantages of both sides in the war. Use the lists as the basis of discussion of the course of the war.

Thomas Paine (1737–1809)

PROFILE

One of the most effective writers on behalf of the patriot cause was Thomas Paine. He had come to America in 1774 from Britain. Working in Philadelphia as a journalist, he wrote appeals to take up the struggle against Britain.

In 1776, Paine published a pamphlet, *Common Sense*, in which he wrote that the rebelling colonists should cut their ties with the British government. Paine said that the cause of America was really the cause of all people, to overturn tyrant rulers. He demanded complete independence and the establishment of a strong union of the former colonies. *Common Sense* became the most widely read patriot pamphlet in the colonies.

During the war, Paine helped to lift the patriots' spirits by writing a series of papers titled *The Crisis*. The first of these began:

These are the times that try men's souls. . . . Tyranny, like hell, is not easily conquered; yet we have this consolation with us, that the harder the conflict, the more glorious the triumph.

After the colonies had won independence, Paine looked for other causes to champion. He urged revolt in Britain and in France. Paine spent his last years in the United States and died in 1809 almost forgotten by the American people.

Where did the early fighting take place?

The main battle took place on Breed's Hill, but history has given prominence to nearby Bunker Hill, the scene of a short action also.

home. The colonies were spread over a huge area, the land was rugged, and roads and means of communication were poor.

Early fighting took place on New England and the northeast area, especially around Boston. Soon after the fighting at Lexington and Concord, American soldiers narrowly lost the Battle of Bunker Hill. The fighting really took place on Breed's Hill, just north of Boston. Then in early 1776, the Continental Army under George Washington set up heavy guns and cannon at Dorchester Heights, hills to the south of Boston. British General William Howe in Boston realized that he could no longer hold the city. He took his troops out of Boston in March.

Thinking that the British would then attack New York, Washington moved his soldiers south to Long Island. The British landed in New York and, in a series of battles, defeated the Americans, driving them out of New York, through New Jersey, and into Pennsylvania. Late in 1776, the Americans crossed the Delaware River east from Pennsylvania into New Jersey. They surprised the enemy and defeated them at Trenton and at Princeton.

Use the map exercise in this chapter on page 145, along with a wall map to discuss the movement of the armies during the war.

The British then made plans to defeat the Americans completely in the northeast during 1777. They wanted to gain control of the Hudson River Valley in New York. To do this, General John Burgoyne and his troops would march south from Canada to the Hudson Valley by way of Albany, New York. Another British force under Colonel Barry St. Leger with Indian support would march east from Lake Ontario to Albany. Still a third force under General Howe would move north from New York City to Albany. This attack would cut New England off from the rest of the colonies.

What was the British Plan of 1777?

The British plan was a failure from the start. General Howe sent forces to capture Philadelphia, instead of Albany. Although he did take Philadelphia, he did not help Burgoyne. With New England farmers rushing to the aid of the Continental Army, St. Leger's forces moving east from Lake Ontario were defeated. All alone, Burgoyne was then defeated at Saratoga in October 1777.

The American victory at Saratoga was considered the turning point of the war. It was important to Americans because it brought France into the war. Benjamin Franklin, who was the colonial representative to France at the time, used the news of victory to persuade the French to enter the war on the side of the colonies. France was a longtime enemy of Britain, and it saw the opportunity to work for Britain's defeat. From this point on, the French, who had already given secret aid to the Americans, began helping them openly. In 1778, French leaders signed a treaty of alliance promising guns, ships, and money to the American colonies.

2.3 Organizing the War. The victory at Saratoga did not solve all the problems the Americans faced. The Continental Congress had a hard time raising money to continue the war. It did not want to pass tax laws, as the British had done. Few colonial legislatures sent money. The government tried printing its own paper money, but most colonists considered it to have no value. The government finally had to borrow as much as $10 million from allied countries like France, Spain, and Holland. Private citizens also came to the aid of the Continental Congress. Wealthy individuals like Haym Salomon and Robert Morris loaned large sums of their money to keep the army in the field.

What problems did the Americans face during the Revolution?

The Major Campaigns of the Revolutionary War (1775-1777)

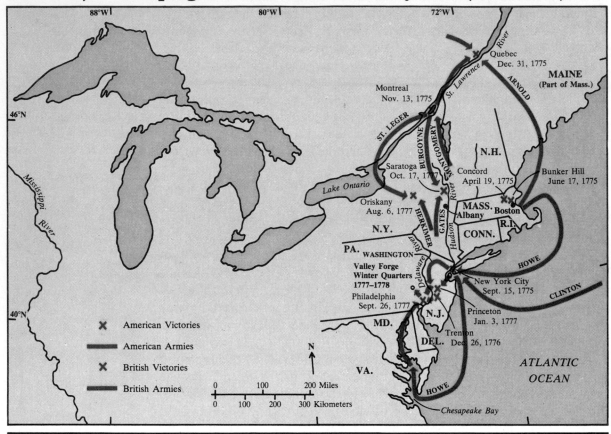

The British hoped to split the colonies by capturing the Hudson River Valley. Where did American armies defeat British armies to prevent the split? Where did British General Howe go instead of going north?

It was largely through the leadership of George Washington that the Continental Army held together. Officially, some 300,000 colonists served in the army during the war. Actually, Washington never commanded more than a few thousand at any one time. Most of his soldiers were often poorly fed and clothed. They suffered terrible hardships in their camp at Valley Forge, Pennsylvania, during the winter of 1777 and early 1778. Most of the men in Washington's army were farmers. They served a few months and then went home to help their families on the farms.

What role did women play in the war?

Few women took an active part in the fighting. Deborah Sampson, a white woman, disguised herself as a man and served in the Continental Army for several months. Deborah Gannet, a black woman, fought and

136　**Winning Freedom**

was later cited for bravery. Some women joined their husbands in camp or on the battlefields, cooking and caring for the ill and wounded. Most women worked at home, tended the farms, ran the plantations, or managed the shops while the men were away at war.

2.4   The War in the West.   In 1778 and 1779, there were a few battles west of the Appalachian Mountains. The British had forts important to the fur trade in the area. The Americans had settlements as far west as the Mississippi Valley. In an area along the Mississippi known as the American Bottoms, settlers established the towns of Cahokia and Kaskaskia. The British and their Indian allies attacked these and other settlements on the frontier.

To protect these colonists, George Rogers Clark gathered about 175 soldiers from Virginia to go into the western lands. Sweeping

Who fought the British in the West?

Prussian Baron von Steuben (left) discusses the war with Washington (right) during the harsh winter at Valley Forge. The baron was one of several foreign-born military officers fighting on the American side. Who was another?

John Trumbull painted "Surrender of Lord Cornwallis at Yorktown." Actually, Cornwallis' second in command surrendered to General Washington's second in command, General Benjamin Lincoln. When was the surrender?

through what today is Illinois and Indiana, Clark's forces overran British posts during the summer and fall of 1778. They struck at one fort, disappeared into the forest, and then struck at another fort miles away. With a victory at Vincennes in 1779, Clark established American control of the area between the Appalachian Mountains and the Mississippi River.

2.5 The War in the South. In the later part of the war, most of the fighting was in the south. British military leaders decided to capture the seaports of Charleston, South Carolina, and Savannah, Georgia. Loyalist support was strong in many areas of the south, and the British hoped to win the area.

Why did the British think they might win in the south?

Loyalists may have formed a majority of the population in South Carolina and Georgia, although no precise figures are known.

As the British army moved inland, American soldiers in small groups tried to break up their advance. Forces led by Francis Marion, Thomas Sumter, and Andrew Pickens stole horses, destroyed supplies, and shot at marching soldiers. Despite some victories, the British were unable to hold any territory.

In 1780 and 1781, the Continental Army fought the British in several major battles, winning at King's Mountain and Cowpens, South

Carolina, and at Guilford Court House, North Carolina. After this last defeat, British General Charles Cornwallis retreated to Virginia. He moved to Yorktown on the Atlantic coast to rest his soldiers and get supplies.

Washington saw a chance to trap Cornwallis. He sent a large Continental force to block the British by land. They were joined by nearly 8,000 French soldiers under the command of the Marquis de Lafayette. Late in August 1781, a French fleet of warships blocked the British from the sea. Cut off from land and sea, Cornwallis surrendered his 7,500 soldiers to Washington. This American victory ended nearly all British hope for winning the war.

Who aided Washington at Yorktown?

The British captured major seaports in the South by 1780. They planned to capture more ports to supply the British armies as they moved north. Why did this plan fail for Lord Cornwallis at Yorktown?

The Major Campaigns of the Revolutionary War (1778-1781)

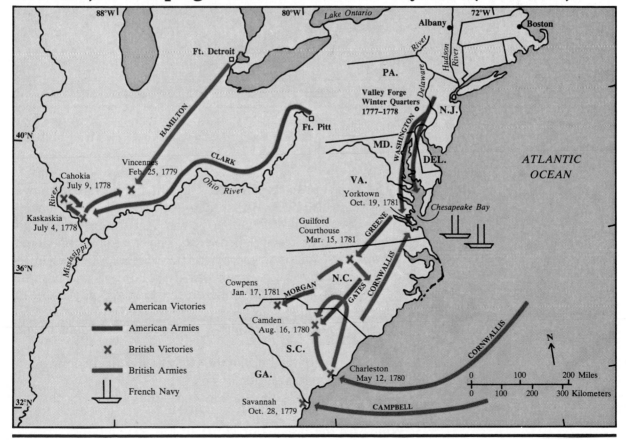

North America in 1763

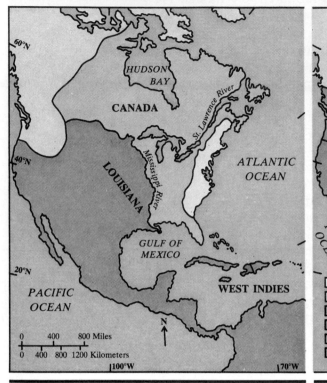

North America in 1783

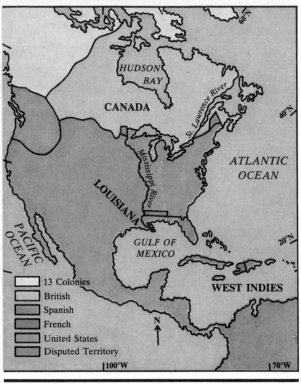

13 Colonies
British
Spanish
French
United States
Disputed Territory

In 1783, which nation gained control of the area to the south of the United States? Which areas did Britain lose? Where were disputed areas after the Treaty of Paris in 1783?

2.6 The Treaty of Paris of 1783.   Some fighting went on over the next two years. In 1783, British and American leaders signed a treaty of peace in Paris, France, ending the war. According to the terms, Britain recognized American independence. The boundaries of the new country were set at Canada in the north, the Mississippi River in the west, and Florida in the south. Spain was given Florida, and both the United States and Britain could trade on the Mississippi. Americans also got fishing rights in the waters off Newfoundland and Nova Scotia. The 13 British colonies had become a new and independent nation.

Point out that the war aim of the United States as stated in the Declaration—independence—was achieved in the Treaty of Paris.

1. Who was the commander of the Continental Army during the American Revolution?
2. Why was the Battle of Saratoga important to the Americans?
3. What was the last major battle of the Revolution?

3. The Meaning of Freedom

The American Revolution brought independence from Britain. It produced certain changes in the government, society, and economy. Independence also set in motion changes in the lives of the American people.

3.1 Political Results.   The most obvious change after the Revolution was the absence of British officials in the new states. Former British political and military leaders went home. After the war, as many as 100,000 loyalists also left the country. Many settled in Canada and the West Indies.

What were the political results of the Revolution?

Each of the 13 colonies had formed state governments during the Revolution. These governments took over when British officials lost their control. Each new state was different from the others in some ways. But they did share certain ideas. The colonies had been using British law and political structures since they were chartered. And they continued to base their state governments in part on the British system.

It is important to make the point that many political practices of the United States are based on British examples. This might make an interesting subject for student research.

The state governments had limited authority because the patriots feared what they saw as the limitless authority of the British government. They did not want their governments to be too strong. In many states, the office of governor was weak, keeping authority out of the hands of one person. Most of the authority was given to the state legislature and its members elected by direct representation.

The Revolution had brought about more demands for participation in government by more citizens. Some of the state governments were under the control of a small group of wealthy people. Voting rights based on wealth and land ownership were gradually relaxed, although they continued to be important in some states.

Women had hoped the war for independence would bring greater rights for them, too. It was a serious concern of Abigail Adams, writing a letter to her husband John at the Continental Congress.

Remember the ladies, and be more generous and favorable to them than your ancestors. Do not put such unlimited power into the hands of the husbands. Remember all men would be tyrants if they could. If particular care and attention is not paid to the ladies we are determined to foment a rebellion, and will not hold ourselves bound by any laws in which we have no voice, or representation.

Despite the hopes of many women, they still could not vote or hold office in the years after the Revolution. In most states, the husbands of

Many of the colonists who supported Britain fled to British-held Canada (left). Some patriots (right) raised a "liberty pole" in celebration of the final break with Britain. How did the Revolution affect the colonists?

married women held legal control over their property and children. Black women as well as black men in America, most of whom were slaves, were unable to take part in political life.

3.2 Social Results. The Declaration of Independence emphasized the importance of human rights. This idea carried over into the American way of thinking after the end of the war. One area in which people applied the idea of human rights was in reforming the treatment of convicted criminals. Conditions in the prisons were improved, and laws which demanded the death penalty for minor offenses were repealed.

The human rights idea was not applied to the slaves, however. During the war, some 5,000 black Americans fought for the Continental Army. At first, many colonial leaders, including Washington, were against recruiting them. After fighting in many battles, Washington praised their bravery under fire. Many black slaves fought hoping to win their own freedom.

What were the social results of the Revolution?

Discuss the difference between independence and freedom. Note the limitations on freedom for blacks, women, and Indians.

After the war, Massachusetts and New Hampshire passed laws ending slavery. Several other states in the north freed slaves on a gradual basis. Within ten years after independence, every state except Georgia had either stopped or limited the importing of new slaves. Still, the market value of the American slaves increased. Some people in the north sold their slaves to owners in the south. Slave owners there were not willing to give up the advantages of using workers who did not have to be paid.

3.3 Economic Results. By the terms of the Treaty of Paris, the United States became one of the largest nations in the world. Its borders stretched from the Atlantic Ocean in the east to the Mississippi River in the west. It was bound by the Great Lakes and Canada in the north and Spanish-owned Florida in the south. The land added to the original colonies made more space available for settlement.

What were the economic results of the Revolution?

Begin the first of a series of map studies on the changing boundaries of the United States.

After the war, the United States took an active role in world trade. America was no longer in business for Britain's needs alone, and its trade with other countries grew. People in manufacturing, which had increased during the war, found new markets in Europe.

The American Revolution led to the end of British restrictions on American trade and industry. It also brought economic problems. Because of the ways the Continental Congress paid for the war, the new government started out deep in debt to allies who had loaned it money. The government's attempt to print more money to meet financial demands lowered the value of the money already in use. America's economic fitness was tested from its start.

1. Why did the Americans limit the authority of the new state governments created during the war?
2. How were slaves affected by the American Revolution?
3. What were the economic problems of the new country after the war?

4. Conclusion

The American states in 1763 had been 13 separate and divided colonies. After the French and Indian War, the changing policies of the British government brought them together to protect what they saw as their natural rights to govern themselves. Their unity helped them to defeat the British in the War of Independence. The government which they set up during the Revolution served its purpose during the war. The question remained whether the 13 states could work together as one nation in peace.

Chapter 5 Review

Main Points

1. After the French and Indian War, Britain passed new laws to control the colonies.
2. The colonists considered the laws harmful to their economic interests.
3. Over several years, hostility mounted and led to open rebellion in 1775.
4. The colonists declared independence in July 1776.
5. After seven years of fighting, the colonial army defeated British forces and secured independence.
6. The Treaty of Paris in 1783 ended the war and set the territorial boundaries of the United States.
7. As a result of the Revolution, more free males began to take part in government.
8. There were few changes in the rights of women and of people held as slaves.
9. Because of large debts to allies who helped to pay for the war, the United States faced major economic problems at the end of the war.

Building Vocabulary

1. Identify the following:

   Grenville Acts
   Townshend Acts
   Boston Massacre
   Boston Tea Party
   Intolerable Acts
   General Thomas Gage

   Paul Revere
   Thomas Jefferson
   July 4, 1776
   Thomas Paine
   George Washington

   General William Howe
   Battle of Saratoga
   George Rogers Clark
   Marquis de Lafayette
   Treaty of Paris of 1783
   Abigail Adams

2. Define the following:

   virtual representation
   direct representation
   direct tax

   boycott
   patriots

   loyalists
   quartered
   minutemen

Remembering the Facts

1. How did the colonists respond to new British laws and regulations on colonial trade and industry?

2. Where did the First Continental Congress meet, and what was its purpose?

3. What was the role of the Sons of Liberty in the conflict with Britain? Why were such groups formed?

4. Which event was the formal statement of the colonists' demand to be independent?

5. What were the advantages and the disadvantages held by the British and the colonists in fighting the war?

6. Which European countries loaned money to the colonies to fight against Britain?

7. What were the main terms of the Treaty of Paris of 1783?

8. What political changes took place in the United States after the war?

9. How did the war influence the lives of blacks and women?

Understanding the Facts

1. Why did Britain change the way it controlled the colonies after the French and Indian War?

2. How were American trade and industry affected by laws passed by the British Parliament after 1763?

3. What were the various views of British policy among the colonists before 1776?

4. How were the colonists able to win the war?

5. How was American life changed as a result of the war and independence?

Using Maps

Tracing Routes.   The map on page 136 shows the United States during the American Revolution from 1775 to 1777. The map on page 139 shows from 1778 to 1781. Symbols, names, and dates give information about major battles of the Revolution from 1775 to 1781. Examine the maps, and answer the following questions.

In answering the questions, you must provide some information concerning directions. To help you, a symbol on the maps shows that north is the direction toward the top of the page. From this symbol, you can decide south, west, and east, as well.

1. Which keys or symbols show the routes followed by American soldiers?

2. Which army won the Battle of Bunker Hill on June 17, 1775?

3. Which direction did Washington's soldiers travel after leaving Trenton?

4. Where were Washington's troops during the winter of 1777 and 1778?

5. How far did Clark's soldiers travel from Fort Pitt to Kaskaskia?

6. Which direction did American soldiers travel to Yorktown?

7. Why was it a problem for Cornwallis to get supplies at Yorktown?

Forming a Union

In this painting of the Constitutional Convention by Thomas Rossiter, George Washington is shown presiding over the delegates. How did Americans govern themselves after they declared independence?

The people of the United States gained their political independence through the Revolution. Each of the former colonies became a state, and together, the states became a nation. Yet the future of the country was far from certain. It was still to be determined how well the states would be able to work together. Close to 3 million people, living along a coast stretching 1,200 miles (1,920 kilometers) from Georgia to Maine, had to learn to govern themselves as one country. There had been democracies before, such as the ones in ancient Greece and medieval Switzerland. None though had ever had so many people scattered over so large an area as the United States.

Have students consider what the size of a country has to do with its unity or effectiveness as a democracy. Consider direct versus representative democracy.

1. The Period of Confederation

During the colonial period, Britain had filled many of the needs of the American people—trade, defense, law, and order. The colonies had been part of a large and secure empire. After they had broken away from the empire, the 13 states tried to fill these same needs for the people. It was important that the new country quickly become strong and united.

Refer students back to Chapter 5, Section 3.1. Have them consider if the structure of the Confederation government also reflected a fear of strong government.

1.1 The Confederation Government. During the war with Britain, the Second Continental Congress was the governing body for the rebelling colonies. In 1777, the congress drew up a plan for government. Known as the Articles of Confederation, the plan was put into effect in 1781. It set up a confederation among the 13 states. The Articles protected the freedom and independence of each state. It also provided a structure for governing the country as a whole.

What was the period following the Revolution called?

The Articles of Confederation set up a one-house congress with representatives from the states. In this legislature, each state had one vote. The Confederation congress had the authority to make war and peace. It also ran the postal service, coined money, set standards of weight and measure, and managed affairs with the Indian peoples. All 13 states had to agree before an *amendment* (a change in the provisions) could be made in the Articles of Confederation. During the time that the congress was not in session, a committee of states managed the day-to-day business of the nation. One delegate from each state made up the committee.

What could the Congress of the Confederation do?

1.2 Western Lands. After the Revolution, American settlers moved into the lands west of the Appalachian Mountains in great

Settlers had begun moving west of the Appalachian Mountains after the French and Indian War, in defiance of British law.

How was land to be divided in the Northwest Territory?

State maps, one from New England and one from a state of the Northwest Territory, may be helpful to show the differences in the divisions of local government, especially townships, as a result of the Land Ordinance of 1785.

numbers. Thousands of people crossed the mountains into Kentucky and Tennessee. No definite plans had been made for this land or for the huge area north of the Ohio River, called the Northwest Territory. With the growing number of settlers, there was a need for order. To answer this need, the Confederation congress passed two *ordinances* (laws)— the Land Ordinance of 1785 and the Northwest Ordinance of 1787. They were based in part on an earlier plan of Thomas Jefferson.

The Land Ordinance of 1785 directed that the Northwest Territory be *surveyed*—examined and measured. The surveyors divided the land into townships along north-south and east-west lines forming six-mile squares. The townships were then divided into 36 sections of 640 acres. Each section was sold to one buyer. In each township, one section was set aside for the support of public education in the township.

Land in the Northwest Territory was to be sold at a price of at least $1 an acre. Because few settlers could afford to buy a whole section, land companies bought much of the land and resold it in smaller lots. The Confederation government often agreed to sell the land to these

Most American families west of the Appalachian Mountains lived in log cabins (left), and they worked small farms. First the land was cleared of trees (right). Then they planted crops. Why did settlers move to the frontier?

148   Forming a Union

The Northwest Territory

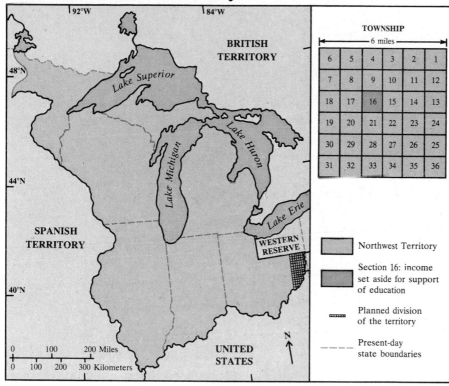

TOWNSHIP

6	5	4	3	2	1
7	8	9	10	11	12
18	17	16	15	14	13
19	20	21	22	23	24
30	29	28	27	26	25
31	32	33	34	35	36

Northwest Territory

Section 16: income set aside for support of education

Planned division of the territory

Present-day state boundaries

Why was the area north of the Ohio River called the Northwest Territory? What states were formed from this area?

companies for only a few cents an acre because the government needed the money to operate.

The township system was not used in the area south of the Ohio River, basically because settlers already lived there. Lands in Kentucky and Tennessee had been divided at random, and the settlers there had set up local governments by 1785. The system established by the Land Ordinance of 1785, however, became the United States policy for organizing new lands.

Why was the township system not used in the South?

In addition to setting up a plan for selling land, the Congress of the Confederation took care of governing the Northwest Territory. It passed the Northwest Ordinance in 1787. This law directed that the congress name a governor, a secretary, and three judges to administer the area.

The ordinance also set up the steps which a territory was to take before becoming a state. Members of the congress agreed that not less than three nor more than five states would be made from the Northwest Territory. When there were 5,000 free adult males of voting age living in

How many states could be made from the Northwest Territory?

In this George Caleb Bingham painting, Daniel Boone (center) is shown escorting settlers through the Cumberland Gap. Boone blazed some of the early trails to the west. How did trailblazers make trips west easier?

Ask how many states were made out of the Northwest Territory. Use the map on page 149. Have the students consider why the government was concerned about the number of states.

Recall that the Fundamental Orders of Connecticut was considered the first written constitution of any kind, but that it was only for a single colony.

How did Britain create problems for the new nation?

the territory, they could elect a legislature for deciding local matters. When there were 60,000 free settlers in an area of the territory, the people could apply to the national government to have the area become a state. This system provided for organizing the Northwest Territory and other areas which would become part of the United States in the future. For this reason, the Northwest Ordinance was considered one of the most important acts passed by the Congress of the Confederation.

1.3 Problems of the Confederation.   The Articles of Confederation was the first United States *constitution*—a written plan of government. The government, guided by this plan, handled the problem of the western lands. Having no strong central organization, it was unable to handle other problems, however. The weaknesses of the Confederation plan of government were seen in both foreign affairs and business at home.

One of the major problems in foreign affairs was relations with Britain. Despite the Treaty of Paris of 1783, British leaders stationed soldiers in forts in the Northwest Territory. Britain hoped to keep on good terms with the Indians in the area to save the fur trade for British merchants. The British government did not favor American trade with the British Empire either. Britain tried to keep Americans from trading directly with the nearby British West Indies, although smuggling kept such trade alive. Attempts to talk over trade agreements with Britain failed. Without British markets, there was a strain on the economy of the new nation.

Spain also created problems for the United States economy. Spanish leaders refused to allow Americans to use the port of New Orleans at the mouth of the Mississippi River. Without this port, western farmers could not ship their goods down the river to the Gulf of Mexico, then to European and other markets.

How did Spain create problems?

Americans were upset that their national government could not solve these problems. The members of the Confederation government complained that they needed funds to support an army or any other program. The government under the Articles of Confederation could not tax its citizens to raise money. The only taxing authority it had was to require postage for mail service. To keep the authority of the national government weak, the states often refused to give it money.

Using a map of the eastern United States, have students consider why, at the time, western farmers would use the Mississippi to ship their products rather than taking them directly to ports on the Atlantic. Individual research projects might tell how long it took a wagon to make such a trip and the cost relative to using the Mississippi River.

One of the most serious problems faced at home also concerned trade. The national government had no authority to control trade among the states. Each state set its own laws. One state could tax products coming in from other states. States argued over control of rivers and harbors. The people of New Jersey paid more for goods because most of their trade came through the port of New York. New York taxed the goods, and that added to the prices. In return, New Jersey taxed New York for a lighthouse built by New York on land owned by New Jersey. Similar disagreements arose between other states.

What was one of the most serious problems at home?

1.4   The Annapolis Convention.   In March 1785, representatives from Virginia and Maryland met to discuss problems between the two states. At this conference held at Mount Vernon, they worked out ways of dealing with navigation rights on their shared waterways, the Potomac River and Chesapeake Bay. The Virginia legislature then invited all the states to send delegates to a larger convention on matters of trade among the states.

This conference met at Annapolis, Maryland, in September 1786. Delegates from only five states—New York, New Jersey, Delaware, Pennsylvania, and Virginia—came to this convention, however. Two delegates at the meeting, Alexander Hamilton of New York and James Madison of Virginia, were eager to have the states consider a complete

Maryland claimed that its boundary took in the Potomac River and claimed the right to tax all Virginia trade using it. Virginia taxed all Maryland trade through the mouth of Chesapeake Bay, within Virginia's boundary.

What was the purpose of the Annapolis Convention?

Only the delegation of
New Jersey was given the
authority to consider
changes in the structure of
the national government.

overhaul of the Articles of Confederation. The members of the Annapolis Convention adopted a report written by Hamilton to hold another convention in Philadelphia. This meeting was supposed to come up with ways to revise the Articles of Confederation so that the government would be able to deal more effectively with the problems of the United States.

1.5 Shays' Rebellion. The Confederation government's money troubles hurt mostly individual citizens. Business began to slow down after the end of the war with Britain. The prices of goods began to rise, and many people could not pay their debts. Taxes rose as the states

Daniel Shays led an army of discontented farmers in an uprising against Massachusetts authorities. At the right, Shays' followers seize the courthouse in Springfield. Many Americans supported the farmers' cause. What effect did Shays' Rebellion have on the country?

Daniel Shays (1747?–1825)

PROFILE

The years following the war with Britain were not easy for most American farmers. Markets shrank, and land taxes rose. Angry Massachusetts farmers organized to oppose some of the state tax laws. One leader of the opposition was Daniel Shays.

Shays had been a captain in the army and fought at Bunker Hill, Ticonderoga, and Saratoga. After the war, he returned to a home deep in debt. He and other landowners asked the state legislature to ease the land taxes. When no action was taken by the summer of 1786, Shays gathered a force of about 500 farmers in a march on the courthouse and armory in Springfield.

The Massachusetts militia stopped the advance and scattered the farmers. Some were arrested. But so many people felt sorry for the farmers' cause that Shays and his followers, at first sentenced to death, were pardoned in 1788.

Shays' uprising influenced the state legislature not to impose new taxes that year. It also passed laws making it possible for people who were bankrupt to keep their household goods and their tools. Equally important, the uprising demonstrated the weakness of the national government under the Articles of Confederation in maintaining a strong economy. After Shays' Rebellion, there came more support for a revision of the government. The plan to revise the Articles led to the framing of a new constitution.

tried to meet their debts and pay for government services. Farmers in states like Massachusetts began to lose their land to banks because they could not make mortgage payments.

In the summer of 1786, some landowners in western Massachusetts revolted against the tax laws. They seized local courthouses in order to keep judges from approving *foreclosures*—taking away of property due to failure to make payments on its debt. Daniel Shays, who had been a soldier in the Revolutionary War, led a group of farmers on a march to a courthouse and an armory in Springfield. The march, with its threat of violence, caused the state legislature to adjourn. Shays' force finally was

Where was Shays' Rebellion?

Have students consider the responsibility of government to aid its citizens versus the need to maintain order and unity.

broken up by the state militia in February 1787. This rebellion brought the economic problems of the country into much sharper focus.

1. What were the two major accomplishments of the Congress of the Confederation?
2. How did Britain violate the terms of the Treaty of Paris of 1783?
3. How was trade between states regulated?
4. What was the basic cause of Shays' Rebellion?

2. Making the Constitution

Before starting this section, have students make a list of changes they might have made in the Articles of Confederation. Compare this later with the changes embodied in the Constitution.

The convention in Philadelphia opened May 25, 1787, when enough delegates arrived to begin work. The meetings were held in the State House, where the Declaration of Independence had been signed. Attending the convention were 55 delegates, elected by the legislatures of 12 states. The leaders of Rhode Island were against any move to strengthen the government, so they did not send delegates.

Most of the convention members were young and came from the landowning upper classes. More than half were college-trained, and many were lawyers. Benjamin Franklin of Pennsylvania, who was 81 years of age, was the oldest. Jonathan Dayton of New Jersey, who was 26 years of age, was the youngest. Franklin and George Washington were the best known of the delegates. But there were some noted leaders not present. Samuel Adams had not been selected to attend. Patrick Henry refused to attend. Thomas Jefferson and John Adams were out of the country, serving as foreign ministers in France and Britain respectively.

Who did not attend the Constitutional Convention? Why?

2.1 Conflicting Plans of Government.   An important question faced the delegates from the beginning of the convention. They had to decide if the Articles of Confederation should be improved or if an entirely new plan of government be written. Many of the delegates had received instructions to work only to improve the Articles. Other delegates felt strongly that a new plan of government was needed.

Who presented the Virginia Plan? the New Jersey Plan?

Four days after the convention opened, Edmund Randolph of Virginia presented 15 resolutions for discussion. These were known as the Virginia Plan and were meant as a design for a new national government. Debate over the Virginia Plan centered on the question of representation in the legislature. Randolph proposed that states not be represented equally. Rather, they should be represented according to either their population or the amount of money each contributed to the

Analyzing Sources of History
SKILL

Historians use many sources of information to understand an event. Written primary sources are often the most reliable record of what happened. Whenever possible, the historian tries to base an interpretation on these sources. Written primary sources include diaries, documents, eyewitness accounts, journals, letters, notes, and reports. These can be published or unpublished sources.

The following selections are written primary sources having to do with the Constitution. When the document was put before the convention on September 17, 1787, the delegates had various reactions.

James Madison of Virginia wrote very detailed notes during the convention. He recorded Benjamin Franklin's last speech to the delegates.

I confess that I do not entirely approve of this Constitution at present; but, sir, I am not sure I shall never approve it; for having lived long, I have experienced many instances of being [made], *by better information or fuller consideration, to change opinions even on important subjects, which I once thought right, but found to be otherwise. . . .*

On the whole, sir, I cannot help expressing a wish that every member of the convention who may still have objections to it would with me on this occasion doubt a little of his own [rightness] *and, to make* [clearly known] *our* [total agreement], *put his name to this instrument.*

George Mason of Virginia did not sign the Constitution. His objection to it is explained in a letter he wrote to George Washington on October 18, 1787.

There is no declaration of rights: (a bill of rights for individuals and states) and the laws of the general government being [higher than] *the laws and constitutions of the several states, the declarations of rights in the separate states are no security.*

Answer the following questions.
1. Which types of written primary sources are these selections?
2. What is Franklin's attitude toward the Constitution?
3. Why did Mason consider a declaration of rights important?
4. Which source would you consider to be more reliable? Why?

national government. With this plan, larger states would have more power.

The Virginia Plan showed clearly that many delegates were open to changing the structure of the government and not just revising the Articles of Confederation. But smaller states, like New Jersey, were against the Virginia Plan. New Jersey's William Paterson presented his own resolution. His plan, called the New Jersey Plan, insisted representation in the legislature remain the same as under the Articles. Each state would be represented equally.

What is a compromise?

2.2 The Great Compromise. The issue of representation was a difficult one. It was settled by *compromise*—a settlement of differences by each side giving up part of what it wants. The delegates decided to have two houses of congress: the Senate and the House of Representatives. Each state was to have two Senators which were to be selected by its legislature. Small and large states, therefore, would be

As delegates signed the Constitution, Benjamin Franklin (center) observed a rising sun on the president's chair and a new day for the country. Not every delegate shared his view. Why did some delegates not sign the Constitution?

equally represented in the Senate. The number of delegates in the House of Representatives would be determined by the number of people in each state. Qualified voters in each state would elect their state's Representatives. The states with the most people would have a stronger voice in the House of Representatives.

Within this so-called Great Compromise was a second compromise which resolved a conflict between slave and free states. Slave states wanted to count all slaves when deciding the population for setting the number of Representatives in the House. Free states did not want slaves figured into the count. It was agreed that three fifths of the number of slaves should be counted to determine the number of **Representatives**. It was also agreed that the slaves were to be counted the same way in deciding each state's share of taxes.

2.3 Other Compromises.   The Great Compromise helped to settle several problems facing the delegates, but there were still others to be solved. Many northern states wanted to give the national government authority to control trade. Southern states feared that such authority might be used to end the slave trade and to create high *tariffs* (taxes on imported goods). The delegates reached a compromise that was acceptable to northern and southern states. The national government was given the exclusive power to regulate trade among states and with other countries, including the power to tax imports. Congress could not, however, put a tax on any export. In addition, Congress could not interfere with the slave trade for 20 years.

Other issues had to be resolved, too. For instance, the delegates decided that the national government was to have three branches or parts. In addition to the legislature, there was to be a national executive branch, headed by a president. The executive branch was to carry out the laws passed by the legislature. The third branch, a national *judiciary*, or court system, also was set up.

The convention met through the summer months of 1787. On September 15, the plan of government was completed. The majority of the delegates signed the Constitution of the United States on September 17. James Madison recorded the event:

While the last members were signing it, Dr. Franklin looked toward the president's chair at the back of which a rising sun happened to be painted, observed to a few members near him that painters had found it difficult to distinguish in their art a rising from a setting sun. "I have," said he, "often and often in the course of the session, and the [changes between] my hopes and fears as to its issue, looked at that behind the president

What compromise was included within the Great Compromise?

The 3/5 compromise shows the strength of the slaveholders who received extra representation for their states, although the slaves themselves had no rights. Consider discussion of the contradiction of claiming slaves as property while counting them as people for purposes of representation.

What were some other compromises?

Stress the importance of compromise in forming the Constitution. Have students consider what they consider the values and limitations of compromise.

without being able to tell whether it was rising or setting. But now at length I have the happiness to know that it is a rising and not a setting sun."

To whom was the Constitution first submitted?

The document was then sent to the Congress of the Confederation. That group submitted it to the states for their approval. Citizens elected special state conventions to consider the Constitution. Nine of the state conventions had to *ratify* (approve) it before the new government could be put into effect.

1. How did the Virginia Plan differ from the New Jersey Plan?
2. What was the Great Compromise?
3. What was the three-fifths compromise?

3. The Struggle for Ratification

Why was acceptance of the Constitution not certain?

Acceptance of the Constitution by the states was not certain. In each state, there were fierce debates over whether to approve the

Eleven states quickly ratified the Constitution, but North Carolina and Rhode Island did not. The *Massachusetts Centinel* urged their acceptance August 2, 1788. Why did this cartoonist want all states to ratify?

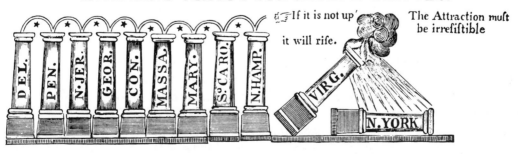

The Ninth *PILLAR* erected !

" The Ratification of the Conventions of nine States, fhall be fufficient for the eftablifhment of this Conftitution, between the States fo ratifying the fame." *Art.* vii.

INCIPIENT MAGNI PROCEDERE MENSES.

If it is not up it will rife.

The Attraction muft be irrefiftible

DEL. PEN. N·JER. GEOR. CON. MASSA. MARY. S°CARO. N.HAMP. VIRG. N.YORK

James Madison (left) and Alexander Hamilton (right) were two Federalist leaders who wrote articles supporting the Constitution. These articles were first published in New York in 1787. What were they called?

Constitution or to keep the Articles of Confederation. Some people feared the authority given to the national government. Many felt that their liberties and the rights of the states were more secure under the Articles of Confederation. They felt that, although the central government was weak, it was also safe.

3.1 Federalists and Anti-Federalists. Two different groups emerged in the struggle to ratify the Constitution. Those in favor of ratification were called Federalists, because they wanted a strong *federal* (national) government. Those against the Constitution were known as Anti-Federalists.

The ranks of the Federalists and the Anti-Federalists had people from every class, area, and economic interest. Well-known figures like George Washington and Benjamin Franklin favored ratification. James Madison, Alexander Hamilton, and John Jay carefully worded the Federalists' ideas in a series of articles for people to read in newspapers. Later the articles were bound together into two books called *The Federalist Papers*. Madison, Hamilton, and Jay tried to convince the people that the Constitution would provide a much better government

Refer students to the Skill Feature on page 155 for further discussion of reaction for and against the Constitution.

Who wrote The Federalist Papers?

The authors of The Federalist Papers wrote under the name "Publius."

Forming a Union 159

Ratification of the Constitution

Date of Ratification	State	Vote
December 7, 1787	**Delaware**	Unanimous
December 12, 1787	**Pennsylvania**	46 For, 23 Against
December 18, 1787	**New Jersey**	Unanimous
January 2, 1788	**Georgia**	Unanimous
January 9, 1788	**Connecticut**	128 For, 40 Against
February 6, 1788	**Massachusetts**	187 For, 168 Against
April 28, 1788	**Maryland**	63 For, 11 Against
May 23, 1788	**South Carolina**	149 For, 73 Against
June 21, 1788	**New Hampshire**	57 For, 47 Against
June 25, 1788	**Virginia**	89 For, 79 Against
July 26, 1788	**New York**	30 For, 27 Against
November 21, 1789	**North Carolina**	194 For, 77 Against
May 29, 1790	**Rhode Island**	34 For, 32 Against

Which state convention was the first to ratify the Constitution? Which state was the last? Which states voted unanimously for ratification? Where was the Constitution narrowly approved?

than the Articles of Confederation. The Federalists were positive in their approach to the change, and they had the advantage of support from Washington and Franklin.

Many of those who were active in the move toward independence in the 1770's supported the Anti-Federalists in 1787. Patrick Henry, Samuel Adams, George Mason, and George Clinton were among those opposing a change in the national government. To them, the new constitution would destroy the rights of the states and individual liberties of the people. They felt that the Constitutional Convention had gone beyond its authority. It was to have improved the Articles of Confederation and nothing more.

What leaders opposed ratification?

3.2 Ratification. The decision to ratify or reject the Constitution began in the state conventions in the fall months of 1787. Before the year was over, Delaware, Pennsylvania, and New Jersey had approved the Constitution. Georgia, Connecticut, and Massachusetts ratified early in 1788. In Massachusetts, Federalist supporters had a tough time winning over the convention led by Samuel Adams. In a compromise measure with the Anti-Federalists, the Federalists promised to help pass a bill of rights as soon as a new government was set up under the Constitution.

What state was first to ratify the Constitution?

Consider having students explain whether they would have voted for or against ratification.

In 1788, enough states voted in favor of ratification to put the Constitution into effect. New Hampshire was the ninth and deciding state. New York and Virginia, however, had not yet acted. Without them, the Constitution would not have the broad support it needed to

Why was it important for New York and Virginia to ratify the Constitution?

succeed. After bitter debate, both states ratified the document during the summer of 1788. By the end of 1788, only North Carolina and Rhode Island had not voted on the Constitution. North Carolina voted in favor of it in 1789. Rhode Island held out until 1790, becoming the last state to approve the new plan of government.

3.3 The Bill of Rights. One of the most important objections to ratifying the Constitution in many states was that it did not include a list of definite individual rights. Laws which limited the authority of the government over the individual had been written into the Constitution. Yet there were those who felt that these personal rights should also be spelled out. Before many of the states approved the Constitution, they insisted that such a list be added to it.

What was one of the strongest objections to ratifying the Constitution?

Soon after the new government began, these rights were written down by Congress. Called together the Bill of Rights, they were approved by the states and added as the first ten amendments to the Constitution on December 15, 1791. Among the basic rights guaranteed to all citizens were freedom of speech, freedom of religion, freedom of the press, and the right to a trial by jury. Also included were the right of assembly, the right to bear arms, and protection from cruel and unusual punishments. The Revolution had been fought for these rights, and Americans felt they must become part of the new government.

Recall the English Declaration of Rights referred to in Chapter 3. The idea of a bill of rights was long held by Americans. The complete text of the Bill of Rights appears in the appendix.

1. Why did the Anti-Federalists oppose the new constitution?
2. What was the purpose of *The Federalist Papers*?
3. How many states were needed to approve the Constitution?
4. What was the Bill of Rights?

4. Conclusion

American leaders created the Constitution of the United States in order to deal with problems which the government under the Articles of Confederation could not solve. A new plan of government was established to change the relationship of the national government to the states. It was also designed to better deal with important foreign problems. Like breaking away from British control, starting a new government in the United States was an uncertain venture. No one could say for sure that the new government would work successfully. But most Americans looked forward to trying government under the Constitution.

Chapter 6 Review

Main Points

1. The future of the United States was uncertain at the end of the war for independence.

2. The central government organized under the Articles of Confederation was a weak union in which each state had an equal vote in the national legislature.

3. The most important legislation passed by the Congress of the Confederation provided for the organization of the Northwest Territory and for the way new states could enter the Union.

4. Government under the Articles of Confederation was unable to handle many important economic problems.

5. Dissatisfaction with the Articles resulted in a convention in Philadelphia and a new plan of government.

6. The new constitution was the product of several compromises.

7. After much debate, the Constitution was ratified by all 13 states.

8. Soon after ratification, a Bill of Rights was added to the Constitution.

Building Vocabulary

1. Identify the following:

   Articles of Confederation
   Northwest Territory
   Annapolis Convention
   Daniel Shays

   Benjamin Franklin
   Virginia Plan
   New Jersey Plan

   Great Compromise
   Federalists
   Anti-Federalists
   Bill of Rights

2. Define the following:

   amendment
   ordinances
   surveyed
   constitution

   foreclosures
   compromise
   tariffs

   judiciary
   ratify
   federal

Remembering the Facts

1. What was the plan for government that was drawn up during the war for independence?

2. What were the provisions of the Land Ordinance of 1785?

3. What were the provisions in the Northwest Ordinance of 1787 for admitting new states?

4. What were the weaknesses of the Articles of Confederation?

5. What was the purpose of the 1787 convention in Philadelphia? What action did the convention take?
6. How did the delegates at the convention bring about agreement among people who had various views on what government should and should not do?
7. When was the Constitution ratified, and when did it go into effect?
8. What were some of the individual rights protected by the Bill of Rights?

Understanding the Facts

1. How did the colonial experience with the British government influence the kind of government established under the Articles of Confederation?
2. Why was the government under the Articles of Confederation not able to handle the problems facing the new nation?
3. How did the Great Compromise combine parts of the Virginia Plan and parts of the New Jersey Plan?
4. What were the major points of disagreement between the Federalists and the Anti-Federalists?
5. What was the purpose of the Bill of Rights?

Using Maps

Scale. Maps are drawings which give a small representation of a much larger area of the earth's surface. In an effort to make them as accurate as possible, reference maps and most thematic maps are drawn to scale. This means that a precise distance on the earth's surface is shown by a much smaller, but also precise, space on a flat surface.

The scale on a map tells the relationship to the actual size. It is usually given as part of the map key. For example, on the map on page 149, the miles of the earth's surface are shown by inches and centimeters.

Study the map, and answer the following questions.

1. On the map, one inch equals how many miles? how many kilometers?
2. Between which parallels of latitude is the Northwest Territory?
3. Between which meridians of longitude is the Northwest Territory?
4. What is the east-west distance across the Northwest Territory measured at 40 degrees north latitude?
5. What is the north-south distance across the Northwest Territory measured at 92 degrees west longitude?
6. What lake extends into the middle of the Northwest Territory? How long is it?
7. Which five states were organized from the Northwest Territory?

The Constitution 7

The Constitutional Convention met at Independence Hall in Philadelphia. What kind of document did the delegates write? What ideas about government did the document reflect?

The Constitution is the fundamental law of the United States. It provides an outline for the basic organization of the national government and sets procedures and limitations for its operation. As drafted by its Framers, the Constitution is a brief document, originally having less than 5,000 words. When drafted and ratified, the Constitution consisted of a short Preamble (introduction) and seven articles, or major sections. The Preamble states the general goals of the governmental system being formed by the Constitution. Articles I through III concern the organization, powers, and duties of the three branches of government—legislative, executive, and judicial. Article IV covers relations between and among the states. Article V provides for an amendment process. Article VI deals with miscellaneous items, and Article VII sets up the procedures for ratification.

What is the fundamental law of the United States?

How many Articles are there in the Constitution?

The complete text of the Constitution appears in the appendix.

1. Basic Principles

At the heart of the Constitution lie a number of basic principles upon which the American political system rests. In forming their ideas about government, the Framers drew upon many sources in their political heritage, including British political philosophy and the ideals of the American Revolution.

1.1 Popular Sovereignty. In the United States, supreme political power rests with the people. Government gets its authority from them and acts only with their consent. This principle of *popular sovereignty* is clearly spelled out in the opening words of the Preamble to the Constitution, which states: "We, the people of the United States . . . do ordain and establish this Constitution. . . ."

1.2 Limited Government. Hand-in-hand with the idea of popular sovereignty goes the principle of *limited government*. Since the authority to rule comes from the people, then it follows that government may exercise only those powers granted to it by the people. No government in the United States—federal, state, or local—has unlimited power.

The Constitution prohibits both the federal and state governments from doing certain things. For example, Article I, Section 9 places several restrictions on the federal government. It cannot tax exports, suspend the writ of habeas corpus during peacetime, or grant titles of nobility. Article I, Section 10 says that the states cannot do such things as make treaties with other countries, coin money, or pass laws which void the obligations of contracts.

From whom does government in the United States get its power?

Refer students back to Chapter 5, Section 2.1 where Jefferson states that government gets its power from the people.

Have students consider the problems which might arise if state governments could make treaties, coin money, or do other such things.

How is government limited in the United States?

The Constitution 165

1.3 Federalism.   The principle of *federalism*—the division of
power between a central government and a number of state
governments—grew out of the American struggle for independence
from Great Britain. When the colonies revolted in 1775, they were
rebelling against the rule of a powerful central government. The
colonists insisted that such a government restricted their conduct of
local affairs. After achieving independence, they were fearful of
creating a strong central government in America.

The problems under the Articles of Confederation convinced many
Americans that some form of government was needed other than a
loose confederation of independent states. Therefore, the Framers of
the Constitution provided for a system of government where political
power is divided between the federal government and the states.

1.4 Separation of Powers.   The Framers of the Constitution
not only divided the powers of government on two levels, but they also
separated the executive, legislative, and judicial functions of the
national government among three branches. This *separation of powers*
was somewhat revolutionary at the time. In 1787, almost every nation in
the Western world was ruled by a monarch. Even the British
parliamentary system did not separate the basic functions of
government. The British Parliament was both the maker and the
administrator of laws.

The separation of powers is clearly stated in three articles of the
Constitution. Article I, Section I says that "All legislative powers . . .
shall be vested in a Congress. . . ." Congress cannot authorize any

other agency or persons to make laws in its place. Article II, Section I provides that "The executive power shall be vested in a President. . . ." The President must see that the laws passed by Congress are carried out and can also recommend new laws. Though assisted by various agencies and bureaus, the President is solely responsible for the exercise of executive power at the national level. Article III, Section I provides that "The judicial power of the United States shall be vested in one Supreme Court, and in such inferior [lower] courts as the Congress may from time to time . . . establish." Judicial power includes interpreting, or determining the meaning of laws.

1.5 Checks and Balances. In drafting the powers and duties of each branch of the federal government, the Framers made certain that

How can the President check Congress and the Supreme Court? How can Congress check the Supreme Court and the President? How can the Supreme Court check the President and Congress?

System of Checks and Balances

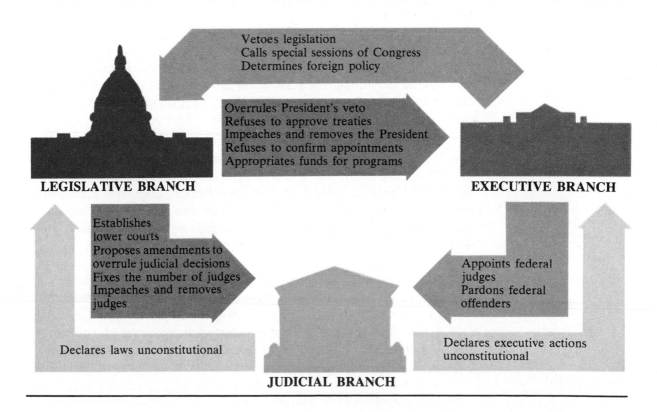

Vetoes legislation
Calls special sessions of Congress
Determines foreign policy

Overrules President's veto
Refuses to approve treaties
Impeaches and removes the President
Refuses to confirm appointments
Appropriates funds for programs

LEGISLATIVE BRANCH

EXECUTIVE BRANCH

Establishes lower courts
Proposes amendments to overrule judicial decisions
Fixes the number of judges
Impeaches and removes judges

Appoints federal judges
Pardons federal offenders

Declares laws unconstitutional

Declares executive actions unconstitutional

JUDICIAL BRANCH

How is balance provided among the branches?

Students should realize that the system of checks and balances has the disadvantage of being somewhat slow and cumbersome but has the advantage of ensuring that too much power is not achieved by one person or group.

no branch was totally independent of the other two. They set up a system of **checks and balances** by which each branch could restrain the power of the other branches. For example, although Congress has the power to pass laws, the President can veto any act of Congress. Congress, on the other hand, can pass a law over the veto of the President by a two-thirds vote of each house. The President has the power to make treaties and appoint ambassadors, judges, and other officials. But treaties and presidential appointments require the approval of the Senate.

1. What are the basic principles of the Constitution?
2. Are popular sovereignty and limited government related? How?
3. How are separation of powers and checks and balances related?

2. Other Principles_____

The principles described in Section 1 pertain to the very nature of the Constitution. That is, they describe the elements which make up the American political system. They are the root of the Constitution. In addition to the basic principles, there are a number of other principles that relate to the Constitution. Though these principles do not lie at the core, they are quite important.

What is the principle of judicial review?

The idea of judicial review was part of the British system of law.

2.1 Judicial Review. One of the great checks in the American governmental system is the principle of *judicial review*. This is the power of the courts to determine if acts of Congress or actions of the President are constitutional. Although the Constitution does not specifically provide for judicial review, it has become one of the most important functions of the courts. Alexander Hamilton wrote in *Federalist Paper #78:*

> *The interpretation of the laws is the proper and peculiar province* [responsibility] *of the courts. A constitution is, in fact, and must be regarded by the judges as, a fundamental law. It therefore belongs to them to ascertain its meaning as well as the meaning of any particular act proceeding from the legislative body.*

See the Profiles of Madison and Marshall on page 175 for historical development of the idea of national supremacy.

2.2 Supremacy of National Law. One principle noted in the Constitution is the **supremacy of national law,** or the concept that national law is superior to state law. Article VI of the Constitution contains the supremacy clause which states that "This Constitution, and the laws of the United States . . . shall be the supreme law of the land. . . ."

What are the two principles of supremacy?

2.3 Supremacy of Civilian Authority. The second important principle regarding supremacy is the idea that the military is subject to civilian authority. Although *supremacy of civilian authority* is not mentioned in the Constitution, it is shown by the fact that the President, a civilian, is commander in chief of the armed forces and only Congress has the power to declare war.

2.4 Additional Principles. There are other major principles which are part of the American political system. Among these are the rule of the majority, the recognition of minority rights, and respect for the worth and dignity of the individual. Although these principles have not been upheld at times, they have given meaning to the operation of government under the Constitution.

What are other important principles of the American political system?

1. How do the basic principles differ from other principles?
2. Which law is considered supreme, national or state?
3. What is the obligation of the majority to the minority?

There are many places throughout the text where basic principles are important. Students should be aware to look for them.

3. Branches of Government

The Framers of the Constitution created three distinct branches of the federal government—legislative, executive, and judicial. Although unique for a national government at the time, this model of government was not unknown. The governments of the states, which had developed from those of the colonies, had such a form.

3.1 Congress. In a democratic system, perhaps the most important function of government is to make the people's will into public policy by means of law. The importance of this can be seen by the fact that the first and longest article of the Constitution deals with the legislative branch. In the American system, it is Congress which is the legislative branch of the federal government.

Who makes law at the national level?

Article I of the Constitution outlines the powers of Congress, the limits of those powers, and a variety of organizational and other matters. In Section I, the Framers created a *bicameral* (two-house) legislature. The lower house is the House of Representatives, and the upper house is the Senate. The creation of a bicameral legislature solved

Recall that the Great Compromise was discussed in Chapter 6, Section 2.2.

This scene of the old House chambers was painted by Samuel F. B. Morse. Voters elect members of the House of Representatives every two years. What are the qualifications for being elected to the House of Representatives?

What are the qualifications of members of Congress?

Have students consider the dangers of having all members of Congress serve the same term and thus come up for reelection at the same time.

the problem of legislative representation and was at the heart of the Great Compromise. Most Americans were familiar with the concept of a two-house legislature. All of the colonial governments except Georgia and Pennsylvania had two-house assemblies. The Framers also favored a bicameral legislature in the belief that one house would act as a check upon the other.

In addition to solving the problem of representation, the Framers had other decisions to make. One of these concerned qualifications for the members of Congress. They decided that members of the House of Representatives must be at least 25 years of age, citizens of the United States for 7 years, and residents of the states from which they are elected. Senators, on the other hand, must be at least 30 years of age, citizens for 9 years, and residents of the states from which they are elected. The Framers also decided that Representatives would serve two-year terms, while Senators would serve six-year terms.

The Framers wanted to make one house of the legislature more responsible to the will of the people and still provide a check on the pressures of public opinion. This was one reason why terms of office differed for Senators and Representatives. In addition, the Framers set up different methods of selecting members to the two houses. Representatives are elected directly by the voters. Although later changed, Senators were originally chosen by state legislatures.

There are still other differences between the House of Representatives and the Senate. Most of these deal with specific powers. For example, all *revenue bills* (tax bills for raising money and bills authorizing the spending of money) must be started in the House of Representatives. Only the Senate approves treaties and confirms presidential appointments. Each house has a different role in the impeachment process. The House of Representatives has the power to *impeach* (bring charges against) the President, Vice-President, and federal judges, and other civil (nonmilitary) officers of the United

What role does each house play in the impeachment process?

What changes were made in the functions of Congress? Who was the executive under the Articles of Confederation? What authority did the Constitution give to the Supreme Court?

Plans of Government

Articles of Confederation		Constitution of 1787
Unicameral legislature	**Legislative**	Bicameral legislature
One vote per state regardless of size or population		One vote per delegate with each state having equal representation in the Senate and represented according to population in the House of Representatives
Determine war and peace		
Send and receive ambassadors		Declare war
Make treaties and alliances		Tax and borrow money
Regulate value of coin		Coin money and regulate value
Set standards of weights and measures		Regulate commerce with foreign countries, between states, and with Indian people
Regulate trade and manage Indian affairs		Set standards of weights and measures
Set up and regulate post offices		Provide post offices and post roads
Direct land and naval forces		Protect copyrights and patents
		Set up minor courts
		Raise, support, and govern army and navy
		Call out militia to stop uprisings and invasions
		Govern the national capital
Committee of States serve when Congress is not in session	**Executive**	One person serves as President
Committee chosen by the Congress; presiding president chosen by Committee		Chosen by electors who are chosen by voters in the individual states
Specific powers authorized by Congress		Directs army and navy as commander in chief
Nine states must agree to the extent of the power		Pardons federal offenders, except in cases of impeachment
		Appoints ambassadors, judges, and federal officers
		Makes treaties and receives ambassadors
		Calls Congress into session in emergencies
		Executes all laws of the country
Congress can set up courts only to hear cases involving piracy or capture at sea	**Judicial**	Congress sits as a court for impeachment
Congress itself sits as a court in deciding disputes between two states		Supreme Court, plus minor courts set up by Congress, hear cases involving national laws, treaties, the Constitution, foreign nations and ambassadors, ships and shipping, two or more states, a state and citizen of another state, citizens of different states, and the national government

States. The Senate tries and removes that person from office upon conviction. Members of Congress are not subject to impeachment, but they can be expelled under the rules established by each house.

3.2 The Presidency. One of the weaknesses of government under the Articles of Confederation was the lack of a strong executive. In drafting the Constitution, the Framers sought to correct this problem. They created the office of the Presidency and gave executive power to one person.

In Article II, the powers and duties of the President are outlined. There is no clearly spelled-out definition of executive power. Because of this, there has been a continuing debate over the power of the Presidency. One side supports a strong chief executive who takes independent action, while the other side favors a President who follows the will of Congress more closely. Nevertheless, the Presidency has become a very powerful position. The power of the office can be seen by the many different functions of the President. For example, the President is the chief of state, or the ceremonial head of the national government. The President is also the chief administrator, the chief diplomat, the commander in chief of the armed forces, and the leader in suggesting new laws.

As the chief administrator, the President is responsible for carrying out and enforcing federal laws. Hundreds of federal departments, bureaus, agencies, and offices carry out the day-to-day affairs of the national government, under the control and direction of the President. The President has the power to issue executive orders to these offices which have the effect of law.

As the chief diplomat, the President is the leader in making American foreign policy. The President carries out this role through the power to make treaties, appoint diplomats, and give recognition to foreign countries.

As commander in chief of the army, the navy, the air force, and the militia of the states when called into federal service, the President is the nation's chief military officer. For the first time, the country had a single, overall military commander to organize the nation's defense in time of peace and direct the nation's military efforts in time of war.

As the leader in suggesting new laws, the President is the most important person in forming the nation's public policy. The President proposes, supports, and often pressures Congress to pass laws. The President is also required to review each bill approved by Congress.

The Framers wanted the method of selecting a President and the qualifications for office to be different from those for members of Congress. They decided that to become President, a person must be at

Who holds executive power at the national level?

Note that Americans went from a strong executive under British rule to a weak executive under the Articles back to a strong executive under the Constitution.

What are some of the roles of the President?

The question of executive power will become especially important as students study the 20th century. It will be useful to recall this section at that time.

Responsibility

CONCEPT

At the time the Constitution was written, citizens understood more about their duty toward government than about government's duty to protect their rights. Citizens in some European countries had no rights which the government respected. With this in mind, the Framers of the Constitution added a list of citizens' rights.

This does not mean citizens had no responsibilities. It means, however, that the Framers thought the citizens would take their duties toward government for granted. There seemed to be no reason to write them down.

Throughout the Constitution, the responsibilities are implied in various articles and amendments. Read the following selections from the Bill of Rights, and identify the implied responsibilities.

Congress shall make no law respecting an establishment of religion, or prohibiting the free exercise thereof; or abridging the freedom of speech, or of the press; or the right of people peaceably to assemble, and to petition the government for a redress of grievances.

A well-regulated militia being necessary to the security of a free state, the right of the people to keep and bear arms shall not be infringed.

The right of the people to be secure in their persons, houses, papers, and effects, against unreasonable searches and seizures, shall not be violated, and no warrants shall issue, but upon probable cause, supported by oath or affirmation, and particularly describing the place to be searched, and the persons or things to be seized.

Excessive bail shall not be required, nor excessive fines imposed, nor cruel and unusual punishments inflicted.

Answer the following questions.
1. What responsibility is implied in each of these selections?
2. Why would the failure of citizens to accept responsibility endanger their rights?
3. What happens in a democracy if the majority of the people must be forced to live up to their responsibilities?

What are the quali-
fications to be
President?

least 35 years of age, a resident of the United States for 14 years, and a native-born citizen. They also set up the electoral college as the method of selecting the President. It was designed to reduce the possibility of people making unwise choices through direct election. The Framers also felt that allowing Congress to choose the President would lessen the independence of the executive branch.

The issue of the electoral
college versus direct election is still being debated
today. It might make a
good subject for further
study and class debate.

Under the electoral college system today, each state has as many presidential electors as that state has Representatives and Senators in Congress. The electors are chosen by methods set up by the legislatures of the states (by popular vote in all 50 states today). These electors, meeting in their own states in early December, cast their ballots for President (and Vice-President since the adoption of the Twelfth Amendment in 1804). The electors in each state are pledged to the candidate who receives the highest number of votes from the people in that state.

How is a President
elected?

Once the presidential electors have voted, the ballots are sealed and sent to Congress, where they are counted in early January. The person receiving a majority of the electoral votes is declared President. If no person has a majority, the House of Representatives chooses the chief executive from among the three candidates receiving the highest number of electoral votes. If no person receives a majority of electoral votes for Vice-President, the Senate makes the choice between the two leading candidates.

The House of Representa-
tives has chosen the President twice—in 1800 and
again in 1824—as students
will read.

3.3 The Courts. As noted by Alexander Hamilton in *The Federalist Papers:* "Laws are a dead letter without courts to expound and define their true meaning and operation." A major weakness of the Confederation government was the lack of a national court system. Under the Confederation government, the laws of the United States had been interpreted by each state as it saw fit. The Framers of the Constitution felt that a national court system was needed if the federal government was to be successful.

What was a major
weakness of the
Articles of
Confederation?

Article III provides the basis for the national judiciary. The organization is simple—one Supreme Court and such inferior (lower) courts as thought necessary by Congress. Congress established the basic court structure with the Judiciary Act of 1789.

Have someone in the class
find out in what federal
court district you live and
where a person would go
for a federal court
appearance.

The national court system exists side-by-side with the court systems of the states. Each of the court systems has its own *jurisdiction,* or authority to hear cases. Most cases in the federal courts begin in the lower courts. They can be appealed to higher courts—all the way to the Supreme Court. There are some cases, however, which begin in the Supreme Court and are decided there. To provide a stable system, and to keep judges from being removed simply because of an unpopular

What is jurisdiction?

James Madison (1751–1836)
John Marshall (1755–1835)
═══PROFILE═══

James Madison and John Marshall disagreed on foreign issues. They disagreed on affairs at home. But both helped to make the Constitution a workable plan for government.

In 1787, Madison was selected by the Virginia legislature to attend the Constitutional Convention. There Madison often showed a deep understanding of past governments, the Articles of Confederation, and the idea of federalism.

Madison favored a strong central government. He supported the new Constitution during the convention and through the ratification process. He served as a member of the Virginia Ratifying Convention. Madison also wrote essays for *The Federalist Papers*.

When the new government began, the voters of Virginia elected Madison to the House of Representatives. In Congress, he proposed to add the Bill of Rights to the Constitution. In 1801, President Thomas Jefferson named him Secretary of State. From 1809 to 1817, Madison was President.

John Marshall's contribution to the working of the Constitution came after the new government had been in operation for several years. In 1801, John Adams named Marshall Chief Justice of the Supreme Court.

The federal legal system was not well established when Adams appointed Marshall. The court had followed the British model. Marshall gave it a fashion of its own. In one ruling, he stated that the United States Supreme Court could decide if an act of the legislature was unconstitutional. This had been the practice in Britain and in the American state courts. Marshall, however, was the first to establish the practice for the federal court.

In disagreements between the federal and state governments, he ruled that the federal government was supreme. These decisions made the new government stronger. During 34 years as Chief Justice, Marshall made the federal government superior to the states and set up the federal judicial system as an equal branch of the government.

Both Madison and Marshall were strong leaders in the branches of the government that they served. Both desired to make the government under the Constitution succeed.

decision, federal judges are appointed for life, providing they properly carry out their duties.

1. What are the two houses that form the Congress?
2. Who elects the President of the United States?
3. Which court is the highest court in the United States?

4. Division of Powers

Paying attention to the chart on division of powers, page 177, will help students deal with a sometimes confusing topic. It might help for them to know that many of the divisions are simply ways of organizing the same powers in several different ways.

What is at the base of the American federal system?

At the base of the American federal system is the division of powers between the national and state governments. The Constitution was written in such a way as to give certain powers to the federal government, leave other powers to the states or to the people, and provide for the sharing of still other powers by both the federal and state governments.

What powers does the federal government have?

4.1 Delegated Powers. The federal government has only those powers delegated (given) to it by the Constitution and no others. There are three kinds of *delegated powers*—expressed, implied, and inherent.

Those powers known as *expressed powers* are formally stated in the Constitution. Examples of the expressed powers of Congress include laying and collecting taxes, borrowing money, regulating trade with foreign countries and among the states, and coining money. Among the expressed powers of the President are granting pardons for crimes against the United States and making treaties and appointments with the approval of the Senate.

What is the base of the implied powers?

Those powers known as *implied powers* are not stated directly in the Constitution, but are suggested or implied by the wording. The basis for the implied powers can be found in Article I, Section 8, which contains the Necessary and Proper Clause. This clause is sometimes called the "Elastic Clause." It states:

> *The Congress shall have power . . . to make all laws which shall be necessary and proper for carrying into execution the foregoing powers, and all other powers vested by this Constitution in the government of the United States, or in any department or officer thereof.*

Two examples of the use of implied powers of Congress are passing draft laws, which is implied by the power to raise armies, and selling treasury bonds, which is implied from the power to borrow money.

Those powers known as *inherent powers* belong to the federal government simply because it is a national government. The powers do not need to be spelled out in so many words. For instance, all national governments have the power to take action to defend their countries, to gain territory, and to regulate immigration.

4.2 Reserved Powers. The federal government is a government of delegated powers, while the states are governments of *reserved powers*. That is, the Constitution reserves to state governments those

What powers are exclusively federal? What powers are reserved to the states? What powers do the federal and state governments share? What powers are denied to the federal government? What are denied to the states?

Division of Powers

Powers Denied to the National and State Governments

Certain Powers Denied to the National Government:

Tax exports
Suspend writ of habeas corpus
Grant titles of nobility

Certain Powers Denied to Both the National and State Governments:

Deny due process of law
Pass ex post facto laws
Pass bills of attainder

Certain Powers Denied to State Governments:

Coin money
Enter into treaties
Void contracts

Powers Divided Between the National and State Governments

Certain Exclusive Powers of the National Government:

Coin money
Conduct foreign relations
Regulate interstate commerce

Certain Concurrent Powers of Both the National and State Governments:

Levy taxes
Provide for the public welfare
Define and punish crimes

Certain Reserved Powers of State Governments:

Create local governments
Provide public education
Direct automobile operation

powers not given to the federal government or denied to the states. For example, the states have the power to set up rules for the operation of public schools. The basis for reserved powers is the Tenth Amendment to the Constitution, which states:

What is the basis of the reserved powers?

> *The powers not delegated to the United States by the Constitution, nor prohibited by it to the states, are reserved to the states respectively, or to the people.*

What are "police powers"?

Probably the most important reserved powers of the states are their so-called *"police powers."* These are the ones that safeguard individual well-being. Under their police powers, states can forbid the practice of medicine without a license, require motor vehicle inspections, establish minimum wage and maximum working hour laws, prohibit gambling, and protect individual rights. Although states can restrict and regulate many things under their police powers, they cannot properly use these powers in an unreasonable or unfair way, nor can they violate constitutional provisions.

An easy example of concurrent powers is the building of state roads and interstate highways.

4.3 Shared Powers.   There are still other powers which may be exercised by both the federal and state governments. These are called shared, or *concurrent powers*. Those powers not prohibited to the states by the Constitution may be used by the states at the same time as the federal government. Among the concurrent powers are the power to tax, to try those accused of crimes, and to provide money to build roads.

What are some limitations on power?

4.4 Limitations on Power.   There are certain limitations on the powers of both the states and the federal government. For example, both the federal and state governments have the power to tax. However, neither level of government can tax the other. If this were possible, they might tax each other so heavily that they would destroy each other and the federal system.

Recall the example of the problems of Virginia and Maryland in Section 1.4, page 151.

Some powers, called *exclusive powers,* belong only to the federal government. Many of the expressed powers are also exclusive powers. Some exclusive powers, such as the coining of money, are denied to the states in the Constitution. If the states were allowed to hold certain powers, such as regulating trade among states, confusion might result.

1. What are the three kinds of delegated powers under the Constitution?
2. What powers are held by both federal and state governments?
3. What powers are held only by the federal government?

5. The Changing Constitution

The Framers of the Constitution realized that future problems of the country could not necessarily be solved with procedures set up in their time. They knew that as the country developed, it would be necessary to change and add to the Constitution. Because of this, they provided for a method of amending the Constitution.

5.1 The Amending Process. Article V states the ways in which the Constitution can be amended. Amendments can be proposed by a two-thirds vote in each house of Congress. Another method is by a national convention called by Congress at the request of two thirds of the state legislatures. To be adopted, amendments must be ratified by either the legislatures in three fourths of the states or by conventions in three fourths of the states. The first ten amendments were added to the Constitution soon after the federal government got started. Sixteen other amendments have been added since then.

How might amendments be proposed? ratified?

In 1789, the United States was a small agricultural country of 3.5 million people. Today the United States is a nation of 237.5 million people and a powerful industrial country. The amendments have allowed the Constitution to keep up with the changes caused by this

Realizing that their plans of government could not cover every situation, the Framers provided the means for change. This is the amendment process. How many ways can the Constitution be changed?

Amending the Constitution

Proposed by

Approved by

Congress
Two-thirds vote required in both Senate and House of Representatives

State Legislatures
Three fourths of all states required

or

or

National Convention
Congress calls a convention at the request of two thirds of the state legislatures

Special Conventions
Three fourths of all states required

growth. All 26 amendments were proposed by a two-thirds vote in each house of Congress. Only the original Constitution and one amendment have been ratified by state conventions. Some amendments, like the Twelfth, which altered the electoral college system, have changed original terms of the Constitution.

5.2 Informal Change. In writing the Constitution, the Framers provided an outline of government. They left the many details of actual government operation to be added later by the various branches of government. Over the years, the Supreme Court, the Congress, the President, and political party practices have influenced the way in which the Constitution would be applied. In a number of cases, for example, Supreme Court rulings have defined and extended the meaning of the Constitution. In one case, the Supreme Court ruled that a person accused of a crime must be informed of certain basic rights, such as the right to remain silent and to have an attorney present during questioning. This ruling extended the provisions of the Fifth Amendment.

Congress, too, has added to basic provisions of the Constitution in order to change or expand the political system. For example, Congress was given the power to tax, but nothing was said about the kinds of taxes, how much they would be, who would pay them, or how they would be collected. All these things have been added through laws passed by Congress.

Like Congress, Presidents have interpreted their constitutional powers in many important ways. As an example, several Presidents, acting as commander in chief, have authorized the use of American military forces without a declaration of war from Congress. The most recent case is the Vietnam War.

Party practices and custom, too, have influenced the ways in which the Constitution has been interpreted and applied. Political parties were not mentioned by the Framers, but they have been an important part of the American political system since the 1790's. A custom that a President would serve no more than two terms was upheld until 1940, when President Franklin D. Roosevelt broke the tradition. The Twenty-second Amendment was then added to the Constitution. This amendment made the custom a formal part of the fundamental law of the land.

1. How does Article V provide for changing the Constitution?
2. What is the role of the Supreme Court in changing the Constitution?

Through what means has the political system changed?

See the Fifth Amendment with the rest of the Constitution in the back of the book.

What custom became a formal amendment?

6. Conclusion

The Constitution of the United States has provided the framework for the nation's government for nearly 200 years. It is the oldest written national constitution still in force in the world today. It has served as the model for the constitutions of many other nations.

The Constitution has lasted so long chiefly because of its flexibility. It was constructed in a way that permitted it to adapt to change and solve new problems. The Framers drew upon their knowledge and experience as they wrote the document. They were familiar with most of the old important historical documents—such as the English Magna Carta, the Mayflower Compact, and the English Bill of Rights. These and other political writings gave them ideas for the principles upon which the Constitution rests. They were aware of the forces at home and abroad which threatened the survival of the young nation. They also recognized the difficulty of writing a document which would guarantee the freedom of the people and still maintain order in the community. Their accomplishment is something in which all Americans can take pride.

After weeks of debate, a draft of the Constitution was submitted to the convention on August 6, 1787. Some discussion continued for another month. The document was signed on September 17. It went into effect in 1789. How does the Constitution continue to be more than just a written document?

Chapter 7 Review

Main Points

1. The Constitution is the fundamental law of the United States and provides for the organization of the national government.

2. Supreme political power rests with the people. The people elect representatives who operate the government.

3. Under the Constitution, government is limited to those powers granted to it by the people.

4. Under the Constitution, power is divided between state governments and the national government.

5. Within the national government, power is divided among the legislative, executive, and judicial branches.

6. Each branch of government has certain checks on the other branches to balance power within the national government.

7. There are a number of other principles besides those that are basic to the Constitution. They include judicial review, supremacy of national law, and supremacy of civilian authority.

8. According to the Constitution, some powers are held by the federal government only, some by the states or the people only, and some are shared.

9. The Constitution may be changed by adding formal amendments to it. It may also be changed informally by court interpretation.

Building Vocabulary

1. Identify the following:

   Framers   electoral college   John Marshall
   Preamble   James Madison   "Elastic Clause"

2. Define the following:

popular sovereignty	supremacy of civilian authority	expressed powers
limited government	bicameral	implied powers
federalism	revenue bills	inherent powers
separation of powers	impeach	reserved powers
checks and balances	jurisdiction	"police powers"
judicial review	delegated powers	concurrent powers
supremacy of national law		exclusive powers

Remembering the Facts

1. What is the source of supreme political power under the Constitution?

2. Which basic principle prevents government under the Constitution

from taking any action it might want to take?

3. What are the two levels of government provided for under the principle of federalism?

4. In providing for the separation of powers, what are the three branches of government in the Constitution?

5. What are the checks that each branch of government has over the others?

6. How do the two houses of Congress differ?

7. What is the role of the President of the United States with regard to the armed forces?

8. Because it is a national government, what are the powers held by the federal government?

9. What powers do the states have under the Constitution?

10. How can the Constitution be changed?

11. Where does the process of changing the written Constitution begin?

Understanding the Facts

1. How was the government created by the Constitution like the colonial government under Britain?

2. In what way was the government set up by the Constitution stronger than that of the Articles of Confederation?

3. How did the Framers of the Constitution attempt to prevent one branch of government from becoming too powerful?

4. Why would a revolution not be needed to change the Constitution?

Using Diagrams

Reading Diagrams. A diagram is a drawing which explains some idea. It is used instead of a written description or with a written description to make clear important points and relationships. The way a diagram is drawn is important to getting across the intended idea.

The diagram on page 167 concerns the government established under the Constitution. Read the title. Examine the drawing and its various parts. Read the written descriptions within the diagram. Then answer the following questions.

1. What does the diagram explain?

2. What are the three branches of government?

3. How does the diagram show the ways one branch of the government can check and balance another branch?

4. How can the legislative branch prevent a person, who was appointed by the executive branch, from taking office?

5. Which branch appoints the people who decide if a law is constitutional or not?

6. Which branch has the authority to remove the President from office?

7. What is meant by checks and balances?

Philadelphia 1750-1775

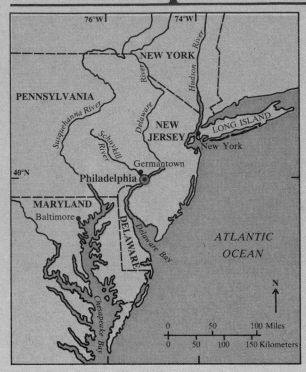

and other Christians in Philadelphia than there were Quakers. Several Jewish families also lived in the city, and many people did not belong to any particular church. The Quakers, however, continued to have a strong influence on the development of the city.

Earning a Living

Philadelphia quickly became a center of business for ·Pennsylvania and the other colonies. There were ironworks, flour mills, yards for building and repairing ships, carriage and wagon shops, and many different ways for people to earn their livings. Farmers brought produce from their rich fields to market. In the city's shops, they purchased candles, shoes, tools, and other goods.

Shipping and trade were the base of Philadelphia's economic growth. James Birket, a visitor to the city in 1759, reported on what he saw.

William Penn laid out the plans for his Pennsylvania "city of brotherly love" in 1682. He located Philadelphia on the west banks of the Delaware River, not far from the Atlantic coast. The city grew quickly and, by the middle of the eighteenth century, was the largest and richest city in the American colonies.

The first settlers of Philadelphia were English Quakers, or members of the Society of Friends. They allowed all other Christians to come there and worship as they pleased. That freedom of religion drew many different groups of people from Europe, and the city's population continued to grow. By 1740, there were more Presbyterians, Anglicans, Roman Catholics, Baptists, Methodists, Lutherans,

There is belonging to this town a great number of ships, and from here a very extensive trade is carried on to all the English islands in the West Indies for bread, flour, pork, hams, Indian corn, buckwheat oats, apples . . . shingles, hoops, bar iron . . . also livestock as sheep, geese, turkeys, ducks and fowl in great plenty; but some of their chief men . . . drive on a very large illegal trade with the French . . . for sugar and molasses, to the great damage of the honest and fair trader.

They have also a good trade for wheat, staves and other things, to Madeira, Lisbon, and several parts of Spain, to say nothing of that extensive trade between them and England for black walnut and other valuable wood of different kinds. . . .

William Penn founded Philadelphia on the west bank of the Delaware River. This is how it looked in 1702. How did its location help its economic and physical growth by the middle 1700's?

Such a busy city could support workers with special skills. Painters, weavers, silversmiths, and cabinetmakers made things that were beautiful as well as useful. There was a need, too, for printed business and legal forms, government notices, and other useful items. By the time Benjamin Franklin arrived in 1723 to look for work, there were already two printers in Philadelphia. He went to work for one of them and, in a few years, became the city's most famous printer. Franklin, as others did, printed a newspaper, pamphlets, and a yearly almanac.

Families often continued to work in the same trade or profession for generations. The Bradfords, for example, were Philadelphia printers for more than 100 years. Cornelia Bradford, in 1740, became the first woman to be a successful printer and bookseller in the city. By the 1770's, presses were turning out seven different newspapers and thousands of books and pamphlets. Philadelphia's printers played a very important part in the exchange of ideas among the American colonists.

Self-improvement

Many of the people in the city enjoyed sharing ideas. Clubs were sometimes formed for "mutual improvement," as Franklin said of the Junto, a club that he and 11 of his friends started in 1727.

. . . we met on Friday evenings. The rules that I drew up required that every member, in his turn, should produce one or more queries [questions] on any point of Morals, Politics, or Natural Philosophy, to be [discussed] by the company; and once in three months produce and read an essay of his own writing, on any subject he pleased. Our debates were . . . in the sincere spirit of inquiry after truth. . . .

According to the social traditions of the times, only men belonged to these clubs. But women were sometimes the topic of the meetings. Carl Bridenbaugh, historian of colonial Philadelphia, wrote about a club that met in October 1766. Its members had chosen to discuss the question of women in politics.

After an animated and extremely serious discussion, in which it was conceded [agreed]

This advertisement appeared in a Philadelphia newspaper in the 1700's. What product is being advertised? Who is selling the product?

Juft imported in the Ship **Myrtilla**, Captain **Bolitho**, from London, and to be fold by
HANNAH BREINTNALL,
At the Sign of the Spectacles, in Second-ftreet, near Black-Horfe Alley,

A Great Variety of the fineft Chryftal Spectacles, fet in Temple, Steel, Leather or other Frames. Likewife true Venetian green Spectacles. for weak or watery Eyes, of various Sorts. Alfo Concave Spectacles, for fhort fighted Perfons; Magnifying and Reading Glaffes; and an Affortment of large and fmall Spy glaffes and Bone Microfcopes, with magnifying and multiplying Glafs, &c. &c. Pocket Compaffes, of different Sizes. &c.   ‖ 10 s. Tbctf.

that women have natural abilities equal to those of men, which might be improved by education, that their lively imaginations would "throw a subject into new lights," that their natural timidity [lack of boldness] would make for prudent [wise] decisions, and that Queen Elizabeth had proved an able ruler, the question was decided in the negative, on the grounds that the use of beauty and female arts would prejudice the public good and that active participation by the ladies [in politics] would "destroy the peace of Families."

Education

Education for women was not a common idea in all of the colonies. But the Quakers believed in a practical education for both boys and girls. Reading and writing were taught without charge if the children's parents were too poor to pay. Those who could pay were expected to do so. Philadelphia's first schools were started by the Quakers and other church groups. Within a few years, night schools opened for young workers eager to advance in business. Good private teachers could always find enough students to fill their classes.

In 1751, the Philadelphia Academy opened for the city's young men. It had been a special project of Franklin's, and he helped decide the subjects that were taught. Families from the lower and middle classes wanted their sons trained for business with English, bookkeeping, and other such practical courses. Upper-class families wanted their sons trained in the arts with foreign languages, philosophy, and classics. As a compromise, Franklin wrote:

. . . it would be well if they could be taught everything that is useful and everything that is ornamental. But art is long and their time is short. It is therefore proposed that they learn

those things that are likely to be most useful and most ornamental, regard being had to the . . . professions for which they are intended.

That same year, David Dove opened a private school for teaching girls some of the more advanced subjects. His school was very successful. Three years later, Anthony Benezet convinced the leaders of the Academy to permit girls to study the same subjects that the boys were offered, but in a separate building.

Benezet was also a pioneer in education for black people. A few black children had been attending the Quaker church schools. In 1750, Benezet opened an evening school for them in his home and paid for the supplies himself. He continued these classes until a group of Quakers took over the costs. They opened a free school to teach reading, writing, and arithmetic to black children in 1770. By the 1790's, Philadelphia had schools for black students taught by black teachers.

City Improvements

The rapid growth of business pushed the city's boundaries outward. The price of land within the city grew higher, and the noise of city traffic grew louder. To avoid the higher land costs, many smaller merchants moved to the edges of town. To avoid the noise and traffic, many of the richer families built their homes in areas outside the city. By the 1770's, Philadelphia had grown from a trade town to a metropolitan city with suburbs, or outlying districts of homes and small businesses.

Although many lived in the suburbs, the people worked to improve the appearance of the city. They supported many plans for the general public. Franklin and the members of the Junto were often involved in these projects. In his writings, Franklin described their "first project of a public nature."

Many of Benjamin Franklin's plans and projects benefited Philadelphia. How did Franklin help to improve city life?

Those who [loved] *reading were* [obliged] *to send for their books from England. . . .* [In 1731] *I* [proposed] *to render the benefit from books more common, by commencing* [beginning] *a public subscription library. . . . So few were the readers at that time in Philadelphia, and the majority of us so poor, that I was not able, with great industry, to find more than fifty persons, mostly young tradesmen, willing to pay down for this purpose forty shillings each, and ten shillings per annum* [year]. *On this little fund we began. The books were imported; the library was opened one day in the week for lending to the subscribers, on their promissory* notes to pay double the value if not duly returned. *The institution soon manifested* [showed] *its utility* [usefulness], *was imitated by other towns, and in other provinces.*

Fires were a problem in the city, and there was no organized way to fight them. In 1737, Franklin wrote and printed a paper about the different causes of fires. He also wrote about ways to deal with them.

This . . . gave rise to a project, which soon followed it, of forming a company [the Union Fire Company] *for the more ready extinguishing of fires, and mutual assistance in removing and securing of goods when in danger. Associates in this scheme* [plan] *were presently found, amounting to thirty. Our articles of agreement* [obliged] *every member to keep always in good order, and fit for use, a certain number of leather buckets, with strong bags and baskets (for packing and transporting of goods), which were to be brought to every fire; and we agreed to meet once a month* [to discuss] *the subject of fires, as might be useful in our conduct on such occasions.*

. . . this went on, one new company being formed after another. . . . The small fines that have been paid by members for absence at the monthly meetings have been [applied] *to the purchase of fire-engines, ladders, fire-hooks, and other useful implements* [tools] *for each company, so that I question whether there is a city in the world better provided with the means of putting a stop to beginning conflagrations* [fires]. . . .

More than 25 years after his first public project, Franklin was still working for the general good of the city. He had convinced the city leaders to keep the streets cleaned and patrolled at night for safety. But he believed that there was more to be done.

Our city, [though] *laid out with a beautiful regularity, the streets large,* [straight], *and crossing each other at right angles, had the disgrace of suffering those streets to remain long* [unpaved] *and in wet weather the wheels of heavy carriages* [plowed] *them into a quagmire* [deep mud], *so that it was difficult to cross them; and in dry weather the dust was offensive. . . .*

After some time I drew a bill for paving the city, and brought it into the Assembly. It was just before I went to England, in 1757 [on colonial business], *and did not pass till I was gone . . . with an additional provision for lighting as well as paving the streets, which was a great improvement. It was by a private person, the late Mr. John Clifton, his giving a sample of the utility of lamps, by placing one at his door, that people were first* [impressed] *with the idea of enlighting all the city.*

Social Improvements

As Philadelphia grew into a rich city, many of its successful people were interested in helping those who were not successful. At first, the Quakers were the strongest influence in this work. Soon church groups, business and social clubs, and many individuals were involved. They supported buildings to house and care for the old, the poor, the widows, and the orphans. They also collected money, food, and clothing.

Dr. Thomas Bond, helped by Franklin, opened a hospital to care for people who were sick and those who had mental illnesses in 1751. Bond needed Franklin's help to raise money because the idea of a hospital was new to most people. Many families of the lower and middle classes never went to doctors, and even the upper classes usually tried old family cures first.

Philadelphia also became a center of resistance to slavery. The Quakers taught that every individual had special dignity and that blacks were people, not property. Their ideas influenced others in the city. In 1775, the people of Philadelphia started the first anti-slavery society in America. Philadelphia was indeed the "city of brotherly love."

1. Who were the first settlers in Philadelphia?
2. What was the base of Philadelphia's economic growth?
3. What contributions did Franklin make to the development of Philadelphia?
4. Why did the suburbs of Philadelphia develop?

Philadelphia's population in 1775 was 40,000. At that time, it was larger than any city in England except for London. After the Revolution, it became the nation's capital. What attracted people to live and work in Philadelphia?

Unit II Review

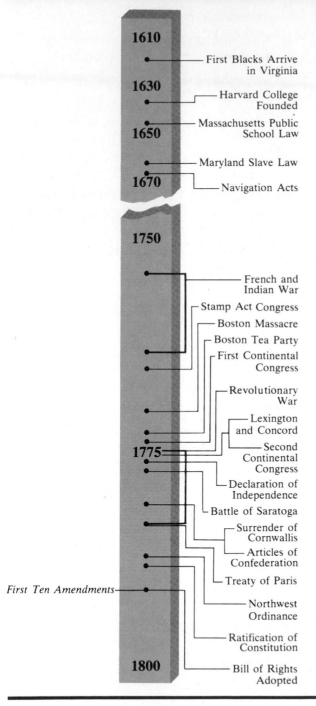

1610
First Blacks Arrive in Virginia

1630
Harvard College Founded

Massachusetts Public School Law

1650

Maryland Slave Law

1670
Navigation Acts

1750

French and Indian War

Stamp Act Congress

Boston Massacre

Boston Tea Party

First Continental Congress

Revolutionary War

Lexington and Concord

Second Continental Congress

1775

Declaration of Independence

Battle of Saratoga

Surrender of Cornwallis

Articles of Confederation

Treaty of Paris

First Ten Amendments

Northwest Ordinance

Ratification of Constitution

1800
Bill of Rights Adopted

Summary

1. The people of the English colonies came from Europe—especially the countries of England, Scotland, and Germany—as well as from Africa.

2. Although many groups contributed to the culture of the colonies, the English language and culture became the standard.

3. British victory in the French and Indian War freed the colonies from a major threat to their security and led them to hope for greater freedom.

4. Disagreements over political and economic matters developed between the colonies and Britain, leading to rebellion in 1775.

5. The colonies declared their independence from Britain, which they won after seven years of warfare.

6. Political rights for many men were expanded as a result of the Revolution, although there were few changes in rights for women or for those people held as slaves.

7. The government of the United States under the Articles of Confederation proved too weak to deal with the problems following the Revolution.

8. Dissatisfaction with the Articles of Confederation led to a convention of delegates from the states which drew up the Constitution as the fundamental law of the United States.

9. Under the Constitution, supreme political power rests with the people, who elect representatives.

Unit Questions

1. How were the experiences of people in the English colonies different from those in Africa and Europe?
2. What were some of the reasons for the development of three distinct regions in the English colonies?
3. How did the ways that the British government viewed their colonies in America differ from the ways that the colonists viewed themselves?
4. Why did the colonists, who thought of themselves as British citizens, revolt against their home country?
5. Why were the colonies able to defeat the powerful British army?
6. What were some of the most important social, political, and economic effects of the Revolution?
7. What were the boundaries of the United States as set by the Treaty of Paris in 1783?
8. How were experiences of Americans under British rule reflected in their distrust for strong central government under the Articles of Confederation?
9. Why did Americans decide to replace the Articles of Confederation with the Constitution?
10. What were the arguments for and against adopting the Constitution?

Suggested Activities

1. Imagine that you are a teenager who came from Europe or Africa during the late 1600's. In keeping a diary, what events might you describe?
2. Compare the Constitution with the rules of organization for one of your school groups. Identify the differences and similarities between the two.
3. As a class, compare life in eighteenth-century Philadelphia with life in your town today. How are they alike? How are they different?

Suggested Readings

Davis, Burke. *Black Heroes of the American Revolution*. New York: Harcourt Brace Jovanovich, 1976. Contributions of blacks in the American Revolution.

Depauw, Linda. *Founding Mothers: Women of America in the American Revolutionary Era*. Boston: Houghton Mifflin Company, 1975. Examines the roles of women in the American Revolution and the conditions which shaped their lives.

Forbes, Esther. *Johnny Tremain*. New York: Dell, 1969. The adventures of a young member of the Sons of Liberty during pre-Revolutionary days in Boston.

Perl, Lila. *Slumps, Grunts, and Snickerdoodles: What Colonial America Ate and Why*. New York: Seabury Press, Inc., 1975. Contains recipes and traces the changes in foods produced and eaten by the colonists.

UNIT III

Democracy

Democracy began as an outgrowth of a new and wide-open environment in the United States. Americans were free to move around the country and within social classes. They were no longer supposed to be grouped together according to ancestry, wealth, or education. Americans claimed that all people were created equal. It was believed that all Americans should be judged on their own merits. The democratic practice of government by all of the people in the United States was a developing process.

Chapter 8   Testing the New Government ____ **194**
Chapter 9   The Growth of Nationalism ____ **214**
Chapter 10 The Age of Jackson ____ **234**
City Sketch   *Washington, D.C. 1800–1825* ____ **252**

Testing the New Government

8

George Washington receives a naval salute in New York harbor after his inauguration. Washington was the unanimous choice for the new office of President. What problems faced the United States and America's first President?

During the first few years after the Constitution was adopted, the future of the new nation was in question. The United States was not yet unified. Most people still felt they were citizens of a certain state rather than citizens of the United States. Many wondered whether the Constitution would work. Some people questioned whether America could last in a world of powerful, unfriendly countries.

George Washington voiced these worries when he said, ". . . the preservation of the sacred fire of liberty and the destiny of the [democratic] model of government . . . [depend] on the experiment intrusted to the hands of the American people." For better or for worse, however, this great American experiment was under way.

You might discuss with the students Washington's use of the word "experiment." Stress that Americans had few precedents from the past to follow as a guide for democratic government.

1. The Beginning

The Constitution provided an outline of government for the country's leaders. They began to create a working government, drawing on this outline plus their experiences in colonial government and the Confederation. As they set about their tasks, these leaders knew that their actions would serve as examples to be followed in years to come.

In studying the beginning of the federal government, refer students to the Constitution to show that actions taken were in line with the plans developed by the Framers.

1.1 The First Election. As soon as the Constitution had been ratified, the new plan for government was set in motion. The first members of the Senate and the House of Representatives were elected. Then state legislatures chose *electors* whose task was to choose the President and Vice-President. In the country's first presidential election, George Washington was selected President, and John Adams was named Vice-President. Early in 1789, the new leaders of the country gathered in New York, the national capital, to begin work.

Who chooses the President?

1.2 The First Executive. As chief executive, President Washington thought his major task was to execute or carry out the policies set by Congress. In practice, the President also became a maker of policies. He did this by setting *precedents*—acts that would serve as examples in later situations. One of the first things Washington did was select people to head the executive departments newly set up by Congress. He named Thomas Jefferson of Virginia as Secretary of State, Alexander Hamilton of New York as Secretary of the Treasury, Henry Knox of Massachusetts as Secretary of War, and Edmund Randolph of Virginia as Attorney General. Washington met with these people and asked for their advice in government matters. They became the Cabinet, or body of advisors, and every President has had one.

What precedents did Washington set?

Washington also made policies in foreign affairs. He gained more power for his office in this field than was stated in the Constitution. It

Washington usually met with the Cabinet members individually. Only later did Presidents begin to meet with their Cabinet members as a group.

George Washington (left) selected the first Cabinet—Edmund Randolph, Thomas Jefferson, Alexander Hamilton, and Henry Knox (from right to left). What area of responsibility did each Cabinet member hold?

How did Washington gain more power for the Presidency in foreign affairs?

What courts were set up by Congress in 1789?

The Supreme Court as set up by the Judiciary Act of 1789 had one Chief Justice and five Associates. It also set up 13 District Courts and three Circuit Courts.

said that the President was to make treaties with other countries with the help and approval of the Senate. At first, Washington tried to do this. When he was *negotiating* (trying to arrange terms) with a group of Indians, he asked the Senate's help. The Senators would not discuss the treaty while Washington was present. They wished to talk it over in private. Washington left, and from then on, he and the Presidents who followed him have negotiated treaties as they think best. Then they have sent the treaties to the Senate for approval.

1.3   A New Court System.   One of the most important goals of the Framers of the Constitution was to make a strong court system. It would protect the rights of the people and keep them from being harmed by governments or by other people. To do this, Congress passed the Judiciary Act of 1789. It set up a system of courts that is still working, although sometimes the numbers of the courts have changed.

The lowest courts in this system were district courts set up to hear cases involving federal law. Next were the circuit courts which hear cases sent to them on *appeal*—the review of a lower court's findings by a higher court. This happens when there is some question about the first court's ruling. The Supreme Court is the highest court in the country and the last court of appeal. Washington chose John Jay of New York as the first Chief Justice of the Supreme Court.

1. Who was the first President to be elected under the Constitution?
2. What were the roles of Thomas Jefferson and Alexander Hamilton in the new government?
3. What was the highest court created by the Framers of the Constitution?

2. The Economy

Those who were forming the new government wanted it to be strong. To keep order at home and to be on equal terms with other countries, the United States had to have a strong economy. During Washington's first term, government leaders wanted to set up an economic program that would make the country prosperous. Alexander Hamilton, the Secretary of the Treasury, drew up such a program.

Who drafted this nation's first economic program?

2.1 Hamilton and the Debt. Alexander Hamilton saw that the new government had little money on hand and was deeply in debt. During the Revolution, the central and state governments had both borrowed money from their citizens and from other countries. These governments owed over $80 million. Hamilton thought that the federal government should repay the money owed to other countries and to its own citizens as well as the debts of the states. He believed that this money had to be repaid if the United States was to establish its credit.

Federal assumption of state war debts led foreign countries to look to the national government for authority rather than the state governments, an important sign of growing strength for the new nation.

Congress agreed to pay money owed to foreign countries. Conflict arose, however, over the plan to pay for the *domestic* (internal or within the country) debts. When the government had borrowed money during the Revolution, it had issued *bonds*—paper notes promising to repay the money in a certain length of time. After the war, many people believed that the government would not be able to pay off the bonds. So their value dropped, and they were bought by *speculators*—people who buy stocks, bonds, or land for the purpose of selling it for a profit later when the price goes up. Hamilton proposed that these bonds be *redeemed* (paid off) at their original value. Those people against the plan felt that the country should not give the speculators the benefit of a large profit. Hamilton convinced Congress that the debts must be paid.

What were the conflicts that arose over paying the debt?

Another part of the debt was owed by several states to American citizens. Hamilton wanted the government to *assume* (take over) these debts. Most of the southern states had already repaid their debts. Members of Congress from the South felt that citizens of their states should not be taxed to repay the debts of other states. A compromise was reached. Southerners agreed that the federal government would

Benjamin Banneker (1731–1806)
══ PROFILE ══

In 1771, Benjamin Banneker was a 41-year-old, black, Maryland farmer. That year, he seriously began to follow a lifelong interest in the sciences. He read about the earth and the heavens. With a simple telescope, he watched the sky. In 1789, he correctly predicted an eclipse of the sun. At a time when most American blacks were slaves and few were educated, Banneker was known as a mathematician and astronomer.

Banneker's talent drew the attention of Thomas Jefferson. It was Jefferson who told President George Washington that Banneker should be a member of the team to plan the new Federal District (later District of Columbia). He was the first black person named to a job by a President of the United States.

In 1791, Banneker began printing an annual almanac. It held not only scientific information, but also reports on social problems. In the 1793 edition, Banneker recommended what amounted to a department of the interior for the United States. He also planned for a league of nations to gain world peace.

Banneker saw his work as evidence that there was no connection between race and ability to learn. He believed his success was due to his free birth and education. In letters to Thomas Jefferson, he stated this and called for more democratic feelings toward blacks.

The capital was transferred from New York to Philadelphia in September 1790. See the City Sketch of Washington, D.C. on page 252.

take over the states' debts. In return, people from the North agreed that the new capital of the United States would be built in the South. Until it was finished, the capital would be in Philadelphia.

2.2 A National Bank. Another part of Hamilton's plan proposed that the federal government establish a central bank for the United States. Hamilton did not want just one bank, but a national banking system. It would provide a place where the government could deposit its money. It would be large enough to lend money to the government as well as to private citizens. Finally, the bank would provide a sound currency.

What was the argument over establishing a national bank?

When the bill to set up the Bank of the United States came up in Congress, there was much debate. Some people argued that the

Constitution did not give the government the power to create a bank. A majority of Congress, however, agreed with Hamilton's plan, and the bank bill was passed in 1791.

2.3   A Tariff Proposal.   Congress wanted to find ways to raise additional money for the federal government. In 1789, it passed a tariff act which placed *duties* (a kind of tax) on certain goods coming into the United States from other countries. Hamilton agreed with those who thought this was a good way to raise money. On December 5, 1791, he gave a *Report on Manufactures* to Congress. In it, Hamilton asked that Congress pass a *protective tariff*—a heavy tax on some manufactured goods imported into the United States. This would make foreign goods more expensive than those produced at home. Americans would then be encouraged to buy the cheaper goods made in the United States. This should encourage the growth of industry. Hamilton's report had little effect, although a slightly higher tariff was passed in 1792.

2.4   The Whiskey Rebellion.   In another proposal, Hamilton asked Congress to place an *excise tax* (tax on goods made and sold inside the country) on whiskey. On March 3, 1791, it was passed. Farmers in the frontier areas of the country thought the tax was very unfair. They often distilled grain into whiskey to sell, and it was a major source of money for them. Many of them began to avoid paying the tax.

Farmers in western Pennsylvania openly refused to pay the tax in 1794. Hamilton felt the authority of the new government was being

The Bank of the U.S. was resented by southern and western farmers for its tight credit policies and by smaller banks for its competition. Loan policies favored eastern business interests.

Why did Hamilton want a protective tariff?

The tariff issue will be important throughout American history. As tariffs protect American business, they raise the cost of imported goods to consumers. This has caused many political battles.

Note that the frontier in 1790 was just west of the Appalachian Mountains.

Where did the Whiskey Rebellion take place?

The first Bank of the United States was built in Philadelphia in 1795. Although Jefferson opposed it, Hamilton thought it would be a step toward creating a secure money system for the country. What was the purpose of a national bank?

A wagon load of whiskey sold for about $220. A wagon load of grain sold for about $36. An excise tax on whiskey meant less profit. Where did resentment toward the tax cause fighting between farmers and federal troops?

challenged. He wanted to show that the new government could enforce its laws. So Hamilton asked Washington to send troops against the resisting farmers. In October 1794, a force of about 13,000 militia marched into Pennsylvania to restore law and order. This show of force soon ended the "Whiskey Rebellion."

2.5 Opposition to Hamilton. Although Hamilton's economic plans were working, they had drawn strong opposition from the beginning. Perhaps the greatest disagreement was over the Bank of the United States. Thomas Jefferson thought the law setting up the Bank of the United States was unconstitutional because the Constitution did not specifically give Congress the power to set up a bank. He understood the Constitution to mean only what it actually said. His view was called a *strict construction* (narrow interpretation). Hamilton understood the Constitution to mean much more than it said. It gave Congress the power "to make all laws necessary and proper" to carry out its work. Hamilton felt this gave Congress the power to set up a bank. This view was called a *loose construction* (broad interpretation). The disagreement marked the start of two ways of understanding the Constitution.

Two political parties were formed out of these differences. One group was the Federalists, led by Hamilton. The other was Democratic-Republicans, usually called Republicans, led by Jefferson. Generally, Hamilton's followers favored a strong national government. They interpreted the Constitution broadly in order to give the federal government as much power as possible. Most Federalists believed that

Who led the opposition to Hamilton's policies?

See Chapter 7, Section 3.1—the Elastic Clause.

What did each of the political parties favor?

people of wealth and education should hold office, and that the economy should be based on industry and trade as well as agriculture. Jefferson's supporters, on the other hand, favored the rights of the states, and they interpreted the Constitution strictly. They believed that average people should lead the country. They thought the economy should be based on agriculture with industry and trade less important.

1. Why did Hamilton insist on paying the national debts?
2. What was the purpose of the Bank of the United States?
3. Why did farmers in western Pennsylvania refuse to pay taxes?
4. Which political parties developed over disagreements on national economic policies?

3. Foreign Affairs

The world situation greatly added to the concerns of the new government. While trying to build a sound economy, it faced growing problems with European countries. Quarrels among these countries threatened to draw the United States into war. Great Britain still had trading posts in the American Northwest and had been capturing some American trading ships in the West Indies. Debates over these issues further divided the country's political parties.

3.1 Staying Neutral.   When Great Britain and France went to war in 1793, the United States found itself in a difficult position. It had signed a treaty of alliance with France in 1778. But the United States did not want to fight another war with Great Britain. The possibility of war widened the differences between Jefferson, who favored the French, and Hamilton, who favored the British. In April 1793, President Washington issued a Proclamation of Neutrality. *Neutrality* means to not take sides in a conflict.

3.2 The Jay Treaty.   The British would not accept America's neutral stand. They seized American ships carrying goods to France. They also began a policy of *impressment*. This meant they were stopping American ships and taking sailors off to force them to work on British ships. Often the British claimed that the sailors were really British citizens who had moved to America.

Hoping to avoid war, Washington sent a peace mission to Great Britain in 1794. It was headed by John Jay, Chief Justice of the Supreme Court. Jay made a treaty with the British. By its terms, Britain agreed to pull out of its posts in the Northwest Territory. The United States

The French Revolution began in 1789 and was admired by many Americans as a new democracy until violence wiped out many of the reforms.

Why did Washington issue the Proclamation of Neutrality?

How did the British interfere with American trade?

The British seized American ships when they suspected that the cargo was going to France. While on board, the British had American sailors pronounce certain words. If an American sailor spoke with an Irish or British accent, he was made prisoner and forced to serve in the British navy. How did the policy of impressment affect relations between the United States and Britain?

agreed that debts owed to British citizens from the Revolution would be paid. Americans who suffered losses from British seizures of ships were also to be paid for damages. The boundary with Canada in the northeast was to be surveyed and set.

The Jay Treaty was approved by the Senate. It had prevented war with Great Britain, but it upset many Americans. Many were angry that the United States had not gained free trade with the West Indies. Others did not want the United States to repay debts owed to Great Britain from the Revolution. Those who were against the policies of Hamilton used the treaty to gain support for their views and further widened the gap between the political parties.

Why were Americans upset with the Jay Treaty?

3.3 The Pinckney Treaty. When Spain learned about the Jay Treaty, its leaders decided to settle their differences with the United States. Because Spain had just signed an agreement with France, it faced war with Great Britain. Spanish officials feared that Britain and the United States might move against its territory in America.

What were the issues underlying the Pinckney Treaty?

Thomas Pinckney, the United States minister to Great Britain, negotiated a treaty with Spain, signed in October 1795. By its terms, Americans were guaranteed the right to navigate the Mississippi River and to use freely the port of New Orleans. They would also be able to transfer goods from river boats to oceangoing vessels without paying duties to Spain. In addition, Spain and the United States set the

Recognizing Main Ideas
SKILL

Some writers use the first sentence in a paragraph to present a main idea. Other writers give background information and conclude with the major point. There are also writers who do not state a main idea, leaving it up to the reader to decide.

Location alone does not determine the main idea for a paragraph, a chapter, or a book. Read the material, and ask what does most of the information explain or describe. When you can answer this, you have begun to identify the main idea.

Read the following selection about the Congress of the United States when Philadelphia was the capital city. It was written by a visitor to Congress in the late 1700's.

On entering the House of Representatives, I was struck with the convenient arrangement. . . . The size of the chamber was about 100 feet by 60. The seats in three rows formed semicircles behind each other, facing the Speaker, who was in a kind of pulpit near the center . . . and the clerk below him. Every member was accommodated for writing, by there being likewise a circular writing desk to each of the circular seats. Over the entrance was a large gallery, into which were admitted every citizen without distinction, who chose to attend; and under the gallery likewise were accommodations for those who were [invited]. *But no person either in the gallery or under it, is suffered to express any mark of applause or discontent at what is dabbled; it being understood they are present in the person of their representative. This has been a great error in the new French government. An attempt, however, was once made to introduce it here (in March last) by clapping of hands, at a speech which fell from Mr.* [Josiah] *Parker. But the whole house instantly rose to resent it, and adjourned their business, being then in a committee and the galleries were closed.*

Over the door I observed a bust of Dr. [Benjamin] *Franklin, the great founder of their liberties, and* [a Framer] *of their present constitution.*

1. What is the main idea of this selection?

2. Is the main idea stated, or must the reader determine it?

3. If it is stated, where does the writer present the idea?

4. Is all the other information used to explain or describe the idea?

boundary between Georgia and Spanish Florida at the 31st parallel. Many Americans were very pleased with the Pinckney Treaty.

3.4 Washington's Farewell. President Washington prepared to leave office in 1796. During his two terms, he had helped establish the new government on a solid foundation. But Washington was troubled. Matters with France were growing worse. The French had been angered by the Jay Treaty. Under the terms of the treaty of 1778, France and the United States were allies. Great Britain was France's enemy.

The importance of Washington to the establishment of the government should again be stressed.

Why did Washington issue a Farewell Address?

President Washington was concerned over the possibility of war with France. In a Farewell Address written in September 1796, he urged future leaders to keep the United States independent when dealing with other nations. Washington said:

The ideas expressed in the Farewell Address will be a cornerstone of American foreign policy, especially toward Europe.

> *The great rule of conduct for us in regard to foreign nations is, in extending our commercial relations to have with them as little* political *connection as possible. . . .*
> *It is our true policy to steer clear of permanent alliances with any portion of the foreign world, so far, I mean, as we are now at liberty to do it. . . .*

Washington went on to admit that temporary alliances are sometimes necessary. Permanent alliances were to be avoided, however.

1. What war in Europe threatened United States neutrality?
2. How did the European war affect American trade?
3. What advice did Washington give in his Farewell Address?

4. The Adams Presidency

The United States faced many challenges following 1796. For the first time under the Constitution, George Washington was not leading the country. During the years from 1788 to 1796, however, the new government had proved it could work. A pattern had been set which promised success in dealing with the future.

4.1 The Election of 1796. The presidential election of 1796 was the first between political parties. John Adams and Thomas Pinckney ran for the Federalists. Thomas Jefferson and Aaron Burr ran for the Democratic-Republicans. The vote was very close. Many people were angry about the Jay Treaty and gave their support to the

Democratic-Republican party. When the votes were counted, Adams received a majority and was elected President. Jefferson received the second largest number of votes and became Vice-President. These two political rivals would share the highest offices in the land. But their first concern was the threat of war with France.

Who followed Washington as President?

4.2   The XYZ Affair.   American relations with France had grown steadily worse during Washington's second term. The French had begun to do more damage to American shipping than had the British. President Adams was determined to avoid war. In 1797, he sent a peace commission to France. The three American commissioners were met by three people representing the French government. They demanded a loan for France and a bribe before allowing official talks to begin with the French government. The commissioners refused and returned to the United States. President Adams reported this to Congress, referring to the French officials as "X, Y, and Z." When news of the XYZ Affair became known, many Americans were angered. Congress voted funds to increase the size of the army and the navy. It seemed only a matter of time before war would break out.

A popular slogan at the time of the XYZ affair was "Millions for defense but not one cent for tribute."

4.3   The Convention of 1800.   A sudden change in the French government helped relations between the two countries. In 1799, an American mission was greeted with friendship by the new leader of France, Napoleon Bonaparte. The Treaty of Morfontaine, better

John Adams (left) defeated Thomas Jefferson (right) in the 1796 presidential election. This campaign offered American voters a choice between political parties. Which party did each candidate represent?

*What were the
agreements made in
the Convention of
1800?*

known as the Convention of 1800, was signed by representatives of the two countries. The United States was released from the Alliance of 1778. In return, the French did not have to pay damages for the American shipping they had destroyed. War had been avoided.

4.4 The Alien and Sedition Acts.   Differences between the Federalists and Democratic-Republicans grew stronger as the election of 1800 drew near. The Federalists worried that they might lose the election. They were alarmed at the growth of the Democratic-Republican party. Much of it came from immigrants joining that party.

In 1798, the Federalists in Congress passed several laws known as the Alien and Sedition Acts. These measures were intended to stop the Democratic-Republicans from gaining more power. One law increased the number of years needed for an *alien* (person who is not a citizen of the country in which he or she lives) to become a United States citizen. New immigrants then would not be able to vote for some years. In another act, the President was given the power to *deport* (send out of the country) any foreigner thought to be dangerous to the nation. The Sedition Act said that anyone guilty of *sedition*—the use of language to stir up rebellion against a government—could be fined and sent to prison. This law was aimed at a group of American newspaper writers who favored the Democratic-Republicans.

Why did the
Democratic-Republican
party oppose Jay's
Treaty? Why did the
Federalist party favor a
pro-British foreign
policy? Who would
most likely support the
Federalist party, a
Pennsylvania wheat
farmer or a
Massachusetts banker?
Who would most likely
support the
Democratic-Republican
party, a South Carolina
tobacco seller or a
Kentucky blacksmith?

Political Parties in the 1790's

Federalist		Democratic-Republican
Favored government control by wealthy and educated citizens	Political Beliefs	Favored the selection of representatives by average citizens
Favored a strong national government		Favored a limited national government
Supported government aid to business, finance, and trade	Economic Beliefs	Supported no special favors to business; preferred farming
Favored a national bank		Favored sound state banks
Supported protective tariffs		Supported duty free imports
Favored British commercial ties and feared the French	Foreign Affairs	Sympathized with the French Revolution
Favored Jay's Treaty		Opposed Jay's Treaty
Strong in New England and seacoast areas	Sources of Strength	Strong in south, southwest, and frontier areas
Manufacturing interests, bankers, and merchants		Farmers, artisans, and skilled workers

The Alien and Sedition Acts were used by the party in office to fight their rivals. Although they did not last, they were laws made at a time when some people thought that strong political actions against the party in office were disloyal and illegal. Slowly people began to understand that party opposition was not only legal but valuable as a check on the party in power.

Discuss the value of opposition to the group in power in a government and the dangers of having no opposition.

4.5 The Kentucky and Virginia Resolutions. The Alien and Sedition Acts were attacked by Democratic-Republicans as unconstitutional. In 1798, Jefferson and Madison wrote papers protesting these acts. Jefferson's ideas were adopted by the legislature of Kentucky and Madison's by Virginia. These papers are known as the Kentucky and Virginia Resolutions.

Students should understand that both views involved interpretation of the Constitution. This issue will be brought up many times as study progresses.

Jefferson and Madison stated that the federal government had been formed by an agreement among the states. They believed in *states' rights*—that each state could decide when an act of the government was unconstitutional. A state could declare a law *null and void* (not binding). The Federalists disagreed. They stated that the government had been formed by the people, and that only the Supreme Court had the power to declare a law unconstitutional. No other state legislatures agreed with Virginia and Kentucky. The questions raised by this issue were important but left to another time to be answered.

What was the basic idea presented in the Resolutions?

4.6 The Election of 1800. The Federalist party was badly divided by 1800. Hamilton and others were angry at President Adams, partly because he had made peace with France. Jefferson had won support for his attack of the Alien and Sedition Acts. In the election, a Democratic-Republican Congress was elected by a slim margin of votes. The results of the presidential election were in question for a while. Originally, the Constitution stated that electors would vote for two names for President. The person receiving the most votes would be President, and the person with the second largest number of votes would be Vice-President. In 1800, however, Jefferson and Aaron Burr, Republican candidate from New York, both received the same number of votes. The tie was settled in the House of Representatives where Jefferson was elected President. In 1804, an amendment was added to the Constitution to keep this from happening again. It said that electors would vote separately for President and Vice-President.

Hamilton used his influence to get several Federalists not to vote, thus allowing the House to choose Jefferson. Hamilton and Burr had long been rivals in New York. In 1804, they fought a duel over insults supposedly made by Hamilton. Hamilton was shot and killed.

Who tied for the Presidency in 1800?

Who settled the issue?

1. Who became President after George Washington?
2. With which country was the United States involved in the XYZ Affair?
3. What was the purpose of the Alien and Sedition Acts?
4. Who won the presidential election of 1800?

Election of 1800

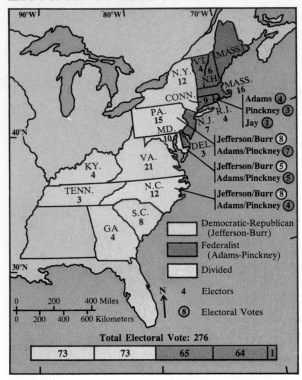

Adams ④
Pinckney ③
Jay ①

Jefferson/Burr ⑧
Adams/Pinckney ⑦

Jefferson/Burr ⑤
Adams/Pinckney ⑤

Jefferson/Burr ⑧
Adams/Pinckney ④

☐ Democratic-Republican
(Jefferson-Burr)

■ Federalist
(Adams-Pinckney)

☐ Divided

4 Electors

⑧ Electoral Votes

Total Electoral Vote: 276

| 73 | 73 | 65 | 64 | 1 |

REPUBLICANS

Turn out, turn out and save your Country from ruin !

From an *Emperor*—from a *King*—from the iron grasp of a *British Tory Faction*—an unprincipled banditti of British speculators. The hireling tools and emissaries of his majesty king George the 3d have thronged our city and diffused the poison of principles among us.

DOWN WITH THE TORIES, DOWN WITH THE BRITISH FACTION,

Before they have it in their power to enslave you, and reduce your families to distress by heavy taxation. Republicans want no Tribute-liars—they want no ship Ocean-liars—they want no Rufus King's for Lords —they want no Varick to lord it over them—they want no Jones for senator, who fought with the British against the Americans in time of the war.—But they want in their places such men as

Jefferson & Clinton,

who fought their Country's Battles in the year '76

A Federalist campaign poster (top right) maintained that Jefferson was unworthy to follow in the tradition of Washington. A Democratic-Republican notice (bottom right) said that the Federalists would lead the nation to ruin. Who won in 1800?

5. Jefferson in Office

When Thomas Jefferson was elected in 1800, it marked the beginning of many years of Democratic-Republican control in the United States. In an inaugural address made at his ***inauguration*** (ceremony of installing a person in office), Jefferson tried to quiet the fears of many Federalists who believed that he would make sweeping changes. He called upon all citizens to work together stating, "We are all Republicans, we are all Federalists."

Why did Jefferson think his election was a "revolution"?

5.1 The "Revolution of 1800." Jefferson liked to call his election the "Revolution of 1800." It showed that, in the United States, one political party could be defeated and the opposition party could take power peacefully. So far as policies were concerned, Jefferson's election was by no means a revolution. He continued the Bank of the United States and many of the policies of the Federalists. The biggest change he made was to cut government costs sharply, mostly by cutting money spent for the army and navy. He also ended the whiskey tax and raised money through customs duties and selling federal land.

5.2 Marbury v. Madison. Early in Jefferson's first term, the Supreme Court decided one of the most important cases in American history. The Federalists had lost control of the executive and legislative branches in the election of 1800. They wanted to make their hold on the judicial branch stronger. Between the election and the inauguration, Congress added to the number of judges and court officers. President Adams then named members of his party to fill these posts.

When Jefferson took office, he told Secretary of State James Madison to hold the papers that would allow the new officials to start their jobs. William Marbury brought suit against Madison to make him turn over the papers on his appointment. The case came before the Supreme Court. Chief Justice John Marshall stated the opinion of the Court in 1803. He said Marbury had a right to the papers, but that the Court could not force Madison to turn them over to him. According to the Judiciary Act of 1789, the Court had the power to give such orders. Marshall said that the Court could not do so because that part of the Judiciary Act was unconstitutional.

The case of *Marbury* v. *Madison* was the first time that the Supreme Court declared an act of Congress to be unconstitutional. In later decisions over the years, the Marshall Court said that the powers of the federal government were above those of the states in cases of constitutional law. All of these decisions made the judicial branch of the government as strong as the executive and legislative branches.

5.3 The Louisiana Purchase. Soon after he became President in 1801, Jefferson learned that Napoleon of France was taking control of Louisiana away from Spain. Louisiana was a huge area stretching from the Mississippi River to the Rocky Mountains. The people of the West depended on the Mississippi River and New Orleans, the gateway to the sea, to get their goods to market. They were afraid that the French would close the Mississippi River and New Orleans to American use.

Napoleon had been planning to build a new French empire in North America. He had to give up those plans, however, when slaves on the Caribbean island of Santo Domingo revolted against French rule. Led by Toussaint L'Ouverture, they established the nation of Haiti. Without the island as a naval base, Napoleon feared that he could not hold Louisiana against the British. So he offered to sell Louisiana to the United States.

This is a good place to make the point of how power passes from one party or person to another. Have students compare this with the process under a monarchy or one-party government.

Chief Justice Marshall was a cousin of President Jefferson.

Who declared an act of Congress unconstitutional?

Recall Chapter 7, Section 2.1, page 168, for judicial review.

The former slaves of Haiti revolted in 1791 and had defeated the French by 1804, becoming the first free black nation in the Western Hemisphere.

From whom was Louisiana purchased?

Refer students to Jefferson's view of the Constitution in Section 2.5 of this chapter.

Although Jefferson favored the purchase, he was worried because the Constitution did not give the federal government power to buy land from a foreign country. As President, however, he did have the power to make treaties with the approval of the Senate. So he decided to sign a treaty to buy Louisiana. In April 1803, an agreement was signed for the purchase of Louisiana. The United States received claim to 827,000 square miles of land for $15 million. This new land doubled the size of the country at that time.

Who served as guides for Lewis and Clark?

5.4 Exploring Louisiana. Very little was known about the area west of the Mississippi River. In 1804, President Jefferson sent a United States Army expedition under Captain Meriwether Lewis and Captain William Clark to explore the new territory. During their travels, they hired Sacajawea, a Shoshoni Indian, and her husband, Toussaint Charbonneau, a French fur trapper, to guide them. The

Note for students that areas on the map showing U.S. territories are part of the United States but have not yet become states.

This map shows the extent of the Louisiana Purchase. The routes of the Lewis and Clark expedition are also shown. Which Americans benefited most from the purchase? How did the purchase affect the size of the United States?

Exploring the Louisiana Purchase, 1806

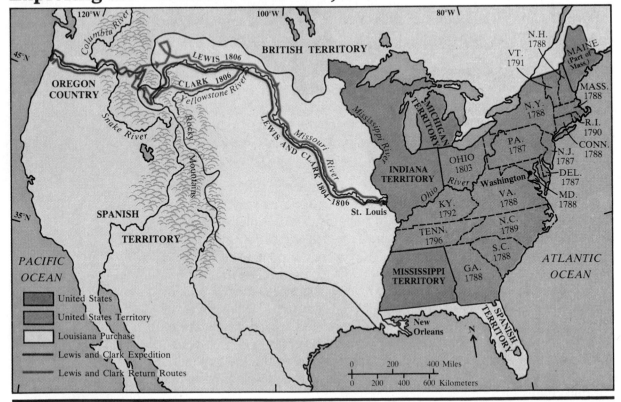

Lewis and Clark commanded an expedition of more than 50 people. Sacajawea, the only woman, joined the group as a guide. Ben York, Lewis' servant, was the only black. The others were soldiers, trappers, and volunteers. When was the trip?

group with Lewis and Clark made its way up the Missouri River and into the wilderness beyond. After crossing the Rocky Mountains, the expedition traveled down the Columbia River, reaching the Pacific Ocean in 1805. Lewis and Clark returned to St. Louis in 1806, bringing with them valuable facts about the lands west of the Mississippi. A whole new frontier was opened to American settlement.

Some 44 other people, soldiers and civilians, went with the expedition, including York, a slave of Clark.

1. What was the biggest change in government made by Thomas Jefferson as President?
2. What was the case in which the Supreme Court first declared an act of Congress unconstitutional?
3. Who led an expedition into Louisiana after its purchase in 1803?

6. Conclusion

The United States under the Constitution was a growing, changing country. In its early years, it faced many problems which the Framers of the Constitution had not expected. Some of the issues raised during these years would not be completely answered for years to come. But the new government had shown that it could withstand change and operate successfully. It had passed its first test. The nation had become established.

Chapter 8 Review

Main Points

1. As the first President of the United States, George Washington established many precedents.

2. Alexander Hamilton's economic program aimed to create a strong national economy.

3. Arguments over Hamilton's program led to the formation of political parties.

4. Foreign policy under Presidents Washington and Adams aimed to keep the United States neutral.

5. The Alien and Sedition Acts were passed in 1798. They were intended to stop the Democratic-Republicans from gaining more power.

6. The election of Thomas Jefferson as President in 1800 showed that control of government could pass peacefully from one party to another.

7. Under President Jefferson, the physical size of the United States increased with the purchase of Louisiana.

Building Vocabulary

1. Identify the following:

George Washington
Cabinet
Judiciary Act of 1789
Supreme Court
Alexander Hamilton
Benjamin Banneker

Whiskey Rebellion
Federalists
Democratic-Republicans
Jay Treaty
Pinckney Treaty

XYZ Affair
Alien and Sedition Acts
Marbury v. *Madison*
Toussaint L'Ouverture
Lewis and Clark Expedition
Sacajawea

2. Define the following:

electors
precedents
negotiating
appeal
domestic
bonds
speculators
redeemed

assume
duties
protective tariff
excise tax
strict construction
loose construction
neutrality

impressment
alien
deport
sedition
states' rights
null and void
inauguration

Remembering the Facts

1. How was George Washington elected as first President?

2. When and where did the new national government begin its work?

3. What were the levels of federal courts created by the Judiciary Act of 1789?

4. What were the main points of Hamilton's economic program?

5. Which political party supported a strict construction of the Constitution? Which supported a loose construction?

6. What were the provisions of the Jay Treaty with Britain in 1794?

7. What did the United States gain in the Pinckney Treaty of 1795?

8. What was the XYZ Affair?

9. How was the tied election of 1800 settled?

10. What was the issue in the case of *Marbury* v. *Madison*?

11. Where did Lewis and Clark explore? Who went with them?

Understanding the Facts

1. Why was George Washington's Presidency important?

2. Why was a strong court system a goal of the Framers of the Constitution?

3. What was the purpose of the Bank of the United States?

4. Why did Jefferson and his followers oppose the plan for a national bank?

5. Why did political parties form in the United States?

6. How did the Pinckney Treaty help farmers in the western United States?

7. Why did Congress pass the Alien and Sedition Acts in 1798?

8. What was the significance of the "Revolution of 1800"?

Using Maps

Direction and Distance. Two often asked questions about places are, What direction is one place from another? and, How far is one place from another? These questions were on the minds of Americans when the Louisiana Territory was purchased. This land was a new frontier that had little exploration before the Lewis and Clark expedition.

Check your understanding of direction and distance by using the map of the Louisiana Purchase on page 210. Using the scale and the direction indicator, answer the following questions.

1. Which direction from the United States was the Louisiana Territory?

2. Which direction provides the most direct route from Washington, D.C., to southern Louisiana?

3. When Lewis and Clark left St. Louis in 1804, which direction did they travel into Louisiana?

4. Which direction did Lewis and Clark travel along the Columbia River going toward the Pacific Ocean?

5. When Clark returned to St. Louis in 1806, what distance did he and his party travel along the Yellowstone River?

6. How far is Washington, D.C., from St. Louis?

7. How far did Lewis and Clark travel up the Missouri River?

The Growth of Nationalism

9

In 1812, the people in Philadelphia celebrated the Fourth of July. Less than half a century after Independence, the Fourth had become a national tradition. How did celebrating Independence Day help to form a national identity?

In the early 1800's, the future of the United States looked promising. The Constitution had proved to be a strong base upon which to build the new nation. The purchase of Louisiana more than doubled the size of the United States and gave people a huge new area in which to settle. Americans looked ahead confidently and expected to carry on their own affairs with no interference from Europe. They had created their own form of government, and they were beginning to create their own identity as a people.

1. The United States and Neutral Rights

President Jefferson began his second term of office in March 1805. He hoped to continue the policies which had brought peace and prosperity to the country during his first term. The United States had gained much from the long war between Great Britain and France. Both European countries bought American goods. Both allowed American merchants to trade with their West Indian islands. Things began to change, however, and foreign relations again became a major concern.

1.1 The Chesapeake Affair. Between 1804 and 1806, France conquered much of Europe. Great Britain, a major enemy of France, controlled the seas. Each nation wanted to limit the other's trade. Both countries stated that they would attack ships heading for the other's ports. Great Britain began to *blockade* (close off) the American coast to stop American ships loaded with goods on their way to France. The British also continued to impress American sailors into the British navy. These acts interfered with *freedom of the seas*—the right of merchant ships in peace or war to move in any waters, except those belonging to a country. The British acts angered people in the United States.

In June 1807, the British warship *Leopard* sailed up to the American warship *Chesapeake*. The British demanded the right to search the American ship for *deserters* (soldiers or sailors who run away from their duty). When the American officer refused, the *Leopard* opened fire. Three sailors were killed, and 18 were wounded. Four other sailors were taken off the ship, accused of being deserters.

1.2 The Embargo. After the attack on the *Chesapeake,* many Americans were ready for war. Jefferson, however, wanted to avoid it. He felt the country was not prepared to fight, because the Democratic-Republicans had reduced the size of the army and navy. Jefferson wanted to stop the British and French from harming

What was the Chesapeake Affair?

It might be interesting for someone in the class to read about conditions aboard ships during this period. This will help students to understand why the British navy was losing some 2,400 sailors a year through desertion.

Ograbme, a snapping turtle, was a favorite cartoon character after 1807. Ograbme is embargo spelled backward. This cartoon shows a turtle grabbing a man who is trying to smuggle a barrel of tobacco onto a British ship. What did the Embargo of 1807 accomplish?

What is an embargo?

Against whom was the Embargo Act directed?

What acts were passed after the repeal of the Embargo Act?

American trade. He decided that the answer was to keep American ships from sailing the seas.

As a result, Congress passed the Embargo Act of 1807. An *embargo* is a law stopping all ships except foreign ships without cargo from leaving the country for foreign ports. Jefferson hoped to win the respect of Britain and France for American rights by refusing to sell them American goods. The policy did not work. The embargo hurt American trade even more than it did that of other countries. Harbors were crowded with ships, and thousands of workers were out of work. Prices dropped as goods had to be stored. Congress soon repealed the act.

James Madison became President in 1808. Soon after the election, the Non-Intercourse Act was passed. It allowed Americans to trade with any country except France and Great Britain. In 1810, Congress passed a new act. Under Macon's Bill Number 2, it was decided that if either Great Britain or France lifted their restrictions on American shipping, America would cut off all trade with the other country. Napoleon agreed to do this, and Madison gave orders forbidding trade with Great Britain. By 1812, Great Britain was so hurt by the boycott that the British repealed their restrictions on American shipping.

1.3 Trouble on the Frontier. There was another reason why Americans were angry with Great Britain besides interference with trade and impressment. The British in Canada were helping the Indians fight American settlers along the western frontier. During this time, more and more settlers were crossing the Appalachian Mountains,

Tecumseh (1765–1813)

PROFILE

As settlers pushed west across the Appalachian Mountains, Indians of the Northwest Territory crowded together for support. They were afraid of losing their land and their ways of life. Tecumseh, chief of the Shawnee people, and his brother Tenskwatawa, the Prophet, tried to bring all the Indian people together to stop the advance of American settlement.

Tecumseh believed that all land, like water and air, belonged to all Indian people. He traveled and spoke with most of the Indian people east of the Rocky Mountains. A gifted speaker, Tecumseh urged the various groups to join together in a confederation. In this way, they could work as one to prevent the loss of their land and secure their future.

In 1808, Tecumseh and the Shawnee people were forced by settlers to move to Indiana from Ohio. While in Indiana, Tecumseh formed a plan of action that led to the Battle of Tippecanoe with United States soldiers in 1811.

When the War of 1812 began, Tecumseh believed that the British leaders were going to support his people's desire to protect their land in the Northwest Territory. So he and his followers joined the British soldiers against the Americans. The next year, United States forces defeated Tecumseh's soldiers at the Battle of the Thames, near Ontario, Canada. Tecumseh died in the battle, and with him, the dream of an Indian confederation died, too.

forcing the Indians to move farther west. As the Indians were crowded together, they were concerned about losing their lands and losing their ways of life.

Tecumseh, the chief of the Shawnees, and his brother, the Prophet, tried to unite several groups of Indians in 1811 in defense against the spread of white settlers. Many Indians along the frontier formed a confederation to try to prevent further loss of land. On November 7, 1811, American forces under General William Henry Harrison fought and defeated the Indians in western Indiana where the Tippecanoe River joins the Wabash River. The Indian defeat in the Battle of Tippecanoe was a major setback for Tecumseh's plans.

What did Tecumseh try to do?

Tecumseh was not present at the Battle of Tippecanoe, being away talking with other Indian groups about the confederation.

1.4 The War Hawks. Many people in the West called for war against Great Britain. They thought that this was the way to stop the British aid to the Indians along the western frontier. Many were also convinced that Spain was giving aid to the Indians in the southeast. Great Britain and Spain were allies, and it seemed that the two countries were working against the United States.

In 1810, several new members were elected to the House of Representatives. They voiced the demands of frontier people, stating that war was the way to protect American interests. Known as "War Hawks," they gained support for their views. Among them were John C. Calhoun of South Carolina and Henry Clay of Kentucky.

1.5 Madison's War Message. On June 1, 1812, President Madison sent a message to Congress. It asked for a declaration of war with Great Britain and stated his reasons. The British had impressed American sailors on the high seas, had blockaded the American coast, had interfered with trade, and had aided the Indians on the frontier. Although Congress was divided over the question of war, a majority in both houses voted in favor of the declaration. War was declared on June 18, 1812. The British had repealed their orders against American shipping two days before, but the news did not reach Congress in time.

1. Who interfered with United States' freedom of the seas?
2. How was the Embargo of 1807 unsuccessful?
3. With whom did the United States go to war in 1812?

2. The War of 1812

Those Americans who were in favor of the War of 1812 felt that the United States needed to force Great Britain to respect American rights. Yet the country was not prepared for war in many ways. The army and navy were small and poorly equipped. Financing the war would be a major problem, because the Bank of the United States had been allowed to go out of existence in 1811. In addition, most of the people in New England were against what they called "Mr. Madison's War."

2.1 America on the Offensive. One advantage for Americans at the beginning of the war was that the British were fighting a war with France in Europe. Because of this, the British could not concentrate their attention on the trouble in America. The United States was therefore able to take the offensive in the first year of the war.

A major American goal in the War of 1812 was to take over Canada. In the late summer of 1812, the United States planned a drive

Major Campaigns of the War of 1812

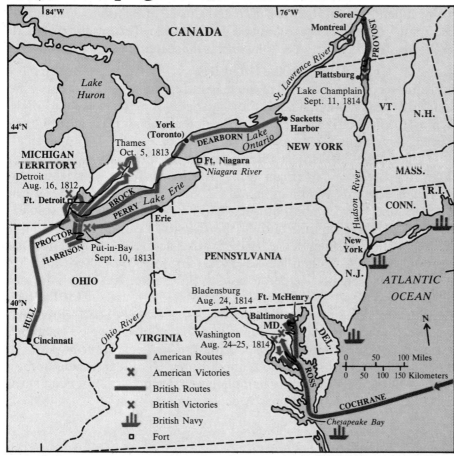

Major Campaigns of the War of 1812

CANADA

Lake Huron

84°W

76°W

Sorel
Montreal
PROVOST
Plattsburg

Lake Champlain
Sept. 11, 1814

VT.   N.H.

44°N

York (Toronto)
DEARBORN Lake Ontario
Sacketts Harbor

St. Lawrence River

Thames
Oct. 5, 1813

NEW YORK

MICHIGAN TERRITORY

Ft. Niagara
Niagara River

MASS.

Detroit
Aug. 16, 1812
Ft. Detroit

BROCK
PERRY Lake Erie
Erie

Hudson River

CONN.   R.I.

PROCTOR
HARRISON
Put-in-Bay
Sept. 10, 1813

New York

N.J.

ATLANTIC OCEAN

OHIO

PENNSYLVANIA

40°N

HULL

Cincinnati

Ohio River

VIRGINIA

Bladensburg
Aug. 24, 1814
Ft. McHenry

Baltimore
MD.

Washington
Aug. 24–25, 1814

DEL.

ROSS

N

0   50   100 Miles
0   50   100   150 Kilometers

American Routes
✕ American Victories
British Routes
✕ British Victories
British Navy
▫ Fort

COCHRANE
Chesapeake Bay

Many Americans believed that Canada would sooner or later become part of the United States, something most people in Canada regarded as a constant threat.

The major battles of the War of 1812 were widely scattered. Washington, the United States capital, and York, the Canadian capital at the time, were key military targets. What was each side trying to do? What was the purpose of the British blockade along the Atlantic coast?

on Canada. One attack was to be from Detroit, another along the Niagara River, and a third aimed at Montreal. All three attacks failed. Detroit fell to the British and Indians. British forces drove back two attacks across the Niagara River. The drive against Montreal ended when the New York militia refused to leave the United States.

The United States had few victories in 1812 except for those won by its small navy. Several American ships were sent out to harass and intercept the British fleet. The U.S.S. *Constitution* destroyed two British ships, earning the nickname "Old Ironsides." The British navy set up a blockade of the American coast early in 1813.

American forces were able to stop the British from taking the Great Lakes area in 1813. On September 10, naval forces led by Oliver Hazard Perry defeated the British at Put-in-Bay. Perry reported the

What was the American goal in the War of 1812?

Have a student who is interested in ships prepare a report on the U.S.S. *Constitution* with attention to improved technology in its construction.

Who was the hero of the Battle of Lake Erie?

The Growth of Nationalism   219

victory by saying, "We have met the enemy and they are ours." This victory gave Americans control of Lake Erie. On October 5, 1813, an army under General Harrison defeated a force of British and Indians at the Battle of the Thames in Canada. In the battle, Tecumseh was killed. With his death, efforts for a lasting Indian confederacy also died.

2.2   Great Britain on the Offensive.   By 1814, the British navy had almost complete control of the seas and commanded the coast of the United States. Until that year, they had been using most of their forces against the French in Europe. With the defeat of Napoleon in 1814, they turned their attention to the war in America.

On August 19, British forces landed on the coast of Maryland. They defeated an American army at Bladensburg, Maryland, and marched toward Washington, D.C. Several thousand American soldiers and government officers fled to Virginia. British soldiers entered Washington and burned the Capitol and the White House, home of the President. The British were acting in revenge for the burning of the Canadian city of York (Toronto) by Americans.

Next the British decided to attack Baltimore. But they were not able to break down the defenses of Fort McHenry just outside the city. During the three-day shelling of the fort, Francis Scott Key, who watched the battle, wrote a poem titled "The Star-Spangled Banner." Later it was set to music and became the *national anthem*—song of praise and patriotism—of the United States. About the same time, a British invasion along Lake Champlain was stopped by American naval forces under Captain Thomas Macdonough.

Why were the British able to take to the offensive?

See more on the burning of the Capitol in the City Sketch on page 256.

Where did the British attack?

Distribute copies of the words of the "Star Spangled Banner" to students. Discuss Key's feelings as reflected in the song.

The bombing of Fort McHenry by the British led Francis Scott Key to observe the "rockets' red glare." Key felt so proud of the way the American forces held out that he wrote a poem. Later his poem was set to music and became the national anthem. How does a national anthem encourage patriotism?

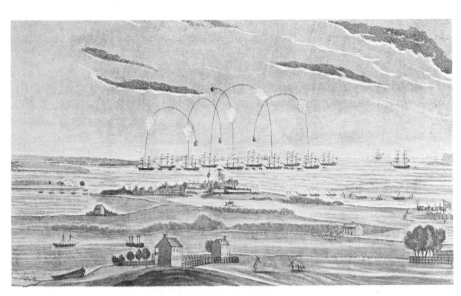

After peace was signed but before the news of it arrived, Americans defeated the British at New Orleans. Andrew Jackson (far right on the white horse) became one of many national heroes during the War of 1812. Dolley Madison and Oliver Hazard Perry were others. How did heroes help a national pride to grow?

2.3   The Battle of New Orleans.   After their failure to take Baltimore, the British prepared to attack New Orleans. They wanted to gain control of the entire Mississippi Valley. British ships sailed from the West Indies with 7,500 soldiers under Sir Edward Pakenham. American forces in New Orleans were led by General Andrew Jackson. Jackson had been fighting Indians in the Mississippi Territory since 1813. His troops had defeated the Indians at the Battle of Horseshoe Bend and had invaded Spanish Florida. They seized Pensacola in November 1814. Some of those who fought with Jackson in Florida were with him as he moved west to New Orleans.

Who commanded American troops in the Battle of New Orleans?

Most of the 5,000 American soldiers with Jackson, including two black battalions, had had little fighting experience. The British soldiers, on the other hand, were well trained and veterans of the war against France. They thought the Americans would not put up much resistance. Joining Jackson in New Orleans were several thousand other soldiers, including many from Kentucky and Tennessee and Jean Laffite from France. The British attacked on January 8, 1815. When the battle was over, about 2,000 British, including General Pakenham, had been killed or wounded. Less than 100 Americans had lost their lives.

American troops were lodged behind earthworks and the British chose to make a head-on attack.

The victory at New Orleans restored some of the national pride which had been lost because of earlier defeats. Many Americans felt they had won the war, but victory in this battle had no effect upon the war's outcome. Because of the slowness of communications, the Battle of New Orleans was fought after the treaty of peace.

What was unique about the Battle of New Orleans?

The American negotiators included John Quincy Adams and Henry Clay. American successes in the battles at Lake Champlain and Baltimore helped convince the British to sign a peace treaty.

What were the results of the War of 1812?

New England continued to trade with Canada throughout the war.

What was the Hartford Convention?

Recall the Virginia and Kentucky Resolutions in Section 4.5, page 207.

What happened to the Federalist party after the War of 1812?

2.4 The Treaty of Ghent. In August 1814, five American representatives had met with British officials in Ghent, Belgium, to discuss peace. For over three months, the two sides could not come to terms. Finally, on December 24, 1814, an agreement was reached to end the war. Neither side could claim victory. Nevertheless, the United States became more independent from European affairs after the war.

The Treaty of Ghent ended the fighting and brought peace. It said nothing, however, about the issues which had caused the war. It did not deal with impressment, blockades, or the United States' right to trade freely. It did return all land boundaries to what they had been when the war began. A commission was set up to decide the northeast boundary between the United States and Canada. Control of the Great Lakes and fishing rights were to be settled at a later date. The treaty was approved by the Senate on February 17, 1815.

2.5 The Hartford Convention. The war had been very unpopular in some parts of the United States. The area of the country most against it was New England. People there made their living by trade, and this was greatly hurt when the war began. New England was the only area of the country where the Federalists were in a majority, and the Federalists led the fight against the war.

When the war dragged on without a victory, New England Federalists became more and more bitter. In December 1814, they held a convention in Hartford, Connecticut. They met to discuss ways of taking action against the war. Some members of the group thought the New England states should *secede,* or break away from the United States. Few of the members agreed with this, however. After much discussion, a report was written. It stated that if a state found a federal law to be unconstitutional, it had the right to protect itself—to declare that law null and void. This idea had appeared earlier in the Kentucky and Virginia Resolutions written by Democratic-Republicans.

The report also included a list of amendments to be added to the Constitution. They would add to the powers of the states and take some power away from the federal government. Because they did not like James Madison, the members of the Convention wanted Presidents to serve only a single term in office. They wanted a two-thirds vote of both houses of Congress before war could be declared or new states could be added to the United States.

The Hartford Convention sent representatives to Washington to present their demands to the government there. When they arrived, however, the people were celebrating news of the Treaty of Ghent and Jackson's victory at New Orleans. The Hartford Convention had met too late to have any effect upon the war. Later it was thought to have been disloyal to the United States, and the Federalists were looked upon as traitors. The power of the party was destroyed after the war.

1. Where were the major American victories in the war?
2. When was the treaty signed to end the war?
3. Which section of the United States opposed the war?

3. The National Spirit

The War of 1812 is sometimes called the "Second War of Independence." From 1789 to 1815, American policies had often been shaped by events in Europe. For 100 years after the Treaty of Ghent, the United States was more independent from Europe and was not directly involved in European wars. This gave Americans a chance to develop their own country. The end of the War of 1812 began a time of strong national pride under the Democratic-Republican party.

3.1 Nationalism and Politics. A spirit of nationalism was behind the message that President Madison presented to Congress in December 1815. *Nationalism* is a feeling of pride in the nation as a whole and loyalty to its goals. Madison called upon Congress to pass several measures to make the country strong and protect its independence. To give the country a sound money supply, Madison asked for a new Bank of the United States. He wanted a protective tariff to help American industry to grow. To improve transportation and help trade, he called for government money to build a system of roads and canals. To better protect the country, he asked that the army and navy be made larger.

It seemed to many people that the Democratic-Republicans had taken over much of the Federalist program. President Madison's ideas meant more power and responsibility for the federal government. However, many people were no longer against this and were in favor of the President's plans. By the time James Monroe took office in March 1817, much of Madison's program had been passed.

In 1816, Congress chartered the Second Bank of the United States for 20 years. When the first Bank had gone out of existence in 1811, many state governments had given bank charters to private individuals. These banks did not always have enough gold or silver to back up their paper money. Its value declined, creating an unstable financial situation. The Second Bank of the United States was strong and had many branches in different states. The money it issued was sound, and it had control over the less stable state-chartered banks.

Discuss what is meant by national spirit or nationalism. Discuss ways in which these are expressed today. Refer students to the Feature on page 227.

What things did President Madison want Congress to pass?

Recall Hamilton's ideas in Chapter 8, Section 2.5.

Why was a new Bank of the United States needed?

Make sure the ideas in this part are understood. They will be of importance again in Chapter 10.

How did the Tariff of 1816 protect American industries?

Congress also passed a new tariff in 1816. As the first real protective tariff, it placed high duties on foreign manufactured goods shipped into the United States. During the War of 1812, it had been hard to get some goods from Europe. As a result, many new factories had been built in America. After the war, the British sent large shipments of goods to sell in the United States. These goods were generally cheaper than those made in America. By having lower prices, the British hoped to drive the new American industries out of business. The Tariff of 1816, however, protected the new American industries by adding to the price of British products.

The building of a good transportation system was important to the United States. Farmers in the West and South needed roads and canals to carry goods to the East where a large amount went on to foreign markets. Northeastern manufacturers needed to move their goods to the West. However, the plan for building roads moved ahead slowly.

What road was built with federal aid?

Only one important route to the West was finished with federal aid. This was the Cumberland, or National, Road which was first planned in

The Erie Canal (left) was the first canal in America. It launched a boom in canal construction that lasted until the mid-1800's. New roads were also built during that time. A stagecoach (right) bounces along an unfinished portion of the National Road. Notice where the canals and roads are located on the map on the next page. How did farmers in the South get goods to markets along the Atlantic coast?

Many roads at this time were "toll roads," built and owned by private companies.

Principal Roads and Canals by 1840

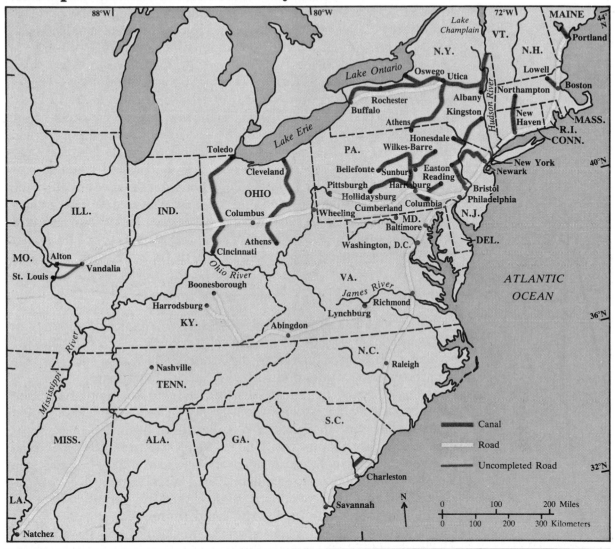

1807. Construction began in 1811, and by 1818, it joined the Potomac and Ohio rivers. Between 1822 and 1838, it was extended through Columbus, Ohio, and Indianapolis, Indiana, to Vandalia, Illinois. Bills for more roads and canals paid for by the federal government were thought to be unconstitutional by Presidents Monroe, Adams, and Jackson over the years. The idea of a national system of transportation had to be set aside for a time. Many of the roads and canals that were built were paid for by the states or by private companies.

Compare a map of the eastern U.S. showing major roads in 1835 with a map showing major roads today. Discuss what this means for communications and for national unity.

Recall the case of *Marbury* v. *Madison* in Chapter 8, Section 5.2.

You may want students to refer to Chapter 7 and to the text of the Constitution that appears in the appendix.

What idea was at the base of the Court's decisions in the early 1800's?

What were the provisions of the Adams-Onís Treaty?

The boundary line between U.S. and Spanish territory is shown in Chapter 13, page 310.

These nations were struggling to become democracies on the American model and were resented by the monarchies of Europe.

Why did Monroe announce the Monroe Doctrine?

3.2 Nationalism and the Courts.   The judicial branch of the government strongly supported nationalism in the early 1800's. Chief Justice John Marshall was the leading figure in the Supreme Court. He had already stated his ideas about the role of the courts and judicial review in his opinion on the 1803 case of *Marbury* v. *Madison*.

In the case of *Fletcher* v. *Peck* in 1810, the Supreme Court ruled that acts of a state government could be voided if they violated provisions of the Constitution. In 1819, the Court ruled in *McCullough* v. *Maryland* that the state of Maryland could not tax the Bank of the United States. This ruling upheld the doctrine of implied powers and the supremacy of the national government. Marshall said that "the power to tax involves the power to destroy," and no state could destroy a national institution. In the case of *Gibbons* v. *Ogden* in 1824, the Supreme Court said that the state of New York could not grant a monopoly to anyone to run steamboats between New York and New Jersey. The opinion of the Court was that only Congress had the power to make laws governing **interstate trade,** or trade between or among states. All of these decisions added to the power of the national government over that of the states.

3.3 Nationalism and Foreign Affairs.   A spirit of nationalism was shown in American foreign policy after the War of 1812. With the problems of Europe involving the United States less and less, the country turned its attention to the Western Hemisphere.

A new time of expansion began after the war. Spain and the United States agreed in the Adams-Onís Treaty of 1819 that Spain would **renounce** (give up) all claims to West Florida and would **cede** (yield or grant) East Florida to the United States. In return, the federal government agreed to pay claims of American citizens against the Spanish government up to $5 million. The United States also gave up its claims to Texas. The two countries also agreed to a boundary between the United States and the Spanish lands to the west.

In the early 1800's, many Spanish colonies in Latin America had won their independence from Spain. Some European countries were thinking about returning these colonies to Spain or possibly taking them over. America wanted the colonies to stay independent. In December 1823, President Monroe announced what was later to become known as the Monroe Doctrine. He said that North and South America should no longer be thought of as "subjects for future colonization" by European countries. The United States would not interfere in European affairs, and Europeans were not to interfere in the affairs of the Western Hemisphere. Monroe's statement was a warning to European nations to keep "hands off" the newly independent Latin American countries. It

Nationalism

CONCEPT

Nationalism is a feeling of pride and devotion to a nation. The spirit of nationalism raises that nation above all others, promoting loyalty to its culture and interests. In the United States, American nationalism uniquely developed among people who came from various countries. These people became proud of the United States and loyal to it.

This feeling of nationalism grew in Mary Jane Watson in the 1820's when she came with her parents to live in Albany, New York. She wrote a letter in 1825 to her grandparents in England. She expressed her feelings about her new country and her confidence in its future.

My Dear Grandparents:

. . . It would be very agreeable for me to see my English friends, but I don't wish to return to England again. I like America much the best; it is a very plentiful country. A person may get a very good living here if they are industrious.

My father is doing very well and is very well satisfied to stay in this country. He has got a cow of his own and nine hogs. . . .

I have been very fortunate. I have got good clothes, and I can dress as well as any [upper-class woman] in Sedlescomb. I can enjoy a silk and white frock, and crepe frock and crepe veil. . . . You cannot tell the poor from the rich here; they are dressed as good as the other. . . .

We want Uncle William to come over to America. . . . [He] must . . . bring all . . . working tools. . . . Don't be discouraged now because some come back. Don't do as Mr. Rolfe did, step on shore and, before you know anything about the place, go right back again.

Any respectable person may get a good living by industry. It is a good place for young people; they can get good wages for their work. . . .

The people here are very good about education, much more than they are in England.

Mother and Father wish to be remembered to you. . . .

Your very affectionate granddaughter,
MARY JANE WATSON

1. How does Watson feel about her new home in the United States?
2. How does what Watson wrote in her letter show nationalism?
3. Why does Watson exaggerate the equality of life in America?

was also a warning to Russia not to move into the Pacific Coast area south of Alaska, which Russia held.

Americans were proud of Monroe's statement, but it was not greatly respected in Europe. At the time the Monroe Doctrine was issued, the United States could not really enforce it. For the most part, European nations left the Latin American countries alone because Great Britain had warned them away. The British had a strong trade with these countries and would use their navy to protect it. It was not until years later that the Monroe Doctrine became a powerful force in foreign affairs. In issuing the Doctrine, however, the United States had shown its political independence and its growing spirit of unity.

Who made the Monroe Doctrine effective in its early years?

1. How was the spirit of nationalism reflected in actions of Congress?
2. Which actions by the Supreme Court showed a feeling of nationalism?
3. How was American nationalism seen in United States foreign policy?

4. The Creation of a National Culture

The growing nationalism after the War of 1812 led to the rise of a truly American culture. From colonial times through the War of 1812, cultural life in the United States was strongly influenced by Europe, chiefly Great Britain. Long after they had won independence, Americans read European literature and admired European art and architecture. In the years after the War of 1812, however, Americans began to create their own art forms.

Who influenced American cultural life prior to 1812?

Select passages from some of the literature of this period and read it to the class as a means of showing the use of American themes.

4.1 American Literature. During the country's first years, most American authors wrote about political matters. Many of them copied British writing because most people in the United States favored British literature. Few publishers would print the works of American authors. After the War of 1812, American authors were inspired by the national feeling. They began to form their own literature. They used settings, characters, and humor that were typically American.

What was unique about Irving's writing?

Washington Irving of New York was one of the first authors to break away from British influence. He was also one of the first Americans to be widely read in Europe. The publication of his major work, the *Sketch Book,* in 1820 showed Irving's skill at short-story writing. In "Rip Van Winkle" and "The Legend of Sleepy Hollow," he

President James Monroe (standing) discusses foreign policy with his Cabinet—John Quincy Adams, William H. Crawford, William Wirt, John C. Calhoun, Samuel L. Southard, and John McLean. What was the major contribution of the Monroe administration to foreign policy?

wrote about life in the Hudson River Valley. He used American forms of speech and action as well as America's history for his works.

One of the country's first major novelists was James Fenimore Cooper of New York. He wrote the "Leatherstocking" tales, including *The Last of the Mohicans, The Pathfinder,* and *The Deerslayer.* In these tales of the early western frontier, Cooper created an American folk hero in the character of "Leatherstocking." His adventure stories became well known in both America and Europe.

Other authors, such as William Cullen Bryant of Massachusetts, wrote poetry. Bryant expressed a love for natural beauty. His poem "Thanatopsis" appeared in 1817. In it, he suggested that by studying nature, people could better understand life and death.

Bryan's poetry expresses a love for what thing?

> So live, that when thy summons comes to join
> The innumerable caravan, that moves
> To that mysterious realm, where each shall take
> His chamber in the silent halls of death,
> Thou go not, like the quarry-slave at night
> Scourged to his dungeon, but, sustained and soothed
> By an unfaltering trust, approach thy grave,
> Like one who draws the drapery of his couch
> About him, and lies down to pleasant dreams.

With such poems as "Thanatopsis" and "To a Waterfowl," Bryant became famous on both sides of the Atlantic Ocean.

If possible, show pictures and slides of artwork of this period showing American themes in painting.

Who were some important American artists that contributed to the growth of the national spirit?

4.2   American Painting and Music.   Like literature, American painting in the country's early years was influenced by Europe. Well-known artists like Benjamin West, John Singleton Copley, and Gilbert Stuart had studied abroad and followed the British style of painting. They most often painted portraits.

After the War of 1812, American artists turned their attention to American themes. In the East, William Sidney Mount painted his Long Island neighbors at work and play. He showed them at barn dances, fishing in their boats, whittling wood, and bowling on the green. George Caleb Bingham left a vivid account of everyday life on the Missouri frontier. He pictured fur traders, riverboat workers, political speakers, and tax-paying citizens. George Catlin was one of several artists who lived and worked among the Indians. He painted scenes of their daily life, at trading posts and on hunting trips.

American painters also found inspiration in the rugged beauty of their country. Thomas Doughty of Pennsylvania was one of the first successful landscape painters and a leader of the "Hudson River

George Catlin (left) always attracted a crowd when he set up his easel. Catlin painted Four Bears (right), a Mandan chief, in 1832. How did Catlin and other artists contribute to what was known about Indians at the time?

School" of painting. This was made up of artists who liked to paint views of the Catskill Mountains and the Hudson River in New York. One of these artists, Thomas Cole of Ohio, became well known for his huge paintings of the mountains and forests of America. The public paid attention to the painting of this time. More Americans attended art shows and bought paintings to hang in their homes.

People also enjoyed the lighter side of cultural life. Almost every large city had more than one theater. Companies of players visited smaller towns, performing in barns, tents, or log cabins. Plays and musicals were most often a part of any steamboat trip. Families bought pianos to play tunes written by Americans. Stephen Foster was one such songwriter. "My Old Kentucky Home" and "O Susanna," written by Foster, were played, sung, or hummed by thousands. American music, like American literature and art, was created for all the people to enjoy.

What other cultural developments occurred in the years after the War of 1812?

4.3 American Architecture. Some Americans showed their pride in America in literature and painting. Others designed private homes and public buildings that would display the spirit of the nation. In the early years, American buildings had been copies of ones in Europe. After Americans had won independence, they wanted buildings in their own styles. At first, Americans borrowed from those of ancient Rome. This was called the "Roman Revival." Thomas Jefferson thought about Roman styles when he planned his home, Monticello, and buildings for the University of Virginia.

A Greek style followed the Roman style. This "Greek Revival" was partly due to American feeling about the Greek revolt against Turkey in 1821. Greek design became the model for public buildings all over the country, including the Capitol in Washington, D.C. It was also used for private homes, such as the plantation houses in the South.

If possible, show pictures and slides of American architecture of this period showing Roman or Greek Revival styles.

1. What settings were used by American writers in the 1800's?
2. What were the themes of American painters after 1812?
3. Which styles were most used by American architects?

5. Conclusion

In the years after the War of 1812, Americans gained confidence in their own abilities and in the future of their country. The war was a turning point after which the American people began to establish a separate identity. The attention of the nation turned from Europe toward America. A new period of national growth and territorial expansion was about to begin.

Chapter 9 Review

Main Points

1. War between France and Britain brought prosperity and problems to America.
2. France and Britain both interfered with United States shipping and trade.
3. An embargo in 1807 failed to force France and Britain to respect the rights of the United States.
4. Under Tecumseh, a confederation of Indians tried to halt the western expansion of American settlers.
5. The United States fought a war with Britain between 1812 and 1814.
6. The Treaty of Ghent, signed on December 24, 1814, ended the war and set the peace terms.
7. Following the war, a spirit of nationalism influenced actions in domestic and foreign affairs.
8. The growth of nationalism led to the development of a unique American culture.

Building Vocabulary

1. Identify the following:

Chesapeake	Andrew Jackson	Monroe Doctrine
Tecumseh	Treaty of Ghent	Washington Irving
War Hawks	Hartford Convention	"Thanatopsis"
"Old Ironsides"	Cumberland Road	Thomas Doughty
Oliver Hazard Perry	*McCullough* v. *Maryland*	Stephen Foster
Francis Scott Key		"Greek Revival"

2. Define the following:

blockade	national anthem	interstate trade
freedom of the seas	secede	renounce
deserters	nationalism	cede
embargo		

Remembering the Facts

1. How did war in Europe affect American trade in the early 1800's?
2. Why did the United States embargo its trade with foreign countries?
3. Which frontier conflict increased tension between Britain and America?
4. What were the major American victories of the War of 1812?
5. Why did people in New England oppose the war?
6. What were the provisions of the Treaty of Ghent in 1814?

7. Which Federalist ideas were adopted by President Madison and his party?
8. What were the provisions of the Monroe Doctrine?

9. Who was the first American author to break away from British styles?
10. What was the "Hudson River School"? Who was its leader?

Understanding the Facts

1. Why did the United States go to war with Britain rather than France?
2. How did poor communications influence both the start of the war and the Battle of New Orleans?
3. Why did the War of 1812 weaken the Federalist party?

4. Why was the War of 1812 called the "Second War for Independence"?
5. What change took place in American culture after the War of 1812?
6. What does the increased nationalism tell about the way Americans thought of themselves and their country?

Using Maps

Tracing Routes.   Certain map skills are needed to gain information from a line of travel on a map. Knowing direction, using the scale, and reading the key make it possible to use a map to trace past events. Use the map on page 219 to answer the following questions about the War of 1812.

1. How are American troops shown on this map?
2. How are British troops shown?
3. What was the starting point for United States soldiers who took part in the western attacks on Canada?
4. Where did the Americans attack Canada?

5. How far did American troops travel on their way to fight in the Battle of the Thames?
6. From which direction did British soldiers move in their approach to Washington, D.C.?
7. How far did British soldiers travel overland to Washington?
8. Which places in the area of Virginia and Maryland, other than Washington, were attacked by British troops?
9. From which direction did the American navy approach York, Canada?
10. Which direction is Plattsburg, New York, from Montreal, Quebec?

The Age of Jackson 10

Andrew Jackson ushered in a new generation of political leaders. Electoral reform sparked greater participation. George Caleb Bingham captures the spirit in this painting, "Verdict of the People." Why was this time called the "Age of Jackson"?

The spirit of nationalism that swept the country after the War of 1812 led to a time of political unity. Because of this, the years that James Monroe served as President were called the "Era of Good Feelings." By 1816, the Federalist party had died, and in 1820, the Democratic-Republican candidate Monroe was reelected without opposition.

What was at the base of the "Era of Good Feelings"?

The political unity was short-lived, however. It had only existed on the surface. New forces were at work which would soon change the American political system. In 1828, these forces put Andrew Jackson in the White House. More than any other person, Jackson stood for the growing power of the American people in government. Because he was so important to the politics of the time, the years from 1828 to 1840 are known as the "Age of Jackson."

Students should understand that the term "Age of Jackson" is used by historians to label this period.

1. The Return of the Two-Party System

After the death of the Federalist party in 1816, the Democratic-Republicans dominated politics. But by 1824, the "Era of Good Feelings" was drawing to a close. Differences began to arise between groups in the party. Both the growing power of the common people and the rivalry among the major sections of the country created conflict in the years between 1824 and 1828. It was during this time that new parties began to take shape.

1.1 The Election of 1824. As the country grew, different sections—the Northeast, South, and West—began to form. Often they had different ideas and concerns. This gave rise to *sectionalism*—rivalry based on the special interests of different areas in a country.

What is sectionalism?

In 1824, each area offered its own candidate for President. Leaders in New England were most interested in business and manufacturing. They wanted John Quincy Adams of Massachusetts as President. People in the west wanted better transportation and cheaper land prices. Both Henry Clay of Kentucky and Andrew Jackson of Tennessee were from the West, although Clay thought of himself as a national figure. People in the South wanted lower taxes on imported goods. They backed either John C. Calhoun of South Carolina or William Crawford of Georgia. Calhoun later withdrew to run for Vice-President. All of the candidates called themselves Democratic-Republicans. The official representative of the party was Crawford.

Recall for students that there were different regions during the colonial period, each with different interests. Discuss the meaning of sectionalism and any evidence that it still exists.

None of the candidates won the necessary majority of electoral votes in 1824. For cases like that, the Constitution states in the Twelfth

The Age of Jackson   235

Although John Quincy Adams (left) and Andrew Jackson (right) posed the same way for these portraits, they had little in common politically. Over what issues did Adams and Jackson disagree? How did they represent a split in their party?

Recall the election of 1800 in Chapter 8, Section 4.6, page 207.

Amendment that the House of Representatives is to choose the President from the top three. Because Jackson had received the largest number of votes, his supporters expected him to be chosen.

Henry Clay, who came in fourth, was out of the running for President. He asked his followers in the House to vote for Adams. Adams was close to Clay in his support of the American System. This was an economic plan that included a national bank, a protective tariff, and a system of roads and canals paid for by the federal government. With Clay's help, Adams was chosen President.

Who was elected President in 1824?

1.2   A Split in the Party.   Shortly after taking office, President Adams named Henry Clay to be Secretary of State. Those people who followed Jackson were angry at this. They charged that a ***corrupt bargain*** had been made between Clay and Adams—that Clay had helped Adams win the election so that, in return, he would get a top post in his ***administration***—the major offices in the executive branch of the government. In 1825, Andrew Jackson left the Senate and began to campaign for President. Members of Congress who supported Jackson worked against Adams and blocked most of his plans.

Why was there a split in the Demo-cratic-Republican party?

Near the end of Adams' term in office, Congress passed the Tariff Act of 1828 to protect certain raw materials and woolen goods. People in the South were strongly against this measure as it would harm their direct trade with England. Northeastern manufacturers favored the tariff because it would protect American industry. Sectional differences like this led to a split in the Democratic-Republican party. Those favoring Jackson became Democrats, while Adams and his followers became National-Republicans. In 1828, there would again be two parties in the election.

1.3 The Election of 1828. Followers of Jackson were determined that he would win the election of 1828. They worked hard to gain support for him all over the country. People in the sections of the country backed Jackson for different reasons. Those in the South thought Jackson believed in states' rights. In the West, people hoped Jackson would use federal money to build roads and canals. They also expected that he would put an end to the Second Bank of the United States. The new Democratic party was strong in certain states of the Northeast, such as Pennsylvania and New York.

For what reasons was Jackson supported?

In the election of 1824, what section of the country voted for Andrew Jackson? What section voted for John Quincy Adams? How did Adams win the election of 1824? Where did Jackson gain support to win in 1828?

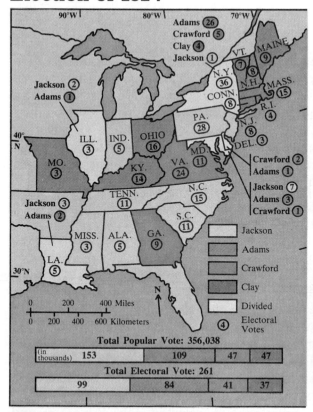

Election of 1824

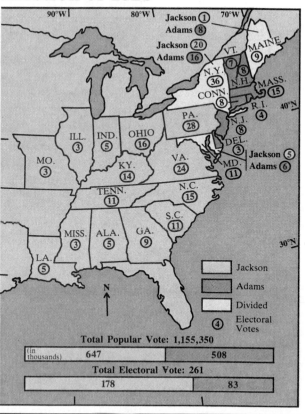

Election of 1828

In 1828, Andrew Jackson received 178 electoral votes to 83 for John Quincy Adams. Jackson won the election with a clear majority. He was the first person from the West to become President. All former Presidents had been from Virginia or Massachusetts.

1. Who were the candidates for President in 1824?
2. Why was the North in favor and the South against a protective tariff?
3. Which party won the election of 1828?

2. Jacksonian Democracy

Thousands of people went to Washington, D.C., for the new President's inauguration. Many of them were average Americans who felt Jackson's election was a victory of the common people. For the first time, the votes of these people—from city workers to farmers—had played an important part in a national election. Jackson was felt to be more truly a choice of the people than any former President.

How was Jackson's victory in 1828 viewed?

2.1 The Jacksonian Ideal.   Andrew Jackson stood for certain things which many Americans regarded with favor. He was an example of the frontier spirit and, like many others, had moved west into Indian lands. He had fought both the Indians and the British and was a military hero as a result of the Battle of New Orleans. He did not have the education or political experience of other Presidents. However, many people saw this as an advantage. Jackson seemed to prove that an ordinary American could become President.

Have students consider why there might be a greater feeling of equality in frontier areas.

2.2 The Growing Power of the People.   Jackson became President at a time when greater numbers of people in the United States were able to take part in politics. The Constitution had allowed each state to decide which of its citizens could vote. Older state laws had limited voting to white males who owned property. Often there were also religious restrictions. Qualifications for *suffrage* (the right to vote) were first changed in the new states west of the Appalachian Mountains. Their laws allowed almost any white male citizen to vote or hold office. The laws of the eastern states changed more slowly.

Where were voting qualifications first changed?

Up to this time, the Presidency had been far-removed from control of the people. Candidates for President and Vice-President had been selected by party leaders in closed meetings, or *caucuses*. Then electors, picked by the state governments, selected the President and

John Floyd (1783–1837)

PROFILE

For most of his life, John Floyd actively supported political causes. He defended frontier interests. He encouraged Americans to settle the Oregon country. He was bitterly against Andrew Jackson. And he could not be moved from his stand for states' rights.

Floyd was born in the Kentucky territory. He studied medicine in Pennsylvania and settled in Virginia where his family first lived. In 1817, he was elected to the United States Congress where he fought for his causes, especially states' rights.

Floyd backed Jackson for President in 1828 because he thought Jackson would name him to a Cabinet post. When this did not happen and when Jackson showed his opposition to states' rights, Floyd became one of Jackson's main enemies.

On November 17, 1832, Floyd wrote in his diary:

Jackson is again elected . . . President of the United States. Should he still pursue his ignorant and violent course, which there is a strong probability he will do, we will never see another President of the United States elected.

Floyd left the federal government discouraged because not many there supported those things he did. Back home in Virginia, he was elected governor and kept up his objection to a strong national government. John Floyd felt the only way to guarantee states' rights was for states to secede from the Union.

Vice-President from among the candidates. By the early 1830's, candidates were nominated by convention, and citizens voted directly for presidential electors.

How were candidates nominated by the early 1830's?

The number of voters had grown by the 1830's, and their influence had become stronger. However, the greater democracy of the Age of Jackson did not extend to women, slaves, or Indians. In fact, while the laws were changing to allow more white males to vote and hold office, laws for slaves were becoming more harsh. Equal opportunity for each person in the country had yet to come.

Slavery will be discussed more fully in Chapter 14.

2.3 The Spoils System. Soon after taking office in 1829, President Jackson began to put members of his own party in government jobs. He believed that changing the people who held these jobs would protect the government from dishonesty. It would also bring about greater democracy in the government. One of the people who agreed with Jackson, William Marcy of New York, was quoted as saying "to the victor belongs the spoils." So the practice of giving government jobs to political supporters came to be known as the *spoils system*. President Jackson called it "rotation in office." Jackson used the spoils system more widely than any former President. He set a pattern which would be followed for many years—sometimes with poor results.

Who coined the idea of a "spoils system"?

Have students consider both advantages and disadvantages of the spoils system.

1. What did Andrew Jackson do before becoming President?
2. Which groups did not have the right to vote?
3. How did President Jackson use the spoils system?

Use the study of President Jackson as an occasion to discuss presidential leadership. Make a list of the things which students consider important in a President and use the list to measure Jackson and other Presidents by it.

3. Jackson's Use of Presidential Power

Andrew Jackson was liked by many voters because of his courage and daring in battle. As the leader of his party, he showed strong will in political battles. Jackson was thought to be a strong President and as such greatly influenced politics in the United States.

3.1 Executive Powers. Other Presidents had respected but not often used the powers of their office. George Washington had thought of himself as the chief executive whose job was to carry out the will of Congress. Jefferson had tried to act inside strict guidelines stated in the Constitution.

How did Jackson differ from earlier Presidents?

Jackson, on the other hand, believed in the powers of his office and did not hesitate to use them. All six former Presidents together had vetoed only nine bills passed by Congress. Jackson alone vetoed 12. Other Presidents had vetoed bills only when they thought them unconstitutional. Jackson vetoed them for political reasons as well. If a decision of the Supreme Court was different from his own views, Jackson felt he should have the last word. At first, few people knew what Jackson's views were on major issues. As events happened, the President's views became clear. Sometimes he was in favor of the rights of the states, and at other times the rights of the federal government.

3.2 States' Rights and Union. President Jackson's power was challenged shortly after he took office. Many people in the South were angry over the Tariff of 1828. During the summer of that year, South Carolina printed the "South Carolina Exposition and Protest." It was

Daniel Webster of Massachusetts (standing) speaks to the Senate. He is answering Robert Hayne of South Carolina (seated center, left of the Senator with his hand on his chin). What was the major issue of the Webster-Hayne debates?

later learned that Vice-President John C. Calhoun was its author. The paper said that each state could decide when an act of Congress was unconstitutional. If it so decided, the state could then declare the law null and void. This plan of *nullification* was much like that set forth earlier in the Kentucky and Virginia Resolutions. It had also been offered by New England Federalists at the Hartford Convention. To get a law passed once a state had nullified it, three fourths of the states would have to ratify it as an amendment to the Constitution.

What is nullification?

People in the South tried to win western support for nullification in 1830, during a debate in the Senate which began over western lands. People in the West were angry because of a bill which would limit the sale of these lands. Robert Hayne of South Carolina said that the Union was a joining of separate states. So the western states could nullify the bill if it became law. Daniel Webster of Massachusetts argued that the Union was a national government of all people in all states. He was against the idea of nullification. Webster said that only the Supreme Court had the right to decide if a law was constitutional.

What were Daniel Webster's thoughts on nullification?

The Webster-Hayne debates did not settle the question. No one was certain which side President Jackson would favor. In April 1830, leaders of the Democratic party held a dinner in honor of the late

Democrats trace the beginning of their party back to Thomas Jefferson.

Thomas Jefferson. At that dinner, Jackson offered a toast: "Our Federal Union: It must be preserved." It was clear that the President agreed with the views of Webster against nullification. Calhoun then rose to speak: "The Union, next to our liberty, most dear." This was a break between the two highest officers of the land. Jackson and Calhoun agreed on many things. But they had sharply different views on the major question of the right of a state to resist federal authority.

Why did Jackson veto the Maysville Road bill?

3.3 The Maysville Road Veto.   President Jackson was a strong nationalist. He also believed in a narrow interpretation of the Constitution. Jackson believed in the absolute power of the federal government in its sphere. However, he wanted to limit that sphere. Shortly after the Jefferson Day dinner, he showed this point of view by vetoing the Maysville Road bill.

Use recent newspaper or magazine articles which show government support for roads and other projects. Have students decide whether Jackson would have supported or opposed each based on his stand on the Maysville Road bill.

In May 1830, Congress passed a bill for the federal government to buy $150,000 worth of stock in the Maysville Road Company. This company planned to build a *turnpike*—a road built by a private company that charged a fee for using it—in Kentucky from Maysville to Lexington. This road would later connect with the National Road in Ohio. Jackson vetoed the measure on the grounds that the federal government should support only national projects. Since the Maysville Road would be built inside the state of Kentucky, it should be a state project. People in the West were upset. They had expected Jackson would favor *internal improvements*. This was a program of building roads, bridges, canals, and railroads during the early 1800's.

3.4 The Nullification Crisis.   In July 1832, Congress passed a new protective tariff. It had lower rates than the Tariff of 1828, but people in the South were not pleased. In November 1832, the South Carolina government passed a bill to nullify the tariff acts of 1828 and 1832. It warned that South Carolina would secede from the United States if the government tried to enforce the law after February 1833. President Jackson was angry at these moves and prepared to send troops into South Carolina.

How was the nullification crisis resolved?

With the country facing a civil war, leaders worked out a compromise. Henry Clay drew up a new tariff which allowed for lower rates over a number of years. Congress also passed the Force Bill. It gave Jackson the power to use the army and navy to uphold federal law. Upon learning of the compromise, South Carolina withdrew its nullification bill. However, the trouble was only ended for a while. The ideas of states' rights and federal authority would arise again.

3.5 Jackson and the Bank.   One of Jackson's biggest political battles was fought over the Bank of the United States. Like many

Reading for Detail
SKILL

It is important to be able to recognize the main idea of any paragraph, chapter, or book. In addition, it is important to understand the information which describes or explains an idea. If you try to put together a bicycle and do not understand the details of the instructions, the wheels might not turn or the gears might not shift.

The first step in reading for detail is to identify the major point. Once the point has been identified, the next step is to recognize the detailed information related to it. Sometimes it helps to ask questions about the main idea—who? what? when? where? how?

The following selection was written in 1832 by a British actor who visited the United States. In her journal, she wrote about a ten-hour carriage trip covering the 100 miles (160 kilometers) between New York and Philadelphia. Read the selection for the detail.

English eye has not seen, English ear has not heard, nor has it entered the heart of English people to conceive the surpassing clumsiness and wretchedness of these . . . inconveniences [coaches]. They are shaped something like boats, the sides being merely leather pieces, removable at pleasure, but which, in bad weather, are buttoned down to protect the inmates from the wet. . . . For the first few minutes, I thought I must have fainted from the intolerable sensation of smothering which I experienced. However, the leather having been removed, and a little more air obtained, I took heart of grace, and resigned myself to my fate. Away wallopped the four horses . . . and away we went after them . . . over the wickedest road, I do think, the cruellest, hard-heartedest road, that ever wheel rumbled upon. Through bog and marsh, and ruts . . . with the roots of trees protruding across our path, their boughs every now and then giving us an affectionate scratch through the windows; and, more than once, a half-demolished trunk or stump lying in the middle of the road lifting us up, and letting us down again, with most awful variations. . . .

1. Who was the traveler?
2. What were the roads and the coach like?
3. When did the writer travel?
4. Where was she traveling?
5. How did the writer feel about the experience?

Race over Uncle Tam's Course.
4ᵈ March 1833

In this anti-Jackson cartoon, the President and Martin Van Buren (left) ride a donkey in a race over the bank issue. They are losing to Henry Clay who supported the Bank of the United States. Actually, Jackson won his fight against the national bank. What was the bank issue?

Who was head of the Second Bank of the United States?

people from the West, he did not like banks and thought paper money was of no value. He had once lost most of his fortune because bank notes he accepted from a Philadelphia merchant were worthless. Jackson thought of the Bank as a monopoly used by the rich and powerful for their own gain. Although the government owned one fifth of its stock, control of the Bank was in the hands of the directors. Jackson said that the Bank was unconstitutional. In doing so, he was showing that he believed in the limited powers of the federal government. Jackson was also ignoring the Supreme Court's ruling in *McCullough* v. *Maryland*, which had upheld the implied powers of Congress.

Early in his first term, Jackson made his views on the Bank known. More and more people were against the Bank, and its head, Nicholas Biddle, became alarmed. He decided to take Henry Clay's advice and ask for a renewal of the Bank's charter four years early. Clay wanted to run for President in 1832. He thought that if Jackson vetoed the bill to renew the Bank charter, it would be unpopular with those who favored the Bank. So Jackson would lose the election. Congress passed the bill, and the President did veto it, attacking special interests and monopolies. Many Americans, however, agreed with Jackson's feeling about the Bank and were pleased by his vote. In 1832, Jackson was reelected by a wide margin.

After the election, Jackson set out to destroy the Bank. He ordered federal money removed from it and placed in certain state banks. These so-called *pet banks* printed large numbers of their own bank notes, often with little thought about the amount of *specie* (gold and silver coin) on hand to back them up. They used this money to start a credit boom. People borrowed the bank notes to buy government land. The land offices deposited this money back into the pet banks where it could be loaned to more people. *Land speculation* (buying up land to sell at a large profit) increased. It was a time of reckless spending and uncontrolled economic growth.

Before Jackson left office, he acted to slow down the wave of land speculation. In July 1836, he wrote the "Specie Circular," which stated that only people who settled the land could pay for it with paper money. Everyone else had to pay for public lands with gold or silver.

How did Jackson destroy the Bank?

Remember that westerners favored easy credit, which was the reason they opposed the Bank of the U.S.

The "Specie Circular" was issued to the Treasury Department to accept only specie in payment for public land.

1. How did President Jackson use the veto power?
2. Where was the strongest support for nullification?
3. How did President Jackson and Vice-President Calhoun differ on the major issues?
4. What brought about the nullification crisis?

4. Jackson and the Indians

Andrew Jackson was from a frontier state—Tennessee. He shared with many Americans at that time the view that the Indians were blocking settlement. As President, Jackson set up a plan for moving the Indian groups to lands west of the Mississippi River. Attempts to uphold the rights of Indians were opposed by the President.

4.1 Government and the Indians. The process of uprooting the Indians had been going on for a long time. Since the beginning of the nation, the United States government had promised to respect Indian rights. But settlers, desiring more and more land, kept moving west. Years of wars brought defeat to Indians trying to stop this advance. Speckled Snake, a Creek chief, spoke to his people in 1829:

Note the double standard applied to the principle of private ownership by European Americans when dealing with Indian lands.

> When the first white man came over the wide waters, he was but a little man. . . . His legs were cramped by sitting long in his big boat, and he begged for a little land. . . .

What were the points Speckled Snake had to make in his speech of 1829?

When he came to these shores the Indians gave him land, and kindled fires to make him comfortable. . . .

But when the white man had warmed himself at the Indian's fire, and had filled himself with the Indian's hominy, he became very large. He stopped not at the mountain tops, and his foot covered the plains and the valleys. . . . Then he became our Great Father. He loved his red children, but he said: "You must move a little farther, lest by accident I tread on you. . . ."

Now he says, "The land you live upon is not yours. Go beyond the Mississippi; there is game; there you may remain while the grass grows and the rivers run."

Will not our Great Father come there also? . . .

Brothers! I have listened to a great many talks from our Great Father. But they always began and ended in this—"Get a little farther; you are too near me. . . ."

Why did Jackson encourage removal?

In 1830, with Andrew Jackson's encouragement, Congress passed the Indian Removal Act. It set up Indian resettlement west of the Mississippi River. The act also gave the President power to negotiate with the Indian groups. During Jackson's two terms, 94 treaties were made. The Removal Act did not say that federal troops could be used to aid in Indian resettlement. Few Americans, however, opposed the use of force against those Indians who refused to move.

4.2   Indian Removals.   Over the next ten years, the Chippewa, Menominee, Iowa, Sioux, Ottawa, and Winnebago Indians of the Great Lakes area signed treaties with the government and moved west. Some Indians, however, offered resistance to the government's policy. In 1832, the Sac and Fox Indians under Chief Black Hawk tried to return to their lands in the Wisconsin Territory and Illinois. In what became known as Black Hawk's War, army troops and the Illinois militia defeated the Indians. The Sac and Fox were forced to remain in the Iowa Territory.

Abraham Lincoln was a member of the Illinois militia in Black Hawk's War.

In the Southeast, the states of Georgia, Mississippi, and Alabama passed laws stating that they had authority over the Indians and Indian lands inside their borders. These laws were aimed at the Creek, Chickasaw, Choctaw, and Cherokee peoples whose rights had been guaranteed by a treaty with the United States. The President, however, supported the states. The Chocktaw, Chickasaw, and Creek Indians moved west.

The Cherokee Indians were the last to leave their lands. Under several treaties with the United States, the Cherokees in Georgia had

In "Choctaw Removal" by Valjean Hessing, people who were forced from their land travel west in the 1830's. The painting shows a journey that one group of Indians called a "Trail of Tears." Why were Indians forced to leave their lands?

been recognized as a nation. They had formed a written language and were printing a newspaper. They were governed under a constitution that set up a legislature, a court system, and a militia. People in Georgia, however, kept moving into Cherokee lands, especially after gold was discovered there. The Cherokees appealed their case to the Supreme Court. In 1832, the Court ruled that the state of Georgia had no authority over the Cherokees. President Jackson, however, refused to back up the decision of the Court. He is reported to have said, "John Marshall has made his decision, now let him enforce it."

The Cherokees were forced to begin their journey west in 1838. White settlers moved in as groups of Cherokee families moved out to begin the 1,000-mile (1,600 kilometer) trip west. More than 4,000 people died on this long, hard journey from cold, lack of food and shelter, and disease. Because they had to stop every few miles to bury their dead, the Cherokee journey west became known as the "Trail of Tears."

In the Florida Territory, many Seminole Indians refused to leave their homeland. Led by Osceola and with the help of escaped slaves, they fought against federal troops. Although Osceola died in 1838, the Seminoles fought on into the 1840's. During these years, many of them were captured and sent west. The remaining Seminoles were finally pushed back into the southern swamps of the Everglades. In 1842, the government agreed that the few hundred left could stay there. During the years of Indian resettlement, more than 100,000 people were forced

Why were the Cherokee Indians one of the last groups to leave their lands?

Recall that Indian groups had been considered nations as far back as Washington's administration.

Why is the Cherokee resettlement known as the "Trail of Tears"?

Osceola was captured after being invited to peace talks at St. Augustine in 1837. He died in prison.

The Age of Jackson   247

west across the Mississippi River. Again, they were promised that they could remain on their new lands forever.

1. What was Jackson's policy regarding the Indian people?
2. What was the decision of the Supreme Court in the case involving the Cherokee Indians?
3. Why were the Cherokees unable to keep their land?

5. The Impact of Jackson Politics

Andrew Jackson decided to leave politics when his second term of office ended. He wanted his policies to continue, however. So he used his influence to have Vice-President Martin Van Buren nominated for President in 1836. Through Van Buren and others, Jackson's ideas would influence American politics for many years.

Who became President after Jackson?

5.1 The Election of 1836. During Jackson's time in office, some important government leaders had been against his policies. In 1834, they formed a new political party. Most of the National-Republicans as well as others who did not like Jackson belonged to it. They thought Jackson was a tyrant and were called Whigs after the party in England that had fought against the king in the 1700's. In 1836, however, Jackson was still liked by most people. That and the seeming prosperity of the country gave a victory to the Democrats. Martin Van Buren became the next President.

Have students look again at Section 3.5, and make sure they understand the causes of the depression.

5.2 The Panic of 1837. Van Buren was hardly settled into the White House when the United States suffered an economic *depression*. This is a period of slow economic activity with prices low and many people out of work. This depression had its roots in the Jackson years.

What was the "Specie Circular" supposed to prevent?

The trouble began shortly after President Jackson wrote the "Specie Circular" in 1836. This had stated that only people who settled land could use paper money to buy it. Few people had gold and silver to pay for land, and sales dropped sharply. Banks had no specie to lend and began to call in loans. Many people could not pay all they owed and lost their land to the bank. Speculators were hit very hard.

Soon the banks faced a panic. People with deposits in the banks tried to take out their money in specie. The banks were not getting enough money from the sale of land to pay these people. Many banks failed. Prices dropped, and business slowed because people bought less. Many workers lost their jobs because fewer goods were being sold. Businesses failed. The Whigs blamed Van Buren and the Democrats for

Voter Participation, 1824–1840

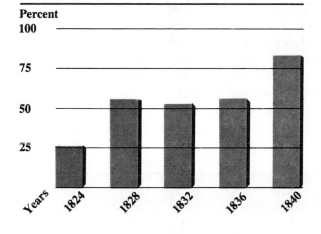

Percent
100

75

50

25

Years 1824 1828 1832 1836 1840

Percent of Eligible Voters, 1840

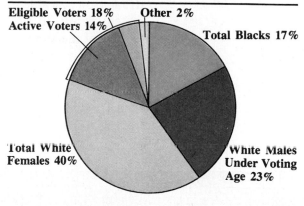

Eligible Voters 18%
Active Voters 14%
Other 2%
Total Blacks 17%
Total White Females 40%
White Males Under Voting Age 23%

What was the increase in voter participation from 1824 to 1840? What were some reasons for the increase? What percent of the total population was eligible to vote in 1840? What percent was not eligible? What percent actually voted?

the Panic of 1837. They accused the President of following the policies of Jackson and doing nothing to end the depression.

5.3 Tippecanoe and Tyler Too. The Whigs hoped to win the election of 1840. They chose William Henry Harrison of Ohio, the hero of the Battle of Tippecanoe, to run for President. John Tyler of Virginia was selected as his running mate. As the Democrats had done with Jackson, the Whigs said that Harrison was an average American, hoping to appeal to many voters.

Harrison was the son of a Virginia plantation owner and one-time governor of the Indiana Territory.

Jackson's policics of the 1830's had a further impact on the election of 1840. The Whigs knew that party leaders could no longer choose a candidate on their own. They had to win over large numbers of people who were allowed to vote. Rallies, parades, and slogans were used to gain support. The Whigs did not write a *platform*, or statement of the policies of the party. Instead, they campaigned with "Tippecanoe and Tyler too." The depression and the organization of the Whigs put Harrison in the White House. The election of 1840 showed how much the political process had changed in the Age of Jackson.

What was different about the election of 1840?

Use pictures and songs of early political campaigns to transmit the flavor of this period.

1. Which new political party was formed after 1832?
2. Whom did the new party nominate for President?
3. How did the Panic of 1837 help elect Harrison?

The Age of Jackson   249

6. Conclusion

Andrew Jackson shaped the history of the time and was shaped by it. Jackson was able to settle, for a time, the question of nullification and states' rights. In the area of Indian affairs, he followed the general feeling of the times. Most Americans believed the Indians were in the way of their settlement and should be moved to the West. Important changes took place in the American political system during the Age of Jackson. Some began before Jackson took office. Others came during his term. One of the most important changes of the Age of Jackson was the greater number of people able to take part in political affairs.

Chapter 10 Review

Main Points

1. John Quincy Adams became President in 1824 in an election settled by the House of Representatives.

2. The election of 1824 led to a split in the Democratic-Republican party.

3. Andrew Jackson, elected in 1828, increased the power of the Presidency.

4. Democracy during the Jackson years provided a greater voice in government for white males. Women, blacks, and Indians did not benefit.

5. Sectional interests produced new conflicts during Andrew Jackson's Presidency.

6. Opposition to President Jackson led to the formation of the Whig party.

7. William Henry Harrison, the Whig candidate, became President in 1840.

Building Vocabulary

1. Identify the following:

"Era of Good Feelings"	John C. Calhoun	Indian Removal Act
American System	Webster-Hayne debates	Black Hawk's War
Andrew Jackson	Force Bill	Trail of Tears
John Floyd	"Specie Circular"	Whigs

2. Define the following:

sectionalism	spoils system	pet banks
corrupt bargain	nullification	specie
administration	turnpike	land speculation
suffrage	internal improvements	depression
caucuses		platform

Remembering the Facts

1. How was the President elected in 1824?
2. Which two political parties formed from the Democratic-Republican party following the election of 1824?
3. How was Jackson different from those who were President before him?
4. Which changes made it possible for more people to vote?
5. What was President Jackson's opinion of nullification?
6. Why did Jackson oppose the Bank?
7. What was the government's policy toward the Indians?
8. Which Indians fought against efforts to move them from their lands?
9. Why was the Whig party created?
10. What was the depression of 1837?

Understanding the Facts

1. Why did rivalries develop among various sections of the United States?
2. Why did Andrew Jackson think he had been cheated in the election of 1824?
3. Why did President Jackson replace government workers with members of his own political party?
4. When did Jackson act as a nationalist? as a supporter of states' rights?
5. Why did Jackson want the Indians to move west of the Mississippi River?
6. How did the Panic of 1837 influence the election of 1840?
7. Why did the Age of Jackson end?

Using Maps

Comparing Maps. Sometimes several maps are used together to show information about similar events at different times. By comparing what is shown on the different maps, additional information can be gained.

The maps shown on page 237 can be used this way. They show the voting patterns by states for the presidential elections in 1824 and 1828. Study each map. Compare the maps, and answer the following questions.

1. In which election did Andrew Jackson win the most states?
2. In which election did Jackson receive a majority of the electoral vote?
3. Which states did not support Jackson in both elections?
4. Where was Jackson's support strong in both elections?
5. Where was Jackson's support weak in both elections?
6. Which states divided their vote?

Washington, D.C. 1800-1825

The United States government moved to the new federal city of Washington in 1800. In that year, the young city was a clear example of the difference that can exist between dreams and reality. In the dreams of government leaders, Washington was a magnificent capital with lovely parks, beautiful public buildings, and grand avenues. In reality, it was a small village of rough fields, half-finished buildings, and muddy paths.

There had been years of debate in Congress over the location of the nation's capital. No state wanted any other state to have special influence over the federal government. Congress had met in eight different cities, four different states. Moving became more difficult as the quantity of needed

records grew. A compromise was finally reached that settled the question of a permanent location for the capital city. When southerners agreed to let the federal government assume the state debts of the Revolution, northerners agreed to have the capital along the banks of the Potomac River.

Two states gave land to the government to form the federal District of Columbia. There, only Congress had control. The District was free of any single state's influence. The capital, built in the District, was available to people from the North, the South, and the rapidly growing West.

Plans

President Washington selected the French engineer, Pierre Charles L'Enfant, to design the federal city in 1791. L'Enfant had come to America to serve in the Revolution. He wanted very much to design a great capital for the new nation. And on paper, his plans for the city of Washington were beautiful.

The survey work of marking the District's boundaries was done by Americans Andrew Ellicott and Benjamin Banneker. Banneker, a free black from Baltimore, was also an astronomer, mathematician, and scientist. The boundaries of the District of Columbia included the cities of George Town in Maryland and Alexandria in Virginia. The capital city itself was located next to George Town, on the Maryland side of the Potomac River. Later Alexandria and the lands across the Potomac were returned to Virginia.

L'Enfant planned Washington so that the three branches of the federal government were located in three separate areas of the city, according to their different constitutional duties. The building for the legislature, the Capitol, was on the highest point of land. A mile and a half away was the President's House, in the center of the executive area. From both of these, streets went out into the rest of the city. Pennsylvania Avenue was planned as a broad, stately connection between them. It would serve for ceremonial processions and would add dignity to the communication between the Congress and the President. The judicial building was to be in a third section of the city, away from these two main areas of traffic. The different buildings would be designed by different architects. By law, there could be no slave labor used to build the capital. Some slaves were hired out to do this work and earned money to buy their freedom.

Wide streets set Washington apart from other cities at the time. In Pierre Charles L'Enfant's plan, what were these boulevards designed to do?

Money Problems

President Washington and the early sessions of Congress did not set aside any money for building the city because they thought it would pay for itself. Government leaders expected many people to move into the area and buy expensive lots for their homes and businesses. Profits from those sales would be used to pay for the public streets and buildings. That idea did not work. Few people came to the city at first, and even fewer of them invested their money in it. The total number of people working for the federal government at that time was very small. It was not easy for others to earn a living in Washington. There was not much business in providing for the needs of those who worked for the government. Carpenters, stonemasons, and people in the building trades even had difficulty finding steady work. Life in the new federal city was certainly not as pleasant or profitable as it was in Philadelphia and the older American cities.

Moving In

With only three months left to serve in his term, John Adams moved into the President's House in 1800. Abigail, his wife, arrived in November and described the city in a letter to her sister.

As I expected to find it a new country, with Houses scattered over a space of ten miles, and trees [and] stumps in plenty with, a castle of a house—so I found it—The Presidents House is in a beautiful situation in front of which is the Potomac. . . . The country around is romantic but a wild, a wilderness at present.

I have been to George Town. . . . It is only one mile from me but a quagmire [deep mud] after every rain. Here we are obliged to send daily for marketing; The capital is near two miles from us. . . . but I am determined to be satisfied and content, to say nothing of inconvenience. . . .

Determined as she was, Abigail did mention some of the problems of living in a huge, unfinished house in another of her letters.

The house is upon a grand and superb scale, requiring about thirty servants to attend and keep the apartments in proper order, and perform the ordinary business of the house and stables. . . . The lighting [of] the apartments, from the kitchen to parlors and chambers, is a tax indeed [so may candles are needed] . . . we are obliged to keep [fires going] to secure us from daily agues [chills and fevers]. . . . bells [to call the servants] are [wholly] wanting, not one single one being hung through the whole house, and promises are all you can obtain. This is so great an inconvenience, that I know not what to do, or

George Washington inspects the unfinished President's House with architect James Hoban. Who was the first President to live in the White House?

how to do it. . . . if they will put me up some bells, and let me have wood enough to keep fires, I design to be pleased. I could content myself almost anywhere three months. . . . We have, indeed, come into a new country.

You must keep all this to yourself, and, when asked how I like it, say that I write you the situation [location] is beautiful, which is true. The house is made habitable, but there is not a single apartment finished. . . . We have not the least fence, yard, or other convenience . . . and the great unfinished audience-room [the East Room] I make a drying-room of, to hang up clothes in. The principal stairs are not up, and will not be this winter.

The Capitol

Members of Congress arrived in Washington after the fall harvest season. They found an unfinished Capitol with a few boarding houses close by it. One wing of the new building was almost completed. Its rooms were shared among the Senate, the House of Representatives, the Supreme Court, the courts of the District, and the new Library of Congress.

Unlike the members of the executive branch, the lawmakers usually came to their sessions alone. They left their families behind since Congress met for only a few months of the year. Most of the members lived in the boarding houses, and their social life generally centered around the dinner tables there. Travel around the city was difficult during the day and dangerous at night. There were no real streets, only fields and a few paths. In most areas, the ground was not even leveled to make walking easier.

Margaret Bayard Smith, wife of the city's first newspaper editor, wrote a letter that

During the War of 1812, 4,000 British soldiers attacked and burned Washington. How did the burning affect the future growth of the city?

described the dangers of traveling at night. Thomas Law, a friend, had built a new house:

This out-of-the-way-house to which Mr. Law removed, was separated from the most inhabited part of the city by fields and waste grounds broken up by deep gulleys or ravines over which there was occasionally a passable road. The election of President by Congress was then pending, one vote given or withheld would decide the question between Mr. Jefferson and Mr. Burr. Mr. Bayard from Delaware held that vote. He with other influential and leading members [of Congress] *went to a ball given by Mr. Law. The night was dark and rainy, and on their attempt to return home, the coachman lost his way, and until daybreak was driving about this waste and broken ground and if not overturned into the deep gullies was momentarily in danger of being so, an accident which would most probably have cost some of the gentlemen their lives, and as it so happened that the company in the coach consisted of Mr. Bayard and three other members of Congress who had a leading and decisive influence in this difficult crisis of public affairs, the loss of either, might have turned the scales . . . and Mr. Burr* [would have] *been elected to the Presidency. . . .*

Slow Growth

During Jefferson's administration, Congress did provide $3,000 to improve Pennsylvania Avenue and to plant trees along it. In general, however, little progress was made in completing the city. Poverty and unemployment were serious problems in Washington from its beginning. By 1802, 40 percent of the city's funds were used to help the poor.

The city's founders had expected a very rapid growth in population, especially by people with money to invest. But in 20 years' time, the total number of people who lived in the capital had increased by just 10,000 people, most of them poor. Free blacks were the only group within Washington that grew quickly in number. The city did allow slavery, and most citizens did not seem to have strong antislavery feelings. But Washington did not force slaves to leave the area when they were freed, as most of the southern states did. The city also had not made laws that stopped the growth of independent churches and schools for blacks. In general, most free black families felt safer in Washington than in other southern American cities. By 1820, the number of free blacks almost equaled the number of slaves. By 1840, their number was four times larger than the number of slaves.

The commerce and industry that was expected by the city's planners did not develop. George Town and Alexandria competed for most of the business in the District.

Congress seldom provided funds for work on the public properties. The experiment of establishing a magnificent federal city seemed to be a failure. Political scientist James Sterling Young suggests that the main problem was a lack of interest on the part of most Americans in a government that was located out of their way.

For the government of Jeffersonian times was not, by any candid [honest] view, one of the important institutions in American society—important as a social presence or important in its impact upon the everyday lives of the citizens. It was, for one thing, too new, an unfamiliar social presence in a society whose ways of living and whose organization of affairs had developed over a century without any national governmental institution. . . .

What government business there was was not, most of it, of a sort to attract any widespread, sustained [long lasting] citizen interest.

Growth was so slow for the capital that some people continued to believe that the federal government should move back to a larger city. To many people, the burning of Washington's government buildings by the British forces in 1814 seemed to be the final blow. Margaret Smith expressed those feelings in her writings:

Thursday. . . . This morning on awakening we were greeted with the sad news, that our city was taken, the bridges and public buildings burnt, our troops flying in every direction. Our little army totally dispersed [scattered].

. . . I do not suppose Government will ever return to Washington. All those whose property was invested in that place, will be reduced to poverty. . . .

Tuesday [August] 30. Here we are, once more restored to our home. . . . The blast has passed by, without devastating this spot. . . . The poor capitol! nothing but its blackened walls remained! 4 or 5 houses in the neighborhood were likewise in ruins. . . . We afterwards looked at the other public buildings, but none were so thoroughly destroyed as the House of Representatives and the President's House. Those beautiful pillars in that Representatives Hall were cracked and broken, the roof, that noble dome, painted and carved with such beauty and skill, lay in ashes in the cellars. . . . In the P.H. [President's House] not an inch, but its cracked and blackened walls remained. That scene, which when I last visited it, was so splendid . . . was now nothing but ashes. . . .

Recovery

But the government did return to Washington. That same September, President and Mrs. Madison moved into a house in the city, and the President worked from there. Members of Congress came back to the city for a special session. They met in the only government building that had not been damaged, the Post Office. There, after three weeks of debate, the House of Representatives voted 83 to 54 to keep the federal government in Washington. City bankers offered a loan to start the work of rebuilding. Three and a half months later, the Senate finally agreed.

Adams to Adams

In 1818, James and Elizabeth Monroe moved into the White House, as it was beginning to be called. Its outside walls had been freshly painted white to cover the marks from the British fire. Both wings of the Capitol were finished by then. Work had

The federal city in 1824 had many grand buildings like the Capitol. It also had many muddy streets. What problems faced lawmakers and their families from around the country who came to live and work in Washington?

begun on the center section. Washington still had no street lights, no sewer system, no city water system. Water was carried from wells in the center of the city or from the nearby creek. There were still open fields where cattle and hogs ran free. But there was a stronger feeling that the federal capital of Washington, D.C., was in place to stay.

John Quincy Adams moved into the White House just 25 years after his parents had lived in it. There was still no fence, but the grounds had been made smoother for walking. Most of the White House rooms were finished enough to be used. Louisa Adams, unlike Abigail, could use the great "audience-room" for public receptions instead of drying the family's clothes in it. A quarter of a century had passed since the government first moved to the District of Columbia. There was still a very strong contrast between the original dream and the reality of the capital city, but a beginning had been made. Washington, as a city, would move a little closer to the dream in the years to come.

1. What was L'Enfant's plan for the capital city?
2. Name the main street which connects the Capitol building and the President's House.
3. How did Congress expect to pay for the building of the capital city?
4. Where did most of the lawmakers live during their stay in Washington?
5. How was Washington affected by the War of 1812?
6. Compare the President's House which Abigail Adams lived in to that of her daughter-in-law, Louisa Adams.

Unit III Review

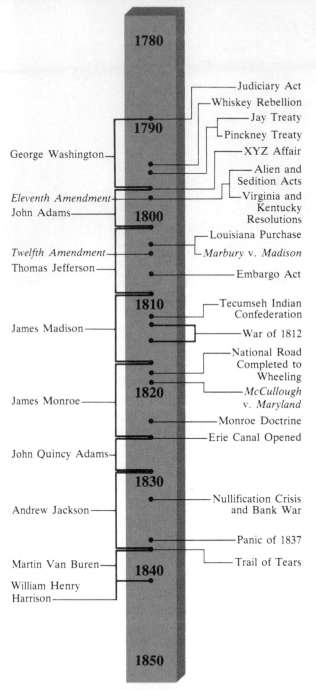

1780

Judiciary Act
Whiskey Rebellion
1790
Jay Treaty
Pinckney Treaty
XYZ Affair

George Washington
Alien and Sedition Acts
Virginia and Kentucky Resolutions

Eleventh Amendment
John Adams
1800

Louisiana Purchase
Marbury v. *Madison*

Twelfth Amendment
Thomas Jefferson
Embargo Act

1810
Tecumseh Indian Confederation
War of 1812

James Madison

National Road Completed to Wheeling
1820
McCullough v. *Maryland*

James Monroe
Monroe Doctrine
Erie Canal Opened

John Quincy Adams
1830

Nullification Crisis and Bank War
Andrew Jackson

Panic of 1837
Trail of Tears

Martin Van Buren
1840
William Henry Harrison

1850

Summary

1. It was not certain at first that the government of the United States would work under the Constitution because many people felt they were citizens of a state rather than of the nation.

2. Under the leadership of President Washington, who set many precedents for later leaders, the government was established on a firm foundation.

3. Because of disagreements over economic policies and foreign affairs, political parties formed around Thomas Jefferson and Alexander Hamilton.

4. The election of Thomas Jefferson as President in 1800 showed that in the United States, political power could be transferred from one party to another peacefully.

5. Under the Presidency of Thomas Jefferson, the size of the United States was doubled through the purchase of Louisiana from France.

6. The United States went to war with Britain in 1812, believing that the British were violating American rights at sea and turning the Indians on the western frontier against Americans.

7. The War of 1812 was followed by a new spirit of nationalism which helped to produce a unique American culture.

8. Democracy expanded for white men during the Age of Jackson, but women, blacks, and Indians benefited little.

9. Sectional differences became stronger during the Age of Jackson, challenging the power of the federal government.

Unit Questions

1. What major problems did the United States face during the first 50 years under the Constitution?
2. What cultural developments after the War of 1812 showed a greater emphasis of the people on democracy?
3. Who do you think won the War of 1812? Why do you think so?
4. What evidence can you give for the growth of nationalism and sectionalism in the country at the same time?
5. Washington, Jefferson, and Jackson are among the great American Presidents. What did each do that had a major influence on the government of the United States?
6. Why was Washington, D.C., made the capital of the country? How did it differ from the other cities which had served as the national capital?
7. What political parties existed in the first 50 years of the United States? Why did each develop?
8. Why did President Jackson, a strong nationalist, not support the position of the federal courts in the case of the Cherokee Indians against the state of Georgia?

Suggested Activities

1. Several new countries have come into existence during the last 50 years. Choose one and compare it with the first 50 years of the United States in terms of how it gained independence, its government, and its economy.
2. Write a poem or the lyrics of a song or draw or paint a picture which you think reflects American culture following the War of 1812.
3. Find out information about the major political parties in the United States today. Perhaps you could invite a representative from each of the major parties to speak to the class about their party's ideas and goals.

Suggested Readings

Blos, Joan. *A Gathering of Days: A New England Girl's Journal, 1830–1832.* New York: Charles Scribner's Sons, 1979. The journal of a teenager tells of life on a farm in New Hampshire.

Davis, Louise. *Snowball Fight in the White House.* Philadelphia: Westminster Press, 1974. Story of a children's Christmas party during the Presidency of Andrew Jackson.

Fisher, Vardis. *Tales of Valor.* Mattituck, New York: American Reprint/Rivercity Press, 1976. Traces Lewis and Clark's expedition into Louisiana.

Fleishman, Glen. *Cherokee Removal 1838: An Entire Nation Is Forced Out of Its Homeland.* New York: Watts, 1971. Looks at the actions taken to force the Cherokees out of Georgia.

UNIT IV

Expansion

Expansion marked a course of history from the earliest days of people in America. The United States was made up of people who had moved to it from many places in the world. Many Americans remained on the move as the United States extended its political borders and grew economically. New reasons for moving continued to arise as new ways of getting there were developed. Advantages and disadvantages resulted from a rapid physical and economic growth in the United States.

Chapter 11   The Promise of America ———— 262
Chapter 12   New Ways and New People —— 280
Chapter 13   From Ocean to Ocean ———— 298
City Sketch New Orleans 1845–1855 ———— 318
City Sketch San Francisco 1845–1855 ——— 322

The Promise of America

Transcendentalists believed in the importance of self-reliance. Henry David Thoreau tried to live this belief near Walden Pond in Massachusetts. How did Thoreau symbolize widespread hope for a better America in the middle 1800's?

The greater democracy during the Jackson years was not just a matter of politics. There was also a spirit of equality and progress that made many Americans feel proud. They wanted to make life in the United States even better for all its people. A move toward reform began in the early 1800's and lasted through the first half of the century. These same years saw a flowering of American culture. The years from the 1820's through the 1850's was a high point for American literature.

1. The Spirit of Perfection

Review the importance of religion in early American history as a background for this section.

The American people had confidence that they could build a better future for America. They believed that people were able to perfect their lives. If each person could improve, then all society could improve. This spirit spread to more and more Americans in the 1820's and 1830's.

1.1 Changing Views on Religion. Religion was one of the bases of the reform movement. Many Americans were changing their ideas about religion. During the 1700's, some churches had taught that only a certain number of people—the *elect*—were chosen by God to be saved and go to heaven. As the country became more democratic, many churches began to teach that people had a duty to improve themselves and the world around them. In this way, they could be saved. These ideas encouraged people to make changes for the better.

How was religion changing in the 1800's?

Beginning in the 1820's, a number of *revivals*—meetings to make people more interested in religion—took place around the country. As part of this, preachers moved around the country giving sermons at large camp meetings most often held outdoors. One of the leading figures at the revivals was Charles Finney. He taught that good works were important, as well as faith. He said that with God's help, it was possible for people to live better lives. His teaching, and that of others like him, caused many Americans to support a wide variety of reforms.

What were revivals?

1.2 New Religious Groups. As more and more people began to change their ideas about religion, a number of new religious groups appeared in the United States. One of the largest was started in New York by Joseph Smith in 1830. It was the Church of Jesus Christ of Latter-Day Saints. The church members were called Mormons. Smith said that he had had *revelations* (special messages) from God. He taught those who followed him that they were God's chosen people. Smith also said that Mormon men could have more than one wife. The Mormons tried to set up ideal societies where they could live in their own way.

Who were the Mormons?

A son of Smith's remained in Nauvoo and set up a separate branch of the church.

Mormons were often *persecuted* (treated cruelly) by other people for what they believed. They were forced to move several times. After living for a short time in Ohio and Missouri, they settled in Illinois. There in 1844, Joseph Smith was killed by an angry crowd. Brigham Young became the new Mormon leader. Driven from Illinois, the Mormons settled in Utah where they established Salt Lake City in 1847. During the next few years, they founded many towns and attracted thousands of new church members from Europe and the eastern United States.

Another new religious group began in western New York. William Miller said that the second coming of Jesus Christ would happen on a certain day in 1843. He asked people who followed him, known as Millerites, to prepare for that day. When the event did not take place on the day given, Miller said that it would happen sometime later.

1.3 A New Philosophy. Another base of the American reform movement was a *philosophy* (a set of ideas) developed largely by Ralph Waldo Emerson of Massachusetts. This was *transcendentalism*. Emerson believed that people could go beyond their limitations and perfect themselves and their society. Transcendentalists thought that every person was worthwhile, and that people had the ability to guide their own lives. Their philosophy was hopeful and encouraged the idea of progress.

What did transcendentalists believe?

Religious camp meetings were common in the 1830's. Large numbers of people gathered to practice their religion and encourage others to join them. Sermons at these meetings often visibly affected the people in the audience. Who was one of the leading revival preachers?

The Oneida Community, like most utopian experiments, believed that perfection could be gained through being industrious. Oneida produced a variety of goods, including silverware. What was the main purpose of utopian communities?

1.4 Utopian Communities.   Some people wanted to remake, rather than reform, the world around them. They thought that the best way to practice their ideas was to withdraw from society into smaller groups. In the 1830's and 1840's, many of these groups set up ideal communities, or *utopias*. They were based on their ideas of how people should live together. Work, property, and wealth were shared.

In 1825, Robert Owen of Great Britain founded a community at New Harmony, Indiana. Brook Farm was started in Massachusetts in 1841. Several well-known transcendentalists lived there for a time. These settlements, however, did not last very long. In some other groups, like the Shakers, religion joined the people closer together. In 1842, the Amana Community was set up as a religious colony in New York. It later moved to Iowa, where its factories still turn out a variety of appliances.

It might be interesting to have students discuss whether they would or would not want to live in a utopian community.

Owen was a factory owner who wanted to start a community where everyone had equal opportunities and there was no private property.

What were some utopian communities?

1. How did religion influence the reform movement?
2. Which new religious groups were started during the middle 1800's?
3. What was transcendentalism?

Sarah Grimké (1792–1873)
Angelina Grimké (1805–1879)

The Grimké sisters played a major role in the antislavery crusade during the 1800's. They both wrote and lectured for the cause. But they were also identified with women's rights. The sisters were perhaps the first to present the case for women's legal and social freedoms in the United States.

Sarah and Angelina Grimké were born in Charleston, South Carolina. Their father was a supreme court judge in a state that strongly supported slavery. It might be expected that the sisters would have shared their father's and their state's views. Instead, they became abolitionists.

Living in South Carolina, they saw directly how owners treated slaves. The Grimké family itself owned slaves. Torn by the cruelty of slavery, the sisters left the South and moved to Philadelphia where they joined the Quakers. The antislavery activities of the Quakers fit the attitudes of the two women.

During the years that followed, they wrote and spoke against holding slaves. Angelina Grimké wrote an *Appeal to the Christian Women of the South*. Sarah Grimké wrote an *Epistle to the Clergy of the Southern States* asking for support for abolition. Because of their personal experience with the slave system, the Grimkés were believable. And because they were careful always to base their beliefs on the Bible, they were doubly effective.

The sisters spoke mainly to women's groups. But Angelina Grimké sometimes lectured to both men and women. Since women were not expected to speak in public to groups of both men and women, the sisters were criticized. Even other abolitionists objected to this activity.

When the Grimkés spoke of their right to speak before mixed groups, they hit at their basic rights as citizens. From this point, their activities included speaking for the rights of women as well as the rights of blacks. Sarah Grimké wrote newspaper articles on "The Province of Women." She also published the book *Letters on the Condition of Women and the Equality of the Sexes*.

Both sisters lived to see slavery ended after the Civil War. But much remained to be done before the rights they sought for blacks and women would gain widespread support.

2. Reforming American Society _____

The spirit of perfection led to the founding of ideal communities for some people. It had a different impact on the country as a whole. Many Americans believed that society could be improved by making its basic institutions better. During the early 1800's, reformers tried to improve almost every area of American life.

2.1 The Antislavery Movement.   Slavery had become more and more rooted in American life since the country's beginning. Some people wanted to *abolish,* or put an end to, it. Known as *abolitionists,* they spoke out against slavery at a time most Americans accepted it.

Some abolitionists formed the American Colonization Society in 1817. They wanted to buy slaves, free them, and send them to a colony in Africa. Free blacks living in the United States would be sent there, too. The Society bought a strip of land on the west coast of Africa and named it Liberia, from a Latin word for "free." Several thousand freed slaves were sent there. The plan, however, was not very successful. It took a great deal of money, and the Society found it difficult to raise enough. Many blacks did not want to go to Africa. In New York, one group wrote:

> *We are content to abide where we are. . . . The time must come when the Declaration of Independence will be felt in the heart, as well as uttered from the mouth, and when the rights of all shall be properly acknowledged and appreciated. . . . This is our home, and this is our country. Beneath its sod lie the bones of our fathers: for it, some of them fought, bled, and died. Here we were born, and here we will die.*

Most early abolitionists wanted to free the slaves slowly. At first, their groups had only a few members. The number grew, however, with the greater democratic feeling of the middle 1800's. One of the strongest supporters of abolition was William Lloyd Garrison. Garrison wanted immediate freedom for all slaves. He felt the government accepted slavery and the Constitution defended it. So Garrison refused to work through the political system. In 1831, he began publishing *The Liberator*, a newspaper which printed his views on slavery. In 1833, Garrison and several others started the American Anti-Slavery Society.

Another group of abolitionists, led by Theodore Weld of Ohio, did not agree with Garrison. Weld had been influenced toward reform by Charles Finney. Weld wanted freedom for all slaves but thought it should be done gradually. Weld and his group were willing to use

What idea did the American Colonization Society put forth?

How did blacks react to the idea?

How did Garrison differ from other abolitionists?

You might have students consider ways in which the Constitution did or did not support slavery.

Beginning in 1831, William Lloyd Garrison published *The Liberator* for 35 years. This is the newspaper masthead. How was the abolitionist movement, based on religious ideas, similar to other reform movements?

politics to gain their ends. In 1840, they formed the Liberty party and chose James G. Birney to run for President. Although the party did not last long, it played a role in the elections of 1844 and 1848.

Many free blacks also worked against slavery. Some, like Frederick Douglass, had been slaves at one time. Douglass had taught himself to read and write before he escaped to the North. There he edited an abolitionist newspaper. He also gave moving speeches around the country for the American Anti-Slavery Society. Sojourner Truth had been a slave on a New York farm. After she was freed by state law in 1827, she traveled in the North, speaking for women's rights as well as against slavery.

For many years, abolitionists were unpopular in both the North and South. This was partly because of the prejudice against black people. *Prejudice* is an attitude or opinion about a person, group, or race which is formed without taking time or care to judge fairly. Angry crowds broke up many antislavery gatherings. In 1837, Elijah Lovejoy, an abolitionist publisher in Alton, Illinois, was killed while trying to save his printing press from being destroyed. The antislavery movement remained small during the 1840's and 1850's. Slowly, however, more and more people came to agree with the views of these people.

2.2   The Struggle for Women's Rights.   During the early years of America's history, women had few legal or political rights. They could not vote or hold public office. When a woman married, any property she held belonged to her husband. There were few educational opportunities, and most professions were closed to women.

Who was Frederick Douglass?

Recall that after the Revolution, most northern states provided for gradual emancipation of all slaves.

Why were abolitionists unpopular?

In the 1840's, some people began to work to improve the position of women. Lucretia Mott and several other women had gone to London to attend an antislavery conference. They were not allowed into the meeting because they were women. So they decided to begin working for equal rights for women. In 1848, the first women's rights convention met in Seneca Falls, New York. Lucretia Mott and Elizabeth Cady Stanton had done most of the organizing for this meeting. Those attending wanted equal political, social, and economic rights for women. They wrote a statement modeled on the Declaration of Independence:

Compare the experiences of Mott with those of the Grimké sisters in the Profile on page 266.

Who were some of the early leaders in the women's rights movement?

> *We hold these truths to be self-evident: that all men and women are created equal. . . .*
>
> *Now, in view of this entire disenfranchisement of one-half the people of this country, their social and religious degradation, in view of the unjust laws above mentioned, and because women do feel themselves aggrieved, oppressed, and fraudulently deprived of their most sacred rights, we insist that they have immediate admission to all the rights and privileges which belong to them as citizens of the United States.*

At first, gains of women's rights were small. However, the reformers did begin to draw people's attention to the cause.

Elizabeth Cady Stanton (left) and Lucretia Mott (right) organized the first women's rights convention at Seneca Falls, New York. What did those women attending the meeting hope to gain?

The Promise of America 269

2.3 New Ideas on Education.

What was education like before the mid-1800's?

Ideas about schools were also changing by the middle of the 1800's. Most schools before then were only for white children. In the South, general education for blacks was not allowed, although some slaves learned to read and write. There were also some independent schools for free black children. Elementary schools for whites were most often church schools. There children learned to read and write about their religions. Private schools were mostly for training young men as church, government, and business leaders. Those private schools and colleges often cost too much for most people.

Why was it difficult to set up public education?

Point out that the groups mentioned here are the ones least able to afford private education for their children.

The struggle to set up public education was not an easy one. Local and state governments were willing to set land aside for schools. But they often did not vote tax money to help run them. When they did, citizens without children objected. Wealthy parents often did not want to pay for the education of poor children. Church schools were opposed to education without religious training.

By the 1830's, this situation was changing. Many Americans began to agree that schools should be free to all children. Citizens needed to be able to read, write, and understand issues in order to vote. Farmers in the West, workers in eastern cities, and newly-arrived immigrants wanted their children to have the chance to improve their lives. There was an increase in the demand for public, tax-supported schools.

Who was an important leader in the public school movement?

One of the most important leaders in the public school movement was Horace Mann of Massachusetts. Mann became the secretary of the Massachusetts Board of Education in 1837. He supported many reforms and laid the base for teaching as a profession. In Mann's day, many

"The Mechanics of Arithmetic" are addition, subtraction, multiplication, and division. Why does this poster from the 1800's present problems in terms of fruits and vegetables? What other subjects did children at the time learn?

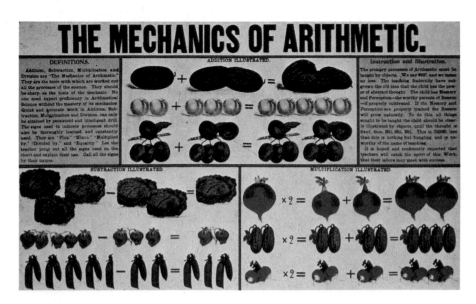

These women graduated from Oberlin College in 1855. Oberlin won nationwide attention with its views on women's rights and slavery. The college admitted women from its founding in 1833. What other schools were open to women?

teachers worked only part-time. They were often students in law or the ministry. Mann wanted well-trained, full-time professionals. He set up schools for training teachers and got higher salaries for teachers.

A number of new and better schools were started under Mann's direction. By 1860, the idea of free public schools was widely accepted in the northern part of the country. Most white children could receive an elementary, and often a high school, education. Private schools remained the major avenue of education in the South.

In the first half of the 1800's, efforts were made to give women more opportunities for education. Up to this time, women had generally not been allowed to enter schools of higher learning. In 1821, Emma Hart Willard opened a Female Seminary at Troy, New York. In 1837, Mary Lyon opened the Mount Holyoke Female Seminary in Massachusetts. A few colleges, such as Oberlin in Ohio, began to allow women to take courses. It took a long time, however, for most people to accept the idea of higher education for women.

The books used by teachers and students during this period were also changing. Noah Webster, sometimes called the "schoolmaster to

What efforts were made to improve educational opportunities for women?

Oberlin was also the first college to admit blacks and was strongly involved in the antislavery movement.

Read to the class and discuss selections from a McGuffey reader or some other textbook of the time.

America," tried to develop a uniform American speech. In 1828, he wrote a dictionary and a speller. Thousands of these books were sold all over the country. Webster and others, like William McGuffey, published readers that contained stories praising American life.

2.4 Helping People With Handicaps.

Improving the lives of persons with handicaps began to receive more attention during the 1830's and 1840's. In 1817, the Reverend Thomas Gallaudet founded a school for people with hearing and speech difficulties in Hartford, Connecticut. It became a model for other schools in many parts of the country. In 1833, Dr. Samuel Howe set up the Perkins Institute for the Blind in Boston. This school also served as a model for others. Howe was a part of the antislavery movement and backed Horace Mann in his work to improve schools. In addition, Howe favored better care for people with mental illnesses.

Howe is another good example of a person involved in more than one area of reform.

Another person interested in the care of people with mental illnesses was Dorothea Dix. In 1841, Dix visited the Cambridge House of Correction in Massachusetts. She was shocked by what she saw there. People were treated as criminals and often kept in cages or chained. Sanitary conditions were very poor. Dix visited other jails and poorhouses, making notes of everything she saw. In 1843, she presented a report to the Massachusetts state legislature.

When discussing the work done to help people with handicaps, students might be asked to find information on present laws in this area.

Slowly, things in Massachusetts improved, and Dix began visiting other parts of the United States. She helped set up a number of hospitals for people with mental illnesses. Dix also tried to get government aid for these hospitals. Congress passed a bill giving land grants to states to help in the care of those with mental illnesses. The bill was vetoed, however, by President Pierce. He felt that this care came under the powers of the states.

What changes were aimed at helping people with handicaps?

2.5 Prison Reform.

In the early 1800's, many Americans became concerned about the cruel treatment of people who had committed crimes. Prison conditions were very harsh. Criminals, debtors, and people with mental illnesses were all housed together. There were long sentences for small crimes, and the death penalty was used often.

Quakers were behind many efforts at prison reform in Pennsylvania.

In the 1820's, efforts were begun to reform the prison system. Pennsylvania built a new prison with a cell for each person. The Auburn Prison near Syracuse, New York, also had separate cells. It allowed the people in the prison time for meals and exercise. In time, those people were given the chance to take part in work and study programs. The emphasis shifted from punishment to reform. Dorothea Dix was one of the people who supported this change.

How did Auburn differ from earlier prisons?

Population Density by 1850

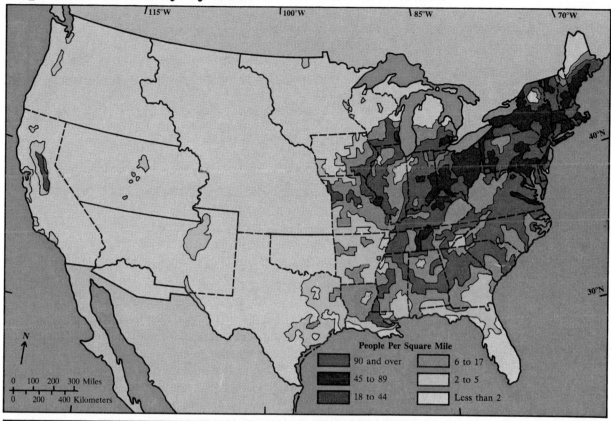

This map shows the average number of people living in every square mile of the United States in 1850. Where were most of the cities located? Where were most of the farms located?

2.6 The Temperance Crusade. One of the most powerful of the reform movements was the drive to limit or put an end to the use of liquor. Some people linked alcohol to crime, poverty, and other problems. They worked to win people over to the idea of *temperance,* or self-control, in drinking. Many groups were formed all over the country. And in 1826, the first national organization was founded. It was called the American Society for the Promotion of Temperance.

Some reformers believed that education was not enough. They wanted laws passed to stop the sale of liquor. One of the leaders in this drive was Neal Dow, the mayor of Portland, Maine. In 1851, largely because of Dow's work, Maine passed the first prohibition law. *Prohibition* means the forbidding by law of the manufacture, shipping,

What was the temperance crusade?

Consider a class discussion of whether or not prohibition laws are undemocratic and the kinds of things that laws should prevent under a democratic government.

How did prohibition differ from temperance?

and sale of alcoholic beverages. Although other states passed laws like Maine's, many were later *repealed* (withdrawn).

1. Who were the abolitionists?
2. What came out of the women's rights convention of 1848?
3. What were the steps taken to improve education?
4. Who worked for reform for people in mental hospitals?

3. American Literature in the Reform Years————

One of the greatest periods for American authors came during the years of growing democracy and reform. The writers of this time were often influenced by the democratic spirit and the spirit of perfection. They wrote about America and its people. They tried different forms and new ideas and themes.

3.1 Transcendentalists. Ralph Waldo Emerson of Massachusetts was one of the most important figures in American thought in the first half of the 1800's. He spent much of his life writing and giving public speeches. In 1837, Emerson spoke at Harvard College. He urged Americans to look to the United States, rather than Europe, for their ideas. He also pointed out how important individualism, self-reliance, and self-improvement are. Many people thought of Emerson's speech as a kind of declaration of independence for American scholars.

Another leading American transcendentalist was Henry David Thoreau. Like Emerson, Thoreau believed in the supreme importance of individual freedom. In 1845, he went to live in a small cabin on the banks of Walden Pond near Concord, Massachusetts. He spent his time thinking and studying nature. Thoreau wrote one of his best works about his life there. Titled *Walden,* it was first printed in 1854.

Another transcendentalist author was Margaret Fuller. She grew up in New England and knew Ralph Waldo Emerson. In 1840, Fuller became the editor of a transcendentalist magazine, the *Dial.* Four years later, she went to New York where she wrote for a major newspaper. Fuller also wrote a book in favor of equal rights for women, titled *Woman in the Nineteenth Century.*

3.2 Poets and Novelists. Born in New England, Nathaniel Hawthorne wrote stories about his Puritan heritage. Hawthorne knew most of the leading transcendentalists and lived at Brook Farm for a time. However, he did not share the views of people there that all people could perfect their lives. His main concern was with the problem

What influenced American writers of the mid-1800's?

Have students consider how individualism, self-reliance, and self-improvement were part of the nation's past.

In what did Thoreau believe?

How did Hawthorne differ from the transcendentalists?

Creativity
CONCEPT

Creativity can be defined as the ability to produce original ideas or things. No one seems to know why one person may be more creative than another. And no one seems to know why creative activity seems to occur at one place over a period of time. Some people say it happens when people recognize a need for something.

In the years between 1820 and 1850, a number of people in the United States recognized the need for a uniquely American literature. One of the literary figures of the time was Ralph Waldo Emerson. The selection which follows is from Emerson's *Nature*, published in 1836.

So shall we come to look at the world with new eyes. It shall answer the endless inquiry of the intellect,—What is truth? . . . What is good? . . . Then shall come to pass what my poet said; 'Nature is not fixed but fluid. Spirit alters, moulds, makes it. . . . Every spirit builds itself a house and beyond its house a world and beyond its world a heaven. Know then that the world exists for you. . . . Build therefore your own world. As . . . you conform your life to the pure idea in your mind . . . a

revolution in things will attend the influx of the spirit . . . [and] the advancing spirit [creates] its ornaments along its path, and carry with it the beauty it visits and the song which enchants it; it shall draw beautiful faces, warm hearts, wise discourse, and heroic acts, around its way, until evil is no more seen. . . .

On August 31, 1837, Emerson delivered "The American Scholar" speech at Harvard College. At that time, he said the following:

Not he is great who can alter matter, but he who can alter my state of mind. They are the kings of the world who give the color of their present thought to all nature and all art, and persuade men by the cheerful serenity of their carrying the matter, that this thing which they do is the apple which the ages have desired to pluck, now at last ripe, and inviting nations to the harvest. The great man makes the great thing.

1. What does Emerson think about creativity?
2. According to Emerson, what should be the world's view of the creative person?

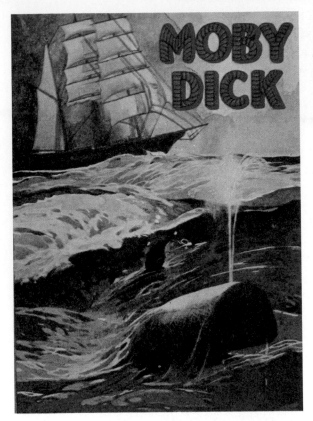 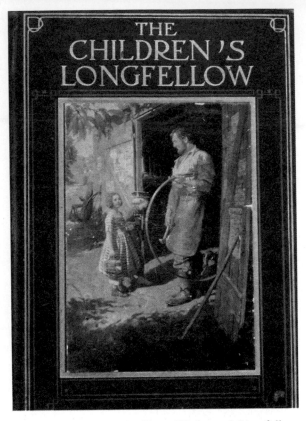

Novels by Herman Melville (left) and books of poetry by Henry Wadsworth Longfellow (right) were popular reading in the middle 1800's. How did literature contribute to a spirit of change in the United States?

Find out if students have read any of the literature mentioned here in another class. Discuss what can be learned about the history of a period through the reading of literature.

of evil in people's lives. This is shown in such works as *The Scarlet Letter* and *The House of Seven Gables*.

Another novelist of the middle 1800's was Herman Melville of New York. He wrote adventure stories often based on his own experiences. Melville had a fairly gloomy view of human nature, as shown in one of his most famous works, *Moby Dick*. Set against the background of a whaling trip, the story deals with the struggle between good and evil. Melville's stories were complex, and he used a great deal of *symbolism*, or the use of one thing to stand for something else. For example, in *Moby Dick*, the white whale stands for evil. Many people had trouble understanding his writing, and Melville was overlooked for many years. Later he came to be thought of as one of America's leading authors.

Edgar Allen Poe wrote mostly poems and short stories. Poe was born in Boston and lived much of his life in Virginia. One of his poems, "The Raven," brought him to people's attention around the country.

Poe is thought of as the creator of detective stories. He also wrote horror tales, such as *The Pit and the Pendulum* and *The Murders in the Rue Morgue*. Poe's stories were complicated. He often used unhappy themes and wrote of the struggle between good and evil. More people read and liked Poe's work in later years than while he was alive.

What is Poe thought to have created?

Walt Whitman was another author of poems. He, perhaps more than any other author of this time, reflected the democratic spirit. Like the transcendentalists, he believed in the individual. One of his most important works was a group of poems called *Leaves of Grass,* first printed in 1855. In it, he praised the growing American nation. Whitman broke with the style of earlier poets. He wrote in *free verse*—poems which do not rhyme. This was one reason why he was not very popular while he was alive. After his death, Whitman became famous as the "Poet of Democracy."

What did Whitman reflect?

Henry Wadsworth Longfellow was one writer who was very popular during his lifetime. A New England poet, Longfellow used American themes in such widely-read tales as *The Courtship of Miles Standish* and *Song of Hiawatha*. Most of his works, including "The Village Blacksmith," appealed to the common people.

Why was Long-fellow popular?

Nearly as well known as Longfellow was John Greenleaf Whittier of Massachusetts. He wrote poems such as "Snow-Bound" and "The Barefoot Boy," based on New England life and legend. Whittier worked in the abolitionist movement, at times helping William Lloyd Garrison. Whittier's *Voices of Freedom* is a group of antislavery poems.

1. Where did Ralph Waldo Emerson think Americans should look for their ideas and themes?
2. Which authors of the middle 1800's reflected transcendentalism in their works?
3. What were some of the major literary works of this time?

4. Conclusion

The growth of democracy and the spirit of perfection influenced society and culture during the first half of the 1800's. Reformers worked to improve their society and shape American social institutions. These years were also important in the development of an American culture. The writers of the time created a national literature and set a standard which served to inspire later writers. These social and cultural forces helped to strengthen the bonds of national unity. However, disagreements over such problems as slavery were beginning, at the same time, to divide the nation.

Chapter 11 Review

Main Points

1. During the first half of the nineteenth century, Americans attempted to reform several aspects of their society.
2. Religion was an important factor in the reform movement of the period.
3. Changes in ideas about religion produced several new religious groups.
4. The movements to get equal rights for women and to abolish slavery made gains but remained small.
5. Public education was well established in the North by 1860. In the South, there were mostly private schools.
6. Major efforts for reform were concerned with the care of people with handicaps and people in prisons.
7. American literary figures wrote about America and its people.
8. American writers experimented with new literary forms.

Building Vocabulary

1. Identify the following:

Charles Finney	William Lloyd Garrison	Auburn Prison
Mormons	Theodore Weld	Neal Dow
Ralph Waldo Emerson	Sojourner Truth	Walden Pond
Brook Farm	Lucretia Mott	Margaret Fuller
Sarah Grimké	Horace Mann	Edgar Allen Poe
Angelina Grimké	Dorothea Dix	Walt Whitman

2. Define the following:

elect	transcendentalism	temperance
revivals	utopias	prohibition
revelations	abolish	repealed
persecuted	abolitionists	symbolism
philosophy	prejudice	free verse

Remembering the Facts

1. Why did many Americans in the 1800's believe they could build a better future?
2. What did the transcendentalists believe about people's ability to perfect themselves and society?
3. Why did people establish utopian communities?
4. Who were the leading abolitionists, and what did they want to accomplish?
5. How were women's rights limited?

6. Which changes took place in public education during the early 1800's?
7. How were people with handicaps treated before the 1800's?
8. Which changes did reformers seek to make for prisons?
9. Who were the leading writers and poets of the middle 1800's?

Understanding the Facts

1. How did the revival movement influence reform?
2. Why did many Americans oppose the Mormons?
3. Why did some utopian communities fail while others lasted?
4. Why was the abolitionist movement small at a time when the country was becoming more democratic?
5. Why were many of the same people in several of the various reform movements in the eary 1800's?
6. Why was public education important in a growing democracy?
7. Why were some reformers opposed to the drinking of liquor?
8. How did the works of writers of this period reflect transcendentalism?

Using Maps

Demographic Maps. The ancient Greeks used the word *demos* to mean people. The Greek word *grapho* meant to write about a certain subject. Combining the two words forms the word *demography* which means the writing about human population.

A demographic map is a map that contains information about human population. The map on page 273 shows population density, the average number of people living in every square mile of an area. The information shown is for various parts of the United States in 1850. Study the map and its key. Answer the following questions.

1. Which section of the United States in 1850 was the most densely populated?
2. Was the most densely populated area north or south of the line of 40° north latitude?
3. Which section of the United States in 1850 was the least densely populated?
4. How would you describe the population for most of the area of the Mississippi River Valley?
5. Which was more densely populated, Michigan or North Carolina?
6. Was the area east of 85° west longitude more densely populated than the area to the west?

New Ways and New People

12

Manufacturing became more important to the American economy beginning with the establishment of Samuel Slater's mill in Rhode Island. How did the rise of industry change both economic and social life in America?

The United States, in the early 1800's, was an agricultural nation. It had been so since its beginning. Most of the people living in the United States were of British background and belonged to one of the Protestant churches. Major changes, however, were taking place that would alter American economic and social life. A new era was about to begin.

1. The Rise of Industry

In the years after the American Revolution, the United States imported most of its manufactured goods. Many Americans agreed with Thomas Jefferson's statement: "Let our workshops remain in Europe." Jefferson and others wanted the United States to stay a country of individually-owned farms.

During these years, some manufacturing was done in homes or small workshops. Manufacturing became more important to the American economy with the coming of the Industrial Revolution. This was a series of great changes that took place in *industry*—the making and selling of goods—starting in the 1700's. It began in Great Britain with new power-driven machines. It later spread to other countries around the world.

1.1 Beginnings in Textiles. As machines began to be used, products were made in factories instead of by one person at home or in a small shop. In the past, the people of the United States had mainly produced raw materials such as cotton, lumber, iron, and wheat. And until the 1800's, artisans like blacksmiths used hand tools to make their products. Shoes, saddles, hats, wagons, nails, flour, and books were all made by hand. People in England had carefully guarded their knowledge of manufacturing. Machinery or plans for it were not allowed to be taken out of the country.

In 1789, Samuel Slater came to America from Great Britain. He had worked in a cotton mill there and knew a great deal about the British *textile,* or cloth-making, machines. Slater had memorized the plans for the machines. With money from a Quaker merchant, Slater built some of these machines. In 1790, he started the first American textile mill on the banks of the Seekonk River in Pawtucket, Rhode Island. Water power was used to drive the machines in the early factories.

During the early 1800's, the country moved steadily away from the system of home manufacture. More and more work was done in the new textile mills. There were few of these, however, until the War of 1812. At this time, trade slowed down, and New England merchants began to

Where was manufacturing done in the late 1700's?

Recall the British policy of mercantilism discussed in Chapter 4, Section 4.2, page 114.

What was the first industry to become industrialized?

Many rivers in New England, flowing from hilly country to the ocean, were well-suited to driving machinery.

Why did New England merchants begin putting money into textiles?

put more money into textiles and less into shipping. They felt that people would buy American-made goods since European products were no longer available. The textile industry grew rapidly during and after the war.

1.2 The Factory System. Slater's mill at Pawtucket, Rhode Island introduced a new way to make goods. It was the *factory system*. Under it, workers came from their homes to buildings called factories where goods were made with power-driven machines. Making a product was divided into separate tasks. Instead of having one trained worker do all tasks, each task was done by a person with less training. Women and children, and later people from foreign countries, provided much of this unskilled labor, especially in the textile mills.

What was the factory system?

At Lowell, Massachusetts, investors set up what they called a model factory. They built boarding houses for the workers, who were mostly young women from New England farms. Hours were long, and the free time of workers was controlled. Time was set aside for some activities, such as the publication of a monthly magazine, *The Lowell Offering*.

Owners of textile mills (left) and other light industries employed many women. Women workers in Lowell, Massachusetts, published *The Lowell Offering* (right), a company magazine. Why did mill owners hire so many women?

Checking Fact and Opinion
SKILL

Fact and opinion are often difficult to separate. What a writer personally feels about a subject can flavor the writing. The reader must recognize the difference between fact and opinion and read with that in mind.

The following selection is from the travel journals of Josiah Quincy. During his lifetime, Quincy became a member of Congress. He also served as mayor of Boston and president of Harvard College. In 1801, he visited Slater's textile mill in Rhode Island. He described the mill scene, blending facts with opinion. As you read the selection, notice the various kinds of information Quincy included.

We found the proprietor very cautious of admitting strangers to view its operations, nor would he grant us the privilege until he had received satisfactory assurances that we were as ignorant and unconcerned about every thing relating to the cotton manufacture as he could wish. All the processes of turning cotton from its rough [form] into every variety of marketable thread . . . are here performed by machinery operating by Water-wheels, assisted only by children from four to Ten years old, and one [supervisor]. Above an hundred of the [children] are employed, at the rate of from 12 to 25 cents for a day's labor. Our attendant was very [enthusiastic about] the usefulness of this manufacture, and the employment it supplied for so many poor children. But an [argument] was [given] on the other side of the question . . . which called us to pity these little creatures, [working] in a [crowded] room, among [fast machinery], at an age when nature requires for them air, space, and sports. There was a dull dejection in the [faces] of all of them. This, united with the deafening roar of the falls and the rattling of the machinery, [satisfied] our curiosity.

Answer the following questions.

1. Which facts did Quincy give about workers in the factory?
2. What was his opinion about using children as workers?
3. Which other opinions did Quincy express?
4. Which other facts are mentioned?
5. How can you tell what is fact and what is opinion?

Factory conditions in Europe influenced Robert Owen to set up the New Harmony community discussed in Chapter 11.

In general, what conditions existed in the early factory system?

Many Americans hoped that factories in the United States following the Lowell plan would be able to avoid the problems which came with the rise of manufacturing in Europe. The Lowell System, however, was not followed. In most other factories, conditions were as bad as those in Europe. Buildings were dirty, and pay was poor. Companies often cut wages as prices were brought down to encourage people to buy their goods. The factory system brought great change into the lives of a people used to farming their own land and making their own decisions.

1.3 Inventions and Industry.   In America, the need for new ways to do things produced a large number of inventions. The rapidly growing manufacturing in the 1800's was aided by the larger number of new machines. In 1800, there were 306 *patents*—licenses to make, use, or sell new inventions—registered with the United States Patent Office. By 1860, there were 28,000 new patents.

In 1793, Eli Whitney developed a machine to remove the seeds from cotton. The machine was called the *cotton gin* (short for "engine"). With it, workers were able to prepare more cotton for shipment to textile mills in a shorter time. The amount of cotton coming out of the South increased greatly, and plantation owners profited.

Why was Whitney an important inventor?

Whitney also used a new system of *interchangeable parts* in the making of firearms. These were parts which were exactly alike. If one part of a gun was damaged, another part of the same type could replace it. This discovery made *mass production* possible. This is a system of producing large numbers of an item quickly by using interchangeable parts. By the 1840's, many kinds of machinery, from clocks to farm equipment, were made in this way.

In 1839, Charles Goodyear discovered a way to cure rubber that made it able to stand great heat or cold. This process, *vulcanization,* made rubber practical for industrial use. In 1844, Samuel F. B. Morse finished his experiments with an electric telegraph by sending a message from Baltimore to Washington, D.C. The telegraph made it possible to send and receive news quickly. Elias Howe invented a machine in 1846 which could sew cloth faster than a person could by hand. Isaac Singer improved the sewing machine in 1851. This speeded up the manufacture of clothing. In 1851, William Kelly discovered a better way to make steel from iron ore. All of these and other inventions helped the growth of industry.

Have students draw up a list of things which, if invented, would improve the quality of life today. Focus on the relationship between the need for an item and its being developed.

1.4 The Machine on the Farm.   Machines had an effect on farming as well as manufacturing. Many of the new inventions made it easier to farm on a large scale. One of the most important was a mechanical reaper for harvesting grain. It was invented in 1831 by Cyrus

Isaac Singer's sewing machine (left) made mass production of clothing possible. With Cyrus McCormick's reaper (right) farmers could plant more crops each year. What other inventions helped to improve the American economy?

McCormick, who later set up a factory to manufacture reapers. In 1847, George Page built a revolving disc harrow which made the job of breaking up the earth for planting easier. John Heath invented a mechanical binder for grain harvesting in 1850. Many of these machines were later improved and had a greater impact on farming after 1860.

What impact did the inventions of the 1830's and 1840's have on farming?

1.5   The Iron Industry.   With more and more machines being used in farming and manufacturing, the need for iron grew. The United States had been producing iron in small mills for many years. The Lehigh, Susquehanna, and Delaware river valleys were early iron centers. Furnaces were set up near sources of wood, which was used in making charcoal. Charcoal was used to heat the furnaces that changed iron ore into crude iron.

Students should learn more about the industries in their area and particularly when and why they were located there.

In 1830, it was discovered that coal could be used instead of charcoal in making iron. The coal fields of Pennsylvania became an important source of fuel. By 1855, iron furnaces were using more coal than charcoal. By 1860, over 500,000 tons of crude iron were produced yearly by over 400 furnaces around the country. The United States became one of the leading iron producers in the world.

When did the United States become one of the leading iron producers in the world?

1. Who built the first textile machines in the United States?
2. Where was the first model factory system?
3. What were the major inventions of the middle 1800's?
4. Which product replaced charcoal in making iron?

2. A System of Transportation

In the early 1800's, it was not easy to get raw materials to factories, goods to markets, and food to the people cheaply and quickly. The rise of manufacturing and greater farming added to the need for better transportation.

2.1 New Roads. The United States had begun to improve transportation by building a system of roads. The National Road and similar projects were finished in the years from 1810 to 1860. By 1860, there were over 88,000 miles (140,000 kilometers) of hard-surfaced roads in the country. Road transportation was slow and costly, however. Goods were moved in wagons pulled by teams of horses. Wagons could carry only small loads and often made several trips.

2.2 The Canal Age. Farmers and manufacturers began to demand cheaper means of transportation. This led to a time of canal building, as boats or barges could carry larger loads at less cost. One of the most important projects during these years was the building of the Erie Canal. It was begun by the state of New York in 1817 and finished in 1825. The Erie Canal linked New York City with Buffalo on Lake Erie by way of Albany on the Hudson River. It opened the farms of the Middle West to the markets of the East.

What was one of the major road projects of the early 1800's?

Refer students to the map of roads and canals on page 225.

What was one of the major canal projects of the early 1800's?

Tools used in building the Erie Canal (left) were powered by animals and groups of workers. To get canal boats over a rocky cliff, a double set of five locks (right) had to be built. Which cities did the Erie Canal link?

By the 1830's, canals were being dug all around the country, though mostly in the North. Pennsylvania developed a system of waterways connecting Philadelphia with other areas of the state. Ohio and Indiana had canals linking the Great Lakes and the Ohio River. New Jersey linked the Delaware and Raritan rivers. Both Virginia and Maryland built canals reaching from the Atlantic coast to farm areas in the western parts of those states. There were few important canals in the South. Several smaller canals were built to make it easier to travel on the rivers there. Generally, these rivers served the needs of the South.

2.3 The First Steamboats. Neither the improvement of roads nor the building of canals solved the problem of slow transportation. In the early 1800's, however, different inventors began to develop new means of transportation which were also faster. The steam engine was invented by Thomas Newcomen by 1708. James Watt, a Scot, patented an improved engine in 1769. His work made the steam engine valuable as a machine for transportation.

Who built the first steamboat?

Robert Fulton of New York adapted the steam engine for use on a boat. In August 1807, Fulton's *Clermont* traveled from New York City to Albany. It was a trip of 150 miles (240 kilometers) up the Hudson River, and it took about 32 hours. Up to this time, boats had not been able to move easily upstream. Soon steamboats were being used in other parts of the country, especially on the Ohio and Mississippi rivers. By 1860, there were nearly 1,000 steamboats in service on the rivers.

As with most inventions, Fulton's work was the result of the efforts of many different people. Fulton brought these ideas together successfully.

Robert Fulton became the first to show that steamboats were a practical method of transportation. What was the name of Fulton's ship? How did his success affect river travel?

The first railroads in the United States linked nearby towns to improve existing means of transportation for goods and passengers. This painting shows the New Jersey Camden and Amboy Railroad in 1834. What other forms of transportation available in the middle 1800's are shown? Notice the railroad routes on the map on the next page. Where were most of the major lines?

2.4 The Coming of the Railroads.   The steam engine was applied to land transportation at about the same time as it was being used in steamboats. An engineer in England, George Stephenson, built a steam-powered locomotive, *The Rocket*. It weighed five tons and could pull a load three times its own weight at 12 miles (19.2 kilometers) an hour. In 1829, *The Rocket* entered a contest with other kinds of locomotives and won. It set the pattern for future locomotive development. This was the beginning of the "railway era."

Who built the first steam locomotive?

By contrast, Fulton's boat hit a top speed of 5 mph in its first run.

In the United States, railroads, as well as early roads and canals, grew out of the commercial rivalry of eastern cities. Merchants in Boston, New York, Philadelphia, Baltimore, and Charleston promoted the building of railroads. They felt that this would bring them more trade. The first successful railroad in the United States was the Baltimore and Ohio. In 1830, Peter Cooper built the first steam locomotive in America, for the Baltimore and Ohio Railroad. It was called the *Tom Thumb*. In Charleston, South Carolina, *Best Friend of Charleston* carried passengers on the first scheduled steam-railroad run in 1830. Harriet Martineau, a visitor from England, wrote about several of her trips by train in the mid-1830's.

What was the first successful railroad in the United States?

. . . my journeys on [the Charleston and Augusta railroad] *were by far the most fatiguing of any I underwent in the country. The motion and the noise are distracting. . . .*

One great inconvenience of the American railroads is that, from wood being used for fuel, there is an incessant shower of large sparks, destructive to dress and comfort. . . . Some serious accidents from fire have happened in this way; and, during my last trip on the Columbia and Philadelphia rail-road, a lady in the car had a shawl burned to destruction on her shoulders; and I found that my own gown had thirteen holes in it. . . .

Nearly all of the early railroads were started to link ports on the east coast with areas farther west. Later they joined major cities

What area had the most developed railroad system by 1850?

Major Railroads in the 1850's

together as well. By 1850, New England had a system of railroads which connected nearly every city in the area. In 1852, the first railroad linking Detroit and Chicago was finished. The Rock Island Line built the first bridge over the Mississippi River in 1856. In the South, lines ran from Charleston and Savannah to Atlanta. However, there were not nearly as many miles of track in the South as in the North and Middle West.

By the mid-1800's, some 30,000 miles (48,000 kilometers) of track had been laid throughout the country. The United States, however, did not yet have a fast transportation system. Backed by different states and private merchants, railroad companies built lines in which the *gauge,* or distance between the rails, varied. This meant that at places where railroads of different gauges came together, goods had to be moved from one car to another. There were other problems, such as the lack of strong bridges and rails. In spite of these drawbacks, railroads were an important step toward faster, cheaper transportation.

With the growing number of railroads came a rise in related industries. There was a greater need for iron, timber, and coal. A communications system also developed along with the railroads. Telegraph lines were set up along the tracks, and the use of the telegraph improved railroad service. Messages could be sent from station to station giving the arrival and departure times of trains.

What were the major problems of railroads in the mid-1800's?

Use pictures of early trains, provide information on schedules, and invite to class someone who can describe a cross-country trip by train.

1. Why was good transportation important for the rise of industry?
2. Why did farmers need good transportation?
3. Which part of the country had the fewest miles of railroad?

3. The Growth of Cities

The factory system and the new industries in the middle 1800's led to a growing number of cities. Towns were built near factories because people had to live close to their work. Older cities grew, and new cities were started as the factories were built. There was a tremendous growth in the number and size of cities before 1860. In 1790, about 5 percent of the population lived in urban areas. By 1860, the number of people living in these areas had reached nearly 20 percent.

3.1 Old Cities and New Cities. In 1790, there were only 24 places in the United States with over 2,500 people. As America began to industrialize, older cities grew. Between 1820 and 1840, New York City's population rose from 123,000 to 312,000. Philadelphia grew from

Population Growth, 1790–1860

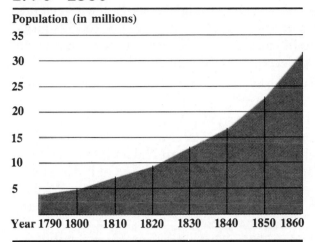

Population (in millions)

Year 1790 1800 1810 1820 1830 1840 1850 1860

Total Estimated Population, 1860

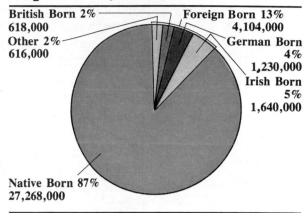

British Born 2%
618,000

Other 2%
616,000

Foreign Born 13%
4,104,000

German Born
4%
1,230,000

Irish Born
5%
1,640,000

Native Born 87%
27,268,000

How did total American population change from the time of the first census in 1790 until 1860? What percent of the population in 1860 was not born in the United States? Where were most immigrants born?

a population of 112,000 to 220,000. The number of people in Baltimore increased from 62,000 to 102,000, while Boston expanded from 42,000 to 93,000 people. New factories, the growth of commerce brought about by the railroads, and foreign trade all played a part in the growth of these older cities.

In general, how much did cities grow from 1790 to 1860?

By 1830, new cities had been started in the West. Cincinnati, Pittsburgh, and Louisville all had populations from 10,000 to 25,000. These cities and others, like St. Louis, were located on rivers. They benefited from such improvements in transportation as the steamboat. Railroads were important to new cities of the West such as Chicago. Chicago was fast becoming one of the leading railroad junctions in the country. By 1860, it had a population of 109,000 and was growing rapidly. Altogether, by 1860, there were 392 places in the United States which had a population of 2,500 or more.

3.2 Benefits and Problems. During the years from 1820 to 1860, people had both benefits and problems from city life. Education and jobs were easier to get than in rural areas. Many of the large cities had libraries, and some offered classes for adults. There were operas and plays for those who could pay to see them.

Use this section as the basis for discussing the benefits and problems of cities today.

What did cities do during the mid-1800's that created problems?

The growing urban centers, however, went beyond the ability of their governments to deal with certain problems. Larger cities stretched

New Ways and New People 291

their borders beyond the point where water, sewage, and other services were available. There was much sickness in areas where poor people lived in crowded *tenements*—apartment houses generally without sanitation, comfort, and safety. The burning of coal made great clouds of smoke that hung over factory towns. In 1833, a visitor to Pittsburgh complained that the smoke caused so much dirt and soot that clean hands and faces were "objects of rare occurrence."

3.3 Improving City Life.   One of the major problems facing people who lived in cities was having enough water. City governments began building waterworks and dams to form *reservoirs*—places where water is collected and stored for use. In 1799, water from the Schuylkill River was carried through log pipes to an area of Philadelphia. With the opening of the Fairmount Waterworks in 1822, all parts of Philadelphia received water through a system of iron pipes. The problem of water supply also became serious in New York City. In 1842, the Croton Dam was built to form a reservoir for the city.

Most towns in the early 1800's did not have adequate lighting for the streets. At first, oil lamps were used. Later oil was replaced by coal gas. Boston began using coal gas for street lighting in 1822. New York City began its use the following year, and Philadelphia did the same in 1837. By the 1850's, gas lighting was common in most of the larger cities.

Another major improvement in city life was the development of professional police and fire departments. In the early 1800's, cities had poorly-paid *night watches*—people who lit the street lamps and called

What was a major problem that people faced living in cities in the mid-1800's?

What were night watches?

Every city lived in fear of fire because most buildings were made of wood. By the 1850's, many cities began to set up fire-fighting departments with public funds. Where was one of the earliest full-time fire departments?

Margaret Gaffney Haughery (1813–1882)

PROFILE

The career of Margaret Gaffney Haughery symbolizes both the drive for business success and the spirit of reform in America during the middle 1800's. Born in Ireland, Haughery's family moved to Maryland when she was five years old. At age nine, her parents died. She was brought up by neighbors, and she never learned to read or write. In 1835, she married. After moving to New Orleans, her husband left her, and her only child died.

Haughery worked at a laundry. She spent her free time with the children at a local orphanage. Using the money she saved, she bought several cows and started her own dairy business. By 1840, she had a dairy of 40 cows. In time, she used her profits to build a home for orphans. During her life, she helped to establish ten other homes for children and for elderly people.

In 1858, Haughery sold the dairy business and opened a bakery. She bought new, steam-powered machinery for it, making it the first bakery in the South to be run by steam. Later it became New Orleans' largest export business, producing and selling packaged crackers.

Even though she was a success in business, Haughery's simple way of life did not change. She liked to give help to people in need. Before she died, Haughery left a large amount of money to continue this help. Most people remembered her as "the Bread Woman of New Orleans."

out the hour of the night. They also sounded the alarm in case of fire. In 1844, New York City authorized a professional police force, and other cities soon followed this example. At first, fire protection for cities was provided by volunteer companies. A full-time fire department was formed in Cincinnati in 1853. This helped set a pattern of fire protection for other cities.

As water systems were built, it became possible to install fire hydrants at convenient locations.

1. What was the largest city in the United States by 1840?
2. What were the benefits of city life?
3. What problems did the city cause?

4. The Changing Population

Many changes were taking place in the United States as the country industrialized. More people took jobs in factories and lived in cities. The population of the country was growing rapidly. There was also an increase in immigration to the United States from other areas of the world. When George Washington became President of the United States in 1789, the nation had nearly 4 million people. By 1810, the population had reached 7 million and by 1850, 23 million. Part of this growth came from a heavy flow of immigration beginning in the 1820's.

4.1 Increasing Immigration. During the years from 1820 to 1840, over 700,000 immigrants landed on the shores of the United States. Nearly 60 percent of these people were German or Irish. A second large movement of immigrants to the United States began in the 1840's. In 1846, the failure of the potato crop in Ireland started a *famine,* a general lack of food in an area causing starvation. During the next 15 years, more than 1 million Irish came to the United States. Thousands of Germans also came between 1840 and 1860. Poor harvest, lack of land and jobs, and desire for political freedom caused them to leave Germany in search of a better life. Altogether, well over 4 million people came to the United States in the years from 1840 to 1860.

The potato was domesticated in South America and taken to Europe after the arrival of Europeans in the New World. The Irish potato crop was largely destroyed by a plant disease in the early 1800's.

What caused the Irish and Germans to immigrate to the United States in large numbers in the mid-1800's?

Many industries actively recruited foreign labor to come to the United States. This British drawing is titled "The Lure of American Wages." What does it suggest about the benefits of working in America?

4.2   Settling in America.   The experiences of the immigrants when they arrived in the United States followed certain patterns. For the most part, people from Germany arrived with some money. Many were able to move to areas where land was available, such as the Middle West. Large numbers of German immigrants settled on farms in Illinois, Missouri, and Wisconsin. Thousands of Germans also settled in cities, especially in the West. Many set up their own businesses. By 1860, nearly half of the population of both Milwaukee and St. Louis was of German descent. Germans made up 30 percent of the population of Cincinnati.

When Irish immigrants landed in the United States, they generally did not have the money to buy farms or land. They often settled in eastern seaports, such as New York, Boston, Philadelphia, and Baltimore. In 1855, there were more than 50,000 Irish living in Boston. Nearly two thirds of the Irish immigrants to America settled in the northeast section of the country. Irish workers were important sources of labor around the country for the factories and for canal and railroad building.

Why did most Irish settle in eastern cities?

4.3   The Nativist Movement.   During the 1830's and 1840's, a movement against the immigrants began in America. Members of the group were known as Nativists because they were native to, or born in, the United States. Most were Protestants of British background. Nativists feared competition for jobs from immigrants who worked for low wages. Nativists also believed that the country was in danger from the large numbers of Catholics coming there to live. Because most Irish immigrants were Catholics, the movement was largely directed against them. There were violent clashes in several cities between Nativist groups and Irish immigrants.

Why did a Nativist movement develop?

Nativists wanted only American-born Protestants to hold political office. They were against both foreigners and Catholics. In the 1850's, a national party was formed. When asked about opposition to immigrants, its members answered, "I know nothing." Because of this, they became known as the Know-Nothings. Under the name of the American party, the Know-Nothings participated in the election of 1856. They lost strength in the years after 1856. Issues like slavery began to push the question of immigration into the background.

Discuss the opposition of immigration in light of the fact that the United States is largely a nation of immigrants.

1. From where did most of the immigrants come during the years between 1820 and 1840?
2. Where did most of these people settle?
3. Which political party was formed in opposition to the immigrants?

5. Conclusion

During the years from 1820 to 1860, the United States experienced a great deal of growth and change. Industry expanded with the introduction of power-driven machinery. Cities were established around newly-built factories. The coming of the railroad revolutionized transportation. Population increased as thousands of immigrants landed in the United States. By 1860, the "old" America had given way to a "new" America.

Chapter 12 Review

Main Points

1. In the first half of the nineteenth century, the United States began to develop industry as an important part of the national economy.

2. The factory system developed first in textiles and spread to other industries.

3. Numerous inventions aided in the growth of industry and transportation.

4. The rise of industry and the improvements in transportation led to the growth of more cities.

5. Life in the cities produced both benefits and problems.

6. Political opposition developed to the large number of immigrants who entered the United States.

Building Vocabulary

1. Identify the following:
   Industrial Revolution
   Samuel Slater
   The Lowell Offering
   Eli Whitney
   Samuel F. B. Morse
   Cyrus McCormick
   Erie Canal
   Robert Fulton
   The Rocket
   Margaret Gaffney Haughery
   Nativists
   Know-Nothings

2. Define the following:
   industry
   textile
   factory system
   patents
   cotton gin
   interchangeable parts
   mass production
   vulcanization
   gauge
   tenements
   reservoirs
   night watches
   famine

Remembering the Facts

1. What were the conditions in the early factories?
2. Which development made mass production possible?
3. How did inventions influence industry?
4. How were a person's rights to an invention legally protected?
5. What new methods of transportation were developed?
6. Which actions were taken to improve life in the cities?
7. What groups of people came to America from 1820 to 1860?
8. Why did Nativists oppose immigrants?

Understanding the Facts

1. Why was the textile industry the first to develop the factory system?
2. How did the factory system differ from the home workshop?
3. Which invention had the greatest effect on agriculture in the South?
4. What were the advantages of using the new inventions over the way things had been done?
5. Why was the iron industry important to most other industries?
6. What effect did new methods of transportation have on other industries?
7. How did the development of factories, farm machinery, and transportation effect the growth of cities?
8. How did the population change as the United States industrialized?

Using Line Graphs

Using Line Graphs. The left illustration on page 291 is called a line graph. A line is used to show the level of the subject of the graph during the years listed across the base line. The sweep and direction of the line provides comparison with the years before and after. The line graph also gives a sense of the trend or direction over the entire period shown.

Using the graph, answer the following questions.

1. What is shown by the graph?
2. How many people were in the United States in 1790?
3. What was the population of the United States in the most recent census before Andrew Jackson became President?
4. What was the population after President Jackson left office?
5. What was the increase in population between 1828 and 1836?
6. Did population become less, stay the same, or increase from 1790 to 1860?
7. Based on the information on the graph, why would you think that the population in 1870 would not be over 100,000,000 people?

From Ocean to Ocean   13

John Charles Frémont, the "Pathfinder," became a living sign of the spirit of manifest destiny. His adventures inspired many Americans to go west. What did people hope to find in the area west of the Mississippi River?

With the Louisiana Purchase in 1803, the United States gained its first area of land west of the Mississippi River. In the years following, Americans began to move into these lands as well as others in the West. Large areas of land were added to the United States in the 1840's and 1850's. Soon the nation extended from the Atlantic Ocean to the Pacific Ocean. Except for Alaska and Hawaii, the United States grew to its present size during these years.

1. The Westward Movement

Americans had begun to explore the lands west of the Mississippi River before many areas to the east of it were settled. The Lewis and Clark expedition of 1804 to 1806 gave people in the United States their first information about the Louisiana Territory. Soon other Americans were exploring and settling lands in the West. Moving across the Mississippi River into the huge area of the West presented exciting challenges and new problems to Americans and the United States.

1.1 Leading the Way West. The United States followed up the Lewis and Clark expedition with others. In 1806, Lieutenant Zebulon Pike traveled up the Arkansas River to the Rocky Mountains in Colorado. Pike's report gave new information about the West. It added to American interest in trade with the Spanish in New Mexico.

Another expedition was led by Major Stephen Long in 1819 and 1820. Long explored the Great Plains along the Platte River to the Rocky Mountains. Both Pike and Long reported that the Great Plains were not fit for settlement because of the lack of rainfall and trees. This led to the common belief that the Great Plains was a "Great American Desert." For years, people were not interested in settling there.

Fur traders and trappers were an even more important source of information about the West. After the United States gained Louisiana, Americans became important in the western fur trade. Prior to that time, the French and Spanish had competed with the British for furs.

The trappers went into the mountains and river areas of the West for beaver. Some time during the year, they met with a representative of a fur-trading company to sell their furs. These furs were later sold by the companies to customers in the East or in Europe. Over the years, the trappers came to know the streams, rivers, mountain passes, and trails of nearly every area in the West. Such trappers as Jim Bridger and Jedediah Smith guided early settlers through the Rocky Mountains to Oregon and California.

Use a topographical map to trace Pike's travels and to consider the nature of the land into which he went.

Where did Pike explore?

What were the early reports about the Great Plains?

Note that the fur trade was forced farther west as the line of settlement moved west.

1.2 Manifest Destiny. Americans moved into the lands west of the Mississippi River for the same reason that they had always moved west—for cheap and plentiful land. Large numbers of settlers started farms in Iowa, Arkansas, and Missouri in the 1820's and 1830's. By the 1840's, much of the Mississippi River Valley was settled, and interest began to grow in lands farther west.

What was the major reason people moved west?

Since colonial times, the settlers in America had believed that they had a right to the lands they settled. Most of them did not spend time talking about the westward movement. However, many would agree that it was helping to extend the democratic way of life. Political leaders and authors sometimes expressed ideas about the westward movement. They reflected the views of many Americans at the time.

What is meant by manifest destiny?

In 1845, a magazine editor first used the term manifest destiny. He wrote that it was the ***manifest destiny,*** or certain fate, of the United States to stretch from ocean to ocean. Many people in all parts of the country agreed with him. They were called ***expansionists*** because they wanted to expand the land area of the United States. People in business wanted ports on the Pacific coast where American ships could stop on their way to trade with Asia. Settlers wanted to live in the fertile lands of Oregon and California. American leaders did not want any European country to control these areas.

Manifest destiny became a popular slogan to reflect hopes which Americans wanted to fulfill. See if the class can think of any other slogans important to American history.

1. Who explored the West in the early 1800's?
2. How did the term manifest destiny come into use?
3. Which groups were in favor of expanding the area of the United States?

2. On to Oregon

Oregon was one of the areas in the West which attracted Americans. It included lands that are now the states of Oregon, Washington, Idaho, and parts of Wyoming and Montana. It stretched from a latitude of 54°40′ in the north to 42° in the south—from the southern tip of present-day Alaska to northern California. Its boundary in the east was the Rocky Mountains and in the west, the Pacific Ocean. The area had been claimed at different times by several countries. Its rich soil, good rainfall, and mild climate became a strong attraction for American settlers.

Students should remember that Canada was a British possession.

2.1 Early Claims. In the early 1800's, Oregon was claimed by four different countries—Great Britain, the United States, Russia, and Spain. Spain gave up its claim to the area in the Adams-Onís Treaty of

1819. It set the boundary between Spanish lands and the Louisiana Purchase. After the Monroe Doctrine was issued in 1823, Russia gave up its claim to Oregon. By the late 1820's, only the United States and Great Britain were still trying to decide who controlled the area.

Both the United States and Great Britain claimed Oregon because both had explored the area and set up trade there. Traders from New England had sailed into the area toward the end of the 1700's. The Lewis and Clark expedition had traveled there. Also, John Jacob Astor's Pacific Fur Company had founded Fort Astoria on the Columbia River in 1811. This was the first permanent American settlement in the Oregon country. James Cook, an English explorer, had visited the Oregon coast in 1788. British claims were helped by the presence of the Hudson's Bay Company. Dr. John McLoughlin ran the company's business from a fort on the Columbia River. Until the 1840's, trappers working for the Hudson's Bay Company controlled the Oregon fur trade.

What was the basis of the American and British claims to Oregon?

2.2 The Canadian Boundary. Great Britain and the United States were not able to settle their differences over Oregon quickly.

Independence Rock in Wyoming was a popular resting place along the Oregon Trail. Many travelers scratched their names on the large landmark to document their journey. How long was the trip from Missouri to Oregon?

Routes to the Far West

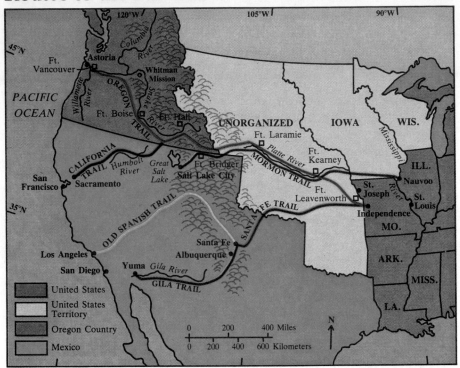

What forts were along the Oregon Trail? How long was the Santa Fe Trail? Where did the Mormon Trail begin and end? What towns were linked by the Gila Trail? Where was the Old Spanish Trail? What river flowed along a section of the California Trail?

What agreement helped to settle much of the U.S.-Canadian boundary?

They did, however, come to agree about the dividing line between the United States and Canada in the west. In the Convention of 1818, the boundary was set at the 49th parallel, running from the Lake of the Woods to the Rocky Mountains. The two countries also agreed to settle the question of Oregon at a later time. For a while, there would be a *joint occupation* of the territory. This meant that people from both the United States and Great Britain could settle in the area.

2.3 Oregon Fever. Events in Oregon soon began to favor the American claim. In the 1830's, missionaries from the United States, led by the Reverend Jason Lee, began to arrive. They settled south of the Columbia River in the Willamette Valley. Farther east on the Columbia River, Marcus and Narcissa Whitman founded a mission at Walla Walla. The experiences of the missionaries interested many people in the United States.

Beginning in the 1840's, "Oregon fever" gripped many Americans. In 1841, the first wagon train made the trip overland from Independence, Missouri, to Oregon. Soon other larger trains were making the 2,000-mile (3,200-kilometer) journey. These pioneers

Compare the movement of Americans into Oregon, Texas, and California with the movement of Europeans to the New World.

followed a path which came to be called the Oregon Trail. The wagon trains crossed the Great Plains, following the Platte River to Fort Laramie, some 600 miles (960 kilometers) from Independence. They crossed the Rocky Mountains at South Pass and went on to Fort Hall. From there, the settlers followed the Snake River to Fort Boise and on to the Columbia River. Moving along it, they made their way to the Willamette Valley. Many of these pioneers started farms there.

How did most pioneers get to Oregon?

In 1846, Francis Parkman traveled through the West. He wrote *The Oregon Trail* in 1849, describing what he had seen.

> *We were late in breaking up our camp . . . and scarcely had we ridden a mile when we saw . . . drawn against the horizon, a line of objects stretching . . . along the level edge of the prairie. An intervening swell soon hid them from sight, until, ascending it . . . we saw close before us the . . . caravan, with its heavy white wagons creeping on in slow procession, and a large drove of cattle following behind. Half a dozen . . . Missourians, mounted on horseback, were . . . shouting among them. . . . they called out to us: "How are ye, boys? Are ye for Oregon or California?"*
>
> *As we pushed rapidly by the wagons, children's faces were thrust out from the white coverings to look at us; while the careworn, thin-featured matron . . . seated in front, suspended the knitting on which most of them were engaged to stare at us with wondering curiosity. By the side of each wagon stalked the proprietor, urging on his patient oxen, . . . inch by inch, on their . . . journey.*

What was the journey to Oregon like?

The journey to Oregon took from four to six months. The people who made it faced dust, rainstorms, and sickness along the trail. Indians sometimes attacked, trying to stop the settlers moving through their lands. Snow was a danger once the wagon trains reached the Rocky Mountains. Often wagon wheels broke or metal tires fell off from the changes in temperatures.

Wagon wheels, made of wood, had a metal "tire" nailed to their surface.

Despite the hardships, there were soon 5,000 Americans living in the Oregon country. All of them lived south of the Columbia River, but they far outnumbered British people in the area. In 1843, they set up a temporary government. These settlers wanted the United States to stop sharing control of the area with Great Britain.

Compare the importance of the presence of a large number of Americans in Oregon to the importance of a large colonial population as a factor in eventual English success in winning North America from the French.

1. Where was the Oregon Trail?
2. Which countries had early claims to Oregon?
3. With which country did the United States jointly occupy Oregon?

3. The Southwest and California

Americans had become more interested in the land of Oregon in the 1840's. At the same time, they were looking to the lands south and west of the Louisiana Territory. These lands belonged to Spain until 1821, when Mexico declared its independence. The area had huge ranches and some mines, which were run by a few wealthy Spanish owners and their workers. The area served chiefly as a border to protect the lands of central Mexico. The Spaniards had not allowed people in these areas to trade with the United States. This began to change, especially after the new Mexican government took over. By the 1820's, Americans were trading and sometimes settling in Texas, New Mexico, and California.

When did Mexico become independent?

3.1 Early Contacts in New Mexico. American trappers had sometimes gone into the settlements of New Mexico for food and supplies. The expedition of Zebulon Pike increased American interest in trade with this area. In 1822, William Becknell led a large caravan from Missouri to Santa Fe along what became known as the Santa Fe Trail. This marked the opening of regular trade between Americans and the people of New Mexico.

What was the Santa Fe Trail?

3.2 Americans in California. Early California was a land of missions and cattle ranches. Most of the people living there were

As this painting suggests, California missions became centers of community life. How did the breakup of the missions affect the people who lived near them?

Mariano Guadalupe Vallejo (1808–1890)

PROFILE

During his life as a military and political leader, Mariano Guadalupe Vallejo saw California change from a thinly settled Spanish outpost into a well-populated American state. Vallejo was born, lived, and died in northern California.

In the 1830's, the Mexican government assigned Vallejo as the commander of a military post at Sonoma, north of San Francisco. His duty was to keep out settlers from the United States and to watch the Russian fur traders along the northern border of Mexican California. Vallejo owned a large section of land near Sonoma. Because of this and his position as military commander, he was one of the most powerful leaders in northern California. However, he could not stop the settlers coming from the United States. He decided to help them find places to settle, since he could not stop them.

In 1836, Vallejo supported his nephew, Juan Bautista Alvarado, in a rebellion against Mexico that led to the proclamation of the "free state" of California. When the United States went to war with Mexico in 1846, Americans with Vallejo's backing declared the Bear Flag Republic. After the war, when California became a state, Vallejo became an important state leader. He was a delegate to the state constitutional convention in 1849 and served in the new state senate.

Indians or the descendants of Spanish colonists. The first American contact with California was by way of the sea.

As early as 1795, ships from New England sailed California waters hunting sea otters. Sometimes these ships stopped to trade with the towns along the coast, although this was illegal. After the area became independent of Spain, an active trade in hides developed with Mexican ranchers. American merchants settled in towns such as Monterey, Los Angeles, and San Diego.

In the 1840's, people from the United States and Europe came to live in California. John Sutter, a Swiss settler, built a fort on the Sacramento River. A few Americans made their way overland to the fort by way of the California Trail. This trail had been started by

Who were the first Americans to settle in California?

trappers and began at Fort Bridger on the Oregon Trail. In a few years, several hundred Americans were living in California. There was talk of adding California to the United States.

During these years, the lands of the Catholic missions were broken up by the Mexican government. The Indians who worked for the missions were supposed to get part of the lands, but they received very little. The breakup of the missions and the large numbers of Americans moving into California affected the Indians. Many died from disease and lack of food. Their population dropped from more than 100,000 to fewer than 50,000.

The story of the founding of the missions is in Chapter 2, Section 2.6, page 54.

3.3 Americans in Texas.   Texas interested the people in the United States chiefly because of its rich soil. In the early 1800's, southern cotton growers had begun migrating west from Virginia, the Carolinas, and Georgia. The soil in these states had become worn out. The farmers looked for better land in the Gulf regions. Louisiana, Mississippi, and Alabama became important cotton-growing states. In the 1820's, planters were looking to Texas as a real source of rich land on which to grow cotton, using slave labor.

People from the Southeast tended to settle the Southwest just as people in the Northeast tended to settle the Northwest.

Why were southerners interested in Texas?

Stephen Austin started a settlement on the Brazos River in Texas in the early 1820's. Under an agreement made with the Mexican government, each of the 300 families which Austin brought to Texas received over 13,000 acres of land. Austin and others like him who brought settlers to Texas were known as *empresarios*—people who organize and take the risk for business deals. In 1825, Mexico began to accept all settlers who would swear their loyalty to Mexico and practice the Catholic religion. The population of Texas grew rapidly. By the early 1830's, there were 30,000 settlers from the United States living in Texas. Most were from the South, and many owned slaves.

Ask students why the Americans in Texas chose not to remain loyal to Mexico. Compare their actions with those of the colonists in deciding not to support Britain.

3.4 The Republic of Texas.   Slavery and other troubles soon led to quarrels between the Americans in Texas and the Mexican government. Mexico had ended slavery and objected to the holding of slaves by Americans living in Texas. At the same time, Mexicans began to wonder whether loyalty of the Texas settlers was to the United States or to Mexico. They tried to stop more Americans from entering Texas.

What things caused quarrels between Americans in Texas and the Mexican government?

In 1834, General Antonio López de Santa Anna became president of Mexico. He wanted the government to control all of Mexico, including Texas, at a time when Texas wanted more freedom in local affairs. When the Texans rebelled in 1835, Santa Anna took steps to stop them. He crossed the Rio Grande with 6,000 soldiers. The main Mexican army under Santa Anna marched toward San Antonio. At the Alamo, a deserted mission in San Antonio, 187 Texans held out for several days against nearly 4,000 Mexican soldiers. The Mexican army

Where was the first battle between Texans and Mexicans fought?

In the Texas war for independence, Sam Houston (left) was the Texans' commander and first president of the republic. Fighting at the Alamo (right) inspired the Texas army. Why did "Remember the Alamo" become a rallying cry for Texas?

finally took the Alamo. In the attack, the defenders, including the famous frontier fighters Jim Bowie and Davy Crockett, were killed. A second Mexican force defeated a Texas army at the town of Goliad and killed over 300 prisoners. "Remember the Alamo" and "Remember Goliad" became important battle cries for Texans.

On March 2, 1836, Texans declared their independence. Sam Houston was placed in charge of the army. On April 21, 1836, Texas troops under his command won a victory that ended the war. They attacked and defeated the larger Mexican army near the San Jacinto River. Santa Anna was captured. He agreed to leave Texas with his army. Texans set up their own government like that of the United States. They chose Sam Houston as their first president.

3.5 The Annexation Issue. Many Americans expected that Texas would be **annexed,** or added, to the United States after winning its independence. Over the next several years, however, the American government avoided the issue. Leaders feared war with Mexico since Mexico had not recognized the independence of Texas. They also did not want to stir up trouble over slavery. When John Tyler became President in 1841, he wanted to annex Texas but could not get Congress to agree. For several years, the people of Texas governed themselves.

Seven Mexican states, including Texas and California, revolted against Santa Anna. See the profile of Vallejo on page 305.

Who commanded the Texas forces?

Point out the issue of sectionalism apparent in the annexation issue.

In the election of 1844, James K. Polk became President of the United States. During the campaign, he had called for the annexation of both Texas and Oregon. Since most people living in Texas were Americans, they wanted Texas to be a part of the United States. Most people expected that when Polk took office in March 1845, Congress would approve the annexation of Texas. However, President Tyler got Congress to agree to annex Texas before Polk took office. On March 1, 1845, Texas became a state.

In his first message to Congress, President Polk called for an end to joint occupation of the Oregon country. He set up talks between both sides. The British government finally proposed the 49th parallel as the dividing line between British and American lands, except for the tip of Vancouver Island. On June 15, 1846, the Senate gave its approval. The United States annexed the area below the 49th parallel. These lands

When was Texas annexed?

Recall in Section 2.2 that the U.S. and Britain had set the boundary at the 49th parallel as far west as the Rocky Mountains.

When was the Oregon dispute settled?

Before the Oregon boundary settlement in 1846, who occupied the Oregon Country? How was the dispute finally solved?

Oregon Boundary

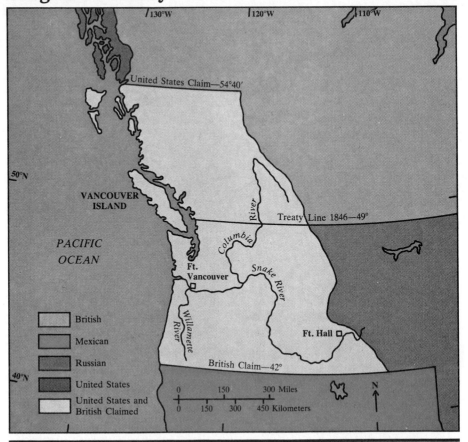

In this daguerreotype (an early type of photograph), American soldiers ride into a Mexican village. The Mexican War was the first American war to be photographed. Why was the Mexican War fought?

later became the states of Oregon and Washington. The final boundary with Canada had been set across the whole continent.

3.6 The Mexican War.   Although the Oregon question was being settled peacefully, there was trouble with Mexico over the annexation of Texas. After Texas became a state, Mexico ended formal government relations with the United States. Conflict grew between the two countries over the Texas-Mexico border. The United States backed the Texas claim that its southern boundary was the Rio Grande. Mexico believed that it was farther north and east, along the Nueces River.

President Polk sent an agent to Mexico to talk about the border dispute and to try to buy California and New Mexico. When Polk heard that Mexican officials would not meet with this agent, he ordered General Zachary Taylor and his troops to the north bank of the Rio Grande. Mexico saw this as an invasion of its land. Polk began preparing a message asking Congress to declare war on Mexico for refusing to meet with his representative.

Before Polk could send the war message, however, word came that Mexican soldiers had crossed the Rio Grande and attacked American forces. The President sent a new war message to Congress. He wrote: "Mexico has passed the boundary of the United States, has invaded our territory, and shed American blood on American soil." On May 13, 1846, Congress declared war on Mexico.

Once war had been declared, the United States Army acted quickly. General Taylor, known as "Old Rough and Ready," crossed

The area disputed with Mexico is shown on the map on page 310.

Have students consider President Polk's message in light of the fact that the boundary had yet to be decided.

What brought about a declaration of war against Mexico?

the Rio Grande and made his way into northeastern Mexico in a series of hard-fought battles. He won an important victory at the Battle of Buena Vista in February 1847.

A second American army was led by General Winfield Scott. Scott was called "Old Fuss and Feathers," because he was such a careful planner. Scott's army moved down the east coast of Mexico by sea and landed at Vera Cruz. The Americans then marched inland and finally captured Mexico City, the capital, on September 14, 1847.

A third American army under the command of Colonel Stephen Kearny marched south from Fort Leavenworth, Kansas, to take Santa Fe. Part of this force then went on to California where a revolt had been staged in 1846 by Americans living there. Helped by Captain John C. Frémont and his United States soldiers, the rebels declared their independence from Mexico. They adopted a flag with a picture of a bear

Outside the original 13 states, how was each section of the country obtained? How many different ways did the United States use to gain land? By which means did the United States gain most of its land?

United States Expansion, 1853

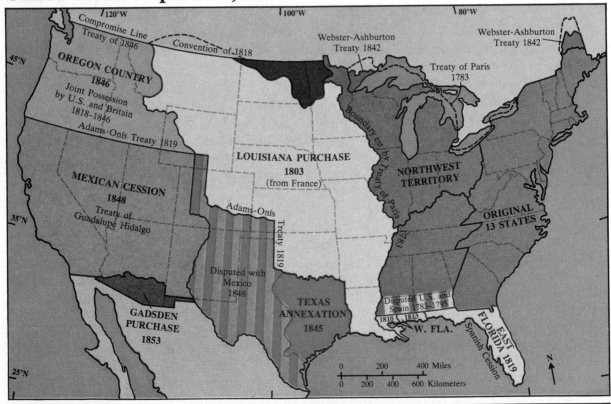

People came from many parts of the world to look for California gold. When was gold discovered in California?

on it as their symbol. For a few days, California became the Bear Flag Republic. Volunteers and sailors from the United States Navy under Commodore John D. Sloat soon took over much of California. There was some resistance from Mexicans living in California. But the Americans, including Kearny's troops, finished the conquest.

What was the Bear Flag Republic?

3.7 The Treaty of Guadalupe Hidalgo.   As the war went on, some Americans began to demand more territory. A few even wanted to annex all of Mexico. Most Americans at least wanted to get California and New Mexico. The government also wanted Mexico to agree that Texas was part of the United States.

President Polk's agent in Mexico, Nicholas Trist, arranged a treaty that spelled out these terms. The Treaty of Guadalupe Hidalgo was signed early in 1848. The United States paid Mexico $15 million for all the land north of the Rio Grande and the Gila River. This area included the present states of California, Nevada, Utah, Arizona, New Mexico, Texas, and parts of Colorado and Wyoming. Several years later, the United States found that the best southern railroad route to the Pacific coast was south of the Gila River. In 1853, the United States paid Mexico $10 million for the strip of land that now forms the southern part of Arizona and New Mexico. This deal was known as the Gadsden Purchase. Including Texas, the United States had gained a huge area of over 1 million square miles. It had good soil, many natural resources, and ports on the coast of California.

Who arranged for the Treaty of Guadalupe Hidalgo?

Have students compare the size of the land gained from Mexico with the Louisiana Purchase and the U.S. after the Treaty of Paris.

3.8 The California Boom.   Once the United States gained control over large areas of the West, Americans began moving into

Mobility

Mobility means the process of moving or being moved. Americans in the 1700's and 1800's were characterized by movement. Artisans traveled from town to town to find work. Entire families moved to the frontier for more land.

Mobility can also mean a change in social or economic positions. This social mobility is the movement within a social class or from one class to another. Social mobility also has been characteristic of American life.

The discovery of gold in 1849 in California made many people rich, changing their social and economic status. The possibility of finding gold lured many people to the West. Read the following selections from the diary of Walter Colton, the founder of the first newspaper in California. Colton lived during the gold rush days.

Monday, May 29. Our town was startled out of its quiet dreams to-day, by the announcement that gold had been discovered on the American Fork [River]. The men wondered and talked, and the women too; but neither believed. . . .

Tuesday, June 20. . . . The excitement produced was intense; and many were soon busy in their hasty preparations for a departure to the mines. The family who had kept house for me caught the moving infection. Husband and wife were both packing up; the blacksmith dropped his hammer, the carpenter his plane, the mason his trowel, the farmer his sickle, the baker his loaf. . . . All were off for the mines. . . . I don't blame [them] a whit; seven dollars a month, while others are making two or three hundred a day! that is too much for human nature to stand. . . .

Thursday, August 16. . . . a man, well known to me . . . worked on the Yuba river sixty-four days and brought back, as the result of his individual labor, five thousand three hundred and fifty-six dollars. . . . a boy, fourteen years of age . . . worked . . . fifty-four days, and brought back three thousand four hundred and sixty-seven dollars.

Answer the following questions.

1. Which examples does Colton provide to show mobility as movement from one place to another?
2. How does he show social mobility?
3. Would the mobility of the people have been the same without gold?

these new lands. One event which drew people to the West was the discovery of gold. In 1848, James Marshall found gold on the property of John Sutter in California. Word spread rapidly. By 1849, large numbers of people were making their way from the East to California by ship or overland. This movement was called the **gold rush**. During 1849, more than 80,000 people came to California from Europe, Mexico, China, and the United States. They were known as **"forty-niners"** because of the year in which most of them came. Gold mining camps were quickly set up in the mountain valleys of central California. San Francisco grew up as an important trading center and source of supplies.

At first, there seemed to be a great deal of gold. Miners often found it near the surface of the earth where it was easy to mine. Only a few people, however, became rich mining for gold. Many were disappointed and returned home. Some left to try their luck in other gold or silver booms in Nevada, Colorado, and later in Montana. Others settled down to farming or business. As a result of the gold rush, the population of California increased rapidly. It became a state in 1850. Similar opportunities would soon bring people to other areas of the West.

Why were the people participating in the California gold rush known as "forty-niners"?

How successful were most miners?

See the San Francisco City Sketch beginning on page 322.

1. Who started the trade between Americans and the people of New Mexico?
2. Who set up the first American settlement in Texas?
3. Who were the military leaders in the Mexican War?
4. What brought people to California in 1849?

4. Indians and the Westward Movement

The movement of people and the expansion of the United States into the lands west of the Mississippi River had a great influence on the Indians of the area. At first, there was little contact between the Indians and the newcomers. As time went on, there was greater contact with the growing numbers of trappers, miners, and settlers moving into the West. This affected the Indians' ways of life and caused the loss of more and more Indian land.

4.1 Changes in Indian Life. The Spanish exploration and settlement in the West had brought many changes in the Indians' ways of life. One of the most important changes came with the introduction of horses into North America. The Spaniards brought horses with them when they explored the Great Plains in the 1500's. Through raids and trading with the Spaniards and each other, many groups of Indians

The introduction of what resulted in a major change in the Indians' ways of life?

acquired horses. With horses, they could hunt buffalo more easily and travel over larger areas of land.

Trade with trappers, hunters, and settlers became important to some groups of Indians. Often, new products were introduced by the traders. One of the most important of these was the gun, which greatly affected the Indians' method of warfare. When forced to move, Indians sometimes had to learn new ways of making a living. Those who had been hunters had to take up farming in order to survive. The greatest change for the Indians of the West was the same as for the Indians of the East—the loss of their land.

4.2   The Indians' Loss of Land.   The trappers who first went to the West did not fight with the Indians. Trappers often worked with them and sometimes married Indian women. They were not there to settle and farm, and so they did not threaten Indian land. As settlers followed the trappers into the lands on which Indian groups lived or used for hunting, conflicts grew. In the 1840's, the federal government was concerned with protecting the wagon trains moving through Indian

This might be a good place to discuss how the creation of opportunities for one group creates serious problems for others—the benefits of westward expansion versus the problems of Indians.

What was at the root of Indian-white conflicts?

George Catlin painted this scene of Plains Indians hunting buffalo. How did horses make the hunt easier? How did horses change the Indians' ways of life? Why was the buffalo important to the Plains Indians?

lands in the Great Plains. It built forts along the Oregon Trail and assigned army troops to them.

In 1851, the Sioux, Cheyenne, Arapaho, and several other Plains groups met with a representative of the United States government. They signed the Fort Laramie Treaty of 1851. Under its terms, the Indians were to receive payment from the federal government in exchange for the settlers' right to pass through their lands. Boundaries were set on the hunting lands of each group. A similar treaty was signed with the Comanches and Kiowas at Fort Atkinson, Kansas, in 1853.

The treaties set boundaries on the lands of the Indians. This made it possible for the United States government to begin keeping Indian groups within certain limits. Eventually, this policy would lead to *reservations,* or separate areas set aside or reserved for the Indians by the government.

What are reservations?

As more and more settlers entered western lands, the government pushed the Indians into ever smaller areas. As land was taken by settlers, many of those Indians who had already been sent from the East to areas of the West were made to move again. Some groups of Indians in more remote areas of Arizona, Montana, and other parts of the West, were not affected much in the years before 1860. However, conflicts continued in the years after 1860 that would affect Indians in all areas.

1. What was the effect of the horse on the Indian people of the Great Plains?
2. What was the significance of the Fort Laramie Treaty of 1851?

5. Conclusion

The huge amount of land added to the United States during the 1840's gave the country a great store of natural resources and provided land for new settlers. In the years before 1860, most settlers passed through the Great Plains and the Rocky Mountains on their way to the Pacific coast. Some also moved into the rich lands of the lower Mississippi Valley.

When the major part of the westward movement was over, the United States was a larger, more powerful country. On the one hand, expansion strengthened the feelings of nationalism. On the other hand, it led to division. The new lands added new states to the nation. This raised the question of slavery again. Balancing the interests of slave and nonslave states would become a greater problem than ever before.

Chapter 13 Review

Main Points

1. Many Americans came to believe that it was the manifest destiny of the United States to expand to the Pacific Ocean.

2. Americans were attracted to the West by the desire for land, gold, and adventure.

3. Settlers moved west over established trails into land occupied by Indians and claimed by Mexico and Britain.

4. American settlers in Texas revolted against Mexico and established an independent country.

5. In the 1840's, the United States annexed Texas and the Oregon country.

6. Mexico's objection to the annexation of Texas led to war with the United States.

7. As a result of victory in the Mexican War, the United States gained control of a huge amount of land north of the Rio Grande and the Gila River. Later it bought the area south of the Gila River in the Gadsden Purchase.

8. Contact with new groups moving into the West caused great changes in the Indians' ways of life.

9. Settlers forced Indians off the land in the West and onto reservations.

Building Vocabulary

1. Identify the following:

Zebulon Pike	Santa Anna	Stephen Kearny
49th parallel	Alamo	John C. Frémont
Marcus and Narcissa Whitman	James K. Polk	Bear Flag Republic
"Oregon fever"	Zachary Taylor	Treaty of Guadalupe Hidalgo
Mariano Guadalupe Vallejo	Winfield Scott	Gadsden Purchase
Stephen Austin		Fort Laramie Treaty

2. Define the following:

manifest destiny	empresarios	gold rush
expansionists	annexed	"forty-niners"
joint occupation		reservations

Remembering the Facts

1. What was the role of explorers and trappers in the westward movement?

2. Why did merchants, settlers, and political leaders want to expand the United States to the Pacific Ocean?

3. Which route did Americans follow in traveling to Oregon?

4. What happened to the Spanish missions in California when Mexico gained its independence from Spain?

5. What did the Mexican government ask of Americans who settled in Texas?

6. How did Texas become independent? How did it become part of the United States?

7. What were the provisions of the Treaty of Guadalupe Hidalgo?

8. Which discovery in California attracted many Americans to that area?

9. What changes did the horse make in the lives of the Plains Indians?

10. What did the government do to protect settlers moving into Indian lands?

Understanding the Facts

1. What attracted Americans to the area west of the Mississippi?

2. With which countries did conflicts develop as Americans moved west?

3. Why did Texas want to be independent of Mexico? Why did it want to join the United States?

4. What were the causes of the war between Mexico and the United States?

5. How did the westward movement of Americans affect the Indians who lived west of the Mississippi River?

6. What was the government policy toward the Indians during the 1850's?

Using Maps

Longitude and Latitude. Laws and treaties often set boundaries in terms of longitude and latitude. One example of this concerned Oregon. The Oregon country in the early 1800's extended from the Rocky Mountains westward to the Pacific Ocean and from latitude 42° to 54°40′. It was claimed by both Britain and the United States. In 1846, an agreeable boundary for the huge area was set.

The map on page 308 provides information concerning the disputed area of Oregon. Review what you know about longitude and latitude. Study the map, and then answer the following questions.

1. Does the line 54°40′ refer to north latitude or south latitude?

2. After the treaty of 1846, 54°40′ set the boundary between which countries?

3. After 1846, 49° set the boundary between which countries?

4. After 1846, 42° set the boundary between which countries?

5. What is the distance north to south from 42° latitude to 49° latitude?

New Orleans 1845-1855

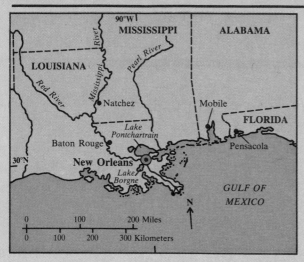

The French settlement of New Orleans was located about 100 miles (160 kilometers) from where the Mississippi River emptied into the Gulf of Mexico. During its early history, New Orleans had been controlled by first France, then Spain, then France again. In 1803, the United States had gotten New Orleans when it bought the Louisiana Territory from France. By the 1840's, New Orleans had become the third largest city in the country and a major southern port.

The Levees

The city was built on low land, almost as low as the river level in some areas. When northern snows melted in the spring, the river overflowed its banks and flooded many parts of the city. Early settlers began building walls of earth, or levees, to keep back the spring floods. In later years, more earth was added to the levees, and the walls grew high and wide. As the levees got wider, warehouses and roads were built on them. Ships and boats of all kinds were tied up at the docks along the levees. There the cargoes, or goods from the ships, were picked up or deposited. In New Orleans, the richest cargoes were usually those like Kentucky tobacco, Ohio flour, and cotton and sugar from plantations in Mississippi, Georgia, and Louisiana. Workers, called stevedores, moved the goods between the ships and warehouses. From New Orleans, the cargoes were carried in larger ships to the West Indies, Central and South America, Europe, and Africa. Goods brought to New Orleans from other countries were loaded onto steamboats and carried up the Mississippi River.

Visitors always found the levee exciting. Oakey Hall, from New York, wrote a description of the activity there in 1851:

A wilderness of ships and steamboats skirt it—if 'tis early morning. If but one short hour after sun-rise, the decks and wharfs are all astir, processions of loaded drays [heavy wagons] are going by. . . . Thousands of hogsheads [barrels], bales, and bags and packages . . . sailors; stevedores; steamboat hands; clerks; planters; wealthy merchants too; running to and fro with [many] projects in their head. . . . A million dollars could not buy the articles of traffic [trade goods] taken in at one glance; articles of traffic that before twenty-four hours have gone by will all have disappeared. . . .

French Influence

Although three different countries had controlled New Orleans at one time or another, France had the most influence over the culture and customs of the people. The children and grandchildren of the early French and Spanish settlers called themselves Creoles. They wanted to set themselves apart from the Anglo-Americans who came to New Orleans. The Anglos were Americans whose culture was most like the Anglo-Saxon people of Britain.

During the mid-1800's, the Creoles continued to follow French customs. French was the language used by the rich. People wore clothes designed after the latest French fashions and decorated their homes with French furniture. Many parents who could afford it sent their children to school in Paris.

The Code of Napoleon was the basis of Louisiana civil law, and legal proceedings were often conducted in French. Through the Creole influence, New Orleans became a center for opera and theater.

Many Peoples and Cultures

New Orleans was an exciting mixture of peoples. There were many blacks in the city, slave and free born. New Orleans was one of the country's main slave markets, yet there were about 10,000 free blacks living in the city. Some of them were very successful in business and the arts. Cecee Macarthy started an import business that was worth more than

Stevedores kept goods moving along the New Orleans levee. River boats carried products up and down the Mississippi River. Ocean ships sailed to and from foreign ports. What goods came through New Orleans?

$150,000 by the time she died in 1845. Armand Lanusse was a famous poet, and inventions of Norbert Rillieux were of value to the sugar industry.

As individuals, free white and black people often respected each other in New Orleans. Free blacks lived on the same city streets as whites. When they could afford it, they sent their children to private schools in America and France. As a group, however, the whites had almost all of the power and wealth. By the 1850's, more laws were passed to limit the rights of free blacks.

The demand for cheap labor drew many immigrants to New Orleans. Many died on the way or of yellow fever once they arrived in New Orleans. Since it had become illegal to import slaves from West Africa, those slaves that were already in New Orleans were too valuable to do heavy work. The European immigrants, especially the Irish, were hired to do the heaviest jobs of draining canals, paving streets, and improving the levees.

Northern visitors were often surprised by the way the people spent their Sundays. Bishop Whipple wrote in his journal:

. . . this is the day of military parade and review . . . a day of pomp and parade. . . .
Shops were open and singing and guitar playing in the streets, for which in New York or Philadelphia one would be put in prison.

Sunday was also a holiday for slaves in New Orleans. Many of them spent their time in Congo Square where they sang and danced in West African tradition. Some blacks in New Orleans continued to practice non-Christian religions brought from Africa and the West Indies. Most blacks attended Christian churches, usually Catholic, sometimes Baptist and Methodist. The Catholic church services were attended by whites and blacks together.

In other services, blacks usually were separated from whites. New Orleans also had a few churches that were only for blacks.

The Young People

Eliza Ripley wrote a book about her life in New Orleans. Her story has many examples of what it was like to grow up in that city.

In 1842 there was a class in Spanish at Mr. Hennen's house. . . . I was ten years old, but was allowed to join with some other members of my family, though my mother protested it was nonsense for a child like me and a waste of money. Father did not agree with her, and after over sixty years to think it over, I don't either. . . . years and years thereafter . . . while traveling in Mexico, some of the señor's teaching came [like a miracle] *back to me, bringing with*

Chocktaw Indians display produce in the French Market. What other nationalities made up the city's population, giving it an international flavor?

it enough Spanish to be of material help in that stranger country.

Ripley and her friends also had private lessons in music, singing, and dancing. Teachers were hired to give children lessons in polite manners. They were expected to learn how to walk gracefully and how to bow and curtsy properly. Ripley later wrote:

Is it any surprise that the miscellaneous education we girls of seventy years ago in New Orleans had access to, [ended] by fitting us for housewives and mothers, instead of [also teaching us to be] writers and platform speakers, doctors and lawyers . . . ?

The Homes

People had candelabras. . . . The candles in those gorgeous stands and an oil lamp on the [usual] center-table were supposed to furnish abundance of light for any occasion. . . . People sewed, embroidered, read and wrote and played chess evenings by candlelight, and except a few near-sighted people and the aged no one used glasses.

. . . Everybody in my early day had black haircloth furniture; maybe that was one reason red curtains were preferred. . . . However, as no moth [ate] it, dust did not rest on its slick, shiny surface, and it lasted forever, it had its advantages. [Many people had] a haircloth sofa, with a couple of hard, round pillows of the same . . . too slippery to nap on. . . .

Butler's pantry! My stars! Who ever heard of a butler's pantry, and sinks, and running water, and faucets inside houses? The only running water was a hydrant in the yard. . . .

Of course, every house had a storeroom . . . lined with shelves. . . . We had wire [boxes] on the back porch and a [metal-lined] box for the ice. . . . Ice was in

Many buildings in New Orleans are very decorative. Which group of people had the most influence on the culture of the people?

general use but very expensive. It was brought by ship from the North. . . .

The population of New Orleans had grown rapidly during the mid-1800's. The people who had lived there for many years were proud of their city.

"How do you like the city?" inquires an old resident. While you hesitate for an answer, himself replies:

"Excellently, of course; fine commercial advantages, eh?—the store-house of the Mississippi Valley—great destiny ahead."

1. Where was New Orleans located?
2. What is a levee?
3. What groups of people lived in New Orleans?
4. What did young people study during this period in New Orleans?

San Francisco 1845-1855

wrote that the paper was closing down because they could not find anyone to work on it. Almost all of the 800 people living in the town had gone off to look for gold.

The whole country . . . resounds with the sordid [greedy] cry of gold! GOLD!! GOLD!!!—while the field is left half planted, the house half built, and every thing neglected . . . one man obtained one hundred and twenty-eight dollars' worth of the real stuff [gold] in one day's washing, and the average for all concerned is twenty dollars per [day]!

People arrived from all over the world—from South America, Europe, Australia, Asia, Mexico, and Canada. They traveled to California by land and by sea.

Golden Opportunities

As thousands of people came to California, new towns were started, and older towns became large cities. Those people who came by sea often landed first at San Francisco. Merchants in the city soon made it a supply center for the miners. One historian wrote in 1855:

A short experience of the mines had satisfied most of the citizens of San Francisco that . . . all was not gold that glittered, and that hard work was not easy. . . . They returned very soon to their old quarters, and found that much greater profits, with far less labor, were to be found in supplying the necessities of the miners. . . .

The miners' work was, in fact, hard and uncomfortable. They usually stood in cold streams for hours to wash, or separate, the gold from the mud and gravel. After the loose

The city of San Francisco began as a village near a Spanish mission run by priests from the order of Saint Francis of Assisi. The village was often called the village of Saint Francis or *pueblo de San Francisco*. It was started halfway up the coast of California. It was built on an arm of land that reached out between the Pacific Ocean and a beautiful bay. A natural deep-water channel connected the bay to the ocean. This made San Francisco one of the finest and safest seaports in the world.

At the end of the Mexican War, California became part of the United States. Once people in the East learned about the rich soil and good weather, they began to move west.

Gold!

By the spring of 1848, the quiet growth of San Francisco ended. Gold had been discovered in the nearby Sierra Nevada Mountains.

San Francisco's *Californian* newspaper printed its last issue in May. In it, the owners "washing" or digging. Everyone who sold anything kept scales on hand to weigh the gold, valued at $16 an ounce.

One person from New York named Levi Strauss arrived in San Francisco in 1850. He had a roll of canvas cloth and some new ideas for making strong work pants. In a few years, miners and farmers alike were buying the famous "Levi's" work clothes.

It was a rare thing to find people doing the same kind of work in San Francisco that they had done before coming to California. People who had been farmers or bankers could as easily earn money as bankers and storekeepers. There seemed to be many different ways to get rich.

All That Glitters

According to some San Francisco historians, "the place and habits of the people" were odd or different because there were so few women and children.

There was no such thing as a home to be found. . . . Both dwellings and places of business were either common canvas tents, or small rough board shanties [poorly built sheds], *or frame buildings of one story. Only the great gambling saloons, the hotels, restaurants, and a few public buildings and stores had any pretensions* [claims] *to size, comfort or elegance. . . .*

City Government

Within a year following the gold rush, the population of San Francisco had grown from 2,000 to 25,000 people. This rapid growth caused the local government to be in a state of confusion. In 1849, there were three different city councils, each claiming to be the official one. A newly elected official discussed the city problems.

Levi Strauss sold canvas work clothes called blue jeans to gold miners. What other businesses began to support the needs of gold miners?

gold was taken up, the miners had to dig for the rest of it. They often slept on the ground at night and seldom cooked a good meal at camp. Most miners suffered from sore hands, sore feet, and sore stomachs. So they came into town for company and comfort, as well as for supplies and news from home.

In a short time, there was more gold in San Francisco than there were goods to buy with it. Storekeepers charged very high prices, and people paid them. Many people made very large fortunes without a bit of

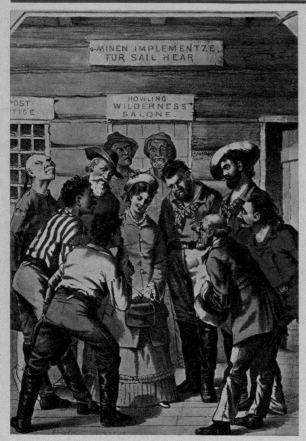

New arrivals in San Francisco were common. People came from all over the world to look for gold. Why were women and children a rare sight?

At this time we are without a dollar in the public treasury, and it is to be feared the city is greatly in debt. . . . You are without a single police officer or watchman, and have not the means of confining [holding] a prisoner for an hour; neither have you a place to shelter, while living, sick and unfortunate strangers who may be cast upon our shores, or to bury them when dead. Public improvements are unknown in San Francisco. In short, you are without a single [thing] necessary for the promotion of prosperity, for the protection of property, or for the maintenance of order.

Law and Order

There was no clear government authority to establish order or to enforce laws. San Francisco was sometimes a very frightening city. Stealing, mugging, and murder were common, and criminals often went unpunished. Fires were a constant danger because of so many canvas tents and wooden buildings. Whole sections of the city burned to the ground in a few hours. Many people believed that some of the fires were set in order to cover up a robbery or murder.

The citizens became angry over the lack of law and order. John Nugent encouraged the forming of a vigilante committee in his newspaper *Herald:*

We are here without jails, . . . without a police sufficiently strong for the circumstances; and . . . with these [shortages] we have a bankrupt city and an incompetent council. On whom must we depend for relieving the town from the desperate and abandoned scoundrels who now infest it? There is clearly no remedy for the existing evil but in the strong arms and stout souls of the citizens themselves. . . . Let us then organize a band of two or three hundred Regulators, composed of such men as have a stake in the town, and who are interested in the welfare of the community. . . . If two or three of these robbers and burglars were caught and treated to lynch law, their fellows would be more careful about future [robberies]. . . .

By early spring, 100 people formed a merchants' night patrol. They divided into street patrols and worked different areas of the city once a week on eight-hour shifts. This merchant patrol was the beginning of the vigilante group which would take the law into its own hands. In early June 1851, a constitution signed by 716 people stated the rules of

San Francisco was a busy seaport by the middle of the 1850's. What became the economic base of the city after the gold rush years?

the vigilante committee. Money to run the group would come from donations from merchants, plus $5 from each member. Most members were well-educated and well-known in the community. They organized the vigilante committee like an army. Their headquarters was called Fort Gunnybags because of the barrier of sandbags placed on three sides of the building and piled eight feet high.

The committee organized a court, called the witnesses, and was judge and jury as well as executioner. Many people were worried about this means of handling the law. But the majority of citizens felt that it was the only way to restore order to the city. The committee was in existence twice during the 1850's. It captured, tried, and hanged several well-known criminals. It forced many others to leave the area. Although there were serious complaints against these groups because they had ignored the established system of law, no legal action was brought against the committee.

Gold to Goods, Again

By the middle of the 1850's, the California miner working alone had little chance of finding a rich strike. The gold was too deep in the earth to be taken out by hand. San Francisco had based its growth on the miners' gold. For a few years, the city suffered a panic and a depression as the supply of new gold grew smaller. Some miners went on to other western territories. Some returned, with or without gold, to their former homes. Many brought their families west and settled down in farming or business.

In the early years of the gold rush, the city was a wild and rough place. But almost overnight, San Francisco had changed from a quiet village into a major center of banking and trade. Ship captains from around the world continued to come to its excellent harbor. And the newly populated western lands continued to offer opportunities to people seeking adventure.

1. Who settled San Francisco?
2. Why is San Francisco such a good port?
3. Why did the population in San Francisco grow so rapidly?
4. Why were there so many fires in San Francisco?
5. Why was a vigilante committee formed?
6. How are San Francisco and New Orleans alike?
7. What kinds of people came to San Francisco and New Orleans? Why did they come?

Unit IV Review

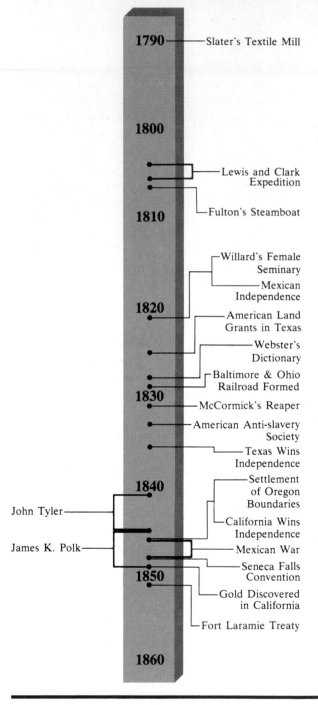

1790 — Slater's Textile Mill

1800

Lewis and Clark Expedition

Fulton's Steamboat

1810

Willard's Female Seminary

Mexican Independence

1820

American Land Grants in Texas

Webster's Dictionary

Baltimore & Ohio Railroad Formed

1830

McCormick's Reaper

American Anti-slavery Society

Texas Wins Independence

Settlement of Oregon Boundaries

1840

California Wins Independence

John Tyler

Mexican War

James K. Polk

Seneca Falls Convention

1850

Gold Discovered in California

Fort Laramie Treaty

1860

Summary

1. The Age of Jackson saw a spirit of greater equality and progress which resulted in movements to improve American society.

2. The spirit of the Age of Jackson brought improvements in public education, better care for people with handicaps, reform of prisons, and demands for temperance, equal rights for women, and the abolition of slavery.

3. The early to middle 1800's was a period of major achievement concerning American literature, with American authors using new forms and themes to write about the country and its people.

4. The United States entered an Industrial Revolution in the early 1800's, beginning with the use of power-driven machinery in textile manufacturing.

5. New inventions helped to increase production in both industry and on the farm.

6. The rise of industry and improvements in transportation spurred major growth of American cities as immigrants and people from farm areas moved to them in search of better opportunities.

7. With a belief in manifest destiny and a desire for more land, Americans fought a war with Mexico, settled Oregon, and expanded their borders from the Atlantic to the Pacific.

8. With the exception of Alaska and Hawaii, the United States grew to its present size by 1853.

Unit Questions

1. Why was American literature in the 1800's, as expressed by writers such as Ralph Waldo Emerson, important to the development of the nation?
2. How were religion, philosophy, and the reform movements of the Jackson years related?
3. In what ways were the rise of industry, the development of a transportation system, and the growth of cities related to each other?
4. What section of the United States underwent the greatest changes as a result of the Industrial Revolution? What section or sections changed little and why?
5. What new territories were added to the country in the years from 1820 to 1850? In what different ways were they added?
6. Do you think that the changes in the nation to 1850 reflected more the philosophy of Thomas Jefferson or of Alexander Hamilton? Explain.
7. What circumstances or events before 1850 do you think clashed with the ideas of equality and progress as expressed in the Age of Jackson?
8. How do New Orleans and San Francisco reflect the expansion of the country in the mid-1800's? In what ways was each important to its section?

Suggested Activities

1. Find out information about when your school system was established. How is the system funded?
2. Using maps which show the country in the period from 1820 to 1850, decide where you would have built a railroad line. Between which points would it run? What would be its major function?
3. Find the size of covered wagons used in the 1840's. Make a list of important items which you think people needed for a move to the West.

Suggested Readings

Eggleston, Edward. *The Hoosier School Master*. Evanston, Illinois: McDougal-Littel & Co., 1977. Fictional account of the life of a rural school teacher in Indiana during the 1840's.

Flory, Jane. *The Golden Venture*. Boston: Houghton Mifflin Co., 1976. An 11-year-old girl's story of her trip and later life in the gold fields of the 1840's.

Nabokov, Peter (ed.). *Native American Testimony: An Anthology of Indian and White Relations. First Encounter to Dispossession*. New York: Thomas Y. Crowell Co., 1978. Firsthand accounts of Indians' views about relations with whites.

O'Dell, Scott. *Carlota*. Boston: Houghton Mifflin Co., 1977. The Mexican War as seen through the eyes of a young girl.

UNIT V

Division

Division along economic, political, and social lines split the United States. Seldom before had a single nation of vast territorial expanse been made up of people with so many various backgrounds and outlooks. In a democratic society which encouraged free and open exchanges of ideas, differences were almost expected to occur. A variety of factors contributed to conflict and strife between people and regions. These same factors contributed to the difficulties in reuniting the nation.

Chapter 14   A Divided Nation _____ 330
Chapter 15   The Civil War _____ 351
Chapter 16   Rebuilding the Nation _____ 373
City Sketch   New York 1860–1865 _____ 394
City Sketch   Atlanta 1860–1865 _____ 398

A Divided Nation   14

The North and South differed socially, economically, and politically. It was the conflict over slavery, however, that threatened to rip the two sections apart. Over what other issues did North and South disagree?

People in the United States had won a victory in the Mexican War and had settled the Oregon question. They had fulfilled what they thought of as the manifest destiny of their country. However, adding new territories also brought problems. The possibility of several new states in the Union raised the question of whether or not these states would allow slavery. Leaders in the North felt that it should not be allowed. Southern leaders, on the other hand, supported the spread of slavery. The struggle between the North and South became bitter, and there was talk of disunion and civil war.

This chapter is designed on a topical basis to cover the sectional issues leading to the Civil War.

1. Sectional Differences

Much of the material here both reviews and expands the material in Chapter 4, Section 3.

Differences between the North and South did not begin or end with slavery. The two areas had been growing apart for more than 50 years. Social, economic, and political differences formed the background for the debate over slavery.

1.1 Social Differences. Different forms of social life had developed in the North and in the South. During colonial times, the sections shared certain social patterns. Most of the people were of British *heritage,* or background. They shared the same language, customs, and law. There were differences even then, however. In general, planters dominated social life in the South, while in the North, no single group set the pattern of living. Education was more widespread in the North than in the South.

How did the North and South differ socially?

In the years before 1860, the North changed more than the South, and the two areas became even less alike. The population of the North grew rapidly. Cities became important. Immigration brought a great variety of people to the northern states. The white population of the South grew slowly. Immigration into the South was also slow, and its impact was slight. The large number of black slaves in the South further set the two sections apart.

1.2 Economic Differences. The North and South also moved in different directions economically. In the early days of the United States, life in both parts of the country centered around farms and small villages. The South remained an agricultural area and did not develop much industry. Although most southern whites had small farms, the most important part of the southern economy was the large plantations. On them, tobacco, rice, sugar cane, and cotton were grown, using slave labor. Economic ideas changed slowly in the South. Southern leaders

How did the North and South differ economically?

The economy of the South was largely dependent on cotton picked by black labor. Notice the number of people who worked in the fields in this Currier and Ives lithograph. Why were so many people needed to produce cotton?

were generally against high taxes, government spending, and federal banks. They fought against raising tariff rates, since the South imported most of its manufactured goods.

After the War of 1812, the northern states rapidly began to build factories. Cities grew with the rise of industry. The building of factories required loans from banks. Northern leaders favored federal banks and government spending. They wanted government aid for building roads and making other transportation better. To protect the growing American industries, they favored higher tariffs on imported goods. While most people in the North also made a living by farming, industry was very important. Labor in the North was done by hired workers rather than by slaves.

1.3 Political Differences. In the country's early years, people in the North and South held similar political views. They believed in a constitutional form of government that placed limits on government actions and officials. They believed in a representative democracy in which government got its authority from the people. They also held a view of federalism that allowed each state to take care of its own affairs, while the federal government took care of national problems. In later

How did the North and South differ politically?

years, however, northern and southern states began to think differently about federalism.

One view was that the rights of states were above those of the federal government. This was the view first put forward in the Virginia and Kentucky Resolutions of 1798. It was later suggested at the Hartford Convention during the War of 1812 and by John C. Calhoun in his theory of nullification in the 1830's. As the debate over slavery became more bitter, many southern leaders came to favor the idea of states' rights. They depended on slavery for their wealth, and they felt that the federal government threatened it.

Remember that these are general statements. Differences of opinion existed within each section. Recall that it was New England which invoked states' rights at the Hartford Convention.

Northern leaders, on the other hand, supported the power of the federal government over that of the states. This view was stated in 1830 by Senator Daniel Webster of Massachusetts, when he argued with Robert Hayne against Calhoun's theory of nullification. People in the North thought that the federal government helped promote national unity and progress.

1. Which section developed an industrial economy?
2. In which section were slaves most important?
3. Which section strongly supported states' rights?

2. The Peculiar Institution

Slavery lay at the heart of the differences between the North and South. Southern whites called it the *"peculiar institution."* This did not mean that they thought slavery was strange or odd, but simply a way of life unique to the South.

What is meant by "peculiar institution"?

2.1 The Slave Trade. The first blacks brought to America were not slaves but indentured servants. They expected to be free after they had finished their terms of service. Later the status of indentured black servants was changed by law to that of slaves. The number of slaves grew slowly until 1713. Then the British took over the slave trade of North and South America, and the number of slaves grew rapidly.

What is the difference between slave and indentured servant?

The demand for slaves in the United States grew even more after the invention of the cotton gin in 1793 by Eli Whitney. In 1808, Congress stopped the importation of slaves. That year, there were about 1 million slaves in the United States. Despite the action of Congress, the system did not die out. Some slaves were smuggled into the country in the years after 1808, and the birthrate for slaves was very high. Between 1820 and 1850, the number of slaves rose from 1.5

The cotton gin is an interesting example of a technological improvement having unforeseen social consequences.

million to over 3 million. Between 1850 and 1860, the number grew from 3 million to almost 4 million.

Most of the slaves brought into the United States came from the west coast of Africa. Many of these landed first in the West Indies and later were moved north. Of the estimated 10 million slaves brought to the New World, one third went to Brazil, and many of the rest went to the Caribbean islands and parts of South America. Only about 5 percent of the people taken from Africa were brought to the United States.

To where in the New World were most slaves brought?

2.2   People in Bondage.   Slaves were given a variety of tasks in the United States. Some worked in mines and others on the railroads. A small number of slaves worked as blacksmiths or carpenters in southern cities. The largest number of slaves, however, worked on plantations. Although some plantation slaves were household workers, most were field hands. They spent long hours growing tobacco, rice, sugar cane, and cotton. Solomon Northup, an escaped slave, told about work on one cotton plantation:

What did most slaves in the United States do?

> The hands are required to be in the cotton fields as soon as it is light in the morning, and, with the exception of ten or fifteen minutes, which is given them at noon . . . they are not permitted to be a moment idle until it is too dark to see, and when the moon is full, they often times labor till the middle of the night. . . .
>
> The day's work over in the field, the baskets are . . . carried to the gin-house, where the cotton is weighed. . . . no matter how much [a slave] longs for sleep and rest—a slave never approaches the gin-house with [a] basket of cotton but with fear. If it falls short in weight . . . [the slave] knows that [he or she] must suffer. And if [the slave] has exceeded it by ten or twenty pounds . . . [the owner] will measure the next day's task accordingly.

Readings from slave narratives can help students explore what it meant and how it felt to be a slave.

Slaves were most often thought of as property. They could be moved around and sold as their owners wished. The sale of slaves was done at *auctions*—public sales where goods or slaves are sold to the person who offers the most money for them. Often families were broken up when children were sold to different owners than those of their parents. Parents were often separated as well.

How were slaves considered property?

Every southern state had *slave codes,* or laws which controlled the lives of blacks. For slaves to learn to read and write was against the law, and their religious teaching was carefully watched. The daily lives of slaves were spelled out in detail. Punishments such as whipping, branding, and even death were given to slaves breaking these laws.

Despite the problems of living in slavery, there is much evidence that strong family ties existed for many slaves.

The number of southern whites who owned slaves was fairly small. Only about one fourth owned slaves or were members of a family which owned them. Also, most slave owners had a small number of slaves. In 1850, over one half of all slave owners had fewer than five slaves. Less than 1 percent had more than 100 slaves. Even the whites who owned no slaves were not in favor of ending the system, however. For the most part, these people believed that slavery was the only way to control blacks and allow blacks and whites to live together.

2.3   Forms of Slave Protest.   Although slaves had no rights, they were still able to work against the system of slavery. They made up songs and stories which helped them cope with their lives. Also, some slaves slowed down their work or damaged their tools. These things had to be done carefully and in secret for fear of punishment.

What forms did slave protests take?

Sometimes slaves revolted against their condition. These revolts almost always ended in failure, and most often resulted in death for those who took part. In 1800, more than 1,000 slaves led by Gabriel Prosser and Jack Bowler planned an attack on Richmond, Virginia. Their plans were discovered, and the leaders, along with some 14 other people, were put to death. In 1822, Denmark Vesey, a free black,

Slaves were regarded by many people as property which could be bought or sold. Like any product, they were advertised (left). Some slaves were sold by slave dealers (right). How was the sale of slaves most often done?

planned an uprising in Charleston, South Carolina. Again, the plans were discovered. Vesey and more than 30 others were put to death.

One slave revolt almost succeeded. It caused great fear among southern whites. The revolt was led by Nat Turner in 1831. Close to 60 white people were killed before Turner's rebellion in Southampton County, Virginia, was ended by state and federal troops. More than 100 blacks lost their lives in the fighting. A number of people, including Turner, were put to death. Fear of other slave revolts led whites to tighten controls over slaves.

Why did the Nat Turner revolt cause such great fear among southern whites?

Escape from slavery was also a form of protest. Since travel by slaves was closely watched, escape was difficult and dangerous. The chance of being caught was great. Slaves tried to leave the South and make their way north across the Ohio River or into Pennsylvania. They could be stopped by whites and asked for papers showing they could travel. Once an owner discovered a slave missing, a hunt began for the slave's capture and return.

What was the Underground Railroad?

Escaped slaves were not really safe until they reached Canada. They were often helped in their escape by people who were against slavery. These people served as **conductors** on a secret escape network known as the Underground Railroad. The slaves were led from one **station,** or safe place, to another until they reached safety. Harriet Tubman, herself a runaway slave, returned to the South many times and helped over 300 people escape to freedom.

2.4 Northern Attitudes Toward Slavery. The feelings of people in the North about slavery were mixed. Not all northern whites

Frederick Douglass (1817–1895)
═══ PROFILE ═══

In 1838, Frederick Douglass fled slavery in Tuckahoe, Maryland, for freedom in New Bedford, Massachusetts. In 1840, at a meeting of the Massachusetts Antislavery Society, Douglass told what freedom meant to him. He so impressed the abolitionists that they hired him to speak about his life as a slave. Douglass worked for the end of slavery and the end of unfair treatment of free black people everywhere.

Douglass wrote his autobiography in 1845. Because of his growing fame, he was concerned that some people might try to send him back to slavery. So he went to Europe for two years.

In England and Ireland, Douglass spoke to abolitionist groups.

With enough money from his book to buy his freedom, Douglass returned to the United States, settling in Rochester, New York. Douglass continued to work for the antislavery movement by starting a newspaper, the *North Star*. And he continued to oppose the discrimination he and other black people faced.

Douglass led attacks on separate seating for blacks and whites on trains and separate schools. He worked hard for equal rights for black people. Douglass was the leading supporter of liberty and justice for American black people in the 1800's.

were against it. Many, perhaps the majority, were prejudiced against blacks, both free blacks in the North and slaves in the South. Of the people who were against slavery, there were some who simply did not want it to spread into new territories or states. Others, the abolitionists, wanted an end to all slavery. Free blacks, such as Sojourner Truth and Frederick Douglass, went even further. They worked for equal treatment of blacks in America.

What were northern attitudes toward slavery?

2.5 Southern Response. The response of southern whites to the move to end slavery took several forms. At first, those people who favored slavery were most upset by abolitionists. Southern leaders felt that these people encouraged slaves to revolt. They tried to keep antislavery speakers out of their states. Post office workers in the South would not deliver mail about abolitionist ideas. In 1836, southern

How did southerners react to abolitionists?

members of the House of Representatives pushed through a *gag rule*. This law prevented the reading of antislavery petitions in the House.

As things grew worse between the North and South, southern leaders began to change their approach. They said that slavery was necessary to the economy of the South and the United States. They pointed out that the export of cotton paid for most of the country's imported goods. Southern whites also argued that slavery had existed in many societies in the past. They said that the working conditions in many northern factories were worse than those of the slaves. They pointed out that some factory workers earned barely enough money to live, while most slaves were well fed, clothed, and given shelter.

What arguments did southerners use to defend slavery?

1. What invention increased the demand for slaves?
2. How did the number of slaves in the United States change between 1820 and 1850?
3. Why did some people who did not own slaves favor slavery?
4. What were the goals of the abolitionists?

3. Slavery and Politics

Before the 1840's, leaders in both the North and South had tried to keep slavery out of politics. Neither of the major parties would take a stand on the issue. Both the Democrats and the Whigs drew support from all areas of the country, and they did not want to lose it. Arguments for and against slavery were presented, for the most part, by reformers or authors. Beginning in the 1840's, however, the slavery question came to dominate politics.

Why would the major parties not take a stand on slavery?

3.1 The Missouri Compromise. Representatives in Congress from the slave and free states had always looked out for the interests of their section. There was an uneasy balance of power in the Senate. Slave states and free states had been admitted in equal numbers and had equal numbers of Senators. In 1819, a bill had come up in Congress for the admission of Missouri as a state. Senator James Tallmadge of New York presented an amendment to the bill which would outlaw slavery in Missouri. Slaves already in Missouri would be *emancipated,* or set free. Southern representatives were against this idea. They felt it would upset the balance of power in the Senate in favor of the North. A deadlock resulted between northern and southern leaders in Congress.

Refer students to the map on page 345 as they read this section.

This might be a good place to again discuss compromise as an important part of the American political process. Consider the effect of the Compromise of 1820 on the North, the South, and slaves living in Missouri.

Henry Clay of Kentucky played a major part in getting both sides to agree to a new compromise bill in 1820. In his plan, Missouri would be

Sectionalism

Slavery was at the heart of the sectional conflict which erupted in the 1840's. It often became an issue in debates in Congress. During the Mexican War, David Wilmot of Pennsylvania told the House of Representatives:

. . . we are fighting this war for Texas and for the South. I affirm it, every intelligent man knows it, Texas is the primary cause of this war; for this, sir, northern treasure is being exhausted and northern blood poured out upon the plains of Mexico. We are . . . cheerfully fighting this war for Texas; and yet we seek not to change the character of her institutions. Slavery is there; there let it remain. . . .

Now, sir, we are told that California is ours; that New Mexico is ours. . . . They are free. Shall they remain free? . . .

Slavery follows in the rear of our armies. . . . Shall this Government depart from its neutrality on this question and lend its power and influence to plant slavery in these Territories? There is no question of abolition here, sir. Shall the South be permitted by aggression, by invasion of the right, by subduing free territory and planting slavery upon it, to wrest

these provinces from northern freemen. . . .

Two years later, Robert Toombs of Georgia told the House:

. . . if by your legislation . . . [the North seeks] to drive us from the territories of California and New Mexico, purchased by the common blood and treasure of the whole people, . . . I am for disunion. . . . The Territories are the common property of the people of the United States. . . . it is your duty, while they are in a territorial state, to remove all impediments to their free enjoyment by all sections and people of the Union, the slaveholder and the non-slaveholder.

Neither person speaks out against the existence of slavery. After you have read these statements, answer the following questions.

1. What is it about slavery over which the two speakers differ?

2. What reflects different views based on the home states of these members of Congress?

3. What are the chances of compromise between the views expressed?

admitted to the Union as a slave state. To balance Missouri, Maine, which had been part of Massachusetts, would become a free state. Slavery would not be allowed in the rest of the Louisiana Territory north of latitude 36°30′, the southern border of Missouri. The Missouri Compromise settled slavery as a political question for the next 25 years.

3.2 The Wilmot Proviso and Popular Sovereignty. The question of slavery in new lands came up again when the United States went to war with Mexico. In August 1846, Representative David Wilmot of Pennsylvania put forth an amendment to a bill in Congress. It would outlaw slavery in any of the lands won from Mexico. Southern representatives were against the Wilmot Proviso, and it failed to pass.

In 1847, Senator Lewis Cass of Michigan came up with a plan called *popular sovereignty.* Under this plan, the people of each territory would decide for themselves whether or not to allow slavery. Cass' idea did not settle the problem.

3.3 The Free-Soil Party. In 1848, the Democrats chose Senator Cass to run for President. The Whigs chose General Zachary Taylor, who was well-known from the Mexican War, as their candidate. Neither party would take a stand against slavery. People in both parties who were strongly against slavery joined with members of the old Liberty party. They formed the Free-Soil party and asked Martin Van Buren to run for President. Members of the Free-Soil party favored the Wilmot Proviso, free homesteads for western settlers, and federal money for internal improvements.

Zachary Taylor was elected President in 1848. Although the Free-Soil party lost, it did serve to bring the question of slavery's expansion to the country's attention. Feelings on both sides grew sharper. When Congress met in 1849, the debate over slavery ended in another deadlock. Northern members refused to vote on any bills until slavery was outlawed in all new lands. Southern members refused to vote for any measure which would not allow slave owners to take their slaves anywhere they wished.

3.4 The Compromise of 1850. The deadlock centered around the lands recently won from Mexico. New states, formed from these areas, could upset the balance in the Senate between the North and South. To prevent trouble, Henry Clay came up with a compromise.

In the Compromise of 1850, California was admitted to the Union as a free state. This would balance Texas, which had been added as a slave state in 1845. The rest of the Mexican lands were formed into two territories, New Mexico and Utah. The people of these areas were to decide about slavery according to the popular sovereignty ideas of Cass.

New Mexico later voted to become a slave territory, and Utah voted to be free. The slave trade was stopped in the District of Columbia. A Fugitive Slave Act was passed. This called for the use of federal officers to catch *fugitive,* or runaway, slaves. Land claimed by both Texas and New Mexico was given to New Mexico. In return, Texas was paid $10 million by the federal government.

1. Which political parties were against the spread of slavery?
2. What was the purpose of the Free-Soil party?
3. What did the North and South gain from the Compromise of 1850?

4. The Road to Disunion

The Compromise of 1850 seemed to be a success. But it did not give the country a long period of peace. Both the North and the South were reaching the point where they were no longer willing to compromise. There were many events in the next ten years which kept the slavery issue before the American people.

Uncle Tom's Cabin (left) was written by Harriet Beecher Stowe (right) to promote the antislavery cause. Over 10,000 copies of it were sold in one week in 1852. Where did this book probably sell the best?

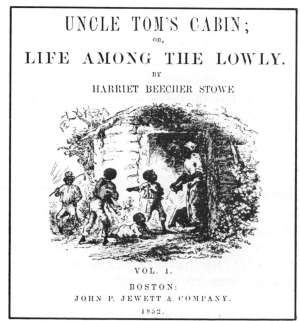

Have students consider
whether the personal lib-
erty laws were themselves
an expression of states'
rights over federal law.

Read to the class sections
of *Uncle Tom's Cabin* to
show its treatment of the
slavery question.

Proslavery settlers adopted
a state constitution in
1857, while free soil settlers adopted a constitu-
tion forbidding slavery
in 1859.

4.1 The Fugitive Slave Act.   One thing which hardened northern opinion against slavery was the new Fugitive Slave Act. It said that federal law officers were to help catch escaped slaves. Anyone helping a slave could be fined or put in jail. The oath of a slave owner was all that was needed to prove that a black person was an escaped slave. No trial was allowed. In response to this act, many northern states passed *personal liberty laws*. These laws stopped state and local officials from obeying the federal fugitive slave laws.

4.2 An American Best-Seller.   In 1852, a book was printed which greatly added to the tensions between the North and South. *Uncle Tom's Cabin* had been written by Harriet Beecher Stowe. It was a dramatic story of slave life. The book was a huge success, selling over 300,000 copies its first year in print. *Uncle Tom's Cabin* was also made into a stage play. Many people were moved by the story and joined the fight to end slavery.

4.3 The Kansas-Nebraska Act.   The brief peace which resulted from the Compromise of 1850 came to an end in 1854. Senator Stephen Douglas of Illinois introduced a bill in Congress to organize the lands north of latitude 36°30′ into the territories of Kansas and Nebraska. Douglas wanted the United States government to help build a railroad from Chicago to the Pacific Ocean. Once the area was organized, the government could give land to companies to build railroads. These companies could then sell land to settlers who would provide business for the railroads.

Douglas wanted to gain the support of southern members of Congress. He said that people in these new areas could decide about slavery on the basis of popular sovereignty. This would repeal that part of the Missouri Compromise which kept slavery from spreading into the area north of latitude 36°30′. Douglas' bill opened the slavery question in Congress again. Southern members favored the bill, while northern members hoped to defeat it. They were not able to do so, however. The Kansas-Nebraska Act became law in May 1854.

4.4 Bleeding Kansas.   Kansas became the center of the battle over slavery. Both the North and South wanted to control the area and sent people to live in Kansas. Antislavery business leaders, such as Amos Lawrence of Boston and Moses Grinnell of New York, formed groups to help people who wanted to move to Kansas. People moved into the area from the free states of Ohio, Indiana, and Illinois. Settlers favoring slavery moved into the area from Missouri.

During local elections, large numbers of people from Missouri crossed into Kansas. They voted for candidates favoring slavery and then returned to their homes. By 1856, there were two governments in the territory—one proslavery and one antislavery. Things in Kansas grew worse. In May 1856, people favoring slavery set fire to the town of Lawrence. Three days later, John Brown and several others killed five people at the proslavery settlement of Potawatomie Creek. In the 1850's, the territory became known as "Bleeding Kansas."

What events led to Kansas becoming known as "Bleeding Kansas"?

4.5   The Election of 1856.   The slavery issue brought the end of the Whig party. Many northern Whigs joined with members of the Free-Soil party and some antislavery Democrats to form another party in 1854. This new Republican party stood for the repeal of the Fugitive Slave Act and the Kansas-Nebraska Act. The party was not in favor of abolition, but it did want to stop the spread of slavery. It drew nearly all of its support from the North.

The Republican party has been called the most successful third party in American history because it became one of the two major parties.

Against the background of violence in Kansas, the end of the Whig party, and the rise of the Republican party, the election of 1856 took place. The Democrats supported the Kansas-Nebraska Act and made no move against slavery. They chose James Buchanan of Pennsylvania to run. They hoped that he would appeal to people in both the North and the South. The Republicans chose John C. Frémont. They came out against the spread of slavery and for adding Kansas to the Union as a free state. Buchanan was elected President in 1856. The Republicans won a surprising number of votes. The election showed the rapid growth of the party, and this alarmed Southern leaders.

Who were the candidates in the election of 1856?

4.6   The Dred Scott Case.   During these years, many people feared that the Union was splitting apart. Leaders in the North and

The Battle of Hickory Point, near Lawrence, Kansas, intensified sectionalism. Fighting resulted when opposing forces struggled for control of Kansas. What forces fought for the territory?

*What was the Dred
Scott case?*

Scott was sold to an abolitionist shortly after the
doctor's death. *Dred Scott
v. Sandford* was a deliberate test case. Scott was
freed by Sandford shortly
after the Supreme Court's
decision.

*What was the Dred
Scott decision?*

Review the constitutional
provisions related to slavery in Article IV, Section
2. Note that they apply to
states and do not mention
territories.

South could not agree about slavery in the territories. The Supreme
Court seemed to offer hope for a solution. It was considering an
important case from a Missouri court about a slave named Dred Scott.

Scott was the slave of an army doctor who lived in Missouri. He had
been taken by the doctor into Illinois, a free state, and into a territory
(later Minnesota) where Congress had forbidden slavery. Scott
believed that he had become free because of his stay in free territory.
One Missouri court held that Scott was free, while the state supreme
court ruled that he was still a slave. The case was taken to the Supreme
Court of the United States.

Two days after President Buchanan took office in March 1857, the
Supreme Court handed down its decision. Chief Justice Roger B. Taney
gave the Court's opinion. He said that Scott was not a citizen. So he did
not have the right to take a case to court. Taney denied Scott's claim that
he was free. Taney also said that the Missouri Compromise was
unconstitutional because Congress had no power to keep slavery out of
territories. Slaves were thought of as property. According to the Fifth
Amendment, a person's property could not be taken away without due
process of law. Taney also said that Congress could not stop citizens
from taking their slaves into free territories.

Southern leaders hailed Taney's decision. They felt that it
supported their views on the spread of slavery. Republicans and many
northern Democrats were strongly against it. The Kansas-Nebraska Act
had said that the people could decide about slavery in each territory.
The Dred Scott case suggested that slavery could not be kept out of
territories, even if the settlers voted against it.

4.7 The Lincoln-Douglas Debates.   Many Democrats, in both
the North and South, hoped to see Stephen Douglas run for President
one day. To them, he seemed the best hope for saving the Union. In
1858, Republican Abraham Lincoln ran against Douglas for election to
the Senate from Illinois. Lincoln challenged Douglas to a number of
public debates, hoping to win votes. The two candidates covered the
important questions of the day.

The most important meeting of the two was at Freeport, Illinois.
There Lincoln asked Douglas to explain his support of both popular
sovereignty and the Dred Scott decision. Lincoln pointed out that the
two positions were in conflict. Popular sovereignty meant that the
people could decide whether or not to have slavery in their territories.
The Dred Scott decision said that the government, and therefore the
people, could not stop slavery in these areas.

*What was the con-
flict that Lincoln
asked Douglas to
explain?*

Douglas stated that the people could keep slavery out if they
wished. If they did not pass laws to protect slavery, it would not last.

Expansion of Slavery

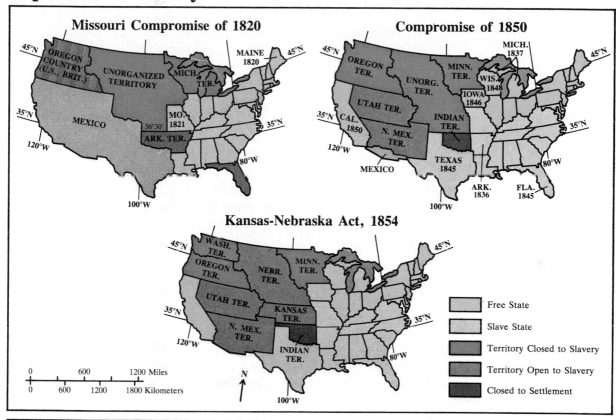

Missouri Compromise of 1820

Compromise of 1850

Kansas-Nebraska Act, 1854

Free State

Slave State

Territory Closed to Slavery

Territory Open to Slavery

Closed to Settlement

What resulted from the Missouri Compromise of 1820? How did the Compromise of 1850 affect the lands obtained from Mexico? Why did antislavery supporters oppose the Kansas-Nebraska Act of 1854?

Douglas won the election, but he lost much of his southern support for the Presidency. Lincoln, on the other hand, gained popularity in many parts of the North.

4.8   John Brown's Raid.   Bitterness between the North and South became even greater in the fall of 1859. John Brown, the Kansas abolitionist, formed a plan to give weapons to slaves and start a war for freedom. Brown and a small band of blacks and whites gathered at Harpers Ferry in what is now West Virginia. There they attacked the federal *arsenal,* a place where weapons are kept. United States troops under Colonel Robert E. Lee captured Brown and his followers after two days of battle. Brown and four others were hanged. The events at Harpers Ferry upset southern slave owners. They feared there would be

What was John Brown's raid?

Some people think of
John Brown as a hero
while others see him as a
murderer and a villain.
Have class members give
their opinions about him
and his actions.

other slave uprisings, planned by people from the North who were
against slavery.

1. What was the Fugitive Slave Act?
2. When was the Republican party founded?
3. Why did many southern owners of slaves favor the Dred
   Scott decision?

5. The Final Break

In 1860, a presidential election was held. Judging by the election of
1856, the question of slavery would be central to the contest. Southern
leaders were determined to see that the Republicans did not win. They
thought the Republican party was a threat to their way of life.

The convention was held
in Charleston as a conces-
sion to proslavery
Democrats.

*What caused the
split in the Demo-
cratic party in 1860?*

5.1 Party Conventions.   The Democrats held their convention
in Charleston, South Carolina, only six months after the death of John
Brown. Southern members feared that Stephen Douglas no longer
favored slavery. They wanted him to accept a platform which protected
slavery in the territories. When Douglas would not do this, delegates
from eight southern states left, ending the convention. Northern
Democrats met in Baltimore, where they chose Stephen Douglas. The
southern Democrats later chose John C. Breckenridge of Kentucky.

Some Whigs and American party members also met at Baltimore.
They formed the Constitutional-Union party. They wanted to gather
support from both North and South and did not take a stand on slavery.
John Bell of Tennessee was their candidate.

In May 1860, the Republican party convention opened in Chicago.
With the Democratic party divided, they hoped to win. They chose
Abraham Lincoln as their candidate. They wanted to stop the spread of
slavery but did not demand that slaves in the South be freed.

See the map on the next
page. Douglas finished
second to Lincoln in pop-
ular votes but won only
12 electoral votes.

*What did the elec-
tion of 1860 show?*

5.2 The Election of 1860.   The election was a four-way race
among Lincoln, Douglas, Breckenridge, and Bell. Lincoln knew that he
could get no support from the South and looked to the major cities in the
North. As a result, he won 180 electoral votes from 18 free states.
Breckenridge won 72 electoral votes from 11 slave states. Douglas and
Bell finished far behind. The election showed how deeply the country
was divided over slavery.

*What was the
southern response
to Lincoln's
election?*

5.3 The Confederate States of America.   Many southern
leaders came to believe that *secession,* or withdrawing from the Union,
was the only answer to Lincoln's election. On December 20, 1860,
South Carolina voted to secede from the Union. Mississippi, Florida,

Election of 1860

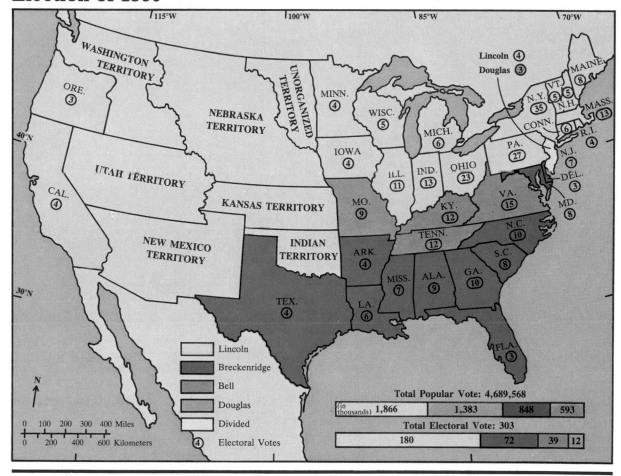

What section supported Abraham Lincoln in the election of 1860? Where was support for John C. Breckenridge the strongest? How was division in the United States over the slavery issue shown in the results of this election?

Alabama, Georgia, and Louisiana voted to leave the United States in January 1861. Texas withdrew in February.

Delegates from six of the seven states met in Montgomery, Alabama, in February 1861. They drew up a constitution for the Confederate States of America. It was much like that of the United States. Under this constitution, most of the power remained with the states. The Confederate congress could not pass laws against slavery or tariffs to protect industry. The delegates at Montgomery elected a president for a single six-year term. They chose Jefferson Davis of

Governor Sam Houston refused to call a legislative session to consider secession, but a special convention was called without his support.

The people shown with Lincoln are (left to right) Edwin Stanton and Salmon P. Chase. Those with Davis are T.R.R. Cobb, Judah P. Benjamin, and (standing) Vice-President Alexander Stevens and military aides.

With the election of Abraham Lincoln (left, seated at the far right) southern states began to leave the Union. The South organized under the leadership of Jefferson Davis (right, seated at the far left). When was the Confederacy established?

Mississippi for this office. Alexander Stephens of Georgia became the vice-president.

1. Who were the candidates for President in 1860?
2. Which states left the Union to form the Confederate States of America?

6. Conclusion

The social, economic, and political differences between the North and the South reached the breaking point over the question of slavery. The election of Abraham Lincoln in 1860 was seen by southern leaders as a signal to leave the Union. They believed that it was no longer possible to live in the same political system as the North. Southern people wanted their own system of government, with a society and an economy based on slavery. It remained to be seen whether the rest of the United States would allow the South to go its own way.

Chapter 14 Review

Main Points

1. For more than 50 years, political, social, and economic differences had been developing between the northern and southern sections of the country.
2. Views on slavery affected the way northerners and southerners came to feel about the nature of the Union.
3. Southern blacks often opposed slavery by revolting or trying to escape.
4. Northern abolitionists opposed slavery and its spread.
5. Owners of slaves considered slavery important to their way of life.
6. In spite of the efforts to compromise, slavery became a national issue.
7. After the election of Abraham Lincoln as President, seven southern states withdrew from the Union.

Building Vocabulary

1. Identify the following:

Nat Turner
Harriet Tubman
Underground Railroad
Frederick Douglass
Henry Clay
Missouri Compromise

Wilmot Proviso
Lewis Cass
Zachary Taylor
Compromise of 1850
Fugitive Slave Act

Harriet Beecher Stowe
Stephen Douglas
Dred Scott
Abraham Lincoln
John Brown
Jefferson Davis

2. Define the following:

heritage
"peculiar institution"
auctions
slave codes
conductors

station
gag rule
emancipated
popular sovereignty

fugitive
personal liberty laws
arsenal
secession

Remembering the Facts

1. What were the political, social, and economic differences which developed between the North and the South?
2. How many slaves were in the United States by 1850?
3. How were the lives of slaves restricted?
4. How did many slaves protest their bondage?
5. What were the abolitionists' attitudes toward slavery?

6. What were the efforts made to keep slavery from becoming a national issue on which people disagreed? What were the results?
7. How did the Kansas-Nebraska Act and the Dred Scott decision affect the efforts to compromise on the slavery issue?
8. What was the position of the Republican party on slavery?
9. Which event led southern states to secede from the Union?

Understanding the Facts

1. Why was states' rights tied closely to the slavery issue?
2. Why did the invention of the cotton gin increase the demand for slaves?
3. How was the life of a free person in the United States different from the life of a slave?
4. Why did neither major political party take a stand on the slavery issue before 1840?
5. Why did the compromises passed by Congress fail to prevent slavery from becoming a major issue in national politics?

Using Maps

Comparing Maps. Using two or more maps of the same area at different times can show change. The three maps on page 345 together show the expansion of slavery in the United States. Each map identifies the status of states and territories regarding slavery from 1820 to 1854. Study the maps, and answer the following questions.

1. Are these reference maps or thematic maps?
2. How many states existed in 1854 that did not at the time of the Missouri Compromise?
3. Were there more slave states or free states in 1820?
4. Were there more slave states or free states in 1850?
5. Were there more slave states or free states in 1854?
6. In 1854, was the total area of slave states and territories larger or smaller than the total area of free states and territories?
7. Considering the size of the area in which slavery was permitted, did the slave states gain or lose between 1820 and 1854?
8. Considering the number of states in which slavery existed, did the slave states gain or lose between 1820 and 1854?

The Civil War 15

Paul Philippoteaux painted this detail of the Battle of Gettysburg. During the war, one of every four soldiers serving in the two armies was killed. Why was the Civil War fought between the North and the South?

By early 1861, seven states of the lower South had seceded from the United States. The federal government faced a crisis. Allowing these states to leave would destroy the Union. But to save the Union, it might be necessary to use force. The use of force, of course, meant civil war for the nation.

1. The Opening Guns

Americans spent several anxious months from the election of Abraham Lincoln in late 1860 to the day he took office on March 4, 1861. Lincoln had not given his views about the South in public, and everyone wondered what he would do. Many people still hoped that a war between the North and the South could be avoided.

1.1 Lincoln's Inauguration. On February 11, 1861, Abraham Lincoln left his home in Springfield, Illinois, to begin the long journey to Washington, D.C. There had been reports that an attempt would be made on his life. So he entered Washington in disguise, after a secret train ride by night.

In his inaugural speech, Lincoln tried to reassure the country. He said that he would do nothing to end slavery in the states where it already existed. He said that he believed the Union was *perpetual,* or everlasting, and that under the law, no state could leave it. Lincoln did not accept the secession of the lower South. To him, the Union was still unbroken. He said that he would carry out the law in all the states and protect government property in the states which were rebelling. Finally, Lincoln stated that he would preserve the Union at all costs.

1.2 The Fort Sumter Crisis. Early in 1861, the Confederate states had taken over many forts, arsenals, and navy yards in the South. Fort Sumter, on an island off Charleston, South Carolina, was one of the few remaining federal strongholds. The Confederacy thought of it as the property of a foreign power on southern soil.

Major Robert Anderson, commander of the fort, let President Lincoln know that he needed help. Lincoln knew that a relief ship sent to the fort might be taken as an act of war by the Confederacy. If he did not send relief, he felt that he would be failing in his duty as President. Lincoln finally decided to send a ship loaded with supplies only. He let South Carolina know what he had decided.

Southern leaders, however, saw this as an act of war. On the morning of April 12, 1861, Confederate cannons at Charleston opened fire on Fort Sumter. After 40 hours, soldiers in the fort surrendered. The firing on Fort Sumter marked the opening of the Civil War.

What did Lincoln try to do in his inaugural address? How?

Remind students of the argument on the nature of the Union and the issue of states' rights.

Note for the students the use of "Confederate states" as an expression of the states' rights point of view.

An earlier attempt was made to reinforce Fort Sumter in January 1860, while Buchanan was still President. The ship was forced to turn back by gunfire from South Carolina militia.

How did Lincoln try to handle the Fort Sumter crisis?

1.3 The Spread of Secession. The attack on the fort helped unify the North. Lincoln felt that the Confederate leaders, and not he, had taken the first step toward war. He issued a call for 75,000 volunteers for the army. The South saw this as a declaration of war. Jefferson Davis, president of the Confederacy, also called for volunteers to fight.

What did Lincoln do following the attack on Fort Sumter?

Until this time, eight slave states had remained with the Union. With President Lincoln's call for troops, Arkansas, North Carolina, Tennessee, and Virginia left the Union. This brought the number of Confederate states to 11. To the Confederates, Virginia was very important. Its large population and economy would benefit the South. With Virginia, the South also gained several experienced army officers, including Robert E. Lee. The capital of the Confederacy was moved from Montgomery, Alabama, to Richmond, Virginia.

Why was Virginia important to the Confederacy?

West Virginia seceded from Virginia in 1861 and was admitted to the Union in 1863. Some groups in Indian Territory backed the Union while others favored the Confederacy. What areas were the Union? What areas were the Confederacy?

Union and Confederacy

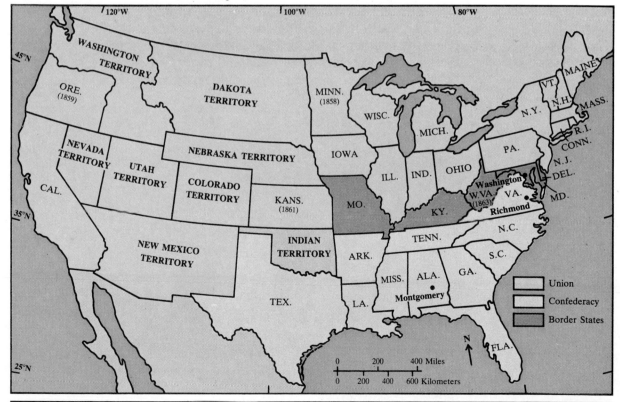

The remaining slave states—Missouri, Kentucky, Delaware, and Maryland—did not secede. These were the **border states,** located between the North and South. There, as in many other places, sentiment was divided. Part of Virginia, for example, refused to secede with the rest of the state. In 1863, 46 western counties joined the Union as the state of West Virginia. Even families were torn apart in this conflict, with some members joining the South, and others fighting for the North.

There was considerable opposition to secession in parts of Georgia, Alabama, and Tennessee, in addition to western Virginia.

1.4 Union Plans and Advantages. The main goal of the leaders of the United States was to save the Union. General Winfield Scott was the commander of the Union army in 1861. He favored what was called the Anaconda Plan, after the snake which crushes its prey to death. The Union would blockade the Confederacy by sea from Norfolk, Virginia, to Texas. This would keep the South from sending out its cotton or bringing in supplies. Another part of the plan was to take over the Mississippi River and divide the South at that point. Also, the Union would invade the South and crush the Confederates there. On the foreign front, the North hoped to keep any European country from recognizing the Confederacy as a separate country. This would lessen the chance of outside aid for the South.

What was the Anaconda Plan?

The North had important advantages over the South. It had over twice the number of people and could raise large armies. Most of the factories which could make arms and other war supplies were in the North. Southern equipment often could not be replaced. The North had

What were the Union's advantages?

Civil War armies used many innovations. In this drawing, Union soldiers set up telegraph lines. The telegraph improved communications among armies moving over great distances. Why were good communications important for an army to be successful?

Union and Confederate Resources, 1860

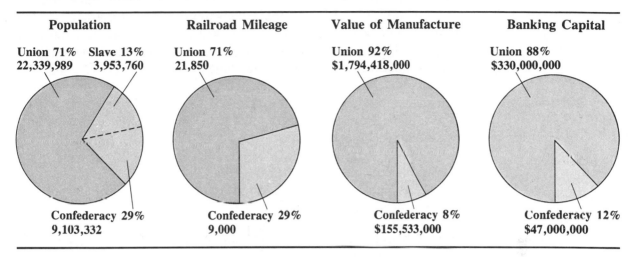

Population	Railroad Mileage	Value of Manufacture	Banking Capital
Union 71% Slave 13% 22,339,989 3,953,760	Union 71% 21,850	Union 92% $1,794,418,000	Union 88% $330,000,000
Confederacy 29% 9,103,332	Confederacy 29% 9,000	Confederacy 8% $155,533,000	Confederacy 12% $47,000,000

The Union had certain advantages over the Confederacy at the beginning of the war. These advantages were based on the resources of the two regions. How were most resources an advantage for the Union and a disadvantage for the Confederacy?

a better railroad system with more than 21,000 miles (33,600 kilometers) of track, to the South's 9,000 miles (15,300 kilometers). Finally, as the United States Navy became larger, the North gained the control of the sea.

1.5   Confederate Plans and Advantages.   The South also had certain advantages in 1861. The Confederates planned to fight a *defensive war.* That is, they would stay in their own area and defend it from attack. The South's army would be close to its cities and could get supplies easily. The soldiers would know the land in which they were fighting. Also, the South had many experienced military leaders. Army officers, such as Robert E. Lee, Thomas "Stonewall" Jackson, Joseph E. Johnston, and A. S. Johnston, had joined the Confederates.

Southern leaders hoped to get help from Europe, especially from France and Great Britain. They believed that British textile mills depended so much on southern cotton that Great Britain would aid the Confederacy to keep trade open. With European help, the South hoped to force the Union to recognize its independence.

1.6   The First Battle of Bull Run.   Many people in the North thought that General Scott's plan to defeat the South was not needed.

What were the Confederacy's advantages?

By the 1850's, more than 80 percent of British cotton came from the U.S. But by the spring of 1861, there was an oversupply. Both Britain and France were able to get cotton from India and Egypt once the war began.

They thought that one quick victory over Confederate forces would end the war. President Lincoln gave in to the pressure for quick action. He allowed General Irvin McDowell to lead an attack on Richmond.

On July 16, 1861, McDowell's army of 30,000 marched out of Washington. They headed for the railroad junction at Manassas, Virginia. There, near a little stream called Bull Run, the Union soldiers met Confederate troops on the morning of July 21, 1861. The southern soldiers under General Pierre Beauregard defeated the Union troops. Retreat turned into flight as McDowell's soldiers headed back toward Washington. For the first time, people in the North began to see that it was going to be a long, hard war.

Confident of victory, spectators and reporters went with the Union army to watch the battle.

Why was the first Battle of Bull Run important?

1. When and where did the Civil War begin?
2. Which states had seceded from the Union after the start of the war?
3. Which slave states remained in the Union?
4. From which European countries did the Confederacy hope to get aid?

2. From Plans to Action

After the Battle of Bull Run, both sides realized that their soldiers would have to have better training before battle. This was especially true of the North. The army of each side was larger than any before in America. The commanders of both the Union and Confederate forces had to learn how to direct groups of soldiers often numbering 50,000 or more. The months after Bull Run were spent in preparation as each side moved to put their plans into action.

What did each side do following the first Battle of Bull Run?

2.1 The War in the West. The Union plan to take control of the Mississippi River met with more success than did the first campaigns in the East. On February 6, 1862, northern troops under Ulysses S. Grant moved up the Tennessee River. With the help of Union ships, they captured Fort Henry. Nearby Fort Donelson on the Cumberland River surrendered to Grant on February 16. The capture of these two forts opened much of the Confederate west to attack.

A number of diaries of Civil War soldiers are available. Students can use these to prepare reports on soldier training.

Grant's army moved south on the Tennessee River to Pittsburg Landing, sometimes called Shiloh. On the morning of April 6, 1862, Confederates under General A. S. Johnston caught the Union army there by surprise. There was heavy fighting, and Grant drove the

Who were the commanders at Shiloh?

The first encounter between ironclad ships happened in March 1862. The Union *Monitor* (left) clashed with the Confederate *Virginia* (right). As part of the Union navy, the *Virginia* had been named the *Merrimac*. What was the result of the battle of the ironclads?

Confederates off. After this Battle of Shiloh, Union forces controlled much of Tennessee and northern Mississippi.

Some 100,000 troops fought at Shiloh, with 23,000 dead and wounded.

2.2 The Naval Campaign. The most important task of the Union navy was to blockade the southern coast. At first, because there were few ships, this did not work well. ***Blockade runners***—people who slipped goods through the blockade—were able to get through without much trouble. However, as the North began to build more and more ships, the blockade was tightened. Some ships were able to get to the South. But for the most part, the Union navy was able to stop southern trade. As the war went on, this had a disastrous effect on the South.

One real threat to the blockade was a Confederate ship, the *Virginia*. In 1861, this ship, then named the *Merrimac,* had been left by retreating Union forces. The Confederates recovered it and named it the *Virginia*. They turned it into an ***ironclad,*** a new kind of battleship covered with thick iron plates. The *Virginia* was based in Norfolk, which was blockaded by the Union navy.

Have an interested student explore the effect of the ironclads on the future of naval warfare.

What was the battle of the ironclads?

On March 8, 1862, the *Virginia* sank several Union ships in Norfolk harbor. The following day, the North sent in an ironclad of its own—the *Monitor*. The two ironclads shot at each other for five hours without doing much damage. The *Virginia* finally withdrew, and the blockade held. This had been the first battle between metal ships.

In April 1862, the Union navy under Admiral David Farragut took New Orleans. This limited Confederate use of the Mississippi River. Then Union troops took Memphis in June. This gave the North control of a great part of the Mississippi River.

Farragut was a good example of a person born in one section fighting for the other. He was born in Tennessee but served in the federal navy for most of his adult life.

2.3   The War in the East.   The campaigns in the East were very important in the Civil War. The Union wanted to capture the Confederate capital at Richmond, Virginia. It also wanted to defeat the Army of Northern Virginia. This was the largest of the South's armies. Fighting against it was the Union's Army of the Potomac.

At first, there was a time of delays and no action. President Lincoln then ordered General George B. McClellan, who led the Army of the Potomac, to begin an operation to take Richmond. With the defeat of the *Virginia,* the Confederate navy could no longer prevent a move

How did the Union appear to be following General Winfield Scott's Anaconda Plan? Where did Confederate armies stop Union army advances? What was the purpose of the Union naval blockade?

Early Civil War (April 1861–July 1862)

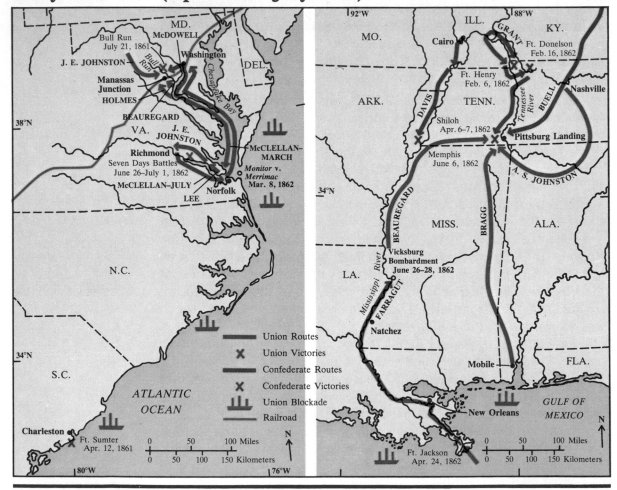

President Lincoln was an active commander in chief. In this Matthew Brady photograph, the President is shown visiting General George B. McClellan (facing the President) after the Battle of Antietam. Why did Lincoln consider Antietam an important Union victory?

against Richmond. So McClellan shipped over 100,000 soldiers by water to the peninsula between the York and James rivers in Virginia. Slow movement by the Union army allowed the Army of Northern Virginia, under General Robert E. Lee, to prepare defenses. After three months of fighting in this Peninsula Campaign, the Union army was forced back to the coast. The North had failed to take Richmond. President Lincoln replaced McClellan as commander of the Army of the Potomac.

Despite the change of command, northern forces in the East suffered one defeat after another. In August 1862, Lee defeated Union troops at the Second Battle of Bull Run. In September 1862, Lee decided to invade the North for the first time. He hoped that the sight of southern soldiers on Union soil might make Great Britain and France recognize and give aid to the Confederacy.

President Lincoln and other northern leaders were worried by the success of Lee's Army of Northern Virginia. Lincoln again made McClellan commander of the Army of the Potomac and ordered him to stop Lee. The two armies fought the Battle of Antietam in Maryland on September 17, 1862. Although McClellan did not win a clear victory, Lee's army withdrew to Virginia. More soldiers died during this one-day battle than during any other single day of the war. *Casualties,* or those people killed or wounded, were around 23,000.

2.4 The Emancipation Proclamation. President Lincoln believed that the war was being fought to save the Union, not to abolish

Initially, the Confederate forces were commanded by Joseph E. Johnston, who was wounded and replaced by Robert E. Lee.

What did Lee hope to achieve by invading the North?

There were greater numbers of casualties in battles other than Antietam, but none greater in a single day.

What was Lincoln's primary purpose in fighting the war?

The Civil War 359

slavery. In 1862, he wrote a letter to Horace Greeley of the New York *Tribune* explaining this view:

> *My* [main] *object in this struggle is to save the Union, and is not either to save or to destroy slavery. If I could save the Union without freeing any slave I would do it; and if I could save it by freeing all the slaves I would do it; and if I could save it by freeing some and leaving others alone I would also do that. . . . I have here stated my purpose according to my view of official duty; and I intend no* [change] *of my oft-expressed personal wish that all men every where could be free.*

Lincoln felt that making abolition the main goal of the war might divide the North. He did not want the slave states of Delaware, Maryland, Kentucky, and Missouri to leave the Union. As the move to end slavery grew stronger, however, Lincoln wanted to keep abolitionist support and still save the Union. He decided to take action against slavery in at least part of the South. This would help unite the North and hurt the Confederacy.

What did the Emancipation Proclamation state?

On September 22, 1862, shortly after the Battle of Antietam, Lincoln issued the Emancipation Proclamation. This ***proclamation,*** or official announcement, said that as of January 1, 1863, all slaves in Confederate lands would be "then, thenceforward, and forever free." This did not apply to the border states or to areas that had already been won back by the North. As Union armies took over more areas in the South, however, thousands of slaves were freed.

Nearly 200,000 blacks, most of whom had been slaves, joined the Union forces. Generally, they were not treated equally. They received lower pay and were often given jobs away from the fighting. However, during the last two years of the war, black soldiers took part in nearly every major battle.

Discuss the Emancipation Proclamation both as an instrument to free slaves and as a propaganda device to win the war.

The Confederacy attempted to recruit slaves into the army toward the end of the war, but the attempt came too late.

1. Which western forts did the Union capture?
2. What were the early Confederate victories?
3. How active were blacks in fighting for the Union?

3. The War on the Home Front _____

The Civil War affected more people than any war in American history up to that time. It was no longer a matter of two small armies deciding the outcome, as in earlier years. The farms and factories on

The Civil War involved much of the population of both North and South. This drawing by Winslow Homer shows women filling cartridges at the Watertown Arsenal in Massachusetts. How else was the war supported on the home front?

both sides had to provide the supplies needed for the huge armies and navies. Because of this, the war touched nearly every town and family in the country. It changed the lives of most Americans.

3.1 People at Home. For people in the North and the South alike, it was a terrible war. They were shocked by the large numbers of people being killed. While soldiers were fighting and dying on the battlefields, those at home did what they could to help the war effort.

In both the North and the South, women set up volunteer aid societies in churches, schools, and homes. They met to raise money, gather food, collect clothing, and roll bandages. Several women, such as Rose O'Neal Greenhow and Belle Boyd, became Confederate spies. In July 1861, Greenhow carried messages to Confederates about General Irvin McDowell's plans. This enabled the South to prepare for the first Battle of Bull Run. Belle Boyd was a messenger for Generals Beauregard and Jackson. She also smuggled medicines into the South and was a blockade runner.

At the beginning of the war, medical services were poor. The only real nursing care came from Catholic religious groups. In June 1861, the War Department made Dorothea Dix superintendent of nurses in the Union armies. Dix helped bring order into the hospitals of the North in spite of prejudice against women in the field of medicine. Clara Barton took medical supplies to the battlefields and nursed wounded soldiers. Mary Ann Bickerdyke brought sanitation and proper food to many Union army hospitals. By the end of the war, at least 3,200 women in both the North and South had served as nurses.

How did the Civil War differ from earlier wars?

Deaths from disease and poor medical treatment claimed 1.5 to 2 times as many soldiers as did deaths from battle.

Greenhow was arrested in her Washington home by the famous detective Allen Pinkerton. Boyd was arrested three times during the war but was released each time, twice sent to the South and once to Canada.

What women played important roles in medical improvements?

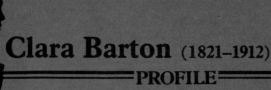

Clara Barton (1821–1912)
PROFILE

Clara Barton's goal in life was to bring comfort to people in trouble. In 1861, Barton began carrying supplies and nursing soldiers wounded in battle. Without help or encouragement from the government, she cared for the injured. She became known as the Angel of the Battlefield.

At the war's end, Barton set up an office to find information on the thousands of soldiers who were missing in action. In 1869, she traveled to Europe to recover from an illness. While in Switzerland, Barton learned of the International Committee of the Red Cross, which cared for the victims of war.

In 1881, Barton organized the American Red Cross. Under her leadership, this group raised money and expanded their efforts to aid victims of flood, fire, disease, and other disasters. Between 1881 and 1904, Barton provided relief without government help in 21 disasters. These included a forest fire in Michigan in 1881 and the Johnstown, Pennsylvania, flood in 1889.

The Red Cross goal was to get quickly to the scene of an emergency with relief—food, clothing, medicine, and materials for shelter. Because of Barton, the Red Cross provides relief in peace as well as in war.

3.2 Profits and Poverty. Some people in the North gained much wealth because of the war. Farms in the Midwest became larger. The need for food grew because the soldiers had to be fed. Crop failures in parts of Europe made markets for American farm goods. Farmers bought more machines to replace workers who had gone off to war.

What was the status of farming during the war?

Some northern industries were hurt by the war, while others benefited from it. Certain textile plants, for example, had to shut down because there was not enough cotton. On the other hand, industries which made iron, cannons, movable bridges, and locomotives did well.

The prosperity brought about by the war was not spread evenly. Poor people and industrial workers usually did not share in the new wealth. Greater profits and higher taxes pushed up the price of many goods, such as food, gas, and firewood. Labor troubles grew as the war went on. Coal miners near Pittsburgh, dry-goods clerks in New York

Discuss the obligations of people on the home front during a war and the issues involved in strikes and large war profits.

City, shopkeepers in Boston, and newspaper workers in Chicago went on strike for higher wages during the war.

Life for people in the South was generally harder than for people in the North. Manufactured goods became scarce, and the price of food rose after the blockade was set up. Shortages became serious as the war dragged on. Butter sold for $15 a pound, bacon was $9 a pound, and potatoes sold for $25 a bushel. Sickness became a problem when the blockade cut off shipments of drugs and other medical supplies.

3.3 Soldiers for the Armies.   At the beginning of the war, there was little problem getting enough soldiers to serve in the armed services. People were excited about the war. Enlistment tents were set up near busy streets, and recruits rushed to join up.

As the war dragged on, the number of volunteers slowed. States offered *bounties*—payments of money to a person for entering the armed services. On April 14, 1862, the Confederate congress passed a law beginning the *draft*. This was a selection of people who would be forced to serve in the military. The Union did the same the following year. The draft was not popular, especially in some parts of the North. On both sides, those drafted could hire someone else to serve for them. Poor people, who could not hire substitutes, thought the draft was

Why was life on the home front more difficult for southerners?

How did the South and the North get troops as the war continued?

Discuss the issue of having a draft in a democratic society and whether or not it is sometimes necessary. Also talk about the issue of paying to escape service as it relates to democracy.

"Come and Join Us Brothers" was a poster issued to urge more blacks to sign on for service in the Union army. Both North and South relied mostly on enlistments for the armed forces. How else were people persuaded to join the armies?

See the New York City Sketch beginning on page 392.

Recall that President Jackson ended the Bank of the U.S. in 1834.

What are greenbacks?

Why was it more difficult for the South to pay for the war?

Have students consider the stand of southern representatives on these issues if secession had not occurred.

What territories were established during the war?

unfair to them. In July 1863, a draft riot took place in New York City. The crowds, 50,000 strong, burned many shops and attacked free blacks. Soldiers were brought in, and the riot ended after four days.

3.4 Financing the War.   Both the North and South were faced with the problem of finding enough money to pay for the war. The federal government borrowed money through the sale of bonds. It taxed the states and set up an income tax for the first time in America's history. It also issued paper money known as *greenbacks* that were not backed by either gold or silver. The government simply promised to redeem them in gold or silver at a later date. A national banking system was set up for the first time since the Age of Jackson.

The South had more trouble paying for the war than the North did. Because it had to buy many supplies from Europe, the South ran out of cash early in the war. It hoped to raise money from European loans, using cotton and other cash crops as guarantees. Very little money, however, was raised in this way. The Confederate government set up a direct tax on the states, but it did not collect much money this way. The lack of cash became so great that the Confederacy began printing paper money which was not backed by gold or silver. The value of the money fell, and by the end of the war, it was almost worthless.

3.5 Congress Without the South.   Republicans in the United States Congress took steps to pass laws which had been blocked before the war by southern members. Kansas came into the Union as a free state in 1861. Colorado, Nevada, and Dakota were admitted as free territories. Nevada then became a state in 1864. A new protective tariff for manufactured goods was passed. The Homestead Act of 1862 provided free land in the West for settlers. Also, two companies were chartered to build a railroad from Omaha, Nebraska, to California.

1. What were the roles of women during the war?
2. Which industries made a profit from the war?
3. How did the North and the South pay for the war?

4. The High Point of the Confederacy

Although the South had many problems, it continued to hold its own in the fighting. There were many people in the United States and in Europe who thought that the North would never be able to defeat the South. The fortunes of the Confederacy reached their high point in late

1862 and early 1863. Then events turned against the South, and the Union began the slow march toward victory.

4.1 Fredericksburg and Chancellorsville. Shortly after the Battle of Antietam, President Lincoln again replaced McClellan as the Union commander in the East. General Ambrose Burnside led the Army of the Potomac in a march south to take Richmond. On December 13, 1862, the Union army attacked Lee's forces at Fredericksburg, Virginia. The Confederates were *entrenched,* or set up in a strong position, on a number of hills south of the town. They defeated the Army of the Potomac, with 11,000 casualties.

Once more, Lincoln changed commanders. In the spring of 1863, the Army of the Potomac under General Joseph Hooker again invaded Virginia. Hooker's forces clashed with Lee's Army of Northern Virginia near the town of Chancellorsville. The battle opened on May 2, and four days later, Hooker had to order his army to retreat. Lee had

Who replaced McClellan as commander of the Army of the Potomac?

Many volunteers on both sides were very young men who were drawn by the excitement of army travel. Where was the Confederate army's farthest northern advance? How far did McClellan's army travel from Washington to Antietam?

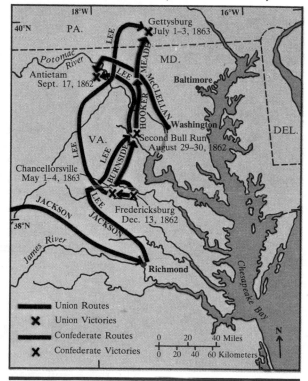

War in the East (1862–1863)

Jackson was shot in the confusion of battle by his own troops.

won another victory for the South. The losses on both sides were great, however. The South, in particular, had lost General Thomas "Stonewall" Jackson. Casualties for both sides were nearly 30,000.

4.2　The Battle of Gettysburg.　　After winning at Fredericksburg and Chancellorsville, Lee decided to invade the North again. He believed that a southern victory on Union soil might force the North to give up the war. It might also persuade Great Britain and France to recognize the Confederacy.

What did Lee hope to accomplish by his second invasion of the North?

Lee's army marched north through the Shenandoah Valley of Virginia into Pennsylvania, heading for Harrisburg. From there, Lee hoped to be able to attack Philadelphia, Washington, or Baltimore. People all over the North were greatly worried. Lincoln replaced General Hooker with General George Meade and ordered him to stop Lee's army. The Army of the Potomac numbered nearly 100,000 against the Confederate army's 75,000.

On July 1, 1863, the two armies met near the small town of Gettysburg, Pennsylvania. For three days, the Confederate troops tried without success to break through the Union lines. On the afternoon of July 3 came the climax of the battle. General George Pickett led 15,000 soldiers against the heart of the Union's defense. "Pickett's Charge," as it was called, ended in failure.

What was Pickett's Charge?

Having suffered nearly 28,000 casualties, the Confederate army retreated. The Union losses were over 23,000 people killed or wounded. Lee's Army of Northern Virginia had suffered a major defeat in one of the most critical battles of the war.

See the Gettysburg Address on the next page.

4.3　The Fall of Vicksburg.　　At about the same time that Lee was defeated at Gettysburg, General Ulysses S. Grant was fighting near the city of Vicksburg, Mississippi. On July 4, 1863, after a six-week siege, Vicksburg fell to Grant. The loss of Vicksburg cut off Arkansas and Texas from the rest of the South. With the fall of Vicksburg, the Mississippi River was completely in Union control.

Grant's Vicksburg campaign was one of the most brilliant of the war and would make an interesting student report.

1. What were the major battles fought in late 1862 and 1863?
2. Which battle stopped the Confederate invasion?
3. Why was the victory at Vicksburg important to the Union?

5. The Road to Appomattox

After the loss at Gettysburg and the fall of Vicksburg, events in the war more and more favored the North. Until these battles, Great

Asking Questions
SKILL

Historians use source material to answer questions they have about the past. The same material, however, can also raise other questions.

On November 19, 1863, at least 50,000 people listened while President Abraham Lincoln spoke at Gettysburg, Pennsylvania. He was part of a dedication ceremony at a new national cemetery. The planners of the ceremony had invited Lincoln but did not expect him to attend while the war continued. The speech Lincoln made is one of the more famous speeches in American history. He said:

Four score and seven years ago our fathers brought forth on this continent, a new nation, conceived in Liberty, and dedicated to the proposition that all men are created equal.

Now we are engaged in a great civil war, testing whether that nation or any nation so conceived and so dedicated, can long endure. We are met on a great battle-field of that war. We have come to dedicate a portion of that field, as a final resting place for those who here gave their lives that that nation might live. It is altogether fitting and proper that we should do this.

But, in a larger sense, we can not dedicate—we can not consecrate—we can not hallow—this ground. The brave men, living and dead, who struggled here, have consecrated it, far above our poor power to add or detract. The world will little note, nor long remember what we say here, but it can never forget what they did here. It is for us the living, rather, to be dedicated here to the unfinished work which they who fought here have thus far so nobly advanced. It is rather for us to be here dedicated to the great task remaining before us—that from these honored dead we take increased devotion to that cause for which they gave the last full measure of devotion—that we here highly resolve that these dead shall not have died in vain—that this nation, under God, shall have a new birth of freedom—and that government of the people, by the people, for the people, shall not perish from the earth.

Read the following questions, and decide which of them is answered by the material. Also decide which questions are raised by reading the material.

1. What did Lincoln think was the meaning of the war?
2. What had happened before Lincoln's speech?
3. Why did he choose to attend?
4. What was the unfinished work about which Lincoln spoke?
5. What is the importance of the speech for us today?

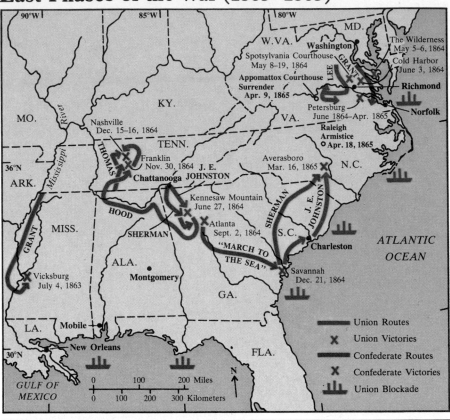

Last Phases of the War (1863–1865)

Map labels:
- The Wilderness May 5–6, 1864
- Cold Harbor June 3, 1864
- Washington
- Spotsylvania Courthouse May 8–19, 1864
- Appomattox Courthouse Surrender Apr. 9, 1865
- Richmond
- Petersburg June 1864–Apr. 1865
- Norfolk
- Raleigh Armistice Apr. 18, 1865
- Nashville Dec. 15–16, 1864
- Franklin Nov. 30, 1864
- Chattanooga
- J. E. JOHNSTON
- Averasboro Mar. 16, 1865
- Kennesaw Mountain June 27, 1864
- Atlanta Sept. 2, 1864
- Charleston
- "MARCH TO THE SEA"
- Savannah Dec. 21, 1864
- Vicksburg July 4, 1863
- Montgomery
- Mobile
- New Orleans
- GULF OF MEXICO
- ATLANTIC OCEAN
- States: MD., W.VA., KY., VA., TENN., MO., ARK., N.C., S.C., MISS., ALA., GA., LA., FLA.

Legend:
- Union Routes
- X Union Victories
- Confederate Routes
- X Confederate Victories
- Union Blockade

Scale:
0 100 200 Miles
0 100 200 300 Kilometers

What did Grant accomplish by capturing Vicksburg? What was the purpose of Sherman's "March to the Sea"? Which series of battles in Virginia led to the Confederate surrender?

What was Grant's plan for victory?

Union forces took Chattanooga in September 1863, which was followed by the important battles of Chickamauga, Lookout Mountain, and Missionary Ridge.

Britain had been thinking about recognizing the Confederacy. After the battles, it dropped the idea. Although the war was far from over, the advantage passed to the Union forces.

5.1 Grant in Command. In March 1864, after his success in the West, Grant was given command of all Union armies. He worked out a plan which would have these armies in the East and West working together. A large army under General William Sherman was to march out of Chattanooga, Tennessee, toward Atlanta. The Army of the Potomac would march on Richmond and Lee. The plan was designed to wear down the Confederates and destroy their will to fight.

5.2 Sherman's March to the Sea. Sherman's army of nearly 100,000 soldiers left Chattanooga in May 1864, moving slowly toward Atlanta. Confederate troops under General Joseph Johnston tried to block the way but were forced back, greatly outnumbered. In September, Sherman's army entered Atlanta. The capture of the city was a great loss to the Confederacy. It was a major manufacturing center and the junction for several important railroads.

Sherman and his soldiers marched from Atlanta toward Savannah, Georgia and the Atlantic Ocean. Along the way, anything that might be used to help the South's war effort was destroyed. Crops, machinery, barns, and bridges were burned, and many miles of railroad track were torn up. On December 22, Sherman entered Savannah. From there, his forces moved north to join Grant in Virginia.

5.3   Grant Against Lee.   At the same time that Sherman was moving through Georgia, General Grant began the march toward Richmond. Grant knew that he had one important advantage—Union losses could be replaced, while those of the South could not. He felt that the war could be won if the larger and better-equipped northern army continued to pressure the Confederates.

Grant led the Army of the Potomac into the wilderness area south of the Rappahannock River in Virginia. Lee's forces won the Battle of the Wilderness which took place on May 5 and 6, 1864. Grant then moved to the southeast and attacked Lee at Spotsylvania Courthouse. On June 3, Grant attacked Lee and was defeated at Cold Harbor. Near the railroad center of Petersburg, Virginia, the two armies dug in against each other again. Months of fighting followed. The number of casualties on both sides was very high in these battles, and Lee's army was slowly being reduced. In the spring of 1865, he decided to break away from Grant. Lee retreated west from Richmond only to find his

What was the "march to the sea"?

See the Atlanta City Sketch beginning on page 398.

What was Grant's advantage over Lee?

Have students report on the lives of Grant and Lee, including their family backgrounds, education, and experiences before the Civil War.

What battles took place between the armies of Grant and Lee?

General Robert E. Lee (right) surrendered the Confederacy's largest and most successful field army to General Ulysses S. Grant (left). As they met, officers from both sides were reunited with old friends and classmates. What did the Civil War accomplish?

army surrounded by federal soldiers. Lee knew his army could not continue to fight. The cause was lost.

On April 9, 1865, Lee and Grant met at the village of Appomattox Courthouse, Virginia. There the terms of surrender were worked out. Lee's forces laid down their arms and returned to their homes. A little over a month later, the last Confederate army under General Kirby Smith surrendered. The Civil War was over.

Who surrendered the last Confederate army?

5.4 With Malice Toward None. Abraham Lincoln had been reelected President of the United States in 1864. As the war ended, he faced the task of rebuilding the country. He spoke of his plans in his second inaugural address.

> *With malice toward none, with charity for all, with firmness in the right as God gives us to see the right, let us strive on to finish the work we are in, to bind up the nation's wounds, to care for him who shall have borne the battle and for his widow and his orphan, to do all which may achieve and cherish a just and lasting peace among ourselves and with all nations.*

What was the tone of Lincoln's second inaugural address?

It should be pointed out that Booth was not performing in the play being watched by the President, although he had appeared previously at Ford's Theater.

5.5 The Assassination of President Lincoln. The plans of the President were cut short, however. On the night of April 14, 1865, only five days after Lee surrendered, President Lincoln went with his wife, Mary Todd Lincoln, to Ford's Theater. They were attending the play, *Our American Cousin*. There, Lincoln was *assassinated*—killed by sudden or secret attack—by John Wilkes Booth, an actor who believed he was helping the Confederate cause. The death of Lincoln would prove tragic for the South. It lessened the chance for an easy peace.

Why was Lincoln's assassination a loss for the South?

1. Who commanded the Army of the Potomac in 1864?
2. When and where was the surrender?
3. When was Lincoln assassinated?

6. Conclusion

The Civil War was a turning point in American history. The North's victory saved the Union and ended the issue of federal authority versus states' rights. The war caused many problems, however. There were areas of the country which had to be rebuilt. There was great bitterness over the war. Sorrow had touched nearly every family in the country. About 2,400,000 soldiers had served in the two armies. Nearly 600,000 of them died. There was also the question of the freed slaves. It remained for them to become a truly equal part of American society.

Chapter 15 Review

Main Points

1. President Lincoln wanted to preserve the Union.

2. The Civil War began when Lincoln ordered supplies to Fort Sumter in South Carolina. Southern leaders then ordered an attack on the fort.

3. When Lincoln called for troops to put down the rebellion, Arkansas, North Carolina, Tennessee, and Virginia seceded. This brought the total of Confederate states to 11.

4. The Union had the advantages of a larger population, more industry, and better transportation.

5. The Confederacy had the advantages of better military leadership and shorter supply lines.

6. The Civil War was a long conflict with many casualties on both sides.

7. The Emancipation Proclamation laid the basis for freeing the slaves as the Union army took over areas formerly under Confederate control.

8. Many blacks fought in the Union army.

9. Many women in the North and the South took over jobs which had been done by men.

10. The Civil War ended when Lee surrendered to Grant at Appomattox Courthouse on April 9, 1865.

11. Lincoln was assassinated by John Wilkes Booth on April 14, 1865.

12. Lincoln's death lessened the chance for a peaceful rebuilding of the nation.

Building Vocabulary

1. Identify the following:

Abraham Lincoln	*Virginia*	Gettysburg
Fort Sumter	Emancipation Proclamation	William Sherman
Robert E. Lee	Belle Boyd	Appomattox Courthouse
Anaconda Plan	Clara Barton	John Wilkes Booth
Ulysses S. Grant		

2. Define the following:

perpetual	ironclad	draft
border states	casualties	greenbacks
defensive war	proclamation	entrenched
blockade runners	bounties	assassinated

Remembering the Facts

1. In his inaugural address, what was President Lincoln's position on slavery?

2. What were the plans of each side to win the war as soon as possible?

3. Why did the Confederacy think it would get financial aid from France and Britain?

4. Where were slaves freed at the time of the Emancipation Proclamation?

5. How did the war affect people on the home fronts?

6. Which political party controlled Congress during the war?

7. When did Lee surrender to Grant?

8. What were the major battles of the Civil War?

9. What prevented President Lincoln from putting his peace plan into operation?

Understanding the Facts

1. Why did Arkansas, North Carolina, Tennessee, and Virginia leave the Union in May 1861?

2. Why did the Union feel it was better prepared to win the war quickly?

3. Why did the Confederacy feel it was better prepared to win the war?

4. What was President Lincoln's purpose in the Emancipation Proclamation?

5. How did each section raise money and soldiers for the war?

6. How did those opposed to fighting avoid becoming soldiers?

7. Why was the Battle of Gettysburg important to both the North and the South?

8. Why did John Wilkes Booth assassinate President Lincoln?

Using Pie Graphs

Reading Pie Graphs. The illustrations shown on page 355 are called pie graphs. The circle, or the whole pie, represents the whole amount of the item being considered. The pie is divided into slices to show what percent of the whole is related to one group or another.

The pie graphs on page 355 consider several important economic factors. They compare the Union and the Confederacy at the time the Civil War began. Study each of the graphs, and answer the following questions.

1. In which of the matters considered is the Confederacy stronger than the Union?

2. In which of the matters considered is the Union stronger than the Confederacy?

3. Is the amount of money needed to fight a war a factor which favored the Union or the Confederacy?

4. Considering all four graphs, was the Union or the Confederacy better equipped to fight the war?

Rebuilding the Nation 16

On the night of April 2, 1865, the Confederate government abandoned Richmond. The city was left in flames. What plans were made for reuniting North and South and for rebuilding the Union?

President Lincoln and other government leaders in Washington faced a grave situation after Lee's surrender at Appomattox. The North's victory meant an end to the Confederacy. Still, the seceded states had to be brought back into the Union. There was the great task of rebuilding the many areas destroyed during the Civil War. And although nearly 4 million slaves had been freed, most of them had no clear idea how they would start making their livings. The United States tried to solve these issues in the years from 1865 to 1877, known as the Reconstruction period.

1. President Versus Congress _____

Over what did Lincoln and Congress quarrel?

Discuss with students what direction can be drawn from the Constitution in deciding whether the President or Congress should control reconstruction.

During the Civil War, Lincoln and Congress had often disagreed about government policy. Some Republican leaders thought the President should be harder on the South in the war. They also felt that Lincoln's plan for *reconstruction,* or rebuilding the Union after the war, was too soft on the South. This led to a struggle between the President and Congress. They could not agree over which branch of government should direct reconstruction and how it would be carried out. Things grew worse when Andrew Johnson took office following Lincoln's death.

When did Lincoln present his plans on reconstruction?

1.1 Lincoln and Congress. After the Union victories at Vicksburg and Gettysburg, President Lincoln had begun to make plans for returning the seceded states to the Union. In December 1863, he presented a *Proclamation of Amnesty and Reconstruction,* which outlined his plans. It said that southern whites should take an oath of loyalty to the United States. They would then be given *amnesty,* or a general pardon by the government. Confederate military and government leaders were not part of this plan. Once 10 percent of the people in each state who had voted in 1860 had taken the oath, that state could begin to form a new government. The new state governments had to recognize the freedom of blacks, but Lincoln did not push for further changes.

How did Lincoln and the Radicals differ on their view regarding the Confederate states?

Many members of Congress thought Lincoln's plan was too mild. One group of Republicans were called Radicals because they wanted to make *radical,* or major, changes. Senators Charles Sumner of Massachusetts and Benjamin Wade of Ohio, as well as Representatives Thaddeus Stevens of Pennsylvania and Henry Winter Davis of Maryland, were Radical Republicans. They were most upset with Lincoln's plan.

Make students aware that the term "radical" is a relative one.

Lincoln felt that the southern states had never been legally out of the Union. So they still had all the rights of states. The Radicals, however, thought that the southern states had left the Union and should be treated as territories. Most Republicans also feared that the Democratic party would come back into power. They wanted to keep the southern states, which had been Democratic, out of the Union as long as possible.

The Radicals in Congress did not like the 10 percent part of Lincoln's plan. They felt it was not only too mild but also allowed the President, not Congress, to control reconstruction. In 1864, Arkansas, Tennessee, and Louisiana were ready to return to the Union under Lincoln's plan. Congress refused to seat their representatives.

Why did the Radicals not like Lincoln's plan?

In July 1864, Congress passed the Wade-Davis Bill. It said that a majority of the white male citizens in each seceded state should take an oath of loyalty to the United States. Then a convention could be held to set up a new state government. Only those who took an oath that they had never willingly aided the Confederacy could vote or serve in these state conventions. This barred anyone who had served as a member of a Confederate government or voluntarily fought for the South. Also, the new state constitution had to abolish slavery. Then, if Congress agreed, the state would be readmitted.

What was the Wade-Davis Bill?

Lincoln kept the Wade-Davis Bill from becoming law through the use of a *pocket veto*. A pocket veto occurs when a President fails to sign a

Have students see Article I, Section 7 of the Constitution to find out what happens if Congress remains in session.

There were no immediate provisions made for slaves freed by the Thirteenth Amendment. Most blacks had neither jobs nor land of their own. Why did some blacks move to cities in the North?

bill presented to him by Congress within ten days of its recess. Lincoln's action further angered the Radicals, and the split between the President and Congress grew wider.

What did the Thirteenth Amendment do?

1.2 The Thirteenth Amendment.   Republicans were concerned that there were still slaves in the border states, in Tennessee, and in parts of certain other states. Lincoln's proclamation in 1863 led to the freeing of slaves only in those areas which were part of the Confederacy. So there were still slaves in some parts of the country. In January 1865, Congress passed the Thirteenth Amendment to the Constitution. It abolished slavery everywhere in the United States. The necessary 27 states ratified it, and on December 18, 1865, the amendment became law.

1.3 Johnson and Congress.   When Lincoln died, the task of reconstruction passed to Andrew Johnson. President Johnson had been born into a poor family in North Carolina and later moved to Tennessee. He entered politics and became known for defending the rights of poor farmers against the large plantation owners. As a Democratic candidate, Johnson was elected to the United States Senate in 1856. When Tennessee left the Union in 1861, he remained in the Senate. In 1864, Johnson was elected Vice-President of the United States.

As President, Johnson was at first on good terms with the Republicans. Because of his record, they thought that he would follow a firm policy toward the South. They were soon disappointed, however. Although Johnson did not like southern planters, he believed in states' rights and cared little about the freed slaves.

Ask students to draw up plans of the things that they think should have been done to help people freed from slavery become productive citizens. Compare these later with the things which were actually done.

What was Johnson's plan for reconstruction?

In May 1865, Johnson set forth a plan of reconstruction much like Lincoln's. According to Johnson's plan, most southern whites would be pardoned once they had taken a loyalty oath. Leaders of the Confederacy and people who had at least $20,000 in cash or property would have to get a special pardon. Seceded states could hold elections for constitutional conventions. These conventions had to repeal their acts of secession. They also had to adopt the Thirteenth Amendment and refuse to pay the debts from the time they were Confederate states. Then new state governments could be formed and members of Congress chosen. By December 1865, the southern states had followed Johnson's plan and were ready to return to the Union.

Students should be aware that $20,000 would represent much more buying power in 1865 than today.

How did Congress react to Johnson's plan?

1.4 Congressional Reaction.   The Radicals were angry because Johnson had formed a plan on his own. They thought that his plan, like Lincoln's, was too soft. The Radicals and other people in the North were also alarmed at the number of former Confederate leaders

Drawing Conclusions
SKILL

What most people in the North knew about the South they read in newspapers or heard in stories. What most people in the South knew about the North they also read or heard. Travelers and writers provided firsthand observations, and readers and listeners provided their own conclusions.

David Macrae, a well-known Scottish writer and church leader, toured the United States in 1867 and 1868. He later wrote a book called *The Americans at Home*. The following selections from that book describe the lives of some southern whites and some former slaves after the Civil War. Read the selections, and based on them, draw some conclusions about the South.

The South had not only wasted her population, but her material resources. I visited districts where the people . . . had dug up every potato in their fields, pulled every apple from their orchards, taken even the blankets from their beds, to make up and send to the . . . army.

. . . I heard of one lady who in January 1865 had 150,000 dollars in Confederate paper [money], and owned slaves that would have sold in 1860 for 50,000 dollars more in gold. . . . she had to go . . . to the [Freedmen's] Bureau shed . . . to get bread to keep her children from starvation.

. . . Men who had held commanding positions during the war had fallen out of sight and were filling humble [jobs]. . . .

The old planters were . . . so poor that they were trying to sell a portion of their land in order to pay the tax upon the rest. . . .

All this talk about the [blacks] being happier in slavery I heard amongst the white people, but rarely if ever amongst the [blacks] themselves. Many of the poorest of them told me that they had to put up with coarser food . . . and poorer clothing . . . and that they had a hard struggle even for that; but the usual wind-up was,—"But thank the Lord, we're free, anyhow."

1. What is Macrae's view of white people in the South?
2. What is his view of the former slaves?
3. Based on this information alone, how would you describe the conditions in the South?
4. Why is one source of information often not enough to draw a proper conclusion?

who had been elected to office. When Congress met, the Republicans blocked the new southern members from taking their seats and prepared to defeat Johnson's plan.

1. Why was there conflict between President Lincoln and the Congress?
2. Who were the Radical Republicans?
3. How did Andrew Johnson view reconstruction?

2. Congressional Reconstruction

While President Johnson was putting forth his plan, Republicans in Congress were drawing up their own plan of reconstruction. They had several goals. The first was to return the southern states to the Union, but under tougher terms than those set by either Lincoln or Johnson. The second was to protect the freedom of blacks in the South. Once those who had been slaves had the right to vote, the Republicans stood to gain their support. This would help the Republicans stay in power. With these goals in mind, the Radicals moved to take charge of reconstruction.

Assign for reports the various Radical Republican leaders in Congress.

2.1 The Freedmen's Bureau. In March 1865, Congress set up the Freedmen's Bureau. It aided all needy people in the South, although *freedmen*—men, women, and children who had been slaves—were its main concern. The Bureau helped blacks set up farms on abandoned lands. It drew up work contracts between black workers and white landowners. The Bureau also set up schools and courts for blacks. John T. Trowbridge, a visitor from the North, described one of the courts.

What did the Freedmen's Bureau do?

> *The freedmen's court is no respecter of persons. The proudest aristocrat and the humblest [worker] stand at its bar on an equal footing. . . .*
>
> *A great variety of business is brought before the Bureau. Here is a [black] man who has printed a reward offering fifty dollars for information to assist him in finding his wife and children, sold away from him in times of slavery: a small sum for such an object, you may say, but it is all he has, and he has come to the Bureau for assistance. . . .*
>
> *[Another] has made a crop; found everything—mules, feed, implements; hired his own help—fifteen men and*

The Freedmen's Bureau was set up to help former slaves adjust to freedom. The work of the Bureau included establishing schools. Why did freed blacks need a basic education?

women; managed everything; by agreement he was to have one half; but owing to an attempt to swindle him, he has had the cotton attached [legally taken away]. . . .

The Bureau was the only direct step taken by the government to help the South and the former slaves economically. In February 1866, Congress passed a bill to add to the powers of the Freedmen's Bureau. According to the bill, the Bureau would continue to work in the South. Blacks there would go on being protected by United States' soldiers. Johnson vetoed the bill on the grounds that it was passed by a Congress in which 11 states were not represented. Later a bill continuing the Freedmen's Bureau for two years was passed over his veto.

Why did Johnson veto the bill to add to the powers of the Freedmen's Bureau?

2.2 Black Codes and the Civil Rights Act.   Soon after the end of the war, southern state governments had begun passing laws, called **black codes,** that limited the rights of blacks. The codes differed from state to state. But there were many similarities. Blacks were not allowed to vote. They could not testify against whites in court, nor could they serve on juries. Blacks could hold only certain kinds of jobs, generally in agriculture. Those who did not have a job were assigned to work for whites. With these restrictions, the lives of the freedmen were not much different from when they were slaves.

What were black codes?

Compare the black codes with the system of laws during slavery.

What did the Civil Rights Act of 1866 provide?

Congress moved to protect the rights of blacks by passing the Civil Rights Act of 1866. This act aimed at protecting freedmen through the courts rather than by military power. Blacks were made citizens, and it became illegal to treat a person differently because of color. This was the first federal law to define citizenship and to safeguard civil rights within the states. President Johnson vetoed the bill on the grounds that it went against states' rights. Congress passed it over his veto.

Why did the Radicals propose the Fourteenth Amendment?

2.3 The Fourteenth Amendment.   The Radicals in Congress feared that the Supreme Court might overturn the Civil Rights Act. To stop this, Congress made the act into a constitutional amendment. In June 1866, the amendment was sent to the states.

Point out that the Fifth Amendment contains a due process clause but that another is included in the Fourteenth Amendment to prohibit the *states* from infringing on individual rights.

The Fourteenth Amendment stated that all persons born in the United States (except Indians) were citizens of the United States and of the states in which they lived. No state could deprive a citizen of life, liberty, or property without due process of law. In addition, every citizen was entitled to equal protection of the laws. States that kept any adult male citizen from voting could lose part of their representation in Congress. Anyone who had sworn to uphold the Constitution and then taken part in a rebellion against the United States could not hold public office. Finally, Confederate debts were said to be illegal.

When was the Fourteenth Amendment adopted?

The only southern state that agreed to ratify the amendment in 1866 was Tennessee. That year Tennessee became the first seceded state to return to the Union. The other southern states felt that citizenship was a matter for each state to decide. They were supported by President Johnson and the northern Democrats. These states did not ratify the Fourteenth Amendment for two more years, until 1868.

2.4 The Reconstruction Acts.   President Johnson decided to go directly to the voters with his ideas about reconstruction. He hoped to talk the people into voting against the Radicals in the congressional elections of 1866. Johnson gave a number of strong speeches around the North in order to gain support. The Republicans, however, won more than a two-thirds majority in each house of Congress. As a result, they could pass any bill over Johnson's veto and so direct the course of reconstruction.

What did the Reconstruction Acts provide?

In March 1867, Congress passed the first of several Reconstruction Acts. Under these acts, the South (except Tennessee) was divided into military districts. Each of the five districts was headed by a general backed by soldiers. The generals were to see that the states held constitutional conventions. Delegates were to be chosen by all adult male voters. Confederate leaders were not allowed to vote or hold office. When the state constitutions had been accepted by Congress and enough of the new legislatures had approved the Fourteenth

Reconstruction of the South

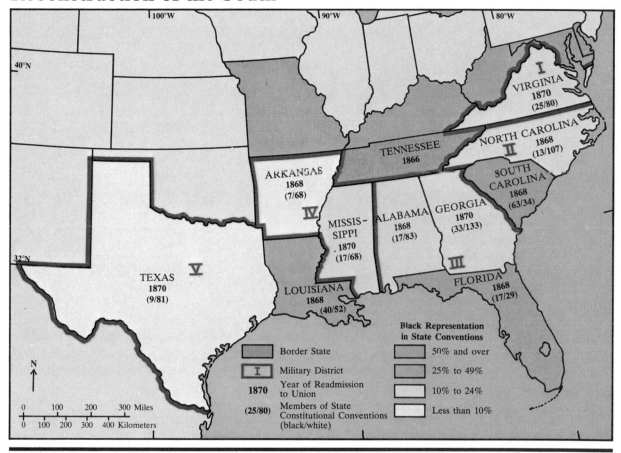

When did Congress pass the first Reconstruction Acts? What process did the former Confederate states follow for readmission into the Union? What was the purpose of establishing military districts?

Amendment, the states would be readmitted. By 1868, the amendment had been adopted. By 1870, all of the southern states had returned to the Union.

2.5 Johnson's Impeachment. The struggle between Congress and Johnson was brought to a head by the Tenure of Office Act, passed in March 1867. *Tenure of office* means the length of time that a person can stay in office. This act stated that the President could not remove a person from federal office without the approval of the Senate. It was passed to check Johnson's power.

Johnson felt that the act was unconstitutional. He hoped to test the case in court. In February 1868, he removed Secretary of War Edwin

What was the Tenure of Office Act?

An officer of the Congress notified President Andrew Johnson of his impeachment (left). Tickets (right) were sold for the trial in the Senate. What was the result of the President's trial?

Why did Johnson remove Stanton from office?

The Tenure of Office Act was not invoked again and was repealed in 1887. Had Johnson been convicted, it might have set the dangerous precedent of removing a President for political reasons.

What was the outcome of Johnson's impeachment?

Stanton from office. The Radicals then charged Johnson with breaking the law. The House of Representatives drew up 11 articles of impeachment against Johnson. Most of these were about the President not following the Tenure of Office Act.

The trial began in March 1868 with Chief Justice Salmon P. Chase presiding and the Senate acting as jury. Many people felt that Johnson was really being tried because he did not get along with the Radicals. The final vote came on May 16, 1868. With seven Republicans voting "not guilty," the final count was 35 to 19. This was just one vote short of the two-thirds majority needed to convict Johnson. Republican Senator Edmund G. Ross of Kansas cast the final and decisive ballot for *acquittal,* or a verdict of not guilty. Johnson served the rest of his term, but he had lost most of his influence.

1. Who was the Freedmen's Bureau meant to help?
2. How did the black codes restrict southern blacks?
3. Which southern state was the first to return to the Union?
4. Why was President Johnson impeached?

3. Reconstruction and the Postwar South _____

People all over the country held different ideas about reconstruction. This was especially true in the South. Opinions there were divided not only between blacks and whites but also among people of different political views. All of these groups had an important impact on reconstruction after the war.

3.1 Southern Blacks and Reconstruction. Most of the blacks living in the South had been slaves before the Civil War. Afterwards, they were free, but most of them owned no land and had no money. Few could read or write. They hoped that reconstruction would bring them land and the chance for an education. These freedmen wanted to be able to vote and hold office in order to have an equal place in southern life.

Under the Reconstruction Acts, black people were allowed to vote for the new state governments. To protect their interests, blacks generally supported the Republicans. Blacks did more than vote, however. For the first time, they held public office in the South. Some black officials were appointed by the military governors. Others were

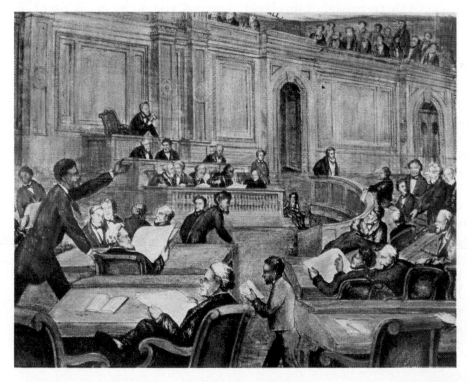

Robert Brown Elliot of South Carolina was a southern black elected to Congress during Reconstruction. What other black leaders filled key positions in state and federal governments?

Who were some
important black
leaders in the
South during
Reconstruction?

elected. Blanche K. Bruce of Mississippi, a former slave, was elected to the United States Senate. He had studied at Oberlin College in Ohio. Hiram P. Revels served as a Senator from Mississippi for one year. He had been trained for the ministry at Knox College in Illinois. Jonathan C. Gibbs, a Dartmouth College graduate, was secretary of state in Florida. He helped to set up Florida's public schools. Francis L. Cardozo, who had attended the University of Glasgow in Scotland, was secretary of state and later state treasurer in South Carolina.

In what state were
blacks a majority in
the state constitu-
tional convention?

Many blacks were elected to public office after the war. But they never really directed reconstruction in the South. Blacks were a minority in all southern state constitutional conventions, except South Carolina. There they outnumbered whites 76 to 48. In Mississippi, for example, there were only 17 blacks out of 100 representatives at the state convention. In Alabama, there were only 8 blacks out of 108. The percentage of blacks in the state legislatures was about the same, and their numbers grew smaller as time passed.

3.2 Southern Whites and Reconstruction.   Most southern whites accepted the defeat of the Confederacy and the abolition of slavery. They were not willing to go much further than that, however. They stood firmly against equal rights for black people. These southern whites did not want black people to vote or to hold office. They wanted blacks only to provide farm labor, under a system much like that of slavery. Most of them opposed the new Republican governments and anyone else seeking to help blacks.

What did most
southern whites
want for blacks?

3.3 Carpetbaggers and Scalawags.   The Republican party in the South was controlled, for the most part, by two groups. People from the North who moved into the South to take part in reconstruction were one group. Many of them carried their belongings in bags made of the same material as carpets. So they were called *carpetbaggers*. Some of them truly wanted to help, while others were just looking for opportunity for personal gain or adventure.

People from the other group were called *scalawags*. They were southern whites who worked with Reconstruction officials. Other southern whites thought of them as traitors. Some scalawags thought what they were doing was the best way to help the South. Others were thinking only of themselves. Some had been Whigs. They wanted to build up southern industry by working with northern Radicals. They hoped this would lessen the South's dependence on agriculture. Many people in the South did not want this change in their way of life. Many scalawags hoped that by influencing the votes of black people, they would reach their goals. When this failed, almost all of them left the Republican party.

3.4 Claims of Corruption.   Many southern whites thought that the new governments in their states were corrupt. To prove this, they pointed to the growth of both state budgets and state debts. In South Carolina, for example, the public debt went from $7 million to $29 million in eight years. Taxes increased about 80 percent in Louisiana and almost 1400 percent in Mississippi. Southern whites generally put the blame on dishonest carpetbaggers and untrained blacks in government.

Although there was corruption in some state governments in the South after the Civil War, the same thing was true for many northern governments. Because of the needs of the people, large-scale spending was needed in the South. Bridges and buildings had to be replaced. Railroad lines had to be repaired and hospitals built. Public schools had to be set up. In 1860, there were only 20,000 children in the public schools of South Carolina. By 1873, there were about 120,000—both black and white. Social services of all kinds had to be provided, often for the first time.

3.5 The Ku Klux Klan.   Many southern whites felt that freed blacks, with the help of northern Republicans, would destroy the South. These people wanted to keep white control in all areas. To do this, it was

Why did people think there was corruption in the Reconstruction governments?

Have students consider why large-scale public spending was not needed in the South before the Civil War.

Why was there large-scale spending?

Have students compare the aims of the KKK with the ideas in the Declaration of Independence and the Preamble to the Constitution.

With the economy of the South in near ruin, many southern whites moved west. How were those who stayed affected by Reconstruction?

"The First Vote" (left), from *Harper's Weekly*, shows a polling place in the South. In 1867, the Ku Klux Klan (right) was organized to frighten black voters from the polls. How else were blacks denied their rights?

necessary to stop northern support for the freedmen. They also wanted to keep blacks from voting and holding office. Since the Reconstruction governments, backed by the army, protected the voting and civil rights of all citizens, some whites turned to secret societies to achieve their goals.

What was the Ku Klux Klan?

One of the strongest of the secret groups was the Order of the Ku Klux Klan. It was formed shortly after the war in Pulaski, Tennessee, by Confederate soldiers. It quickly spread to many parts of the South. Robed and hooded, members of the Klan rode through the land trying to scare blacks and their supporters, especially agents of the Freedmen's Bureau. Blacks were kept from voting by threats, beatings, and sometimes killings.

Nathan Bedford Forrest, a former Confederate cavalry officer, became the first head of the KKK.

1. What did the former slaves hope to gain from reconstruction?
2. Whom did southern blacks generally support during Reconstruction?
3. How did southern whites feel about new legislation during Reconstruction?
4. Why was the Ku Klux Klan formed?

4. The End of Reconstruction

By the late 1860's, Radical reconstruction was well under way in the South. It seemed likely to continue in the years ahead. In the 1870's, however, many Americans began to grow tired of the problems presented by reconstruction.

4.1 The Election of Grant. In 1868, the Republicans chose the Union army general, Ulysses S. Grant, to run for President. Democrats selected Horatio Seymour, former governor of New York. The Republicans stood by reconstruction, while the Democrats favored an end to it. They favored pulling United States soldiers out of the South. They wanted to pardon former Confederates and return all rights to the states.

What position did each party take in the election of 1868?

The campaign that year was a heated one. Republicans pointed to their war record. They reminded people that it had been members of the Democratic party in the South who had started the Civil War. Republicans claimed to have saved the Union. They pictured theirs as the party of patriotism.

Republicans wanted to ensure black votes for the future while the Democrats wanted the ex-Confederate states returned to the Union to strengthen their party.

The Republicans won the election of 1868. Grant won in 26 states, with an electoral vote of 214 to Seymour's 80. The popular vote, however, was much closer—3,012,833 for Grant and 2,703,249 for Seymour. Grant received around 400,000 votes from blacks. This showed how important the black vote could be.

In the North, many states had chosen not to let blacks vote, although the new state governments in the South had been forced to do so. This was changed by the Fifteenth Amendment. It said that no state could keep a person from voting because of color. The amendment was approved by enough states to become law on March 30, 1870.

What did the Fifteenth Amendment prohibit?

4.2 Grant and Reconstruction. Once in office, President Grant took a strong stand in favor of Radical reconstruction and black rights. He approved the Force Act, passed in May 1870, as well as the Ku Klux Klan Act of 1871. These laws gave Grant the power to use troops to end violence against blacks and Republican governments. Many arrests were made and the Klan began to lose its power.

Slowly, however, national backing for Radical policies began to weaken. By the end of his first term in office, President Grant had lost interest in sending soldiers into the South to protect Republicans and blacks. After his reelection in 1872, he stopped sending them.

4.3 Other Interests, Other Concerns. Congress, too, was becoming less concerned with supervising the South and helping the

Charlotte Forten (1837–1914)

PROFILE

In late 1861, Union army forces captured a group of islands off the coast of South Carolina and Georgia. Thousands of slaves had been left there as their owners fled from the northern soldiers. Many government leaders and abolitionists saw this as a chance to show that former slaves could live successfully as free citizens. The Port Royal Experiment gave educational and medical aid to the freed slaves on the islands. Charlotte Forten was one of the teachers who volunteered to help. She taught there from 1862 to 1864.

Forten was born in Philadelphia. She studied in Salem, Massachusetts, from 1854 to 1856. For two years, she taught elementary school there. In 1858, Forten moved back to Philadelphia where she lived with her family until going to Port Royal.

Forten kept a journal of her years on the Sea Islands. In it, she expressed her commitment to help the former slaves. She also reveals her own feelings as a young black woman growing up in a mostly white country.

This morning a large number—Superintendents, teachers and freed people, assembled in the little Baptist church. It was a sight that I shall not soon forget—that crowd of eager, happy black faces from which the shadow of slavery had forever passed. "Forever free!" "Forever free!" Those magical words were all the time singing themselves in my soul. . . .

What was occurring in the northern attitude toward reconstruction in the 1870's?

freedmen. For one thing, some of the most important Radical leaders were gone. By 1870, Davis, Wade, and Stevens had either retired or died. In May 1872, Congress passed an amnesty law. It allowed most former Confederate officials to vote and hold office. It also ended the Freedmen's Bureau.

The general public in the North had heard enough about reconstruction. There were other problems which attracted their attention. Among them were the Indian wars in the West, and a plan for the United States to buy Santo Domingo. There were also talks with the British over damage caused the North by Confederate ships built in Great Britain.

4.4 Scandals Under Grant. Tales of scandal in the federal government under Grant also drew people's attention away from the South. Grant had been a great army leader, but he had not had much experience in politics. Some people tried to take advantage of this for their own gain.

Americans learned that in September 1869, Jay Gould and Jim Fisk, both millionaires, had bought enough gold to control its price. Fisk and Gould tried to get President Grant not to sell government gold. This would drive up the price of gold. Grant refused. Fisk and Gould then spread a rumor that the government had agreed not to sell, and the price rose. Fisk and Gould sold their supply of gold at a higher price. Soon after, the government released $4 million. This drove the price down and ruined many people. They blamed the government and President Grant for their losses.

What did Gould and Fisk attempt to do?

This is called "cornering the gold market."

In 1872, the Crédit Mobilier scandal broke. The Crédit Mobilier construction company was formed by leaders of the Union Pacific Railroad. This company received contracts to build the railroad and charged very high prices. The costs were picked up by other stockholders in the railroad. The money, however, really went to the leaders and to some members of Congress who had accepted stock in the company for certain favors.

Who was involved in the Crédit Mobilier scandal?

Recall that the railroad was approved by Congress. See Chapter 15, Section 3.5, page 364.

Later in Grant's term, Secretary of the Treasury W. A. Richardson was found to be dishonest. He was forced to leave office. It was also discovered that President Grant's private secretary, Orville Babcock, was a part of what was called the "Whiskey Ring." This was a group of revenue officers and distillers formed to cheat the government out of tax money. By the time the Whiskey Ring was discovered, the government had lost millions of dollars. In 1876, the head of the War Department, W. W. Belknap, resigned from office. He was about to be impeached for taking bribes.

Evaluate Lincoln, Johnson, and Grant as Presidents, using the criteria developed earlier.

4.5 The Election of 1876. These scandals hurt the Republican party, which had already lost most of its power in the South. By 1875, only three states—Louisiana, Florida, and South Carolina—remained under Republican control.

Against this background, the election of 1876 took place. At their convention, the Republicans chose Governor Rutherford B. Hayes of Ohio, a former Civil War general. The Democrats picked Governor Samuel Tilden of New York. Both candidates were interested in reform.

What southern states were under Republican control in 1876?

Who were the candidates in the election of 1876?

Tilden won a majority of the popular vote, but a question arose over the electoral vote. Both the Republicans and the Democrats claimed victory in South Carolina, Florida, and Louisiana. In Oregon, one vote was also in question. Congress set up a commission to award the votes. It had 15 members—five from the House, five from the Senate, and five from the Supreme Court. The commission finally voted eight to seven to give the 20 votes in question to Hayes.

The Democrats reached a compromise with the Republicans accepting the commission's decision. The Democrats accepted Hayes as President. In return, federal soldiers were removed from the South. The Compromise of 1877 was an agreement between northern Republicans and southern Democrats. It spelled the end of the period of Reconstruction.

How was the election decided?

The House of Representatives was unable to come to a decision and a serious political crisis was brewing because of the vacancy in the Presidency.

Who won the popular vote in the election of 1876? Which candidate had the most electoral votes? What delayed the final outcome of this election? What made this election different from those before it?

Election of 1876

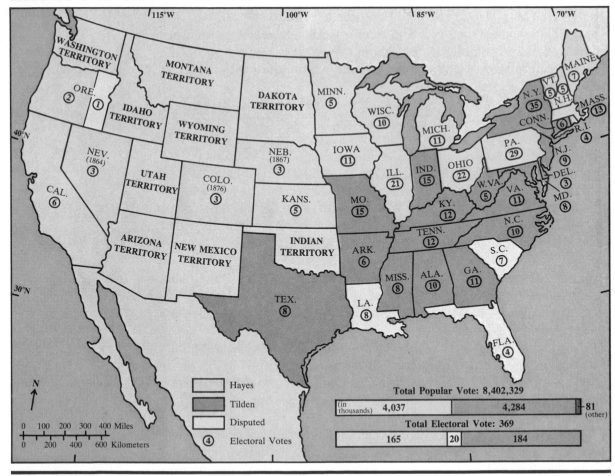

4.6 The Plight of Southern Blacks. The real losers in the Compromise of 1877 were southern blacks. The last Radical governments in the South were no longer protected by the federal government. They were soon taken over by the Democrats. People in the South called these Democrats the "Redeemers," or saviors, of the South.

As southern Democrats came into power, blacks began to lose their political rights. Some were kept from voting by violence. Others were threatened with the loss of their jobs or homes. Efforts were made to control those few who were allowed to vote.

It was almost impossible for blacks to prevent the loss of their rights because they did not have economic power. The Radical promise of free land had never been carried out, and most blacks had no cash or credit to buy land. Only a small number were able to rent farms. So many southern blacks had to hire out as laborers on farms or plantations owned by whites.

A system called *sharecropping* became the way of life for many freedmen. Instead of receiving wages or paying rent, blacks and some whites worked small pieces of land owned by someone else. In return, they received a share of a season's crops. Many landowners gave the farmers supplies and housing. Whatever the sharecroppers owed the landlord was taken out of their earnings at the end of the season. This system often put the sharecroppers into debt from which they never escaped.

1. How did President Grant view reconstruction?
2. What effect did the scandals during Grant's term of office have?
3. When did Reconstruction end?
4. How did the Compromise of 1877 affect southern blacks?

Again note for the class the use of words which have special or one-sided meanings, in this case the use of "Redeemers." It reflects the point of view of southern whites against that of blacks.

In Section 3.1, students considered the importance of political power to a group. Have them also consider the importance of economic power to achieving an equal place in society.

What was the system of sharecropping?

5. Conclusion

By the end of Reconstruction, the South was once more a part of the Union. Southern whites were again in control of southern state governments. Blacks had lost many of their newly gained political rights. The South had restored its economy. It had begun to industrialize, although agriculture was still important. Blacks, though legally free, were still workers tied to the land. Their struggle for equal rights would last for many years.

Chapter 16 Review

Main Points

1. President Lincoln and the Congress differed on how reconstruction of the South was to be carried out.
2. The Thirteenth Amendment, ratified in December 1865, freed all slaves.
3. Johnson's plan for reconstruction was much like Lincoln's.
4. Congress' plan for reconstruction would restore the South to the Union and protect the rights of former slaves.
5. The Fourteenth Amendment protected the rights of all people born or naturalized in the United States.
6. Conflict between Congress and President Johnson led to the President's impeachment. The Senate failed by one vote to convict Johnson of the charges.
7. Blacks voted and participated in the Reconstruction governments.
8. The Fifteenth Amendment was passed to protect the rights of blacks to vote.
9. Many people in the South opposed citizen rights for blacks. Blacks lost many of these rights when Democrats gained control of state governments in the South.

Building Vocabulary

1. Identify the following:

Andrew Johnson	Freedmen's Bureau	Ku Klux Klan
Radical Republicans	Civil Rights Act of 1866	Ulysses S. Grant
Charles Sumner	Fourteenth Amendment	Charlotte Forten
Wade-Davis Bill	Blanche K. Bruce	Crédit Mobilier
Thirteenth Amendment		Rutherford B. Hayes

2. Define the following:

reconstruction	freedmen	acquittal
amnesty	black codes	carpetbaggers
radical	tenure of office	scalawags
pocket veto		sharecropping

Remembering the Facts

1. What was President Lincoln's plan for reconstructing the South?
2. Which slaves were freed by the Thirteenth Amendment?
3. How did Johnson become President? What was his plan for reconstruction?
4. What was the congressional plan for the reconstruction of the South?

5. Why was the Freedmen's Bureau organized?
6. What were the protections provided by the Fourteenth Amendment?
7. What was the role of the former slaves in politics during Reconstruction? In which states were they most active?
8. What did the Ku Klux Klan do against blacks and against the Radical Republicans?
9. What scandals broke during Grant's term as President?
10. What did the North and the South gain from the Compromise of 1877?

Understanding the Facts

1. How did presidential reconstruction differ from congressional reconstruction?
2. Why did Congress think President Johnson would follow a firm policy toward the South?
3. What charges were brought against Johnson by the House of Representatives? How were they decided?
4. Why did states in the South pass black codes?
5. Why was it important for blacks to vote? Why did southern whites object?
6. Why was there no major effort to provide land for freed slaves?

Using Maps

Thematic Maps. Maps are often used to show information on a variety of themes. They combine geographic information with information that could also appear in a table or on a chart.

The thematic map on page 381 deals with the reconstruction of the South after the Civil War. It contains geographic data and additional theme information. Study the map carefully, and answer the following questions.

1. What are the geographic divisions of the South shown on the map?
2. Which information on the map might have been placed in a chart?
3. Which military district shown on the map was composed of three states?
4. Which military district was composed of only one state?
5. Which state was not in any military district? Why not?
6. Which state had the largest number of black members of its constitutional convention?
7. In how many states did black members outnumber white members?
8. Based on the information in this map, who controlled the conventions that drew up the southern state constitutions?

New York 1860~1865

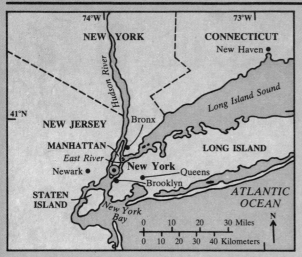

A group of American Indians sold an island off the northeastern coast of their lands to the Dutch West India Company in 1626. The Company had established a fort and trading post at the tip of the island which was located in a large bay. The island was named Manhattan after the Indians who sold it. The Dutch called the settlement New Amsterdam.

In 1664, New Amsterdam came under the rule of the English who changed its name to the City of New York. The English held it until the end of the Revolutionary War. The new government of the United States took its first census in 1790. By that time, Manhattan was home to more than 33,000 people. Under Dutch, English, and American rule, the city had grown as a center of trade.

In 1860, on the eve of the Civil War, New York was the biggest, richest city in the entire United States. More than 800,000 people lived on Manhattan, and hundreds of thousands more lived in nearby cities like Brooklyn, Queens, and the Bronx. Almost half the people living on the island had come to the United States from other countries. The City of New York was the biggest center of immigration in America.

First Impressions

In the spring of 1861, an English news writer visited the United States to report on the possibility of war between the North and South. William Russell's visit took him first to New York and then to other cities in the North and South. Russell returned to New York in July, after the war had started.

. . . the first thing which struck me was the changed [look] of the streets. Instead of peaceful citizens, men in military uniforms [crowded] the pathways, and [so many] United States' flags floated from the windows and roofs of the houses as to [give] the impression that it was a great holiday festival. . . . [In March,] it was very rarely I ever saw a man in soldier's clothes. . . . Now, fully a third of the people carried arms, and were dressed in some kind of martial garb.

The change in manner, in tone, in argument, is most remarkable. I met men to-day who last March argued coolly . . . about the right of Secession. They are now furious at the idea of such wickedness. . . .

Reactions

Once the question of war was decided, the people of New York joined in support of the Union cause. They acted quickly to organize and equip the soldiers, and they gave help to the families of those who volunteered to serve. There were thousands of volunteers, especially among the immigrant groups. To the poorest of them, army service meant pay. To most of the immigrants, it was also proof of loyalty to their new country.

Through religious, social, and government organizations, the people of the city played an important part in the war. They raised money for special payments to those who volunteered to join the army. They arranged for improved health care and sanitary conditions in the distant army camps. By the spring of 1862, people realized that "the show time of the war has passed away, and it has become a matter of sober business." Edward Dicey also wrote:

In many a house that I have been into, I have found the ladies busy in working for the army . . . but there is little talk or fuss made about it. There are few balls or large parties this season, and the opera is not regularly open. . . . but

Printing House Square was the center of the New York newspaper industry. What were some of the newspapers? What was their role in the Civil War?

work is plentiful, and the distress, as yet, has not gone deep down.

Young People

The daily lives of the younger people in the city changed little during the war years. Most of them kept up their studies, and Dicey was very impressed by the schools they attended.

The instruction is entirely [free]—everything, down to the pens and ink, being provided by the State. Education is not compulsory [required by law]; but the demand for it is so great that . . . the school benches are always more than filled. . . . The teachers in all the classes, except two or three . . . are women. . . . Reading, writing, ciphering [arithmetic], geography, grammar, history, book-keeping for the boys, and moral philosophy [the study of right and wrong] for the girls, were the [main subjects]. . . .

Besides the State schools, there are several free public schools, kept up by voluntary contributions [from church members]. . . . In the classes I went through . . . were representatives of almost every foreign nation . . . the majority were Germans, Irish, and [blacks]. . . . they learn to read and write [American English]. . . .

The Cost of Living

By the summer of 1863, the slow and deadly progress of the war had changed life for many of the city's people. Some of those in business became very rich from war trade. But the pay of ordinary soldiers was quickly spent by families as the cost of living increased. Taxes rose, rents went up, and food became very expensive.

Even the lowest-paying jobs became very important to the city's immigrants who held most of them. The Emancipation Proclamation had upset many workers, especially the Irish who had most of the unskilled, low-paying jobs. These people were afraid that freed blacks would come north to find work. Many of the workers had been the first to volunteer to fight for the Union. They were not so willing, however, to fight for the freedom of slaves.

The Draft Riot

Some political leaders and news writers in the city did not agree with the way President Lincoln ran the war. In 1863, they especially attacked the order to draft soldiers. The first list of drafted men was published on Sunday, July 12. It was made up mostly of poor people; many of them also supported the Democratic party. Some Democratic party leaders had

To protest the Conscription Act of 1863, some people in New York set fire to a building storing draft records. Why did people challenge the draft law?

claimed that it was unconstitutional for the government to force a state citizen to serve in a federal army. They charged that the number of Democrats on the draft list was too high.

Monday morning, a large crowd of people gathered in front of the draft office. Some of them believed that men had been drafted for political reasons. Others were afraid of losing their jobs to blacks. Many were tired of high prices and low pay.

By Monday afternoon, the crowd had changed into a violent mob. Men, women, and some children began to attack the draft office. They set fire to the records, books, and furniture. They beat the people who tried to stop them. From the draft office, the mob went to attack the shops and homes of antislavery leaders. They caught black people on the street and beat them, sometimes killing them. A home for black orphans was burned to the ground, and one child died in the fire.

After four days, the riot was finally ended with the help of federal and state soldiers and special groups of volunteer citizens. Many people had lost their lives, and over $1.5 million worth of property had been destroyed.

Joy and Sorrow

In some sections of New York, many people were making a great deal of money from the war. They enjoyed spending it. New theaters opened, and large new houses were built. Richly dressed men and women rode in expensive carriages along Fifth Avenue to Central Park.

George Templeton Strong, who lived on Manhattan all his life, recorded some of the events of April 1865 in his diary. Strong was walking down Wall Street on April 3 when the news came that Richmond had been captured by Union troops.

An enormous crowd soon blocked [the street]. . . . *Never before did I hear cheering that came straight from the heart . . . given because people felt relieved by cheering and hallooing. . . .*

I walked about on the outskirts of the crowd, shaking hands with everybody. . . . Men embraced and hugged each other . . . retreated into doorways to dry their eyes and came out again to flourish their hats and hurrah. . . .

It was not long, however, before joy turned into sadness. Two weeks later, Strong wrote:

April 15. . . . LINCOLN . . . ASSASSINATED LAST NIGHT!!!! . . . Tone of [angry] *feeling* [is] *very like that of four years ago when the news came of Sumter.*

. . . No business was done today. Most shops are closed and draped with black and white muslin [cloth].

Homecoming

As the war came to an end, soldiers who were not given other duties were allowed to go home. A news writer reported on their return to New York.

Some came by sea, but most by railways to Jersey City, and thence across the ferry to Pier No. 1. They landed near the open space by the Battery [the old Dutch fort area] *and marched up town. . . .* [Some freed blacks], *acting as water-carriers,* [walked] *in the rear. . . . Regiments known in the city were of course more warmly greeted than strangers passing through. . . . Heavy losses had been sustained. . . . The New York 52nd regiment, for example, came back less than three hundred strong, having had on its muster rolls, during the war, two thousand six hundred names.*

Broadway was a busy street in the 1860's. It was spared from battle during the war. How were the people of New York affected by the Civil War?

Many families had lost their fathers, brothers, and husbands. Some soldiers returned from the war badly wounded or crippled. These families faced a difficult future. Others looked at the rebuilding of the South as a new business adventure. They faced the future with confidence. The lives of the people of New York had been changed by the war in many ways.

1. What was the City of New York's original name?
2. Describe New York City on the eve of the Civil War.
3. Why did the immigrants volunteer for the Union army?
4. Describe Wall Street on April 3, 1865, when Richmond had been captured.

Atlanta 1860~1865

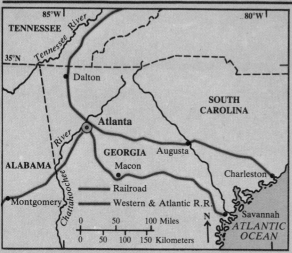

In the 1840's, two railroads in northeastern Georgia met at a town called Marthasville on the Chattahoochee River. Railroad promoters renamed the town Atlanta. The town began to grow very quickly. Property sales multiplied as new people came to start businesses. There was a medical college, but Atlanta did not have a public school system. White children attended private schools or took private lessons. There were very few free black families in the city, and slave children were not allowed to study. There were churches, factories, warehouses, banks, hotels, and restaurants. Doctors and lawyers settled in Atlanta, and newspaper offices opened. By 1860, Atlanta had a population of nearly 6,000 people and was one of the most important cities in the South.

Civil War Service

Atlanta was the chief supply center for the Confederate army during most of the Civil War. Its factories made many of the weapons used by the South. The four main railroad lines through the city carried soldiers and supplies to the front lines of the war. Some of Atlanta's people had moved north when the war first started. Many more of them stayed, raising money for weapons and supplies and caring for wounded soldiers. As the war dragged on, Atlanta grew so important to the Confederate cause that it became a main target of General Sherman's Union troops.

Early in the summer of 1864, Union soldiers pushed the Confederate troops into Georgia and across the Chattahoochee River. By July, General Hood's outnumbered troops prepared to defend Atlanta. Hood encouraged most of the families in the city to leave. Many of them did, and merchants and bankers sent their extra supplies to other cities for safekeeping. In August, Sherman's Union guns opened fire on the city.

Surrender

After several weeks of Union attack, the Confederates were forced to abandon Atlanta. Before leaving the city, Hood ordered his soldiers to burn all the army supplies that they could not carry with them. He did not want to leave weapons for the enemy to use. Sherman's soldiers entered Atlanta on September 2, 1864.

Sherman ordered the citizens to leave their homes and turned Atlanta into an armed Union camp. The city had been captured, but the war was not over. By November, Sherman's plans for marching through Georgia to Savannah were complete. He ordered his troops to destroy the railroad and telegraph lines and the bridges into northern Georgia and Tennessee. Atlanta was not to serve the Confederates as a supply base again.

When the Union troops prepared to leave the city, they gathered cattle and food supplies to take with them. Sherman told his officers that the army of more than 62,000 soldiers would have to "live off the land" when those supplies were gone. Orders were given to burn warehouses and factories before leaving the city. A Union soldier wrote about that day.

. . . it soon became [clear] that these fires were but the beginning of a general [blaze] which would sweep over the entire city and blot it out of existence . . . the soldiers [took] what they wanted before it burned up. . . . new fires began to spring up . . . noises rent the air . . . soldiers on foot and horseback raced up and down the streets while the buildings on either side were solid sheets of flame. . . . The night,

Union troops entered Atlanta in September 1864. Why was the capture and occupation of this southern city an important Union army objective?

for miles around was bright as mid-day; the city of Atlanta was one mass of flame. . . .

Coming Home

Three weeks after the Union army had burned Atlanta, General W. P. Howard of the Georgia troops came to inspect the damage. He reported to the governor:

Could I have arrived ten days earlier, with a guard of 100 men, I could have saved the State and city a million dollars.

There were about 250 wagons in the city on my arrival, loading with pilfered plunder [stolen goods]; pianoes, mirrors, furniture of all kinds, iron, hides without number, and . . . other things, very valuable at the present time. This exportation of stolen property had been going on ever since the place had been abandoned by the enemy.

Kate Massey from Atlanta wrote about some of the difficulties that families faced upon their return to the city.

People lived in anything they could find. Some families were housed in old freight cars. Some used discarded army tents. . . .

. . . A young woman [who needed a new dress] took several old ones, ripped, raveled, carded, spun, and wove them into new material. Then she made her dress. . . . Some children's shoes were made with wooden soles.

A few people found their homes unburned when they reached the city. Octavia Hammond wrote to neighbors about the condition of their property.

Your flowers are still alive and I think the grass lots have a notion to come up. If it were possible to [find] material we would have your lots enclosed for you to save them from wagons, horses and cattle. But the plank is not

General William Tecumseh Sherman made his mark on Atlanta by ordering it destroyed. What did Sherman hope to accomplish by burning the city?

to be had. . . . We have no garden at all, but I am afraid Ma will plant the front yard in cabbage, onions and peas. If she does I will [give you some]. . . .

Action!

Enough people had returned to Atlanta by December that regular elections were held for mayor and city council. The council then elected people to jobs like tax collector, city doctor, and police officers. The newly-elected treasurer reported that the city had less than $2 in cash. Supplies of money and goods were low, but the people of Atlanta had energy and courage. A visiting news writer reported on their activities a few months later.

From all this ruin . . . a new city is springing up with marvelous [speed]. . . . streets are alive from morning till night with . . . hauling teams and shouting men,— with loads of lumber and loads of brick and loads of sand,—with piles of furniture and hundreds of packed boxes . . . with carpenters and masons,—with rubbish removers and house-builders . . . all bent on building and trading and swift fortune making.

Union Blue Again

By early spring, a few private schools had opened, and the medical college was preparing to hold classes again. But April was a month filled with bad news for the citizens of Atlanta. On the ninth, they learned that General Lee had surrendered to General Grant. On the twenty-sixth, General Johnston surrendered to General Sherman. For Atlanta, and for the whole South, the Civil War was over. Early in May, the city again became a military post for the United States army. This time, citizens were encouraged to stay and to continue rebuilding the city.

In many ways, the Union troops were helpful to the people of Atlanta. They were a strong influence on law and order, and they brought Northern money to the city. In the months that followed, the federal government was a great help to the poor of the city. Atlanta's leaders were concerned about the large numbers of Southerners who came to the city for help. The editor of the Atlanta *Daily Intelligencer* wrote in September about these people.

There is a population in and on the suburbs of this city . . . of families who have been stripped of everything, and whose [working men] went into the war and have never returned. . . . they simply exist. . . . With barely food [enough] to keep soul and body together. . . .

Others . . . were driven from their homes in other states and places, and have never been able to return to them. . . . These people may be seen in any direction on the outskirts of town, and in the hurry and bustle of business it becomes us not to forget them. Strained, as our people are . . . surely something may be spared [for these others]. . . .

Another [group], *larger and increasing . . . are huddled together in most* [awful poverty]. *. . . our feelings are not so keenly aroused in their behalf. We* [mean] *the recently liberated slaves. . . .*

. . . the good of society, and the [lessening] *of crime, demand . . .* [we do something for them] *speedily!*

Freedom

Almost all groups of people faced hardships after the war. The recently freed slaves also faced terrible prejudice. Some white Southerners supported the ideas of freedom for blacks. Very few of them were willing to accept the idea that any blacks should have full voting rights as citizens of the United States.

To most black people, freedom meant joy mixed with fear. Many came to the city because they had nowhere else to go. As Frederick Douglass said, "They were sent away empty-handed, without money, without friends and without a foot of land to stand upon."

A few black people had been trained in skills or as household servants. They often found work in the city, although they did not receive the same pay as white workers. Thousands of blacks had known only field work. They came to the city because they were curious or to find family and friends. Many came from fields ruined by war, and they needed the food that was given out by the army and the government.

Even with the terrible hardship they faced, blacks preferred their new roles as free people. Margrett Nillin, a former slave, explained when asked about it:

What do I like best, to be slave or free? . . . Well, it's this way, in slavery I own nothing and never own nothing. In freedom I can own the house and raise the family. All that causes me worry—and in slavery I had no worries—but I take the freedom.

Unlike New York, war ravaged both the city and the people of Atlanta. What did the people do to build a new city from the ruins of the old city?

1. How did Atlanta get its name?

2. What did the Union troops do in Atlanta during the war? after the war?

3. Describe the problems that faced the people of Atlanta after the war.

4. Compare the school systems of New York and Atlanta.

5. What roles did New York and Atlanta play in the Civil War?

Unit V Review

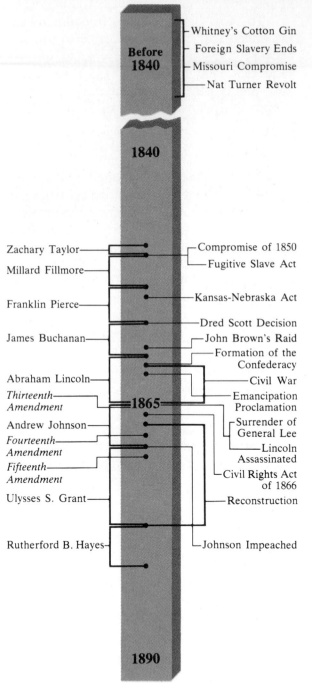

Before 1840
- Whitney's Cotton Gin
- Foreign Slavery Ends
- Missouri Compromise
- Nat Turner Revolt

1840

Zachary Taylor
Millard Fillmore
- Compromise of 1850
- Fugitive Slave Act

Franklin Pierce
- Kansas-Nebraska Act

James Buchanan
- Dred Scott Decision
- John Brown's Raid
- Formation of the Confederacy

Abraham Lincoln
Thirteenth Amendment
- Civil War
- Emancipation Proclamation

1865

Andrew Johnson
Fourteenth Amendment
Fifteenth Amendment
- Surrender of General Lee
- Lincoln Assassinated
- Civil Rights Act of 1866

Ulysses S. Grant
- Reconstruction

Rutherford B. Hayes
- Johnson Impeached

1890

Summary

1. Strong sectional differences had been developing between the North and South since the beginning of the nation.

2. The most important difference dividing the two sections—the institution of slavery—took on greater importance as the issue arose of slavery's expansion into new territories of the West.

3. Despite many attempts to keep the slavery issue out of politics, it became the leading question of the late 1850's, giving rise to the Republican party.

4. The victory of Abraham Lincoln and the Republican party in the election of 1860 was followed by the secession of 11 states from the Union.

5. The Union and Confederacy fought a long civil war which caused great loss of life and much damage in the South.

6. Following the Union victory in the war, wide differences in opinion arose over the efforts at reconstruction and over whether Congress or the President would guide reconstruction.

7. Congress, led by the Radical Republicans, took over reconstruction, passing laws to protect freed blacks.

8. Southern whites fought against rights for freed blacks, who were left without land or money to protect their position in southern society.

9. When federal support for freed blacks faded, white-controlled Democratic governments took over southern states, bringing an end to Reconstruction.

Unit Questions

1. Why did westward expansion before 1860 contribute to the sectional crisis between the North and the South?

2. Why did many Americans feel that slavery clashed with the ideas in the Declaration of Independence? How did white southerners deal with the ideas of slavery and the ideals of the Declaration of Independence?

3. How was the Republican party different from the Whigs or Democrats in its support? How was this important in 1860?

4. What were the major reasons why the North was able to win the war?

5. What was the position of the Confederacy toward President Lincoln's belief that the Union was perpetual? Did the position of the Southern states change during Reconstruction and how?

6. How did the Republican party use reconstruction for its own advantage?

7. What were the successes and failures of the war and reconstruction as far as the rights of blacks were concerned?

Suggested Activities

1. Write a brief statement showing how each of the following people might have reacted to news of the Dred Scott decision: a slave, a slave owner, a free black, and an abolitionist.

2. Locate poems and songs written during or about the Civil War. Try to include those which were about people from both the South and the North. Select several, and present them to the class.

3. Organize a discussion or class debate on the following—Do you think that reconstruction should have been controlled by Congress or the President?

Suggested Readings

Davis, Burke. *Mr. Lincoln's Whiskers.* New York: Coward, McCann, & Geoghegan, Inc., 1979. Discusses Lincoln's election as President and advice given him to grow a beard.

Ellis, Keith. *The American Civil War.* New York: G. P. Putnam, Sons, 1971. Discusses the leaders, battles, and events of the war.

Keith, Harold. *Rifles for Watie.* New York: Thomas Y. Crowell Co., 1957. The story of a young soldier during the Civil War.

Sterling, Dorothy. *The Trouble They Seen: Black People Tell the Story of Reconstruction.* Garden City, New York: Doubleday, 1976. Blacks give eyewitness accounts of reconstruction to Congress.

Students should understand that many small areas were unsettled, that there was no clear line of frontier.

Discuss the terms segregation, discrimination, and prejudice. Show how each was reflected in the Jim Crow laws. The *Plessy* v. *Ferguson* case was one of the most important civil rights cases in American history.

Conclusion

Reconstruction to the Present

As it moved into the latter 1800's, the United States was almost 100 years old. After the Civil War, the country was experiencing change. In the next hundred years, there would be more change—in society, in culture, and in the economy. These changes would bring new challenges to America and Americans.

1. The Watershed Years

In the years between 1865 and 1900, many Americans experienced changes in their way of life. At the same time, the nation's attention was centered on new issues—on renewed settlement of the West, on industrialization, and on growth, prosperity, and reform.

1.1 Settlement of the Last Frontier. In 1865, only the trans-Mississippi West remained to be settled. Settlement of this last frontier took place during the 1860's, 1870's, and 1880's. First came miners in search of gold, silver, and other precious minerals. Then came ranchers looking for open range to graze their herds. Finally came homesteaders in search of land to farm.

Settlement often resulted in conflict, the greatest being between the Indians and white settlers and lasting until the late 1880's. One by one, Indian nations were defeated by federal troops and moved to reservations. There, their traditional ways of life often came to an end.

1.2 Blacks in the Late 1800's. Blacks had made great gains immediately after the Civil War. Once Reconstruction ended, however, some southern whites looked for ways to take away rights guaranteed to blacks under the Fourteenth and Fifteenth Amendments. All voters were required to pay a poll tax and pass a literacy test before voting. Southern states also passed *segregation* laws, called "Jim Crow" laws, to separate blacks from whites in schools; in public places such as hotels and restaurants; and on all forms of public transportation.

During the latter 1800's, the Supreme Court supported states' rights and defended segregation. In 1873, it ruled that the Fourteenth Amendment applied only to certain situations, that the rights of citizens were the responsibility of the state, and that the Fourteenth Amendment did not prohibit individuals and private businesses from practicing segregation. In 1896, in *Plessy* v. *Ferguson,* it upheld a Louisiana law that

This is a good place to discuss the concept of free enterprise and competition and the problems presented by trusts and monopolies in such a system.

Discuss the economic principle of supply and demand. Use the increased farm production and falling prices as an example.

permitted railroads to have separate cars for blacks and whites. This put forth the idea that states could legally separate people by race if equal facilities were provided for each group.

1.3 Industrialization. The process of industrialization, which began in the 1820's, quickened after the Civil War. Between 1865 and 1900, large industry was so important that the period became known as the "Age of Big Business." Large-scale industrialization was possible because the country had a large labor supply and an abundance of natural resources needed for industrial production. New inventions also helped by providing machinery that increased productivity, while an extensive railroad network made possible transport of raw materials and manufactured goods.

Putting these advantages to work, a number of American business leaders organized gigantic companies. In 1867, John

D. Rockefeller founded the Standard Oil Company that eventually controlled 90 percent of the nation's oil-refining business. Andrew Carnegie took similar steps to control the steel industry, while Gustavus Swift and Phillip Armour dominated the meat-packing industry. Through *corporations* (businesses in which investors own shares of stock) and *trusts* (organizations made up of several companies in an industry run as one company), business leaders were able to raise and control millions of dollars for investment. Their efforts were supported by the government's *laissez-faire* policy under which it refrained from setting rules for business conduct.

This industrialization affected the economy. Among the first to feel the change were farmers. Although they produced more products, farm prices dropped and farm costs rose. To gain reforms, many farmers joined organizations like the Patrons of

One of the best-known Currier and Ives prints of the West is "Across the Continent." It was painted by Fanny Palmer. What images does Palmer use to promote the benefits of the West?

Reconstruction to the Present   405

City government was not provided for in the Constitution and is controlled by state legislatures. Perhaps students can investigate their local area's type of government.

Use examples of labels on food and medicine to show the results of the Food and Drug Act. Discuss what might happen without such laws.

Husbandry, or the Grange. In 1892, farmers joined with others seeking reform to form a new political party called the Populist party. Its members called for such democratic political reforms as the *secret ballot* for voting.

Farmers, however, were not the only ones affected by the rise of Big Business. Urban factory, mill, and mine workers, complaining about low wages, long hours, and poor working conditions, engaged in many disputes and strikes. Seeking reforms, they organized into unions such as the Knights of Labor and the American Federation of Labor (AFL).

At the same time, concerned church groups and social organizations began helping the poor and underprivileged. Social workers, such as Lillian Wald and Jane Addams, established *settlement houses,* or neighborhood centers that offer services to the poor, and crusaded for better housing and public health. Newspaper and magazine writers, known as *muckrakers,* criticized certain policies of Big Business and exposed corrupt practices.

1.4 The Progressive Movement. By 1900, industrialization had helped to create more opportunities for many Americans. At the same time, however, it had created severe problems for some. During the late 1800's and early 1900's, reformers proposed so many solutions that the period became known as the Progressive Era.

Many Progressive reforms were put into practice first at local and state government levels. Many cities introduced such new forms of government as the commission and city-manager systems. Many states passed such measures as the *direct primary* (whereby

voters select candidates for public office) and *workman's compensation* (insurance protection to workers injured on the job). Soon, the reforms spread to the national level. The Interstate Commerce Act of 1887, for example, set up the Interstate Commerce Commission (ICC) to regulate railroads. The Sherman Antitrust Act of 1890 attempted to control trusts and monopolies.

Progressives found a supporter at the national level in Theodore Roosevelt, who had become President following the assassination of William McKinley in 1901. Roosevelt was not opposed to Big Business, but thought that, to protect the interests of the people, it should be regulated. After his election in 1904, Roosevelt pushed for passage of Progressive laws. The Pure Food and Drug Act and the Meat Inspection Act set up controls to protect the American consumer. The Hepburn Act empowered the ICC to set maximum railroad rates. Roosevelt also supported the conservation movement to protect the nation's natural resources.

The Progressive movement slowed down when William Howard Taft became President, but returned with Woodrow Wilson's election as President in 1912. Wilson proposed the New Freedom program. It included lowering tariff rates, establishing a graduated income tax, and setting up a national banking network under the Federal Reserve System.

Wilson also sought to end the hold that business monopolies had on the economy. In 1914, the Federal Trade Commission (FTC) was set up to put a stop to unfair business practices, and the Clayton Antitrust Act was passed to strengthen government control of

Immigrants were welcomed for cheap labor by employers. Yet the newcomers were resented for working for low pay by many Americans. Discuss some of the problems that were faced by the immigrants.

Pluralism
CONCEPT

From colonial times, the American population has been made up of various nationalities, races, and religions. The people who came to America tried to maintain their old world traditions while living in American society. Because of this, America became characterized by pluralism—several independent ethnic groups within a common society.

Despite the accepted idea of a pluralistic America, some Americans in the late 1800's felt that some immigrants would hurt the United States as a whole. There were hostile reactions to certain newcomers. A mood of fear led to many laws aimed at controlling immigration to the United States.

In 1896, Senator Henry Cabot Lodge of Massachusetts argued for a bill to establish a literacy test. The bill was designed to exclude all immigrants who could not read or write 25 words of the Constitution in any language.

It is found, in the first place, that the illiteracy test will bear most heavily upon the Italians, Russians, Poles, Hungarians, Greeks, and Asiatics, and very lightly, or not at all, upon English-speaking emigrants or Germans, Scandinavians, and French.

In other words, the races most affected by the illiteracy test are those whose emigration to this country has begun within the last twenty years and swelled rapidly to enormous proportions, races with which the English-speaking people have never hitherto assimilated, and who are most alien to the great body of the people of the United States.

President Grover Cleveland disagreed with Lodge's view and vetoed the bill.

It is said . . . that the quality of recent immigration is undesirable. The time is quite within recent memory when the same thing was said of immigrants who, with their descendants are now numbered among our best citizens. . . .

In my opinion, it is . . . safe to admit . . . immigrants who, though unable to read or write, seek among us only a home and opportunity for work. . . .

1. Which groups did Senator Lodge hope to exclude? Why?
2. What was President Cleveland's argument opposing literacy tests?
3. What is the connection between the concept of pluralism and the idea of democracy?

restraint of trade. Other legislation also was passed to help farmers and workers. However, the Progressive movement did not benefit blacks and other minorities.

1. What was the pattern of settlement of the last frontier?

2. How did the status of blacks change during the late 1800's?

3. Who were the critics of Big Business?

4. What reforms took place under the Progressives?

2. Rise to World Power

At the same time the nation was recovering from the Civil War and adjusting to changes brought by industrialization, the United States became interested in expansion overseas. American interest and involvement in foreign affairs kept growing. By 1920, the United States was both a leading industrial nation and a major world power.

2.1 The Spanish-American War. During the late 1880's, Americans began looking beyond their country. Some were interested in overseas markets. Others saw foreign lands as sources for raw materials. Still others wanted to expand American influence around the world.

It was not until 1895, however, when Cubans revolted against Spanish rule, that the United States became seriously involved in foreign affairs. Already angered by exaggerated news accounts of Spanish atrocities against Cuban civilians, Americans became outraged when, on February 15, 1898, the battleship *U.S.S. Maine* exploded in Havana harbor. On April 20, Congress passed a resolution demanding that Spain withdraw from Cuba. On April 25, the United States declared war on Spain.

Actual fighting began on May 1 in the Philippines, a Spanish colony in the Pacific,

when Admiral George Dewey steamed into Manila Bay, destroyed the Spanish Pacific fleet, and captured Manila. In the Caribbean, American troops landed at Santiago, Cuba, and after winning battles at El Caney and San Juan Hill, forced Spanish forces there to surrender.

In August, an *armistice,* or truce, was reached, and, in December, a peace treaty was signed. Spain agreed to recognize Cuban independence. The United States received Puerto Rico and Guam as payment for war damages and bought the Philippines for $20 million.

2.2 Foreign Policy in the Early 1900's. The Philippines were important to the United States because they were close to China. At the time, Great Britain, France, Germany, Russia, and Japan were claiming parts of China as their own *spheres of influence,* or zones of control over trade. American business people believed that, with the Philippines as a base, they could gain a greater share of the China trade.

In 1899, Secretary of State John Hay sent notes to the major powers asking them to keep Chinese ports open to all countries. In March 1900, he announced the powers had agreed to an "Open Door" policy. In July, he issued a second note, stating that the

United States Acquisitions, 1858–1917

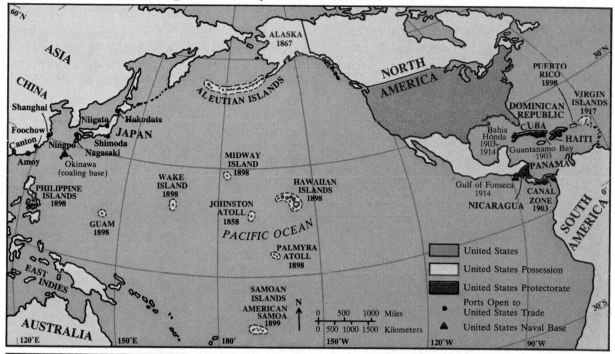

United States was committed to preserving China's territorial integrity.

With interests in both the Pacific and Caribbean, the United States wanted a canal across Central America to allow ships to travel from one ocean to the other without sailing around South America. It offered Colombia $10 million for a strip of land across the Isthmus of Panama. Colombia, however, refused the offer.

In November 1903, Panama revolted against Colombian rule. President Roosevelt sent American warships to the area to prevent Colombian troops from landing to put down the revolt. The United States then recognized the new Republic of Panama and signed the Hay-Bunau-Varilla Treaty. It gave the United States the right to build a canal in Panama. In 1914, the Panama Canal was completed.

Acquiring the Panama Canal was part of Roosevelt's strong foreign policy, known as **big stick diplomacy** because of Roosevelt's willingness to threaten to or to use force to protect American interests. The 1904 Roosevelt **corollary,** or addition, to the Monroe Doctrine, said that the United States would intervene in Latin America to keep order and to protect life and property.

Roosevelt's successor, William Howard Taft, took a different approach. He encouraged American businesses to invest

Reconstruction to the Present   409

Prior to World War II, there was no term "World War I." It was known as the Great War.

Students could research the many advances in technology represented by the weapons used in World War I.

money in other countries. Through this *dollar diplomacy,* he hoped the United States would be able to influence the policies of other countries without using force.

When Wilson became President, he promised to change the direction of American foreign policy by replacing military force and economic pressure with friendship, fair play, and democracy. Despite this, Wilson sent American troops into the Caribbean to prevent disorder and violence and got involved in the political affairs of Mexico. Soon, however, events in Europe forced Americans to focus attention on a much greater conflict than that in Mexico.

2.3 The World at War. By the early 1900's, two alliances had formed in Europe. One was the Triple Entente, made up of Great Britain, France, and Russia. The other was the Triple Alliance, made up of Germany, Austria-Hungary, and Italy. Members of each were bound to defend their allies in case of war.

Both Russia and Austria-Hungary wanted to control the Balkans. In June 1914, Archduke Franz Ferdinand, heir to the Austrio-Hungarian throne, was assassinated. This incident turned existing tensions into war. By 1915, Germany and Austria-Hungary, now known as the Central Powers, were at war with the Triple Entente, now known as the Allied Powers. The Central Powers were supported by Bulgaria and the Ottoman Empire (Turkey). The Allies were supported by many countries including Italy, which had switched sides.

When World War I first began in Europe, the American people were divided. Those of British heritage wanted to help the Allies, while those of German heritage supported the Central Powers. Though the official policy of the nation was one of neutrality, gradually most Americans began to favor the Allies. The sinking without warning of unarmed passenger ships by German submarines did much to turn public opinion against Germany.

In 1916, Germany pledged not to sink passenger vessels without warning. For nearly a year, relations between the United States and Germany improved. Then, on January 31, 1917, Germany announced that its submarines would sink on sight all ships in the waters around Great Britain. This announcement increased tensions between Berlin and Washington. Official concern became even stronger when it was learned that the German minister to Mexico had offered to make an alliance with Mexico in the event of war with the United States.

In March, German submarines sank several American merchant ships. On April 2, Wilson went before a joint session of Congress to ask for a declaration of war against Germany. On April 6, the United States joined the Allies to "make the world safe for democracy."

2.4 America in World War I. To make certain the country met the needs of the military, the federal government took a number of actions. Congress passed a *selective service* act, or draft, to provide enough troops to fight. It also established a number of agencies to regulate the economy and to make more effective the war effort. The War Industries Board fixed prices, set standards, and decided what goods should be produced. The Food Administration and

If possible, display posters used during World War I to mobilize the home front. Discuss how each aimed to influence people.

Have students consider the wisdom of Wilson's refusal to compromise and allow changes in the treaty affecting the League.

the Fuel Administration monitored food and fuel production and consumption. The United States Railroad Administration ran the nation's railways as a single system.

In order to pay the costs of war, Congress passed the War Revenue Act. It made the income tax the major source of war revenue and raised postal rates and excise taxes. The government also sponsored rallies and parades to sell war bonds to the public.

The first American troops to take part in combat arrived in France in June 1917. Called the American Expeditionary Force (AEF), they were led by General John Pershing. At first, they were used only as replacements for British and French soldiers. Finally, the AEF was allowed to fight as one army. Before the war came to an end in 1918, the Americans fought in major battles throughout France.

2.5 Planning for Peace. Long before the fighting ended, Wilson had begun to prepare for the peace conference. In an effort to prevent future wars, he drew up a plan known as the Fourteen Points. Among other things, his plan called for freedom of the seas in peace and war, an end to secret treaties and alliances, and equal trading rights for all nations. It also called for a limitation on armaments, a just settlement of colonial claims, and the right of self-determination for all countries. The fourteenth point called for the formation of a League of Nations responsible for preserving peace.

In December 1918, Wilson went to Paris for the peace conference. He found that the other Allied leaders wanted to punish Germany and would not accept his plan. In

The Versailles Treaty was signed in the Hall of Mirrors at the Versailles Palace outside of Paris. There Wilson presented his Fourteen Points. What part of his peace plan was accepted by the other Allied leaders?

the final treaty, known as the Versailles Treaty and signed on June 18, 1919, Germany was held responsible for starting the war, forced to pay huge war damages, and made to disarm. But Wilson's League of Nations was incorporated into the treaty.

Wilson returned home to find many Senators did not approve of the treaty. Some Republicans were angry that he had not consulted with them before finalizing it. Others feared the League of Nations could draw the United States into future wars to protect foreign nations. When Wilson refused to support changes in the treaty, Senate leaders warned that it would not get Senate approval. In September 1919, Wilson decided to take his case to the people. While

Reconstruction to the Present   411

Have each student write a brief paper on the possibility for success in outlawing war and for preventing wars from taking place.

The first KKK is discussed in Chapter 16, Section 3.5, pages 385-386. Have students compare the first KKK with the one of the 1920's.

on tour, he suffered a disabling stroke. During his illness, the Treaty of Versailles went down to defeat in the Senate.

1. Why did Americans become more involved in world affairs?

2. Why did the United States want a canal across Panama?

3. What caused most Americans to favor support of the Allies?

4. Why did the Senate oppose the Treaty of Versailles?

3. Prosperity and Depression

World War I had brought about many changes in American thinking and ways of life. In fact, some Americans began to think there had been too much change. Elected President in 1920, Republican Warren Harding summed up most people's feelings in his call for a return to "normalcy"—to the practices and values of the past.

3.1 Disarmament. Though membership in the League of Nations had been blocked by rejection of the Versailles Treaty, the Harding administration wanted to show it supported world peace. It called for an international conference on the Limitation of Armaments. At that conference, nine treaties were signed. In one, the United States, Great Britain, Japan, France, and Italy agreed to stop building warships for 10 years and to limit total tonnage.

Encouraged by the Washington conference, many people came to believe it was time to outlaw war altogether. In 1928, 62 nations signed the Kellogg-Briand Treaty, pledging not to resort to war as the means of settling conflicts.

3.2 Intolerance and Civil Rights. Meanwhile, in the aftermath of World War I, many Americans became *intolerant,* or not willing to respect the beliefs, practices, or

behavior of others. Many were angry at those who criticized the United States or followed different ways of life. Others were frightened that the communist movement which had overthrown the Russian government in 1917 would spread to the United States. Because Communists were known as "reds," this fear became known as the Red Scare. Because of it, Congress passed a series of laws during the 1920's placing a quota on the number of people allowed to enter the United States as immigrants in a given year.

Not all intolerance, however, was directed at foreigners in the 1920's. Reorganized in 1915, a new Ku Klux Klan, which used threats and violence against those who opposed it, spoke out against blacks, Catholics, and Jews. Publicity and government investigations, however, resulted in a sharp decline in Klan membership by 1930.

Even with the growth of intolerance, some gains were made in the area of civil rights. Women, for example, acquired the vote with the adoption of the Nineteenth Amendment in 1920. In 1924, Congress passed the Curtis Act, which made citizens of all Indians living in the United States. Hispanics gained greater educational op-

Someone in the class might enjoy compiling a list or collecting photos of the different new inventions made in the 1920's.

Discuss the reasons why people adopt celebrity heroes. Have someone list some of the heroes of the 1920's and the heroes of today. Discuss why these people became heroes.

portunities through the efforts of such groups as the Order of the Sons of America, founded in Texas in 1921. The National Association for the Advancement of Colored People (NAACP), founded in 1909 by William E. DuBois, won some legal battles. In 1927, for example, in *Nixon* v. *Herndon,* the Supreme Court ruled that states could not keep blacks who wanted to vote from taking part in primaries.

3.3 Life in the 1920's. For many Americans, the 1920's were years of prosperity. The aftermath of World War I saw an end to government restrictions on business. Business people, working mostly through the Republican party, pushed hard for free enterprise.

One key reason for the nation's prosperity was the growth of new industries. The development of the automobile in particular produced new factories, more jobs, and changes to the American way of life.

Though government worked to promote business, little attention was directed at reform. Meanwhile, scandal rocked the Harding administration. The nation was shocked by the Teapot Dome affair in which Secretary of the Interior Albert B. Fall illegally leased federal oil reserve lands to private oil companies.

Above all, however, the 1920's was a time of sharp contrast in life-styles. Some Americans continued to live in rural areas and to believe that hard work, thrift, and religion were the best values. Others, particularly the young residing in urban areas, sought a more exciting and fast-paced life.

While new inventions like home appliances freed people from time-consuming tasks, the automobile allowed them to move about more easily. More Americans began to do things "for fun." For the first time, the American people created a "celebrity cult" out of entertainers and athletes. *Jazz*—a new form of music that incorporated harmony with black African rhythm—swept the nation and symbolized the times. Other new forms of entertainment, like the radio and "talking" motion pictures, quickly drew large audiences. Spectator sports, such as professional baseball, football, and boxing, became especially popular.

Both the excitement and problems of the 1920's were reflected in the arts.

Painter Aaron Douglas was one of many black artists whose works came to be part of the cultural movement called the Harlem Renaissance. What did these artists try to express?

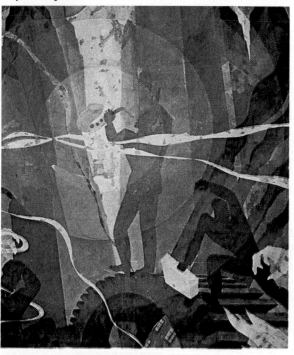

Remind students that there have been many depressions in U. S. history. Recall the one discussed in Chapter 10, Section 5.2, pages 248 and 249.

The New Deal program can be thought of as a two-part program—Emergency Measures and Long-Range Planning.

American painters explored new ways of portraying life that pleased some while shocking others. American writers wrote of disillusionment with the postwar era and traditional values. Black authors and artists gave birth to a movement known as the Harlem Renaissance that sharply depicted what it meant to be black in a predominantly white America.

3.4 The Great Depression. In 1929, the nation's economic boom suddenly came to an end, and a depression set in that lasted through the 1930's. As the worst economic collapse in American history, it became known as the Great Depression.

The problems that led to the Great Depression began in the early 1920's. For one, American farmers produced more crops than they could sell. As a result, farm prices fell so low that many farmers could not pay their debts. For another, prosperity was not equally shared. Wealthy people became wealthier, while most working people did not earn enough to buy the new goods being produced. As a result, industrial production began to slow down.

Because Americans were so sure of prosperity, however, many speculated in the stock market. Throughout the late 1920's, stock prices soared. Then, in October 1929, prices began to decline until on October 29, when the bottom fell out. Stock prices plunged to a fraction of their previous value, and countless numbers of Americans lost their life savings.

The stock market crash immediately affected other areas of the economy. Banks closed, factories shut down, and people lost their jobs. By 1932, more than 13 million Americans were unemployed. Some were forced to wander around the country looking for work. Others had to live in makeshift shacks and survive on charity.

Like many, President Herbert Hoover, who was elected in 1928, at first thought the economy would soon improve. He asked business leaders to keep their factories open and not to cut workers' wages. But as the Depression deepened, he realized other measures were necessary. In 1931, he suggested a government agency be set up to offer credit to various lending institutions. But he would not allow the federal government to provide direct aid to the people. This, he believed, would destroy such time-honored American values as self-reliance and individualism.

In an atmosphere of desperation, the 1932 election was held. Democrat Franklin D. Roosevelt easily defeated Hoover, and the Democrats gained control of both houses of Congress.

3.5 The New Deal. On taking office, Roosevelt adhered to his campaign promise of a New Deal and immediately proposed a number of legislative actions designed to achieve relief and recovery. Programs such as the Civilian Conservation Corps (CCC), the Civil Works Administration (CWA), the Public Works Administration (PWA), and the Works Progress Administration (WPA) provided work for people. The Federal Emergency Relief Administration (FERA) gave direct aid to the states for work projects and relief. The Agricultural Adjustment Administration (AAA) aimed at raising prices by getting farmers to grow less, and the Farm Credit Administration (FCA)

Each federal project was funded for a set number of years, after which Congress voted to extend it or let it die. Students should be aware that the function and authority of each of the

programs here was slightly different from any other. Have students research and list all of the New Deal programs.

The United States Economy

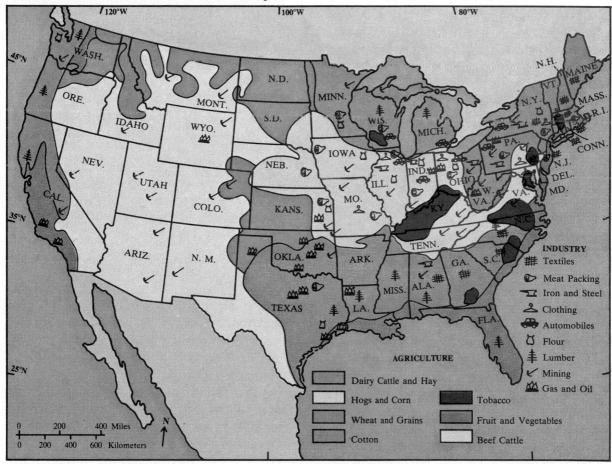

helped farmers get low interest loans. The National Recovery Administration (NRA) worked with industries to set up codes of fair competition, limit production, and to maintain price levels.

The New Deal also was aimed at reform—at improving American life and safeguarding against future depressions. Since most reforms, however, did not come

into being until 1934 or later, this part of Roosevelt's program is referred to as the Second New Deal.

One of the most controversial reforms was the 1933 Tennessee Valley Authority (TVA), the federal government's first and largest attempt at regional planning. It sought to develop the Tennessee Valley by providing flood control through construction

Reconstruction to the Present   415

of a number of dams and a massive program of rural electrification.

Recognizing the New Deal could not succeed without labor's support, the Roosevelt administration also took a number of steps to strengthen labor. The National Industrial Recovery Act of 1933 gave workers the right to organize. The National Labor Relations Board (NLRB), set up by the Wagner-Connery Act of 1935, was given power to define unfair labor practices and to settle disputes between labor and business. The Fair Labor Standards Act of 1938 set a maximum work week of 40 hours and a minimum hourly wage of 40 cents.

Finally, in 1935, Congress enacted a Social Security Act. *Social security* provided unemployment insurance for workers laid off their jobs. It made payments to older people who had retired. It provided aid for the disabled, the blind, and dependent children who had no means of support. Funds for the program came from taxes on business payrolls and workers' earnings.

The New Deal, however, was not without critics or problems. Some Americans believed it went against American principles, or did not go far enough to help the disadvantaged. Some business leaders attacked it as socialism. People, like Senator Huey Long, thought it should initiate programs to share the nation's wealth.

In time, some of those unhappy with the New Deal took their cases to court, where the National Industrial Recovery Act and the Agricultural Adjustment Act of 1933 were struck down. The rulings angered Roosevelt, who feared the Supreme Court might rule against other New Deal programs. As a result, after his reelection in

Responses to Roosevelt's New Deal varied. Some praised his programs, while others criticized them. How does this cartoonist portray Roosevelt's New Deal programs?

1936, he proposed a plan to overhaul the federal court system. Although Congress defeated the plan, the retirement of several conservative Justices allowed Roosevelt to appoint a number of Justices more supportive of New Deal legislation.

The New Deal did not end the Great Depression, but it did give millions of Americans some relief and hope. More importantly, it changed the role of the federal government regarding the economy. Since then, both the government and the President have been viewed as keepers of the nation's well-being.

1. Against whom was intolerance directed in the 1920's?
2. What were some of the changes in life-styles during the 1920's?
3. What factors helped bring about the Great Depression?
4. What were the aims of the New Deal?

There was a long history of anti-Semitism in Germany and other European countries. Hitler used this prejudice to gain political power.

Unlike World War I, World War II was a war of movement, with the large-scale use of armor and motorized infantry units.

4. The World in Conflict _____

While the United States was trying to pull out of the Great Depression, European and Asian nations were trying to recover from the effects of World War I. In the process, several turned to undemocratic governments. In 1922, Benito Mussolini set himself up as an absolute dictator in Italy. In the early 1930's, Adolf Hitler did likewise in Germany, militarists took control in Japan, and Joseph Stalin tightened his hold on the Soviet Union. Soon, world peace once again was threatened.

4.1 The Beginnings of War. In 1935, Italy invaded the African country of Ethiopia. A year later, in violation of the Versailles Treaty, the German army marched into the demilitarized Rhineland. By 1938, Hitler's intent to make Germany master of Europe became clearer with the occupation of Austria and the demand that the German-speaking Sudetenland of Czechoslovakia be made part of Germany.

Like Mussolini, Hitler rose to power by promising to restore the country to a position of world prominence. As leader of the Nazi party, he gained popular support by appealing to national pride and by blaming Germany's problems on the Jews. Once in power, he and the Nazis began a systematic campaign to destroy the Jewish people. In time, most were forced into *concentration camps* (prison camps) where ultimately over 6 million were killed.

At the same time Germany was making aggressive moves in Europe, Japan was seeking to expand its power in Asia. In 1931, it invaded Manchuria and set up a "puppet government." Then, in 1937, it attacked China proper.

The western democracies did little to halt this growing aggression. In fact, British and French leaders appeased Hitler by signing the Munich Pact, which allowed a takeover of Czechoslovakia in 1938. But then, when Hitler broke his pledge and ordered German forces to invade Poland in September 1939, Great Britain and France did declare war. Not much occurred until the spring of 1940, when the German army launched a *blitzkrieg,* or lightning war. Within weeks, the Germans swept through Denmark, the Netherlands, Belgium, and Norway. By June, France had surrendered, and Britain was left alone to fight the Germans.

During the 1930's, many Americans were against being drawn into another war in Europe. By 1939, however, most supported aiding the Allies (Britain, France, and later the Soviet Union). In 1940, the United States gave the British 50 destroyers in return for rights to lease naval and air bases in the Caribbean. Then, following reelection to a third term, Roosevelt persuaded Congress to pass a Lend Lease Act that made it possible for the Allies to obtain armaments on credit.

Meanwhile, in Asia, Japan continued to expand. Fearful for its Pacific bases, the United States placed an embargo on war materials being exported to Japan. At about the same time, Congress passed the nation's first peacetime draft. The Japanese move into French Indochina in 1941 strained Japanese-American relations even further.

Have students consider the reasons people of Japanese ancestry were sent to relocation centers while those of German and Italian ancestry were not.

Production of such goods as household appliances and automobiles was halted from 1942 to 1945.

While talks were going on between the two nations, Japanese militarists were making plans for war. On December 7, 1941, Japanese naval and air forces launched a sneak attack against Pearl Harbor. The next day, Roosevelt sought and got a declaration of war against Japan. Three days later, Congress recognized that a state of war also existed with Japan's Axis allies, Germany and Italy.

4.2 America at War. Following Pearl Harbor, Japanese forces quickly swept through Malaya, invaded the Dutch East Indies, and captured the Philippines and other Pacific islands. Two important naval battles—Coral Sea and Midway—stopped the Japanese advance toward Australia and Hawaii. Meanwhile, German and Italian troops were making gains in Europe and Africa. British troops at El Alamein finally prevented the Axis powers from taking Egypt and the Suez Canal, while the Soviet Union, which had been attacked in June of 1941, halted the German push into Russia at Stalingrad.

On entering the war, American leaders recognized that the major war effort needed to be directed toward Germany's defeat. Once again, the federal government took the lead in mobilizing the nation. In early 1942, the Office of Price Administration (OPA) was created to set prices and to control consumption. The War Production Board (WPB) was set up to supervise industrial production. In its zeal to protect America, however, the government mistreated people of Japanese ancestry living on the West Coast by moving over 100,000 to *relocation centers* (internment camps) in the interior of the country.

Wartime shortages led to rationing. Tires, for example, were salvaged in a drive to collect and reuse rubber. What other controls were set up to help in the war effort?

The great demand for production ended the Great Depression. Because so many men were in the military, for the first time women went to work in war plants as riveters, welders, and the like. By 1944, war production had increased so greatly that American industry gave the Allies a decided advantage over the Axis in war materials.

Ways had to be found to raise funds to finance the war effort. Nearly 40 percent of the cost came from increased taxes. A goodly amount also came from the sale of war bonds.

4.3 Road to Victory. By the summer of 1942, the Allies began to strike back against the Axis. In the Pacific, the Americans launched an island-hopping, two-pronged offensive. In Africa, the British and Americans combined forces to drive the Germans out. In 1943, Allied forces crossed the Mediterranean, took Sicily, and attacked the Italian mainland. Meanwhile, the Rus-

Have students compare the size of the Normandy invasion with an operation of the American Revolution or the Civil War.

The League of Nations was officially disbanded in April 1946. Have students research more fully the two world organizations and compare them.

sians, after entrapping the entire German Sixth Army at Stalingrad, went on the offensive on the eastern front.

Pressed by Soviet leaders to open a second front sooner, Allied forces under the command of General Dwight Eisenhower finally launched a massive invasion of Western Europe on June 6, 1944 (D-Day). Within weeks, they broke through German coastal defenses at Normandy, raced across France, liberated Paris, and moved into Belgium.

The Germans made one last attempt to halt the Allied advance on the western front in December 1944. Their defeat in the resulting Battle of the Bulge opened the way for Allied forces to cross the Rhine into Germany. On April 25, 1945, American and Russian troops met at Torgau on the Elbe River. Two weeks later, on May 8, German military leaders agreed to unconditional surrender, and the war in Europe was over.

At the time the Allies were preparing to invade Western Europe, American forces were also moving forward in the Pacific. By the summer of 1944, they had captured several major island groups. Then, in October, forces under the command of General Douglas MacArthur recaptured the Philippines. The taking of Iwo Jima in February 1945, and Okinawa in April, gave the Americans bases from which to begin daily bombing raids on Japan.

In April, President Roosevelt died, and Harry Truman became President. Knowing how costly in American lives the invasion of Japan would be, Truman ordered the use of a new secret weapon—the atomic bomb. The destruction and killing caused by the bombing of Hiroshima on August 6, and

Nagasaki three days later, led the Japanese to surrender. On September 2, formal terms were signed aboard the battleship *Missouri,* and World War II ended.

4.4 Planning the Peace. Allied political leaders had met several times to discuss war strategies and plans for peace. In 1943, at Teheran, Iran, President Roosevelt, Prime Minister Winston Churchill, and Premier Joseph Stalin talked about setting up a new international organization to keep the peace once war was over. They met again in the Soviet town of Yalta on the Black Sea in early 1945 to formalize peace plans and set the date for a San Francisco conference to draw up the Charter for the United Nations. During the summer of 1945, Truman met with Churchill and Stalin at Potsdam, Germany. There the decision was made to divide Germany into four zones, with the United States, Great Britain, the Soviet Union, and France controlling one zone each. Berlin, which lay within the Soviet zone, was to be shared by all four Allied powers.

Delegates from 50 countries drew up the United Nations charter. The UN was organized into six *organs,* or parts—the General Assembly, the Security Council, the Economic and Social Council, the International Court of Justice, the Trusteeship Council, and the Secretariat. In 1946, it set up headquarters in New York City.

4.5 The Cold War in Europe. Cooperation between the western democracies and the Soviet Union began to break down soon after Potsdam. During 1946, rather than permitting free elections as pledged at Yalta, the Soviet Union set up satellite communist governments in Eastern Europe.

Reconstruction to the Present   419

The establishment of two governments in Germany marked the unofficial recognition of respective areas of control of Soviet and Allied governments.

The fighting in the Korean War was the first military action by the UN to stop aggression. Discuss the use of war to stop aggression.

The western powers viewed this as another Soviet attempt to spread communism. Tensions quickly evolved into a *cold war,* in which each side was willing to use any means short of military action to expand its influence.

In 1947, in the Truman Doctrine, the United States adopted a policy of *containment* to limit the spread of communism. The United States pledged to help any country in danger of being taken over by Communists. The same year, a plan was set forth to help restore Europe's economy. Known as the Marshall Plan, it offered economic aid to all European countries.

The chief struggle between the western powers and the Soviet Union came over Germany, where the western powers were trying to form a self-governing, economically strong German state. The Russians were against this. To force the western powers to alter their plans and withdraw from Berlin, the Russians blockaded all land and water routes into Berlin in June 1948. The western powers responded with an airlift to supply the city. In May 1949, the Russians lifted the blockade, and Germany was divided into two separate nations.

That same year, alarmed by a communist takeover in Czechoslovakia and the Berlin blockade, the United States and 11 other western democracies signed a treaty creating the North Atlantic Treaty Organization (NATO). They agreed that an attack on any one would be viewed as an attack on all. The Soviet Union responded by forming a similar pact with the communist nations of Eastern Europe.

4.6 Communism in Asia. Conflicts in the postwar world were also found in Asia.

Symboling the division caused by the Cold War is the Bradenburg Gate that is a major checkpoint between East and West Berlin. How has the Cold War affected American foreign policy?

In 1947, civil war erupted in China between Nationalists led by Chiang Kai-shek and Communists led by Mao Tse-tung. By 1949, the Communists gained control, setting up the People's Republic of China and driving the Nationalists to the island of Formosa, present-day Taiwan.

East-West tensions were further heightened by events in Korea. On June 25, 1950, the North Korean army invaded South Korea in an effort to unite the country under communist rule. Truman ordered the American military to support South Korea. The UN Security Council, calling on members to aid South Korea, created an international force under the command of General MacArthur. When UN forces drove the North Koreans across the 38th parallel, 250,000 Communist Chinese troops entered the fighting and drove them back south of the 38th parallel.

MacArthur wanted to attack China itself. Truman, not wanting to risk nuclear war with the Soviet Union, decided to maintain a limited war policy. When MacArthur objected, Truman replaced him. In the spring of 1951, UN troops again drove the communist forces north across the 38th parallel, where the war became bogged down in a stalemate. Finally, in July 1953, both sides agreed to an armistice, and the Korean War ended almost where it began—

at the 38th parallel. Some Americans were upset that no clear victory had been won. However, communist expansion in the Far East had been checked.

1. What event led to the outbreak of World War II?

2. What event brought the United States into World War II?

3. What caused the Japanese to surrender?

4. What event brought about the Korean War?

5. Contemporary America

Since the end of World War II, the United States has faced challenge and endured change. International crises, economic strains, domestic turmoil, and technological advancements have all played a part in shaping a society different from that of earlier times.

5.1 International Crises. In 1953, Dwight Eisenhower became President. Like Truman, he wanted to contain the spread of communism. He believed in a *domino theory* whereby the neighbors of a communist country in time would fall to communism. In 1954, to limit the spread of communism in Southeast Asia, he supported the United States joining Great Britain, France, Australia, New Zealand, Pakistan, and the Philippines to form the Southeast Asia Treaty Organization (SEATO). In 1957, fearful of events in the Middle East, he announced the Eisenhower Doctrine, in which he promised to aid any Middle Eastern nation threatened by communist attack. During his last year in office, he

broke off diplomatic relations with Fidel Castro's communist government in Cuba.

Meanwhile, the United States and the Soviet Union agreed to a policy of *coexistence*—recognition of the willingness of each to live in peace. In 1955, Eisenhower and other western leaders met with Soviet Premier Nikita Khrushchev in Geneva to discuss a softening of world tensions. Despite the Suez Crisis and Hungarian Revolt in 1956, tensions eased until 1960 when an American U-2 spy plane was shot down photographing Soviet military bases.

After Kennedy became President in 1961, Soviet-American relations worsened. That year, East Germany, with Russian backing, erected the Berlin Wall to prevent East Germans from fleeing to the West; and Cuban exiles, trained and supplied by the U. S. Central Intelligence Agency (CIA), attempted to invade Cuba. In 1962, when the Soviet Union began installing offensive missiles in Cuba, Kennedy ordered a naval quarantine. Khrushchev, however, finally

Since the middle to late 1950's, relations between the People's Republic of China and the Soviet Union had cooled, and by the late 1970's, the two were enemies. This perhaps prompted the two countries to seek better relations with the United States.

agreed to remove the missiles in exchange for an American pledge not to invade Cuba.

Soon American attention was again directed to Southeast Asia where, during the late 1950's, war had broken out in South Vietnam. Communist rebels, supported by communist North Vietnam, sought to overthrow the Diem regime. After Kennedy's assassination in 1963, President Lyndon Johnson steadily increased the amount of military support to South Vietnamese anticommunist forces. By 1968, over 500,000 American troops were taking part in the war.

When American opposition to the Vietnam War became extremely bitter,

Americans aided South Vietnam in its war against communist rebels. As the fighting went on, tens of thousands of refugees fled their homes seeking refuge from the ravages of war. What happened to South Vietnam after 1973?

Johnson declined to run for reelection. Nevertheless, the new President—Richard Nixon—continued to support the fighting while seeking a solution. Though he ordered American troops to invade Cambodia in 1970 and Laos in 1971 in an attempt to cut communist supply routes, he put forth a policy of *Vietnamization,* or the gradual withdrawal of American combat forces. In January 1973, a peace settlement finally was reached. But it did not prevent the North Vietnamese from reuniting the country under communism in 1975.

During the Vietnam War, the United States and Soviet Union began taking actions to improve relations. Under a policy of *détente,* or accommodation to relax Cold War tensions, they signed a Nuclear Nonproliferation Treaty and a Strategic Arms Limitation Treaty (SALT I). In 1969, Nixon became the first American President to visit Moscow. Three years later Nixon also was the first to visit the People's Republic of China, which the United States formally recognized in 1979.

In 1977, James Carter became President. He emphasized human rights and peaceful solutions to world problems. Through his efforts, Egyptian and Israeli leaders worked out a number of agreements that sought to reduce tensions in the Middle East. Carter also brought about a treaty to turn control of the Panama Canal over to Panama by the year 2000. In November 1979, however, hostile Iranian students seized the American embassy in Teheran and took 65 Americans as hostages, a crisis which Carter seemed unable to resolve.

In 1980, Ronald Reagan was elected President. Promising to concentrate less on human rights and more on reducing the dangers of terrorism, he announced a greatly expanded national defense program, reinstituted a hard-line approach with the Soviet Union, and openly supported Latin American governments favorable to the United States and hostile to communism.

5.2 Changing Economic Patterns. At the same time the United States was coping with international crises, it was also trying to deal with internal economic changes. When after World War II the nation changed from a wartime to peacetime economy, Truman wanted to carry on the programs of the New Deal. After his reelection in 1948, he proposed a Fair Deal, calling for federally sponsored programs in health care, education, and low-income housing, and increases in social security benefits.

In 1952, Eisenhower became the first Republican to be elected to the White House in 20 years. Though many Republicans wanted government to play a less active role in the economy, he made no move to end most social programs. Instead, he expanded social security and low-cost housing and launched a massive road-building program. At the same time, he supported private enterprise.

The idea of using federal power to raise the economic level of the people was renewed by Kennedy. Calling for a New Frontier, he advocated greater aid for health, education, and welfare. Johnson, in his plans for a Great Society, called for a "war on poverty" and got the Economic Opportunity Act passed to help the poor improve job skills and obtain a better education.

By the time Nixon became President in 1969, government spending, combined with the costs of the Vietnam War, had boosted prices to new levels. To stop inflation, Nixon announced a New Economic Policy aimed at cutting government spending and instituting voluntary wage and price controls. He announced a New Federalism, under which state and local governments took over many federal responsibilities. He also proposed *revenue sharing,* whereby the federal government turned over part of its revenue to state and local governments.

Despite the efforts of Nixon and his successor, Gerald Ford, inflation continued to rise. When some oil-producing countries forced up the cost of crude oil in 1973, prices rose even higher. This rising inflation, combined with high interest rates, the energy crisis, and rising unemployment, plagued President Carter, and his failure to control them helped lead to the 1980 election of Ronald Reagan.

Since the beginning of the New Deal, national economic policy had emphasized high taxes and large-scale government spending for social programs. Reagan, determined to limit the federal government's role, sharply cut personal income taxes; reduced the amount of federal money for health, education, and welfare; and urged private groups to provide more social services. He also put an end to government controls on and regulations of several industries, encouraged more mining and drilling for energy resources, and urged development of coastal waters and wilderness areas. In 1984, Reagan was reelected by a landslide that reflected his personal popularity and the impact of his economic policies.

Compare the Civil Rights Act of 1866 with the Civil Rights Act of 1964. Discuss why the 1964 law was necessary when it contained much the same as the first law.

Trace with the class the changing approach used by blacks to protest and improve their position in American society from the slave period to the 1960's.

5.3 Civil Rights and Social Unrest. After World War II, civil rights became an important national issue for the first time since Reconstruction. In 1946, President Truman appointed a Commission on Civil Rights which paved the way for major changes later.

The first change came with Eisenhower's appointment of Earl Warren as Chief Justice in 1953. Under Warren, the Supreme Court took a more liberal attitude toward decisions regarding individual rights. In 1954, in *Brown v. Board of Education of Topeka,* it ruled that segregated public schools were "inherently unequal" and thus unconstitutional. At first, southern whites protested the decision, but after the federal government intervened to enforce court orders, it came to be accepted.

When it became clear, however, that court action alone would not end segregation, blacks and others turned to more direct action. In December 1955, Dr. Martin Luther King, Jr., led a boycott against Montgomery (Alabama) city buses to end segregated seating. In 1960, black students began "sit-ins" in North Carolina to end segregation in restaurants and other businesses. In 1957 and 1960, to promote black voting rights, Congress passed Civil Rights Acts.

By the 1960's, the movement to improve equality for minorities gained momentum. The Twenty-fourth Amendment outlawed poll taxes for voting. The Warren Court handed down a number of decisions to protect the rights of accused people. The Civil Rights Act of 1964 made it illegal to discriminate against people in public places and in employment and set up the Equal Employment Opportunity Commission (EEOC) to investigate complaints. The Voting Rights Act did away with literacy tests for voters and allowed federal officers to register people to vote in areas where local authorities were keeping them from doing so. And the Open Housing Act of 1968 barred discrimination in the sale and rental of housing.

The gains made in civil rights did not come about easily. Throughout the 1960's and much of the 1970's, activists led demonstrations supporting one cause or another. Some were peaceful, like the massive March

Martin Luther King, Jr., spoke of his dream for American blacks during the March on Washington in 1963. What civil rights acts were passed in the 1960's to protect rights of blacks?

Sandra Day O'Connor (1930-   )
Geraldine A. Ferraro (1935-   )

═══PROFILE═══

A little over 100 years ago Justice Joseph Bradley denied a woman a license to be a lawyer because, he said, a woman should fulfill her mission in life as a home maker. Sandra Day O'Connor and Geraldine A. Ferraro believed women can be successful career people as well as homemakers. Both became lawyers, raised families, and took steps women had not taken before.

O'Connor grew up in the Southwest and went to Stanford University Law School. She served as a county attorney in California and later, with her husband and three sons, settled in Arizona to open a law office there. In 1965, she became assistant attorney general for Arizona. From 1969 to 1974, she served as a state senator and became the first woman to be voted majority leader of a state legislature.

In 1974 O'Connor was elected to the Maricopa County Superior Court. She held that post until 1979, when she was appointed to the Arizona Court of Appeals. In September, 1981, O'Connor was appointed by President Reagan to the United States Supreme Court.

Geraldine Ferraro grew up in the East. She graduated from Marymount College and put herself through Fordham University Law School while teaching elementary school. Ferraro and her husband live in New York City where they raised three children. In 1974, she was hired as an assistant district attorney. In 1978, Ferraro was elected to the House of Representatives where she served through 1984.

In June 1984, Geraldine Ferraro was nominated as the Democratic candidate for the Vice Presidency. Though defeated in the general election, she conducted her campaign with vigor and dignity.

O'Connor's appointment to the Supreme Court and Ferraro's nomination for the Vice Presidency by a major political party broke traditions that had been in existence since the formation of the federal government. Each was the first woman to be so honored. Their actions marked yet another step in the struggle of women for full equality in the United States.

Have students see the text of the Twenty-fifth Amendment in the Appendix.

Have students recall the concept of sectionalism on page 339, and have them consider if there are any sectional issues of importance today.

on Washington in 1963, where over 200,000 gathered at the Lincoln Memorial to hear Dr. King's dreams for American blacks. Others resulted in violence, rioting, and destruction.

Not all protests of the 1960's were directed at securing rights for blacks, however. Hispanics, women, and others organized to obtain greater equality. Nor were all protests directed solely at expanding civil rights. Many demonstrations were conducted by anti-war activists protesting America's involvement in Vietnam.

Social unrest peaked during the Nixon administration. Most Americans were shocked to learn that the President was involved in a political coverup that came to be known as the Watergate Affair. The affair began in 1972 when burglars, acting under orders from White House staff members, broke into Democratic committee headquarters. Disclosures made in the Senate investigation that followed led to House impeachment proceedings in 1974. These, in turn, resulted in Nixon being the first President to resign office, and Gerald Ford being the first President never elected to the Presidency or Vice Presidency.

5.4 A Changing Society. Since World War II, the United States has experienced a technological revolution. During the late 1940's, television came of age as a new medium for entertainment and communication. By the 1960's, events occurring anywhere could be viewed by Americans as they were happening.

In 1957, the Soviet Union shocked the American scientific community by successfully launching an artificial satellite into orbit around the earth. In response, the National Aeronautics and Space Administration (NASA) was established in 1958. By 1969, when Neil Armstrong took "one step for man, one giant leap for mankind" by stepping onto the moon, it reached the goal set by President Kennedy.

Other scientists, meanwhile, were finding cures for such life-threatening diseases as polio. Still others were creating new inventions that would automate manufacturing processes and alter business procedures and practices. Perhaps no invention has had greater impact on American business than the computer. With the advent of the automatic copying machine, micro-computer, and word processor, businesses entered the "age of electronics."

At the same time the nation was advancing technologically, other factors were affecting American life. During the postwar years, millions of Americans began moving to the suburbs. Soon, shopping malls and office complexes dotted the countryside. Suburban living was different than urban life. People, for example, became more dependent on the automobile as the basic means of transportation, and the road system grew rapidly.

The mass exodus to the suburbs caused hardships for many cities, especially industrial centers in the Northeast and Midwest. Left with a high percentage of the unemployed, poor, and aged, they faced ever-increasing demands for costly social services and renewal projects. In addition, many people began moving from colder climates to the *sun belt* (warm, sunny regions of the United States). By the 1960's, California replaced New York as the most populous

This is a good place to point out that the diversity in American society, as reflected in politics, styles of living, and the composition of the population, is reflected in a diverse culture.

Discuss the word "trend." Review in detail the various areas in American life in which trends seem to be evident.

James Irwin commanded the 1971 Apollo 15 mission that landed on the moon. Here he appears with a lunar rover completing experiments. Besides space achievements, what other scientific advances are part of the nation's technological revolution?

heritage, beliefs, and ideas. This diversity was reflected in the arts. Not only did authors like Alex Haley in *Roots* and Betty Friedan in *The Feminine Mystique* portray sharply the needs and feelings of different groups, but literature itself became more diversified—from action-packed spy stories to futuristic science fiction.

Like literature, American music and painting came in many different styles and treated many different themes. By the 1960's, rock and country-western music became Big Business. Abstract Expressionism produced one of the first American art styles to have impact worldwide.

In addition to becoming diverse, American culture become popularized both at home and abroad. Professional sports are now Big Business, and more Americans than ever before are participating in physical fitness activities. Travel for pleasure and business is commonplace.

state, and cities like Houston, Dallas, Los Angeles, Phoenix, and San Antonio were among the twenty largest.

Changes in basic life-styles were also reflected by cultural changes. New groups entered the country, each bringing its own

1. Since World War II, at what has much of American foreign policy been directed?
2. How does Reagan differ from most of his post-World War II predecessors regarding economic policy?
3. What gains were made in civil rights during the 1960's?
4. How has American society changed since World War II?

Conclusion

Today the United States faces a great many challenges. These range from social issues, such as poverty, to economic ones, such as budget deficits. Some challenges, like the need to provide equal rights and

opportunities for all Americans, are not new. All, however, point up the need for change—a factor to which Americans have been exposed and have adjusted since the country's beginnings.

Conclusion Review

Main Points

1. The growth of industry created both new opportunities and new problems for the American people.
2. Reform efforts to correct problems that resulted from the growth of industry took place on the local, state, and federal levels.
3. America became a world power as a result of the Spanish-American War.
4. The United States entered World War I in 1917 to make the world safe for democracy.
5. The development of new industries contributed to the economic boom of the 1920's.
6. The Great Depression began in 1929 and lasted through the 1930's.
7. Roosevelt's New Deal included emergency measures to provide relief and recovery and long-range measures to prevent future depressions.
8. The Japanese attack on Pearl Harbor brought the United States into World War II. It took nearly four years from then to defeat the Axis powers.
9. Tensions between the United States and the Soviet Union evolved into a cold war.
10. Since World War II, much of American foreign policy has centered on containing the spread of communism.
11. Since World War II, the nation has endured economic and domestic strains, and technological advancements.

Building Vocabulary

1. Identify the following:

"Jim Crow" laws	Harlem Renaissance	Hiroshima
John D. Rockefeller	Great Depression	United Nations
Progressives	New Deal	Great Society
Theodore Roosevelt	Franklin Roosevelt	New Federalism
Versailles Treaty	TVA	Dr. Martin Luther King, Jr.

2. Define the following:

segregation	workman's compensation	intolerant	cold war
corporations	armistice	jazz	containment
trusts	spheres of influence	social security	domino theory
laissez-faire	big stick diplomacy	concentration camps	coexistence
secret ballot	corollary	blitzkrieg	Vietnamization
settlement houses	dollar diplomacy	relocation centers	détente
muckrakers	selective service	organs	revenue sharing
direct primary			sun belt

Remembering the Facts

1. How did southern state governments prevent blacks from voting in the late 1800's?
2. What made large-scale industrialization possible after the Civil War?
3. What efforts were made to regulate big business in the late 1800's?
4. What were some of Wilson's ideas for the peace treaty in 1918?
5. What was a major reason for the nation's prosperity during the 1920's?
6. How were Americans affected by the Great Depression?
7. What part did women play during World War II?
8. What caused the Cold War?
9. How did blacks attempt to gain their civil rights during the 1950's and 1960's?
10. What technological changes have occurred that changed our society since World War II?

Understanding the Facts

1. How have the lives of black Americans changed between 1877 and the present?
2. What was American foreign policy based on during the early 1900's? Has it changed over the years? How?
3. Was the progressive movement successful in bringing about reform? Why or why not?
4. How do Reagan's economic policies differ from those of Roosevelt's New Deal?
5. Do you think the tactics of protest groups used in the 1960's and 1970's were effective? Why or why not?
6. How do life-styles in the 1920's compare with those of today?

Using Maps

Thematic Maps. Thematic maps can show a variety of information about an area. It can be political, social, cultural, or economic, in addition to geographic. The map on page 415 shows the distribution of industry and agriculture in the United States. Industrial areas are shown with symbols. Agricultural areas are color keyed. Use the map to answer the following questions.

1. What seems to be the main industry of the South?
2. Where is the center of meat-packing activity located?
3. Why are meat-packing plants close to the areas of cattle and hogs?
4. What is the principal industry of the Rocky Mountain area?
5. Where does there appear to be more industry than agriculture?

Houston 1960-1985

Located 50 miles (80 kilometers) inland from the Gulf of Mexico, Houston has grown from a small ranch town into a large American city. Once green with trees and grass, it has become a mass of concrete, steel, and glass in just a short time. Old buildings stand in the shadows of new high-rise apartments, stores, and offices. The city has grown outward in all directions.

The Beginning

John and Augustus Allen founded Houston in 1836. They named the new town after Sam Houston, commander of the Texas forces and president of the Republic of Texas. For a while, the town was the capital of Texas.

Houston, like other towns, had large areas of rich land where cotton could be grown. Nearby forests were good sources for building materials. Narrow marshy channels of water called bayous surrounded Houston, making water transportation possible. Later, when railroads were built, the city was on the main route between New Orleans and the West.

A Seaport

Realizing a need for better transportation of goods, business people early in the twentieth century started a campaign to collect funds to widen the Buffalo Bayou. This was a channel of marshy land leading to the Gulf of Mexico. Over many years, business people gradually gained what they wanted—a deeper waterway. This waterway was called the Houston Ship Channel. Beginning in 1914, large oceangoing vessels could load and unload in Houston.

The Houston Ship Channel has been widened and deepened twice since its opening. Walter Farnsworth was captain of the first oceangoing ship to go through the channel. He looked at it 40 years later:

Over there was a cemetery. . . . They must have moved it to straighten the channel. And see that sugar and molasses plant [factory], *that was all red clay. And when we got into port they had to tie up our lines to trees, and took eight days to unload our cargo. It's all a little hard to believe now.*

From Houston, ships carried cargoes of cotton, lumber, and sometimes rice to many countries. With the discovery of oil in fields near the city, petroleum and products made from it became the largest cargo.

Other industries producing metals, electronic equipment, machinery, and foods, moved to Houston. The costs of fuel, raw materials, and transportation were lower there than in many other areas of the country. Wages were also lower, but so was the cost of living. For these reasons, both workers and business leaders moved to Houston in large numbers.

Space City, U.S.A.

In 1961, Houston was chosen by the National Aeronautics and Space Administration (NASA) to be the site for a new center for the government program for putting astronauts into space. The city was chosen because it had excellent land, air, and sea transportation available. The seaport "provided an excellent means of transporting bulky space vehicles to other NASA locations, especially Cape Canaveral." The airport offered all-weather jet service. The warm climate of southeastern Texas permitted year-round outside work. Many local industries could provide needed supplies, and engineers, scientists, and other skilled workers already lived in the area. There were many universities and research laboratories in the city.

President John Kennedy visited the Space Center after construction began in 1962. He said:

[During the next five years] *your city will become the heart of a large scientific and engineering community. . . .* [In that time] *the National Aeronautics and Space Administration expects to double the number of scientists and engineers in this area. . . .*

His prediction came true. Rice University became the first school in the nation to have a department of Space Science. Many more industries and science firms moved to the city. New jobs were created. NASA workers

Houston registered a 31 percent population gain in the 1960's. Its growth, however, has been constant since its founding in 1836. What industries and improvements have contributed to Houston's growth?

Technicians at the Johnson Space Center follow the progress of a spacecraft on their monitors. When was Houston selected as the site for the space center?

and others moved into the area. Houston became known as "Space City, U.S.A."

The People of Houston

A large number of the people living in Houston have come from other parts of Texas and the United States. Some have come from other countries. Since so many people of different cultures live in the city, organizations have been formed to help them. One example is the League of United Latin American Citizens (LULAC). It was founded in the 1950's to help Mexican Americans, Latin Americans, and other Spanish-speaking citizens adjust to life in the United States.

The major goal of the LULAC is to help stop discrimination and prejudice against these citizens. This is partly done by helping people find jobs and helping them learn English. The "School of 400" was started to help Spanish-speaking children learn at least

400 English words. The LULAC also gives scholarships to students going to college or technical school.

Blacks in Houston in the 1960's and 1970's still worked at less-skilled, lower-paying jobs and lived in the poorest housing in the city. But the growing awareness of the civil rights movement helped to improve people's lives in many ways. In 1980, two women and a Mexican American man were elected to Houston's city council for the first time. Two new black members were also elected to the council. Although there were still barriers, blacks and other minority groups began to advance professionally and politically.

Taking the Opportunity

The rise of Barbara Jordan to national prominence was one example of the new opportunities for women and blacks in the 1960's and 1970's. Born in Houston in 1936, Jordan is the daughter of a Baptist minister who also worked as a warehouse clerk. Jordan went through the segregated schools of Houston. She was an outstanding student at Texas Southern University and then attended Boston University Law School. Looking back on her childhood, Jordan said:

When I was growing up, we didn't focus on being poor and black. Segregation was there. It was the way of life, and if you were fortunate and would just drive hard enough, you might be able to break out of it a little bit.

In 1962, Jordan ran for the Texas House of Representatives and lost. She learned that "It was necessary to be backed by money, power, and influence." She commented:

I considered abandoning the dream of a political career in Texas and moving to some section of the country where a black woman

candidate was less likely to be considered a novelty. I didn't want to do this. I am a Texan; my roots are in Texas. To leave would be a cop-out. So I stayed, and 1966 arrived.

In 1966, Jordan had gained the needed support and was elected to a seat in the Texas Senate. Barbara Jordan was the first black to be elected to such a seat since 1883. She was a hardworking member of the state senate and won election to the United States House of Representatives in 1972. Looking back, she said, "I'm glad I stayed in Texas."

Always Growing

Constant building has been the chief characteristic of Houston. New people meant more building, and the city was always growing. When the city's population reached 1 million in the 1950's, Jesse Jones, a Texas millionaire who helped to build Houston, commented:

I always said that someday Houston would be the Chicago of the South and it is. Railroads built this town, the port made it big, cotton and cattle kept it rich, oil boomed it, and now we're the chemical capital of the world. Growing, growing, growing, that's Houston.

Houston continued to grow into the 1980's. One news magazine reported:

It's Boomtown, U.S.A.—the fastest-growing city in the country and a dazzling

The oil industry in Texas began not far from Houston at Spindletop Spring in 1901. Today, oil refineries continue to be built in the area. How has oil made Houston a boomtown?

monument to free enterprise. It has low taxes, low unemployment and a high-rise downtown that has turned Houston into the industrial and cultural capital of the Sun Belt. Every week, more than 1,000 new residents stream into this Klondike-on-the-bayou, and it may soon pass Philadelphia as the nation's fourth largest city. But some Texas-size headaches are developing in Houston. "The '70's were boom years and we were able to keep booming without many problems," says city-council member Ben Reyes. "Now, we'll either have to act or let the city start deteriorating."

The city and other nearby local governments helped attract industry to the Houston area through favorable tax policies. They also made it easier for people to build in Houston by not having any zoning laws. Anyone could put up buildings, shopping centers, or factories wherever they could buy land. Houston has been the only large American city without zoning laws.

No zoning means little, if any, planning, and this has caused problems for Houston. Every year, floods cause millions of dollars worth of damage. There is no city-wide plan to control such flooding. There are no city or state income taxes, and property taxes are very low. With little money and a city sprawling in every direction, city services such as fire and police protection are spread very thin. City officials admit that 25 percent of Houston's streets are unlighted, 400 miles (640 kilometers) are unpaved, and 29 percent of the poor live in substandard housing.

The Astrodome is the world's first all-purpose, air-conditioned, domed stadium. It rises 208 feet above the flat plains and is surrounded by more than 30,000 parking spaces. How has the automobile affected Houston?

Houston's skyline is mostly the result of recent construction. How do these clean-lined skyscrapers contrast with conditions in other parts of the city that have resulted from Houston's rapid physical growth?

Welfare payments are $40 per child per month.

Traffic is another major problem for Houston in the 1980's. "This is not a city for pedestrians," an economist wrote. "It was built for people on wheels." Public transportation service has been poor because 95 percent of the people in Houston use cars. Despite efforts to improve service, city buses carry fewer and fewer passengers as they move slowly among the many automobiles. A newspaper writer said, "A kingly elephant hemmed in by a flood of . . . mice could feel no more helpless than a bus driver in downtown traffic."

Many attempts have been made to solve Houston's traffic problems. One solution is called "CarShare." Drivers with similar schedules and needs are matched by a computer so they can form car pools.

As a rapidly growing city of the space age, Houston has had many problems. But it also has many advantages. Its economy is very strong and the resources to solve the problems are available. It is truly "Boomtown, U.S.A."

1. How was Houston started?
2. What helped industry to grow in Houston?
3. Why was the city selected for the Space Center?
4. What has caused problems for Houston?
5. What are some of the problems Houston must face?
6. Why is Houston called "Boomtown, U.S.A."?

Epilogue

The Epilogue provides a concise wrap-up for the students to this course of American history by outlining some of the major changes which have occurred in the development of the American nation.

For nearly 400 years, Americans experienced periods of political, economic, and social change. In spite of enormous challenges, they adapted to preserve a spirit of independence and to protect an ideal for democratic government.

During the 1600's and 1700's, most Americans lived on farms of varying size scattered along the Atlantic coast of North America. Colonial life centered around small villages and towns. Only a few larger cities served as trade centers. From this rural, agrarian society came one nation in 1776. With the Constitution, life in America reorganized around federal and state capitals, and concerns slowly became more national.

By the early 1800's, not only was American political life changing but also American economic life was changing. Labor that had been done mostly by hand or animal power was being done with the force of steam. By the 1900's, electricity and gasoline power provided the force to drive machines. Steamboats, trains, automobiles, and airplanes became the products of a continuing industrial revolution in the United States.

As the United States aged, it grew dramatically. The lure of the country's natural resources—land, lumber, water, minerals—drew more people to the United States and across the continent that the country occupied. Total population rose, the number of cities increased, and American life continued to change. From a small, rural republic, the United States grew into an industrial giant with worldwide influence and concerns.

The attitudes of the American people kept pace with the physical expansion of the country. Americans believed progress and opportunity were unlimited. By the twentieth century, Americans called for equality for all people. Many thought that it was within the power of the United States to abolish poverty, wipe out hunger and disease, and see that all people were secure in their old age. They sought an American dream for the world.

But continued opportunity had its challenges. Midway through the twentieth century, perhaps signaled by the explosion of the atomic bomb in 1945, the United States entered a new phase. After a history of plenty, Americans began to experience scarcity. Once again the American people have had to adapt to preserve and protect their ideals and principles to the realities of a changing world.

Readings

After the Ice Age   438
Secrets of the Mayas   438
An Indian's View   439
Columbus Sees America   439
Cortés Meets Montezuma   440
Marquette on the Mississippi   441
Lost Colony Mystery Solved?   442
Discovering an Edible America   443
Religious Toleration in Maryland   444
City Life   445
Massachusetts School Law   446
Albany Plan of Union   447
Disunity in the Colonies   447
The Edenton Tea Party   448
In the Name of Liberty   449
Debate on American Independence   449
Winter at Valley Forge   451
Northwest Ordinance   452
Objections to the Constitution   453
Federalist Number 15   454
Popular Sovereignty   455
The United States Constitution
  as a Model for Other Nations   456
Judicial Review   457
Washington's First Inaugural   458
Hamilton's Opinion
  on the Bank Issue   459
Jefferson's Opinion
  on the Bank Issue   460

Lewis and Clark Journals   461
Our National Anthem   461
The Monroe Doctrine   462
In Defense of American Ways   463
Jackson's Inaugural   464
Nullification Ordinance   465
Trail of Tears   466
The Liberator   467
For a National Language   468
Temperance Crusade   469
Working Women of Lowell   470
On the National Road   471
City Tenant Housing   472
Narcissa Whitman's Diary   472
Travis's Last Appeal   474
Smallpox Destroys the Mandans   475
Rebirth of Slavery   475
Slave Auction   476
"Darling Nelly Gray"   477
In Defense of the South   478
On the Eve of War   478
A Patriotic Song of the South   479
A Patriotic Song of the North   480
Civil War Medical Corps   481
Coming to Terms   482
Columbia in Ruins   483
Lincoln's Reconstruction Policy   484
Texas Rejoins the Union   486

UNIT I

Opportunity

The First Americans   1

After the Ice Age

It is sometimes difficult to imagine the changes that took place as a result of the Ice Age. The following passage describes the effects of the Ice Age on some of the animals in North America.

Musk-ox and reindeer . . . followed the Great Ice into the North forever. Various horses came—strange creatures with several toes—mammoths and mastodon, camels, giant bison, enormous bears. . . . Many returning animals remain, but these have disappeared. Some, like the mammoth, must have vanished just before the white man came. Indeed, it is by no means impossible that, while Columbus was skirting the American coast, the last of the mammoths were dying in Kentucky.

A few of the lesser glacial animals survive to this day in a few favored spots in the United States, which still approximate conditions of the Ice Age. The great [Kodiak] bear is one. Even more interesting is the little White Mountain butterfly, which, when the Great Ice was withdrawing, fluttered up into the colder air on Mount Washington in New Hampshire and one other peak—in Colorado. There, to this day, their descendants remain, the two colonies separated by thousands of miles, prisoners on the peaks which, to the little grey butterflies, are life-saving islands of cold amid the deadly warm air of the modern valleys. Nowhere else in North America does this strange winged relic of the Ice Age appear, until you reach Labrador, where it can still find the cold it grew to love in the days of the great glacier.

From John Bakeless, *The Eyes of Discovery* (Philadelphia: J. B. Lippincott Company, 1950), p. 18. Reprinted by permission.

Questions

1. What animals mentioned in the passage are familiar to you? Describe or draw them.
2. Why do you think many animals followed the glaciers or sought out cold climates?

Secrets of the Mayas

The Mayas' control of Middle America suddenly came to an end, and no one knows for certain why. There have been many suggestions, however. One theory has been presented by Maya specialist Richard Adams of the University of Texas at San Antonio. Adams's theory is based on the existence of a sophisticated network of canals built by the Mayas.

The ancient canal system represented a vast improvement over the "slash and burn" agriculture practiced by many tropical societies. Slash-and-burn farmers cut down all the trees in a region, burned them to deposit minerals in the soil and cultivated the area for one or two years before moving on. The Maya method, in contrast, permitted long-term high yields of corn, beans, squash and other crops. Maya farmers dug series of two parallel canals in swamplands, throwing the excavated earth onto the space between the canals to form raised, level islands of soil. The technique provided plants with just the right amount of water, while channeling away excess moisture that would otherwise have caused roots to rot.

Space technology made the discovery possible. Looking for Maya sites, archeologists flew over the thick jungles in a plane carrying a radar device originally designed to map the surface of Venus. The radar scan revealed an enormous lattice of gray lines [exposing the canals]. "There were intricate patterns all over Guatemala," says Walter Brown of the Jet Propulsion Laboratory in Pasadena, Calif., which developed the radar. . . .

Archeologists caution that considerable fieldwork remains before the new find is fully confirmed. Still, they are already speculating that it might provide clues to the other major Maya mystery—why the civilization declined so [rapidly]. Adams suggests that the canal network implies the existence of a centralized bureaucracy, which might have broken down swiftly in the face of drought, flood, warfare or other calamities. But whatever the cause of the Maya collapse, the complex system of waterways may have helped to keep the civilization alive for centuries.

Adapted from "The Mayas' Secret: A Canal Network," *Newsweek*, June 16, 1980, p. 46. Reprinted by permission.

Questions

1. Why did the Mayas build canals?
2. What does Adams suggest was the relationship between the canals and the collapse of the Mayas' civilization?

An Indian's View

Many of the earliest inhabitants of North America created stories to explain how they came to live in a particular area. The following selection is from the legends of the Lakota people of the Great Plains. It was written down in the 1930's by Chief Luther Standing Bear.

Our legends tell us that it was hundreds and perhaps thousands of years ago since the first [person] sprang from the soil in the midst of the great plains. The story says that one morning long ago a lone man awoke, face to the sun, emerging from the soil. Only his head was visible, the rest of his body not yet being fashioned. The man looked about, but saw no mountains, no rivers, no forests. There was nothing but soft and quaking mud, for the earth itself was still young. Up and up the man drew himself until he freed his body from the clinging soil. At last he stood upon the earth, but it was not solid, and his first few steps were slow and halting. But the sun shone and ever the man kept his face turned toward it. In time the rays of the sun hardened the face of the earth and strengthened the man and he bounded and leaped about, a free and joyous creature. From this man sprang the Lakota nation and, so far as we know, our people have been born and have died upon this plain; and

Indian scouts view a European ship.

no people have shared it with us until the coming of the European. So this land of the great plains is claimed by the Lakotas as their very own. We are of the soil and the soil is of us.

From Chief [Luther] Standing Bear, *Land of the Spotted Eagle* (Boston: Houghton Mifflin Co., 1933), pp. 44-45. Reprinted by permission.

Questions

1. For most of the people of North America, the holiness of the land was very important. Why was this true?
2. What was the Lakotas' claim to the land of the Great Plains?

New World— 2
New Opportunities

Columbus Sees America

On October 9, 1492, Christopher Columbus made a promise to his crew. He said that if land was not found within three days, he would turn back to Spain. After the next two days, land had not yet been sighted. But signs of land, such as tree branches and flowers, floated near the expedition's three ships. The following selection by historian Samuel Eliot Morison describes the events of October 11 and 12, 1492, when the Columbus expedition saw land in America for the first time.

At 10 P.M. [on October 11], an hour before moonrise, Columbus and a [sailor], almost simultaneously, thought they saw a light "like a little wax candle rising and falling." Others said they saw it too, but most did not; and after a few minutes it disappeared. Volumes have been written to explain what this light was or might have been. To a [sailor] it requires no explanation. It was an illusion, created by overtense watchfulness. When uncertain of your exact position, and straining to make a night landfall, you are apt to see imaginary lights and flashes and to hear nonexistent bells and breakers.

On rush the ships, pitching, rolling, throwing spray—white waves at their bows and white wakes reflecting the moon. *Pinta* is perhaps half a mile in the lead, *Santa María* on her port quarter, *Niña* on the other side. Now one, now another forges ahead, but they are all making the greatest speed of which they are capable. With the sixth glass of the night watch, the last sands are running out of an era that began with the dawn of history. A few minutes now and destiny will turn up a glass the flow of whose sands we are still watching. Not since the birth of Christ has there been a night so full of meaning for the human race.

At 2 A.M., October 12, Rodrigo de Triana, lookout on *Pinta,* sees something like a white cliff shining in the moonlight, and sings out, *Tierra! tierra!* "Land! land!" Captain Pinzón verifies the landfall, fires a gun as agreed, and shortens sail to allow the flagship to catch up. As *Santa María* approaches, the Captain General [Columbus] shouts across the rushing waters, "Señor Martín Alonso, you *did* find land! Five thousand maravedis for you as a bonus!"

Questions

1. What did Columbus and some of his crew see the night of October 11, 1492?

2. Why do you think Samuel Eliot Morison considers the sighting of America so important?

Cortés Meets Montezuma

The defeat of the Aztecs by Hernando Cortés and his soldiers brought Spanish control to the mainland of the Americas in 1519. Fifty years after the event Bernal Díaz, who served under Cortés, wrote an account of the conquest of Mexico. In the following excerpt, Díaz describes the first meeting between Cortés and Montezuma, the Aztec ruler.

When Cortés saw, heard, and was told that the great Montezuma was approaching, he dismounted from his horse, and when he came near to Montezuma each bowed deeply to the other. Montezuma welcomed our Captain, and Cortés, speaking through [his interpreter], answered by wishing him very good health. Cortés, I think, offered Montezuma his right hand, but Montezuma refused it and extended his own. Then Cortés brought out a necklace which he had been holding. It was made of those elaborately worked and colored glass beads . . . and was strung on a gold cord and dipped in musk to give it a good odor. This he hung round the great Montezuma's neck, and as he did so attempted to embrace him. But the great princes who stood round Montezuma grasped Cortés's arm to prevent him, for they considered this an indignity.

Then Cortés told Montezuma that it rejoiced his heart to have seen such a great prince, and that he took his coming in person to receive him and the repeated favors he had done him as a high honor. After this Montezuma made him another complimentary speech, and ordered two of his nephews who were supporting him, the lords of Texcoco and Coyoacan, to go with us and show us our quarters. Montezuma returned to the city with the other two kinsmen of his escort, the lords of Cuitlahuac and Tacuba; and all those grand companies of . . . dignitaries who had come with him returned also in his train. And as they accompanied their lord we observed them marching with their eyes downcast so that they should not see him, and keeping close to the wall as they followed him with great reverence. Thus space was made for us to enter the streets of Mexico without being pressed by the crowd.

Spanish interest in Mexico centered chiefly on the gold and other wealth of the Aztec people.

Who could now count the multitude of men, women, and [children] in the streets, on the roof-tops and in canoes on the waterways, who had come out to see us? It was a wonderful sight and, as I write, it all comes before my eyes as if it had happened only yesterday.

Adapted from Bernal Díaz, *The Conquest of New Spain*, J. M. Cohen, tr. (Baltimore: Penguin Books Inc., 1963), pp. 217-218. Reprinted by permission.

Questions

1. Describe the first meeting between Cortés and Montezuma.

2. Why do you think relations between the Aztecs and the Spanish were friendly?

Marquette on the Mississippi

Throughout the 1600's and 1700s, Jesuit missionaries lived and worked in New France. Every year, each Jesuit wrote a report of his activities. These reports made up a yearly Relation, *which was sent to the chiefs of the Jesuit community in France and Rome. Today, these* Relations *form the basis of what is known about discoveries, explorations, and conditions in North America before the interior of the continent was settled.*

Father Jacques Marquette wrote the following excerpt from the Jesuit Relations. *In 1673, Marquette and explorer Louis Joliet led an expedition in search of the Northwest Passage. Along the way, they became the first French to explore the Mississippi River.*

On the following day, the tenth of June, two Miamis who were given us as guides embarked with us, in the sight of a great crowd, who could not sufficiently express their astonishment at the sight of seven frenchmen, alone and in two Canoes, daring to undertake so extraordinary and so hazardous an Expedition.

We knew that, at three leagues from Maskoutens, was a River which discharged into Missisipi. We knew also that the direction we were to follow in order to reach it was west-southwesterly. But the road is broken by so many swamps and small lakes that it is easy to lose one's way, especially as the River leading thither is so full of wild oats that it is difficult to find the Channel. For this reason we greatly needed our two guides, who safely Conducted us to a portage of 2,700 paces, and helped us to transport our Canoes to enter That river; after which they returned home, leaving us alone in this Unknown country, in the hands of providence.

Thus we left the Waters flowing to Quebeq, 4 or 500 Leagues from here, to float on Those that would thenceforward Take us through strange lands. . . . After mutually encouraging one another, we entered our Canoes.

The River on which we embarked is called Meskousing [Wisconsin]. It is very wide; it has a sandy bottom, which forms various shoals that render its navigation very difficult. It is full of Islands Covered with Vines. On the banks one sees fertile land, diversified with woods, prairies, and Hills. There are oak, Walnut, and basswood trees; and another kind, whose branches are armed with long thorns. We saw there neither feathered game nor fish, but many deer, and a large number of cattle. Our Route lay to the southwest, and, after navigating about 30 leagues, we saw a spot presenting all the appearances of an iron mine; and, in fact, one of our party who had formerly seen such mines, assures us that The One which We found is very good and very rich. It is Covered with three feet of good soil, and is quite near a chain of rocks, the base of which is covered by very fine trees. After proceeding 40 leagues on This same route, we arrived at the mouth of our River; and, at 42 and a half degrees of latitude, We safely entered Missisipi on The 17th of June, with a Joy that I cannot Express.

From Reuben Gold Thwaites, ed., *The Jesuit Relations and Allied Documents: Travels and Explorations of the Jesuit Missionaries in New France 1610-1791* (Cleveland: The Burrows Brothers Company, 1900), Vol. 59, pp. 105 and 107. Original spelling included.

Questions

1. Of what value to future explorers was Marquette's detailed description of his voyage?

2. At approximately what degree of latitude does the Wisconsin River enter the Mississippi River? How can you explain Marquette's error?

English Settlement in North America   3

Lost Colony Mystery Solved?

For nearly four centuries the fate of Roanoke, England's first American colony, has intrigued the world. The letters CRO cut into a tree and the word CROATOAN carved into a doorpost remain the only clues to the whereabouts and condition of the settlers of the so-called "lost colony." Here Adolph Dial, chairman of the Department of American Indian Studies at Pembroke State University in North Carolina, and a Lumbee Indian, explores possibilities of what became of the Roanoke colonists.

Q Professor Dial, what happened to the Lost Colony? Did it really disappear without a trace?

A No. There is overwhelming evidence that after the colonists were left on their own and possibly faced starvation, they joined friendly Indians and eventually intermarried with them. Those Indians, now called the Lumbees, are centered in what is now southeastern North Carolina. Very strong oral tradition handed down from one generation to the next holds that the Lumbees are the colonists' descendants.

Q What evidence is there of that?

A For one thing, the Englishmen who returned to the site of the abandoned colony on Roanoke Island found the word CROATOAN carved in wood. The colony's returning governor, John White, took that as a sign the group had moved to an Indian area called Croatan, which was occupied by the Hatteras Indians, who are ancestors of the Lumbees. The notion seemed to be in keeping with a plan to move that White had discussed with the colonists three years earlier. White was not unduly concerned about the group's safety, but he was unable to locate them before a storm forced him to leave.

Q Were there contacts between the Lumbees and any other early settlers?

A Yes. An adventurous man named Morgan Jones claimed to have walked across the Carolinas in the 1660s, and he said he was captured and then befriended by Indians who spoke English. His description of the area sounds like Robeson County, N.C., the heart of the Lumbee settlement. Then when the first big wave of Scottish immigrants reached the Cape Fear Valley in the 1730s, they were astonished to find a group of English-speaking people already living there in European-style houses and tilling the soil in the European fashion. Many of them were blue-eyed and light-haired.

Those people had—and their descendants still have—English family names that were exactly the same as the lost colonists had, such as Brooks, Sampson, and Jones.

Q What happened to the language?

A They had apparently integrated so completely that, even though they continued to prize the Indian part of their heritage, too, they passed along the English language in the form that was spoken in the 16th century.

Nearly 100 years ago, historian Stephen Weeks studied this Robeson County group and was struck by their extraordinary old speech patterns. He noted that they began telling the old traditions this way: "Mon [man], my fayther told me that his fayther told him. . . ."

Q If all this has been known so long, why is there still a widespread idea that the Lost Colony was wiped out?

A It suits the purpose of some romantics who are more intrigued by a supposedly unsolved mystery than the facts. The legend defies the findings of travelers and historians who have been saying for hundreds of years that the descendants of the lost colonists were alive and well in North Carolina.

Q Are there any clues as to what happened to Virginia Dare, the first English baby born in America?

A Yes. The oral traditions are clear that her family survived and that the Dials around here may be her descendants. Even today, if you pronounce *Dare* with a Southern accent, it sounds very much like *Dial*. And I believe that I am a descendant of Virginia Dare, too.

Questions

1. On what does Professor Dial base his belief concerning the survival of the Roanoke colonists?

2. In addition to Dial's explanation, how else could you explain that the Lumbee Indians in the 1730's had European customs?

Discovering an Edible America

The North American continent amazed the first Europeans who saw it. Here was a beautiful place varied in landforms and rich in natural resources. In spite of all the hardships the early colonists endured, including starvation, they still found the energy to write down impressions of their new land. In the book, The Eyes of Discovery, *historian John Bakeless recounts the colonists' enthusiasm for discovering new edible foods. Bakeless also relates stories about dangers in experimenting with unknown American fruits and plants.*

Most of the fruits and plants pleased the colonists. They found "cherries," which were "much like a Damson." . . . Strawberries seemed "much fairer and more sweete then ours." . . . Some of the omnipresent wild grapes were nearly as big as English cherries. . . . William Strachey thought it wonderful "to behold the goodly vines. . . ."

[A number of Virginia colonists, however, who once] gathered a mess of young Jimson weed "for a boil'd Salad" were dangerously affected. A contemporary account says that they suffered from amnesia and temporary insanity for eleven days. . . .

[Other] colonists were not quite so painfully surprised by strange plants and strange fruit as was John Josselyn, who went out for a walk in the wild country near Scarborough, Maine, about 1638. On a tree, he "chanc't to spye a fruit as I thought like a pine Apple," which was "of an Ash Colour." It was a queer-looking fruit, to be sure, and remarkably big; but Josselyn had seen so many strange things in this new country that he was not greatly surprised. He grasped it—only to be stung by an emerging swarm of furious hornets, so severely that his companions could hardly recognize his swollen face. When he recovered from his stings, Josselyn pondered on the odd substance of which the big grey nest was made. It was, of course, paper, but Josselyn did not realize that: "Of what matter its made no man knows; Wax it is not, neither will it melt nor fry, but will take fire suddenly like Tinder."

From John Bakeless, *The Eyes of Discovery* (Philadelphia: J. B. Lippincott Company, 1950), pp. 191 and 193. Reprinted by permission.

Questions

1. With which kinds of fruits and plants were the colonists most likely to experiment?

2. Why do you think Josselyn did not recognize the material of the hornets' nest?

Religious Toleration in Maryland

The Maryland colony, which was settled mostly by Protestants, became a haven for Catholics. In time, conflicts between the two groups led to the passage of the Toleration Act of 1649. This colonial law was an important step toward religious freedom in America. As a result, Maryland became a refuge for many different Protestant sects as well as for Catholics.

Forasmuch as in a well-governed and Christian commonwealth, matters concerning religion and the honor of God ought in the first place to be taken into serious consideration and endeavored to be settled, *be it therefore ordered and enacted* . . . that whatsoever person or persons within this province and the islands thereunto belonging shall henceforth [speak disrespectfully about]

The first colonial legislature met in 1619.

God . . . or deny our Savior Jesus Christ to be the Son of God, or shall deny the Holy Trinity—the Father, Son, and Holy Ghost—or the Godhead or any of the said three Persons of the Trinity or the unity of the Godhead, . . . shall be punished with death and confiscation or forfeiture of all his or her lands and goods to the Lord Proprietary and his heirs. . . .

And whereas the enforcing of the conscience in matters of religion has frequently fallen out to be of dangerous consequence in those commonwealths where it has been practised, and for the more quiet and peaceable government of this province, and the better to preserve mutual love and amity among the inhabitants thereof, be it, therefore . . . ordered and enacted . . . that no person or persons whatsoever within this province . . . professing to believe in Jesus Christ, shall from henceforth be in any way troubled, molested, or discountenanced for or in respect of his or her religion, nor in the free exercise thereof . . . nor in any way compelled to the belief or exercise of any other religion against his or her consent, so as they be not unfaithful to the Lord Proprietary, or molest or conspire against the civil government. . . .

And that all and every person and persons that shall presume contrary to this act . . . directly or indirectly either in person or estate willfully to wrong, disturb, trouble, or molest any person whatsoever within this province professing to believe in Jesus Christ for, or in respect of, his or her religion . . . shall be compelled to pay [triple] damages to the party so wronged or molested, and for every such offense shall also forfeit 20 [shillings]. . . . Or if the party so offending shall refuse or be unable to recompense the party so wronged, or to satisfy such fine or forfeiture, then such offender shall be severely punished by public whipping and imprisonment.

Adapted from W. H. Browne, ed., *Proceedings and Acts of the General Assembly of Maryland, January 1637/8-September 1664* (Baltimore: 1883), Vol. 1, pp. 244-247.

Questions

1. How did the Maryland Toleration Act not provide freedom of religion to people of all faiths?

2. How did this law provide for equal protection for both men and women?

UNIT II

Independence

Colonial Society 4

City Life

Throughout the colonial period, America was primarily rural. By the 1700's, however, the number of towns began to increase. Towns attracted artisans and merchants and people of varied social classes. Although towns contained less than 10 percent of the colonial population, they had an important influence in America's early political, economic, and social life.

The typical colonial town had narrow streets, with the houses immediately bordering them. With the possible exception of Philadelphia, New Haven, and Charleston, the main streets were crooked, and the cross-streets did not intersect them at right angles. By the time of the Revolution most towns had named their streets and adopted a house-numbering system "for the benefit of strangers." Traffic problems mounted with the increased use of stagecoaches, private coaches, business carts, and other vehicles. . . .

[With the growth of towns,] problems emerged that affected the welfare of all the inhabitants. Prevention of fire was one, and laws concerning smoking, the type of building materials used, the regular cleaning of chimneys, and curfews had to be passed to safeguard lives and property. Generally, each town was divided into fire wards, with the residents volunteering to fight blazes in their vicinity. . . .

Police protection was another municipal problem. . . . Constables were the major law enforcement officials in the daytime, but after nightfall the male residents had to take their turn serving on "night watch.". . .

Lighting of the streets was always a problem, which helps to account for the greater need of a night watch. At first, the responsibility for lighting was placed upon the residents; for example, housekeepers were ordered to keep candles or lamps in their front windows during the winter months, and the owner of every seventh home had to have a lantern outside. As the eighteenth century progressed, however, town governments gradually assumed the task of street lighting.

From *Colonial America*, Second Edition, by Oscar Theodore Barck, Jr. and Hugh Talmage Lefler. Copyright © 1968 by Macmillan Publishing Company. Used by permission of the publisher.

Questions

1. What role did local government have in colonial towns?

2. Compare colonial practices of fire prevention and police protection with those currently used in your own town.

Massachusetts School Law

In most English colonies, education was closely related to religion. The first colleges—Harvard, William and Mary, and Yale—were established to train ministers. By the 1640's, however, a new approach to education was being taken in New England. This was the public school system.

In 1642, Massachusetts had passed the first American law requiring families in the colony to educate their children. The school law of 1647, which appears here, took an important step in developing the schools by requiring every town of 50 or more families to provide a teacher.

It being one chief project of that old deluder Satan to keep men from the knowledge of the Scriptures, as in former times by keeping them in an unknown tongue, so in these latter times by persuading from the use of tongues, that so at least the true sense and meaning of the original might be clouded by false glosses of saint-seeming deceivers, that learning may not be buried in the grave of our fathers in the church and commonwealth, the Lord assisting our endeavors:

It is therefore ordered that every township in this jurisdiction, after the Lord has increased them to the number of 50 householders, shall then forthwith appoint one within their town to teach all such children as shall resort to him to write and read, whose wages shall be paid either by the parents or masters of such children, or by the inhabitants in general, by way of supply, as the major part of those that order the prudentials of the town shall appoint; provided those that send their children be not oppressed by paying much more than they can have them taught for in other towns.

And it is further ordered that where any town shall increase to the number of 100 families or householders, they shall set up a grammar school, the master thereof being able to instruct youth so far as they may be fitted for the university, provided that if any town neglect the performance hereof above one year that every such town shall pay £5 to the next school till they shall perform this order.

From Nathaniel B. Shurtleff, ed., *Records of the Governor and Company of the Massachusetts Bay in New England* (Boston: 1853), Vol. 2, p. 203.

Questions

1. According to this law, why was it important for people to be able to read in Massachusetts?

2. Who paid the teachers in Massachusetts?

Albany Plan of Union

In the summer of 1754, delegates from seven colonies met at Albany, New York, to discuss the common defense of the American colonies. War with France was about to break out. During the meeting, Benjamin Franklin, who was concerned with overall colonial unity, presented a plan for intercolonial government. The plan shows that even before the Revolution, some colonial leaders favored an American federation. The following excerpts are from the Albany Plan of Union. This document holds some of the same ideas that are found in the United States Constitution. There are, however, major differences.

It is proposed that humble application be made for an act of Parliament of Great Britain, by virtue of which one general government may be formed in America, including all the said colonies, within and under which government each colony may retain its present constitution, except in the particulars wherein a change may be directed by the said act, as hereafter follows.

1. That the said general government be administered by a president-general, to be appointed and supported by the crown; and a Grand Council, to be chosen by the representatives of the people of the several colonies met in their respective assemblies. . . .

10. That the president-general, with the advice of the Grand Council, hold or direct all Indian treaties in which the general interest of the colonies may be concerned; and make peace or declare war with Indian nations. . . .

15. That they raise and pay soldiers and build forts for the defense of any of the colonies and equip vessels of force to guard the coasts and protect the trade on the ocean, lakes, or great rivers; but they shall not impress men in any colony, without the consent of the legislature.

16. That for these purposes they have power to make laws and lay and levy such general duties, imposts, or taxes as to them shall appear most equal and just (considering the ability and other circumstances of the inhabitants in the several colonies), and such as may be collected with the least inconvenience to the people; rather discouraging luxury than loading industry with unnecessary burdens. . . .

25. That the particular military as well as civil establishments in each colony remain in their present state, the general constitution notwithstanding; and that on sudden emergencies any colony may defend itself and lay the accounts of expense thence arising before the president-general and General Council, who may allow and order payment of the same, as far as they judge such accounts just and reasonable.

Adapted from Jared Sparks, ed., *The Works of Benjamin Franklin* (Boston: Tappan, Whittemore, and Mason, 1836), Vol. 3, pp. 36-55.

Questions

1. List three similarities of the Albany Plan and the United States Constitution.

2. How are those elements of the Albany Plan listed above different from elements of the Constitution?

Disunity in the Colonies

During the years 1759 and 1760, an English traveler named Andrew Burnaby visited the American colonies. After his return home to London, he wrote a book about his journey. It was published in the critical year of 1775. The following excerpt from Burnaby's book seems to reveal that the colonists were in no condition to unite against the British in a war for independence.

Fire and water are not more heterogeneous than the different colonies in North America. Nothing can exceed the jealousy and emulation which they possess in regard to each other. The inhabitants of Pennsylvania and New York have an inexhaustible source of animosity, in their jealousy for the trade of the Jerseys. Massachusetts Bay and Rhode Island, are not less interested in that of Connecticut. The West Indies are a common subject of emulation to them all. Even the limits and boundaries of each colony are a constant source of litigation. In short, such is the difference of character, of manners, of religion, of interest, of the different colonies, that I think, if I am not wholly ignorant of the human mind, were they left to themselves there would soon be a civil war from one end of the continent to the other; while the Indians and [blacks] would, with better reason, impatiently watch the opportunity of exterminating them all together.

From *Burnaby's Travels Through North America,* with Introduction and Notes by Rufus Rockwell Wilson (New York: A. Wessels Company, 1904), pp. 152-153.

Questions

1. According to Burnaby, what caused jealousy among the colonies?

2. What did Burnaby feel would be the final fate of the colonies?

3. Do you think Burnaby's readers in 1775 took the American Revolution seriously?

Winning Freedom 5

The Edenton Tea Party

The Tea Act of 1773, which gave the East India Company the sole right to sell tea directly to the colonies, angered nearly all Americans. In response to it, a number of "tea parties" followed. The most famous one took place in Boston. A tea party in North Carolina, however, had special significance.

The so-called Edenton Tea Party became one of the earliest instances of political activity on the part of women in the American colonies. On October 25, 1774, fifty-one women from five Carolina counties met at Edenton, North Carolina. Led by Penelope Barker, they signed a resolution supporting the action of the First Provincial Congress of North Carolina. The congress had adopted a plan not to drink British tea nor buy British-made clothing. The signed resolution was mailed to Britain where the London newspapers published it. The resolution also appeared in many colonial newspapers.

As we cannot be indifferent on any occasion that appears nearly to affect the Peace and Happiness of our Country, and as it has been thought necessary, for the publick Good, to enter into several particular Resolves, by a Meeting of Members deputed from the whole Province, it is a Duty which we owe, not only to our near and dear Connections, who have concurred in them, but to ourselves, who are essentially interested in their Welfare, to do every Thing as far as lies in our Power to testify our sincere Adherence to the same; and we do therefore accordingly subscribe this Paper, as a Witness of our fixed Intention and solemn Determination to do so.

Abigail Charlton	M. Payne
F. Johnston	Elizabeth Johnston
Margaret Cathcart	Mary Bonner
Anne Johnston	Lydia Bonner
Margaret Pearson	Sarah Howe
Penelope Dawson	Lydia Bennet
Jean Blair	Marion Wells
Grace Clayton	Anne Anderson
Frances Hall	Sarah Matthews
Mary Jones	Anne Haughton
Anne Hall	Elizabeth Beasley
Rebecca Bondfield	Mary Blount
Sarah Littlejohn	Elizabeth Creacy
Penelope Barker	Elizabeth Patterson
Elizabeth P. Ormond	Jane Wellwood

Mary Woolard	Sarah Vallentine
Sarah Beasley	Elizabeth Crickett
Susannah Vail	Elizabeth Green
Elizabeth Vail	Mary Ramsay
Elizabeth Vail	Anne Horniblow
Mary Creacy	Mary Hunter
Mary Creacy	Teresia Cunningham
Ruth Benbury	Elizabeth Roberts
Sarah Howcott	Elizabeth Roberts
Sarah Hoskins	Elizabeth Roberts
Mary Littledle	

From *Virginia Gazette,* November 3, 1774.

Questions

1. What were the women resolving to do?
2. Why do you think certain names appear more than once?

In the Name of Liberty

In the years preceding American independence, some colonists felt that Britain had been just in dealing with the colonies. These people were known as loyalists. Among the patriots, loyalists were very unpopular. Because of their political beliefs, loyalists were often persecuted in the name of liberty. The following account, taken from a letter written by a loyalist, describes a patriot attack on a loyalist family.

Between 12 & 1 o'Clock he was wakened by a knocking at the Door, he got up, enquired the person's name and business, who said he had a letter to deliver to him, which came Express from New York. My Brother puts on his Clothes, takes his drawn Sword in one hand, & opened the Parlor window with the other. The Man asked for a Lodging—said he [my brother], I'll not open my door, but give me the letter. The man then put his hand, attempting to push up the window, upon which my Brother hastily clamped it down, instantly with a bludgeon several violent blows were struck which broke the Sash, Glass & frame to pieces. The first blow aimed at my Brother's

Head, he Providentialy escaped, by its resting on the middle frame, being double, at the same time (though before then, no noise or appearance of more Persons than one) the lower windows, all round the House (excepting two) were broke in like manner. My Brother stood in amazement for a Minute or 2, & having no doubt that a number of Men had broke in on several sides of the House, he retired Upstairs.

You will believe the whole Family was soon alarmed, but the horrible Noises from without, & the terrible shrieks within the House from Mrs. H: & Servants which struck my Ears on awakening, I can't describe, & shall never forget.

I could imagine nothing less than the House was beating down, after many violent blows on the Walls & windows, most hideous Shouting, dreadful [curses], & threats ensued. Struck with terror & astonishment, what to do I knew not, but got on some Clothes, & went to Mrs. H: room, where I found the Family collected, a Stone thrown in at her window narrowly missed her head. When the Ruffians were retreating with loud [cheers] & one cried he will fire,—no says another, he daren't fire, we will come again says a third—Mr. and Mrs. H: left their House immediately & have not lodged a night since in it.

Adapted from Ann Hulton, *Letters of a Loyalist Lady* (Cambridge: Harvard University Press, 1927), pp. 22-24. Reprinted by permission. Original spelling included.

Questions

1. Why was the family and their home attacked?
2. What do you think the patriots were trying to accomplish?

Debate on American Independence

Richard Henry Lee presented a resolution for American independence to the Second Continental Congress on June 7, 1776. At that time, most members of Congress agreed that the colonists should eventually separate from Britain. However, they did not agree about when to declare their independence. The following excerpts from Thomas Jefferson's account of the congressional debates offer some insight into the concerns of the early Americans.

Saturday, June 8

It was argued . . . that, though they were friends to the measures themselves and saw the impossibility that we should ever again be united with Great Britain, yet they were against adopting them at this time; . . .

That the people of the middle colonies (Maryland, Delaware, Pennsylvania, the Jerseys, and New York) were not yet ripe for bidding [farewell] to British connection, but that they were fast ripening and in a short time would join in the general voice of America; . . .

That some of [the colonies] had expressly forbidden their delegates to consent to such a declaration, and others had given no instructions and, consequently, no powers to give such consent;

That if the delegates of any particular colony had no power to declare such colony independent, certain they were the others could not declare it for them, the colonies being as yet perfectly independent of each other; . . .

That if such a declaration should now be agreed to, these delegates must retire, and possibly their colonies might secede from the Union;

That such a secession would weaken us more than could be compensated by any foreign alliance;

That in the event of such a division, foreign powers would either refuse to join themselves to our fortunes, or, having us so much in their power as that desperate declaration would place us, they would insist on terms proportionably more hard and prejudicial; . . .

That it was prudent to fix among ourselves the terms on which we should form alliance before we declared we would form one at all events;

And that if these were agreed on and our Declaration of Independence ready by the time our ambassador should be prepared to sail, it would be as well as to go into that Declaration at this day.

On the other side it was urged . . . that no gentleman had argued against the policy or the right of separation from Britain, nor had supposed it possible we should ever renew our connection; that they had only opposed its being now declared;

That the question was not whether, by a Declaration of Independence, we should make

A committee of five delegates, led by Thomas Jefferson, presents the Declaration of Independence to the Second Continental Congress.

ourselves what we are not, but whether we should declare a fact which already exists;

That, as to the people or Parliament of England, we had always been independent of them, their restraints on our trade deriving [power] from our [assent] only and not from any rights they possessed of imposing them, and that so far our connection had been federal only and was now dissolved by the commencement of hostilities;

That, as to the King, we had been bound to him by allegiance, but that this bond was now dissolved by his assent to the last act of Parliament, by which he declares us out of his protection, and by his levying war on us, a fact which had long ago proved us out of his protection, it being a certain position in law that allegiance and protection are reciprocal, the one ceasing when the other is withdrawn; . . .

That the people wait for us to lead the way;

That *they* are in favor of the measure, though the instructions given by some of their *representatives* are not;

That the voice of the representatives is not always consonant with the voice of the people, and that is remarkably the case in these middle colonies; . . .

That it would be vain to wait either weeks or months for perfect unanimity, since it was impossible that all men should ever become of one sentiment on any question, . . .

That a Declaration of Independence alone could render it consistent with European delicacy for European powers to [negotiate] with us, or even to receive an ambassador from us;

That till this they would not receive our vessels into their ports, nor acknowledge the [judicial decisions] of our Courts of Admirality to be legitimate in cases of capture of British vessels; . . .

That to wait the event of this campaign will certainly work delay, because, during this summer, France may assist us effectually by cutting off those supplies of provisions from England and Ireland on which the enemy's armies here are to depend; or by setting in motion the great power they have collected in the West Indies, and calling our enemy to the defense of the possessions they have there.

Adapted from H. A. Washington, ed., *The Writings of Thomas Jefferson* (Washington, D.C.: 1853-1854), Vol. 3, pp. 12-26.

Questions

1. List three reasons why some members of Congress opposed the adoption of the Declaration of Independence in June 1776.

2. List three reasons why some members of Congress favored the adoption of the Declaration of Independence in June 1776.

Winter at Valley Forge

The courage of the continental army was severely tested during the winter of 1777-1778. Shortages of food, clothing, and blankets made life for most soldiers difficult. The ordeal weakened and discouraged even the best trained troops. Many deserted or simply went home when their enlistments expired.

Albigence Waldo served with Washington's army that winter at the encampment at Valley Forge, Pennsylvania. Waldo recorded his feelings that winter in his diary. His thoughts were shared by most of the army. An excerpt from Waldo's war diary appears here.

Dec. 14th. [1777]—[British] Prisoners & Deserters are continually coming in. The Army who have been surprisingly healthy hitherto—now begin to grow sickly from the continued fatigues they have suffered this Campaign. Yet they still show spirit of [courage] & Contentment not to be expected from so young Troops. I am Sick—discontented—and out of humor. Poor food—hard lodging—Cold Weather—fatigue—Nasty Cloaths—nasty Cookery— . . . I can't Endure it—Why are we sent here to starve and freeze—What sweet [happiness] have I left at home;—A charming Wife—pretty Children—Good Beds—good food—good Cookery—all agreeable—all harmonious. Here, all Confusion—smoke Cold—hunger & filthyness—A pox on my bad luck. Here comes a bowl of beef soup—full of burnt leaves and dirt, sickish enough to make a hector spue,—away with it Boys—I'll live like the Chameleon upon Air. Poh! Poh! crys Patience within me—you talk like a fool. Your being sick Covers your mind with a Melanchollic Gloom, which makes every thing about you appear gloomy. See the poor Soldier, when in health—with what chearfullness he meets his foes and encounters every hardship—if barefoot—he labours thro' the Mud & Cold with a Song in his mouth extolling War & Washington—if his food be bad—he eats it nothwithstanding with seeming content—blesses God for a good Stomach—and [whistles] it into digestion. But harkee Patience—a moment—There comes a Soldier— His bare feet are seen thro' his worn out Shoes—his legs nearly naked from the tatter'd remains of an only pair of stockings—his Breeches not sufficient to cover his Nakedness—his Shirt hanging in Strings—his hair dishevell'd—his face meagre—his whole appearance pictures a person forsaken & discouraged. He comes, and crys with an air of wretchedness & dispair—I am Sick—my feet lame—my legs are sore—my body cover'd with this tormenting Itch—my Cloaths are worn out—my Constitution is broken—my former Activity is exhausted by fatigue—hunger & Cold—I fail fast I shall soon be no more! and all the reward I shall get will be—"Poor Will is dead."

People who live at home in Luxury and Ease, quietly possessing their habitations, Enjoying their Wives & families in peace—have but a very faint Idea of the unpleasing sensations, and continual Anxiety the Man endured who is in a Camp, and is the husband & parent of an agreeable family. These same People are willing we should suffer every thing for their Benefit & advantage—and yet are the first to Condemn us for not doing more!!

From "Diary Kept at Valley Forge by Albigence Waldo, Surgeon in the Continental Army. 1777-1778," *The Historical Magazine,* May 1861, pp. 131-132. Original spelling included.

Questions

1. What are Waldo's greatest complaints?
2. Explain why Waldo is not an objective observer to the events at Valley Forge.

Forming a Union 6

Northwest Ordinance

The Northwest Ordinance laid the basis for the organization of new territorial governments and set a precedent for the method of admitting new states to the Union. It also had what might be called a bill of rights. There was even a specific provision outlawing slavery. The selection that follows is from the Northwest Ordinance.

ARTICLE I

No person demeaning himself in a peaceable and orderly manner shall ever be molested on account of his mode of worship or religious sentiments in the said territory.

ARTICLE II

The inhabitants of the said territory shall always be entitled to the benefits of the . . . trial by jury, of a proportionate representation of the people in the legislature, and of judicial proceedings according to the course of the common law. . . .

ARTICLE III

Religion, morality, and knowledge being necessary to good government and the happiness of [society], schools and the means of education shall forever be encouraged. The utmost good faith shall always be observed toward the Indians; their lands and property shall never be taken from them without their consent. . . .

ARTICLE IV

The said territory, and the states which may be formed therein, shall forever remain a part of this

Confederacy of the United States of America, subject to the Articles of Confederation . . . and to all the acts and ordinances of the United States. . . . The navigable waters leading into the Mississippi and St. Lawrence, and the carrying places between the same, shall be common highways, and forever free, as well to the inhabitants of the said territory as to the citizens of the United States, and those of any other states that may be admitted into the Confederacy, without any tax, impost, or duty therefor.

ARTICLE V

There shall be formed in the said territory not less than three nor more than five states. . . . And whenever any of the said states shall have 60,000 free inhabitants therein, such state shall be admitted by its delegates into the Congress of the United States, on an equal footing with the original states, in all respects whatever. . . .

ARTICLE VI

There shall be neither slavery nor involuntary servitude in the said territory, otherwise than in the punishment of crimes, whereof the party shall have been duly convicted.

Adapted from B. P. Poore, ed., *The Federal and State Constitutions, Colonial Charters, and Other Organic Laws of the United States,* 2nd edition (Washington, D.C.: Government Printing Office, 1877), Vol. 1, pp. 429-432.

Questions

1. What freedom did Article I of the Northwest Ordinance provide?

2. How did Article II of the Northwest Ordinance protect Americans in the territories from unjust persecution?

3. What was the attitude of the authors of the Northwest Ordinance toward schools and education?

Objections to the Constitution

The Constitutional Convention originally met only to improve the Articles of Confederation. Eventually, it wrote an entirely new Constitution. This new Constitution added strength to the powers of the federal government. Many people did not favor a powerful central government, however. These so-called Antifederalists felt that such a government would destroy the rights of the states and the individual liberties of their citizens. The following letter, which was written by two Antifederalist delegates to the Constitutional Convention, outlines the Antifederalist viewpoint.

We beg leave, briefly, to state some [valid] reasons which, among others, influenced us to decide against a consolidation of the states. These are reducible into two heads:

1. The limited and well-defined powers under which we acted and which could not, on any possible construction, embrace an idea of such magnitude as to assent to a general Constitution, in subversion of that of the state.

2. A conviction of the impracticability of establishing a general government, pervading every part of the United States, and extending essential benefits to all.

Our powers were explicit and confined to the sole and express purpose of revising the Articles of Confederation, and reporting such alterations and provisions therein as should render the federal Constitution adequate to [that which is required] of government and the preservation of the Union.

From these expressions, we were led to believe that a system of consolidated government could not in the remotest degree have been in contemplation of the legislature of this state; for that so important a trust as the adopting measures which tended to deprive the state government of its most essential rights of [supreme power], and to place it in a dependent situation, could not have been confided by implication; and the circumstance, that the acts of the Convention were to receive a state [approval] in the last resort, forcibly [confirmed] the opinion that our powers could not involve the subversion of a Constitution which, being immediately derived from the people, could only be abolished by their express consent, and not by a legislature possessing authority vested in them for its preservation. Nor could we suppose that, if it had been the intention of the legislature to [nullify] the existing Confederation, they would, in such pointed terms, have directed the attention of their delegates to the revision and amendment of it in total exclusion of every other idea.

Reasoning in this manner, we were of opinion that the leading feature of every amendment ought to be the preservation of the individual states in their uncontrolled constitutional rights. . . .

Exclusive of our objections originating from the want of power, we entertained an opinion that a general government, . . . by reason of the extensive territory of the United States, the dispersed situation of its inhabitants, and the insuperable difficulty of controlling or counteracting the views of a set of men (however unconstitutional and oppressive their acts might be) possessed of all the powers of government, and who, from their remoteness from their constituents, and necessary permanency of office, could not be supposed to be uniformly [moved] by an attention to their welfare and happiness; that, however wise and energetic the principles of the general government might be, the extremities of the United States could not be kept in due submission and obedience to its laws, at the distance of many hundred miles from the seat of government; that, if the general legislature was composed of so numerous a body of men as to represent the interests of all the inhabitants of the United States in the usual and true ideas of representation, the expense of supporting it would become intolerably burdensome; and that if a few only were vested with a power of legislation, the interests of a great majority of the inhabitants of the United States must necessarily be unknown, or, if known, even in the first stages of the operations of the new government, unattended to.

These reasons were, in our opinion, conclusive against any system of consolidated government; to that recommended by the Convention, we suppose most of them very forcibly apply.

Adapted from Jonathan Elliott, ed., *The Debates in the Several State Conventions on the Adoption of the Federal Constitution* (Philadelphia: J. B. Lippincott, 1861), Vol. 1, pp. 480-482.

Questions

1. What specific power was given to the delegates of the Constitutional Convention?

2. According to Antifederalists, what right of the state governments was taken away by the new Constitution?

3. What factor did the size of the United States play in the Antifederalist opposition to increased federal power?

4. How did earlier conflicts with Britain influence Antifederalist Americans?

Federalist Number 15

In the New York debate over ratification of the new Constitution, the Antifederalists were well organized. Led by Governor George Clinton, the Antifederalists held a clear majority going into the state convention. Victory seemed within their grasp. The Federalists, however, had Alexander Hamilton on their side. Hamilton, along with John Jay and James Madison, defended the new Constitution in a series of widely read essays printed in New York newspapers. Later, these essays were collected and published in a famous work, The Federalist Papers—*a classic in American political literature. The following passage is from the fifteenth essay, which Hamilton wrote. In it, he denounces the failures of the government under the Articles of Confederation.*

We may indeed with propriety be said to have reached almost the last stage of national humiliation. There is scarcely anything that can wound the pride or degrade the character of an independent nation which we do not experience. Are there engagements to the performance of which we are held by every tie respectable among men? These are the subjects of constant and unblushing violation. Do we owe debts to foreigners and to our own citizens contracted in a time of imminent peril for the preservation of our political existence? These remain without any proper or satisfactory provision for their discharge. Have we valuable territories and important posts in the possession of a foreign power which, by express stipulations, ought long since to have been surrendered? These are still retained to the prejudice of our interests, not less than of our rights. Are we in a condition to resent or to repel the aggression? We have neither troops, nor treasury, nor government [for the Union]. Are we even in a condition to remonstrate with dignity? The just imputations on our own faith in respect to the same treaty ought first to be removed. Are we entitled by nature and compact to a free participation in the navigation of the Mississippi? Spain excludes us from it. Is public credit an indispensable resource in time of public danger? We seem to have abandoned its cause as desperate and irretricvable. Is commerce of importance to national wealth? Ours is at the lowest point of declension. Is respectability in the eyes of foreign powers a safeguard against foreign encroachments? The imbecility of our government even forbids them to [negotiate] with us. Our ambassadors abroad are the mere pageants of mimic sovereignty. Is a violent and unnatural decrease in the value of land a symptom of national distress? The price of improved land in most parts of the country is much lower than can be accounted for by the quantity of waste land at market, and can only be fully explained by that want of private and public confidence, which are so alarmingly prevalent among all ranks and which have a direct tendency to depreciate property of every kind. Is private credit the friend and patron of industry? That most useful kind which relates to borrowing and lending is reduced within the narrowest limits, and this still more from an opinion of insecurity than from a scarcity of money. To shorten an enumeration of particulars which can afford neither pleasure nor instruction, it may in general be demanded, what indication is there of national disorder, poverty, and insignificance that could befall a community so peculiarly blessed with natural advantages as we are, which does not form a part of the dark catalogue of our public misfortunes?

This is the melancholy situation to which we have been brought by those very maxims and counsels which would now deter us from adopting the proposed Constitution; and which, not content with having conducted us to the brink of a precipice, seem resolved to plunge us into the abyss that awaits us below.

Adapted from Alexander Hamilton, James Madison, and John Jay, *The Federalist, on the New Constitution* (Philadelphia: M'Carty and Davis, 1826), pp. 78-80.

Questions

1. According to Hamilton, what were the weaknesses of the Confederate government?
2. Why do you think that Hamilton considers the Confederate government dangerous for the United States?

The Constitution 7

Popular Sovereignty

Popular sovereignty is the idea that all political power ultimately belongs to the people. The United States Constitution is based upon popular sovereignty. Under the Constitution, Americans have the power to create, change, or even abolish the government if it fails to meet their expectations. In the following passage, Constitutional Convention Representative James Wilson explains why popular sovereignty is important to the Constitution.

In all governments, whatever is their form, however they may be constituted, there must be a power established from which there is no appeal, and which is, therefore, called absolute, supreme, and uncontrollable. The only question is where that power is lodged—a question that will receive different answers. . . .

But were we to ask some politicians who have taken a faint and inaccurate view of our establishments where does this supreme power reside in the United States, they would probably answer, in their constitutions. This, however, though a step nearer to the fact is not a just opinion; for, in truth, it remains and flourishes with the people; and under the influence of that truth we, at this moment, sit, deliberate, and speak. In other countries, indeed, the revolutions of government are connected with war and all its [accompanying] calamities. But with us, they are considered as the means of obtaining a superior knowledge of the nature of government, and of accomplishing its end. That the supreme power, therefore, should be vested in the people is, in my judgment, the great [cure] of human politics. It is a power [important] to every constitution, inalienable in its nature, and indefinite in its extent. For I insist, if there are errors in government, the people have the right not only to correct and amend them but, likewise, totally to change and reject its form; and under the operation of that right, the citizens of the United States can never be wretched beyond retrieve. . . .

Then let us examine, Mr. President, the three species of simple government. . . . In a monarchy, the supreme power is vested in a single person; in an aristocracy, it is possessed by a body not formed upon the principle of representation but enjoying their station by descent, by election among themselves, or in right of some personal or territorial qualification; and lastly, in a democracy, it is inherent in the people, and is either exercised by themselves or by their representatives. Each of these systems has its advantages and its disadvantages. The advantages of a monarchy are strength, [speed], and unity; its disadvantages are expense, tyranny, and war. The advantages of an aristocracy are experience and the wisdom resulting from education; its disadvantages are the dissension of the governors and the oppression of the people. The advantages of a democracy are liberty, caution, industry, fidelity, and an opportunity of bringing forward the talents and abilities of the citizens, without regard to birth or fortune; its disadvantages are dissension and [foolishness], for the assent of many being required, their exertions will be feeble and their [plans] too soon discovered.

To obtain all the advantages and to avoid all the inconveniences of these governments, was the leading object of the late [Constitutional] Convention. Having therefore considered the formation and principles of other systems, it is natural to inquire—Of what description is the Constitution before us? In its principles, sir, it is purely democratical; varying, indeed, in its form in order to admit all the advantages and to exclude all the disadvantages which are incidental to the known and established constitutions of government. But when we take an extensive and accurate view of the streams of power that appear through this great and comprehensive plan, . . . we shall be able to trace them all to one great and noble source, THE PEOPLE.

From John Bach McMaster and Frederick D. Stone, eds., *Pennsylvania and the Federal Constitution 1787-1788* (Philadelphia: The Historical Society of Pennsylvania, 1888), pp. 218-231.

Questions

1. According to the Constitution, who holds the supreme power in the government of the United States?

2. Who holds the supreme power in each of the following: (a) a monarchy, (b) an aristocracy, and (c) a democracy?

3. According to James Wilson, what are the advantages of a democracy?

The United States Constitution as a Model for Other Nations

The United States Constitution has been guiding America's government for more than two centuries. In addition, it has greatly influenced the constitutions of many other nations. In the following excerpt, a contemporary scholar and worldwide constitution specialist describes why the United States Constitution serves as a model for so many others.

The United States Constitution is this nation's most important export. It was meant to be, has been since even before its [declaration], and continues to be. It *could* not help but be . . . and it *cannot* help but be. . . .

What made the United States Constitution so great, so admired, and so imitated? The establishment of a supreme law of the land was no innovation. . . . It was not the concept of limited government that fascinated foreign statesmen. Even the notions of establishing a republic, having a president, or the radical concept of popular sovereignty were already commonplace. . . .

The genius of America's [Founders] consisted in creating the machinery to translate constitutional philosophy into constitutional reality. Their device was the constitutional convention or constituent assembly. This has been the most significant and most followed precedent in constitutional development, for in this way a nation is formed and gets its constitution (save in those instances where the former colonial power grants independence and bestows a constitution for independence). The constituent assembly institutionalized democracy. It legalized and legitimized revolution, enabling men to do what they had not yet been able to do peacefully and legally—to alter or abolish government and institute new governments deriving their authority from the consent of the governed. . . .

Another reason for the Constitution's serving as a world model is the simple fact that it was the first constitution. It has been readily available for examination for nearly two centuries. . . . Thus, just by being first, the United States Constitution inevitably influenced constitutionalism. Every nation possessing a one-document constitution or committed in principle to having one—all but six countries—invariably has followed the United States model. . . .

[Yet another] reason for the great influence of the Constitution abroad is the widespread publication and distribution of literature. This literature is often distributed in the course of [recruiting others] and features a dedication to constitutionalism and the rule of law.

From the earliest days of the American revolutionary movement, its leaders were conscious that they were doing something of worldwide significance. They had convinced themselves that they were creating a new Eden, not only for America but for all of humanity. They had a story to tell and a message to deliver. They were [recruiters of others] and advocates seeking to justify, legitimize, and legalize their revolution. Consequently, their Declaration of Independence, their Articles of Confederation, their state constitutions, and all of the other [supports] of the United States Constitution were widely distributed abroad.

Adapted from Albert P. Blaustein, "The United States Constitution: A Model in Nation Building," *National Forum: The Phi Kappa Phi Journal,* Fall 1984, pp. 14-16. Reprinted by permission.

Questions

1. Why was the use of a constitutional convention significant?

2. List two reasons why the United States Constitution serves as a world model.

Judicial Review

Judicial review provides, for the judicial branch, an important check on the executive and legislative branches of the United States government. This policy allows the courts to determine the constitutionality of the acts of Congress or the actions of the President. Because it is not specifically stated in the Constitution, judicial review had to be defined by the Supreme Court. The first test of judicial review occurred in 1801, when the Court declared an act of Congress unconstitutional. The following excerpt from Chief Justice John Marshall's decision defends the Court's power of judicial review.

It is, emphatically, the province and duty of the Judicial Department to say what the law is. Those who apply the rule to particular cases must of necessity expound and interpret that rule. If two laws conflict with each other, the courts must decide on the operation of each. So if a law be in opposition to the Constitution, if both the law and the Constitution apply to a particular case, so that the court must either decide that case conformably

George Washington takes the presidential oath.

to the law, disregarding the Constitution, or conformably to the Constitution, disregarding the law, the court must determine which of these conflicting rules governs the case. This is of the very essence of judicial duty. If, then, the courts are to regard the Constitution, and the Constitution is superior to any ordinary act of the legislature, the Constitution, and not such ordinary act, must govern the case to which they both apply. . . .

It is also not entirely unworthy of observation that in declaring what shall be the supreme law of the land, the Constitution itself is first mentioned, and not the laws of the United States generally, but those only which shall be made in pursuance of the Constitution have that rank.

Thus, the particular phraseology of the Constitution of the United States confirms and strengthens the principle, supposed to be essential to all written constitutions, that a law repugnant to

the Constitution is void and that courts, as well as other departments, are bound by that instrument.

From William Cranch, ed., *Reports of Cases Argued and Adjudged in the Supreme Court of the United States* (Washington, D.C.: Government Printing Office, 1804), Vol. 1, p. 137.

Questions

1. According to Chief Justice John Marshall, what is the duty of the judicial department?

2. If a law conflicts with the Constitution, which will be supported by the Supreme Court?

3. How does judicial review check the power of the executive and legislative branches of the United States government?

UNIT III

Democracy

Testing the New Government   8

Washington's First Inaugural

George Washington became President of the United States on April 30, 1789. The first President under the Constitution was inaugurated in New York, the temporary capital of the new government. One of the many witnesses to the events of that day was Pennsylvania Senator William Maclay. He recorded his observations in a diary, from which the following passage is taken.

The President was conducted out of the middle window into the gallery [overlooking Wall Street], and the oath was administered by the Chancellor [the highest judicial officer in the state of New York]. Notice that the business done was communicated to the crowd by proclamation, etc., who gave three cheers, and repeated it on the President's bowing to them.

As the company returned into the Senate chamber, the President took the chair and the Senators and Representatives their seats. He rose, and all arose also, and [he] addressed them. This great man was agitated and embarrassed more than ever he was by the leveled cannon or pointed musket. He trembled, and several times could scarce make out to read, though it must be supposed he had often read it before. . . . When he came to the words *all the world,* he made a flourish with his right hand, which left rather an ungainly impression. I sincerely, for my part, wished all set ceremony in the hands of the dancing-masters, and that this first of men had read off his address in the plainest manner, without ever taking his eyes from the paper, for I felt hurt that he was not first in everything. He was dressed in deep brown, with metal buttons, with an eagle on them, white stockings, a bag [for his back hair], and sword.

From the hall there was a grand procession to Saint Paul's Church, where prayers were said by the Bishop. The procession was well conducted and without accident, as far as I have heard. The militia were all under arms, lined the street near the church, made a good figure, and behaved well.

The Senate returned to their chamber after service, formed, and took up the address. Our Vice-President called it *his most gracious speech.* I can not approve of this. . . . In the evening there were grand fireworks. The Spanish Ambassador's house was adorned with transparent paintings; the French Minister's house was illuminated, and had some transparent pieces; the Hall was grandly illuminated, and after all this the people went to bed.

From Edgar S. Maclay, ed., *Journal of William Maclay* (New York: D. Appleton & Co., 1890), pp. 9-10.

Questions

1. What events at Washington's inaugural did Maclay seem to like?

2. What was it about Washington's public speaking manner that Maclay criticized?

Hamilton's Opinion on the Bank Issue

The establishment of a national bank was a controversial issue in the 1790's. Alexander Hamilton favored the idea and presented a plan to Congress. In 1791, a bill covering most of Hamilton's plan passed Congress and was sent to President Washington for his signature. But Washington was unable to decide if a national bank was constitutional. He asked his advisors for their opinions on the issue. In the end, Hamilton's view was most persuasive. On February 25, 1790, Washington signed the bill creating the bank. Portions of Hamilton's opinion follow.

It is not denied that there are *implied* as well as *express powers,* and that the *former* are as effectually delegated as the *latter.* . . .

It is conceded that *implied powers* are to be considered as delegated equally with *express ones.* Then it follows, that as a power of erecting a corporation may as well be *implied* as any other thing, it may as well be employed as an *instrument* or *means* of carrying into execution any of the specified powers, as any other *instrument* or *means* whatever. The only question must be in this, as in every other case, whether the mean to be employed, or, in this instance, the corporation to be erected, has a natural relation to any of the acknowledged objects or lawful ends of the government. Thus a corporation may not be erected by Congress for superintending the police of the city of Philadelphia, because they are not authorized to *regulate* the *police* of that city. But one may be erected in relation to the collection of taxes, or to the trade with foreign countries, or to the trade between the States, or with the Indian tribes; because it is the province of the federal government to *regulate* those objects and because it is incident to a general *sovereign* or *legislative* power to *regulate* a thing, to employ all the means which relate to its regulation to the best and greatest advantage. . . .

It leaves, therefore, a criterion of what is constitutional and of what is not so. This criterion is the *end,* to which the measure relates as a *mean.* If the *end* be clearly comprehended within any of the specified powers, and if the measure have an obvious relation to that *end,* and is not forbidden by any particular provision of the Constitution, it may safely be deemed to come within the compass of the national authority. . . .

A hope is entertained that it has, by this time, been made to appear, to the satisfaction of the President, that a bank has a natural relation to the power of collecting taxes—to that of regulating trade—to that of providing for the common defence—and . . . that the incorporation of a bank is a constitutional measure.

Adapted from John C. Hamilton, ed., *The Works of Alexander Hamilton* (New York: G. P. Putnam's Sons, 1885), Vol. 3, pp. 184-185, 192, 218-219.

Questions

1. According to Hamilton, were implied or express powers more effective?

2. What question does Hamilton suggest to determine whether a power is implied?

3. Why does Hamilton state that the federal government has the power to establish a national bank?

Jefferson's Opinion on the Bank Issue

Thomas Jefferson strongly opposed the idea of a national bank. He felt that such a bank was the first step toward unlimited national power. The following excerpts from Jefferson's report to George Washington further describe his views on this subject.

I consider the foundation of the Constitution as laid on this ground: That "all powers not delegated to the United States, by the Constitution, nor prohibited by it to the States, are reserved to the States or to the people." To take a single step beyond the boundaries thus specially drawn around the powers of Congress, is to take possession of a boundless field of power, no longer susceptible of any definition.

The incorporation of a bank, and the powers assumed by this bill, have not, in my opinion, been delegated to the United States, by the Constitution.

I. They are not among the powers specially enumerated. . . .

II. Nor are they within either of the general phrases, which are the two following:—

1. To lay taxes to provide for the general welfare of the United States, . . . [Congress is] not *to do anything they please* to provide for the general welfare, but only to *lay taxes* for that purpose. . . . It was intended to lace them up straitly within the enumerated powers, and those without which, as means, these powers could not be carried into effect. . . .

2. The second general phrase is, "to make all laws *necessary* and proper for carrying into execution the enumerated powers." But they can all be carried into execution without a bank. A bank therefore is not *necessary,* and consequently not authorized by this phrase.

It has been urged that a bank will give great facility or convenience in the collection of taxes. Suppose this were true: yet the Constitution allows only the means which are *"necessary,"* not those which are merely "convenient" for effecting the enumerated powers. If such latitude of construction be allowed to this phrase as to give any non-enumerated power, it will go to every one, for there is not one which ingenuity may not torture into a *convenience* in some instance *or other.* . . . Therefore it was that the Constitution restrained them to the *necessary* means.

Adapted from Albert E. Bergh and Andrew A. Lipscomb, eds., *The Writings of Thomas Jefferson* (Washington, D.C.: The Thomas Jefferson Memorial Association, 1903), Vol. 3, pp. 146-149.

Questions

1. According to Thomas Jefferson, which powers belong to the federal government?

2. Why did Thomas Jefferson oppose a national bank?

3. If Thomas Jefferson could have been convinced that a national bank was more convenient for tax collection, would he have favored it? Why or why not?

Lewis and Clark Journals

Before the Lewis and Clark expedition began in May 1804, co-commanders Meriwether Lewis and William Clark assigned one member of the crew as rouster *keeper. His duty consisted of maintaining an official record of military details and orders issued during the expedition. In addition, Lewis and Clark wanted each sergeant to keep a private record of day-to-day events. They also encouraged enlisted men to keep journals to guarantee that at least one written account of the journey survived. As a result, the Lewis and Clark expedition became one of the best documented journeys of exploration in American history. The following selection is William Clark's impression of seeing the Rocky Mountains for the first time.*

May 26th *Sunday* 1805

We set out early and proceeded as yesterday. . . . I took one man and walked out this morning, and ascended the high countery to view the mountains which I thought I saw yesterday, from the first sumit of the hill I could plainly see the Mountains on either side which I saw yesterday and at no great distance from me. . . . I crossed a Deep holler and [ascended] a part of the plain elivated much higher than where I first viewed the above Mountains; from this point, I beheld the Rocky Mountains for the first time with certainty. . . . those points of the rocky Mountain were covered with *Snow* and the Sun Shown on it in such a manner as to give me a most plain and satisfactory view. whilst I viewed those mountains I felt a secret pleasure in finding myself so near the head of the heretofore conceived boundless Missouri [River]; but when I reflected on the difficulties which this snowey barrier would most probably throw in my way to the Pacific Ocean, and the sufferings and hardships of my self and party in them, it in some measure counterballanced the joy I had felt in the first moments in which I gazed on them.

Adapted from Reuben Gold Thwaites, ed., *Original Journals of the Lewis and Clark Expedition, 1804-1806* (New York: Dodd, Mead & Company, 1904), Vol. 2, pp. 81-82. Original spelling included.

Questions

1. According to Clark, what were the most striking features of the Rocky Mountains?

2. Why did Clark view the mountains with both pleasure and sorrow?

The Growth of Nationalism   9

Our National Anthem

America's national anthem, "The Star-Spangled Banner," was inspired by the British attack on Fort McHenry during the War of 1812. On the night of the attack, Francis Scott Key, a young Baltimore lawyer, had gone to the ship of the British admiral. He went with several friends to seek the release of a prominent doctor who had been captured by the British. Because of the attack, Key had to stay in the ship in Baltimore harbor. He spent the night watching the bombardment of the fort.

At dawn, Key was unable to tell if the attack was successful. Then a break in the mist revealed the American flag still flying over the fort. The sight stirred him to write the words of "The Star-Spangled Banner," first printed with the title, "Defence of Fort McHenry." The words were put to the tune of a then-common English song, "The Anacreon in Heaven." It became popular at once. But it was not until 1931 when Congress officially declared "The Star-Spangled Banner" as our national anthem. The original words follow here.

O! say can you see, by the dawn's early light,
What so proudly we hail'd at the twilight's last gleaming,
Whose broad stripes and bright stars through the perilous fight,
O'er the ramparts we watched, were so gallantly streaming?
And the Rockets' red glare, the Bombs bursting in air,
Gave proof through the night that our Flag was still there;
O! say, does that star-spangled banner yet wave
O'er the Land of the free and the home of the brave!

On the shore, dimly seen through the mists of the deep,
Where the foe's haughty host in dread silence reposes,
What is that, which the breeze o'er the towering steep,

As it fitfully blows, half conceals, half discloses?
Now it catches the gleam of the morning's first beam,
In fully glory reflected, now shines on the stream.
'Tis the star-spangled banner; O! long may it wave
O'er the land of the free and the home of the brave.

And where is that band who so vauntingly swore
That the havoc of war and the battle's confusion,
A home and a country should leave us no more?
Their blood has washed out their foul footsteps' pollution.
No refuge could save the hireling and slave,
From the terror of flight, or the gloom of the grave:
And the star-spangled banner in triumph doth wave
O'er the land of the free and the home of the brave.

O! thus be it ever when freemen shall stand,
Between their loved homes and the war's desolation,
Blest with victory and peace, may the Heaven-rescued land
Praise the power that hath made and preserved us a nation!
Then conquer we must, for our cause it is just,
And this be our motto—"In God is our trust!"
And the star-spangled banner in triumph shall wave,
O'er the land of the free and the home of the brave.

From *Baltimore Patriot*, September 20, 1812.

Francis Scott Key watches the bombing of Ft. McHenry.

Questions

1. To whom or what does Key direct his attention in the song?

2. Sing all four verses as part of a class or group project. In your opinion, what makes it sound like a patriotic song?

The Monroe Doctrine

In an 1823 address to Congress, President James Monroe proclaimed what has become known as the Monroe Doctrine. Written by John Quincy Adams, Monroe's Secretary of State, the doctrine was designed to end European influence in the Western Hemisphere. In addition, it showed the world the American spirit of strength and unity and became a cornerstone of United States foreign policy.

The American continents; by the free and independent condition which they have assumed and maintain, are henceforth not to be considered as subjects for future colonization by any European powers. . . .

We should consider any attempt on their part to extend their system to any portion of this hemisphere as dangerous to our peace and safety. With the existing colonies or dependencies of any European power we have not interfered and shall not interfere. But with the Governments who have declared their independence and maintained it, and whose independence we have, on great consideration and on just principles, acknowledged, we could not view any [interference] for the purpose of oppressing them, or controlling in any other manner their destiny, by any European power in any other light than as the manifestation of an unfriendly disposition toward the United States. . . . Our policy in regard to Europe, which was adopted at an early stage of the wars which have so long agitated that quarter of the globe, nevertheless remains the same, which is, not to interfere in the internal concerns of any of its powers; to consider the government [in power] as the legitimate government for us; to cultivate friendly relations with it, and to preserve those relations . . . meeting in all instances the just claims of every power, submitting to injuries from none. But in regard to those [American] continents circumstances are eminently and conspicuously different. It is impossible that the allied powers should extend their political system to any portion of either continent without endangering our peace and happiness; nor can anyone believe that our southern brethren, if left to themselves, would adopt it of their own accord. It is equally

impossible, therefore, that we should behold such [interference] in any form with indifference.

Adapted from James D. Richardson, ed., *A Compilation of the Messages and Papers of the Presidents 1789-1897* (Washington, D.C.: Government Printing Office, 1896), Vol. 2, pp. 209, 218-219.

Questions

1. According to the Monroe Doctrine, what areas were off-limits to Europeans hoping to establish new colonies?

2. What did President Monroe propose to do about existing European colonies?

3. What was U.S. policy, regarding Europe and its governments, at the time of the Monroe Doctrine?

4. Why did President Monroe oppose further European colonization of the Americas?

In Defense of American Ways

Timothy Dwight was a New England minister who served as president of Yale University from 1795 to 1817. Each fall, Dwight travelled throughout New England. When he returned home, he wrote about what he saw and thought during his trip. Like other writers at the time, Dwight recorded his observations in the form of letters to imaginary friends. The following passage is from one of Dwight's letters. It is a defense of American life and culture which at the time were frequently criticized by many foreign visitors. Dwight's letter was written to an imaginary friend in Great Britain.

Of the numerous English [people], who have visited these states, I have seen not a small number. The manners of these, of every rank, and some of them have been persons of considerable distinction, have, with a small number of exceptions, been less unassuming, less civil, more distant, more self-complacent, and more forbidding, than those of my own countrymen in similar spheres of life. . . .

A principal reason, why your countrymen complain of disobliging conduct in mine, is, that they provoke this treatment. [An English traveller, when entering an inn], treats the inn-keeper as if he were his servant; perhaps I might say with truth, his slave; and it is remarkable, that they are the only people, who exhibit this treatment. Unused to it from others, the inn-keeper bears it impatiently from them. Whether this behaviour of the traveller is proper, and defensible, I shall not now stop to inquire. It is not customary; and for this reason, at least, unwelcome. As every New-England [person] feels entirely independent; it is not strange that he should not brook what he considers as unmerited abuse. A little civility would have commanded every effort of the inn-keeper to please [the English traveller]. . . .

We are complained of as inquisitive. We are so; but very rarely, I suspect, in any such manner, as to justify the complaints. I have mentioned the extent, to which I have travelled in New-England and New-York, during the last sixteen years; . . . but do not remember that I have been once . . . met with a single incivility. . . .

The import of these observations is applicable in a greater or less degree to very many things in this country. Our government, our laws, our religion, our manners, the state of arts and manufactures, our literature, our science, our climate nay even the state of vegetation are . . . more or less misapprehended, by every foreign [traveller] who passes through the country. . . .

You will naturally object to these observations, that these things are chiefly the same with those in Great Britain, or very similar. You will say, that our government is the same with yours, except some slight shades of difference; that our religion is the same in all its varieties; that our manners are the same; and that this is true of our whole state of society. . . . [But] there are more differences in the state of things in the two countries than an Englishman can possibly preconceive. . . .

Our common people are far better educated than yours, both in the school, and in the church; and for this very good reason, that they are all at school, and almost all at church. All of them can read, write, and keep accounts. Almost all of them do read; and many of them, much. . . . To [end] the subject, there is a vein of practical good sense, the most valuable of all intellectual possessions, running through the people of New-England, which may be considered as their [most characteristic feature].

Adapted from Timothy Dwight, *Travels; in New-England and New-York* (New Haven: privately published, 1822), Vol. 4, pp. 341-346.

Questions

1. How does Dwight defend the criticisms that Americans are impolite and too inquisitive?

2. How does Dwight explain the differences between the American and English people?

The Age of Jackson   10

Jackson's Inaugural

The inauguration of Andrew Jackson was unlike that of any earlier President. People from all over the country came to Washington to witness the event. But boisterous crowds threw the inaugural reception into disarray. Jackson himself was escorted away for his safety. To Supreme Court Justice Joseph Story, who was present, it seemed the beginning of "the reign of King Mob." For some, however, it represented the triumph of the common people. The following selection is from an account of Jackson's inaugural by an eyewitness, Margaret Bayard Smith.

The *Majesty of the People* had disappeared, and a rabble, a mob, of boys, . . . women, children, scrambling fighting, romping. What a pity what a pity! No arrangements had been made no police officers placed on duty and the whole house had been inundated by the rabble mob. We came too late. The President, after having been *literally*

Andrew Jackson's election was often viewed as a triumph for the common people.

nearly pressed to death and almost suffocated and torn to pieces by the people in their eagerness to shake hands with Old Hickory, had retreated through the back way or south front and had escaped to his lodgings at Gadsby's. Cut glass and china to the amount of several thousand dollars had been broken in the struggle to get the refreshments, punch and other articles had been . . . insufficient, ice-creams, and cake and lemonade, for 20,000 people, for it is said that number were there, tho' I think the estimate exaggerated. Ladies fainted, men were seen with bloody noses and such a scene of confusion took place as is impossible to describe,—those who got in could not get out by the door again, but had to scramble out of windows.

From Margaret Bayard Smith, *The First Forty Years of Washington Society,* Gaillard Hunt, ed. (New York: Charles Scribner's Sons, 1906), pp. 295-296.

Questions

1. Where was President Jackson while all of the inaugural activity was taking place?

2. What do you think she meant by saying "the *Majesty of the People* had disappeared"?

Nullification Ordinance

Most southern states disliked the protective tariffs of 1828 and 1832 because they forced people to pay higher prices for imported goods. In November 1832, a South Carolina state convention nullified the tariffs within its state and threatened to leave the Union if the federal government tried to collect the taxes. The following excerpts are from South Carolina's nullification ordinance.

An ordinance to nullify certain acts of the Congress of the United States purporting to be laws laying duties and imposts on the importation of foreign commodities.

Whereas, the Congress of the United States, by various acts purporting to be acts laying duties and imposts on foreign imports, but in reality intended for the protection of domestic manufacturers and the giving of bounties to classes and individuals engaged in particular employments, at the expense and to the injury and oppression of other classes and individuals, . . . *And whereas,* the said Congress, exceeding its just power to impose taxes and collect revenue for the purpose of effecting and accomplishing the specific objects and purposes which the Constitution of the United States authorizes it to effect and accomplish, has raised and collected unnecessary revenue for objects unauthorized by the Constitution;

We, therefore, the people of the state of South Carolina, in Convention assembled, do declare and ordain, . . . that the several acts and parts of acts of the Congress of the United States purporting to be laws for the imposing of duties and imposts on the importation of foreign commodities . . . are unauthorized by the Constitution of the United States and violate the true meaning and intent thereof, and are null, void, and no law, nor binding upon this state, its officers, or citizens. . . .

And it is further ordained that it shall not be lawful for any of the constituted authorities, whether of this state or of the United States, to enforce the payment of duties imposed by the said acts within the limits of this state. . . .

And we, the people of South Carolina, to the end that it may be fully understood by the government of the United States and the people of the co-states, that we are determined to maintain this, our ordinance and declaration, at every hazard, *do further declare,* that we will not submit to the application of force on the part of the federal government to reduce this state to obedience; but that we will consider the passage by Congress of any act . . . to coerce the State, shut up her ports, destroy or harass her commerce, or to enforce the acts hereby declared to be null and void, otherwise than through the civil tribunals of the country, as inconsistent with the longer continuance of South Carolina in the Union.

And that the people of this state will thenceforth hold themselves absolved from all further obligation to maintain or preserve their political connection with the people of the other states and will forthwith proceed to organize a separate government.

Adapted from Thomas Cooper, ed., *The Statutes at Large of South Carolina* (Columbia, S.C.: 1836), Vol. 1, pp. 329-331.

Questions

1. According to the Nullification Ordinance, why did the United States government tax foreign imports?

2. How did the people of South Carolina justify their Nullification Ordinance?

3. What did South Carolina threaten to do if the United States government tried to enforce the taxes within the state?

Trail of Tears

Early in the 1800's, white settlers in the east urged the federal government to move the Indians to areas west of the Mississippi River. This call for Indian resettlement was especially strong in Georgia, where gold had been discovered within the Cherokee territory. Although recognized as a separate nation by several U.S. treaties, the Cherokee people were eventually forced to leave their lands.

The Cherokees made a 1,000-mile (1,600-kilometer) journey west during the winter of 1838-1839. Over 4,000 Cherokee Indians died before they reached Indian Territory, the present-day state of Oklahoma. Because of the great sadness felt by the Cherokee people, their forced journey became known as the "Trail of Tears." An eyewitness account of the plight of the Cherokee people is given below.

On Tuesday evening we fell in with a detachment of the poor Cherokee Indians

. . . about eleven hundred Indians—sixty wagons—six hundred horses, and perhaps forty pairs of oxen. We found them in the forest camped for the night by the road side . . . under a severe fall of rain accompanied by heavy wind. With their canvas for a shield from the inclemency of the weather, and the cold wet ground for a resting place, after the fatigue of the day, they spent the night . . . many of the aged Indians were suffering extremely from the fatigue of the journey, and the ill health consequent upon it . . . several were then quite ill, and one aged man we were informed was then in the last struggles of death. . . . The last detachment which we passed on the 7th embraced rising two thousand Indians with horses and mules in proportion. The forward part of the train we found just pitching their tents for the night, and notwithstanding some thirty or forty wagons were already stationed, we found the road literally filled with the procession for about three miles in length. The sick and feeble were carried in wagons—about as comfortable for traveling as a New England ox cart with a covering over it—a great many ride on horseback and multitudes go on foot . . . on the sometimes frozen ground, and sometimes muddy streets, with no covering for the feet except what nature had given them. . . . We learned from the inhabitants on the road where the Indians passed, that they buried fourteen or fifteen at every stopping place, and they make a journey of ten miles per day only on an average. . . . When I past the last detachment of those suffering exiles and thought that my native countrymen had thus expelled them from their native soil and their muchloved homes, and that too in this inclement season of the year in all their suffering, I turned from the sight with feelings which language cannot express. . . . When I read in the President's Message that he was happy to inform the Senate that the Cherokees were peaceably and without reluctance removed—and remember that it was on the third day of December when not one of the detachments had reached their destination; and that a large majority had not made even half their journey when he made that declaration, I thought I wished the President could have been there that very day in Kentucky with myself, and have seen the comfort and the willingness with which the Cherokees were making their journey.

From *New York Observer*, January 26, 1839.

Questions

1. How did the Cherokee Indians travel from Georgia to the Indian Territory?
2. List three hardships faced by the Cherokees along the "Trail of Tears."

UNIT IV

Expansion

The Promise of America 11

The Liberator

By 1830, it was clear that the antislavery reformers were not reaching their goals. At this point, William Lloyd Garrison appeared with a much more radical approach. He was against gradual emancipation and colonization. Through his newspaper, the Liberator, *founded in 1831, Garrison demanded slavery's immediate and total abolition. In the first issue, he made his position clear.*

I am aware that many object to the severity of my language; but is there not cause for severity? I *will be* as harsh as truth and as uncompromising as justice. On this subject I do not wish to think, or speak, or write with moderation. No! No! Tell a [person] whose house is on fire to give a moderate alarm; tell him to moderately rescue his [spouse] from the hands of the ravisher; tell the [parent] to gradually extricate [a] babe from the fire into which it has fallen;—but urge me not to use moderation in a cause like the present. I am in earnest; I will not equivocate; I will not excuse; I will not retreat a single inch—AND I WILL BE HEARD. The apathy of the people is enough to make every statue leap from its pedestal and to hasten the resurrection of the dead.

From *Liberator,* January 1, 1831.

Questions

1. Use one word to describe Garrison's position.
2. With what does Garrison compare the danger of slavery?

For a National Language

During the early 1800's, Noah Webster promoted uniformity in the national language. With his dictionaries and spelling books, Webster urged the same pronunciation and spelling of American English wherever it was spoken or written. The following excerpt from Webster's The Elementary Spelling Book *reflects his argument for a national language.*

It is an important object, in this great country, to have a uniform national language, to which all foreigners settling in the country, should conform. In the early days of our independence, much was done to promote this object, by Webster's Spelling Book; for the principal instrument of creating and preserving uniformity, must be a Spelling Book which is used by all classes of children. This book has more influence than all others, on a national language; and the effects of the general use of Webster's book, for more than fifty years, are visible at this day, in the remarkable uniformity of pronunciation among the citizens of the United States. This fact has been remarked by foreigners in the speeches of members of Congress. . . .

Webster's books are all printed with uniform [spelling and pronunciation], and as his large

In the 1800's, most Americans put education high on the list of priorities to attain a successful and powerful United States.

dictionary is admitted in Great Britain as well as in the United States, to be the best English dictionary, and as it is everywhere used in colleges, courts of law, Congress, and by all the higher classes of scholars, as a standard work, there is great propriety in using his elementary work in all our schools. This is the opinion of many of the most distinguished men in the United States. Several years ago, more than a hundred members of Congress expressed this opinion in the following words:—

"The subscribers highly appreciate Dr Webster's purpose and attempt to improve the English language, by rendering its [spelling and pronunciation] more simple, regular, and uniform, and by removing difficulties arising from its [irregularities]. It is very desirable that one standard dictionary should be used by the millions of people who are to inhabit the vast extent of territory belonging to the United States, as the use of such a standard may prevent the formation of dialects in states remote from each other, and impress upon the language *uniformity* and *stability*. It is desirable, also, that the [learning] of the language should be rendered easy, not only to our own citizens, but to foreigners who wish to gain access to the rich stores of science which it contains. We rejoice that the American dictionary bids fair to become such a standard, and we sincerely hope that the Author's elementary books for primary schools and academies will commend themselves to the general use of our fellow-citizens."

From Noah Webster, *The Elementary Spelling Book* (New York: G. F. Cooledge & Brother, 1843), pp. i-ii.

Questions

1. What did Noah Webster try to promote with his *Spelling Book*?

2. Why would a widely used elementary spelling book have more influence than other types of books, on a national language?

3. Why did Congress suggest the use of one standard dictionary?

Temperance Crusade

The temperance crusade was one of the many reform movements in the 1820's and 1830's. It developed to promote self control in the use of alcoholic beverages. Many temperance crusaders believed that excessive drinking was the cause of crime, poverty, and other social evils. Some wanted to outlaw alcoholic beverages altogether. The following speech was written by the Right Reverend Charles P. McIlvaine. It is typical of the literature circulated by temperance groups throughout America at that time.

Our country is free; *with a great price obtained we this freedom.* We feel as if all the force of Europe could not get it from our embrace. Our shores would shake into the depth of the sea the invader who should presume to seek it. One solitary citizen led away into captivity, scourged, chained by a foreign enemy, would rouse the oldest nerve in the land to indignant complaint and league the whole nation in loud demand for redress. And yet it cannot be denied that our country is enslaved. Yes, we are groaning under a most desolating bondage. The land is trodden down under its polluting foot. Our families are continually dishonored, ravaged, and bereaved; thousands annually slain and hundreds of thousands carried away into a loathsome slavery, to be ground to powder under its burdens or broken upon the wheel of its tortures.

What are the statistics of this traffic? Ask the records of [hospitals] and they will answer that one-third of all their [patients] were sent there by intemperance. Ask the keepers of our prisons and they will testify that, with scarcely an exception, their horrible population is from the schools of intemperance. Ask the history of the 200,000 paupers now burdening the hands of public charity and you will find that two-thirds of them have been the victims, directly or indirectly, of intemperance. Inquire at the gates of death and you will learn that no less than 30,000 souls are annually passed for the judgment bar of God, driven there by intemperance.

How many slaves are at present among us? We ask not of slaves to man but to intemperance. . . . They are estimated at 480,000! And what does the nation pay for the honor and happiness of this whole system of ruin? *Five times as much every year as for the annual support of its whole system of government.* These are truths, so often published, so widely sanctioned, so generally received, and so little doubted, that we need not detail the particulars by which they are made out. . . .

Another assertion is equally unquestionable. *The time has come when a great effort must be made to exterminate this unequaled destroyer.* . . . It is too late to put off any longer the effort for deliverance. It is granted by the common sense and urged by the common interest; every feeling of humanity and every consideration of religion enforces the belief that the time has come when a great onset is imperiously demanded to drive out intemperance from the land. . . .

The reformation of the land is in the power of public opinion. . . . In order to exert ourselves with the best effect in the promotion of the several objects in this great cause to which young [people] should apply themselves, let us associate ourselves into *temperance societies.* . . . Let temperance societies be multiplied. Every new association is a new battery against the stronghold of the enemy, and gives a new impulse to the hearts of those who have already joined the conflict. Let us arise, and be diligent, and be united; and may the God of mercy bless our work.

From Charles P. McIlvaine, "The Scourge of Intemperance," *Tracts of the American Tract Society* (New York: n.d.), Vol. 7, No. 244, pp. 1-23.

Questions

1. According to the author, what social evils are a result of intemperance?

2. What does the author suggest to combat the evils of intemperance?

New Ways and New People   12

Working Women of Lowell

In the 1800's, Francis Cabot Lowell and several partners established what they considered to be a model factory at Lowell, Massachusetts. Important to the Lowell model was control of the time spent by workers, who were mostly young women from New England farms. When not working, the young women were provided opportunities to attend classes, join "improvement societies," and publish their own monthly magazine, The Lowell Offering. *As a major benefit of working at the Lowell factory, young women were able to earn and spend their own money. The following passage explains why this was important.*

It must be remembered that at this date [1840] women had no property rights. A widow could be left without her share of her husband's (or the family) property. . . . A woman was not supposed to be capable of spending her own or using other people's money. In Massachusetts, before 1840, a woman could not legally be treasurer of her own sewing-society, unless some man were responsible for her. . . . Thus it happened, that if a woman did not choose to marry, or, when left a widow, to re-marry, she had no choice but to enter one of the few employments open to her, or to become a burden on the charity of some relative.

In almost every New England home could be found one or more of these women, sometimes welcome, more often unwelcome, and leading joyless, and in many instances unsatisfactory, lives. The cotton-factory was a great opening to these lonely and dependent women. . . . For the first time in this country woman's labor had a money value. She had become not only an earner and a producer, but also a spender of money, a recognized factor in the political economy of her time. And thus a long upward step in our material civilization was taken; woman had begun to earn

Advances in manufacturing changed America's economic life. Earliest improvements took place in the textile industry.

and hold her own money, and through its aid had learned to think and to act for herself.

Adapted from Harriet Hanson Robinson, *Loom and Spindle or Life Among the Early Mill Girls* (New York: Thomas Y. Crowell, 1898), pp. 41-42.

Questions

1. Compare and contrast women's economic rights before 1840 and today.
2. What benefits were provided the women who worked at the Lowell factory?

On the National Road

The National Road was the first major highway into the interior of the United States. Like the Erie Canal, it opened up new areas to settlement and travel. The following passage describes a New York traveler's first impressions of the National Road in 1835.

About thirty miles from Wheeling we first struck the national road. It appears to have been originally constructed of large round stones, thrown without much arrangement on the surface of the soil, after the road was first levelled. These are now being ploughed up, and a thin layer of broken stones is in many places spread over the renovated surface. . . . It yields like snow-drift to the heavy wheels which traverse it, and the very best parts of the road that I saw are not to be compared with a Long Island turnpike. Two-thirds indeed of the extent we traversed were worse than any artificial road I ever travelled, except perhaps the log causeways among the new settlements in northern New-York. . . . There is one feature, however, in this national work which is truly fine,—I allude to the massive stone bridges which form a part of it. They occur, as the road crosses a winding creek, a dozen times within twice as many miles. . . . They are monuments of taste and power that will speak well for the country when the brick towns they bind together shall have crumbled in the dust.

These frequently recurring bridges are striking objects in the landscape, where the road winds for many miles through a narrow valley. They may be seen at almost every turn spanning the deep bosom of the [narrow passage], and reflected with all their sombre beauty in the stream below.

From Charles Fenno Hoffman, *A Winter in the West* (New York: Harper & Brothers, 1835), Vol. 1, pp. 47-49.

1. According to the author, what properties of the National Road made it difficult to travel?

2. What feature of the National Road did the author find appealing?

City Tenant Housing

Between 1850 and 1860, the population of United States cities increased over 75 percent. This sharp rise in urban population caused a variety of social problems; the most serious was housing. New York was one of the many states that worked to improve the conditions in its cities. In 1857, a New York legislative committee published a report on its study of the housing problem. Excerpts from its report are found below.

We could tell of one room, 12 feet by 12, in which were five resident families comprising twenty persons, of both sexes and all ages, with only two beds, without partition or screen, or chair or table; and all dependent for their support upon the sale of chips gleaned from the streets, at 4 cents a basket; of another apartment, . . . an attic room, 7 feet by 5, containing scarcely an article of furniture but a bed, on which lay a fine-looking man in a raging fever, without medicine, drink, or suitable food, his toil-worn wife engaged in cleaning the dirt from the floor, and his little child asleep on a bundle of rags in the corner; of another of the same dimensions, in which we found, seated on low boxes around a candle placed on a keg, a woman and her eldest daughter . . . sewing on shirts, for the making of which they were paid 4 cents apiece, and even at that price, out of which they had to support two small children, they could not get a supply of work; of another room, about as large, occupied by a street ragpicker and his family, the income of whose industry was about $8 per month; of another apartment, scarce larger . . . warmed only by a tin pail of lighter charcoal placed in the center of the floor . . . and in one corner lay the body of a woman who had died the day before of disease, her orphan children sleeping near on a pile of rags. . . .

(Proceeding from the lower point of New York City) we came, first, to [a reconstructed tenant house]. . . . The dilapidation of this entire building is extreme; its rickety floors shook under the tread, and portions of the wall, black and mildewed, were continually breaking off, while nearly every vestige of mortar had disappeared from some of the rooms, leaving only smoke-discolored lathing, through which thick moisture was constantly oozing. A poor woman who occupied an apartment on the second floor complained that this last discomfort was incessant. "The ould ceiling," she said, "is ould as meself, and it's full uv the *dhrop* it is," *i.e.*, it was soaked with water that entered through the broken roof whenever it rained. Indeed, the committee were assured (and from appearances the fact could not be doubted) that in wet weather the upper floors of this ruinous habitation were completely flooded, and the poor occupants were obliged to move their drenched beds from spot to spot as the dropping became too troublesome to permit sleep.

From *Report of the Select Committee Appointed to Examine Into the Condition of Tenant Houses in New-York and Brooklyn,* New York State Assembly Documents 205, March 9, 1857.

Questions

1. Describe three housing problems the committee discovered among the tenant houses.

2. Why do you think people lived in the tenant houses described?

From Ocean to Ocean   13

Narcissa Whitman's Diary

Narcissa Prentiss Whitman had the distinction of being one of the first white women to cross the Rocky Mountains. The following selections are

Although glamorized by artists and writers, the trail to the West was often difficult for the American pioneers.

from her diary. They offer a view of life on the trail to Oregon in the 1830's.

[July] 27th [1836] Had quite a level route today. Came down Bear River and encamped on Tommow's [Thomas] Fork, a small branch. . . . We are still in a dangerous country but our company is large enough for safety. Our cattle endure the journey remarkably well. They are a source of great comfort to us in this land of scarcity, they supply us with sufficient milk . . . which is indeed a luxury. We are obliged to shoe some of them on account of sore feet. Have seen no buffalo since we left Rendezvous. Had no game of any kind except a few messes of Antelope which John's Father gave us. We have plenty of dry Buffalo meat which we purchased of the Indians & dry it is for me. I can scarcely eat it, it appears so filthy, but it will keep us alive, and we ought to be thankful for it.

We have had a few meals of fresh fish also, which relished well. Have the prospect of obtaining plenty in one or two weeks more. Found no berries. Neither have I found any of Ma's bread. . . . Do not think I regret coming. No, far from it. I would not go back for a world. I am contented and happy notwithstanding I sometimes get very hungry and weary.

Have six weeks steady journeying before us. Will the Lord give me patience to endure it. Feel sometime as if it was a long time to be traveling. Long for rest, but must not murmur. . . .
[August] 13th Sat. . . . We have come at least fifteen miles & have had the worst route in all the journey for the cart, we might have had a better one, but for being misled by some of the company who started out before their leaders. It was two o'clock before we came into camp. They are preparing to cross the Snake River.

The river is divided by two islands into three branches & is fordable. The packs are placed upon the top of the highest horses & in this way crossed without wetting. . . . The last branch we rode as much as a half mile in crossing & against the current too which made it hard for the horses the water being up to their sides. Husband had considerable difficulty in crossing the cart. (Both the cart & the mules were capsized in the water and the mules entangled in the harness.) (They) would have drowned, but for a desperate struggle to get them ashore. Then after putting two of the strongest horses before the cart & two men swimming behind to steady it, they succeeded in getting it over. I once thought that crossing streams would be the most dreadful part of the journey. I can now cross the most difficult stream without the least fear.

Reprinted by permission of the Publishers, The Arthur H. Clark Company, from *First White Women Over the Rockies,* by Clifford Merrill Drury. Vol. 1, pp. 74-75, 85-86.

Questions

1. Why were the cattle a particular comfort to Narcissa Whitman?
2. What caused the greatest difficulty for the Whitmans in crossing streams?

Travis's Last Appeal

The Battle of the Alamo was fought early in 1836 at a mission in San Antonio, Texas. On March 6, a force of nearly 4,000 Mexican soldiers defeated 187 Texans who were defending the mission. On March 3, Lieutenant Colonel William Barrett Travis, commander of the Texans, sent out his last appeal to the Texas government for reinforcements.

March 3, 1836

In the present confusion of the political authorities of the country, and in the absence of the commander-in-chief, I beg leave to communicate to you the situation of this garrison. . . .

From the 25th to the present date, the enemy have kept up a bombardment. . . . During this period the enemy have been busily employed in encircling us with entrenched encampments on all sides. . . . Notwithstanding all this, a company of thirty-two men, from Gonzales, made their way into us on the morning of the 1st [of the present month], at 3 o'clock, and Col. J. B. Bonham (a courier from Gonzales) got in this morning at 11 o'clock, without molestation. I have so fortified this place, that the walls are generally proof against cannon balls; and I still continue to intrench on the inside, and strengthen the walls by throwing up the dirt. . . . The spirits of my men are still high, although they have had much to depress them. We have [struggled] for ten days against an enemy whose numbers are variously estimated at from fifteen hundred to six thousand. . . . I sent an express to Col. Fannin, which arrived at Goliad on the next day, urging him to send us reinforcements—*none have yet arrived.* I look to the *colonies alone* [Texas] for aid: unless it arrives soon, I shall have to fight the enemy on his own terms. I will, however, do the best I can under the circumstances; and I feel confident that the determined valor, and desperate courage, heretofore [demonstrated] by my men, will not fail them in the last struggle: and although they may be sacrificed to the vengeance of a gothic enemy, the victory will cost the enemy so dear, that it will be worse for him than a defeat. I hope your honourable body will hasten on reinforcements, ammunition, and provisions to our aid, as soon as possible. . . .

If these things are promptly sent and large reinforcements are hastened to this frontier, this neighborhood will be the great and decisive battle ground. The power of Santa Anna is to be met here, or in the colonies; we had better meet them here, than to suffer a war of desolation to rage in our settlements. . . .

The bearer of this will give your honorable body, a statement more in detail, should he escape through the enemies lines—*God and Texas—Victory or Death!*

Your obedient servant,

W. BARRETT TRAVIS,

Lieut. Col. Comm.

P.S. The enemies troops are still arriving, and the reinforcement will probably amount to two or three thousand.

T.

From Mary Austin Holley, *Texas* (Lexington, Ky.: 1836), pp. 351-353. Original spelling included.

Questions

1. Why do you think this letter has stirred much patriotism among Americans?
2. Why did Travis choose to face the Mexican army here and at this time?

Smallpox Destroys the Mandans

The influence of white culture on the Indians was at times very brutal. Diseases against which the Indians had no resistance frequently exterminated whole tribes. The following account of the effects of smallpox on the Mandan people was written by George Catlin, an American artist. Catlin lived and worked among the Mandan for eight years in the 1800's.

The disease was introduced into the country by the Fur Company's steamer from St. Louis; which had two of their crew sick with the disease when it approached the Upper Missouri, and imprudently stopped to trade at the Mandan village, which was on the bank of the river, where the chiefs and others were allowed to come on board, by which means the disease got ashore.

I am constrained to believe, that the gentlemen in charge of the steamer did not believe it to be the small-pox; for if they had known it to be such, I cannot conceive of such imprudence, as regarded their own interests in the country, as well as the fate of these poor people, by allowing their boat to advance into the country under such circumstances.

It seems that the Mandans were surrounded by several war-parties of their more powerful enemies the Sioux, at that unlucky time, and they could not therefore disperse upon the plains, by which many of them could have been saved; and they were necessarily inclosed within the piquets of their village, where the disease in a few days became so very malignant that death ensued in a few hours after its attacks; and so slight were their hopes when they were attacked, that nearly half of them destroyed themselves. . . . The first symptom of the disease was a rapid swelling of the body, and so very virulent had it become, that very many died in two or three hours after their attack, and that in many cases without the appearance of the disease upon the skin. Utter dismay seemed to possess all classes and all ages, and they gave themselves up in despair, as entirely lost. There was but one continual crying and howling and praying to the Great Spirit for his protection during the nights and days; and there being but few living, and those in too appalling despair, nobody thought of burying the dead. . . . That such a proportion of their community as that above-mentioned, should have perished in so short a time, seems yet to the reader, an unaccountable thing; but in addition to the causes just mentioned, it must be borne in mind that this frightful disease is everywhere far more fatal amongst the native. . . .

So have perished the friendly and hospitable Mandans, from the best accounts I could get; and although it may be *possible* that some few individuals may yet be remaining, I think it is not probable; and one thing is certain, even if such be the case, that, as a nation, the Mandans are extinct, having no longer an existence.

From George Catlin, *Illustrations of the Manners, Customs and Conditions of the North American Indians* (London: Henry G. Bohn, 1848), Vol. 2, pp. 257-258.

Questions

1. How did the Mandan people come to be infected with smallpox?
2. What situation resulted in the rapid spread of the disease among all of the Mandan people?

UNIT V

Division

A Divided Nation   14

Rebirth of Slavery

Some historians have said that had it not been for certain developments, slavery might have gone completely from the United States by the 1800's. Historian Carl N. Degler explains in the following passage why slavery did not die. It was, in fact, reborn.

The prospects for [an end to slavery] were [favorable] in the latter part of the eighteenth century, inasmuch as tobacco, the staple of the slave-manned plantations of the South, was becoming an increasingly unprofitable crop. Should the economic and libertarian forces of the period pull in the same direction long enough, it was felt by many and hoped by even more, the anomaly of slavery among a people who believed that "all [people] were created equal" would soon cease to exist.

But toward the very end of the eighteenth century, two historical developments combined to infuse a new vigor into American slavery. The first and most important of these was the mechanization of English manufacturing, or the Industrial Revolution. Among the earliest industries to respond to mechanization was cotton textile manufacturing, with the immediate consequence of a [steep] increase in the demand for raw cotton, which in turn drove the price to very high levels. Prior to the Revolution no cotton of measurable quantities had been grown on the American mainland, though the West Indies had long exported the snowy "wool." The new rise in cotton prices, however, offered great incentive for the American production of the fiber. States like Georgia and South Carolina found that long-fiber cotton, which was readily separated from the seed, could be grown along their [coasts] and coastal islands. But efforts to expand cultivation of this sea-island cotton to the interior lands failed. The only cotton which would grow successfully on the uplands was a type in which the fiber tenaciously adhered to the seed, a fact which rendered its separation a tedious and expensive process even with slave labor.

With such economic incentive for ingenuity, it was inevitable that soon some device would be invented which would quickly and cheaply separate the short-fiber cotton from its seed. The inventor and the invention arrived in 1793 in the form of Eli Whitney and his gin. Immediately recognized as the answer to the ambitious planters' prayers, the gin and the unflagging English demand for cotton provided the necessary encouragement for the development of the Cotton Kingdom on the lands of western Georgia and South Carolina and in the new lands to the west. Intent upon reaping their profits as quickly as possible, the planters turned to the plantation and the . . . slave as the most [speedy] means of production. Slavery was reborn, soon to flourish as never before.

From Carl N. Degler, *Out of Our Past: The Forces That Shaped Modern America,* revised edition (New York: Harper & Row, Publishers, 1959, 1970), pp. 161-162. Reprinted by permission.

Questions

1. What two historical developments in the 1700's combined to infuse new vigor into American slavery?

2. Why would American slavery have ended without these developments?

Slave Auction

Slavery was called "peculiar" because it existed in only one part of the country by the 1800's. It became concentrated in the South, where cotton and other crops required much hand labor. The selection that follows is from the autobiography of Louis Hughes, a man born into slavery in 1832 and sold many times before being freed.

I was sick a great deal—in fact, I had suffered with chills and fever ever since Mr. Reid bought me. He, therefore, concluded to sell me, and, in November, 1844, he took me back to Richmond, placing me in the Exchange building, or auction rooms, for the sale of slaves. The sales were carried on in a large hall where those interested in the business sat around a large block or stand, upon which the slave to be sold was placed, the auctioneer standing beside him. When I was placed upon the block, a Mr. McGee came up and felt of me and asked me what I could do. . . . Virginia was the mother of slavery, and it was held by many that she had the best slaves. So when Mr. McGee found I was born and bred in that state he seemed satisfied. The bidding commenced, and I remember well when the auctioneer said: "Three hundred eighty dollars—once, twice and sold to Mr. Edward McGee." He was a rich cotton planter of Pontotoc, Miss. As near as I can recollect, I was not more than twelve years of age, so did not sell for very much.

Adapted from Louis Hughes, *Thirty Years a Slave: From Bondage to Freedom* (Milwaukee: South Side Printing Company, 1897), pp. 11-12.

Questions

1. Selling slaves was profitable for some people. Do you think the ability to make a profit kept slavery alive in the South?

2. Why did Hughes call Virginia "the mother of slavery"?

"Darling Nelly Gray"

One of Benjamin R. Hanby's most famous songs was "Darling Nelly Gray." He composed it in 1856 when he was a sophomore at Otterbein College in Westerville, Ohio. An observer at the time thought that "Darling Nelly Gray" may have swayed antislavery sentiment even more than Uncle Tom's Cabin, *commenting "a book must be read from cover to cover, but a song leaps from heart to heart."*

A runaway slave named Joe Selby was Hanby's inspiration for the song. Selby had been making his way from Kentucky to Canada along the underground railroad in 1842 when he stopped at the Hanby house in Ohio. Hanby was nine years old at the time but remembered how ill Selby was when he arrived. Hanby also remembered how desperately Selby wanted to find a job in order to buy the freedom of his fiancée, Nelly Gray. Selby soon died, but the fugitive's story lived in Hanby's mind for 14 years until he wrote the following lyrics.

There's a low green valley on the old Kentucky shore,
    Where I've whiled many happy hours away,
A-sitting and a-singing by the little cottage door,
    Where lived my darling Nelly Gray.

Chorus
O my poor Nelly Gray, they have taken you away,
    And I'll never see my darling any more;
I'm sitting by the river and I'm weeping all the day,
    For you've gone from the old Kentucky shore.

When the moon had climbed the mountain, and the stars were shining too,
    Then I'd take my darling Nelly Gray,
And we'd float down the river in my little red canoe,
    While my banjo sweetly I would play.

One night I went to see her, but "She's gone!" the neighbors say,
    The white man bound her with his chain;
They have taken her to Georgia for to wear her life away,
    As she toils in the cotton and the cane.

My canoe is under water and my banjo is unstrung,
    I'm tired of living any more;
My eyes shall look downward and my song shall be unsung
    While I stay on the old Kentucky shore.

My eyes are getting blinded and I cannot see my way;
    Hark! there's somebody knocking at the door.
Oh I hear the angels calling, and I see my Nelly Gray,
    Farewell to the old Kentucky shore.

O my darling Nelly Gray, up in heaven there, they say,
    That they'll never take you from me any more;
I'm a-coming, coming, coming, as the angels clear the way,
    Farewell to the old Kentucky shore.

"Darling Nelly Gray" (Boston: Oliver Ditson Co., 1856). Reprinted courtesy of the Westerville Historical Society.

Questions

1. What happened to Nelly Gray?

2. Why do you think Joe Selby had to leave Kentucky in order to hope to see Nelly Gray again?

Many slaves fled north along the underground railroad.

In Defense of the South

Judah Philip Benjamin has been called "the brains of the Confederacy" by many historians. During the Civil War, he served in Jefferson Davis's cabinet as Attorney General, Secretary of War, and Secretary of State. Before the war, however, he was one of the most respected members of the United States Senate. While still a Senator from Louisiana, Benjamin spoke on February 4, 1861, in the Senate chamber in defense of the South. The following passage is from that speech. Note that his reference to "Hampden" in the closing paragraph is to John Hampden, who in 1637 challenged King Charles I in an English court over the right of the king to rule without the consent of the people.

We are told that . . . the South is in rebellion without cause, and that her citizens are traitors.

Rebellion! The very word is a confession; an avowal of tyranny, outrage, and oppression. It is taken from the despot's code, and has no terror for other than slavish souls. When, sir, did millions of people, as a single man, rise in organized, deliberate, unimpassioned rebellion against justice, truth, and honor? Well did a great Englishman exclaim on a similar occasion:

"You might as well tell me that they rebelled against the light of heaven; that they rejected the fruits of the earth. Men do not war against

their benefactors; they are not mad enough to repel the instincts of self-preservation. I pronounce fearlessly that no intelligent people ever rose, or ever will rise, against a sincere, rational, and benevolent authority. . . . Infatuation is not a law of human nature. When there is a revolt by a free people, with the common consent of all classes of society, there must be a *criminal* against whom that revolt is aimed."

Traitors! Treason! Ay, sir, the people of the South imitate and glory in just such treason as glowed in the soul of Hampden; just such treason as leaped in living flame from the impassioned lips of [Patrick] Henry; just such treason as encircles with a sacred halo the undying name of [George] Washington!

From *The Congressional Globe*, 36th Congress, 2nd session, February 5, 1861.

Questions

1. With what event in American history did Benjamin compare Southern secession?
2. Do you think that Benjamin agreed that the South was in rebellion?

The Civil War 15

On the Eve of War

The thought of secession excited many people in the South. They felt that they had long been oppressed by the federal government and were finally standing united to defend their rights. The following selection was written by Augusta Killock, a young woman living in Chatham County, Georgia. Her letter to her brother, George, a student at Virginia Military Institute, captures a sense of excitement on the eve of civil war.

The Retreat
Chatham Co.
Republic of Georgia
Jan. 22nd [1861]

To George J. Kollock Jr.
V.M.I.
Lexington, Virginia

Dear Brother, I suppose you have seen by the papers that our good State has seceded, and that now we are a *free & independent people*. . . . The whole city has been wild with excitement ever since Sumter was taken, & has just begun to get a little quiet, but I suppose we must prepare for hot times now, that is if the Federal Government persists in the insane policy of coercion. It is the most absurd thing I ever heard of, & I rather think if they attempt it, they will find to their cost, that it is not quite so easy to subdue us as they fancied. They will be obliged to exterminate us. Of course you know that our troops have possession of Pulaski. We cannot have any parties, (though in truth no one has any heart for them) because all the beaux are down at the Fort. Detachments of the Guards, Blues, & Oglethorpe are down there all the time. Eddie Kollock either has joined or is about to join, a new company commanded by Col. Jones, the Pulaski Guards. If there is any war Uncle George is pledged to join another new corps, under Capt. Gallie, called the Savannah Artillery. In it are all the old men in the city, I believe. Think of Uncle G! You must know he is the only Unionist in the family, except Uncle William & James W., but Coercion has turned even him out. George J. has joined the Huzzars. The latter corps has adopted what they call a "service uniform" which consists of a plain pair of dark blue pants, with a duck-tail, tight fitting sack coat of the same, buttoned up the front with large silver buttons of the corps. Both garments are made of *Georgia cassimere*. The pretty dress uniform has been laid aside for a year, on account of the expense, which you know deterred many from joining the corps, & it is surprising how many recruits they have had, they now number 75 or more active members. Father says if there is war he will join again. There are three other new companies, the "Savannah Rifles," The "Blue Caps," Bob Grant commanding, (would you not like to join that corps) & the "Rattlesnakes." These three include all the rowdies in town, I believe. The Rattlesnakes was originally a secret society, a sort of vigilance committee I think, & the most extraordinary notices used to appear in the papers, for instance "Attention, Rattlesnakes! Come out of your holes, and meet at the Canal bridge, at 9 o'clock this evening.

By order of President Grand Rattle
POISON FANG, Secretary"
Then the next day the notice would be to "crawl into your holes."

Fights & weddings are the order of the day. Notwithstanding the times there have been more weddings this winter than for several years. . . . My Christmas presents were not ready to send on in Mothers box, so they will have to go in the next. All are quite well here except Mother, she was complaining yesterday, but seems quite bright today. Goodnight, it is getting late. Love to you both. Yr. affectionate sister.

P.S. Fido is quite well, so is Pluto.

From "Letters of the Kollock and Allied Families," *The Georgia Historical Quarterly,* September 1950, pp. 229-231. Reprinted by permission of The Georgia Historical Society.

Questions

1. Do you think Augusta Kollock was for or against secession?
2. What did Kollock mean by citing her return address as "Republic of Georgia"?

A Patriotic Song of the South

According to General Robert E. Lee, "it is impossible to have an army without music." During the Civil War, the largest collection of war-related songs in American history was produced. These songs often captured the thoughts and feelings of the American people. The most frequently published Confederate song was "The Bonnie Blue Flag." Harry McCarty wrote the song to commemorate an early Confederate flag. The lyrics to McCarty's song are given below.

We are a band of brothers, and native to the soil,
Fighting for the property we gain'd by honest toil;

And when our rights were threaten'd, the cry rose near and far,
Hurrah for the Bonnie Blue Flag, that bears a Single Star.

Chorus
Hurrah! Hurrah! for Southern Rights, Hurrah!
Hurrah! for the Bonnie Blue Flag, that bears a Single Star.

As long as the old Union was faithful to her trust,
Like friends and like brothers, kind were we and just;
But now, when Northern treachery attempts our rights to mar,
We hoist on high the Bonnie Blue Flag, that bears a Single Star.

First, gallant South Carolina nobly made the stand;
Then came Alabama, who took her by the hand;
Next, quickly Mississippi, Georgia and Florida,
All rais'd on high the Bonnie Blue Flag that bears a Single Star.

Ye men of valor, gather round the Banner of the Right,
Texas and fair Louisiana join us in the fight;
Davis, our loved President, and Stephens, statesman rare,
Now rally round the Bonnie Blue Flag that bears a Single Star.

And here's to brave Virginia! the Old Dominion State
With the young Confederacy at length has linked her fate;
Impell'd by her example, now other states prepare
To hoist on high the Bonnie Blue Flag that bears a Single Star.

Then here's to our Confederacy, strong we are and brave,
Like patriots of old, we'll fight our heritage to save;
And rather than submit to shame, to die we would prefer,

So cheer for the Bonnie Blue Flag that bears a Single Star.

Then cheer, boys, cheer, raise the joyous shout,
For Arkansas and North Carolina now have both gone out;
And let another rousing cheer for Tennessee be given—
The Single Star of the Bonnie Blue Flag has grown to be Eleven.

———
From *Heart Songs* (Boston: The Chapple Publishing Company, Ltd., 1909), pp. 60-61.

Questions _____

1. In the first verse of "The Bonnie Blue Flag," the songwriter refers to "property we gained by honest toil." What is the "property" to which he refers?

2. "The Bonnie Blue Flag" specifically mentions the eleven Confederate states. What are they?

A Patriotic Song of the North

Patriotic songs of the Civil War played an important role in the lives of the soldiers and their families. Loneliness, boredom, combat experiences, and uncertainty about the future led soldiers to search for the simple pleasures inherent in music. Many songs, including the Union's "The Battle Cry of Freedom," produced powerful emotions and memories.

"The Battle Cry of Freedom" was written by professional songwriter and music publisher, George F. Root. He wrote the song a few hours after President Lincoln called for Union troops to fight in Virginia. "The Battle Cry of Freedom" sold over 350,000 copies and was one of the most popular songs in the Union.

Yes, we'll rally the flag, boys, we'll rally once again,
Shouting the battle cry of Freedom,
We will rally from the hillside, we'll gather from the plain,
Shouting the battle cry of Freedom.

Chorus
The Union forever, Hurrah boys, Hurrah!
Down with the traitor, Up with the star;
While we rally round the flag, boys, Rally once
    again,
Shouting the battle cry of Freedom.

We are springing to the call of our brothers gone
    before,
    Shouting the battle cry of Freedom,
And we'll fill the vacant ranks with a million
    freemen more,
    Shouting the battle cry of Freedom.

We will welcome to our numbers the loyal true and
    brave,
    Shouting the battle cry of Freedom,
And altho' they may be poor, not a man shall be a
    slave,
    Shouting the battle cry of Freedom.

So we're springing to the call from the East and
    from the West,
    Shouting the battle cry of Freedom,
And we'll hurl the rebel crew from the land we love
    the best,
    Shouting the battle cry of Freedom.

From *Heart Songs* (Boston: The Chapple Publishing Company
Ltd., 1909), pp. 17-18.

Questions

1. How could a song such as "The Battle Cry of
   Freedom" help the Union's cause?

2. Both the Union and the Confederacy sang of
   their fights for freedom. What meaning did the
   term "freedom" hold for each of these groups?

Civil War Medical Corps

In A Stillness at Appomattox, *Civil War
writer Bruce Catton describes the final years of the
war in Virginia. In the passage that follows, Catton
gives readers a vivid account of the medical
conditions in the Union army after the Battle of the
Wilderness in 1864.*

The best was not very good. . . . There were
just thirty army doctors on hand to look after the
7,000 wounded, all of whom by now needed
attention very badly; needed at the very least to be
bathed and given fresh clothing and hot soup, and
to have their bandages changed. Practically none
of these things could be done, partly because of a
woeful shortage of help and partly because the
medicines, fresh dressings, and food that were on
hand were strictly limited to the little that had been
carried in the wagons. The man who got so much as
hardtack and a drink of water that day was in luck.
It took more than twenty-four hours just to get the
men out of the wagons. A good many of them died,
which meant that some of the attendants had to
ignore the living and serve on burial details.

The doctors did their best, and some of the
stretcher-bearers finally turned out to be fairly
useful, and it might not have been so bad if they
could once have got the situation stabilized. But
the army kept pumping new streams of wounded
men in on them faster than the ones they already
had could be cared for, and although the men who
were trying to cope with this in-gathering of misery
worked until they were gray-faced and stupid with
fatigue, they kept falling farther and farther
behind. It was as if war, the great clumsy machine
for maiming people, had at last been perfected.
Instead of turning out its grist spasmodically, with
long waits between each delivery, it was at last able
to produce every day, without any gaps at all.
Since the medical service had never been up
against anything like this before—had never
dreamed of anything like it, in its wildest
[dreams]—there was bound to be trouble.

One doctor wrote that for four days in a
row—including most of the intervening hours—he
did nothing whatever but amputate arms and legs,
until it seemed to him that he could not possibly
perform another operation. Yet hundreds of cases
were waiting for him, and wounded men kept
stumbling in, begging almost tearfully to have a
mangled arm taken off before gangrene [infection]
should set in. "It is a scene of horror such as I never
saw," he cried. "God forbid that I should ever see
another." A day or two later he had found no end
to it: "Hundreds of ambulances are coming into

A tattered Confederate flag flies over Fort Sumter. Held from April 1861 to February 1865, the fort remained a symbol of Southern independence.

town now, and it is almost midnight. So they come every night."

Excerpt from *A Stillness at Appomattox* by Bruce Catton. Copyright 1953 by Bruce Catton. Reprinted by permission of Doubleday & Company, Inc.

Questions

1. Did medical care suffer from lack of knowledge or lack of resources?

2. Why do you think amputation was the most common means of treating an infected arm or leg?

Coming to Terms

The Hampton Roads Conference of February 1865 was an attempt to negotiate an end to the Civil War. The following letter, written by President Abraham Lincoln to Secretary of State William Seward, was intended to provide Seward with guidelines for the negotiations. At the last minute, however, Lincoln decided to attend the Conference.

Lincoln and Seward met with representatives of the Confederate States, Vice-President Alexander H. Stephens, Senator R. M. T. Hunter, and former Supreme Court Justice John A. Campbell aboard the steamer transport River Queen. *The talks lasted four hours, but there were no positive results. The leaders of the Confederacy wanted armistice first, and talk of a reunion later. Lincoln insisted upon the guidelines outlined in the following letter.*

Hon. William H. Seward,   Executive Mansion,
Secretary of State: Washington,
                                        January 31, 1865

You will proceed to Fortress Monroe, Va., there to meet and informally confer with Messrs. Stephens, Hunter, and Campbell. . . .

You will make known to them that three things are indispensable, to wit:

1. The restoration of the national authority throughout all the States:

2. No receding by the Executive of the United States on the slavery question from the position assumed thereon in the late annual message to Congress and in preceding documents.

3. No cessation of hostilities short of an end of the war and the disbanding of all forces hostile to the Government.

You will inform them that all propositions of theirs not inconsistent with the above will be considered and passed upon in a spirit of sincere liberality. You will hear all they may choose to say and report it to me.

You will not assume to definitely consummate anything.

Yours, etc.,
Abraham Lincoln

From Arthur B. Lapsley, ed., *The Writings of Abraham Lincoln* (New York: G. P. Putnam's Sons, 1906), pp. 308-309.

Questions

1. What three things did Lincoln require, before he would agree to end the Civil War?

2. Why do you think that the Hampton Roads Conference was unsuccessful?

Rebuilding the Nation 16

Columbia in Ruins

Southern cities such as Atlanta, Charleston, and Columbia suffered the greatest devastation during the war. One description of the extensive war damage was written by Sidney Andrews, a reporter for the Chicago Tribune *and the* Boston Daily Advertiser. *Andrews toured the ruins of the major Southern cities in the fall of 1865. The following passage is an excerpt from his report on Columbia, South Carolina.*

It is now a wilderness of ruins. Its heart is but a mass of blackened chimneys and crumbling walls. Two thirds of the buildings in the place were burned, including, without exception, everything in the business portion. Not a store, office, or shop escaped; and for a distance of three fourths of a mile on each of twelve streets there was not a building left. "They destroyed everything which the most infernal Yankee ingenuity could devise means to destroy," said one gentleman to me; "hands, hearts, fire, gunpowder, and behind everything the spirit of hell, were the agencies which they used." I asked him if he wasn't stating the case rather strongly; and he replied that he would make it stronger if he could. The residence portion generally escaped conflagration, though houses were burned in all sections except the extreme northeastern.

Every public building was destroyed, except the new and unfinished state-house. This is situated on the summit of tableland whereon the city is built, and commands an extensive view of the surrounding country, and must have been the first building seen by the victorious and on-marching Union army. From the summit of the ridge, on the opposite side of the river, a mile and a half away, a few shells were thrown at it, apparently by way of reminder, three or four of which struck it, without doing any particular damage. With this exception, it was unharmed, though the workshops, in which were stored many of the architraves, caps, sills, &c., were burned,—the fire, of course, destroying or seriously damaging their contents. The poverty of this people is so deep that there is no probability that it can be finished, according to the original design, during this generation at least.

The ruin here is neither half so eloquent nor touching as that at Charleston. This is but the work of flame, and might have mostly been brought about in time of peace. Those ghostly and crumbling walls and those long-deserted and grass-grown streets show the prostration of a community,—such prostration as only war could bring.

From Sidney Andrews, *The South Since the War* (Boston: Ticknor and Fields, 1866), pp. 33-34.

Questions

1. What seems to have been the major target of the Union army in its attack on Columbia?
2. How was much of the city destroyed?

Lincoln's Reconstruction Policy

Under President Lincoln's plan for reconstruction, Arkansas, Tennessee, and Louisiana were ready to return to the Union in 1864. Congress, however, refused to seat their Representatives and Senators. The Radical Republicans within Congress felt that Lincoln's requirements were much too lenient. Among other things, Congress wanted to require fifty percent of the white males in each state to pledge their loyalty to the United States before their state government could be set up. President Lincoln only required that ten percent of the state's voters from 1860 take an oath of loyalty. In the following passages from his last public address, Lincoln defends his position.

FELLOW-CITIZENS:—We meet this evening not in sorrow, but in gladness of heart. The evacuation of Petersburg and Richmond, and the surrender of the principal insurgent army, give hope of a righteous and speedy peace. . . . By these recent successes, the reinauguration of the national authority—reconstruction—which has had a large share of thought from the first, is pressed much more closely upon our attention. It is fraught with great difficulty. Unlike a case of war between independent nations, *there is no authorized organ for us to treat with*—one one [person] has authority to give up the rebellion for any other [person]. We simply must begin with and mould from disorganized and discordant elements. Nor is it a small

Because much of the fighting during the Civil War took place in the South, devastation there was widespread. Factories, railroads, and whole sections of cities were destroyed.

additional embarrassment that we, the loyal people, differ among ourselves as to the mode, manner, and measure of reconstruction. . . . We all agree that the seceded States, so called, are out of their proper practical relation with the Union, and that the sole object of the Government, civil and military, in regard to those States, is to again get them into their proper practical relation. I believe that it is not only possible, but in fact easier, to do this without deciding or even considering whether those States have ever been out of the Union, than with it. Finding themselves safely at home, it would be utterly immaterial whether they had been abroad. . . . The amount of constituency, so to speak, on which the Louisiana government rests, would be more satisfactory to all if it contained fifty thousand, or thirty thousand, or even twenty thousand, instead of twelve thousand, as it does. It is also unsatisfactory to some that the elective franchise is not given to the [black] man. I would myself prefer that it were now conferred on the very intelligent, and on those who serve our cause as soldiers. Still, the question is not whether the Louisiana government, as it stands, is quite all that is desirable. The question is, Will it be wiser to take it as it is and help to improve it, or to reject and disperse? Can Louisiana be brought into proper practical relation with the Union sooner by sustaining or by discarding [its] new State government? Some twelve thousand voters in the heretofore Slave State of Louisiana have sworn allegiance to the Union, assumed to be the rightful political power of the State, held elections, organized a State government, adopted a Free State constitution, giving the benefit of public schools equally to black and white, and empowering the Legislature to confer the elective franchise upon the [black] man. This Legislature has already voted to ratify the Constitutional Amendment recently passed by Congress, abolishing slavery throughout the nation. These twelve thousand persons are thus fully committed to the Union and to perpetuate freedom in the State—committed to the very things, and nearly all things, the nation wants— and they ask the nation's recognition and its assistance to make good this committal. Now, if we reject and spurn them, we do our utmost to disorganize and disperse them. We, in fact, say to the white [people]: You are worthless or worse; we will neither help you nor be helped by you. To the blacks we say: This cup of liberty which these, your old masters, held to your lips, we will dash from you, and leave you to the chances of gathering the spilled and scattered contents in some vague and undefined when, where, and how. If this course, discouraging and paralyzing both white and black, has any tendency to bring Louisiana into proper practical relations with the Union, I have so far been unable to perceive it. If, on the contrary, we recognize and sustain the new government of Louisiana, the converse of all this is made true. We encourage the hearts and nerve the arms of twelve thousand to adhere to their work, and argue for it, and [recruit] for it, and fight for it, and feed it, and grow it, and ripen it to a complete success. The [black people], too, in seeing all united for [them, are] inspired with vigilance, and energy, and daring to the same end. Grant that [they desire] the elective franchise, will [they] not attain it sooner by saving the already advanced steps toward it, than by running backward over them? Concede that the new government of Louisiana is only to what it should be as the egg is to the fowl, we shall sooner have the fowl by hatching the egg than by smashing it. Again, if we reject Louisiana, we also reject one vote in favor of the proposed amendment to the National Constitution.

From Arthur B. Lapsley, ed., *The Writings of Abraham Lincoln* (New York: G. P. Putnam's Sons, 1906), pp. 362-367.

Questions

1. Why was reestablishing national authority in the South more difficult than forming a peace treaty with an independent nation?

2. Why did Lincoln want to admit Louisiana back into the Union, even though it had not met all of the requirements proposed by Congress?

3. What policies did the proposed state government of Louisiana adopt toward blacks?

Texas Rejoins the Union

In order to be reinstated to the Union, each seceded state had to meet specific guidelines. Among the requirements for readmittance were the abolition of slavery and obedience to the laws of the Constitution. Early in 1866, Texas passed several resolutions aligning it with the Union. Thus, on August 20, 1866, President Andrew Johnson proclaimed the insurrection in Texas to be at an end. Passages from Johnson's proclamation appear below.

And whereas, the laws can now be sustained and enforced in the said State of Texas, by the proper civil authority, State or Federal, and the people of the said State of Texas, like the people of the other States before named, are well and loyally disposed, and have conformed or will conform in their legislation to the condition of affairs growing out of the amendment of the Constitution of the United States, prohibiting slavery within the limits and jurisdiction of the United States; . . .

And whereas, adequate provision has been made by military orders, to enforce the execution of the acts of Congress, aid the civil authorities, and secure obedience to the Constitution and laws of the United States within the State of Texas, if a resort to military force for such purpose should at any time become necessary;

Now, therefore, I, ANDREW JOHNSON, President of the United States, do hereby proclaim and declare that the insurrection which heretofore existed in the State of Texas is at an end, and is to be henceforth so regarded in that State, as in the other States before named, in which the said insurrection was proclaimed to be at an end, by the aforesaid proclamation of the second day of April, one thousand eight hundred and sixty-six.

And I do further proclaim that the said insurrection is at an end, and that peace, order, tranquility, and civil authority now exist in and throughout the whole of the United States of America.

In testimony whereof, I have hereunto set my hand and caused the seal of the United States to be affixed.

Done at the city of Washington this twentieth day of August, in the year of our Lord one thousand eight hundred and sixty-six, and of the Independence of the United States of America the ninety-first.

Andrew Johnson

From George P. Sanger, ed., *The Public Statutes at Large of the United States of America from the Organization of the Government in 1789, etc.* (Boston: 1868, 1873), Vol. 14, pp. 814-817.

Questions

1. At the time of President Johnson's proclamation, what was the position of the Texas legislature concerning slavery?

2. Why did President Johnson proclaim that "peace, order, tranquility, and civil authority now exist in and throughout the whole of the United States"?

Atlas and Historical Data

United States	488	The World	496
Climate	490	North America	498
Land Use	490	South America	499
Mineral Resources and Deposits	491	Eurasia	500
Industry and Manufacturing	491	Africa	502
The American People	492	The States of the Union	503
The American Society	493	Presidents and Vice Presidents	504
The American Economy	494	American Political Parties	505
The Government Sector	495		

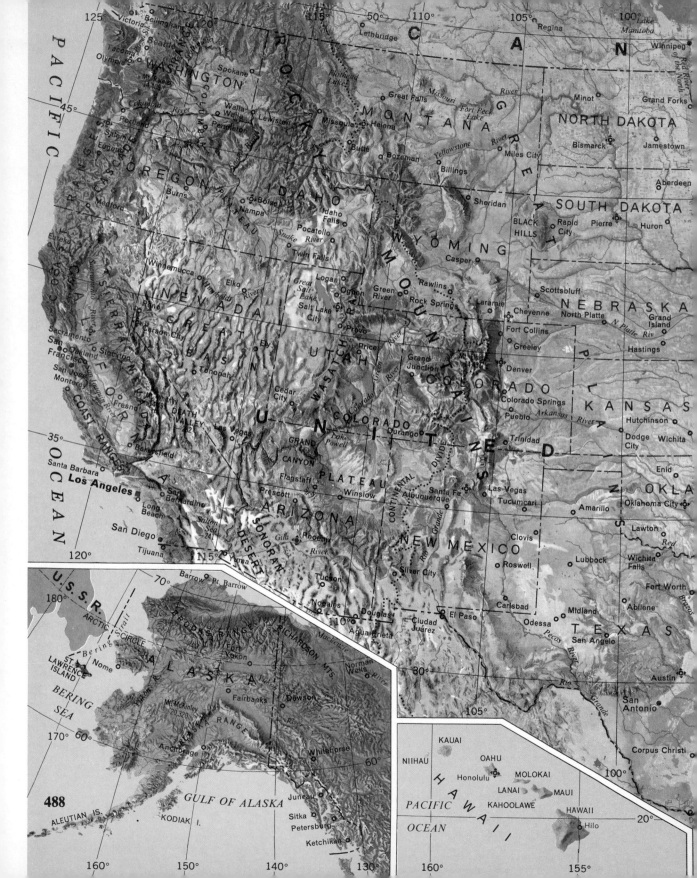

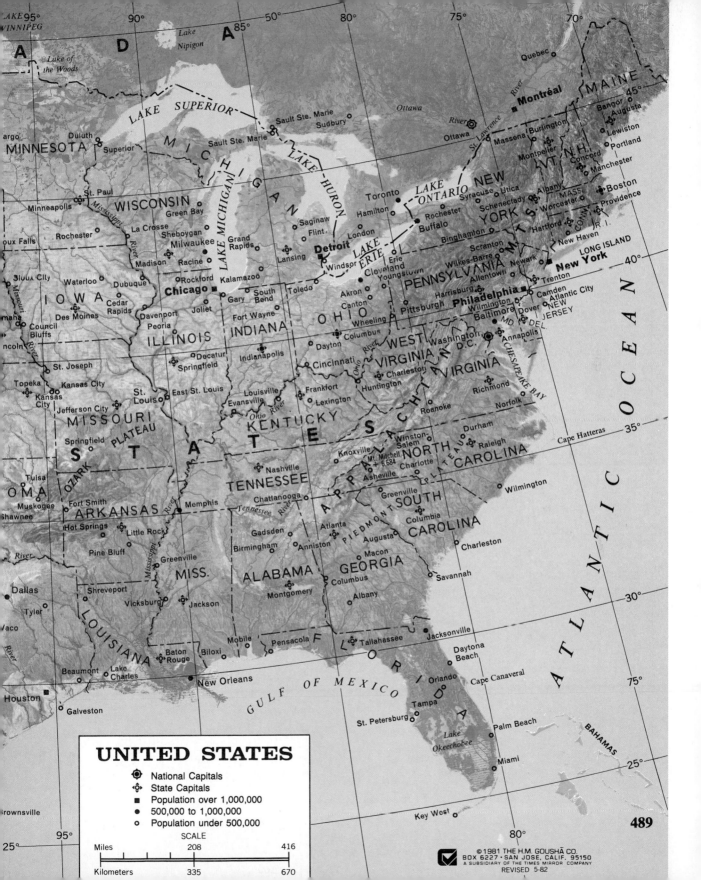

UNITED STATES

◈ National Capitals
✪ State Capitals
■ Population over 1,000,000
● 500,000 to 1,000,000
○ Population under 500,000

SCALE

Miles |—————| 208 |—————| 416

Kilometers |—————| 335 |—————| 670

489

© 1981 THE H.M. GOUSHĀ CO.
BOX 6227 • SAN JOSE, CALIF. 95150
A SUBSIDIARY OF THE TIMES MIRROR COMPANY
REVISED 5-82

CLIMATE

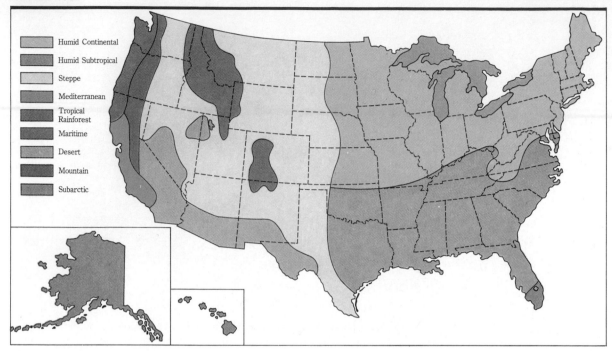

- Humid Continental
- Humid Subtropical
- Steppe
- Mediterranean
- Tropical Rainforest
- Maritime
- Desert
- Mountain
- Subarctic

LAND USE

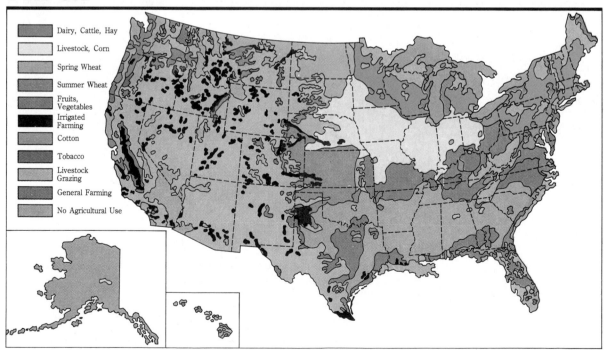

- Dairy, Cattle, Hay
- Livestock, Corn
- Spring Wheat
- Summer Wheat
- Fruits, Vegetables
- Irrigated Farming
- Cotton
- Tobacco
- Livestock Grazing
- General Farming
- No Agricultural Use

MINERAL RESOURCES AND DEPOSITS

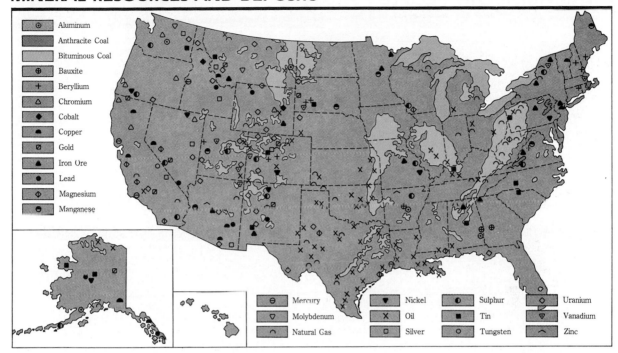

Symbol	Mineral
⊙	Aluminum
	Anthracite Coal
	Bituminous Coal
⊕	Bauxite
+	Beryllium
△	Chromium
◆	Cobalt
▲	Copper
▨	Gold
▲	Iron Ore
●	Lead
◐	Magnesium
⊖	Manganese

Symbol	Mineral		Symbol	Mineral		Symbol	Mineral		Symbol	Mineral
⊖	Mercury		▼	Nickel		◐	Sulphur		◇	Uranium
▽	Molybdenum		✕	Oil		■	Tin		▽	Vanadium
⌒	Natural Gas		▢	Silver		○	Tungsten		⌒	Zinc

INDUSTRY AND MANUFACTURING

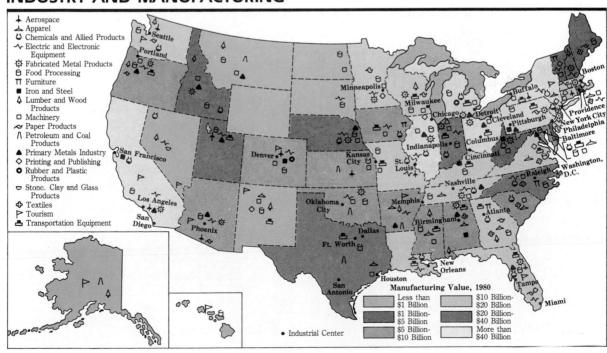

- ✈ Aerospace
- ⊥ Apparel
- ↻ Chemicals and Allied Products
- ∿ Electric and Electronic Equipment
- ✿ Fabricated Metal Products
- ◷ Food Processing
- ⊓ Furniture
- ■ Iron and Steel
- ⚐ Lumber and Wood Products
- ▢ Machinery
- ～ Paper Products
- ⋀ Petroleum and Coal Products
- ▲ Primary Metals Industry
- ◇ Printing and Publishing
- ✪ Rubber and Plastic Products
- ▽ Stone, Clay and Glass Products
- ✚ Textiles
- ▷ Tourism
- ⛴ Transportation Equipment

Manufacturing Value, 1980

Less than $1 Billion	$10 Billion– $20 Billion
$1 Billion– $5 Billion	$20 Billion– $40 Billion
$5 Billion– $10 Billion	More than $40 Billion

● Industrial Center

Seattle, Portland, Minneapolis, Milwaukee, Chicago, Detroit, Cleveland, Buffalo, Pittsburgh, Providence, New York City, Philadelphia, Baltimore, Boston, Columbus, Cincinnati, Indianapolis, St. Louis, Kansas City, Denver, San Francisco, Los Angeles, San Diego, Phoenix, San Antonio, Ft. Worth, Dallas, Houston, New Orleans, Oklahoma City, Memphis, Nashville, Birmingham, Atlanta, Raleigh, Washington, D.C., Tampa, Miami

491

THE AMERICAN PEOPLE

POPULATION

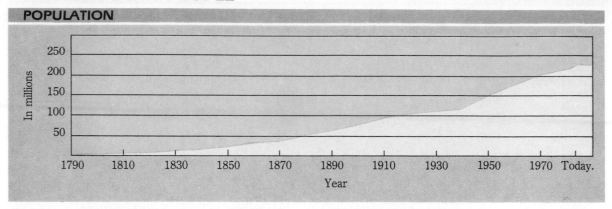

DISTRIBUTION BY AGE

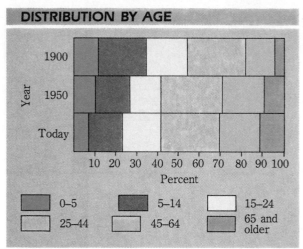

POPULATION BY RACE AND ORIGIN

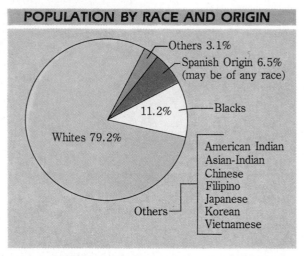

BIRTH AND DEATH RATE

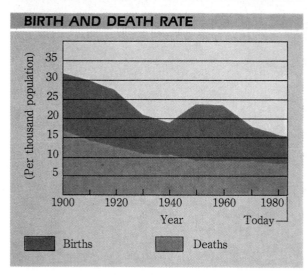

LIFE EXPECTANCY AT BIRTH

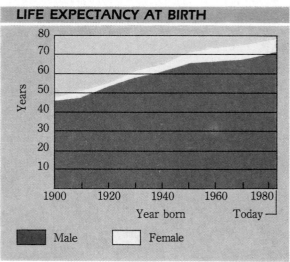

THE AMERICAN SOCIETY

EDUCATION

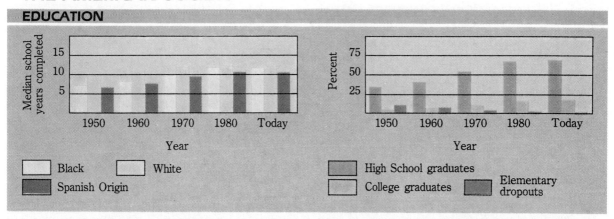

Black · White · Spanish Origin

High School graduates · College graduates · Elementary dropouts

HEALTH CARE EXPENDITURES

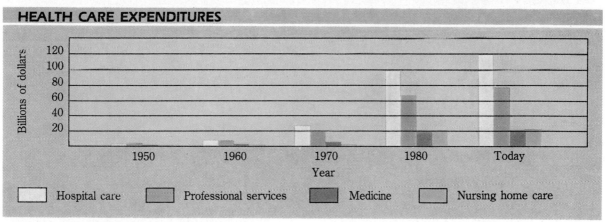

Hospital care · Professional services · Medicine · Nursing home care

CENSUS OF RELIGIOUS GROUPS

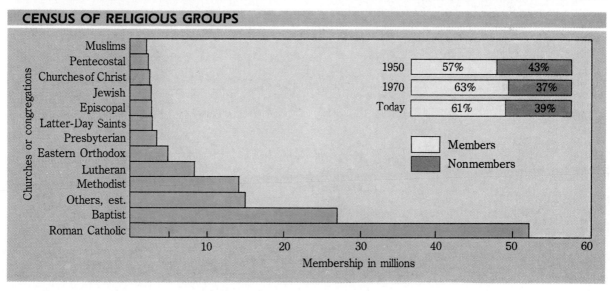

THE AMERICAN ECONOMY

GROSS NATIONAL PRODUCT

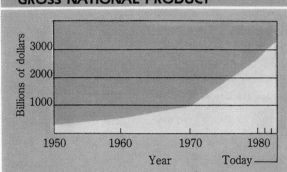

Billions of dollars

1950   1960   1970   1980

Year   Today

MEDIAN INCOME OF FAMILIES

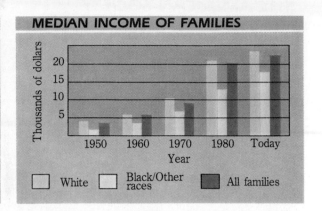

Thousands of dollars

1950   1960   1970   1980   Today

Year

☐ White   ☐ Black/Other races   ■ All families

AMERICA AT WORK

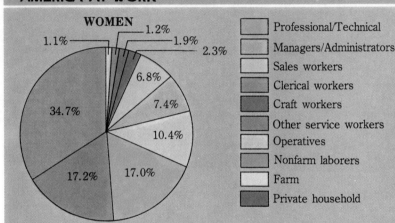

WOMEN

1.1%   1.2%   1.9%   2.3%
6.8%
7.4%
34.7%   10.4%
17.2%   17.0%

☐ Professional/Technical
☐ Managers/Administrators
☐ Sales workers
☐ Clerical workers
☐ Craft workers
☐ Other service workers
☐ Operatives
☐ Nonfarm laborers
☐ Farm
■ Private household

MEN

0.1%   3.9%
6.1%
20.7%   6.3%
7.1%
16.5%   8.8%
15.9%   14.6%

PURCHASING POWER OF THE DOLLAR

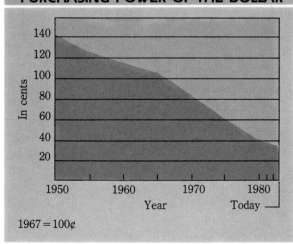

In cents

140
120
100
80
60
40
20

1950   1960   1970   1980

Year   Today

1967 = 100¢

CONSUMER AND WHOLESALE PRICES

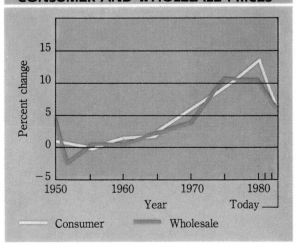

Percent change

15
10
5
0
−5

1950   1960   1970   1980

Year   Today

── Consumer   ── Wholesale

494

THE GOVERNMENT SECTOR

PUBLIC EMPLOYEES

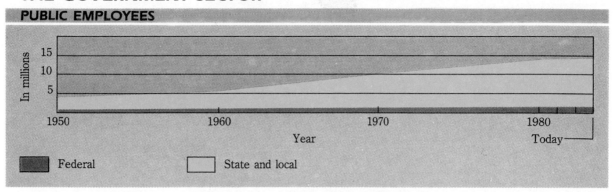

FEDERAL GOVERNMENT RECEIPTS AND EXPENDITURES

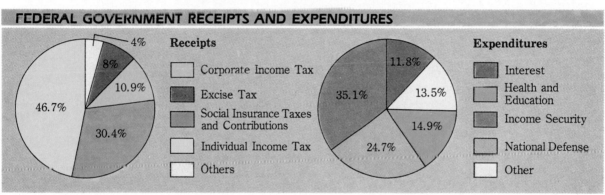

EXPENDITURES BY STATE AND LOCAL GOVERNMENT

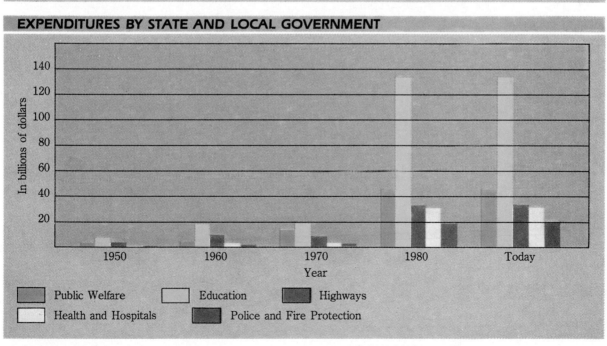

ARCTIC OCEAN

ALASKA (UNITED STATES)

CANADA

NORTH AMERICA

UNITED STATES

Ottawa

New York

Washington, D.C.

Los Angeles

MEXICO

ATLANTIC

Mexico City

BAHAMAS

CUBA

DOMINICAN REPUBLIC

HAITI

JAMAICA

BELIZE

HONDURAS

GUATEMALA

EL SALVADOR

NICARAGUA

COSTA RICA

PANAMA

TRINIDAD AND TOBAGO

Caracas

VENEZUELA

GUYANA

SURINAME

FR. GUIANA

Bogotá

COLOMBIA

EQUATOR

ECUADOR

SOUTH

BRAZIL

AMERICA

Lima

Brasília

BOLIVIA

PARAGUAY

Santiago

URUGUAY

Buenos Aires

ARGENTINA

PACIFIC

OCEAN

OCEAN

INTERNATIONAL DATE LINE

HAWAII (U.S.)

ARCTIC

ICELAND

UNITED KINGDOM

IRELAND

DEN

NETH

BEL

London

France

Par

PORTUGAL

SPAIN

Madrid

MOROCCO

ALGERIA

MAURITANIA

MALI

A F

CAPE VERDE

SENEGAL

GAMBIA

GUINEA-BISSAU

GUINEA

VOLTA

BENIN

SIERRA LEONE

LIBERIA

CAMER

EQUAT. GU

GAE

CAB (ANG

OCEAN

PRIME MERIDIAN

THE WORLD

SCALE IN MILES AND KILOMETERS

One inch 1800 miles

One centimeter 1140 kilometers

Mercator Projection

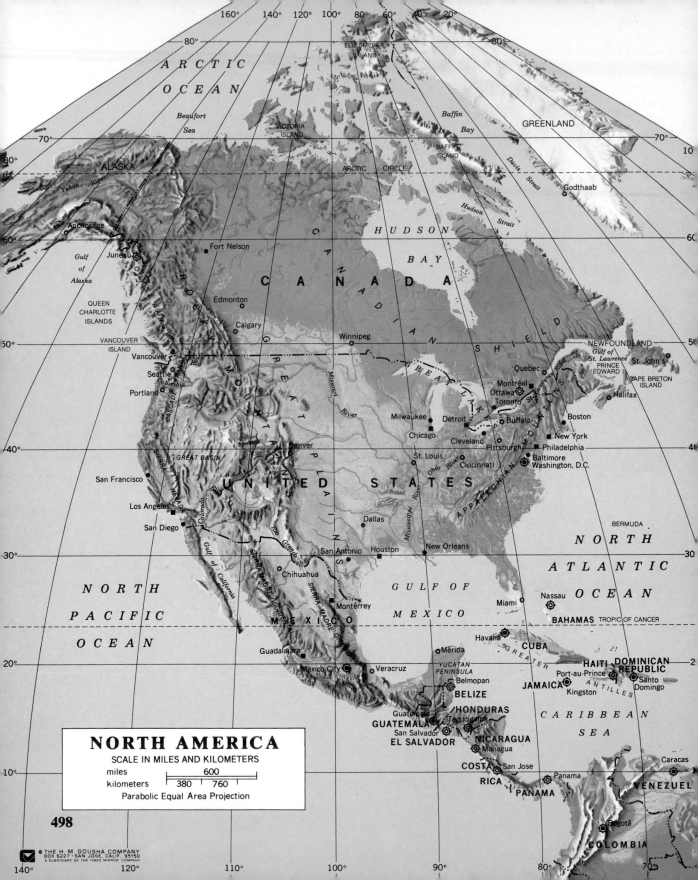

NORTH AMERICA

SCALE IN MILES AND KILOMETERS

miles 600

kilometers 380 760

Parabolic Equal Area Projection

498

© THE H. M. GOUSHA COMPANY
BOX 6227 · SAN JOSE, CALIF. 95150
A SUBSIDIARY OF THE TIMES MIRROR COMPANY

SOUTH AMERICA
SCALE IN MILES AND KILOMETERS

miles · 600
kilometers · 380 | 760
Parabolic Equal Area Projection

© THE H. M. GOUSHA COMPANY
BOX 6227 · SAN JOSE, CALIF. 95150
A SUBSIDIARY OF THE TIMES MIRROR COMPANY

499

160° 170° 180°

AN

Laptev
Sea

70°

Verkhoyansk

S I B E R I A

River

60°

KAMCHATKA PENINSULA

KOLYM MOUNTAINS

STANOVOY MOUNTAINS

Sea of Okhotsk

ovosibirsk   Krasnoyarsk

SOCIALIST   REPUBLICS

Lake Baikal

Irkutsk

SAYAN MOUNTAINS

Lake
Balkhash

50°

Khabarovsk

KURIL

ISLANDS

Amur River

Pinkiang
(Harbin)

Alma Ata

Ulan Bator

HOKKAIDO

MONGOLIA

GOBI
DESERT

M A N C H U R I A

Shenyang
(Mukden)

Vladivostok

NORTH
KOREA

J A P A N

40°

NAN SHAN

TAKLA
MAKAN

PAMIR

Beijing
(Peking)

Luda
(Dairen)

Pyongyang

Sea
of Japan

HONSHU

Islamabad

KUNLUN MOUNTAINS

C H I N A

Tianjin
(Tientsin)

Yellow
Sea

Seoul

SOUTH
KOREA

Pusan

Kyoto

Tokyo

Lahore

PLATEAU OF TIBET

Lhasa

Xi'an
(Sian)

TSINLING SHAN

He

Qingdao
(Tsingtao)

Kobe   Osaka

SHIKOKU

AKISTAN

Delhi

HIMALAYAS

Mekong River

Chang Jiang

Wuhan
Wuhan

Nanjing
(Nanking)

Shanghai
(Shanghai)

KYUSHU

East
China
Sea

30°

achi

New
Delhi

Lucknow

NEPAL

Mt. Everest
29,141 ft.

BHUTAN

Brahmaputra R.

SZECHWAN
BASIN

Chongqing
(Chunking)

Tungting
Hu

OKINAWA

THAR
DESERT

Ganges

Katmandu

River

NAGA HILLS

Taipei

Kanpur

BANGLA-
DESH

Dacca

Xi Jiang

Guangzhou
(Canton)

TAIWAN

Ahmadabad

Calcutta

Red River

TROPIC OF CANCER

Nagpur

Jaipur

Mandalay

Hanoi

Victoria
(Hong Kong)

20°

Bombay   Pune

WESTERN

I N D I A

Bay of Bengal

BURMA

Irrawaddy R.

Gulf of
Tonkin

S O U T H

AN

Hyderabad

GHATS

Rangoon

Vientiane

L A O S

VIETNAM

C H I N A

REPUBLIC
OF THE
PHILIPPINES

Bangalore

EASTERN

Madras

THAILAND

Bangkok

S E A

Manila

GHATS

CAMBODIA

Tonle Sap

Phnom Penh

10°

SRI LANKA

Gulf of
Siam

Ho Chi Minh City
(Saigon)

Colombo

MALDIVES

MALAY

PENINSULA

MALAYSIA

BRUNEI

NDIAN   OCEAN

Strait of Malacca

Kuala
Lumpur

501

SINGAPORE

Singapore

0°

EQUATOR

REPUBLIC OF INDONESIA

70°   80°   90°   100°   110°   120°   130°

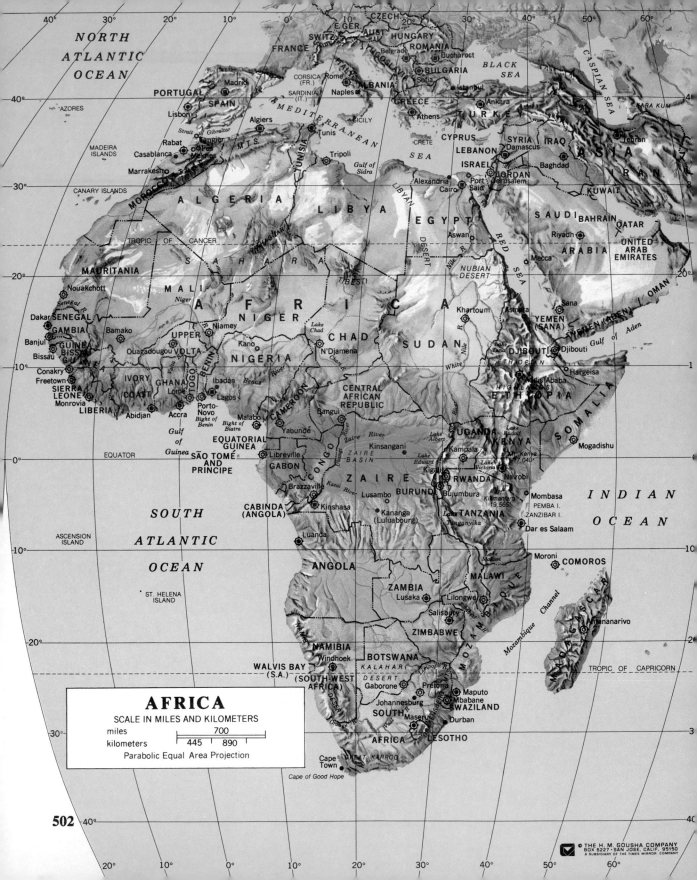

AFRICA

SCALE IN MILES AND KILOMETERS

miles 700

kilometers 445 890

Parabolic Equal Area Projection

502

THE STATES OF THE UNION

STATE	CAPITAL	ENTERED UNION	POPULATION 1980	PCT. CHANGE FROM 1970	AREA IN SQ. MILES
Alabama	Montgomery	1819	3,890,061	+12.9	51,609
Alaska	Juneau	1959	400,481	+32.4	586,412
Arizona	Phoenix	1912	2,717,866	+53.1	113,909
Arkansas	Little Rock	1836	2,285,513	+18.8	53,104
California	Sacramento	1850	23,668,562	+18.5	158,693
Colorado	Denver	1876	2,888,834	+30.7	104,247
Connecticut	Hartford	1788	3,107,576	+2.5	5,009
Delaware	Dover	1787	595,225	+8.6	2,057
Florida	Tallahassee	1845	9,739,992	+43.4	58,560
Georgia	Atlanta	1788	5,464,265	+19.1	58,876
Hawaii	Honolulu	1959	965,000	+25.3	6,450
Idaho	Boise	1890	943,935	+32.4	83,557
Illinois	Springfield	1818	11,418,461	+2.8	56,400
Indiana	Indianapolis	1816	5,490,179	+5.7	36,291
Iowa	Des Moines	1846	2,913,387	+3.1	56,290
Kansas	Topeka	1861	2,363,208	+5.1	82,264
Kentucky	Frankfort	1792	3,661,433	+13.7	40,395
Louisiana	Baton Rouge	1812	4,203,972	+15.3	48,523
Maine	Augusta	1820	1,124,660	+15.2	33,215
Maryland	Annapolis	1788	4,216,446	+7.5	10,577
Massachusetts	Boston	1788	5,737,037	+0.8	8,257
Michigan	Lansing	1837	9,258,344	+4.2	58,216
Minnesota	St. Paul	1858	4,077,148	+7.1	84,068
Mississippi	Jackson	1817	2,520,638	+13.7	47,716
Missouri	Jefferson City	1821	4,917,444	+5.1	69,686
Montana	Helena	1889	786,690	+13.3	147,138
Nebraska	Lincoln	1867	1,570,006	+5.7	77,227
Nevada	Carson City	1864	799,184	+63.5	110,540
New Hampshire	Concord	1788	920,610	+24.8	9,304
New Jersey	Trenton	1787	7,364,158	+2.7	7,836
New Mexico	Sante Fe	1912	1,299,968	+27.8	121,666
New York	Albany	1788	17,557,288	−3.8	49,576
North Carolina	Raleigh	1789	5,874,429	+15.5	52,586
North Dakota	Bismarck	1889	652,695	+5.6	70,665
Ohio	Columbus	1803	10,797,419	+1.3	41,222
Oklahoma	Oklahoma City	1907	3,025,266	+18.2	69,919
Oregon	Salem	1859	2,632,663	+25.9	96,981
Pennsylvania	Harrisburg	1787	11,866,728	+0.6	45,333
Rhode Island	Providence	1790	947,154	−0.3	1,214
South Carolina	Columbia	1788	3,119,208	+20.4	31,055
South Dakota	Pierre	1889	690,178	+3.6	77,047
Tennessee	Nashville	1796	4,590,750	+16.9	42,244
Texas	Austin	1845	14,228,383	+27.1	267,339
Utah	Salt Lake City	1896	1,461,037	+37.9	84,916
Vermont	Montpelier	1791	511,456	+15.0	9,609
Virginia	Richmond	1788	5,346,279	+14.9	40,817
Washington	Olympia	1889	4,130,163	+21.0	68,192
West Virginia	Charleston	1863	1,949,644	+11.8	24,181
Wisconsin	Madison	1848	4,705,335	+6.5	56,153
Wyoming	Cheyenne	1890	470,816	+41.6	97,914
District of Columbia			637,651	−15.7	67

PRESIDENTS AND VICE PRESIDENTS

President	Born	Died	Term of Office	Party	State*	Vice-President
George Washington	1732	1799	1789–1797	Federalist	Va.	John Adams
John Adams	1735	1826	1797–1801	Federalist	Mass.	Thomas Jefferson
Thomas Jefferson	1743	1826	1801–1809	Republican	Va.	Aaron Burr
						George Clinton
James Madison	1751	1836	1809–1817	Republican	Va.	George Clinton
						Elbridge Gerry
James Monroe	1758	1831	1817–1825	Republican	Va.	Daniel D. Tompkins
John Quincy Adams	1767	1848	1825–1829	Republican	Mass.	John C. Calhoun
Andrew Jackson	1767	1845	1829–1837	Democratic	Tenn.	John C. Calhoun
						Martin Van Buren
Martin Van Buren	1782	1862	1837–1841	Democratic	N.Y.	Richard M. Johnson
William H. Harrison	1773	1841	1841	Whig	Ohio	John Tyler
John Tyler	1790	1862	1841–1845	Whig	Va.	
James K. Polk	1795	1849	1845–1849	Democratic	Tenn.	George M. Dallas
Zachary Taylor	1784	1850	1849–1850	Whig	La.	Millard Fillmore
Millard Fillmore	1800	1874	1850–1853	Whig	N.Y.	
Franklin Pierce	1804	1869	1853–1857	Democratic	N.H.	William R. King
James Buchanan	1791	1868	1857–1861	Democratic	Pa.	John C. Breckinridge
Abraham Lincoln	1809	1865	1861–1865	Republican	Ill.	Hannibal Hamlin
						Andrew Johnson
Andrew Johnson	1808	1875	1865–1869	Democratic	Tenn.	
Ulysses S. Grant	1822	1885	1869–1877	Republican	Ill.	Schuyler Colfax
						Henry Wilson
Rutherford B. Hayes	1822	1893	1877–1881	Republican	Ohio	William A. Wheeler
James A. Garfield	1831	1881	1881	Republican	Ohio	Chester A. Arthur
Chester A. Arthur	1830	1886	1881–1885	Republican	N.Y.	
Grover Cleveland	1837	1908	1885–1889	Democratic	N.Y.	Thomas A. Hendricks
Benjamin Harrison	1833	1901	1889–1893	Republican	Ind.	Levi P. Morton
Grover Cleveland	1837	1908	1893–1897	Democratic	N.Y.	Adlai E. Stevenson
William McKinley	1843	1901	1897–1901	Republican	Ohio	Garret A. Hobart
						Theodore Roosevelt
Theodore Roosevelt	1858	1919	1901–1909	Republican	N.Y.	Charles W. Fairbanks
William H. Taft	1857	1930	1909–1913	Republican	Ohio	James S. Sherman
Woodrow Wilson	1856	1924	1913–1921	Democratic	N.J.	Thomas R. Marshall
Warren G. Harding	1865	1923	1921–1923	Republican	Ohio	Calvin Coolidge
Calvin Coolidge	1872	1933	1923–1929	Republican	Mass.	Charles G. Dawes
Herbert Hoover	1874	1964	1929–1933	Republican	Cal.	Charles Curtis
Franklin D. Roosevelt	1882	1945	1933–1945	Democratic	N.Y.	John Garner
						Henry Wallace
						Harry Truman
Harry Truman	1884	1972	1945–1953	Democratic	Mo.	Alben Barkley
Dwight Eisenhower	1890	1969	1953–1961	Republican	N.Y.	Richard Nixon
John F. Kennedy	1917	1963	1961–1963	Democratic	Mass.	Lyndon Johnson
Lyndon Johnson	1908	1973	1963–1969	Democratic	Texas	Hubert Humphrey
Richard Nixon	1913		1969–1974	Republican	N.Y.	Spiro Agnew
						Gerald Ford
Gerald Ford	1913		1974–1977	Republican	Mich.	Nelson Rockefeller
Jimmy Carter	1924		1977–1981	Democratic	Ga.	Walter Mondale
Ronald Reagan	1911		1981–	Republican	Cal.	George Bush

*State of residence at election

504

POLITICAL PARTIES IN POWER

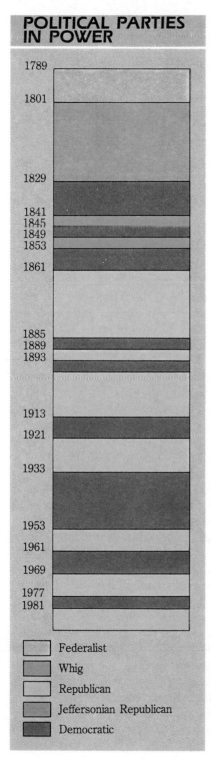

1789
1801
1829
1841
1845
1849
1853
1861
1885
1889
1893
1913
1921
1933
1953
1961
1969
1977
1981

- Federalist
- Whig
- Republican
- Jeffersonian Republican
- Democratic

THIRD PARTY MOVEMENTS

PARTY	STRONGEST SHOWING	ISSUE	STRENGTH
Anti-Masonic	1832	Against secret societies	Pa., Vt.
Liberty	1840–44	Anti-Slavery	North
Free Soil*	1848	Anti-Slavery	N.Y., Ohio
American (Know Nothing)*	1856	Anti-Immigrant	Northeast, South
Constitutional Union*	1860	Preservation of the Union	Ky., Tenn., Va.
Greenback	1876–80	"Cheap Money" 8-Hour Work Day	National
Prohibition	1884	Anti-Liquor	National
Union Labor	1888	Pro-Industrial Worker	Northeast
Populist*	1892	Free Coinage of Silver	South, West
Socialist	1900–20	Collective Ownership	National
Progressive (Bull Moose)*	1912	End High Tariffs, Women's Suffrage	Midwest, West
Farmer Labor	1924	Social Security, Farm-Labor Support	Iowa, Minn.
Progressive*	1924	Labor Reform	Midwest, West
Socialist	1928–48	Liberal Reforms	National
Communist	1932	Working Class Control	West, Northeast
Union	1936	Anti-New Deal	National
States' Rights (Dixiecrats)	1948	Pro-Segregation	South
Progressive	1948	Anti-Cold War	Cal., N.Y.
American Independent*	1968	States' Rights	South
American	1972	Law and Order	West
Libertarian	1980	Limited Government	National

*Received more than 10% of the popular votes cast.

The Declaration of Independence

In Congress, July 4, 1776
The Unanimous Declaration of the Thirteen
United States of America

When in the course of human events, it becomes necessary for one people to dissolve the political bands which have connected them with another, and to assume among the powers of the earth, the separate and equal station to which the laws of nature and of nature's God entitle them, a decent respect to the opinions of mankind requires that they should declare the causes which impel them to the separation.

We hold these truths to be self-evident, that all men are created equal, that they are endowed by their Creator with certain unalienable rights, that among these are life, liberty, and the pursuit of happiness. That to secure these rights, governments are instituted among men, deriving their just powers from the consent of the governed; that whenever any form of government becomes destructive of these ends, it is the right of the people to alter or to abolish it, and to institute new government, laying its foundation on such principles, and organizing its powers in such form, as to them shall seem most likely to effect their safety and happiness. Prudence, indeed, will dictate that governments long established should not be changed for light and transient causes; and accordingly all experience hath shown, that mankind are more disposed to suffer, while evils are sufferable, than to right themselves by abolishing the forms to which they are accustomed. But when a long train of abuses and usurpations, pursuing invariably the same object, evinces a design to reduce them under absolute despotism, it is their right, it is their duty, to throw off such government, and to provide new guards for their future security. Such has been the patient sufferance of these colonies; and such is now the necessity which constrains them to alter their former systems of government. The history of the present King of Great Britain is a history of repeated injuries and usurpations, all having in direct object the establishment of an absolute tyranny over these states. To prove this, let facts be submitted to a candid world.

He has refused his assent to laws, the most wholesome and necessary for the public good.

He has forbidden his governors to pass laws of immediate and pressing importance, unless suspended in their operation till his assent should be obtained; and when so suspended, he has utterly neglected to attend to them.

He has refused to pass other laws for the accommodation of large districts of people, unless those people would relinquish the right of representation in the legislature, a right inestimable to them and formidable to tyrants only.

He has called together legislative bodies at places unusual, uncomfortable, and distant from the depository of their public records, for the sole purpose of fatiguing them into compliance with his measures.

He has dissolved representative houses repeatedly, for opposing with manly firmness his invasions on the rights of the people.

He has refused for a long time, after such dissolutions, to cause others to be elected; whereby the legislative powers, incapable of annihilation, have returned to the people at large for their exercise; the state remaining in the meantime exposed to all the dangers of invasion from without and convulsions within.

He has endeavored to prevent the population of these states; for that purpose obstructing the laws for naturalization of foreigners, refusing to pass others to encourage their migrations hither, and raising the conditions of new appropriations of lands.

He has obstructed the administration of justice, by refusing his assent to laws for establishing judiciary powers.

He has made judges dependent on his will alone, for the tenure of their offices, and the amount and payment of their salaries.

He has erected a multitude of new offices, and sent hither swarms of officers to harass our people, and eat out their substance.

He has kept among us, in times of peace, standing armies without the consent of our legislatures.

He has affected to render the military independent of and superior to the civil power.

He has combined with others to subject us to a jurisdiction foreign to our constitution, and unacknowledged by our laws; giving his assent to their acts of pretended legislation:

For quartering large bodies of armed troops among us;

For protecting them, by a mock trial, from punishment for any murders which they should commit on the inhabitants of these states;

For cutting off our trade with all parts of the world;

For imposing taxes on us without our consent;

For depriving us, in many cases, of the benefits of trial by jury;

For transporting us beyond seas to be tried for pretended offenses;

For abolishing the free system of English laws in a neighboring province, establishing therein an arbitrary government, and enlarging its boundaries so as to render it at once an example and fit instrument for introducing the same absolute rule into these colonies;

For taking away our charters, abolishing our most valuable laws, and altering fundamentally the forms of our governments;

For suspending our own legislatures, and declaring themselves invested with power to legislate for us in all cases whatsoever.

He has abdicated government here, by declaring us out of his protection and waging war against us.

He has plundered our seas, ravaged our coasts, burned our towns, and destroyed the lives of our people.

He is at this time transporting large armies of foreign mercenaries to complete the works of death, desolation, and tyranny, already begun with circumstances of cruelty and perfidy scarcely paralleled in the most barbarous ages, and totally unworthy the head of a civilized nation.

He has constrained our fellow citizens taken captive on the high seas to bear arms against their country, to become the executioners of their friends and brethren, or to fall themselves by their hands.

He has excited domestic insurrections among us, and has endeavored to bring on the inhabitants of our frontiers, the merciless Indian savages, whose known rule of warfare is an undistinguished destruction of all ages, sexes, and conditions.

In every stage of these oppressions we have petitioned for redress in the most humble terms: our repeated petitions have been answered only by repeated injury. A prince, whose character is thus marked by every act which may define a tyrant, is unfit to be the ruler of a free people.

Nor have we been wanting in our attentions to our British brethren. We have warned them from time to time of attempts by their legislature to extend an unwarrantable jurisdiction over us. We have reminded them of the circumstances of our emigration and settlement here. We have appealed to their native justice and magnanimity, and we have conjured them by the ties of our common kindred to disavow these usurpations, which would inevitably interrupt our connections and correspondence. They too have been deaf to the voice of justice and consanguinity. We must, therefore, acquiesce in the necessity which denounces our separation, and hold them, as we hold the rest of mankind, enemies in war, in peace friends.

We, therefore, the representatives of the United States of America, in General Congress, assembled, appealing to the Supreme Judge of the world for the rectitude of our intentions, do, in the name and by authority of the good people of these colonies, solemnly publish and declare, that these united colonies are, and of right ought to be, free and independent states; that they are absolved from all allegiance to the British Crown, and that all political connection between them and the State of Great Britain is and ought to be totally dissolved; and that as free and independent states, they have full power to levy war, conclude peace, contract alliances, establish commerce, and to do all other acts and things which independent states may of right do. And for the support of this declaration, with a firm reliance on the protection of Divine Providence, we mutually pledge to each other our lives, our fortunes, and our sacred honor.

John Hancock, **President**

New Hampshire
Josiah Bartlett
William Whipple
Matthew Thornton

Massachusetts
Samuel Adams
John Adams
Robert Treat Paine
Elbridge Gerry

New York
William Floyd
Philip Livingston
Francis Lewis
Lewis Morris

New Jersey
Richard Stockton
John Witherspoon

Francis Hopkinson
John Hart
Abraham Clark

Pennsylvania
Robert Morris
Benjamin Rush
Benjamin Franklin
John Morton
George Clymer
James Smith
George Taylor
James Wilson
George Ross

Delaware
Caesar Rodney
George Read
Thomas M'Kean

Maryland
Samuel Chase
William Paca
Thomas Stone
Charles Carroll
of Carrollton

Rhode Island
Stephen Hopkins
William Ellery

Connecticut
Roger Sherman
Samuel Huntington
William Williams
Oliver Wolcott

Virginia
George Wythe
Richard Henry Lee

Thomas Jefferson
Benjamin Harrison
Thomas Nelson, Jr.
Francis Lightfoot Lee
Carter Braxton

North Carolina
William Hopper
Joseph Hewes
John Penn

South Carolina
Edward Rutledge
Thomas Heyward, Jr.
Thomas Lynch, Jr.
Arthur Middleton

Georgia
Button Gwinnett
Lyman Hall
George Walton

508

The Constitution of the United States

Preamble

We the People *of the United States, in order to form a more perfect union, establish justice, insure domestic tranquillity, provide for the common defense, promote the general welfare, and secure the blessings of liberty to ourselves and our posterity, do ordain and establish this* CONSTITUTION *for the United States of America.*

The Preamble is an introduction that explains why the Constitution is necessary and lists the purposes and goals to be achieved.

Article 1   Legislative Branch

Section 1 Congress

All legislative powers herein granted shall be vested in a Congress of the United States, which shall consist of a Senate and House of Representatives.

Section 1 grants Congress the sole power to make law at the national level. It also established a bicameral legislature.

Section 2 House of Representatives

1. The House of Representatives shall be composed of members chosen every second year by the people of the several states, and the electors in each state shall have the qualifications requisite for electors of the most numerous branch of the state legislature.

2. No person shall be a representative who shall not have attained to the age of twenty-five years, and been seven years a citizen of the United States, and who shall not, when elected, be an inhabitant of that state in which he shall be chosen.

Section 2 set the House term at two years, provided for the popular election of Representatives, and set the qualifications which must be met to hold the office.

3. Representatives and direct taxes shall be apportioned among the several states which may be included within this Union, according to their respective numbers, which shall be determined by adding to the whole number of free persons, including those bound to service for a term of years, and excluding Indians not taxed, three fifths of all other persons. The actual enumeration shall be made within three years after the first meeting of the Congress of the United States, and within every subsequent term of ten years, in such manner as they shall by law direct. The number of representatives shall not exceed one for every thirty thousand, but each state shall have at least one representative; and until such enumeration shall be made, the State of New Hampshire shall be entitled to choose three; Massachusetts, eight; Rhode Island and Providence Plantations, one; Connecticut, five; New York, six; New Jersey, four; Pennsylvania, eight; Delaware, one; Maryland, six; Virginia, ten; North Carolina, five; South Carolina, five; and Georgia, three.

In regard to income taxes, the direct tax requirement was voided by the 16th Amendment. The 3/5 reference to slaves was cancelled by the 13th and 14th Amendments.
A census has been taken every 10 years since the first in 1790. The current size of the House—435 members—was established by law in 1929. Since then, there has been a reapportionment of seats based on population shifts rather than an addition of seats because of population growth.

4. When vacancies happen in the representation from any state, the executive authority thereof shall issue writs of election to fill such vacancies.

A vacancy in the House is filled through a special election called by the state's governor.

5. The House of Representatives shall choose their Speaker and other officers; and shall have the sole power of impeachment.

Only the House may impeach, or charge, federal officials with not carrying out their duties.

509

Section 3 Senate

1. The Senate of the United States shall be composed of two senators from each state, chosen by the legislature thereof, for six years; and each senator shall have one vote.

2. Immediately after they shall be assembled in consequence of the first election, they shall be divided as equally as may be into three classes. The seats of the senators of the first class shall be vacated at the expiration of the second year, of the second class at the expiration of the fourth year, of the third class at the expiration of the sixth year, so that one third may be chosen every second year, and if vacancies happen by resignation, or otherwise, during the recess of the legislature of any state, the executive thereof may make temporary appointments until the next meeting of the legislature, which shall then fill such vacancies.

Section 3 set the Senate term at six years and provided for one third of the membership to be selected every two years. In addition, a state's governor can fill a vacancy by temporary appointment until the next general election. State legislative selection of Senators was ended with ratification of the 17th Amendment.

3. No person shall be a senator who shall not have attained to the age of thirty years, and been nine years a citizen of the United States, and who shall not, when elected, be an inhabitant of that state for which he shall be chosen.

Like those for the House, the only constitutional requirements that must be met for membership in the Senate deal with age, citizenship, and residency.

4. The Vice-President of the United States shall be President of the Senate, but shall have no vote, unless they be equally divided.

The Vice-President is the presiding officer of the Senate. The Vice-President may (but is not required to) vote only when there is a tie vote on a bill or issue.

5. The Senate shall choose their other officers, and also a President *pro tempore,* in the absence of the Vice-President, or when he shall exercise the office of President of the United States.

6. The Senate shall have the sole power to try all impeachments. When sitting for that purpose, they shall be on oath or affirmation. When the President of the United States is tried, the Chief Justice shall preside; and no person shall be convicted without the concurrence of two thirds of the members present.

Only the Senate may try persons impeached by the House. The Chief Justice presides in the trial of a President. Conviction requires a two-thirds vote of "guilty" by the members present.

7. Judgment in cases of impeachment shall not extend further than to removal from office, and disqualification to hold and enjoy any office of honor, trust, or profit under the United States; but the party convicted shall nevertheless be liable and subject to indictment, trial, judgment, and punishment, according to law.

Punishment is limited to removal from office and, if the Senate chooses, barring of future office-holding; but a person impeached can still be tried in court and held accountable under the law for any crimes committed.

Section 4 Congressional Elections and Meetings

1. The times, places, and manner of holding elections for senators and representatives shall be prescribed in each state by the legislature thereof; but the Congress may at any time by law make or alter such regulations, except as to the places of choosing senators.

Although the time, place, and manner of holding elections is left to the states, Congress can set regulations. In 1872, Congress set the first Tuesday after the first Monday in even numbered years as the date for congressional elections.

2. The Congress shall assemble at least once in every year, and such meeting shall be on the first Monday in December, unless they shall by law appoint a different day.

Congress must meet at least once a year. The opening date was changed to January 3 by the 20th Amendment.

Section 5 Congressional Powers and Duties

1. Each house shall be the judge of the elections, returns, and qualifications of its own

members, and a majority of each shall constitute a quorum to do business; but a smaller number may adjourn from day to day, and may be authorized to compel the attendance of absent members, in such manner, and under such penalties, as each house may provide.

Each house has the power to exclude, or to refuse to seat, a member elect. This power was limited in 1969 to judgment of constitutional qualifications only by a Supreme Court ruling in *Powell* v. *McCormack*. Technically to conduct business, 218 members must be present in the House and 51 in the Senate. The quorum rule is seldom enforced, however, in handling of routine matters.

2. Each house may determine the rules of its proceedings, punish its members for disorderly behavior, and, with the concurrence of two thirds, expel a member.

Each house sets its own rules. There are a few unique ones. Under the "seniority" rule, committee chairmanships go to the majority party member who has served the longest on the committee. Under "senatorial courtesy," the Senate will refuse to confirm a presidential appointment if a Senator from the appointee's state and of the same party as the President objects to the appointment. One notable difference between the two houses in rules governing proceedings concerns debate. Debate is limited to one hour per member in the House, whereas in the Senate, a member can hold the floor indefinitely.

Though both houses can censure (rebuke) or expel members for misconduct, both have rarely been used.

3. Each house shall keep a journal of its proceedings, and from time to time publish the same, excepting such parts as may in their judgment require secrecy; and the yeas and nays of the members of either house on any question shall, at the desire of one fifth of those present, be entered on the journal.

In addition to the journals, a complete official record of everything said on the floor, as well as the roll call votes on all bills or issues, is available in the *Congressional Record* published daily by the Government Printing Office.

4. Neither house, during the session of Congress, shall, without the consent of the other,

adjourn for more than three days, nor to any other place than that in which the two houses shall be sitting.

Neither house may recess for more than 3 days without consent of the other, nor may it conduct business in any place other than the Capitol.

Section 6 Privileges and Restrictions of Members

1. The senators and representatives shall receive a compensation for their services, to be ascertained by law, and paid out of the Treasury of the United States. They shall in all cases except treason, felony, and breach of the peace, be privileged from arrest during their attendance at the session of their respective houses, and in going to and returning from the same; and for any speech or debate in either house, they shall not be questioned in any other place.

To strengthen the federal government, the Framers set congressional salaries to be paid by the U.S. Treasury rather than by members' respective states. Originally, members were paid $6 per day. In 1981, salaries are $79,125 for the Speaker, $65,000 for the President pro tem and floor leaders, and $60,663 for regular members. Members also receive numerous monetary benefits such as travel allowances, free postage ("franking" privilege), and a special tax exemption for maintaining a second home in Washington, D.C.

The "immunity" privilege is of little importance today. The Framers included it as a safeguard against the British colonial practice of arresting legislators to keep them from performing their duties. More important is immunity from slander or libel for anything said on the floor or published in official publications.

2. No senator or representative shall, during the time for which he was elected, be appointed to any civil office under the authority of the United States, which shall have been created, or the emoluments whereof shall have been increased, during such time; and no person holding any office under the United States shall be a member of either house during his continuance in office.

A person cannot serve in Congress and hold another government position at the same time.

Section 7 The Legislative Process

1. All bills for raising revenue shall originate in the House of Representatives; but the Senate may propose or concur with amendments as on other bills.

All money bills must originate (begin) in the House. Money bills include two types—tax bills for raising revenues and appropriation bills for spending funds.

2. Every bill which shall have passed the House of Representatives and the Senate shall, before it become a law, be presented to the President of the United States; if he approve he shall sign it, but if not he shall return it, with his objections, to that house in which it shall have originated, who shall enter the objections at large on their journal, and proceed to reconsider it. If after such reconsideration two thirds of that house shall agree to pass the bill, it shall be sent, together with the objections, to the other house, by which it shall likewise be reconsidered, and if approved by two thirds of that house, it shall become a law. But in all such cases the votes of both houses shall be determined by yeas and nays, and the names of the persons voting for and against the bill shall be entered on the journal of each house respectively. If any bill shall not be returned by the President within ten days (Sundays excepted) after it shall have been presented to him, the same shall be a law, in like manner as if he had signed it, unless the Congress by their adjournment prevent its return, in which case it shall not be a law.

Paragraph 2 of Section 7 outlines the basic requirements for enacting legislation. These are (1) bills must be approved in like form by both houses, (2) be submitted to the President for his signature, and (3) be approved (signed) by the President. Vetoed bills must be returned to Congress with objections for reconsideration. They can be enacted into law by a two-thirds vote of both houses. Should the President fail to sign a submitted bill within 10 days, it automatically becomes law unless Congress has adjourned. If Congress has adjourned, then the bill fails to become law (pocket veto). Unlike some governors, the President cannot veto certain items. He must veto a bill in its entirety.

3. Every order, resolution, or vote to which the concurrence of the Senate and House of Represen-

tatives may be necessary (except on a question of adjournment) shall be presented to the President of the United States; and before the same shall take effect, shall be approved by him, or being disapproved by him, shall be repassed by two thirds of the Senate and House of Representatives, according to the rules and limitations prescribed in the case of a bill.

The Framers included this paragraph to prevent Congress from passing joint resolutions instead of bills to avoid the possibility of a presidential veto. A bill is a draft of a proposed law, whereas a resolution is a formal expression of opinion, on a matter. There are 3 types of resolutions—simple, concurrent, and joint. Only joint resolutions, which have the same effect as bills when passed, require the President's signature.

Section 8 Legislative Powers

Almost all of Congress' legislative powers are found in this section.

The Congress shall have power:

1. To lay and collect taxes, duties, imposts, and excises, to pay the debts and provide for the common defense and general welfare of the United States; but all duties, imposts, and excises shall be uniform throughout the United States;

Congress may tax only for public purposes, and it must exercise its power with respect to all other constitutional provisions. Taxes must be uniform— the same rate—throughout the country. That is, the federal excise on whiskey must be the same in Florida as it is in Illinois.

2. To borrow money on the credit of the United States;

When need arises, Congress can borrow funds. The most common means of borrowing is through the sale of bonds. There is no constitutional limit on the amount Congress can borrow, though Congress has placed a ceiling (which it periodically revises) on the amount the federal government can go into debt.

3. To regulate commerce with foreign nations, and among the several states, and with the Indian tribes;

Congress has exclusive power to control foreign and interstate commerce. Like its taxing power,

Congress' commerce power has expanded over time and today is quite broad. Congress can exercise control over not only the exchange of goods (buying, selling, and transporting) but also the means (the carriers) by which they are traded. And it can use its power to encourage, promote and protect, as well as to prohibit, restrain, and restrict.

4. **To establish a uniform rule of naturalization, and uniform laws on the subject of bankruptcies throughout the United States;**

Naturalization is the process by which immigrants become citizens. Bankruptcy is the process by which debtors are relieved of debt obligations when they cannot pay in full.

5. **To coin money, regulate the value thereof, and of foreign coin, and fix the standard of weights and measures;**

The U.S. monetary system is based on the decimal system, with dollars as the base unit. In setting standards of weight and measures, Congress adopted the English system in 1838 and the French metric system in 1866.

6. **To provide for the punishment of counterfeiting the securities and current coin of the United States;**

Counterfeiting is punishable by a fine up to $5000 and/or imprisonment up to 15 years.

7. **To establish post offices and post roads;**

Since colonial times, the postal service has been a government monopoly. Until 1970, it operated as an executive department. That year Congress established it as an independent agency, headed by an 11-member board of governors.

8. **To promote the progress of science and useful arts, by securing for limited times to authors and inventors the exclusive right to their respective writings and discoveries;**

The works of authors (writers, poets, composers, dramatists, artists) are protected by copyrights. Today a copyright extends for the life of an author plus 50 years. The works of inventors are protected by patents which vary in length of protection from 3 1/2 to 17 years. Patents are obtainable on processes as well as products.

9. **To constitute tribunals inferior to the Supreme Court;**

This clause gave Congress the power to create the federal court system under the Supreme Court.

10. **To define and punish piracies and felonies committed on the high seas, and offenses against the law of nations;**

Federal law extends to those traveling on American ships on the high seas.

11. **To declare war, grant letters of marque and reprisal, and make rules concerning captures on land and water;**

Only Congress can declare war. But the President, as commander in chief, can use the armed forces as much as he chooses.

Letters of marque and reprisal, authorizing private parties to attack enemy vessels in time of war, have been forbidden under international law since 1856.

12. **To raise and support armies, but no appropriation of money to that use shall be for a longer term than two years;**

The restriction on funding was intended to ensure the army would always be subject to civilian control.

13. **To provide and maintain a navy;**

Rules and procedures for the navy are similar to those for the other armed services.

14. **To make rules for the government and regulation of the land and naval forces;**

Under this provision, Congress has established the uniform Code of Military Justice.

15. **To provide for calling forth the militia to execute the laws of the Union, suppress insurrections, and repel invasions;**

Militia refers to the National Guard. It may be federalized (called into federal service) by either Congress or the President.

16. **To provide for organizing, arming, and disciplining the militia, and for governing such part of them as may be employed in the service of the United States, reserving to the states respectively**

the appointment of the officers, and the authority of training the militia according to the discipline prescribed by Congress;

When federalized, the National Guard is subject to the same rules and regulations that Congress has set for the armed services.

17. To exercise exclusive legislation in all cases whatsoever over such district (not exceeding ten miles square) as may, by cession of particular states, and the acceptance of Congress, become the seat of the government of the United States, and to exercise like authority over all places purchased by the consent of the legislature of the state in which the same shall be, for the erection of forts, magazines, arsenals, dock-yards, and other needful buildings;—and

In order to check state interference and to avoid interstate jealousy, the Framers provided for a national seat of government outside of any state. The District of Columbia was the result of a compromise over Hamilton's plan on the assumption of state debts. Washington himself marked out the exact 10-mile square, which was reduced to 69 square miles when Congress returned to Virginia its portion of donated land in 1846.

18. To make all laws which shall be necessary and proper for carrying into execution the foregoing powers, and all other powers vested by this Constitution in the government of the United States, or in any department or officer thereof.

This provision is the basis of Congress' implied powers. Any implied power, however, must be related to an expressed power and must be constitutional in all other respects.

Section 9 Powers Forbidden the United States

1. The migration or importation of such persons as any of the states now existing shall think proper to admit, shall not be prohibited by the Congress prior to the year one thousand eight hundred and eight, but a tax or duty may be imposed on such importation, not exceeding ten dollars for each person.

Paragraph 1 contains the agreement the Framers reached regarding regulation of the slave trade in exchange for Congress' exclusive control over interstate commerce.

2. The privilege of the writ of habeas corpus shall not be suspended, unless when in cases of rebellion or invasion the public safety may require it.

The writ of habeas corpus is a court order to release or to bring an individual before the court to determine if that person should be charged with a crime. It is intended to prevent persons from being imprisoned for no reason. The writ may be suspended only during wartime. It was suspended twice—during the Civil War and during World War II in Hawaii. The Hawaiian suspension was later held unconstitutional in *Duncan* v. *Kahanomoku*.

3. No bill of attainder or ex post facto law shall be passed.

A bill of attainder is a law that is directed against an individual or group and provides punishment without a trial. An ex post facto law is one which prescribes punishment for an act committed before the law's enactment.

4. No capitation, or other direct, tax shall be laid, unless in proportion to the census or enumeration herein before directed to be taken.

A capitation tax is a direct tax imposed on individuals. The income tax, authorized by the 16th Amendment, is the exception to this prohibition.

5. No tax or duty shall be laid on articles exported from any state.

The prohibiting of the taxing of exports was part of the Commerce Compromise.

6. No preference shall be given by any regulation of commerce or revenue to the ports of one state over those of another; nor shall vessels bound to, or from, one state, be obliged to enter, clear, or pay duties in another.

This prohibition prevents Congress from favoring one state or region over another in the regulation of trade.

7. No money shall be drawn from the treasury, but in consequence of appropriations made by law; and a regular statement and account of the receipts

and expenditures of all public money shall be published from time to time.

8. No title of nobility shall be granted by the United States: And no person holding any office of profit or trust under them, shall, without the consent of the Congress, accept of any present, emolument, office, or title, of any kind whatever, from any king, prince, or foreign state.

Section 10 Powers Forbidden the States

1. No state shall enter into any treaty, alliance, or confederation; grant letters of marque and reprisal; coin money; emit bills of credit; make any thing but gold and silver coin a tender in payment of debts; pass any bill of attainder, ex post facto law, or law impairing the obligation of contracts, or grant any title of nobility.

2. No state shall, without the consent of the Congress, lay any imposts or duties on imports or exports, except what may be absolutely necessary for executing its inspection laws; and the net produce of all duties and imposts, laid by any state on imports or exports, shall be for the use of the treasury of the United States; and all such laws shall be subject to the revision and control of Congress.

3. No state shall, without the consent of Congress, lay any duty of tonnage, keep troops, or ships of war in time of peace, enter into any agreement or compact with another state, or with a foreign power, or engage in war, unless actually invaded, or in such imminent danger as will not admit of delay.

Article 2   Executive Branch

Section 1 President and Vice-President

1. The executive power shall be vested in a President of the United States of America. He shall hold his office during the term of four years, and, together with the Vice-President, chosen for the same term, be elected, as follows:

2. Each state shall appoint, in such manner as the legislature thereof may direct, a number of electors, equal to the whole number of senators and representatives to which the state may be entitled in the Congress: but no senator or representative, or person holding an office of trust or profit under the United States, shall be appointed an elector.

Congress. No member of Congress or federal officer may be an elector.

3. The electors shall meet in their respective states, and vote by ballot for two persons, of whom one at least shall not be an inhabitant of the same state with themselves. And they shall make a list of all the persons voted for, and of the number of votes for each; which list they shall sign and certify, and transmit sealed to the seat of the government of the United States, directed to the President of the Senate. The President of the Senate shall, in the presence of the Senate and House of Representatives, open all the certificates, and the votes shall then be counted. The person having the greatest number of votes shall be the President, if such number be a majority of the whole number of electors appointed; and if there be more than one who have such majority, and have an equal number of votes, then the House of Representatives shall immediately choose by ballot one of them for President; and if no person have a majority, then from the five highest on the list the said house shall in like manner choose the President. But in choosing the President, the votes shall be taken by states, the representation from each state having one vote; a quorum for this purpose shall consist of a member or members from two thirds of the states, and a majority of all the states shall be necessary to a choice. In every case, after the choice of the President, the person having the greatest number of votes of the electors shall be the Vice-President. But if there should remain two or more who have equal votes, the Senate shall choose from them by ballot the Vice-President.

Coupled with the previous paragraph, Paragraph 3 outlines the original method of selecting the President and Vice-President. It has been replaced by the method outlined in the 12th Amendment. It should be noted, however, that there has been considerable change in the machinery created by the Framers. For example, the Framers did not envision the rise of political parties, the development of nominating systems (primaries and conventions), or the broadening of democracy whereby electors would be elected rather than chosen by state legislatures.

4. The Congress may determine the time of choosing the electors, and the day on which they shall give their votes; which day shall be the same throughout the United States.

Congress set the first Tuesday after the first Monday in November of every fourth year (leap year) as the general election date for selecting presidential electors in 1845.

5. No person except a natural-born citizen, or a citizen of the United States, at the time of the adoption of this Constitution, shall be eligible to the office of President; neither shall any person be eligible to that office who shall not have attained to the age of thirty-five years, and been fourteen years a resident within the United States.

The only constitutional qualifications to be President are provided here. Though not expressly stated, the qualifications to be Vice-President are the same, since the Vice-President could succeed to the office of President.

6. In case of the removal of the President from office, or of his death, resignation, or inability to discharge the powers and duties of the said office, the same shall devolve on the Vice-President, and the Congress may by law provide for the case of removal, death, resignation, or inability, both of the President and Vice-President, declaring what officer shall then act as President, and such officer shall act accordingly, until the disability be removed, or a President shall be elected.

Until the adoption of the 25th Amendment, the succession of the Vice-President was based on a precedent set by John Tyler in 1841. In 1947, Congress established an official line of succession when there is no Vice-President to qualify. First in line is the Speaker of the House.

7. The President shall, at stated times, receive for his services a compensation, which shall neither be increased nor diminished during the period for which he shall have been elected, and he shall not receive within that period any other emolument from the United States, or any of them.

Originally, the President's salary was $25,000 per year. In 1981, it is $200,000. Like members of

Congress, the President also receives numerous fringe benefits including a $50,000 taxable expense account, a $40,000 nontaxable allowance for travel and entertainment, and living accommodations in two residences (the White House and Camp David). It has been estimated that to live like the President, an individual would need an income after taxes of $10 million per year.

8. Before he enter on the execution of his office, he shall take the following oath or affirmation:—"I do solemnly swear (or affirm) that I will faithfully execute the office of President of the United States, and will, to the best of my ability, preserve, protect, and defend the Constitution of the United States."

The oath of office is generally administered by the Chief Justice, but can be administered by any official authorized to administer oaths. All President-elects except Washington have been sworn into office by the Chief Justice. Only Vice-Presidents Tyler, Coolidge, and Lyndon Johnson in succeeding to the office have been sworn in by someone else.

Section 2 Powers of the President

1. The President shall be commander in chief of the army and navy of the United States, and of the militia of the several states, when called into the actual service of the United States; he may require the opinion, in writing, of the principal officer in each of the executive departments, upon any subject relating to the duties of their respective offices, and he shall have power to grant reprieves and pardons for offenses against the United States, except in cases of impeachment.

As commander in chief, the President exercises broad military power. All military personnel is subordinate to the President.

The provision the President "may require the opinion. . ." is the constitutional base for the Cabinet.

Like his other powers, the President's judicial powers are limited. Presidential clemency is limited to those accused or convicted of federal crimes. A reprieve is a delay in carrying out a sentence. A pardon is a legal absolution of responsibility for a crime. The President can also commute (reduce) and parole (suspend the completion of) an imposed sentence.

2. He shall have power, by and with the advice and consent of the Senate, to make treaties, provided two thirds of the senators present concur; and he shall nominate, and by and with the advice and consent of the Senate, shall appoint ambassadors, other public ministers and consuls, judges of the Supreme Court, and all other officers of the United States, whose appointments are not herein otherwise provided for, and which shall be established by law; but the Congress may by law vest the appointment of such inferior officers, as they think proper, in the President alone, in the courts of law, or in the heads of departments.

The President is the chief architect of American foreign policy. He alone is responsible for the conduct of foreign relations, or dealings with other countries. Though requiring Senate approval, a treaty is ratified (signed upon approval) by the President. If it is not ratified or made public, an approved treaty is voided, and Congress cannot override the President's decision to kill it. A treaty has the same legal force as an act of Congress. In addition to treaties, the President can make binding agreements (executive agreements) with other countries under his ordinance power. Executive agreements do not require Senate approval.

Most federal positions today are filled under the rules and regulations of the civil service system. Most presidential appointments serve at the pleasure of the President. Removal of an official by the President is not subject to congressional approval, but the power can be restricted by conditions set in creating the office.

3. The President shall have power to fill up all vacancies that may happen during the recess of the Senate, by granting commissions which shall expire at the end of their next session.

Presidential appointments requiring Senate approval are made on a temporary basis if the Senate is in recess.

Section 3 Duties of the President

He shall from time to time give to the Congress information of the state of the Union, and recommend to their consideration such measures as he shall judge necessary and expedient; he may, on extraordinary occasions, convene both houses, or either of them, and in case of disagreement between them with respect to the time of adjournment, he may adjourn them to such time as he shall think proper; he shall receive ambassadors and other public ministers; he shall take care that the laws be faithfully executed, and shall commission all the officers of the United States.

Today the President is the chief designer of the nation's major legislative program. Presidential recommendations are put forth in the State of the Union address, the Budget Report, and special messages dealing with specific proposals.

The provision to "receive ambassadors . . ." is the constitutional basis of the President's power to extend and to withdraw diplomatic recognition of a foreign government.

All military commissions (appointments as officers in the armed forces) require presidential authorization and congressional approval.

Section 4 Impeachment

The President, Vice-President and all civil officers of the United States, shall be removed from office on impeachment for, and conviction of, treason, bribery, or other high crimes and misdemeanors.

Presidential appointees can be removed by the impeachment process as well as by presidential request of resignation.

Article 3   Judicial Branch

Section 1 United States Courts

The judicial power of the United States shall be vested in one Supreme Court, and in such inferior courts as the Congress may from time to time ordain and establish. The judges, both of the Supreme and inferior courts, shall hold their offices during good behavior, and shall, at stated times, receive for their services, a compensation, which shall not be diminished during their continuance in office.

Section 1 created a national judiciary. Congress established the national court system in 1789. Today there are 10 judicial circuits, with a Court of Appeals in each, and 90 judicial districts. At least one district with a District Court is in every state. Other constitutional courts include: (1) the Court of Claims,

established in 1855; (2) the Customs Court, established in 1890; and (3) the Court of Customs and Patent Appeals, established in 1910. There is also various special, or legislative, courts that handle cases arising out of the exercise of particular congressional powers but do not exercise the judicial power of the United States.

Federal judges are appointed by the President with Senate approval, and nearly all hold office during good behavior for life.

Originally, judges' salaries were $3500 ($4000 for the Chief Justice). In 1981, Supreme Court Justices are paid $75,960 (the Chief Justice $79,125); Court of Appeals judges $60,663; and District Court judges $57,528.

Section 2 Jurisdiction

1. The judicial power shall extend to all cases, in law and equity, arising under this Constitution, the laws of the United States, and treaties made, or which shall be made, under their authority;—to all cases affecting ambassadors, other public ministers, and consuls;—to all cases of admiralty and maritime jurisdiction;—to controversies to which the United States shall be a party;—to controversies between two or more states;—between a state and citizens of another state;—between citizens of different states;—between citizens of the same state claiming lands under grants of different states; and between a state, or the citizens thereof, and foreign states, citizens or subjects.

Jurisdiction is the right of a court to try a case. Federal courts have jurisdiction over a case because of its subject matter or the parties involved. In regard to subject matter, federal courts try cases that: (1) arise under the Constitution, acts of Congress, or treaties, or (2) are part of admiralty law (matters that arise on the high seas or navigable waters within the country) or maritime law (matters that arise on land but are directly related to water). Since adoption of the 11th Amendment, a state cannot be sued in federal court by a foreign citizen or a citizen of another state.

The judicial power of the United States includes civil cases (private wrongs that arise under common law or equity) as well as criminal cases. Common law is the rules and principles that developed in England from decisions made on the basis of custom. Equity is a branch of law that provides legal remedy when strict application of common law results in an injustice. The main difference is that common law deals with wrongs that have occurred, whereas equity seeks to prevent them from occurring.

2. In all cases affecting ambassadors, other public ministers and consuls, and those in which a state shall be party, the Supreme Court shall have original jurisdiction. In all other cases before mentioned, the Supreme Court shall have appellate jurisdiction, both as to law and fact, with such exceptions, and under such regulations as the Congress shall make.

The Supreme Court has both original and appellate jurisdiction. Original jurisdiction refers to cases to be tried for the first time. Appellate jurisdiction refers to cases to be reviewed after being tried in a lower court. The vast majority of cases the Supreme Court hears are on appeal. Its decisions are by majority opinion.

3. The trial of all crimes, except in cases of impeachment, shall be by jury; and such trial shall be held in the state where the said crimes shall have been committed; but when not committed within any state, the trial shall be at such place or places as the Congress may by law have directed.

All people accused of committing a crime for which they can be tried in federal court are guaranteed the right of trial by jury in the state where the crime takes place.
This provision makes it possible for there to be jury trials in the Supreme Court in cases of original jurisdiction. To date, there has been only one jury trial, however—that of *Georgia* v. *Brailsford* in 1794.

Section 3 Treason

1. Treason against the United States shall consist only in levying war against them, or in adhering to their enemies, giving them aid and comfort. No person shall be convicted of treason unless on the testimony of two witnesses to the same overt act, or on confession in open court.

Treason is the only crime specifically defined in the Constitution, and Congress cannot alter or amend the criteria for conviction. The charge can be levied against American citizens at home or abroad and resident aliens.

2. The Congress shall have power to declare the punishment of treason, but no attainder of treason shall work corruption of blood, or forfeiture except during the life of the person attainted.

Congress has set the punishment for treason to be from a minimum of 5 years imprisonment and a $10,000 fine to a maximum of death. No person convicted of treason has ever been executed by the United States. John Brown was executed by Virginia for treason against that state.

Article 4 Relations Among the States

Section 1 Official Acts

Full faith and credit shall be given in each state to the public acts, records, and judicial proceedings of every other state. And the Congress may by general laws prescribe the manner in which such acts, records, and proceedings shall be proved, and the effect thereof.

States must honor the laws, records, and court decisions of other states. Regarding judicial proceedings, there are two exceptions. (1) One state does not have to enforce another state's criminal code, and (2) one state does not have to recognize another state's grant of a divorce if legitimate residence was not established by the person obtaining the divorce.

Section 2 Privileges of Citizens

1. The citizens of each state shall be entitled to all privileges and immunities of citizens in the several states.

A state may not deny to its citizens or the citizens of another state the rights enjoyed by citizens of the United States. In other words, a resident of one state may not be discriminated against unreasonably by another state.

2. A person charged in any state with treason, felony, or other crime, who shall flee from justice, and be found in another state shall, on demand of the executive authority of the state from which he fled, be delivered up, to be removed to the state having jurisdiction of the crime.

The process of returning a fugitive to the state where a crime has been committed is known as extradition. Most requests are routinely processed, but the Constitution does not absolutely require that a fugitive be surrendered. A governor can refuse to honor the request for extradition if it will result in an injustice to the fugitive.

3. No person held to service or labor in one state, under the laws thereof, escaping into another, shall, in consequence of any law or regulation therein, be discharged from such service or labor, but shall be delivered up on claim of the party to whom such service or labor may be due.

This provision applied to fugitive slaves. It was cancelled by the 13th Amendment.

Section 3 New States and Territories

1. New states may be admitted by the Congress into this Union; but no new state shall be formed or erected within the jurisdiction of any other state; nor any state be formed by the junction of two or more states, or parts of states, without the consent of the legislatures of the states concerned as well as of the Congress.

Only Congress can admit states to the Union. New states are admitted on the basis of equality with older states. The general process, as outlined by the Northwest Ordinance of 1787, is: (1) a territory seeking statehood petitions Congress, (2) Congress passes an enabling act directing the drafting of a state constitution, (3) a territorial constitutional convention drafts a constitution which is approved by popular vote and submitted to Congress, and (4) Congress passes an act of admission.

Though a new state cannot be carved out of an existing state without its consent, there has been one unusual exception—West Virginia, which was admitted in 1863 after Virginia had seceded.

Texas provides another interesting case. It was the only state that was an independent republic at the time of its admission and the only state admitted by joint resolution rather than by an act. In addition, by terms of its admission, Texas could subdivide itself into 5 states, if it so chooses.

2. The Congress shall have power to dispose of and make all needful rules and regulations respecting the territory or other property belonging to the United States; and nothing in this Constitution shall be so construed as to prejudice any claims of the United States, or of any particular state.

Congress has the power to control all property belonging to the United States. It can set up governments for territories, establish national parks and forests, authorize reclamation projects, and exercise eminent domain (taking of private property for public use through condemnation).

Section 4 Protection of the States

The United States shall guarantee to every state in this Union a republican form of government, and shall protect each of them against invasion; and on application of the legislature, or of the executive (when the legislature cannot be convened) against domestic violence.

Though the Constitution does not define "republican form of government," the Supreme Court has held it to mean one in which the people choose their own representatives to run the government and make the laws in accord with delegated power.

The federal government can use whatever means are necessary to prevent foreign invasion and to put down domestic violence.

Article 5 The Amendment Process

The Congress, whenever two thirds of both houses shall deem it necessary, shall propose amendments to this Constitution, or, on the application of the legislatures of two thirds of the several states, shall call a convention for proposing amendments, which, in either case, shall be valid to all intents and purposes, as part of this Constitution, when ratified by the legislatures of three fourths of the several states, or by conventions in three fourths thereof, as the one or the other mode of ratification may be proposed by the Congress; provided that no amendment which may be made prior to the year one thousand eight hundred and eight shall in any manner affect the first and fourth clauses in the ninth section of the first article; and that no state, without its consent, shall be deprived of its equal suffrage in the Senate.

There are 4 methods for amending the Constitution—2 of proposal and 2 of ratification. To date, all amendments have been proposed by Congress and only the 21st has been ratified by convention instead of by state legislature. There is one prohibition against change—that is, no state can be denied its equal representation in the Senate.

Article 6   General Provisions

1. All debts contracted and engagements entered into, before the adoption of this Constitution, shall be as valid against the United States under this Constitution, as under the Confederation.

This provision assured the nation's creditors that the new federal government would assume the existing financial obligations (debt) of the country.

2. This Constitution, and the laws of the United States which shall be made in pursuance thereof; and all treaties made, or which shall be made, under the authority of the United States, shall be the supreme law of the land; and the judges in every state shall be bound thereby, anything in the Constitution or laws of any state to the contrary notwithstanding.

The Supremacy Clause guarantees federal law will take priority over state law in cases of conflict. To be valid, however, any law must be constitutional.

3. The senators and representatives before mentioned, and the members of the several state legislatures, and all executive and judicial officers, both of the United States and of the several states, shall be bound by oath or affirmation to support this Constitution; but no religious test shall ever be required as a qualification to any office or public trust under the United States.

Almost all government officials must affirm or take an oath to uphold the Constitution. No religious qualification can be set as a requirement for holding public office.

Article 7   Ratification

The ratification of the conventions of nine states shall be sufficient for the establishment of this Constitution between the states so ratifying the same.

To become operable, 9 states were required to ratify. Delaware was first and New Hampshire ninth, but not until Virginia (10th) and New York (11th) ratified, was the Constitution assured of going into effect.

Done in convention by the unanimous consent of the states present the seventeenth day of September in the year of our Lord one thousand seven hundred and eighty-seven, and of the independence of the United States of America the twelfth. In witness whereof we have hereunto subscribed our names.

Of the 55 delegates who attended the Constitutional Convention, only 38 signed the document. The 39th signature—that of John Dickinson—was written by George Read at Dickinson's request. Elbridge Gerry of Massachusetts and Edmund Randolph and George Mason of Virginia refused to sign. 13 delegates left the convention prior to its end. Rhode Island sent no delegates to the convention.

George Washington, **President and Deputy from Virginia**

New Hampshire
John Langdon
Nicholas Gilman

Massachusetts
Nathaniel Gorham
Rufus King

Connecticut
*William Samuel
    Johnson*
Roger Sherman

New York
Alexander Hamilton

New Jersey
William Livingston
David Brearley
William Paterson
Jonathan Dayton

Pennsylvania
Benjamin Franklin
Thomas Mifflin
Robert Morris
George Clymer
Thomas Fitzsimons
Jared Ingersoll
James Wilson
Gouverneur Morris

Delaware
George Read
Gunning Bedford, Jr.
John Dickinson
Richard Bassett
Jacob Broom

Maryland
James M'Henry
*Daniel of St. Thomas
    Jenifer*
Daniel Carroll

Virginia
John Blair
James Madison, Jr.

North Carolina
William Blount
*Richard Dobbs
    Spaight*
Hugh Williamson

South Carolina
John Rutledge
Charles C. Pinckney
Charles Pinckney
Pierce Butler

Georgia
William Few
Abraham Baldwin

Attest: *William Jackson,* **Secretary**

The first 10 amendments are known as the Bill of Rights. They were proposed by Congress during its first session and were adopted in body in 1791. Originally, the prohibitions limited only the federal government. But many of the guarantees have been extended against state action by the Due Process Clause of the 14th Amendment.

Amendment 1 Freedoms of Expression

Congress shall make no law respecting an establishment of religion, or prohibiting the free exercise thereof; or abridging the freedom of speech, or of the press; or the right of the people peaceably to assemble, and to petition the government for a redress of grievances.

The 1st Amendment protects 5 basic civil liberties—freedom of religion, of speech, and of the press and the rights to assemble peacefully and to petition for redress of grievances. Like all civil rights, however, these liberties are not absolute; they must be exercised in a manner relative to the rights of others.

Under the guarantee of religious freedom, the government cannot establish an official religion or place restrictions on religious beliefs. Though the 1st Amendment does create a separation of church and state, the amendment does not prohibit the government from expressing a friendly attitude toward or encouraging religion.

Freedoms of speech and of the press guarantee to all individuals the right to express themselves freely, both orally and in writing, and to free and unrestricted discussion of public affairs. However, one can still be held accountable under the law for false and malicious use of words—whether oral (slander) or written (libel). Then, too, some forms of censorship for national security or the public good are permissible, even though Congress and the states cannot censor ideas before they are expressed.

The rights to assemble and petition guarantee the means to protest, including the right to demonstrate. Without them, free expression would be limited. But notice that these rights, too, are limited. Public meetings and picketing must be peaceable. Ones that result in violence can lawfully be broken up.

Amendment 2 Right to Keep Arms

A well-regulated militia being necessary to the security of a free state, the right of the people to keep and bear arms shall not be infringed.

The right to keep and bear arms is not free from government restriction. The federal government and the states can and do regulate the possession and use of firearms, such as requiring the licensing of guns and prohibiting the carrying of concealed weapons.

Amendment 3 Quartering of Troops

No soldier shall, in time of peace, be quartered in any house, without the consent of the owner, nor in time of war, but in a manner to be prescribed by law.

Like the 2nd Amendment, this amendment was designed to prevent what had been common practice by the British during the colonial period. It is of little importance today, even though Congress could authorize the boarding of troops in private homes during wartime.

Amendment 4 Searches and Seizures

The right of the people to be secure in their persons, houses, papers, and effects, against unreasonable searches and seizures, shall not be violated, and no warrants shall issue, but upon probable cause, supported by oath or affirmation, and particularly describing the place to be searched, and the persons or things to be seized.

This amendment prohibits unreasonable searches and seizures. However, the police do not need a warrant for a search and seizure if they are a witness to a crime or are in hot pursuit of a criminal. Nor do they need one to search a movable object, such as a car, since it could vanish while a warrant is sought.

There are two types of unreasonable searches and seizures—(1) those made without warrants when warrants are required, and (2) those that do not comply with the elements of the warrant. For it to be proper, a warrant must be issued by a court (judge), there must be good reason for its use, and it must describe in specific terms the place to be searched and the person or thing to be seized. Evidence secured by an improper search and seizure is inadmissible in any court.

Amendment 5 Rights of the Accused

No person shall be held to answer for a capital, or otherwise infamous crime, unless on a presentment or indictment of a grand jury, except in cases arising in the land or naval forces, or in the militia, when in actual service in time of war or public danger; nor shall any person be subject for the same offense to be twice put in jeopardy of life or limb; nor shall be compelled in any criminal case to be a witness against himself, nor to be deprived of life, liberty, or property, without due process of law; nor shall private property be taken for public use, without just compensation.

The 5th Amendment protects the legal rights of people in criminal proceedings.

No person may be brought to trial for a felony without first being charged with a specific crime by a grand jury. Since a grand jury action is not a trial, but hearing to determine if a crime has been committed and if there is sufficient evidence to have the accused stand trial, a grand jury's decision does not have to be unanimous. And since they are not trials, grand jury hearings are not made public.

No person may be tried for the same crime twice. But there are exceptions to the prohibition against double jeopardy. For example, if a person commits an act which violates both federal and state law, that person can be tried for that crime in both federal and state courts. Also, in a recurring crime, like bigamy, double jeopardy does not apply.

People may not be forced to give testimony against themselves. However, the prohibition against self-incrimination does not bar voluntarily testifying against one's self. The protection applies to any proceedings where testimony is legally required.

Due process involves the "how" and "what" of government action. Thus, there are two forms—procedural and substantive. In procedural due process, the government must act fairly in its relations with people. In substantive due process, it must proceed under fair laws in its dealings with people.

Government cannot take private property for public use without payment of a fair market price.

Amendment 6 Criminal Proceedings

In all criminal prosecutions, the accused shall enjoy the right to a speedy and public trial, by an impartial jury of the state and district wherein the crime shall have been committed, which district shall have been previously ascertained by law, and to be informed of the nature and cause of the accusation; to be confronted with the witnesses against him; to have compulsory process for obtaining witnesses in his favor, and to have the assistance of counsel for his defense.

The 6th Amendment protects the procedural rights of people in criminal proceedings.

The right to a speedy and public trial was to prevent a person from languishing in jail or being tried by a secret tribunal. But a trial must not be so speedy as to prevent time for preparing an adequate defense nor so public that mob rule prevails.

A trial can be moved from the district where the crime was committed (a motion for a change in venue) if public prejudice might affect the impartiality of the trial.

A person must be informed of the charges for an arrest. After being arrested, an accused is brought before a judge for arraignment, a determination if formal charges by a grand jury will be sought.

The right to confront witnesses guarantees an accused the right to cross-examination (direct rebuttal to testimony given). Though testimony can be given by deposition when witnesses for legitimate reasons cannot be present in court, it carries less weight because it is not subject to cross-examination.

A witness can be compelled to testify by means of a subpoena, a writ commanding that person to appear in court. Failure to comply with a subpoena will result in being held in contempt of court.

Though one can act as one's own counsel, all people are entitled to counsel. If one cannot afford counsel, the government must provide one from the public defender's office. The right to counsel includes police interrogation as well as trial.

Amendment 7 Jury Trial

In suits at common law, where the value in controversy shall exceed twenty dollars, the right of trial by jury shall be preserved, and no fact tried by a jury shall be otherwise re-examined in any court of the United States than according to the rules of common law.

Civil suits involve parties contesting private matters. Unlike criminal cases in which it is always the prosecutor, the government may or may not be a party in a civil suit. When a party, it can be either the plaintiff (the party wronged) or the defendant (the party being held accountable).

Amendment 8 Excessive Punishments

Excessive bail shall not be required, nor excessive fines imposed, nor cruel and unusual punishments inflicted.

Bail is security (money) put up to obtain the release of an accused from jail pending trial. Bail is set by the court at the time of arraignment. Failure to appear for trial is ground for forefeiture of the bail to the government.

For it to be unconstitutional, a punishment must be both cruel and unusual. Like bails and fines, a punishment must not be unreasonably severe in relation to the crime. Rarely have bails, fines, and punishments been contested as violating the 8th

Amendment, since most are imposed in accordance with what is prescribed by law.

Amendment 9 Rights of the People

The enumeration in the Constitution of certain rights shall not be construed to deny or disparage others retained by the people.

The Constitution does not specifically list all rights of the people. This amendment protects the peoples unenumerated rights.

Amendment 10 Reserved Powers

The powers not delegated to the United States by the Constitution, nor prohibited by it to the states, are reserved to the states respectively, or to the people.

The 10th Amendment safeguards the reserved powers of the states. But with the adoption of the 14th Amendment, a state's reserved powers, particularly its police powers, are subject to closer scrutiny. State practices that infringe upon personal liberty will be viewed as violating the guarantee of due process against arbitrary or unreasonable state action.

Amendment 11 Suits Against States

The judicial power of the United States shall not be construed to extend to any suit in law or equity, commenced or prosecuted against one of the United States by citizens of another state, or by citizens or subjects of any foreign state.

Adopted in 1798, the 11th Amendment changed a provision in Article 3, Section 2. It resulted from strong opposition to the Supreme Court's ruling in *Chisholm* v. *Georgia* in which the Court held that if a state could bring suit against citizens of another state, then certainly citizens of another state could bring suit against a state. The ruling was seen as weakening state sovereignty.

Under the 11th Amendment, foreign citizens or citizens of another state must sue a state in its courts in accordance with its law.

Amendment 12 Election of President and Vice-President

The electors shall meet in their respective states and vote by ballot for President and Vice-President, one of whom, at least, shall not be an inhabitant of the same state with themselves; they shall name in their ballots the person voted for as President, and in distinct ballots the person voted for as Vice-President, and they shall make distinct lists of all persons voted for as President, and of all persons voted for as Vice-President, and of the number of votes for each, which lists they shall sign and certify, and transmit sealed to the seat of the government of the United States, directed to the President of the Senate;—the President of the Senate shall, in the presence of the Senate and House of Representatives, open all the certificates and the votes shall then be counted;—the person having the greatest number of votes for President, shall be the President, if such number be a majority of the whole number of electors appointed; and if no person have such majority, then from the persons having the highest numbers not exceeding three on the list of those voted for as President, the House of Representatives shall choose immediately, by ballot, the President. But in choosing the President, the votes shall be taken by states, the representation from each state having one vote; a quorum for this purpose shall consist of a member or members from two thirds of the states, and a majority of all the states shall be necessary to a choice. And if the House of Representatives shall not choose a President whenever the right of choice shall devolve upon them, before the fourth day of March next following, then the Vice-President shall act as President, as in the case of the death or other constitutional disability of the President.—The person having the greatest number of votes as Vice-President, shall be the Vice-President, if such number be a majority of the whole number of electors appointed, and if no person have a majority, then from the two highest numbers on the list, the Senate shall choose the Vice-President; a quorum for the purpose shall consist of two thirds of the whole number of senators, and a majority of the whole number shall be necessary to a choice. But no person constitutionally ineligible to the office of President shall be eligible to that of Vice-President of the United States.

Adopted in 1804, the 12th Amendment changed the procedure for electing the President and Vice-President as outlined in Article 2, Section 1, Paragraph 3.

To prevent a reoccurrence of the election of 1800, the 12th Amendment specifies that the electors are to cast separate ballots for each office. Other changes include: (1) a candidate must receive a majority of the electoral votes cast rather than votes from a majority of the electors, (2) a reduction from 5 to the 3 highest candidates receiving votes among whom the House is to choose if no candidate receives a majority of the electoral votes, and (3) provision for the Senate to choose the Vice-President from the 2 highest candidates if neither has received a majority of the electoral votes.

The electoral system has been subject to criticism for many years. For example, in any presidential election, it is possible for a candidate to capture fewer popular votes than an opponent and still win a majority of the electoral votes. In fact, both Hayes (in 1876) and Harrison (in 1888) did so. Then, too, electors are not legally bound to vote for the choice of the people in two thirds of the states.

The 12th Amendment does place one restriction on electors. Though never tested, it prohibits electors from voting for 2 candidates (President and Vice-President) from their home state.

Amendment 13 Slavery

Section 1. Neither slavery nor involuntary servitude, except as a punishment for crime whereof the party shall have been duly convicted, shall exist within the United States, or any place subject to their jurisdiction.

Section 2. Congress shall have power to enforce this article by appropriate legislation.

Adopted in 1865, the 13th Amendment ended slavery in the United States. It also prohibits peonage (binding of a person to perform a personal service due to debt). Not all involuntary servitude (forced labor) is prohibited, however. In addition to imprisonment for crime, the Supreme Court has held that the draft (selective service) is not a violation of the amendment.

Amendment 14 Rights of Citizens

Section 1. All persons born or naturalized in the United States, and subject to the jurisdiction thereof, are citizens of the United States and of the state wherein they reside. No state shall make or enforce any law which shall abridge the privileges or immunities of citizens of the United States; nor shall any state deprive any person of life, liberty, or property, without due process of law, nor deny to any person within its jurisdiction the equal protection of the laws.

Adopted in 1868, the 14th Amendment is one of the most important. It is the basis for numerous Supreme Court decisions, particularly relating to civil rights.

Until its adoption, the Constitution contained no definition of citizen, despite the fact that "citizens" are mentioned in numerous provisions. Citizenship may be acquired by birth or by naturalization. Citizenship by birth may be either *jus soli* (the law of the soil; born in the United States or its territories) or *jus sanguinis* (the law of blood; that is, born to American citizens).

In addition to defining citizenship and extending it to blacks, Section 1 prohibits states from denying privileges and immunities of citizenship to any citizen. The guarantee of due process was intended to prevent states from denying blacks their civil rights. The guarantee of equal protection of the laws prohibits states from making unreasonable distinctions between different groups of people. Its purpose is to prevent arbitrary classification and discrimination in laws or executive actions.

Section 2. Representatives shall be apportioned among the several states according to their respective numbers, counting the whole number of persons in each state, excluding Indians not taxed. But when the right to vote at any election for the choice of electors for President and Vice-President of the United States, representatives in Congress, the executive or judicial officers of a state, or the members of the legislature thereof, is denied to any of the male inhabitants of such state, being twenty-one years of age, and citizens of the United States, or in any way abridged, except for participation in rebellion, or other crime, the basis of representation therein shall be reduced in the proportion which the number of such male citizens shall bear to the whole number of male citizens twenty-one years of age in such state.

Section 2 abolishes the three-fifths compromise as worded in Article 1, Section 2, Paragraph 3. In addition to an attempt to guarantee blacks the right to vote, it also provides the government with the power to reduce a state's representation in the House in proportion to that state's improper disfranchisement of qualified voters.

Section 3. No person shall be a senator or representative in Congress, or elector of President or Vice-President, or hold any office, civil or military, under the United States, or under any state, who, having previously taken an oath, as a member of Congress, or as an officer of the United States, or as a member of any state legislature, or as an executive or judicial officer of any state, to support the Constitution of the United States, shall have engaged in insurrection or rebellion against the same, or given aid or comfort to the enemies thereof. But Congress may by a vote of two thirds of each house, remove such disability.

Section 3 was aimed at punishing the leaders of the Confederacy. By 1872, most were permitted to return to political life, and in 1898, amnesty was granted to all still living.

Section 4. The validity of the public debt of the United States, authorized by law, including debts incurred for payment of pensions and bounties for services in suppressing insurrection or rebellion, shall not be questioned. But neither the United States nor any state shall assume or pay any debt or obligation incurred in aid of insurrection or rebellion against the United States, or any claim for the loss or emancipation of any slave; but all such debts, obligations and claims shall be held illegal and void.

Like Section 3, Section 4 dealt with matters directly related to the Civil War. It validated the debt of the United States, prohibited assumption of any of the Confederate debt, and prohibited payment for any loss resulting from freeing of the slaves.

Section 5. The Congress shall have power to enforce, by appropriate legislation, the provisions of this article.

Amendment 15 Black Suffrage

Section 1. The right of citizens of the United States to vote shall not be denied or abridged by the United States or by any state on account of race, color, or previous condition of servitude.

Section 2. The Congress shall have power to enforce this article by appropriate legislation.

Adopted in 1870, the 15th Amendment replaced Amendment 14, Section 2 in guaranteeing blacks the right to vote. Yet, despite its prohibition against both the federal government and the states, blacks were disfranchised by many states following Reconstruction. By such means as poll taxes, literacy tests, "grandfather clauses," and white primaries, blacks were successfully prevented from participating in political life in much of the South until well into the 20th century. Not until the 1960's did Congress take firm action to enforce the guarantee of the 15th Amendment and end voter discrimination.

Amendment 16 Income Tax

The Congress shall have power to lay and collect taxes on incomes, from whatever source derived, without apportionment among the several states, and without regard to any census or enumeration.

Adopted in 1913, the 16th Amendment provided an exception to the restrictions placed on direct taxation by Article 1, Section 2, Paragraph 3, and Section 9, Paragraph 4. Like the 11th Amendment, it was adopted to reverse a Supreme Court ruling. Although there had been a temporary income tax during the Civil War, the tax's constitutionality was not tested until it was reinstated by the Wilson-Gorman Tariff Act of 1894. The Court held that it was unconstitutional since it was a direct tax imposed without apportionment or regard to enumeration in *Pollack* v. *Farmer Loan and Trust Company.*

Under the amendment, Congress has levied a tax on income derived from all sources, including wages, salaries, interest, dividends, rents, royalties, commissions, bonuses, and tips. The income tax applies to business income as well as personal income. It is a "progressive" tax—that is, the rate increases as income increases. In addition to its power to levy taxes on income, Congress has the authority to provide for its enforcement. It has provided stiff penalties for both tax evasion and tax fraud.

Amendment 17 Election of Senators

Section 1. The Senate of the United States shall be composed of two senators from each state, elected by the people thereof, for six years; and each senator shall have one vote. The electors in each state shall have the qualifications requisite for electors of the most numerous branch of the state legislatures.

Section 2. When vacancies happen in the representation of any state in the Senate, the executive authority of such state shall issue writs of election to fill such vacancies: Provided, that the legislature of any state may empower the executive thereof to make temporary appointments until the people fill the vacancies by election as the legislature may direct.

Section 3. This amendment shall not be so construed as to affect the election or term of any senator chosen before it becomes valid as part of the Constitution.

Adopted in 1913, the 17th Amendment provided for the direct election of Senators by the people and replaced their method of selection as outlined by Article 1, Section 3, Paragraphs 2 and 3.

The governor of a state can fill a vacancy by calling a special election or, if authorized by the state legislature, making a temporary appointment until the next general election.

Amendment 18 National Prohibition

Section 1. After one year from the ratification of this article the manufacture, sale, or transportation of intoxicating liquors within, the importation thereof into, or the exportation thereof from the United States and all territory subject to the jurisdiction thereof for beverage purposes is hereby prohibited.

Section 2. The Congress and the several states shall have concurrent power to enforce this article by appropriate legislation.

Section 3. This article shall be inoperative unless it shall have been ratified as an amendment to the Constitution by the legislatures of the several states, as provided in the Constitution, within seven years from the date of the submission hereof to the states by the Congress.

Adopted in 1919, the 18th Amendment established national prohibition by barring the manufacture, sale, and transportation of alcoholic beverages throughout the United States.

Although it evolved out of the temperance movement, prohibition was not taken seriously until the late 1800's when a number of southern and western states allowed the citizens of local communities to decide by election if their communities should permit or prohibit the sale of liquor. It received great impetus during World War I when Congress enacted legislation restricting manufacture due to the demand for grain to feed the Allies.

Note the 18th Amendment was the first to specify the method of ratifying and to set a time limit on ratification. It also was the first to provide for enforcement by both Congress and the states.

Amendment 19 Woman Suffrage

Section 1. The right of citizens of the United States to vote shall not be denied or abridged by the United States or by any state on account of sex.

Section 2. Congress shall have power to enforce this article by appropriate legislation.

Adopted in 1920, the 19th Amendment established woman suffrage on a nationwide basis and indirectly established the right of women to hold public office. Prior to its adoption, some western states did allow women to vote. Wyoming (in 1890) was the first.

Amendment 20 Change of Terms, Sessions, and Inauguration

Section 1. The terms of the President and Vice-President shall end at noon on the 20th day of January, and the terms of senators and representatives at noon on the 3rd day of January, of the years in which such terms would have ended if this article had not been ratified; and the terms of their successors shall then begin.

Section 2. The Congress shall assemble at least once in every year, and such meeting shall begin at noon on the 3rd day of January, unless they shall by law appoint a different day.

Section 3. If, at the time fixed for the beginning of the term of the President, the President-elect shall have died, the Vice-President-elect shall become President. If a President shall not have been chosen before the time fixed for the beginning of his term, or if the President-elect shall have failed to qualify, then the Vice-President-elect shall act as President until a President shall have qualified; and the Congress may by law provide for the case wherein neither a President-elect nor a Vice-President-elect shall have qualified, declaring who shall then act as President, or the manner in which one who is to act shall be selected, and such person shall act accordingly until a President or Vice-President shall have qualified.

Section 4. The Congress may by law provide for the case of the death of any of the persons from whom the House of Representatives may choose a President whenever the right of choice shall have devolved upon them, and for the case of the death of any of the persons from whom the Senate may choose a Vice-President whenever the right of choice shall have devolved upon them.

Section 5. Sections 1 and 2 shall take effect on the 15th day of October following the ratification of this article.

Section 6. This article shall be inoperative unless it shall have been ratified as an amendment to the Constitution by the legislatures of three fourths of the several states within seven years from the date of its submission

Adopted in 1933, the 20th Amendment changed the start of congressional terms (from March 4 to Jan. 3) and presidential and vice-presidential terms (from March 4 to Jan. 20) following general elections.

It is known as the "Lame Duck" Amendment because it shortened the time between the general election and the date newly-elected officials took office and eliminated "lame ducks" (defeated Representatives and Senators) from continuing to serve in Congress for 4 months during a new session (which began in December prior to the amendment's adoption).

The amendment also provided for presidential succession in case of death or disability of a President-elect.

Amendment 21 Repeal of National Prohibition

Section 1. The eighteenth article of amendment to the Constitution of the United States is hereby repealed.

Section 2. The transportation or importation into any state, territory, or possession of the United States for delivery or use therein of intoxicating liquors, in violation of the laws thereof, is hereby prohibited.

Section 3. This article shall be inoperative unless it shall have been ratified as an amendment to the Constitution by conventions in the several states, as provided in the Constitution, within seven years from the date of the submission hereof to the states by the Congress.

Adopted in 1933, the 21st Amendment repealed national prohibition (the 18th Amendment). It is the only amendment that has repealed a prior amendment. To date, it is the only amendment ratified by state conventions. And it repealed national prohibition, but not prohibition. States still maintain their power to prohibit the manufacture and sale of alcoholic beverages. Note also that the transporta-

tion of liquor into a "dry" state is a federal crime as well as a state crime.

Amendment 22 Presidential Tenure

Section 1. No person shall be elected to the office of the President more than twice, and no person who has held the office of President, or acted as President, for more than two years of a term to which some other person was elected President shall be elected to the office of the President more than once. But this article shall not apply to any person holding the office of President when this article was proposed by the Congress, and shall not prevent any person who may be holding the office of President, or acting as President, during the term within which this article becomes operative from holding the office of President or acting as President during the remainder of such term.

Section 2. This article shall be inoperative unless it shall have been ratified as an amendment to the Constitution by the legislatures of three fourths of the several states within seven years from the date of its submission to the states by the Congress.

Adopted in 1951, the 22nd Amendment limited the number of terms a person can be elected as President to two. Thus, it formalized the two-term tradition established by Washington, which was broken by Franklin Roosevelt.

Notice that it is possible for a person to serve more than two terms, or 8 years. In fact, Lyndon Johnson was a case in point. Johnson, who assumed the Presidency following the assassination of John F. Kennedy, was eligible to run for reelection in 1968. Had he chose to run and won, he could have served 9 years, 1 month, and 28 days. Note, too, the amendment was not applicable to Harry Truman, President at the time of the amendment's ratification.

Amendment 23 Presidential Electors for D.C.

Section 1. The District constituting the seat of government of the United States shall appoint in such manner as the Congress may direct:

A number of electors of President and Vice-President equal to the whole number of senators and representatives in Congress to which the District would be entitled if it were a state, but in no event more than the least populous state; they shall be in addition to those appointed by the states, but they shall be considered, for the purposes of the election of President and Vice-President, to be electors appointed by a state; and they shall meet in the district and perform such duties as provided by the twelfth article of amendment.

Section 2. The Congress shall have power to enforce this article by appropriate legislation.

Adopted in 1961, the 23rd Amendment provided for the choosing of electors for the District of Columbia. Until its adoption, residents of the District were excluded from presidential elections.

By the wording of the amendment, the District is limited to 3 electors, the same number as the least populous state. If the District was a state, it would be entitled to 4 electors based on its probable representation in Congress.

Amendment 24 Prohibition of Poll Tax

Section 1. The right of citizens of the United States to vote in any primary or other election for President or Vice-President, for electors for President or Vice-President, or for senator or representative in Congress, shall not be denied or abridged by the United States or any state by reason of failure to pay any poll tax or other tax.

Section 2. The Congress shall have power to enforce this article by appropriate legislation.

Adopted in 1964, the 24th Amendment prohibits both the federal government and the states from denying a qualified voter the right to vote in federal elections for failure to pay any tax. The amendment did not prohibit states from imposing a poll tax as a voting qualification in state and local elections. However, the Supreme Court held the poll tax to be a denial of the Equal Protection Clause of the 14th Amendment and, therefore, unconstitutional in *Harper* v. *Virginia State Board of Elections* in 1966.

Amendment 25 Presidential Succession and Disability

Section 1. In case of the removal of the President from office or his death or resignation, the Vice-President shall become President.

Section 2. Whenever there is a vacancy in the office of the Vice-President, the President shall nominate a Vice-President who shall take the office upon confirmation by a majority vote of both houses of Congress.

Section 3. Whenever the President transmits to the President pro tempore of the Senate and the Speaker of the House of Representatives his written declaration that he is unable to discharge the powers and duties of his office, and until he transmits to them a written declaration to the contrary, such powers and duties shall be discharged by the Vice-President as Acting President.

Section 4. Whenever the Vice-President and a majority of either the principal officers of the executive departments, or of such other body as Congress may by law provide, transmit to the President pro tempore of the Senate and the Speaker of the House of Representatives their written declaration that the President is unable to discharge the powers and duties of his office, the Vice-President shall immediately assume the powers and duties of the office of Acting President.

Thereafter, when the President transmits to the President pro tempore of the Senate and the Speaker of the House of Representatives his written declaration that no inability exists, he shall resume the powers and duties of his office unless the Vice-President and a majority of either the principal officers of the executive departments, or of such other body as Congress may by law provide, transmit within four days to the President pro tempore of the Senate and the Speaker of the House of Representatives their written declaration that the President is unable to discharge the powers and duties of his office. Thereupon Congress shall decide the issue, assembling within 48 hours for that purpose if not in session. If the Congress, within 21 days after receipt of the latter written declaration, or, if Congress is not in session, within 21 days after Congress is required to assemble, determines by two thirds vote of both houses that the President is unable to discharge the powers and duties of his office, the Vice-President shall continue to discharge the same as Acting President; otherwise, the President shall resume the power and duties of his office.

Adopted in 1967, the 25th Amendment clarifies Article 2, Section 1, Paragraph 6. Until its adoption, the assumption of the office of the President by the

Vice-President because of vacancy was based upon the precedent set by John Tyler following the death of William Henry Harrison in 1841. The 25th Amendment clearly states the Vice-President assumes the office of President should it become vacant. Nine times in American history it has become vacant—four times because of natural deaths (Harrison in 1841, Taylor in 1850, Harding in 1923, and Franklin Roosevelt in 1945); four times because of assassinations (Lincoln in 1865, Garfield in 1881, McKinley in 1901, and Kennedy in 1963); and once because of resignation (Nixon in 1974).

The amendment also provides for the Vice-President becoming acting President should the President become disabled. There are two procedures covering presidential disability—(1) the President can voluntarily declare to the Speaker and President pro tem in writing that he (or she) is unable to discharge the duties of the office; or (2) the Vice-President and the Cabinet can do so when the President cannot.

The 25th Amendment also provides for filling the office of the Vice-President by presidential appointment and congressional approval should it become vacant. Eighteen times in American history there has been a vacancy—9 times because of assumption to the Presidency (Tyler in 1941, Fillmore in 1850, Andrew Johnson in 1865, Arthur in 1881, Theodore

Roosevelt in 1901, Coolidge in 1923, Truman in 1945, Lyndon Johnson in 1963, and Ford in 1974); 7 times through death (Clinton in 1812, Gerry in 1814, King in 1853, Wilson in 1875, Hendricks in 1885, Hobart in 1899, and Sherman in 1912); and 2 times by resignation (Calhoun in 1832 and Agnew in 1973).

Gerald Ford is the first person to be appointed Vice President by a President, with Nelson Rockefeller being the second. Ford also became President following Nixon's resignation. Thus, he is the only person to hold both offices having never been elected to either.

Amendment 26 Eighteen-Year-Old Vote

Section 1. The right of citizens of the United States, who are eighteen years of age or older, to vote shall not be denied or abridged by the United States or by any state on account of age.

Section 2. The Congress shall have power to enforce this article by appropriate legislation.

Adopted in 1971, the 26th Amendment lowered the voting age to 18. Note, however, that the amendment does not prohibit any state from allowing citizens less than 18 to vote if it so chooses. Thus, the amendment does not, in fact, establish a minimum voting age.

Glossary

Glossary

A

abolish put an end to something

abolitionists people who wanted to put an end to slavery

acquittal verdict of not guilty

administration major offices in the executive branch of government

adobe sun-dried brick

agriculture planned growing of food

alien person who is not a citizen of the country in which he or she lives

alliances unions for specific purposes

amendment change in, or addition to, a document

amnesty general pardon by the government

annexed added new land to a territory

appeal review of a lower court's findings by a higher court

armada fleet of warships

armistice agreement to stop fighting

arsenal place where weapons are kept

artisans skilled workers

assassinated killed by sudden or secret attack

assume take over a debt

auctions public sales where goods or slaves were sold to the persons who offered the most money for them

B

bay body of water that is partly enclosed by land and has a wide outlet to the sea

bayou many small marshy creeks and river tributaries that flow through a delta region

bicameral two-house

big stick diplomacy Theodore Roosevelt's foreign policy based on the idea that the United States would be willing to use force to protect American interests

black codes laws that limited the rights of blacks, passed by the southern states during Reconstruction

blitzkrieg very fast attack, usually using both ground and air forces

blockade closing off an area to prevent certain things from going in or coming out

blockade runners people who slipped goods into or out of a blockaded port

bonds certificates bearing a written promise to repay with interest in a certain length of time an amount of money borrowed

border states states located between the North and South in the Civil War in which sentiment about slavery was divided

bounties payments of money to a person for entering the armed services

boycott refusal to buy or use certain products as a means of protest

C

carpetbaggers name given to people from the North who moved to the South during Reconstruction, usually for the purpose of gaining money through political power

casualties persons wounded or killed

caucuses meeting of members of a political party or group to make plans or select candidates

cede yield or grant land

census count of the number of people in a place

charter official paper giving permission for settlements and trade in a certain area

checks and balances system written into the Constitution that allows each branch of government to check on, or balance, the power of the other branches

chernozem rich topsoil with a lower layer of lime

coexistence countries recognizing the rights of each other to live in peace

cold war war in which there is no fighting, but each side uses means short of military action to expand its influences

colonies settlements in other lands made by people still tied to the rule of their home countries

compact agreement

compromise settlement of differences by each side giving up part of what it wants

concentration camps prison camps, especially those of the Nazis during World War II

concurrent powers powers that are shared by the federal and state governments

conductors persons who secretly helped runaway slaves escape on the Underground Railroad

confederation loose union of peoples or groups for shared support and action

conifers cone-bearing evergreen trees

conquistador Spanish conqueror in the Americas in the 1500's

constitution written plan of government

containment policy of limiting Soviet expansion and the spread of communism

corollary statement or policy that adds to an earlier statement or policy

corporations businesses in which groups of investors own shares of stock

corrupt bargain agreement influenced by bribes

coterminous United States the United States excluding Alaska and Hawaii

cotton gin machine which is used to remove seeds from cotton

coureurs de bois early French settlers who hunted and trapped alone in the deep forests of North America, often following Indians' ways of life

cultures ways of life

D

deciduous trees trees that shed their leaves

defensive war war fought by a country remaining in its own territory and defending it from attack

delegated powers powers given to the federal government by the constitution

delta low flatland area usually shaped like a triangle at the mouth of the river

deport force a person to leave a country

depression period of slow economic activity with prices low and many people out of work

deserters soldiers or sailors who run away from their duty

detente relaxing of cold war tensions between the United States and the Soviet Union

direct primary   nominating election

direct representation   representation in which members represent only the people in the area from which they were elected

direct tax   tax that must be paid to the government and is not included in the price of goods

dollar diplomacy   Taft's foreign policy of investing American money in foreign countries in an attempt to maintain economic power in those countries without using force

domestic   internal or within a country

domino theory   idea that countries bordering a country that falls to Communist control will soon also fall

draft   selection of people who would be forced to serve in the military

duties   taxes on imports

E

elect   certain number of people chosen by God to be saved and go to heaven

electors   persons chosen by the voters to vote for President and Vice-President

emancipated   set free

embargo   law stopping all ships except foreign ships without cargo from leaving the country for foreign ports

empire   many different peoples and lands ruled by one government or leader

empresarios   people who organize and take the risk for business deals

entrenched   set up in a strong position

environment   surrounding land, water, and air

excise tax   tax on goods made and sold inside the country

exclusive powers   powers that belong only to the federal government

expansionists   people who wanted to expand the land area of the United States

exporting   sending goods for foreign sale

expressed powers   powers of the federal government stated in the Constitution

F

factory system   system in which workers in buildings known as factories made goods with power-driven machines

fall line line where the land drops off sharply from the Piedmont to the coastal plain, creating steep waterfalls along fast moving rivers

famine general lack of food in an area causing starvation

federal having to do with the central government in a system where states are joined under one central control but keep some governing powers

federalism division of power between a central government and a number of state governments

foreclosures taking away of property due to failure to make payments on its debt

"forty-niners" name given to the people who left the East to move to California during the 1849 gold rush

freedmen men, women, and children who had been slaves and were freed after the Civil War

freedom of the seas right of merchant ships in peace or war to move in any waters, except those belonging to a country

free verse poems that do not rhyme

frontier new area to explore or develop

fugitive runaway

G

gag rule law preventing the reading of antislavery petitions in the House

gauge distance between the rails on railroad tracks

glaciers heavy, giant sheets of solid ice that move slowly across the land

gold rush movement of people from the eastern United States to California after gold was discovered there

greenbacks paper money that was not backed by gold or silver

growing season time when it is possible to grow crops

H

heritage background

hogans small, round houses of the Navaho Indians, made of mud and logs

I

immigrated came to live in a country

impeach charge a person with a crime while that person is holding a government office

implied powers powers of the federal government not directly stated in the Constitution but implied by the wording

importing bringing in goods from other countries to sell

impressment stopping of American ships and forcing of American sailors to work on British ships

inauguration ceremony of installing a person in office

indentured servants people who bound themselves to work for others for a certain time

indigo vegetable dye used on cloth

industry making and selling of goods

inherent powers powers of the federal government that belong to it because it is a national government

initiative method by which citizens can propose new laws at any time

intendant head of the sovereign council of New France

interchangeable parts parts that are exactly alike

interior drainage water flows into lakes or rivers in the area itself rather than flows out to sea

intermontane between mountains

internal improvement programs that are used to make a country better, such as the building of roads, bridges, and canals

interstate trade trade between two or more states

intolerant not willing to respect the beliefs, practices, or behavior of others

investors people who buy shares in a company

ironclad kind of battleship covered with thick iron plates

J

jazz kind of music that has syncopated rhythms and developed from ragtime and blues music during the late 1920's

joint occupation agreement between Great Britain and the United States that people from both nations could settle in the Oregon territory

joint stock companies companies formed by a group of people for the purpose of selling stock to raise money for a business venture

judicial review power to judge whether or not acts of Congress and actions of the President are constitutional

judiciary branch of government responsible for the court system

jurisdiction authority of a court to hear certain cases

K

kayak small, canoelike boat used by the people of the Arctic

kiva round underground room used by the Pueblo Indians for ceremonies, meetings, and work

L

lagoon a shallow body of water connected to a larger one

laissez-faire French term that refers to an economy in which the government does not make rules for business

land bridge narrow strip of land between Asia and North America in the Ice Ages

land speculation buying up land to sell at a profit

legislature lawmaking body

liberalism a belief that government should take as large a role as necessary to promote freedom, equal justice, and equal opportunity

limited government idea that government may exercise only those powers granted to it by the people

long houses large, rectangular homes of the Iroquois Indians, made of wood poles and bark

loose construction broad interpretation of the Constitution to mean more than what it says

loyalists American colonists who remained loyal to England during the Revolution

M

manifest destiny certain fate of the United States to stretch from ocean to ocean

manufacturing making goods by hand or machine

mass production system of producing large numbers of an item quickly using interchangeable parts

meeting houses Puritan places of worship

mercantilism economic policy to increase a country's wealth by increasing its manufacturing and exports, by taxing imports, and by establishing colonies to provide raw materials and new markets

mesas flat tops of high hills

minutemen patriot soldiers who could be ready for duty at a moment's notice

missionaries church workers sent to teach Christianity to non-Christians

monopoly exclusive control of trade

mounds large hills of earth that were part of the religion of some Eastern Woodlands Indians

muckrakers authors who criticized Big Business and government in the early 1900's

N

national anthem song of praise and patriotism

nationalism feeling of pride in the nation as a whole and loyalty to its goals

negotiating discussing in order to reach an agreement or to work out terms

neutrality position of taking no side in a conflict

night watches people who lit street lamps and called out the hour of the night

null and void not binding

nullification idea that a state may cancel a federal law within its own borders

O

ordinances rules or laws

organs parts of an organization

P

patents licenses to make, use, or sell new inventions

patriots those who love their country and strongly support its authority and interests

"peculiar institution" name given slavery by Southern whites, meaning that it was a way of life unique to the South

perpetual everlasting

persecuted treated cruelly by others

personal liberty laws laws to stop state and local officials from obeying the federal fugitive slave laws

pet banks name given to state banks that received money President Jackson withdrew from the Bank of the United States

philosophy set of ideas

planters owners of large farms known as plantations

platform statement of the policies of a political party

pocket veto veto of a bill that occurs when the President fails to sign a bill presented to the President by Congress within ten days of Congress's recess

podzol a leached, acidic bottom ground soil

"police powers" powers set aside for the states that safeguard individual well-being

popular sovereignty idea that a government receives its authority from the people; used before the Civil War to allow settlers in a new area to decide whether or not slavery would be allowed in their territory

potlatch special feast of the Northwest Coast Indians in which the chief proved how rich he was

precedents acts that serve as examples in later situations

prejudice attitude or opinion about a person, group, or race that is formed without taking time or care to judge fairly

proclamation official announcement

prohibition forbidding by law of the manufacture, shipping, and sale of alcoholic beverages

proprietary colonies type of colony operated under a charter granted to the proprietor by the king

proprietors friends of the king that were given grants to start colonies in America

protective tariff heavy tax on imported goods, protecting goods made at home by making imported goods more expensive

pueblos apartmentlike buildings in which whole villages of Pueblo Indians lived

Q

quartered given a place to live

R

radical   extreme or sudden changes from the usual; a person who favors extreme changes in beliefs, habits, or institutions

radiocarbon dating   a method to measure the amount of radiocarbon left in such remains as bones, wood, and cloth that enables scientists to estimate the age of the remains

ratify   give formal approval to a law

reconstruction   rebuilding, especially the Union after the Civil War

redeemed   paid off a loan or a bond

relocation centers   camps in the United States in which people of Japanese ancestry were kept during World War II

renounce   give up claims

repealed   withdrawn, usually referring to a law

reservations   separate areas set aside or reserved for the Indians by the United States government

reserved powers   powers that are not given to the federal government but are reserved to state governments

reservoirs   places where water is collected and stored for use

revelations   special messages from God

revenue bills   tax bills for raising money and bills authorizing the spending of money

revenue sharing   plan in which the federal government gives part of its revenues to state and local governments

revivals   meetings to make people more interested in religion

rituals   forms of service or ceremonies

royal colony   type of colony under the direct control of the king

rural   country

S

sachems   chiefs of the Iroquois Indians

scalawags   name given to southern whites who supported the Republican party after the Civil War

secede   withdraw from an organization, a group, or the Union

secession   withdrawing from the Union

secret ballot   an official ballot distributed only at the polling place and marked in secret

sectionalism   rivalry based on the special interests of different areas in a country

sedition   use of language to stir up rebellion against a government

segregation   separation of blacks from whites in schools, in public places, and on all forms of public transportation

selective service   a draft that selects men for military service

separation of powers   division of power among the three branches of government

settlement houses   places established in the late 1800's and early 1900's as meeting centers or places of education for the poor, immigrants, minorities, and others

sharecropping   system in which people farm land they do not own in return for a share of the crop

slave codes   laws that controlled the lives of slaves

slaves   people who are the property of their owners

social security   program of government aid for older, disabled, or unemployed citizens

sound   a long, narrow inlet of the sea

specie   gold or silver coin

speculators   people who buy stocks, bonds, or land for the purpose of selling it for a profit later when prices rise

spheres of influence   areas of control over trade

spoils system   practice of giving government jobs to political supporters

states' rights   idea that each state could decide if an act of the government is unconstitutional

station   safe places that were part of the Underground Railroad

strict construction   narrow interpretation of the Constitution to mean just what it says

suffrage   right to vote

sunbelt   southeast and southwest parts of the United States where the weather is sunny and warm much of the time

supremacy of civilian authority   principle that the military is subject to civilian authority

supremacy of national law   principle that national law is superior to state law

surveyed   examined and measured land

symbolism   use of one thing to stand for something else

T

tariffs   taxes on imported goods

temperance   self-control, usually in the use of alcoholic beverages

tenements apartment houses generally without sanitation, comfort, and safety

tenure of office length of time that a person can stay in office

textile woven fabric; cloth

tipis cone-shaped homes of the western Plains Indians, made of poles and buffalo hides

totem poles large wooden posts carved with figures of faces and animals, showing the family history and titles of the family leader of some Northwest Coast Indians

town meeting gathering of all eligible voters in a town to debate political issues and pass laws

transcendentalism idea that people could go beyond their limitations and perfect themselves and their society

travois small platforms fastened to two poles, used by the Western Plains Indians

triangular trade triangular pattern of trade of molasses from the West Indies, rum from New England, and slaves from Africa

trusts organizations of several companies that are run as one company

turnpike road built by a private company that charged a fee for using it

U

umiak a large, canoelike boat used by the people of the Arctic

urban city

utopias ideal communities

V

vetoed refused to approve

viceroys persons ruling colonies as direct representatives of the home country

Vietnamization program in which American troops equipped and trained the South Vietnamese to take over the fighting so that Americans could withdraw

virtual representation representation in which members represent all people in an area or country

vulcanization process that makes rubber able to stand great heat or cold

W

wickiups homes of the Apache Indians made from frames of thin poles covered with animal skins

wigwams small, rounded homes of some Eastern Woodlands Indians

workman's compensation law that provides funds for workers hurt on the job

Index

Index

A

AAA (Agricultural Adjustment Administration), 414
Abolition, 267
Abolitionists, 337; Southern responses to, 337
Abstract Expressionism, 427
Adams, Abigail, 253-254
Adams, John Quincy, 235-238, 257
Adams, John, 130, 132, 154, 195, 204-205, 207, 209, 225, 253
Adams, Louisa, 257
Adams, Samuel, 127, 154, 160
Adams-Onís Treaty of 1819, 226, 300-301
Addams, Jane, 406
Adobe, 31
AEF (American Expeditionary Force), 411
AFL (American Federation of Labor), 406
"Age of Big Business," 405
Agricultural Adjustment Act of 1933, 416
Agricultural Adjustment Administration (AAA), 414
Agriculture, 24; Aztec, 26; Beginning, 24; Colonial, 103-105, 109, 111-112; Defined, 24; Eastern Woodlands Indian, 37; Great Depression, 414; Inca, 28; Indian, 89; Pilgrim, 93-94
Alamo, capture of, 306-307
Alaska, 17, 23

Alden, John, 95
Aleutian Islands, 36
Aleuts, 36
Alexander VI, Pope, 48
Alien and Sedition Acts, 206-207
Allegheny Plateau, 6
Allen, Augustus, 430
Allen, John, 430
Allied Powers (Triple Entente), 410
Alvarado, Juan Bautista, 305
Amana Community, 265
Amendments, See Constitution, United States,
America; See also Middle America, North America, South America; Settlement, 23, 26, 28-38
American Expeditionary Force (AEF), 411
American Federation of Labor (AFL), 406
American Party, 295
American Revolution, 122-137, 139, 141, 143; Beyond Appalachians, 137; Economic results, 143; End, 140; Financing of, 135; in the South, 138; Mississippi Valley, 137; Political results, 141; Social results, 142
"American Scholar, The," 274-275
American Society for the Promotion of Temperance, 273
American System, 236
Anasazi, 31
Andes Mountains, 28

Andros, Sir Edmund, 85
Anglican Church, See Church of England, 67
Annapolis Convention of 1785, 151-152
Anti-Federalists, 159-160
Anti-Semitism, 412
Antislavery Movement, 266-268
Antislavery Societies, 189; American, 267-268; Massachusetts, 337
Appalachian Highlands, 5-6
Appalachian Mountains, 6
Appalachian Plateau, 6
Appalachians; Settlement west of, 147-148
Appeal, to Supreme Court, 196
Appomattox Courthouse, Lee's surrender at, 370
Architecture; American, 231; Aztec, 26; Eastern Woodlands Indian, 37-38; Indian, 32, 34; Iroquois, 38; Pueblo, 31
Arctic Circle, 11
Arctic, 36
Arizona, 23
Armour, Phillip, 405
Arms, right to bear, 161
Armstrong, Neil, 426
Army of Northern Virginia, 358-359, 365
Army of the Potomac, 358-359, 365
Art; 1920's, 413-414; 1960's, 427; Abstract Expressionism, 427; Nineteenth century, 230-231

Articles of Confederation, 147, 150-152, 154, 156, 159-160, 166; Compared to Constitution, 171; *See also* Confederation, Congress of

Artifacts, Eskimo, 36

Artisans; Aztec, 26; Eastern Woodlands Indian, 38; Inca, 29

Astor, John Jacob, 301

Atahualpa, 52

Atlanta, Georgia, 398-401

Atomic bomb, 419

Austin, Stephen, 306

Austria-Hungary, World War I, 410

Automation, 426

Automobile; Effect of, 426; Industry, 413

Axis, 418

Aztecs, 26, 28, 51; Religion, 28; Traders, 28; Wars, 28

B

Babcock, Orville, 389

Balboa, Vasco Nuñez de, 49

Balkans, World War I, 410

Baltimore, Maryland, 76

Bank of the United States, 198-200, 209; Second, 223, 226, 237, 242, 244-245

Banking system, National, 198

Banks, closing, 414

Banneker, Benjamin, 198, 252

Barlowe, Arthur, 88

Barton, Clara, 361-362

Baseball, 413

Battle at El Alamein, 418; at El Caney, 408; at San Juan Hill, 408

Battle of Antietam, 359-360; of Breed's Hill, 134; of the Bulge, 419; of Bull

Run, 355-356, Second, 359; of Bunker Hill, 134; of Chancellorsville, 365-366; of Cold Harbor, 369; of Concord, 130, 134; of the Coral Sea, 418; of Cowpens, 138; of Fredericksburg, 365-366; of Gettysburg, 366; of Guilford Court House, 139; of Lexington, 130, 134; of Midway, 418; of New Orleans, 221; of Princeton, 135; of Saratoga, 135; of Shiloh, 356; of Spotsylvania Courthouse, 369; of Stalingrad, 418-419; of Thames (Canada), 220; of Tippecanoe, 217; of Trenton, 135; of Vicksburg, 366; of Wilderness, 369;

Bear Flag Republic, *See* California, 305

Beauregard, Pierre, 356

Becknell, William, 304

Bell, John, 346

Benezet, Anthony, 187

Bering Strait, 16, 17

Berlin Airlift, 420

Berlin Blockade, 420

Berlin Wall, 421

Best Friend of Charleston, 288

Biddle, Nicholas, 244

Big stick diplomacy, 409

Bill of Rights, 155, 160-161 *See also* Constitution, United States

Bill of Rights, English, 181

Bingham, Caleb, 230

Birket, James, 184

Birney, James, 268

Black Codes, 379

Black Hawk, 246

Black Hawk's War, 246

Blackfoot, 32

Blacks; Achievements, 432; after Reconstruction, 391, 404-405; Compromise of 1877, 391; Education, 187; Freedom in South after Civil War, 378; Literature, 414; Military service, 221; Music, 413; Progressive movement, 408; Reconstruction, 378, 380, 383-384; Right to vote, 413; Role in Civil War, 360; Votes in 1868 election, 387

"Bleeding Kansas," 342-343

Blind education, 272

Blitzkrieg, 417

Blockade; Berlin, 420; British of American ports, 215

Bonaparte, Napoleon, *See* Napoleon

Bond, Dr. Thomas, 188

Bonds, 197

Booth, John Wilkes, 370

Boston, 74, 94; American Revolution, 134; Massacre, 127; Tea Party, 128

Bowie, Jim, 307

Bowler, Jack, 335

Boxing, 413

Boycott, 125-127, 130; of British goods by U.S., 216

Boyd, Belle, 361

Braddock, General Edward, 119

Bradford, Cornelia, 185

Bradford, William, 73, 92-95

Bradstreet, Anne, 106

Brazil, exploration, 49

"Bread Colonies," 111

Breckinridge, John C., 346

Bridenbaugh, Carl, 186

Bridger, Jim, 299
Britain; and France, 117;
Army in American
Revolution, 133; Colonial
policies, 123; Land
policies, 123; Navy in
American Revolution, 133;
Relations with, 150,
201-202, 215-216; *See also*
England; Great Britain;
Trade with, 151
British Empire, 130;
in North America, 123
Brook Farm, 265, 274
Brown, John, 343;
Raid on Harpers Ferry,
345-346
Brown v. *Board of
Education of Topeka* 1954,
424
Bruce, Blanche K., 384
Bryant, William Cullen, 229
Buchanan, James, 343
Burgoyne, General John,
135
Burnside, Ambrose, 365
Burr, Aaron, 204, 207

C

Cabinet, First, 195
Cabot, John, 67
Calhoun, John C., 218, 235,
241-242, 333
California Trail, 305
California Trough, 10-11
California; and slavery, 340;
Bear Flag Republic, 305,
311; Settlement, 300, 304,
313
Calvert, George, Lord
Baltimore, 76
Cambodia, United States
invades, 422

Canada, 56, 59, 79;
Boundary with, 309
Canals; Aztec, 26; Inca, 29;
United States, 225, 236,
242, 286-287
Canoes, 34-35
Cape Cod, Massachusetts, 95
Cape Cod Bay, 73, 92
Cardozo, Francis L., 384
Carnegie, Andrew, 405
Carolina Grant, *See* North
Carolina, South Carolina
Carpetbaggers, 384
Carter, James (Jimmy),
422-423
Cartier, Jacques, 56-57
Cascade Mountains, 10
Cass, Lewis, 340
Castro, Fidel, 421
Catlin, George, 230
Cavelier, Robert (Sieur de
La Salle), 59-60
CCC (Civilian Conservation
Corps), 414
Census, Inca, 29
Central Intelligence Agency
(CIA), 421
Central Plains, 7
Champlain, Samuel de, 57
Charles I (England), 77
Charles II (England), 77,
114
Charleston, 79
Chase, Salmon P., 382
Checks and balances,
167-168; Chart, 167
Chernozem, 8
Chesapeake Affair, 215
Chiang Kai-shek, 420
Chile, 28
China, 409; Civil war, 420;
Communists, 420; Japan
invades, 417; Nationalists,
420; Nixon visits People's
Republic, 422; People's

Republic, 408, 420, 422;
Trade, 408
Church of England, 67, 72,
80
Church of Jesus Christ of
Latter-Day Saints
(Mormons), 263-264
Churchill, Winston, 419
CIA (Central Intelligence
Agency), 421
Cibola, Seven Cities of, 53
Cincinnati, 291
Cities; Fire departments,
293; Growth, 290-293;
Police forces, 293;
Problems, 291-292; Safety,
292; Street lighting, 292;
Water supply, 292
City Sketch, 88-95, 184-189,
252-257, 318-325, 394-401,
430-435
Civil rights, 404, 405; 1920's,
412; Demonstrations, 424;
Hispanics, 412; Post-World
War I, 412; Post-World
War II, 424
Civil Rights Act of 1866,
379-380
Civil Rights Act of 1957, 424
Civil Rights Act of 1960, 424
Civil Rights Act of 1964, 424
Civil War, 352, 369; Black
soldiers in, 360; Blockade,
357; Blockade runners,
357; Border states, 354;
Colorado, 364;
Confederate advantages,
355; Confederate
successes, 364-365;
Congress in, 364; Dakota,
364; Draft, 363; Draft
riots, 364, 396; European
aid to Confederacy, 355;
Farming in, 362;
Financing, 364; Great
Britain, 368; Greenbacks,

364; Home front, 360-361; in East, 358-359; in West, 356; Ironclads in, 357; Kansas in, 364; Labor troubles, 362; Lee's surrender, 370; Life in South, 363; Medical care, 361; Mississippi River, 366; Naval campaign, 357; Nevada, 364; Profiteering, 362; Railroads, 355, 364; Sherman's March to the Sea, 368-369; Slave states, 353-354; Slavery, 352-353; Union, 353, 359; Union advantages, 354; West Virginia, 354; Women's role, 361

Civil Works Administration (CWA), 414

Civilian Conservation Corps (CCC), 414

Clark, George Rogers, 137-138

Clark, William, 210

Clay, Henry, 218, 235-236, 244, 338, 340

Clayton Antitrust Act of 1914, 406, 408

Clermont, 287

Cleveland, Grover, 407

Clifton, John, 188

Climate; Great Lakes, 12; Great Plains, 14; Intermontane Plateaus and Basins, 14-15; Mediterranean, 15; Midwest, 12; Northeast, 11; Rocky Mountains, 14; Southeast, 11; Southwest, 14-15; United States, 15; West Coast, 15

Clinton, George, 160

Clothing, Eskimo, 36

Coal, 285

Coastal Plains, 3-5; Atlantic, 3-5; Gulf, 5

Coexistence, 421

Coining of money, 178

Cold war, 419-420, 422

Cole, Thomas, 231

College of New Jersey, See Princeton University, 110

Colombia, 28; Panama Canal role, 409

Colonial population, 105

Colonial society, 100-105, 107-108

Colonies, 45; Daily life, 103; Dutch, 61-63; English, 66–77, 79-82, 84, Government, 85, Population, 101, Religion, 101, Self-government, 82, Settlement, 83; French, 57-61; Middle, 110; New England, 108; Population, 103-104; Proprietary, 75-77, 79; Regions of, 108; Royal, 77, 79, 82; Scotch-Irish, 102; Southern, 112; Spanish, 53-54; Swedish, 62-63; Women's role, See Women, Role in colonial society

Colonists and Indians, See Indians and colonists

Colonists; African, 102, 105, 107; and English king, 114; English, 101; European, 102; German, 102; Scots, 101

Colorado River, 9

Columbia River, 9, 211

Columbia River Valley, Settlement, 303

Columbia University, 111

Columbus, Christopher, 46-49, 67

Commerce, Interstate, 157, 226; Under Articles of Confederation, 151

Commission on Civil Rights, 424

Common Sense, 132, 134

Communication; Inca, 30; Plains Indians, 33

Communism, Satellite governments, 419

Communists; Berlin, 420; Czechoslovakia, 420; See also Soviet Union

Compromise of 1850, 340, 342

Compromise of 1877, 390

Computers, 426

Concentration camps, Germany, 417

Concept; Creativity, 275; Mobility, 312; Nationalism, 227; Pluralism, 407; Responsibility, 173; Sectionalism, 339

Concurrent powers, 178

Confederacy, See also South, Confederate States of America

Confederate States of America; Formed, 346-347

Confederation, 147, 174, 195; Congress of, 150; Tax power, 151; Weaknesses, 150, 153-154; See also Articles of Confederation

Congress, 172; Established in Constitution, 166; Library of, 254; Plan for Reconstruction, 378; Qualifications for, 170; Structure, 169

Conical projection, 13

Connecticut, 75, 82

Conservation movement, 406

Constantinople, capture of, 44

Constitution, 164-172, 174, 178

Constitution, United States, 150, 154-155, 181, 195; 10th Amendment, 178; 12th Amendment, 207; 13th Amendment, 376; 14th Amendment, 380-381, 404, Due process clause, 380, Equal protection clause, 380; 15th Amendment, 387, 404; 19th Amendment, 412; 24th Amendment, 424; Adopted, 158; Amendment, 179; and change, 179; and power, 178; Compared to Articles of Confederation, 171; Compromises in, 157; Congress, 170, 172; Due process, 380; Equal protection, 380; Foreign policy, 172; Interpretation of, 200-201; Powers under, 176-177; Presidency, 172; Principles in, 168-169; Ratification, 158-161; Revenue, 170; Slavery, 157; Treaties, 171

Constitutional Convention of 1787, 154-158

Constitutional-Union Party, 346

Continental Army, 134, 136, 139; Black soldiers, 142

Continental Association, 130

Continental Congress; First, 128-130; Second, 130, 132, 135, 143, 147

Convention of 1800, 205-206

Convention of 1818, 302

Cook, James, 301

Cooke, Francis, 92, 95

Cooper, James Fenimore, 229

Copley, John Singleton, 230

Copying machines, 426

Cornwallis, Charles, 139

Coronado, Francisco Vásquez de, 53

Corporations, 405

Cortés, Hernando, 51-52

Cotton gin, 333

Council for New England, 72

Council of the Indies, 53

Courts, Federal, 174, 196

Crawford, William, 235

Creativity, 275

Credit Mobilier scandal, 389

Creoles, 319

Croatoan, 68

Crockett, Davy, 307

Cromwell, Oliver, 77

Crusades, 43

Cuba, 421; Soviet missiles in, 421-422; Spanish-American War, 408

Culture, Influenced by environment, 30

Cultures, 23

Cumberland Plateau, 6

Cumberland Road, 224-225

Cumberland Valley, 6

Curtis Act of 1924, 412

Cuzco, 52

CWA (Civil Works Administration), 414

Cylindrical projection, 13

Czechoslovakia, Germans take land, 417

D

D-Day, World War II, 419

Dallas, Texas, 427

Dare, Virginia, 68

Dartmouth College, 109

Davis, Henry Winter, 374, 388

Davis, Jefferson, 347, 353

Davis, John, 68

Dawes, William, 130

Dayton, Jonathan, 154

Deaf, education, 272

Death penalty, 142

Debt, national, 197

Declaration of Independence, 132, 142, 154

Declaratory Act, 126

Delaware, 81

Delaware River, 62

Delegated powers, 176-178

Democracy, defined, 190

Democratic-Republican Party, 200-201, 205-206, 222, 235

Democrats, 237

Demonstrations; Anti-Vietnam War, 426; Civil rights, 424

Deregulation, 423

DeSoto, Hernando, 53

Détente, 422

Dewey, George, 408

Dial, 274

Dias, Bartolomeu, 46

Dictatorships, 417

Dinosaurs, 16

Dinwiddie, Robert, 118

Direct Primary, 406

Disarmament, 412

District of Columbia, 252, 257

Division of powers, 176-177

Dix, Dorothea, 272, 361

Dollar diplomacy, 410

Dominican Republic, 49

Dominion of New England, 85

Domino theory, 421

Doughty, Thomas, 230

Douglas, Stephen, 342, 344, 346

Douglass, Frederick, 268, 337

Dove, David, 187

Draft, 363

Draft riots, 364, 396; Civil War, 363-364; World War I, 410

Drake, Sir Francis, 68

Dred Scott case, 343-344

DuBois, William E., 413

Duane, James, 130

Due process, 14th Amendment, 380

Dutch East India Company, 61

Dutch East Indies, World War II, 418

Dutch West India Company, 61, 94

E

East India Company, 128

Eastern Europe, Cold War, 419

Economic Opportunity Act, 423

Education, 187; Colonial, 108-112, 186; Free public, 270; Ideas on, 270

EEOC (Equal Employment Opportunity Commission), 424

Eisenhower, Dwight, 419, 421; Domestic programs, 423

Eisenhower Doctrine, 421

Election; Decided in House of Representatives, 235-236; First, 195

Electoral College, 174

Elizabeth I (England), 67-69

Ellicott, Andrew, 252

Emancipation, 338

Emancipation Proclamation, 359-360

Emma Willard Female Seminary, Troy, New York, 271

England, 67; and France in North America, 123; and Spain, 68-69; Church of, See Church of England; Colonies, See Colonies, English; See also Britain; Great Britain

Equal Employment Opportunity Commission (EEOC), 424

Equal protection, 14th Amendment, 380

Erie Canal, 286

Eskimos, 36

Ethiopia, 417

Europe, Invasion, World War II, 419

Exclusive powers, 178

Executive, Federal; Established, 157; See also Presidency

Expansionists, 300

Exploration, 45; Dutch, 61-62; English, 67-68; French, 56-60; Portuguese, 45-46, 56; Spanish, 47-49, 51-54; Swedish, 62-63

Explorers, European, Chart, 50

Expressed powers, 176

F

Factory system, 282, 284

Fair Deal, 423

Fair Labor Standards Act of 1938, 416

Fall, Albert B., 413

Family, Colonial, 107

Farm Credit Administration (FCA), 414

Farming; Beginning, 24; Organizations, 405-406; Prices, 414; See also Agriculture, 24

Farragut, David, 357

FCA (Farm Credit Administration), 414

Federal Reserve System, 406

Federal Trade Commission (FTC), 406

Federalism, 166

Federalist Papers, The, 159, 168, 174

Federalists, 159-160, 200-201, 206, 222-223, 235

Feminine Mystique, The, 427

Ferraro, Geraldine A., 425

Finney, Charles, 263, 267

Fishing, Colonial, 109

Fisk, Jim, 389

Fletcher v. Peck, 226

Flood control, 415-416

Florida, 49, 79, 119; Annexation, 226

Floyd, John, 239

Food Administration (World War I), 410

Food; Eastern Woodlands Indian, 37; Eskimo, 36; Indian, 90

Football, 413

Force Act of 1870, 387

Force Bill, 242

Ford, Gerald, 423, 426

Formosa, See Taiwan, 420

Fort Atkinson Treaty of 1853, 315

Fort Christina, 63

Fort Donelson, 356

Fort Duquesne, 118-119

Fort Henry, 356

Fort Laramie Treaty of 1851, 315

Fort McHenry, 220

Fort Sumter fired on, 352
Forten, Charlotte, 388
Forty-hour week, 416
"Forty-niners," 313
Foster, Stephen, 231
Fourteen Points, 411
France; in American
    Revolution, 135; in North
    America, 59-61, 117;
    Relations with, 204-206;
    Surrenders, World War II,
    417; World War I, 410
Francis I (France), 56
Franklin, Benjamin, 118,
    132, 135, 154-155, 157,
    159, 185-188
Franz Ferdinand, Archduke,
    410
Free-Soil Party, 340
Freedmen, 383, 386
Freedmen's Bureau, 378-379
Freedom of; Assembly, 161;
    Press, 161; Religion, 67,
    72-76, 85, 101, 161;
    Speech, 161
Frémont, John C., 310, 343
French and Indian War,
    118-119, 123
Friedan, Betty, 427
Friends, Society of, 79-80,
    110, 114, 184, 186,
    188-189
Frobisher, Martin, 68
Frontenac, Count, 59
Frontier; Indian warfare on,
    216-217; Western, 113
FTC (Federal Trade
    Commission), 406
Fuel Administration (World
    War I), 411
Fugitive Slave Act, 342-343
Fuller, Margaret, 274
Fulton, Robert, steamboat,
    287
Fur trade, 94

G

Gadsden Purchase, 311
Gage, Thomas, 130
Gallaudet, Thomas, 272
Galloway, Joseph, 130
Gama, Vasco da, 46
Gannet, Deborah, 136-137
Garrison, William Lloyd,
    267, 277
George III (England), 123,
    126, 130, 132
Georgia, 81; Indians in, 246
Germans; Immigration to
    United States, 294-295
Germany; Anti-Jewish
    campaign, 417;
    Concentration camps, 417;
    Division after World War
    II, 419; Invades Belgium,
    417, Denmark, 417,
    Netherlands, 417, Norway,
    417, Poland, 417;
    Occupies Rhineland, 417,
    Sudetenland, 417; World
    War I, 410; World War II,
    418
Gettysburg Address, *See*
    Abraham Lincoln, 367
Gibbons v. *Ogden,* 226
Gibbs, Jonathan C., 384
Gilbert, Sir Humphrey, 68
Glaciers, 15-16
Glorious Revolution of 1688,
    85
Gobi Desert, 17
Gold Rush, 322, 324-325;
    California, 312-313
Goodyear, Charles,
    vulcanization, 284
Gorges, Sir Ferdinando, 77
Gould, Jay, 389
Government; Branches, 169;
    Colonial, 110; Established,
    195-197; Inca, 30; Limited,
    165; Representative, 125

Grand Canyon, 9
Grange (Patrons of
    Husbandry), 406
Grant, Ulysses S., 356, 366,
    368-369; and
    Reconstruction, 387;
    Elected President, 387;
    Scandals during presidency
    of, 389
Great Basin, 34
Great Britain; World War I,
    410; *See also* England;
    Britain
Great Compromise, 156-157,
    170
Great Depression, 413-416;
    New Deal, 416
Great Lakes, 7;
    Climate, 12
Great Plains, 7-8;
    Climate, 14
Great Salt Lake, 9
Great Society, 423
Great Valley, 6
"Greek Revival," 231
Greeley, Horace, 360
Greenhow, Rose O'Neal,
    361
Greenland, 36
Grenville, George, 123
Grenville Acts, 124-125
Grimké, Angelina, 266
Grimké, Sarah, 266
Grinnell, Moses, 342
Guam, Spanish-American
    War, 408

H

Haiti, Independence, 209
Haley, Alex, 427
Half Moon, 61
Hamilton, Dr. Alexander, 80

Hamilton, Alexander, 151-152, 159, 168, 174, 195, 197-202, 207
Harding, Warren, 412-413
Hariot, Thomas, 88
Harlem Renaissance, 414
Harrison, William Henry, 217, 220, 249
Hartford Convention, 222-223, 241, 333
Harvard College, 109
Hat Act of 1732, 117
Haughery, Margaret Gaffney, 293
Hawkins, Sir John, 68
Hawthorne, Nathaniel, 274, 276
Hay-Bunau-Varilla Treaty, 409
Hay, John, 408
Hayes, Rutherford, 389-390
Hayne, Robert, 241, 333
Heath, John, binder, 285
Henry IV (France), 57
Henry VII (England), 67
Henry VIII (England), 67
Henry the Navigator, Prince, 45
Henry, Patrick, 125, 130, 154, 160
Hepburn Act, 406
High Plains, *See* Great Plains
Hiroshima, Atomic bombing of, 419
Hispanic Rights, 426, 432
Hitler, Adolf, 417
Hohokam, 31
Homestead Act of 1862, 364
Hooker, Joseph, 365-366
Hooker, Thomas, 75
Hoover, Herbert, 414
Hopi, 31–32
Hospitals, *See also* medicine, 188

Hostages, United States in Iran, 422
House of Representatives, 169; Composition, 156-157; Powers, 170-171; Qualifications for, 170
House of Seven Gables, The, 276
Housing; Arctic, 36; Eastern Woodlands Indian, 37; Indian, 32, 34; Iroquois, 38
Houston, Sam, 307, 430
Houston Ship Channel, 430
Houston Space Center, 431
Houston, Texas, 427, 430-435
Howard, W. P., 399
Howe, Elias, sewing machine, 284
Howe, Samuel, 272
Howe, William, 134-135
Hudson, Henry, 61
Hudson River, 61
"Hudson River School" of painting, 230-231
Hudson River Valley, in American Revolution, 135
Hudson's Bay Company, 301
Huguenots, 81
Human rights, United States policy on, 423
Humans; First in North America, 16-17
Hungarian Revolt of 1956, 421
Hunters, Indian, 32
Hutchinson, Anne, 75

I

ICC (Interstate Commerce Commission), 406
Ice Age, 15-17

Illinois; in American Revolution, 138; Indians in, 246
Immigration; Asian, 23; Early, 23; German, 294-295; Irish, 294-295; Quotas, 412
Impeachment; Andrew Johnson, 382; Charges against Richard Nixon, 426
Implied powers, 176
Impressment, 201, 215
Incas, 28, 52; Religion, 29
Indentured servants, 104-105, 107
Independence, 98, 140, 141; and state governments, 141; and women, 141
Indian Removal Act of 1830, 246
Indian wars in West, after Civil War, 388
Indian policy, 314-315
Indiana, in American Revolution, 138
Indians; Alaskan, 35; and Colonists, 72-73, 113-114; and English settlers, 70-71, 91-94; and French settlers, 57-61; and Fur trade, 314; and Horses, 313; and Jacksonian Democracy, 239; and Spanish settlers, 53; and Westward Movement, 313-315; Arapaho, 315; Cayuga, 38; Cherokee, 37, 246-247; Cheyenne, 32, 315; Chickasaw, 37, 246; Chinook, 34; Chippewa (Ojibwa), 35, 246; Choctaw, 37, 246; Chumash, 34; Citizenship, 412; Comanche, 32, 315; Conflict with settlers, 404;

Cree, 35; Creek, 37-38, 245-246; Crow, 32; Eastern Woodlands, 37, 39; Far North, 35; Federal Government and, 245; Forced removal, 246; Fox, 37, 246; Great Basin, 34; Haida, 34; Hopewell, 38; Huron, 37, 57-58; in American Revolution, 135; in California, 306; in Iowa, 246; in New England, 114; in Pennsylvania, 114; Iroquois, 37-38, 57-59; Kiowas, 315; Land, 314-315; Menominee, 246; Miami, 37; Modoc, 34; Mohawk, 38, 57; Natchez, 37; Nootka, 34; Northwest, 34, 151; Ojibwa (Chippewa), 35; Oneida, 38; Onondaga, 38; Ottawa, 35, 246; Pawtuxet, 73; Pequot, 114; Plains, 32-33, 315; Pomo, 34; Power on frontier, 123; Powhatan, 37, 70-71, 88-91; Reservations, 315; Resettlement, 247-248; Sac, 246; Sauk, 37; Seminole, 37, 247; Seneca, 38; Shawnee, 37, 217; Shoshoni, 210; Sioux, 246, 315; Tanaina, 35; Tlingit, 34; Wampanoag, 73, 114; West, 404; Winnebago, 37, 246; Yokut, 34

Industrial Revolution, *See* Industry, Rise of, 281

Industrial growth, 405 1920's, 413

Industry; Iron, 285; Rise of, 281-295; Textile, 281-282

Inflation, 1970's, 423

Inherent powers, 176-177

Interior Highlands, 8

Interior Plains, 7

Intermontane Plateaus and Basins, 9; Climate, 14-15

Interstate Commerce Act of 1887, 406

Interstate Commerce Commission (ICC), 406

Intolerable Acts, 128, 130

Intolerance, 1920's, 412

Inventions, 284; 1920's, 413

Iranians, seize American hostages, 422

Irish immigration to United States, 294-295

Irish potato famine, 294

Iron, 285

Iron Act of 1750, 117

Iroquois, League of, 39, 57

Irving, Washington, 228

Italy; Invades Ethiopia, 417; World War I, 410; World War II, 418

Iwo Jima, World War II, 419

J

Jackson, Age of, 239, 249

Jackson, Andrew, 221, 225, 235-240, 242, 244, 248; and Indians, 245-247; Bank of the United States, 245; Economic policies, 249; Popularity, 238; "Specie Circular," 245; Veto, 240

Jackson, Thomas "Stonewall," 355, 366

Jacksonian Democracy, 238

James I (England), 70, 72-73

James II (England), 79, 82, 85

James VI (Scotland), *See* James I (England), 70

James, Duke of York, 79, 81; *See also* James II (England)

Jamestown, 70, 73, 82, 113

Japan; Attacks Pearl Harbor, 418; Invades China, 417, French Indochina, 417, Malaya, 418, Manchuria, 417; Militarism, 417-418; Surrender, World War II, 419; U.S. relations, 417

Japanese-Americans, relocation World War II, 418

Jay Treaty of 1794, 201-202, 204

Jay, John, 159, 201; U.S. Chief Justice, 196

Jazz, 413

Jefferson, Thomas, 132, 148, 154, 195, 200-201, 204-205, 207-208, 210, 215; Architecture, 231; President, 208

Jewish settlers, 110

"Jim Crow" laws, 404-405

Jogues, Father Isaac, 58

Johnson, Andrew, 374, 376; Impeachment, 381-382, acquittal, 382; Plan for Reconstruction, 376

Johnson, Lyndon, 422-423; Domestic programs, 423

Johnston, A. S., 355-356

Johnston, Joseph, 355, 368

Joint stock companies, 70

Joliet, Louis, 59

Jones, Jesse, 433

Jordan, Barbara, 432-433

Judicial Review, 168, 209

Judiciary Act of 1789, 196, 209

Judiciary, Federal, Established, 157

Junto Club, 185-188

Jury, Right to trial by, 161

K

Kansas, Slavery in, 342-343
Kansas-Nebraska Act, 342-344
Kayak, 36
Kearny, Stephen, 310-311
Kellogg-Briand Treaty of 1928, 412
Kelly, William, 284
Kennedy, John F., 421, 426; Domestic programs, 423
Kentucky and Virginia Resolutions, 207, 222, 241
Key, Francis Scott, 220
Khrushchev, Nikita, 421
King, Martin Luther, Jr., 424, 426
King George's War, 117
King Philip (Wampanoag), 114
King William's War, 117
King's Mountain, Battle of, 138
Kino, Father Eusebio, 54
Knight, John, 68
Knights of Labor, 406
Know-Nothings, 295
Knox, Henry, 195
Korean War, 420-421
Ku Klux Klan, 385, 386; 1920's, 412
Ku Klux Klan Act of 1871, 387

L

Labor disputes, 416
Labor organizations, *See* Unions
Labor; Great Depression, 416; New Deal, 416; Workman's compensation, 406
Labrador, 68

Lafayette, Marquis de, 139
Laffite, Jean, 221
Laissez-faire, 405
Land Ordinance of 1785, 148-149
Land bridge, 16-17
Land ownership, 53
Language, Plains Indians, 33
Lanusse, Armand, 320
Laos, United States invades, 422
La Salle, Sieur de (Robert Cavelier), 59-60
LasCasas, Fr. Bartolomé de, 54
Last frontier, 404
Law, Indian, 90
Lawrence, Amos, 342
League of Nations, 411-412; United States opposition, 411
League of United Latin American Citizens (LULAC), 432
"Leatherstocking Tales," 229
Leaves of Grass, 277
Lee, Jason, 302
Lee, Richard Henry, 132
Lee, Robert E., 345, 353, 355, 359, 365-366, 369; Surrenders to Grant, 370
Legislature, Federal, Established, 157
Lehigh Valley, 6
Lend-Lease Act, 417
L'Enfant, Pierre Charles, 252
Levis, 323
Lewis and Clark Expedition, 210-211, 299, 301
Lewis, Meriwether, 210
Liberator, The, 267
Liberty, Religious, *See* Freedom of religion, 73
Library of Congress, 254
Lifestyle, 1920's, 413
Lima, Peru, 52-53

Limited war, 421
Lincoln, Abraham, 344, 352, 358-360, 365; Abolishes slavery, 360; Assassination, 370, 397; Election, 346, 348; Gettysburg Address, 367; Issues Emancipation Proclamation, 359; Plan for Reconstruction, 374-376; Re-election 1864, 370; Second Inaugural Address, 370; Views on Slavery, 360; Views on Union, 360
Lincoln-Douglas Debates, 344-345
Literacy test, Citizenship, 407
Literature; 1960's, 427; American, 228, 274; Black, 106; Colonial, 106; Women's, 106
Livingston, Robert, 132
Llamas, 28
Lodge, Henry Cabot, 407
London Company, 70-72
Long houses, 38
Long, Huey P., 416
Long, Stephen, 299
Longfellow, Henry Wadsworth, 131, 277
Lord Protector, *See* Cromwell, Oliver, 77
Lost Colony, The, 68
Louisiana, 59; And Spain, 119
Louisiana Purchase, 209-210
Louisiana Territory, 299
Louisville, 291
L'Ouverture, Toussaint, 209
Lovejoy, Elijah, 268
Loyalists, Colonial, 127, 141
LULAC (League of United Latin American Citizens), 432
Lyon, Mary, 271

M

MacArthur, Douglas, 419-421
Macarthy, Cecee, 319
Macdonough, Thomas, 220
Macon's Bill Number 2, 1810, 216
Madison, Dolley, 256
Madison, James, 151, 155, 157, 159, 175, 207, 209, 218, 222-223, 256
Magellan, Fernando, 49
Magellan, Strait of, 68
Magna Carta, 181
Maine, 77
Malaya, World War II, 418
Manchuria, Japan invades, 417
Manhattan, 61-62
Manifest Destiny, 300-301
Mann, Horace, 270-272
Manufacturing; Colonial, 104, 111; English, 68
Mao Tse-tung, 420
Map projections; Conical, 13; Cylindrical, 13; Mercator, 13
Maps, Distortion, 13
Marbury v. *Madison,* 209, 226
March on Washington, 1963, 424, 426
Marcy, William, 240
Marion, Francis, 138
Marquette, Father Jacques, 59
Marshall Plan, 420
Marshall, Chief Justice John, 175, 209
Martineau, Harriet, 288
Maryland, 82; Colonial, 75-76
Mason, George, 155, 160
Mason, John, 77
Massachusetts, 77

Massachusetts Bay Colony, 74, 82, 85, 95; Government, 75
Massasoit, 73, 93
Mayas, 25
Mayflower, 73, 92
Mayflower Compact, 73, 181
Maysville Road Veto, 242
McClellan, George B., 358-359, 365
McCormick, Cyrus, reaper, 284-285
McCullough v. *Maryland,* 226, 244
McDowell, Irvin, 356
McGuffey, William, 272
McKinley, William, 406
McLoughlin, John, 301
Meade, George, 366
Meat Inspection Act, 406
Meat-packing industry, 405
Medicine, 188; Conquest of polio, 426
Melville, Herman, 276
Mental hospitals, 272
Mercantilism, 114, 117
Mercator projection, 13
Merchants, *See* trade, 104
Merrimac, 357
Mesas, 31
Mexican War, 309-311, 322
Mexico, 51; and Texas, 306; Early, 26
Micro-computers, 426
Middle America, 25, 28
Middle Colonies, Government, 110
Millerites, 264
Minimum wage, 416
Mining, 404
Minuit, Peter, 61
Minutemen, 130
Missionaries, 54
Missions; French, 58; Spanish, 54
Mississippi River, 8; and Spain, 53; Trade on, 151

Missouri Compromise, 338, 340, 342, 344
Missouri Plateau, 8
Mittelberger, Gottlieb, 104
Mobility, 312
Moby Dick, 276
Molasses, 109
Molasses Act of 1733, 117
Monitor, 357
Monroe, Elizabeth, 256
Monroe, James, 223, 225-226, 256
Montcalm, General Louis, 119
Monroe Doctrine, 226, 228, 301; Roosevelt Corollary, 409
Montezuma, 51
Montgomery bus boycott, 424
Monticello, 231
Montreal, capture of, 119
Moon landing, U.S., 426
Mormons, *See* Church of Jesus Christ of Latter-Day Saints, 263
Morris, Robert, 135
Morse, Samuel F. B., telegraph, 284
Mott, Lucretia, 269
Mount, William Sidney, 230
Mount Holyoke Female Seminary, 271
Mount Rainier, 10
Mount St. Helens, 10
Mount Whitney, 10
Movies, 413
"Mr. Madison's War," 218
Muckrakers, 406
Mullins, Priscilla, 92, 95
Munich Pact, 417
Murders in the Rue Morgue, 277
Music, American, 230-231
Muslims, 43-44
Mussolini, Benito, 417

N

NAACP (National Association for the Advancement of Colored People), 413
Nagasaki, Atomic bombing of, 419
Napoleon, 205, 209
Napoleonic Wars, 215
NASA (National Aeronautics and Space Administration), 426, 431
Nat Turner's Rebellion, 336
National Aeronautics and Space Administration (NASA), 426, 431
National anthem, 220
National Association for the Advancement of Colored People (NAACP), 413
National Bank, 198, 236; *See also* Bank of the United States, 236
National banking system, 406
National culture, 228-230
National Industrial Recovery Act of 1933, 416
National Labor Relations Board (NLRB), 416
National Recovery Administration (NRA), 415
National-Republicans, 237, 248
National road, 224-225, 242, 286
National states, 45
Nationalism, 214-228
Nativist movement, 295
NATO (North Atlantic Treaty Organization), 420
Nature, 275
Nauset, 95
Navigation Acts, 114, 124
Nazis, 417

Netherlands, *See* Dutch, 61
Neutrality, United States, in Napoleonic Wars, 201
New Amsterdam, 62, 394
New Deal, 414-416, 423; Opposition, 416; Results, 416; Second, 415; Supreme Court, 416
New Economic Policy, 423
New England; Dominion of, 85; Indians, 114; *See also* Colonies, New England
New Federalism, 423
New France, 58-61
New Freedom, 406
New Frontier, 423
New Hampshire, 77, 82
New Harmony, Indiana, 265
New Jersey, 79
New Jersey Plan, 156
New Mexico, 23; and slavery, 340-341
New Netherland, 61-63, 79
New Orleans, Louisiana, 202, 318-321
New Spain, 53
New Sweden, 62-63, 79
New York, 79, 394, 397; National capital, 195
Newcomen, Thomas, steam engine, 287
Newfoundland, 67-68
Nixon, Richard, 422; China visit, 422; Domestic programs, 423; Impeachment charges, 426; New Economic Policy, 423; Resignation, 426; Watergate burglary coverup, 426
Nixon v. *Herndon,* 413
NLRB (National Labor Relations Board), 416
Non-Intercourse Act of 1808, 216
"Normalcy," 412
Norse, *See* Vikings, 43

North America, 30-32, 36
North Atlantic Treaty Organization (NATO), 420
North Carolina, 79; Settlement, 88
North Star, 337
North-South Differences, 336, 338, 340, 348; Economic, 331-332; Industry, 332; Political, 332-333; Slavery, 333-335; Social, 331
Northwest Ordinance of 1787, 148-150
Northwest Passage, 56, 59, 68
Northwest Territory, 148-151, 201
Nova Scotia, 56, 59
NRA (National Recovery Administration), 415
Nuclear Non-proliferation Treaty, 422
Nullification, 241-242, 333
Nurses in Civil War, 361

O

O'Connor, Sandra Day, 425
Oberlin College, 271
Office of Price Administration (OPA), World War II, 418
Oglethorpe, James, 81
Ohio Valley, 113, 117, 128
Oil prices 1970's, 423
Oil-refining industry, 405
Oil reserves, Teapot Dome affair, 413
Okinawa, World War II, 419
"Old Ironsides," 219
Olive Branch Petition, 130
Oneida Community, 265
OPA (Office of Price Administration), 418
Open Door policy, 408

Open Housing Act of 1968, 424
Order of the Sons of America, 413
Oregon, 301, 309; Annexation, 308; Boundary with Canada, 301–302, 308-309; Settlement, 300; Trial, 303, 306, 315
"Oregon fever," 302
Osceola, 247
Ottoman Empire, 410
Owen, Robert, 265
Ozark Plateau, 8

P

Pacific Coastal Ranges, 9-10
Pacific Fur Company, 301
Pacific Northwest, first inhabitants, 23
Paine, Thomas, 132, 134
Painting; Abstract Expressionism, 427; American, 230-231
Panama, 49, 52
Panama Canal, 409; Treaty, 422
Panic of 1837, 248-249
Papagos, 31
Papal Line of Demarcation, 48
Parkman, Francis, 303
Parties, Political, 200, 206
Patents, 284
Paterson, William, 156
Patriots, Colonial, 127
Patrons of Husbandry (Grange), 405-406
Pearl Harbor, Attacked, 418
"Peculiar Institution," 333
Penn, William, 79-81, 114, 184
Pennsylvania, 79-80; and Indians, 114; Settlement, 81; University of, 111

Perry, Oliver Hazard, 219
Pershing, John, 411
Personal liberty laws, 342
Peru, 28, 51-53
Philadelphia, Pennsylvania, 81, 184, 189; in American Revolution, 135
Philadelphia Academy, 186
Philadelphia College, *See* Pennsylvania, University of, 111
Philip II (Spain), 69
Philippines; Spanish-American War, 408; World War II, 418
Philosophy, American, 264
Pickens, Andrew, 138
Pickett, George, 366
"Pickett's Charge," 366
Pike, Zebulon, 299, 304
Pilgrims, 73, 92-93, 95; Government, 73
Pimas, 31
Pinckney, Thomas, 204
Pinckney Treaty of 1795, 202
Pit and the Pendulum, The, 277
Pitt, William, 119
Pittsburgh, Pennsylvania, 291
Pizarro, Francisco, 52
Plains of Abraham, 119
Plan of Union, 1754, 118
Planning, regional, 415-416
Plantations, 331, 334
Plessy v. *Ferguson,* 404-405
Pluralism, 407
Plymouth, 73-74, 77, 82, 92-95; Government, 73
Plymouth Colony, 72, 93
Plymouth Company, 70
Pocahontas, 71
Podzol, 8
Poe, Edgar Allen, 276-277
Poland, Germany invades, 417
Police powers, 178

Polio, conquest of, 426
Polk, James K., 308-309
Poll taxes, outlawed, 424
Ponce de León, Juan, 49
Popular Sovereignty, 165; Slavery, 340
Population changes, 294-295, 426
Populists, 406
Potlatch, 34-35
Potsdam Conference, 419
Powers, under United States Constitution; Concurrent, 178; Delegated, 176-178; Exclusive, 178; Expressed, 176; House of Representatives, 170; Implied, 176, 244; Inherent, 176-177; Limitations on by Constitution, 178; Police, 178; Reserved, 176-178; Senate, 170
Powhatan, 70-71
Preamble, Constitution, 165
Prejudice; Anti-Black, 412; Anti-Catholic, 412; Anti-Jewish, 412
Presidency, 172
President; Commander-in-chief, 172; Qualifications, 172; Resignation, 426
Princeton University, 110-111
Prisons, reform, 272
Proclamation of 1763, 124
Proclamation of Amnesty and Reconstruction, 374
Profile, 425
Progressive Era, 406
Progressive movement, 406, 408
Prohibition, 273-274
Prophet, The (Shawnee Indians), 217

Proprietary Colonies, *See* Colonies, Proprietary
Prosser, Gabriel, 335
Public Works Administration (PWA), 414
Pueblos, 31-32
Puerto Rico, Spanish-American War, 408
Puget Trough, 10
Punishment, cruel and unusual, 161
Pure Food and Drug Act, 406
Puritans, 72-74, 77, 94, 108; Religion, 75
PWA (Public Works Administration), 414
Pyramids, Aztec, 26

Q

Quakers, *See* Friends, Society of
Quebec; Capture, 119; Settlement, 57, 117
Quebec Act, 128
Queen Anne's War, 117
Quincy, Josiah, 283

R

Radical Republicans, 374-375, 382; and Reconstruction, 376, 378
Radio, 413
Radiocarbon dating, 17
Railroads; Baltimore and Ohio, 288; Building, 288-290; Influence on cities, 291
"Rain shadow," 9
Raleigh, Sir Walter, 68, 88
Ranching, 404
Randolph, Edmund, 154, 195

Reagan, Ronald, 422-423; Domestic policies, 423
Rebellion, Nat Turner's, 336
Reconstruction Acts, 380, 383
Reconstruction, 374-376, 378, 391, 404; and President Grant, 387; Congressional Radicals and, 374; Corruption during, 385
Red Scare, 1920's, 412
"Redeemers," 391
Reformation, English, 67
Religion, Freedom of, *See* Freedom of Religion
Religion; Colonial, 108, 110, 112; Eastern Woodlands Indian, 38; Inca, 29; Indian, 90-91; Mayas, 26; Navaho, 32; Nineteenth century, 263; Plains Indians, 33; Pueblo, 32; Puritan, 74
Religious groups, new, 263
Religious revivals, 263
Relocation centers, Japanese-Americans, 418
Representation; Direct, 125; Virtual, 125
Republican Party, 343
Reserved powers, 176-178
Responsibility, 173
Restoration, English, 77
Revels, Hiram P., 384
Revenue; Constitution, 170; Sharing, 423
Revere, Paul, 130-131
"Revolution of 1800," 208-209
Revolution, *See* American Revolution
Rhineland, Germany occupies, 417
Rhode Island, 75, 82
Rice University, 431

Richardson, W. A., 389
Richmond, Virginia, Confederate Capital at, 358
Rights of the accused, 424
Rillieux, Norbert, 320
Ripley, Eliza, 320-321
Roads, 236; Funding, 242, 286
Roanoke Island, 68, 88
Rockefeller, John D., 405
Rocky Mountains, 8-9; Climate, 14
Rolfe, John, 71
"Roman Revival," 231
Roosevelt corollary, 409
Roosevelt, Franklin D., 414, 416; Death, 419; Great Depression, 414-415; World War II, 418
Roosevelt, Theodore, 406; Panama Canal, 409
Roots, 427
Ross, Edmund G., 382
Rum, 109
Russia, World War I, 410
Rutgers University, 111

S

Sacajawea, 210
Salomon, Haym, 135
SALT I, *See* Strategic Arms Limitation Treaty, 422
Salt Lake City, Founded, 264
Samoset, 93
Sampson, Deborah, 136
San Antonio, Texas, 427
San Francisco, California, 54, 322-325
San Joaquin Valley, 11
Santa Anna, Antonio López de, 306-307
Santa Fe Trail, 304
Santo Domingo, 388

Satellite, 426
Scalawags, 384
Scott, Dred, *See* Dred Scott
Case, 343
Scott, Winfield, 310
SEATO (Southeast Asia
Treaty Organization), 421
Secession, 346-347, 353
Secota, 88-91
Secret ballot, 406
Sectional differences, 331
Sectionalism, 235, 339
Segregation, 404-405;
Education, 424; Outlawed
in education, 424
Selective Service, *See* Draft
Senate, 169; Composition,
156-157; Powers, 170-171;
Qualifications for, 170
Seneca Falls Declaration,
269
Separation of powers, 157,
165-167
Separatists, 92
Serra, Father Junípero, 54
Servants, Indentured, *See*
Indentured servants
Settlement houses, 406
Settlement in New World,
See Colonies
Settlement; Colonial, Spread
of, 123; West of
Appalachians, 149-150
Settlers and Indians, *See*
Indians
Seymour, Horatio, 387
Shakers, 265
Sharecropping, 391
Shays, Daniel, 153
Shays' Rebellion, 152-154
Shenandoah Valley, 6
Sherman, Roger, 132
Sherman, William, 368-369;
Atlanta, 398-399; March
to the Sea, 368-369
Sherman Antitrust Act of
1890, 406

Shiloh, *See* Battle of Shiloh
Shipbuilding, 109
Shopping malls, 426
Sierra Nevada Mountains, 10
"Sit-ins," 424
Sketch Book, 228
Skill, 27, 55, 78, 115, 131,
155, 243, 283, 367, 377
Slater, Samuel, 281-283
Slave codes, 334
Slave trade, 46, 102, 109,
157, 333, 334; Ban on
importation of slaves, 333;
District of Columbia, 341;
End of, 143; Origins, 54
Slavery, 34, 102, 107, 109,
268, 295, 333-334, 336,
341, 346; Abolished by
13th Amendment, 376;
Abolished by Lincoln,
359-360; after American
Revolution, 142-143; Civil
War, 352-353;
Constitution, 157;
Defenses, 338; Extent,
335; Great Compromise,
157; Louisiana Territory,
340; Missouri
Compromise, 340; New
England, 106; New
Orleans, 320; New World,
53; Northern attitudes,
336; Opposition, 189, 267,
See also Antislavery
movement, Abolition;
Origins, 105; Politics, 338;
Texas, 306; Utah, 340;
Washington, D.C., 255
Slaves; African, 54; Aleut,
36; Auctions, 334;
Colonial, 112; Escaped,
336; Fugitive, 341; in
Jacksonian Democracy,
239; Indian, 34, 53;
Iroquois, 38; Origins, 334;
Protests, 335-336;

Punishments, 334, *See also*
Fugitive Slave Act;
Working Conditions, 334
Smith, Jedediah, 299
Smith, John, 70
Smith, Joseph, 263-264
Smith, Margaret Bayard,
254, 256
Smuggling, 151
Snowshoes, 35
Social Security, 416
Social Security Act of 1935,
416
Sons of Liberty, 127-128
South America, 25, 28-30
"South Carolina Exposition
and Protest," 240
South Carolina, 79;
Threatens secession 1832,
242
South; and Reconstruction,
384-385
Southeast Asia Treaty
Organization (SEATO),
421
Southwest; Climate, 14-15;
First inhabitants, 23;
Settlement, 304
Soviet Union, 419-420;
Cuba, 421; First satellite,
426
Soviet missiles in Cuba,
421-422
Space City U.S.A., 431-432
Spain; and England, 68-69;
Empire in America, 54;
Relations with, 151
Spanish Armada, 69
Spanish-American War, 408
"Specie Circular," 245, 248
Speckled Snake, 245
Spheres of influence, 408
Spoils system, 239-240
Sports, spectator, 413
Squanto, 73, 93
St. Augustine, Florida, 49

St. Leger, Colonel Barry, 135
Stalin, Joseph, 417, 419
Stalingrad, World War II, 418
Stamp Act of 1765, 124-125
Stamp Act Congress, 125
Standard Oil Company, 405
Standish, Miles, 73, 92, 95
Stanton, Edwin M., 381-382
Stanton, Elizabeth Cady, 269
"Star-Spangled Banner, The," 220
States' rights, 207, 240, 376, 404
States, from Northwest Territory, 149
Steamboats, 287
Steel industry, 405
Stephens, Alexander, 348
Stephenson, George, locomotive: *The Rocket,* 288
Stevens, Thaddeus, 374, 388
Stock market crash, 414
Stowe, Harriet Beecher, 341-342
Strategic Arms Limitation Treaty (SALT I), 422
Strauss, Levi, 323
Strict construction, 200
Stuart, Gilbert, 230
Submarine warfare, World War I, 410
Suburbs, 426
Sudetenland, Germany occupies, 417
Suez Canal, World War II, 418
Suez Crisis of 1956, 421
Suffrage qualifications, 238
Sugar Act of 1764, 124
Sumner, Charles, 374
Sumter, Thomas, 138
Sunbelt, 426, 434
Sun worship, 29
Superior Highlands, 8

Supremacy; of civilian authority, 169; of national law, 168
Supreme Court, United States, 174, 196; New Deal, 416
Sutter, John, 305
Swift, Gustavus, 405

T

Taft, William Howard, 406, 409-410
Taiwan, 420
Talkies, 413
Tallmadge, James, 338
Talon, Jean, 59
Taney, Roger B., 344
Tariff Act of 1828, 236, 240, 242
Tariff Act of 1832, 242
Tariff of 1816, 224
Tariff, Protective, 199, 236
Tax; Tea, 127; Whiskey, 199
Taxation, and American Revolution, 125, 127
Taylor, Zachary, 309, 340
Tea tax, 127
Teapot Dome, 413
Technological Revolution, 426
Tecumseh, 217, 220
Teheran Conference, 419
Telegraph, 284, 290
Television, Importance, 426
Temperance crusade, 273-274
Tennessee Valley Authority (TVA), 415
Tenochtitlán, Mexico, 51-52
Tenure of Office Act of 1867, 381-382
Texas; Annexation, 307-308; Mexico, 307; Republic of, 306-307; Slavery, 340; U.S., 306

Texas Southern University, 432
Thoreau, Henry David, 274
Three-fifths compromise, 157
Tilden, Samuel, 389-390
Time line, 78, 96, 190, 258, 326, 402
"Tippecanoe and Tyler too," 249
Tobacco, 71, 79
Toleration Act, Maryland, 76
Tom Thumb, 288
Toombs, Robert, 339
Tordesillas, Treaty of, 48
Totem Poles, 34
Town meeting, 108
Townshend Acts, 126-127
Trade; Africa, 46; Aztecs, 28; Colonial, 104, 111-112, 117; England, 68-69; Far East, 43, 45; French, in North America, 60-61; Fur, 61-63, 299; Growth, 43; Interstate, *See* Commerce, Interstate, 151; Plains Indians, 33; Policy in colonies, 114; Routes, 43, 45-46; United States, 143; With Asia, Dutch, 61; World, 143; *See also* Exploration, Slave Trade, Triangular trade
Traders, Muslim, 46
"Trail of Tears," 247
Transcendentalism, 264, 274
Trans-Mississippi West, 404
Transportation, 287; Eskimo, 36; National system, 224-225, 286
Treaty-making procedure, 196
Treaty of Ghent 1814, 222-223; of Guadalupe Hidalgo, 311; of Morfontaine 1799, *See*

Convention of 1800; of Paris 1763, 119; of Paris 1783, 140, 143, 150-151; of Versailles 1919, 412

Treaty power, 171

Triangular trade, 109-110; *See also* Slave trade

Triple Alliance, 410

Triple Entente (Allied Powers), 410

Trist, Nicholas, 311

Tropic of Cancer, 11

Truman, Harry, 419-421, 423; Civil rights, 424; Domestic programs, 423

Truman Doctrine, 420

Trusts, 405

Truth, Sojourner, 268, 337

Tudor, Henry, *See* Henry VII (England), 67

Turkey, *See also* Ottoman Empire, 410

TVA (Tennessee Valley Authority), 415

Two party system, 235

Tyler, John, 249, 307

U

United States; Central America, 409; Climate, 15; Cuban policy, 421; Eastern Woodlands, 37; Economy, 423; Expansion, 408; Foreign policy, 408-409, 417-423; Geography, 2-11; Great Basin, 33-34; Great Plains, 32-33; Ice Age, 15-17; Invades Cambodia, 422; Invades Laos, 422; Japanese relations, 417; Latin America, 423; Middle East policy, 421;

Moon landing, 426; Northwest, 34; Prehistoric, 15, 17; Southwest, 30-32; U-2 spy plane, 421; Weather and climate, 11-17; World War I, 410; World War II, 417

U.S.S. *Maine*, 408

U.S.S. *Constitution*, 219

Umiak, 36

Uncle Tom's Cabin, 342

Undemocratic governments, 417

Underground Railroad, 336

Unemployment, Great Depression, 414

Union movement, 406

Union of states, argument over, 241

Union, and Civil War, 387

Unions, 406

United Nations; Charter, 419; Location, 419; Structure, 419

United States Railroad Administration (World War I), 411

Utopian communities, 265

V

Vallejo, Mariano Guadalupe, 305

Valley Forge, 136

Van Buren, Martin, 248, 340

Venezuela, 53

Verrazano, Giovanni da, 56-57

Versailles Treaty of 1919, 411; Violated, 417

Vesey, Denmark, 335

Vespucci, Amerigo, 47-48

Veto power, growth, 240

Vietnam War, 422; United States opposition, 422, 426

Vietnamization, 422

Villages, Eastern Woodland Indian, 37

Virginia, 68, 72, 79; Indians, 113

Virginia Company, 70

Virginia Plan, 156

Virginia and Kentucky Resolutions of 1798, 333

Virginia, See *Merrimac*, 357

Voting Rights Act, 424

W

Wade, Benjamin, 374, 388

Wade-Davis Bill of 1864, 375

Wages, 406

Wagner-Connery Act of 1935, 416

Wald, Lillian, 406

Walden, 274

War Hawks of 1812, 218

War Industries Board (World War I), 410

War Production Board (WPB), World War II, 418

War Revenue Act (World War I), 411

War bonds, World War I, 411; World War II, 418

War of 1812, 218-224

"War on Poverty," 423

Warren, Earl, 424

Wars of the Roses, 67

Wars, Aztec, 28

Washington, George, 130, 134-136, 139, 154, 159, 195-196, 201; Farewell Address, 204; French and Indian War, 118

Washington, D.C., 252, 254, 257; Burning, 256; Design, 252
Washington, State of, 309
Watergate burglary coverup, 426
Watt, James, steam engine, 287
Webster, Daniel, 241-242, 333
Webster, Noah, dictionary, 271
Webster-Hayne debates, 241
Weld, Theodore, 267
West, Benjamin, 230
West Coast, climate, 15
West Indies, 47
West; Indians, 404; Trails to, 302
Western lands; After Revolution, 147; *See also* Appalachians, Settlement west of
Westward Movement, 299-315
Wheatley, Phillis, 106
Whigs, 248-249; End of, 343
Whiskey Rebellion, 199-200
"Whiskey Ring," 389
Whiskey tax, 209
White House, 256
White, John, 68, 88
Whitman, Walt, 277
Whitman Mission, 302
Whitney, Eli, 333; Cotton gin, 284
Whittier, John Greenleaf, 277
Willamette Valley, 303
Willard, Emma Hart, 271
William II (England), *See* William and Mary
William and Mary, 85
William and Mary College, 112
William of Orange, *See* William and Mary

Williams, Roger, 75
Wilmington, Delaware, 63
Wilmot, David, 339
Wilmot Proviso, 340
Wilson, Woodrow, 406, 410, 412; Fourteen Points, 411; League of Nations, 411; Mexico, 410; Peace conference, 411; World War I, 411
Winthrop, John, 75
Wisconsin, Indians in, 246
Wolfe, General James, 119
Women; Achievements, 432; and independence, 141; Education, 186-187, 271; Equality, 425-426; in American Revolution, 136; in Jacksonian Democracy, 239; Poets, 106; Right to vote, 107, 412; Rights of, 141-142, 266, 268-269, 426; Role in American Revolution, 136, Civil War, 361, colonial society, 106-108, Iroquois, 38, Pueblo, 32; Work, 418; World War II, 418; Writers, 106
Women's suffrage, 107, 412
Woolen Act of 1699, 117
Word processors, 426
Work day, length, 406
Work ethic, 108
Work week, 416
Work, colonial, 103-104
Workman's compensation, 406
Works Progress Administration (WPA), 414
World War I, 410; Allies, 410; Balkans, 410; Central Powers, 410; Draft, 410; Submarine warfare, 410; U.S. role, 410

World War II, 417; Africa, 418; Battle of Stalingrad, 419; D-Day, 419; Dutch East Indies, 418; Eastern front, 419; Ends, 419; Europe, 419; Home front, 418; Iwo Jima, 419; Japanese-Americans relocated, 418; Malaya, 418; Okinawa, 419; Opponents, 417; Pacific, 418-419; Philippines, 418; Russia, 419, Sicily, 418; Starts, 417; U.S., 417; Victory, 418; War Bonds, 418; War Production Board, 418; Women, 418
WPA (Works Progress Administration), 414
WPB (War Production Board), 418

X

XYZ Affair, 205

Y

Yale College, 109
Yalta Conference, 419
Young, Brigham, 264
Young, James Sterling, 256
Yukatan Peninsula, 25

Z

Zuñi, 31-32

Acknowledgments

Thanks are due to the following authors and publishers for the material quoted on the pages indicated:

Unit I

P. 49: Adapted from Major, R. H. (trans. and ed.). *Select Letters of Christopher Columbus.* London: The Hakluyt Society, 1870. **p. 73:** Adapted from *The Mayflower Compact.* **pp. 88-91:** Lorant, Stefan (ed.). *The New World.* New York: Duell, Sloan & Pearce, 1946. Reprinted by permission. **pp. 92-94, 95:** Bradford, William *Of Plymouth Plantation 1620-1647.* Ed. Samuel Eliot Morison. New York: Alfred A. Knopf, Inc., 1952. Reprinted by permission. **p. 94:** Pory, John. Altham, Emmanuel, and DeRasieres, Isaack. *Three Visitors to Early Plymouth.* Ed. Sydney V. James, Jr. Plimoth Plantation, Inc., 1963. Reprinted by permission.

Unit II

P. 105: Mittelberger, Gottlieb. *Journey to Pennsylvania.* Ed. and trans. Oscar Handlin and John Clive. Cambridge, Massachusetts: The Belknap Press of Harvard University Press, 1960. **p. 106:** Ellis, John Harvard (ed.). *The Works of Anne Bradstreet.* Gloucester, Massachusetts: Peter Smith, 1867. **p. 106:** Wheatley, Phillis. *Poems and Letters.* Ed. Chas. Fred. Heartman. Miami, Florida; Mnemosyne Publishing Co., Inc., 1969. **p. 115:** Crèvecoeur, J. Hector St. John. *Letters from an American Farmer.* New York: Albert & Charles Boni, 1904. **p. 115:** Nevins, Allan. *The Emergence of Modern America 1865-1878.* New York: The Macmillan Company, 1927. **p. 131:** Longfellow, Henry W. *Paul Revere's Ride.* Portland, Maine: L. H. Nelson Company, 1905. **p. 131:** Adapted from O'Brien, Harriet E. (comp.). *Paul Revere's Own Story.* Privately printed by Perry Walton, 1929. **p. 134:** Fast, Howard. *The Selected Works of Tom Paine.* New York: The Modern Library, 1943. **p. 141:** Adapted from Butterfield, L. H. (ed.). *Adams Family Correspondence.* Vol. I. Cambridge, Massachusetts: The Belknap Press of Harvard University Press, 1963. **pp. 155, 157-158:** Donovan, Frank. *The Benjamin Franklin Papers.* New York: Dodd, Mead & Company, 1962. **p. 155:** Schrag, Peter. *The Ratification of the Constitution and the Bill of Rights.* Boston: D. C. Heath and Company, 1964. **p. 168:** Hamilton, Alexander, Madison, James, and Jay, John. *The Federalist Papers.* New York: The New American Library, 1961. **p. 184:** Adapted from Birket, James. *Some Cursory Remarks.* New Haven: Yale University Press, 1916. **pp. 186, 187-188:** *The Life and Letters of Benjamin Franklin.* Eau Claire, Wisconsin: E. M. Hale & Company. Reprinted by permission. **p. 186:** Bridenbaugh, Carl and Jessica. *Rebels and Gentlemen.* New York: Oxford University Press, 1942. **pp. 186-187:** Van Doren, Carl. *Benjamin Franklin.* New York: The Viking Press, 1938.

Unit III

P. 203: Wansey, Henry. *The Journal of an Excursion to the United States of North America in the Summer of 1794.* London, 1796. **p. 204:** *Washington's Farewell Address.* **p. 227:** Cobbett, William. *The Emigrant's Guide.* London: Mills, Jowett, and Mills, 1829. **p. 229:** Bryant, William Cullen. *Thanatopsis.* New York: G. P. Putnam's Sons, 1878. **p. 239:** Ambler, Charles H. *The Life and Diary of John Floyd.* Richmond: Richmond Press, Inc., 1918. **p. 243:** Adapted from Kemble, Frances Anne. "Boat, Stage, Railroad, and Canal (1832-1833)." As quoted in Bushnell, Albert Hart. *American History Told by Contemporaries.* New York: Macmillan Co., 1901. **pp. 245-246:** Armstrong, Virginia Irving (comp.). *I Have Spoken.* Chicago: The Swallow Press Inc., 1971. **pp. 253-254:** Adapted from Mitchell, Stewart (ed.). *New Letters of Abigail Adams.* Boston: Houghton Mifflin Company, 1947. **p. 254:** Adapted from Beston, Henry. *American Memory.* New York: Farrar & Rinehart, 1937. **pp. 255, 256:** Adapted from Smith, Mrs. Samuel Harrison. *The First Forty Years of Washington Society.* Ed. Gaillord Hunt. New York: Charles Scribner's Sons, 1906. Reprinted by permission. **p. 256:** Young, James Sterling. *The Washington Community 1800-1828.* New York: Columbia University Press, 1966.

Unit IV

P. 267: *The Liberator,* Vol. I. No. 7. page 1, February 12, 1831. Boston, Massachusetts. **p. 269:** *History of Woman Suffrage.* Elizabeth C. Stanton *et al.,* eds., Vol. I, New York, 1881. **p. 275:** Emerson, Ralph Waldo. *Nature, Addresses, and Lectures.* Boston: Houghton Mifflin and Company, 1855. **p. 283:** Quincy, Josiah. "Travel Journal (June 1801)" *Massachusetts Historical Society Proceedings* (May 1888). **p. 289:** Martineau, Harriet. *Society in America.* New York: Saunders and Otley, 1837. **p. 303:** Parkman, Francis. *The Oregon Trail.* Chicago: The John C. Winston Company, 1931. **p. 312:** Colton, Rev. Walter. *Three Years in California.* New York: A. S. Barnes & Co., 1850. **pp. 318, 321:** Hall, A. Oakey. *The Manhattaner in New Orleans.* New York: J. S. Redfield, 1850. **p. 320:** Quoted in Searight, Sarah. *New Orleans.* New York: Stein and Day, 1973. **pp. 320-321, 321:** Ripley, Eliza. *Social Life in Old New Orleans.* New York: D. Appleton and Company, 1912. **pp. 322, 323, 324:** Soulé, Frank, Gihon, John H., and Nisbet, James. *The Annals of San Francisco.* New York: D. Appleton and Company, 1845. **p. 324:** Bancroft, Hubert Howe. *Popular Tribunals,* Vol. I. San Francisco: The History Co., 1887.

Unit V

P. 334: Northup, Solomon. *Twelve Years a Slave.* Eds. Sue Eaken and Joseph Logsdon. Baton Rouge: Louisiana State University Press, 1968. **p. 339:** U. S. *The Congressional Globe,* 29th Cong., 2d Sess., 1847. **p. 339:** U.S. *The Congressional Globe.* 31st Cong., 1st Sess., 1850. **p. 360:** From a public letter in 1862 to Horace Greeley of the New York *Tribune.* **p. 367:** *The Gettysburg Address.* **p. 370:** *Lincoln's Second Inaugural Address.* **p. 377:** From *The Americans at Home* by David Macrae. Published in 1952 by E. P. Dutton, and reprinted with their permission. **pp. 378-379:** Trowbridge, J. T. *The South: A*

Tour of Its Battle-fields and Ruined Cities. New York: Arno Press, Inc., 1969. **p. 388:** Billington, Ray Allen (ed.). *The Journal of Charlotte Forten.* London: Collier-Macmillan Ltd., 1953. **p. 394:** Russell, William Howard. *My Diary North and South.* Vol. II. London: Bradbury and Evans, 1863. **p. 395:** Dicey, Edward. "Three Weeks in New York." *Macmillan's Magazine,* (April 1862), pp. 458, 461-463. **p. 397:** Nevins, Allan, and Thomas, Milton Halsey (eds.). *The Diary of George Templeton Strong.* New York: The Macmillan Company, 1952. **p. 397:** Skinner, John E. Hilary. "After the Storm." As quoted in Still, Bayard. *Mirror for Gotham.* Washington Square: New York University Press, 1956. **p. 399:** Coulter, E. Merton. *Georgia, A Short History.* Chapel Hill: University of North Carolina Press, 1947. **p. 399:** From the *Macon Daily Telegraph and Confederate,* December 12, 1864. As quoted in Garrett, Franklin M. *Atlanta and Environs.* Vol. I. Athens: University of Georgia Press, 1954. **p. 399:** Massey, Kate. "A Picture of Atlanta in the Late Sixties." *The Atlanta Historical Bulletin,* 1940-41. **pp. 399-400:** From a letter on file at the Atlanta Historical Society. As quoted in Garrett, Franklin M. *Atlanta and Environs.* Vol. I. Athens: University of Georgia Press, 1954. **p. 400:** Thompson, C. Mildred. *Reconstruction in Georgia.* New York, 1915. As quoted in Garrett, Franklin M. *Atlanta and Environs.* Vol. I. Athens: University of Georgia Press, 1954. **pp. 400-401:** From the *Daily Intelligencer,* September 13, 1865. As quoted in Garrett, Franklin M. *Atlanta and Environs.* Vol. I. Athens: University of Georgia Press, 1954. **p. 401:** Adapted from Rawick, George P. (ed.). *American Slave.* As quoted in Litwack, Leon F. *Been in the Storm So Long.* New York: Alfred A. Knopf, Inc., 1979. **pp. 430, 433:** "Greater Houston: Its First Million People—and Why" *Newsweek.* July 5, 1954, p. 39. **p. 431:** Oates, Stephen B. *Visions of Glory.* Norman, Oklahoma: University of Oklahoma Press, 1970. **pp. 432, 432-433:** Jordan, Barbara. "How I Got There." *Atlantic Monthly,* March 1975. **pp. 433-434:** "A City's Growing Pains." *Newsweek.* January 14, 1980, p. 45.

Photo Credits

Cover

Courtesy of the Library of Congress

Introduction

Page 2, Ed Cooper/H. Armstrong Roberts; 6, Robert Shay; 9, Tom Bean; 10(l), Tom Till; 10(r), Bob Taylor/FPG; 14(l), Larry Burton; 14(r), David M. Dennis; 16, Stephen J. Krasemann/DRK Photo.

Unit 1

Pages 20-21, Courtesy of the Pilgrim Society, Plymouth, Massachusetts; 22, R.S. Michaud/Woodfin Camp and Associates; 24(t), Museum of the American Indian; 24(b), National Museum of Man, National Museums of Canada; 25, David M. Dennis; 28, British Museum; 29, Vladimir Bibic; 31, Michele Wigginton; 33, Courtesy of the Edward E. Ayer Collection, The Newberry Library, Chicago; 37, John Carter Brown Library, Brown University; 39, Ohio Office of Travel and Tourism; 42, New York Public Library; 45(l), Smithsonian Institution; 45(r), Peabody Museum of Salem; 47(l), File Photo; 47(r), Historical Pictures Service; 52, American Museum of Natural History; 54, Arizona Department of Administration; 57, By permission of the Huntington Library, San Marino, Calif.; 58, 63, 66, Historical Pictures Service; 71, The Bettman Archive; 72, Thomas L. Williams; 74, Pilgrim Society; 76, Historical Pictures Service; 81, Pennsylvania Academy of the Fine Arts, Joseph and Sarah Harrison Collection; 88, 90, 91, British Museum; 93, Historical Pictures Service; 94, Courtesy of John Hancock Mutual Life Insurance Co.; 95, Plymouth Plantation.

Unit 2

Pages 98-99, Historical Pictures Service; 100, New York Public Library; 104(l), William L. Clements Library, Univ. of Michigan; 104(r), Historical Pictures Service; 105, File Photo; 107, The Metropolitan Museum of Art, Gift of Mrs. A. Wordsworth Thompson, 1899; 109, Massachusetts Historical Society; 111, Free Library of Philadelphia; 112, Collection of Carolina Art Association/Gibbes Art Gallery; 118, State Historical Society of Wisconsin; 122, Courtesy of the Joseph Dixon Crucible Co. & the Fort Ticonderoga Museum; 124(lb), Library of Congress; 124(rt), (br), Historical Pictures Service; 126, By Permission of the Huntington Library, San Marino, Calif.; 127, Library of Congress; 133, 137, Historical Pictures Service; 138, Yale University Art Gallery; 142(l), Historical Pictures Service; 142(r), Kennedy Galleries, Inc.; 146, Courtesy of Indepen-

dence National Historical Park Collection, Philadelphia; 148(l), The Newberry Library, Chicago; 148(r), The Brooklyn Museum, Dick S. Ramsay Fund; 150, Washington University Gallery of Art, St. Louis; 152, 156, 158, Historical Pictures Service; 159(l), National Portrait Gallery, Smithsonian Institution; 159(r), Historical Pictures Service; 164, Historical Society of Pennsylvania; 166, Historical Pictures Service; 170, In the Collection of the Corcoran Gallery of Art; 181, File Photo; 185, Library of Congress; 186, Library Company of Philadelphia; 187, Smithsonian Institution; 189, New York Public Library.

Unit 3

Pages 192-193, Historical Society of Pennsylvania; 194, 196, Historical Pictures Service; 199, New York Public Library; 200, 202, Historical Pictures Service; 205(l), National Portrait Gallery, Smithsonian Institution; 205(r), File Photo; 208, Courtesy of the New York Historical Society; 211, 214, Historical Pictures Service; 216, Courtesy of the New York Historical Society; 220, Maryland Historical Society, Baltimore; 221, Historical Pictures Service; 224(l), Courtesy of the New York Historical Society; 224(r), Museum of Fine Arts, Boston; 229, 230(l), The Bettmann Archive; 230(r), National Museum of American Art, Smithsonian Institution, Gift of Mrs. Sarah Harrison; 234, Collection of the Boatman's National Bank of St. Louis; 236(l), Historical Pictures Service; 236(r), National Portrait Gallery, Smithsonian Institution; 241, Historical Pictures Service; 244, Boston Public Library; 247, The Philbrook Art Center; 253, Library of Congress; 254, Smithsonian Institution; 255, 257, The Bettmann Archive.

Unit 4

Pages 260–261, U.S. Department of the Interior; 262, John Hancock Mutual Life Insurance Co.; 264, Whaling Museum; 265, Oneida Community Historical Committee; 268, Courtesy of the New York Historical Society; 269(l), Sophia Smith Collection, Smith College; 269(r), Historical Pictures Service; 270, Reprinted by permission from Lithopinion No. 11 © 1968, Amalgamated Lithographers of America; 271, Oberlin College Archives; 276, PHOTRI; 280, Smithsonian Institution; 282(l), Yale University Art Gallery; 282(r), Courtesy of Lowell National Historical Park; 285(l), Courtesy of the Singer Co.; 285(r), State Historical Society of Wisconsin; 286(l), Canal Museum, Syracuse, N. Y.; 286(r), The Bettmann Archive; 287, I. N. Phelps Stokes Collection, New York Public Library; 288, Kennedy Galleries; 292, Library of Congress; 294, Museum of the City of New York; 298, U.S. Naval Academy Museum; 301, Denver Public

Library; 304, The Society of California Pioneers; 307(l), Courtesy Chicago Historical Society; 307(r), The Granger Collection; 309, Yale University Library; 311, California State Library; 314, Library of Congress; 319, The Bettmann Archive; 320, Smithsonian Institution; 321, The Historic New Orleans Collection, 533 Royal St.; 323, Levi Strauss and Co.; 324, 325, Courtesy, The Bancroft Library, Univ. of California.

Unit 5

Pages 328-329, West Point Museum; 330, Courtesy of Chicago Historical Society; 332, Library of Congress; 335(l), New York Public Library; 335(r), National Archives; 336, Philbrook Art Center; 341(l), New York Public Library; 341(r), File Photo; 343, Kansas State Historical Society; 348(l), File Photo; 348(r), Historical Pictures Service; 351, Courtesy The National Park Service; 354, 357, The Granger Collection; 359, Historical Pictures Service; 361, The Bettmann Archive; 363, Historical Pictures Service; 365, Library of Congress; 369, Appomattox Court House National Historical Park; 373, The Granger Collection; 375, 379, Historical Pictures Service; 382, Library of Congress; 383, 385, 386, Historical Pictures Service; 395, Historical Pictures Service; 396, The Granger Collection; 397, Museum of the City of New York; 399, Atlanta Historical Society; 400, The Bettmann Archive; 401, National Archives.

Conclusion

Page 405, The Granger Collection; 411, Bildarchiv Preussischer Kulturbesite; 413, File Photo; 416, © 1935 (renewed 1963) by Condé Nast Publications, Inc.; 418, The Bettmann Archive; 420, M. Scheller/Black Star; 422, Magnum; 424, UPI; 427, NASA; 431, File Photo; 432, NASA; 433, UPI; 434, Texas Department of Highways; 435, Gerald D. Hines Interest, Inc.

Readings

Page 349, U.S. Naval Academy Museum; 441, Rare Books and Manuscript Division, New York Public Library, Astor, Lenox and Tilden Foundations; 444, Virginia State Library; 446, Susan Marquart; 450, Yale University Art Gallery; 458, The Bettmann Archive; 462, 465, Library of Congress; 468, The Granger Collection; 471, The Bettmann Archive; 473, Library of Congress; 478, The Brooklyn Museum; 482, Museum of the Confederacy; 484, Library of Congress.

1 2 3 4 5 6 7 8 9 10 11 12 13 14 15—95 94 93 92 91 90 89 88 87 86 85